RSAC

APR 0 0 2011

SHI'ISM

SHI'ISM

A Religion of Protest

Hamid Dabashi

The Belknap Press of Harvard University Press
Cambridge, Massachusetts
London, England
2011

Copyright © 2011 by the President and Fellows of Harvard College
All rights reserved
Printed in the United States of America

Library of Congress Cataloging-in-Publication Data

Dabashi, Hamid
Shi'ism : a religion of protest / Hamid Dabashi.
p. cm.
Includes bibliographical references and index.
ISBN 978-0-674-04945-1 (alk. paper)
1. Shi'ah—History. 2. Shi'ah—Doctrines—History. I. Title.
BP192.D33 2010
297.8'209—dc22 2010038963

For and from the serenity of my inner sanctum:

my wife Golbarg

and my children Kaveh, Pardis, Chelgis, and Golchin

(and of course for Bashu and Dazzle: our little strangers)

Shokr-e Izad keh beh eqbal-e kolah-gusheh-ye gol
Nekhvat-e bad-e dey-o showkat khar akher shod

Praised be the Lord that thanks to the blossoming tip of the rose's hat
The arrogance of winter and the might of the thorn are ended at last

Hafez

CONTENTS

Prelude xi
Preface xv

Introduction 1

I

DOCTRINAL FOUNDATION

1 Death of a Prophet 29
2 Birth of a Revolutionary Faith 47
3 The Karbala Complex 73

II

HISTORICAL UNFOLDING

4 In the Battlefields of History 103
5 In the Company of Kings, Caliphs, and Conquerors 132
6 At the Dawn of Colonial Modernity 159

III

VISUAL AND PERFORMING ARTS

7 Shi'ism and the Crisis of Cultural Modernity 207
8 On *Ressentiment* and the Politics of Despair 228
9 An Aesthetic of Emancipation 241

IV

CONTEMPORARY CONTESTATIONS

10 The Un/Making of a Politics of Despair 263
11 Toward a New Syncretic Cosmopolitanism 277
12 Contemporary Sites of Contestation 296

Conclusion 309

Note on Transliteration 327
Arabic and Persian Glossary 328
Schools of Theology, Philosophy, and Political Thought 338
Chronology 344
Notes 348
Further Reading 385
Acknowledgments 390
Index 393

Maps and illustrations follow p. 227

It is a little remarkable, that . . . an autobiographical impulse should twice in my life have taken possession of me, in addressing the public . . . The truth seems to be, however, that when he casts his leaves forth upon the wind, the author addresses, not the many who will fling aside his volume, or never take it up, but the few who will understand him better than most of his schoolmates or lifemates . . . To this extent and within these limits, an author, methinks, may be autobiographical, without violating either the reader's rights or his own.

Nathaniel Hawthorne, "The Custom House":
Introductory to *The Scarlet Letter,* 1850

PRELUDE

Shi'ism is a festive gathering, a festival, a feast, a constellation of moral manners, a commitment, a conviction, a mobile memory—the centerpiece of it the iconic unsheathing of a dagger, for real, for sure, always half-drawn from its worn-out sheath. Always ready to change its own metaphors, Shi'ism is also a raised lantern of hope in desperation, a green flag, a red marker of martyrdom, sacrifice, renewal, resurrection. Shi'ism is the shimmering memory of an event, a dream, a single traumatic incident, condemned forever to try to remember itself: in vain. Shi'ism is the doomed damnation of thinking one has seen and had a vision and then trying for a lifetime, a history, the span of a cosmic universe to remember it, to realize it—all in futility. Shi'ism is the Islamic version of the myth of Sisyphus—condemned to roll the fiction of its own reality up the hill, against the grain of history, then watch it hopelessly roll down to the ground zero of its cyclical desperation for salvation. Shi'ism is crimson in color for its ritual remembrance of the cold-blooded murder of the Prophet's grandson, Hossein ibn Ali; green in its memory of the providential assurances that all will one day be well, the mayhem of the world be damned; white, full of blank determination to wear the shroud of *shahadat* [to bear witness with your life] just before descending to death—into nullity, nonentity, just before rising up again to be a witness, to bear witness (again), thus to account for who and what you were, we are, we ought to be, for what we did right, what we did wrong, whether we were righteous or not. Shi'ism is a blind faith, a reasoned reassurance, a moral mandate, an intellectual tapestry, a way of (not) resting your case with history, the world; it is the meaningful magic that holds your passing days together, your whispering nights full of saintly silences and replete with suggestive gestures of revolt. Shi'ism is a religion of mothers' hopes, bloodied by fathers' vengeance, paid for by sons and daughters of a meaningful death. Shi'ism speaks Persian, prays in Arabic, whispers in Urdu, sings in Turkish, plays in mimetic remembrances of things past—perpetually *à la recherche du temps perdu.*

Shi'ism is a religion of protest, born and bred on the backbone of a combative history—a history gone (for Shi'is) awry. A prophet is born, a messenger is sent, the messenger comes and the messenger goes, the divinity reveals itself, a community is dutifully formed, a faith is declared triumphant, and a belief (a doctrine) takes shape that does not want to let go of the charismatic memory, the ecstatic moment, the embracing persona of the Prophet—so it invests it in another man, a good man, a blessed man, a divinely ordained man to lead His community. But history does not concur, the community does not follow, the majority (the minority thinks) errs. Shi'ism, in believing that Ali ibn Abi Talib should have succeeded Prophet Muhammad ibn Abdullah, takes what has happened in history as the erring side of reality. "The time" for the Shi'is is thus always "out of joint." And cursed spite that ever they were "born to set it right."

Shi'ism is a poem, an elegy, a eulogy, an epic, a panegyric pausing for a moment for history to recollect itself and start anew. Shi'ism is Karbala. In a battle that took place on the 10th of October 680 (10 Muharram 61 on the Islamic calendar), the Prophet's grandson Imam Hossein and seventy-two of his closest comrades and companions were murdered by the reigning Muslim caliph Yazid ibn Mu'awiyah. How did that happen? Muslims killing Muslims—so early in what was now an "Islamic" history? And killing whom—the Prophet's own flesh and blood? Predicated on that tragedy, Shi'ism is the summoned metaphysics of sustainable belief, a suspension of doubt—absolute and final surrender to one overarching truth [*Haq*]—in peace. As the letter of the law dictates and matters of metaphysics prevail (whence reason resigns and a supreme—motherly—serenity of surrender prevails), Shi'ism is the undying belief in the Absolute Unity and the Absolute Otherness of One Almighty God—Omnipotent, Omniscient, Omnipresent, Merciful, Compassionate, Forgiving.

This God for the Shi'is has an essence [*dhat*] and countless attributes [*sifat*]. One of His attributes is wisdom, another justice. Shi'is (as all other Muslims) believe that this Almighty Providence, in His infinite wisdom and justice, has sent periodic emissaries—from Adam through Noah, Abraham, Moses, and Jesus, down to the Last and Most Noble of them all (their Seal) Prophet Muhammad—so that mankind can be led to the Right Path. And yet (and there is the Shi'i rub), the death of the last Prophet, Shi'is believe (unlike all other Muslims, and with that belief they part ways with their Sunni brothers and sisters), left the prophetic seal vacant. Thus with His cousin and son-in-law, Ali ibn Abi Talib, began the cycle of Twelve (or Five or Seven according to other Shi'is) infallible imams, or leaders, who have brought the prophetic cycle to a culminating conclusion. These imams are in possession of the true meaning of the Qur'an, having learned it, chest to chest [*sineh beh sineh*], from one heart to another, from the Prophet Muhammad himself. Justice [*'Adl*] and an equally abiding belief in bodily resurrection in the Final Day of Judgment [*Ma'ad*] are as definitive to Shi'i doctrinal beliefs as are the belief in the Absolute Unity of God (their monotheistic *Tawhid*) and belief in His Divine Providence to send his emissaries to guide people to do the right things (their epistolary *Nubuwwah*)—and the fact that these prophets have in turn left behind infallible interpreters of their revelations (their sacerdotal *Imamah*).

Vindictive, Shi'ism is revolt: from Imam Hossein in Karbala to Ayatollah Khomeini in Iran, to Muqtada al-Sadr in Iraq, to Hassan Nasrallah in Lebanon. Shi'ism is to say "No!" Where it thrives, Shi'ism is a majority with a minority complex. It is not just that Shi'ism is political; politics is Shi'i in its quintessence. If the German sociologist of the Weimar era Max Weber defined politics in terms of (what he always parenthetically considered) legitimate violence, Shi'ism sublates violence from the domain of politics into the site of the metaphysics—for Shi'ism was born (not just politically but also metaphysically) when its very first imam, Ali ibn Abi Talib, was murdered by an assassin, and when Ali's son, the Prophet's grandson, the supreme heroic figure of Shi'ism, Imam Hossein ibn Ali, and his companions were massacred in Karbala. Violence breeds violence, and a persecuted minority thus formed sublates its received and perceived violence into the burning fuel of its ethics and politics, aesthetics and metaphysics. Something of that violence is written in the rectangular precision with which Shi'i designers and architects cut and paste the most exquisite tapestry of colors and designs on the mosaics at the top of the cupola covering the sanctity of their saints and martyrs.

Shi'ism, in the end, is a paradox. It thrives and is triumphant when it is combative and wages an uphill battle; it loses its moral authority and defiant voice the instant it succeeds and is in power. It is, paradoxically, only in power when it is not in power—when it in power, it lacks legitimacy, authority, audacity.

PREFACE

It would be useful if at the very outset I were to share with you the road we will follow in this book. I have divided my book into four major parts, each having three chapters. In the first part, I introduce the historical origin of Shi'ism and the principles of its doctrinal foundations. Here I discuss the historical birth of Shi'ism early in Islamic history and the formation of the doctrinal principles on which it is founded. In the second part, I give you a detailed account of the historical unfolding of Shi'ism from its origin in the seventh century to its encounter with European colonial modernity early in the nineteenth century. For the sake of simplicity I use only the common (Christian) calendar to avoid crowding my prose with too many comparative calendars. You should just know that Muslims have their own calendar, which is a lunar calendar and begins with the migration of Prophet Muhammad from Mecca to Medina in 622 CE. In the third part you will notice a major epistemic shift in my narrative from doctrinal and historical to an aesthetic manifestation of the faith, a manifestation that I propose categorically splits the Shi'i consciousness into two uneven segments—a politics of despair on one side and an aesthetic of formal emancipation on the other. This split, I will argue, is by far the most traumatic experience of Shi'ism in modernity, something that has never been diagnosed before, and an event I wish to articulate in some analytical detail. Most Shi'i scholars and scholars of Shi'ism (these are two different things) are so productively lost in the thicket of its doctrinal and historical details that they have had no time or inclination to see through this split. I have—and I wish to show and tell what I have seen. In the fourth and final part of my book, I will drive you through the political crescendo of Shi'ism in its modern context, analyzing the contemporary sites of contestation in Iran, Iraq, and Lebanon in particular. Here I will demonstrate the thematic exhaustion of political Shi'ism and argue that the contemporary reunification of its exhausted politics and its alienated aesthetics is the premise of a renewed cosmopolitan modernity.

At the heart of this book is a provocative diagnosis about Shi'ism. My principal contention is that Shi'ism is predicated on a rather perplexing paradox—that it is morally triumphant when it is politically defiant, and that it morally fails when it politically succeeds. This permanently revolutionary disposition (and thus my designation of Shi'ism as a religion of protest), I argue, has been a defining paradox of Shi'ism from the outset and all through its medieval history. It might have achieved a resolution in the formation of a public space during the all-important Safavid empire in the sixteenth century but did not because of the demise of that empire in the eighteenth century following a major Afghan invasion. Once again in the nineteenth century, during a massive revolutionary uprising known as the Babi movement against the Qajar dynasty, opportunities presented themselves for this paradox to be resolved in the formation of an even larger and more expanded and potent public space. Again historical circumstance, which I will explain in detail, prevented that possibility. Finally, after repeated attempts at the formation of such a public space, where a public reason could have been cultivated and this Shi'i paradox potentially resolved, and under the added pressure of European colonialism, the Shi'i collective consciousness gave in, normatively collapsed, and underwent a major schizophrenic split, with its politics of desperation going one way and its aesthetic of emancipation another. Its politics became incessantly belligerent and defeatist while its aesthetics became excessively formalized and self-alienating, self-diagnosed as decidedly "secular." This notion of secularism, I contend, was engineered under colonial duress, because the most radical, in fact the most iconoclastic and sacrilegious ideas, ideas infinitely more subversive of the dominant notions of the sacred than seen before under secularism, were generated and maintained by Muslims throughout their histories. Shi'ism itself is in fact the most glaring example of this subversiveness. My contention is that as the Shi'i politics became increasingly nativist, its twin aesthetics went in the opposite direction and became universal, though in a vacuous and self-alienating way that dubs itself "secular." My final argument is that once again history has provided Shi'ism with the possibility of a normative return to its full-bodied self-realization—an opportunity for its creative and critical apparatus to come together in a renewed cosmopolitan context. My intention in this book is to expose that schizophrenic split and thus bring it to the collective consciousness of Shi'is at large, and to do so in the public domain, addressing it and redressing it at one and the same time.

This central thesis, however, is not all I offer in this book. As I pave my way toward the articulation of my thesis, I intend to alter the very language of thinking, speaking, and writing about Islam and Shi'ism. I contend that the very language we have been using about Islam and Shi'ism is an occupied territory and needs to be liberated for a wider and more welcoming feast. Shi'i scholastic writing and Orientalist discursive disposition have combined and pretty much cornered the market, stifling the way we are led to think about the world of Islam. I intend to break through the thick and fortified borders between the sacred and the secular, the personal and the public, and discuss Shi'ism in a language and latitude, tone and trajectory, yet unheard of. You will read, in both thick and thin brushstrokes, about revolutionary woman poets and bearded old scholars, about monarchical potentates and revolutionary rabble-rousers, about learned theologians and iconoclastic philosophers. The way I write about Shi'ism crosses the rigid boundaries between the sanctimonious and the sacrilegious, carefully balanced to pave the way toward a hidden path to its body and soul.

My principal project in this book is to bring to the Shi'i collective mind this historical repression and that particular language of revealing it—visiting upon it the idea that after repeated attempts at resolving its central paradox by way of cultivating a public reason in a public space, Shi'ism undergoes a schizophrenic split. Its aesthetic sensibilities turn formal and wayward (and have been misdiagnosed as "secular") while its politics have turned inward and become self-destructive. I do realize that this is something of an unsettling idea.

Let me now turn to my introductory chapter, where I lay out the first and most critical cornerstone of my argument by way of a friendly conversation with Sigmund Freud, through the intermediary work of my own late teacher Philip Rieff, the great Freudian scholar. The point of this belated conversation, as you will see, is to make my case for Shi'ism as a religion of protest, a *son-religion* as I will call it, a religion predicated on the guilt of having killed the primordial son, as opposed to a *father-religion,* a religion based on the guilt of having killed the primordial father, as Freud theorized. Looking at the origin of Shi'ism through a Freudian lens is a rather iconoclastic proposition requiring a certain amount of delicacy and care. But let me not get ahead of myself; let me find a better and more graceful way to tell you my story and make my case.

SHI'ISM

INTRODUCTION

Masjed-e Bushehri-ha in Ahvaz, the city in which I was born and raised in southern Iran in the early 1950s, was legendary for its Muharram ceremonies. Masjeds, or mosques as they are called in English, are not just where people gather to pray and recite the glory of their Almighty God and his chosen prophets and saints. They are a veritable social institution, architecturally written ever so gracefully into the fabric of urbanism around the Muslim world. They are very much like churches and cathedrals in major European cities, and entirely unlike Protestant churches in rural or suburban America, which are usually located on a very prominent hill, visible from afar, and preside mercifully over the devotedly humbled landscape. Mosques, on the other hand, just like Masjed-e Bushehri-ha, which I frequented as a child with my parents in Ahvaz, were a spatial extension of your peace and comfort zones, where you knew you were home, a bigger home, with a larger family of friendly faces about you, embracing you.

The mosque my parents frequented most during the sacred months of Muharram and Safar was called Masjed-e Bushehri-ha because it was founded by the Bushehri residents of Ahvaz. My late father, Khodadad Dabashi, who worked for the Iranian National Railroad [*Rah-Ahan-e Sartasari-ye Iran*], was originally from the southern coastal city of Bushehr. In this mosque in Ahvaz gathered all the Bushehri natives who had emigrated to the provincial capital of the oil-rich Khuzestan in search of work. This was mostly a working-class mosque. There were of course many other mosques in Ahvaz catering to and established by other migrant workers from around the country. For example, Masjed-e Isfahani-ha was established and frequented mostly but not exclusively by the Isfahani natives now living in Ahvaz, along with many other provincial laborers in search of better jobs and more rewarding opportunities. This mosque was in fact closer to our home in Ardeshir Avenue in the older part of Ahvaz, *Ahvaz Qadim,* as we locals called it, as opposed to *Ahvaz Jadid,* which was the new part of Ahvaz and located on the opposite side of the Karun River. Ahvaz Jadid was the more posh and green part of the city, housing the upper-middle-class portion of the social structure. It contained almost exclusively governmental buildings from the Reza Shah Pahlavi era inspired by Albert Speer's architecture.

Not just for us Bushehris (though my mother Zahra Parvizi Motlaq was originally from Dezful and I had an equal claim to that part of Khuzestan as well) but also for most other people in Ahvaz, there was something particularly attractive, pulsating, and at moments exceedingly exciting about the Muharram ceremonies at Masjed-e Bushehri-ha. The pivotal event at the heart of this mosque and at the zenith of Karbala commemoration during the month of Muharram was the beautiful manner—rhythm and choreography—in which the Bushehris performed their *sineh zani.* At the Isfahanis' mosque, for example, people —mostly young men—just poured into the middle of the courtyard, bared their upper torsos, and began randomly beating their chests to the melodic suggestions of a cantor, with no particular rhyme or rhythm to their chest-beating and bodily movements or, even more important, to the organization of their gathering. At the Bushehris' mosque the situation was entirely different. We were party and witness to a beautifully choreographed combination of what effectively amounted to our version of opera and ballet.

A Ceremony of Innocence

The balletlike ritual of dancing and ceremonious chest-beating while rhythmically circumambulating the chief cantor of the mosque was not the only major attraction at the Masjed-e Bushehri-ha during the holy months of Muharram and Safar. There were many other exciting events, such as a whole panoply of regular and visiting preachers who would ascend the pulpit and deliver speeches on various social (and at times political) issues and conclude with mournfully recounting one or another episode of the Karbala story. Most of the political theology with which my generation of Iranians was born and raised was uttered and articulated on these sorts of pulpits, when preachers took advantage of the slightest opportunities to criticize the Pahlavi monarchy. The period I describe here is in the mid- to late 1950s, long before Ayatollah Khomeini would lead successive uprisings against the Pahlavi regime until he finally toppled it in the late 1970s. A certain Ayatollah Boroujerdi was the chief Shi'i cleric of the land at this time, and by disposition he had an apolitical and acquiescent character. But for me these ceremonies were not overwhelmingly or even primarily political in nature. It would be more than a decade later, when I was a college student in Tehran, that the figure of Imam Hossein in Karbala would begin to fade in and out with that of Che Guevara in Sierra Maestra. Paramount in the air during these sacred months was the communal, collective gathering of a people to remember the most traumatic moment of their faith, as it happened hundreds of years ago in Karbala, which had by now assumed cosmic and metaphysical proportions and import. The chief protagonist of the Karbala story was Hossein ibn Ali, the son of Ali ibn Abi Talib, the First Shi'i Imam, the grandson of Prophet Muhammad. At the head of a small band of his comrades, Hossein ibn Ali had revolted against the reigning caliph in the year 61 on the Islamic calendar (680 CE). They were abandoned by his supporters in Kufa and were subsequently massacred by Yazid ibn Mu'awiyah's army, led by his general Shimr ibn Dhi al-Jawshan. Next to Imam Hossein, or Seyyed al-Shuhada [The Prince of Martyrs], as he is affectionately known, were his half brother Abbas, a valiant warrior, and his courageous and eloquent sister Zaynab (or Zeynab as we pronounced her name in Persian). These names and their heroic adventures and tragic ends were the dramatis personae of a cosmic opera, composed by the collective will of a people over centuries and millennia of communal remembrance, recited ritually, annually, piously, since time immemorial.[1]

Toward evening, when the *sineh zani* was over and the preachers had ascended the pulpits to offer their social commentaries, political criticism, and above all mournful remembering of the events of Karbala while countless rounds of sweetened Ceylon tea were offered and taken, then people had a chance to rest and relax. Suddenly there was a commotion at one corner of the mosque, adjacent to the kitchen, where a variety of musical instruments, including my absolute favorite, a rather long antelope horn; a *dammam* (a bass drum made from wood, rope, and animal skin); an oversize set of cymbals; and various other instrumental odds and ends, were played in unison by members of the mosque (with uneven and at times dubious claims on musicianship). Their music was syncopated and measured to the beat of the drum, and as the pious band played they danced rhythmically, making a complete tour around the vast courtyard. Others watched and followed them, and women and younger children watched with excitement and even joy from the rooftop.

No doubt this musical part of the Muharram ceremony was meant to convey a sense of a mourning procession, a processional requiem, but nevertheless there was a frivolity and playfulness in the act—or at least so it appeared to those who participated in it with much expectation and were visibly excited (and even delighted, I might say) when it started. This part of the Muharram ceremony at the Bushehris' mosque was (most probably) influenced by African music. In the southern part of Iran, particularly in the coastal regions of the Persian Gulf where Bushehr is located, is a syncretic culture heavily influenced by four concurrent traits: Indian from the east, African from the south, Arabic from the west, and Iranian from the north. From our cuisine to our dress and costumes, to our physical features, to our local cultures, music, dance, and even linguistic proclivities, we are made of these four distinct cultural traits. My own last name, Dabashi, is most probably Sanskrit in origin and means "two languages"—a "bilingual" or an "interpreter." My sense is that in the specific manner of dancing and musicianship that are interwoven with our Shi'i ceremonial practices, we are heavily influenced by African, particularly East African, dance and music.

Early in the morning of Ashura, from each mosque in the city would pour out an initially jubilant but intermittently mournful procession of *sineh zanan* (those who rhythmically beat their chest), *zanjir zanan* (those who do the same with a handful of chains beating their back), *alamdaran* (heavy and powerful men carrying huge masts with flags and other religious icons), *noheh khanan* (cantors), and their respective constituencies of mosque-goers. They would come out of the mosques and congregate in a major intersection of the city, between Pahlavi Avenue and Si Metri Avenue, as we called them at the time. I am sure these names have changed now. They marched ritually and ceremoniously toward the older part of the city and the mausoleum of Ali ibn Mahziyar (a local saint buried in an old cemetery). This was by far the most spectacular event of our entire year: block after block, for as far as the eye could see and then beyond, cantors would sing moving oratorios on loudspeakers fixed on long masts, leading a band of (for example) *zanjir zanan*, all dressed in black shirts and black trousers, with the back side of their shirts held with pins that could be opened and the back exposed so that the blows would hit the exposed bare shoulders and keep the rest of their upper torso covered when they rhythmically lifted the two heavy handfuls of chains and forcefully or gently (depending on the tempo of the oratorios that accompanied them) brought them down on their back as they danced back and forth with the melodic syncopation of the cantor. An almost endless, seemingly seamless succession of colorful crowds, a combustion of operatic fervor, choreographed ballets, and tragic zeal, all with epic proportions and cosmic expanse—always sad, sometimes amusing, at times funny, and always with an overriding sense of being part of a drama in which we were actors and spectators at the same time, young and old. Through that play we felt we were part of an immense celestial gathering of our cosmic universe. We were stars dancing in the heavens.

While these spectacular events were progressing around the city (mainly in the old part of Ahvaz, the working-class Ahvaz Qadim neighborhood), inside the Masjed-e Bushehri-ha the scene was no less charged —replete with a panoramic pandemonium reminiscent of the Ashura of some fourteen hundred years ago. Mr. Mahmoudi, the widely popular cantor of religious hymns in our mosque, was now singing the most moving and powerful lyrics lurking in his mind and memory, cast on his soaring soul and carved on his heavy heart; the concentric circles of half-naked men gathered around him and rhythmically beating their chests to his melodic moods were now larger and more crowded than ever; women had pulled their veils over their heads and were crying and gently beating their chests; older men (men busy with various chores in the mosque) were visibly sad, somber, some sobbing, and many pounding their foreheads with their palms as they stood by for a moment or moved around the epicenter of the courtyard; children were frightened, amused, reverential, and wide-eyed all at the same time. Meanwhile, behind the main walls of the mosque in a spacious sidebar of the courtyard there was some serious cooking taking place. The pots that I have seen on these occasions placed over heaps of burning logs and charcoal, boiling with water for basmati rice or sizzling with vegetable oil for minced lamb, chickpea, and tomato stew, I have never seen since. The same pots were used in massive wedding ceremonies, and I have also seen them in some old photographs as well as in a few Iranian movies. This whole commotion began early in the morning of Ashura and was dutifully proceeding while the mourning was in progress in the main courtyard of the mosque. It all came to a crescendo on *Zohr-e Ashura.*

Zohr-e Ashura (exactly noon, when the sun is perpendicular over Earth) is by far the most electrifying moment of the day on Ashura, for Imam Hossein was reportedly beheaded precisely at that hour. It was at this time that Mr. Mahmoudi would hit his absolute highest pitch and let out his most mournful melodies, the *sineh zanan* around him would move around fastest and beat their chests hardest—and on very rare occasions (I have not personally witnessed this, but I know for a fact that it was done), *qameh zanan* would start inflicting excruciating wounds with a sharp saber on their shaven heads. *Qameh* literally means "saber," and *qameh zani* is by far the most violent, gruesome, quite rare, and at times grisly aspect of the Ashura ceremonies. Exceedingly devout men, young and old, would gather in a part of the courtyard or in an isolated room and at the highest moments of their frenzy lift a sharp saber they had been holding in their hands (and rhythmically moving around with it to the mournful oratorios of a cantor) and bring it down forcefully on their purposefully shaven head, causing blood to gush from their slit flesh and fractured bones. I have seen gruesome pictures of *qameh zani,* and as a child I was in mosques and other religious gatherings where there was intimation of *qameh zani* in the vicinity. I have seen men with the scarring signs of *qameh zani* on their shaved heads, but I have never witnessed it. There was always an air of mystery and secrecy about this particular ritual, and women and children were kept out of sight. Pouring ashes over the gushing wound of the *qameh zani* is considered the supreme sign of piety and identification with the pains and suffering of Imam Hossein and his family and friends on the day of Ashura.

The height of the self-flagellating moments on Zohr-e Ashura would seamlessly fade into by far the most spectacular feat of eating and drinking I have ever seen. As the mourners were reaching the height of their frenzy, the feast would be readied—a massive, supersized banquet of eating and drinking, a colorful carnival of food and soft drinks and eating and talking, and then gearing for some more eating and drinking and giving and taking and gathering of body and soul. Long white cloths [*sofreh*] would be spread in the courtyard, magnificent trays of steaming rice would be placed in the adjacent centers of the spread, and sizeable bowls full of the lamb, chickpea, and tomato stew [*khoresht-e qeymeh*] would be placed very close together on the edge of the sofreh, so that one person could sit in front of it with two friends on each side. This food was considered to be sacred and miraculous. My father would give me a generous pot full of rice and another full of stew to take home to my mother. During the summers, when I accompanied my parents and younger brother to the holy city of Mashhad in the northeastern part of Iran, where the Eighth Shi'i Imam is buried under a magnificent mausoleum, the same sanctity would be given to the food that the Astan-e Qods-e Razavi would offer the pilgrims. Devout people who had come as pilgrims from all over Iran and all over the Muslim world would dry this food piously on the rooftops of hotels where they were staying. Then they took it home with them to their cities as a precious souvenir and enjoyed its medicinally miraculous benefits. The pious Shi'is believe in the sanctity of this food, blessed by the memory of the Prince of Martyrs Hossein ibn Ali.

A Sobering Frivolity

Even when I was a child, the conflicting emotions and sentiments that Muharram ceremonies and the Ashura celebrations in particular generated and sustained in us baffled me—the pleasure we took, as a people, a community, a public gathering in who and what we were, commemorating as we did the murder of our heroic origin, the guilt that underwrote that pleasure, and above all the paradox that this colliding confluence of pleasure and guilt entailed. Here we were, commemorating by far the most traumatic and tragic events of the history of our faith as a people, as Shi'is, and yet there was an unmistakable air of joyous frivolity, of playfulness—a gaiety of soul, an open-ended exhilaration, a sense of freedom from inhibitions and reticence—about the whole spectacle. Public acts of mourning, to be sure, were as pious and genuine as an old greengrocer standing reverentially at the closed door of his modest shop as the Ashura procession went by, clad in the black color of mourning for Imam Hossein. He is buttoned up all the way to his thin and white-bearded neck in a worn-out suit that hangs from his bony frame, quietly crying with both his eyes closed. These acts of mourning were as loud and violent as the gruesome acts of *qameh zani*. And yet woven into these profound acts of somber piety was a running theme of jovial merriment. People were genuinely happy, in a state of blissful generosity, casually humorous, publicly affectionate, unusually forgiving, bighearted, joyous, embracing of each other and their habitual flaws. It was, as my old teacher Philip Rieff would say, an entirely "remissive occasion," right at the heart of a sacred order Rieff held paramount in the making of any culture. Things were done and accepted that were otherwise and ordinarily unacceptable. People forgave their enemies, embraced their foes, welcomed strangers, went soft on their demands in a business deal, were more gentle in their expectations from a poor boy who had asked for the hand of their daughter in marriage. Debts were forgiven, credit was renewed, investments were daring and generous, markets were expanded, fears were conquered, goods were abundant —the whole economy of emotions and feelings and sentiments became munificent, openhanded, large, expansive, fortuitous. In the innermost sanctity of our pious remembrances of heroisms past, we became heroically present in our generously expanded emotive universe. We did not put it in these political terms in our childhood, but we would later learn that this was the absolute best time to launch a cataclysmic revolution.

Whence that sobering frivolity, wherefore that somber generosity of spirit, and above all how was it that in the midst of remembering the most tragic and traumatic event of our culture and religion we were also jovial? The doctrinal codification of Muharram ceremonies into Shi'i iconography of martyrdom and sacrifice has now made it almost impossible to probe or suggest pre-Islamic, or perhaps more ancient, or even archaic origins and sentiments at the roots of its festive gathering.[2] For the last fourteen hundred years (but particularly since the sixteenth century—since the commencement of the Safavid dynasty in Iran) the Muharram ceremony has been a Shi'i ritual through and through, with manifestations ranging from India through Iran, Iraq, and Lebanon, and all the way around the world in Trinidad.[3] The drama of Karbala is now successfully written into the poetics, lyrics, dramatics, and ethics of redemptive suffering at the heart of Shi'ism as a world religion.[4] That it may have more archaic and primeval roots is now considered something of a sacrilegious proposition, and scarce any scholar ventures in that hazardous direction. To be sure, the older Iranian origins of aspects of the Karbala celebrations have been suggested, and the similarities between the mourning for Imam Hossein and those of Zarer and Seyavash in pre-Islamic and *Shahnameh* sources have been pointed out by a number of scholars.[5] One such scholar, for example, has suggested:

> The ritual mourning festivals of the Ta'ziyeh-type have clear precedents in pre-Islamic Persia. The passion of Siyavush bears too close a resemblance to the Ta'ziyeh of the Imam [Husayn] in ritual, imagery, and emotive underpinnings to be ignored in an explanation of the emergence of the genre. Whereas Zarer's elegiac epic may be considered Zoroastrian in conception, the funerary rites of Siyavush pre-date the Zoroastrian reform and belong, like many other old practices and beliefs, to the pagan traditions of Eastern Iran.[6]

But now the sacred aura and the ritual sanctity of the Karbala commemorations have assumed entirely sacerdotal proportions for the Shi'is and thus have been placed categorically outside the domain of theoretical speculations.

In a succession of social-anthropological studies ranging from *Totem and Taboo* (1913) to *Future of an Illusion* (1927), *Civilization and its Discontents* (1929), and *Moses and Monotheism* (1939), Sigmund Freud extended his psychoanalytic theories into active speculation about the origin of societies, cultures, religions, and civilizations. In the very first volume of *Totem and Taboo,* Freud daringly proposes a course of development from elementary forms of totemism toward the formation of advanced world religions, particularly in terms of the systematic mutation of "totemic sacrifice and the relation of son to father."[7] In varied forms of totemic gatherings, Freud observes, "the mourning is followed by demonstrations of festive rejoicing: every instinct is unfettered and there is licence for every kind of gratification." By way of further explanation, he adds, "a festival is a permitted, or rather an obligatory excess, a solemn breach of a prohibition. . . . Excess is of the essence of a festival; the festive feeling is produced by the liberty to do what is as a rule prohibited."[8]

The "totem meal" that the Shi'is partake on Zohr-e Ashura, if we were to follow Freud's argument through, is instrumental for the community "to stress their identity with" Imam Hossein as the subject of their sacrifice and mourning—both at the same time. During the course of the meal (through and not despite it), the sacred and heroic memory of the imam is simultaneously recollected, mourned, and celebrated. Freud considered the communal gatherings at such moments as "sanctification through participation in a common meal," and further added "the sense of guilt, which can only be allayed by the solidarity of all the participants, also persists." On such occasions, Freud then observes, the figure of the deity/father/hero becomes the object "with whom those who consume the meal become identified."[9] Freud then connects the serving of the totem meal to the ritual mutation of the father/hero figure into the God/Father figure. Freud's assumption is that "the totem" is nothing other than "a surrogate of the father," and that "the root of every form of religion [is] a longing for the father." The murder of the primal father, Freud further suggests, ultimately fails to generate the democratic aspiration of multiple sons succeeding him, and thus in their failure to reap the benefit of the murder they reverse and have a collective sense of remorse, and thus "their longing for him [the murdered father] increased."[10]

The possibility of looking at the feast on the Zohr-e Ashura as a "totem meal," and Muharram ceremonies in general as a collective act of atonement with a communal sense of primordial guilt, opens up the field of understanding the ritual, and provides a whole new manner of looking at the Karbala event not simply as a historical tragedy giving birth to a ritual drama but in fact as a central and enduring trauma of the faith. Freud's central concern is to link the "festive joy" and "the mourning over the death" of what is both the object of the mourners' veneration and the subject of their sacrifice—they mourn over the death of the hero and yet do so in an atmosphere of festive gathering of their emotions. To begin with, and as Freud is quick to point out, the community acquires a profound sense of "sanctity by consuming the totem," or the totemic meal that corporeally stands for him. This is a community-building proposition, in which members of the faith "reinforce their identification with it [the totemic object] and [through that] with one another." But there is a transformative element in the fact of taking in the meal (standing for the flesh and blood of the hero), and thus "their festive feelings and all that follows from them might well be explained by the fact that they have taken into themselves the sacred life of which the substance of the totem is the vehicle."[11]

According to Freud, "psychoanalysis has revealed that the totem animal is in reality a substitute for the father; and this tallies with the contradictory fact that, though the killing of the animal is as a rule forbidden, yet its killing becomes a festive occasion—the fact that it is killed and yet mourned." Freud extends this father complex all the way to his Oedipal theories, underlining the totemic constitution of the father figure as the originary moment of the ambivalence, whereby the founding father of the culture is at once murdered, mourned, and venerated. Admitting that his theory "may seem fantastic," Freud proposes to "bring together the psychoanalytic translation of the totem with the fact of the totem meal," reaching out for a theory of the primal horde whereby the Oedipal rivalry posits the band of brothers against a possessive and overbearing father.[12] Operating totally within the realm of pure theoretical speculation and at a primal moment of prehistory, Freud proposes the hypothesis that at this primary moment the band of brothers in fact gang up against their father, kill and devour him, and that "the totem meal, which is perhaps mankind's earliest festival, would thus be a repetition and a commemoration of this memorable and criminal deed, which was the beginning of so many things—of social organization, of moral restrictions and of religion."[13]

Are we during the Muharram ceremonies witness to a much distanced and recodified version of a primeval reenacting of the founding moment of social formations? Are Muslim Shi'is reconstituting their historical bonds through a communal ritual much more ancient than their recorded history? If so, what does that mean for the nature and disposition of the society that is today formed around such rituals, or the culture that they entail? For Freud, this was a theoretical exercise in figuring out social-anthropological antecedents for father complexes among children and neurotic patients—but also an attempt at a theory of morality, for at the root of his speculative sociology lies the fundamental category of "guilt": having killed, devoured, and gotten rid of the father, the sons now develop a sense of "deferred obedience," when the dead shadow of the father becomes in fact far more powerful than he might have ever been living and in person. The remorseful sons "thus created out of their filial sense of guilt the two fundamental taboos of totemism, which for that very reason inevitably corresponded to the two repressed wishes of the Oedipus complex" (murder and incest).[14]

What Freud was ultimately after was a social-anthropological (or perhaps even historical) theory of guilt and repression, at a communal and collective level. The strong identification of the band of brothers with their father is at the root of the incest taboo, and thus the strongest survival instinct at the root of what Freud terms "deferred obedience." This identification with the father in turn becomes the *conditio sine qua non* of the most basic human morality and subsequent religious organization of the community that historically succeeds this primeval phase. Freud is conscious of the power of repression in the civilizing function of totemism, for "totemism helped to smooth things over and to make it possible to forget the event [the band of brothers murdering their father in order to inherit his power over the community] to which it owed its origin." Freud's pronouncement about this originary moment of totemic trauma is categorical, universal, and compelling: "Totemic religion arose from the filial sense of guilt, in an attempt to allay that feeling and to appease the father by deferred obedience to him. All later religions are seen to be attempts at solving the same problem."[15]

Was this a primeval event that gave birth to world religions (Judaism, Christianity, Islam, for example), that was then recodified in overwhelmingly sacred and untouchable terms—so much so that the originary event was forever repressed? Or does every one of these religions reenact this primal moment in its own historical terms? Freud does impart a sense of historical recycling of the primal event, and this he offers via a comparative religious historiography. "When Christianity first penetrated into the ancient world," he offers,

> it met with competition from the religion of Mithras and for a time it was doubtful which of the two deities would gain the victory. In spite of the halo of light surrounding his form, the youthful Persian god [Mithras] remains obscure to us. We may perhaps infer from the sculptures of Mithras slaying a bull that he represented a son who was alone in sacrificing his father and thus redeemed his brothers from their burden of complicity in the deed. There was an alternative method of allaying their guilt and this was first adopted by Christ. He sacrificed his own life and so redeemed the company of brothers from original sin.[16]

So if we witness in Mithraism one son killing the father and redeeming the band of brothers, and in Christianity one son sacrificing himself and redeeming the brothers, then specific historical recurrences seem to reenact the primal murder, though with variations on the Freudian theme. In the case of Christianity, the figure of Christ is in fact doctrinally three in one: the Father, the Son, and the Holy Ghost. Thus in reconfiguring the "father-complex," Christ is in fact suicidal, infanticidal, and patricidal (as Freud would say) all at the same time. Sticking to his theory, though, Freud still insists, even in the case of Christianity, "if this sacrifice [of Christ the son] of a life brought about atonement with God the Father, the crime to be expiated can only have been the murder of the father."[17] In the case of Christianity, Freud further adds: "The very deed in which the son offered the greatest possible atonement to the father brought him at the same time to the attainment of his wishes *against* the father. He himself became God, beside, or, more correctly, in place of, the father. A son-religion displaced the father-religion."[18]

Given these historical recurrences of the primal murder, it is not then surprising that Freud narrows in on the Christian conception and practice of communion (which has the closest possible similarity to the Karbala commemoration, the communal meal at the Zohr-e Ashura in particular) as the most immediate and historically updated version of the "totemic meal." Continuing with his observation about Christianity becoming a son-religion, Freud observes:

> As a sign of this substitution the ancient totem meal was revived in the form of communion, in which the company of brothers consumed the flesh and blood of the son—no longer the father—obtained sanctity thereby and identified themselves with him. Thus we can trace through the ages the identity of the totem meal with animal sacrifice, with theanthropic human sacrifice and with the Christian Eucharist, and we can recognize in all these rituals the effect of the crime by which men were so deeply weighed down but of which they must none the less feel so proud. The Christian communion, however, is essentially a fresh elimination of the father, a repetition of the guilty deed. We can see the full justice of [J. G.] Frazer's pronouncement that "the Christian communion has absorbed within itself a sacrament which is doubtless far older than Christianity."[19]

From Golgotha to Karbala

If that be the case, and if Christianity is closest to Islam (and Shi'ism) in history, Passion (of Christ or Hossein), and ritual remembrances of their founding figure, then what about the drama/trauma of Karbala? How does that event pan out against the Freudian theory of primal murder and its ritual remembrance as the guilt-ridden kernel of its morality and normativity?[20]

The most important feature of Shi'ism, if we are to follow Freud's theory of totem and taboo, and the murder of the primal father as the origin of a guilt-ridden morality and normativity, is that Shi'ism is *not* a father-religion but in fact a son-religion. In this regard it is very similar to Christianity: it is the figure of a son (either Ali or Hossein) that is at the center of its traumatic narrative, and yet it is significantly dissimilar to Christianity in the sense that this particular son-figure (either Ali or

Hossein) does not have himself killed (as Freud suggests Christ does) but is killed by the father-figures. Thus Shi'ism cannot be considered a father-religion subconsciously aware of the guilt of patricide (the classical case of totem and taboo as Freud theorized it). It is instead a son-religion subconsciously aware of the guilt of infanticide (a religion of subsequent fathers afflicted by the guilt of having killed their son). This suggestion is corroborated by a succession of historical facts. For obvious historical reasons, we cannot take the father-figure of Muhammad as the center of either Islamic or Shi'i traumatic entry into history because he was not murdered but greatly loved, admired, feared, and emulated. His divine revelations and exemplary conduct are the principal sources of morality and normativity in Islam and Shi'ism alike. But we can certainly take Ali as the inaugural figure of Shi'ism and consider his murder in the year 661 as the traumatic point of departure for Shi'ism, for he was in fact a symbolic son-figure to Prophet Muhammad (his younger cousin and his son-in-law). Ali was violently opposed by the patriarchal legacy that preceded and in turn succeeded the Prophet, actively engaged in warfare by followers of the paternal figure of Uthman ibn Affan (the Third Rightly Guided Caliph of Muslims in general), and ultimately murdered by other Muslims adhering to alternative takes on the Prophet's legacy (the Kharijites)—all done in the name of a different reading of Prophet Muhammad's message and his prophetic legacy. We can also take Hossein ibn Ali—Ali's son and the Prophet's grandson—as the primary figure of the Shi'i trauma. He was opposed, fought against, and ultimately murdered by adherents of Umayyad tribal patrimonialism, again in the name of a more triumphant reading of Muhammad's prophetic legacy.[21]

The entire Karbala syndrome is quintessentially narrated around the trauma of infanticide and the guilt that is incumbent upon it. How could Muslims kill their beloved Prophet's own grandson so cold-bloodedly so soon after the death of the Prophet? That has been the running (guilt-ridden) leitmotif of generations of Muslim hagiography commemorating the Battle of Karbala. One could think through this leitmotif of the Karbala syndrome via any one of its key stories. For example, the story of Muslim ibn Aqil offers a major dramatic turning point in the saga in which we see the centrality of guilt at the heart of the Muharram chronicle.[22] Responding to the Kufans' repeated request that he come to their city to assume leadership of the anti-Umayyad movement but wary of their willingness to join his cause in earnest, Imam Hossein and his most devoted comrades head toward Kufa. Hossein sends his trusted warrior Muslim ibn Aqil in advance to assess the scene and the Kufan readiness to join his revolt. Upon his arrival in Kufa, Muslim ibn Aqil seeks haven at the house of another comrade of Imam Hossein, Hany ibn Urwah, but they are both arrested by Ubaydullah ibn Ziad, the governor of Kufa, and summarily executed. Their severed heads are thrown off the roof of the governor's palace into the Kufan crowd, who in turn run away in fear, never to think of joining any revolutionary cause again. If the story of Muslim ibn Aqil is at the heart of the sense of betrayal and guilt that defines the drama of Karbala, the cold-blooded murder of his two infant sons, Muhammad and Ibrahim, by the governor of Kufa is a premonition of what would soon happen to Imam Hossein and his children, and thus the paramount paradigmatic event of the entire Karbala syndrome—infants and young children murdered by their parental generation. Such a diagnosis extends also to Ali Asghar, Imam Hossein's youngest son, who is equally paradigmatic in marking the Karbala trauma as quintessentially a dramatic upstaging of infanticide.

What emerges from the story of Muslim ibn Aqil is the dramaturgical premonition that the people of Kufa are the simulacrum of the Muslim community at large (across time and space), ready in disguise to deceive and kill their own son-figure (in lieu of the Freudian father-figure). It is also from this story that we learn that the weapons of war that Hossein ibn Ali possesses and carries into the Battle of Karbala originally belonged to his grandfather, the Prophet himself, and thus symbolically (and instrumentally) identify the (grand) son with the (grand) father. Finally, in the story of Muslim ibn Aqil, Imam Hossein's envoy to Kufa has a premonition of the Kufans' betrayal of his soon-to-be martyred master. How, one might ask, is Muslim ibn Aqil so certain that the Kufans will betray and kill Hossein ibn Ali? One answer is that he has a saintly premonition of things to come; another that this is a case of divine predestination or a belief that (in its Shakespearean diction) "there's a divinity that shapes our ends." But an equally compelling dramaturgical factor (given the performative aspects of the play in front of live audiences) is that in Ta'ziyeh performances, the actor playing Muslim ibn Aqil is talking with and to the Shi'i audience watching this play. He is already aware of what will happen next—and thus effectively (dramatically) identifies the audience with the Kufans, reinflicting upon them the pain of vicarious guilt. Such an awareness was visible during the Islamic Revolution of 1979, when Iranian revolutionaries anticipated the arrival of Ayatollah Khomeini from Najaf in Iraq via Neauphle-le-Château in France and expressed their thoughts in a huge banner: *"Ma Ahl-e Kufa Nistim"* [We are not the people of Kufa]. If Muslim ibn Aqil is in fact talking to the audience, then the audience is effectively implicated in the crime—the audience *becomes* the Kufans. The guilt of Kufans betraying Imam Hossein transfuses and becomes the guilt of all Shi'is across history for having betrayed their martyred imam and thus in effect having "murdered" him. The entire drama of Ta'ziyeh thus emerges as the ceremonial reenactment of and atonement for having killed their bravest son.

The Shi'i version of the primal murder, prototypical to a son-religion version of the Freudian theory in his *Totem and Taboo,* posits the feast of Ashura as the functional equivalent of the Shi'i "communion." This reading of Shi'ism as a son-religion, predicated on a succession of ritual mourning over the murder of son-figures (from the Prophet's son-in-law Ali, to Ali's son Hossein, to Hossein's son Ali Asghar), thematically tallies perfectly with a similar theme in Persian national epic, particularly with the stories of Seyavash, the son of King Kavus, and Sohrab, the son of Rostam, in Ferdowsi's *Shahnameh.* In both the Seyavash and the Sohrab stories of the *Shahnameh,* the son-heroes are killed by their respective fathers, King Kavus and Rostam. Seyavash was killed via the circuitous way of being falsely accused by his stepmother Sudabeh of trying to rape her, then leaving his father's kingdom and getting killed while in the service of his arch-nemesis; Sohrab was killed by the father himself, inadvertently. In both these cases, Seyavash and Sohrab are the figurative counterparts of Imam Hossein, son-heroes tragically killed by their father-figures to sustain the dramatic course of the narrative history.[23] One can also trace another, non-Iranian tradition for this murder of the son, as evident in the Muslim Eid al-Adha (the Festival of Sacrifice), which is a commemoration of Abraham's willingness to sacrifice his son as commanded by God. (Muslim tradition names Ishmael as this son who was to be sacrificed, whereas the Judeo-Christian tradition names Isaac for the same purpose.) In either case, the substitution of a lamb for the son is a perfect text analogue for the Freudian totem theory, though in reverse. The son has not murdered his father, but the father is about to murder his son.

I have opted to follow this line of argument, the Freudian idea of son-religion, and see the theory to its logical conclusion. Alternatively we could abandon Freud altogether and follow the argument through Gilles

Deleuze's equally if not even more compelling reading of Leopold von Sacher-Masoch, in his *Coldness and Cruelty* (1969). In this case the son is actually substituting his body for the body of the father and by inflicting pain on his own body vicariously punishes the father. At this initial stage of looking at Shi'ism through such lines of thinking I opt to stay the course with Freud. But the idea of the murdered son bodily substituting for the father, whereby in the Shi'i (and Persian) culture the Oedipal complex is turned upside down and pseudo-masochistic, opens up a whole new line of investigation.[24]

The Civilizing Guilt

My turn to Freud for an understanding of the central trauma of Shi'ism was very much predicated on my childhood experiences of Karbala commemorations but later equally rooted in my reading of Freud through the work of my own teacher Philip Rieff, with whom I closely studied for some seven years as a graduate student at the University of Pennsylvania. Long after my early encounter with Shi'i ceremonies, and while working my way through Freud's psychoanalysis of guilt via Philip Rieff's sociology of culture, this evident paradox at the heart of the Muharram ceremony gradually assumed newer, more theoretically potent implications for me. At the heart of the Muharram ceremony is a profound sense of guilt for generation after generation of Shi'is who bemoan their inability to help Imam Hossein in his battle against the reigning caliph Yazid ibn Mu'awiyah. But there is something more palpable and pronounced about this sense of guilt, an ahistorical identification with the people of Kufa, the city that had promised to join Imam Hossein in his battle against Yazid, but did not. It was indeed a bizarre, belated, and much "deferred," as Freud would say, sense and mode of guilt-ridden identification. Why would generations of Shi'is, hundreds of years after Imam Hossein was murdered and dead, identify with people who did not support him, and try to prove that "*Ma Ahl-e Kufa Nistim*" [We are not Kufans], as a leading banner during the Islamic Revolution of Iran in 1979 said?[25] A prolonged sense of guilt, a paramount manifestation of introverted and overt violence, and above all a sustained sense of festivity were perhaps the most paramount and enduring aspects of Muharram ceremony, by far the most significant Shi'i ritual of collective atonement in Islamic history and doctrine—and I wondered why.

In his own work, beginning with *Freud: The Mind of the Moralist* (1959) and concluding posthumously with his *Charisma* (2008) and the multivolume *Sacred Order/Social Order* (2006–2008), Rieff had become increasingly preoccupied with the central civilizing function of guilt and repression in the cultural formation of what he called "the sacred order." Much of my own reading of Freud was under the influence of Rieff's theory of culture and the manner in which he had extended Freud's psychoanalysis of collective guilt into a powerful condemnation of contemporary (for Rieff "remissive") culture, under which palpitated a deeply engaging theory of cultural formations that originated in a collective sense of guilt and resulted in a civilizing function of repression. "A culture without repression, if it could exist," Rieff believed, "would kill itself in closing the distance between any desire and its object. Everything thought or felt would be done, on the instant . . . In a word, culture is repressive."[26]

Central to Rieff's theory of culture was Freud's psychoanalytic of collective guilt as the originary sentiment at the roots of all cultural formations, on which Freud perhaps best speculates in the last essay of *Totem and Taboo* (1913), "The Return of Totemism in Childhood." Rieff's theory of culture remained obscure and limited in circulation during his own lifetime and accessible only to a handful of his own students.[27] Rieff's political conservatism (which gained little foothold among generations influenced by progressive politics between the late 1950s to the early twenty-first century) was perhaps in part accountable for this obscurity, though that conservatism was a mere shadow of his much more ambitious theoretical project of a post-Judaic articulation of the sacred that went positively archeological in its search for the hidden and repressed layers of subterranean convictions and sacred pronouncements. "No society can exist," Rieff believed, "none of its very particular moralities conveyed, except through distortions and distancings of passions achieved in the repressive design of their conveyance into consciousness."[28] Rieff probed into the making of those "distortions and distancings" through a theory of culture that was launched from the site of what he called "the psychological man," namely from the Freudian citation of the guilt-ridden repressed, which a lucrative and triumphant therapeutic industry has sought to cure, curate, medicate, and treat. By detecting and arguing a site of morality in Freud, Rieff zeroed in on the borderline between what he argued to be a civilizing pathology on one side and a liberating barbarism on the other. "Repression," he said, "is truth experienced negationally." In his writing, he balanced tantalizingly on the borderline, where he could theorize better, but his political demeanor and social conservatism actively obscured his far more liberating theoretical acuity.[29]

Rieff's principal concern with Freud (and thus their mutual insights into the working of collective guilt in making a sacred memory operative) was with the nodal complexity of the civilizing function of guilt and the revelatory nature of repression.[30] Rieff's critique of modernity was far less about what he considered its *remissive* culture than with its extension of that remissive occasion into much wider domains than any sacred order could tolerate and not break. With the transgressive and remissive forces he thought operative in a culture and toward its inhibitions, Rieff always negotiated a careful and caring balance between moral absolutism (which he dreaded) and licentious anarchy (to which he was always attracted more as a psychoanalyst and a sociologist than as a moral police officer). The therapeutic culture, he thought, was too much on the side of saccharine solutions, sunny-side-up delivery from civilizing guilt and release from creative repression. This mutation of critical theory into a lucrative industry, Rieff was convinced, was not what Freud had intended. Rather, the psychoanalytic industry had brought the "psychological man" (of vintage modernity) and "the economic man" (of Enlightenment origin) together to break down the fortitude of the "religious" (for Rieff, Judeo-Christian-Islamic) and the "political" (Greek) man—as Rieff understood them to have been formed from the Greek, to Judeo-Christian-Islamic, to Enlightenment precedents of the Freudian master narrative of neurosis. Whereas in *Freud: The Mind of the Moralist* (1959), Rieff was consistently analytical in his grasp of guilt and repression as the inner and hidden circles of the civilizing trajectory, by the time he wrote *The Triumph of the Therapeutic* (1966), he was full throttle into a critique of (rational, capitalist, consumerist, agnostic) modernity and the rise of the psychoanalytic industry—an industry in which the psychological man and the culture of remissive occasions had successively sought to overcome the civilizing inhibitions. By the time he wrote and published his *Fellow Teachers* (1973), Rieff's language had become positively prophetic, revelatory, aphoristic. (It was at this time when, as his student, I read Nietzsche and Kierkegaard closely and together.) When the second edition of *Fellow*

Teachers came out (1984), Rieff opted to give it a subtitle, *Of Culture and Its Second Death,* and wrote a new preface for the book. (At this time he was diagnosed with acute angina and was terribly concerned about his health and mortality.)

"Every order of actual existence," Rieff believed, "individual and collective, character and culture, derives from the recurrent splitting motion by which master passions are kept at a civilizing distance from direct enactment. Repression, not sublimation, represents the ruling power of culture."[31] That repression, for both Rieff and Freud, was the negational machinery of cultures and their civilizing inhibitions. However, Freud sought to identify and expose them, whereas Rieff thought it necessary, even imperative, for them to remain concealed. Freud created a psychoanalytic discipline out of exposing and examining guilty conscience and its repressive concealments. Rieff crafted a theory of culture out of dwelling on the borderline of revealing and (as he used to say) reveiling them. "Repression lets there be done on a deep but narrow front what is not to be done more broadly."[32] He was, if I were to reduce him to a formula, in favor of those doings of repression on the "deep and narrow front," while sublating the doing of them "more broadly" in an aesthetic theory of cultural creativity—albeit hidden behind a cultural conservatism that put people off and prevented them from reading him more closely. From this civilizing sense of guilt and its ensuing creative repression, Rieff developed a theory of culture always predicated on the centrality of the sacred: "Even toward the end of his career as a theoretical man, Freud never ceased to write out his hidden grievance against the sense of guilt as the agency of the sacred in its juridical function."[33] Rieff had no normative or moral conception of this guilt—but always a combination of analytical distance and aesthetic sensibility: "In its purity, the sense of guilt is unnatural; it does not receive except to reject; it does not feel except to judge. Other senses are openings out; the sixth sense, of guilt, is a closing in. Every other sense participates in the sixth. To give a major example: as the eye closes, so innocence ends—too often and automatic for counting."[34]

In Rieff's theory of culture dwells an enduring psychoanalysis of guilt, informing a sociology of repression—all made possible by detecting in Freud what the psychoanalytic industry had lucratively left behind. To make that sociology of the civilizing repression possible, this is how Rieff understood and extended Freud's theory of enabling/disabling guilt:

> He [Freud] supposed guilt the normal attitude of an individual toward authority, social as well as individual. One of his favorite theses is that human beings have an ineradicable social heritage of guilt. The great religions are attempts to solve the problem of guilt: they are all "reactions to the same great event," the murder of the primal father, "with which civilization began and which, since it occurred, has not allowed mankind a moment's rest." Religion attempts to appease the sense of guilt; at the same time, only by perpetuating it (by such commemorative repetitions of the parricidal act as the Christian communion) does the authority of the faith continue. Morality too stands under the sign of guilt. The best behavior of which we are capable is "at bottom" an attempt "to conciliate the injured father through subsequent obedience." The social and religious meaning of guilt is summed up by Freud in the following formula: society was "based on complicity in the common crime; religion was based on the sense of guilt and remorse attached to it, while morality was based partly on the exigencies of this society and partly on the penance demanded by the sense of guilt." The sense of guilt is thus the pivot for Freud's conception of morality and religion. Religion . . . proceeds by "fomenting an ever-increasing sense of guilt" . . . Man is a remorseful killer, and religion is the history of his guilt.[35]

Rieff's own moral and theoretical project was to ask the one important question that Freud (and next to him Otto Rank) did not ask, and perhaps did not wish to ask: "but why guilt at all? The animals feel none . . . But Freud refused to go the one step further, to admit the universality of guilt . . . Whatever so evidently tore man out of the context of nature was itself repressed."[36] Rieff's project was to uncover this repression of the repression, Freud's own repression, his having discovered a theory of the sacred, "a vision of the highest," as Rieff used to call it, and yet being too repressively worldly and analytical to see or suggest it.

The Pain and Pleasure of a Paradox

The ritual gathering of Shi'is every Muharram and Safar on the Islamic calendar reenacts their history in the morality play of their habitual repression of the guilt that has brought them together as a people, a culture, a universe of significant affiliation with the cosmic character of who they are. The ritual is paradoxically joyous, mournfully playful, introverted while gregarious. To understand it, we need nothing more than one layer of de-codification from its heavily codified Shi'i historiography, into the more archaic manners and modes of guilt-invested occasions of civil, civic, communal, and civilizational formations, for which Freud and Rieff offer one possible line of investigation in detecting a manner of deferred obedience that keeps a community of believers on its moral toes. Cultures for Rieff, following neurosis for Freud, began with sons murdering their fatherly figures, incurring guilt, and then spending a history living with the civilizing consequences of that repressed guilt and its remorseful implications. But how would that idea pan out with Muslim history? Muslims certainly did not kill Muhammad, but they did kill his beloved grandson Hossein. So Islam as a civilizing act began not with the killing of the father but with the murder of the son. This is how Shi'ism may begin to make sense, in a theory of culture that underwrote a psychoanalysis of guilt, as a son-religion, which multiplied by its deferred obedience results in a youthful religion launched against successive generations of fathers for having killed their sons and widowed their daughters. The masculinist and phallogocentric character of this entire line of argument will have to be corrected via a critical rereading of the sort that Luce Irigaray, for example, offers—particularly given the fact that mothers are the primary carriers and transmitters of cultures in contexts and narratives that I offer here.[37]

What Shi'ism as a son-religion amounts to is a combustive combination of deferred obedience and the guilt of infanticide coming together to make a revolutionary faith, antiauthoritarian and quintessentially distrustful of the authority of father-figures in position of power. Under these cultural circumstances, sons are legitimate as long as they are afraid of being killed by their fathers, who are in a position of power, and are fighting against their institutional authority. The instant the sons come to power, the sons themselves become usurpers of power, renewed father-figures, and as such identify with the fathers they have always fought (and even forced into exile or killed). Thus they become resentful of the youthful vigor with which their own sons are fighting them. This disabling/enabling paradox is the engine of Shi'ism in history, of history in Shi'ism—as a religion of protest.

Shi'ism is a festive occasion of ritually remembering its murderous myth of origin in ever more forgetful ways. The combined effect of a deferred obedience, as Freud understood it, and infanticide, as opposed to what Freud prototypically considered the patricidal origin of all religions and cultures, has cast Shi'ism into a state of permanent deferral, constituting a deferred future that is guilt-ridden not for having killed the father but for having murdered the son (the Prophet's grandson in Karbala). In political terms this has amounted to a state of permanent revolutionary defiance. In specifically political terms, this mythic disposition of Shi'ism has turned it into a charismatic semiotics of defiant signs, categorically cast against the historically legislated signifiers of meaning, permanence, and institutions. Thus while Islam as a world religion has gone through its history apace, Shi'ism has been on its periphery fomenting dissent. Seen in this light, I propose Shi'ism as the dream/nightmare of Islam itself as it goes about the world. It represents a promise made but yet undelivered to itself and to the world. As a religion of protest, Shi'ism is a total and complete narrative, its own closure, opposed and as opposed to the worldly character of Islam. Shi'ism thus resists paradigmatic shifts by way of a disabling/enabling paradox written into its myth of origin.

There is thus a fundamental twist to the Freudian theory of deferred obedience when we apply it to Shi'ism, for in Shi'ism what we see is the exact opposite of deferred obedience. Instead we witness a permanent state of deferred defiance—a defiance in the making, a defiance to come. What the Shi'is have deferred in the aftermath of the murder of their primordial son is not obedience—it is defiance. Because the central trauma of Shi'ism is the killing of a primordial son and not a primordial father, Shi'ism has remained a quintessentially youthful religion, the religion of the young revolutionaries defying the patriarchal order of things. This is not to disregard the paramount significance of the patristic generation of Shi'i jurists, a handful of old men who gathered mainly in medieval Baghdad and wrote the jurisprudential backbone of the faith under exceedingly dire circumstances, but to place that fact next to the enduring revolutionary zeal that produced the revered pages of the Shi'i theology with blood and in the battlefields of its combative history—Karbala, in other words, writ large.

Seen in this light, Shi'ism, I propose, was born out of a major historical trauma, early in Islamic history, the trauma of killing the son in lieu of the father, in which case redemption becomes ipso facto an impossibility. At the heart of Shi'ism remains the trauma of a denial—that Ali was denied his right to succeed the Prophet as his divinely ordained deputy; and a trauma of betrayal—that Hossein was invited to Kufa to lead the anti-Umayyad rebellion to reclaim his murdered father's right but was left to be murdered along with a handful of his closest comrades.

Times for the Shi'is ever since have been out of joint, and they believe themselves sent to set it right—from then to eternity, until the End of Time, when the Mahdi, the Messiah, comes and takes the matter in his own hands.

After a long and arduous medieval history, raising the banner of revolt across the Muslim lands, Shi'ism reached colonial modernity in the nineteenth and twentieth centuries ready for a sustained course of combative contestation with its evolving history.[38] Today in Iraq and Lebanon, and above all in Iran, Shi'ism seems to have ceased to be a mere branch within the larger context of Islam. It has emerged as a global claim demanding the most urgent political attention. Shi'ism is now in its combative mode again—always reminiscent of its traumatic birth in early Islamic history. The combative Hezbollah in Lebanon claims Shi'ism, as do the ruling ayatollah in Iran, and as does the defiant Mahdi's Army resisting the imperial domination of their homeland in Iraq. All declare their active loyalties to a religion of protest that has defined their revolutionary progeny for almost fourteen hundred years.

Today on the battleground of Shi'ism in contemporary history we are witness to the death of a metaphor constitutional to a religion of protest—the death of Karbala as the defining allegory of a people. Today, that defining metaphor has been de-sedimented, either over-aestheticized (in the work of such globalized artists as Abbas Kiarostami and Shirin Neshat) or else over-politicized (in the work of militant rebels such as Muqtada al-Sadr and Shaykh Hassan Nasrallah). The critical balance and the creative transmutation of the two into each other is overwhelmed by the enormity of events that Shi'is face. Today, the central metaphor of Shi'ism has metastasized and broken down into either scholastic learning with no intellectual bearing on the epistemic predicament of a postmodern world, or else a militant adventurism with no political tolerance for its rival claims to opposing adventurous imperialism of the sort operative from Central Asia to North Africa.

The fundamental challenge facing Shi'ism today is that it now operates outside its historic cosmopolitan context, and it has been transmuted (just like the triumphalist imperialism it opposes) into a singular and contrapuntally triumphalist religion, and as such it has lost its expansive and emancipatory character, for the measure of violence in it is no longer conducive to a moral imperative of embracing the world and seeking to right its wrongs.[39] At its normative, scholastic, political, and intellectual height during the Safavid period (1501–1722), Shi'ism was integral to a cosmopolitan culture that had a transcendent humanism written into its worldly character. But in its most recent combative mood during the nineteenth and twentieth centuries, Shi'ism had to thrive in a cosmopolitanism of a different sort and compete with Third World socialism and anticolonial nationalism for the soul and trust of millions of disenfranchised masses to stand and oppose their tormentors. Today Shi'ism has lost that cosmopolitan character, that universal conception of itself, that catholicity of learning definitive to its medieval claim on most pious convictions. And yet, as on battlegrounds extended from Iran to Iraq to Lebanon, Shi'ism is identified with violent uprisings and militant resistance against an imperial domination of the globe. A normative alterity that has always been the contrapuntal character trait of Shi'ism is fomenting dissent among the Iranian youth, in the midst of the Iraqi artists, and in the defiant soul of the Lebanese militia fighting against the military invasion and occupation of their homeland. Thus in Shi'ism today is also evident the budding signs of a renewed cosmopolitanism, reaffirming its worldliness, with an alterity written to its emerging theology, a resolution of the Shi'i paradox in the parallax of a world at odds with itself.

Memories and Dreams, Facts and Fantasies

On Si-Metri Avenue between our home in Ardeshir Street and the Masjed-e Bushehri-ha on the opposite side of Meydan-e Mojassameh in Ahvaz, there used to be an almost inconspicuous *saqqa-khaneh*. Saqqa-khaneh is a peculiar Shi'i institution. It is a small cubicle of a water station where passersby can stop and have a drink of water for free. This particular saqqa-khaneh in my hometown was a grand architectural structure rendered in miniature. It was covered externally with modest blue, green, and white tiles and decorated with Persian calligraphy, all singing the praises of the Prince of Martyrs Imam Hossein, the most prominent of which was "*Fada-ye Lab-e Teshnat Ya Aba Abdullah!*" [Were I to Sacrifice my Life for your Thirsty Lips, Oh Imam Hossein!] The tradition has it that Imam Hossein and his family and friends were all killed during warm days near Karbala and while they were thirsty.[40] As a result water and thirst have assumed iconic significance for the Shi'is. There was a small copper faucet extending from one of the walls of this saqqa-khaneh facing the street from which the passersby could have a sip of water, quench their thirst, remember the day of Karbala, whisper under their breath the same formulaic recollection, *"Fada-ye Lab-e Teshnat Ya Aba Abdullah!"* and then go about their business. I remember that this saqqa-khaneh had a very tiny door behind which occasionally an old man sat comfortably in front of a tray full of lit candles surrounded by green and black draperies, with perhaps a suggestion of red somewhere too. There were copper bowls of various sizes, plus an assortment of religious objects, odds and ends and amulets for which I could never imagine any particular use. The old man, the covered tray with the lit candles, the aging draperies, and all those strange objects were part and parcel of each other, woven and written into each other, like a visual whisper, suggestive and symbolic, allegorical and simply too significant to signify anything in particular, but everything together comprised an ensemble, the scattered and collected paraphernalia of a sanctity creating an organic world of fear and trust at the same time together, a comforting haven that looked like a menacing cave. That this saqqa-khaneh actually existed and that from that copper fountain I drank water on countless occasions throughout my childhood, and that upon finishing my sip of water I whispered my most sincere *"Fada-ye Lab-e Teshnat Ya Aba Abdullah!"* I am absolutely certain, but of actually glimpsing its interior and seeing that old man staring at a sea of lit candles, I am not. Maybe I actually saw it, maybe I have dreamt it, imagined it, or perhaps (and most probably) confabulated all these things—a glimpse of reality flowering in time into introverted branches of my memories and coming to fruition in my mind.

On the porous borderlines of memories and dreams, facts self-evident and fantasies made significant, realities banal and passing feeding their own transmutations into enduring signposts of a meaningful life, and then above all visions of things otherwise unseen, dwells a knowledge of self as the microcosmic evidence of the universe one inhabits. This evidence has been the cornerstone of Shi'i theology, philosophy, mysticism, and drama. *"Man 'Arafa Nafsahu"* (Shi'is believe in their innermost mystic convictions), *"faqad 'Arafa Rabbahu"* [Know Thyself to Know Thy Lord]. All Shi'i theology is at its heart a response to an anthropology, a knowledge of the human, the all-too-human. It is useless to read (Shi'i as any other) theology, philosophy, mysticism, and drama abstracted from the quest for an anthropology—a knowledge of the selfsame human who philosophizes—to which they are all, after all, a dialogical response.

I

DOCTRINAL FOUNDATION

1

DEATH OF A PROPHET

Some of the most cherished memories of my late childhood and early adolescence are from summer trips I took with my parents and younger brother Aziz, at times in the company of my Aunt Batul and my cousins Sharifeh, Fattaneh, and Hossein, to the holy city of Mashhad in the province of Khurasan, in the northeastern part of Iran. If you were to draw a line on an Iranian map diagonally from where we lived in Ahvaz (in the southwest), you would find Mashhad. Because my father worked for the Iranian National Railroad, among his annual benefits were roundtrip train tickets during the summer for him and his family from our hometown to anywhere on the national railroad network. Soon after school was over in early July, we would travel from Ahvaz to Qom, because my mother was convinced that if we did not first pay our respects to Hazrat-e Ma'sumeh's shrine, we could not go on to Mashhad, our ultimate destination. If we failed to perform our most pious duties in Qom, as soon as we arrived in Mashhad, Imam Ali al-Rida, our Eighth Shi'i Imam, who has been buried there for some twelve hundred years, would ask (in the metaphysical language and universe in which my mother was always in conversation and communion with her favorite prophets, imams, and saints) why it was that we did not first go to visit his sister in Qom?

Among the most popular items to purchase for souvenirs and as *soghati* [gifts for friends and family] from Mashhad were *tasbih* [colorful rosaries], *ja-namaz* [prayer rugs], loads of saffron, clothing items, black or colorful pieces of garment for chador, and, particularly popular, pictures (or *temsal,* "likenesses," as we were instructed to call them) of Prophet Muhammad and Imam Ali, printed on pieces of cloth or woven into carpets of various sizes and textures. *Temsal-e Mobarak-e Haz-*

rat-e Peyghambar [The Noble Likeness of the Holy Prophet] and *Temsal-e Mobarak-e Hazrat-e Amir* [The Noble Likeness of the Holy Prince (of Believers)—the honorific title of Ali ibn Abi Talib] were among the most cherished items purchased as souvenirs and soghati. In the Mashhad bazaar we were never allowed to call these transactions "purchases," however. We would ask not "How much does this cost?" but *"Hedyash chand misheh?"* [How much would the "gift" be for this?]

There was something peculiar about these temsals of Prophet Muhammad and Imam Ali: they looked almost identical. They were in a roundabout way the pious Iranian artists' visions of holy Arab male features. They both sported green turbans, signs of their identical hallowed sanctity. Muhammad's picture would ordinarily feature a copy of the Holy Qur'an in his hand, whereas Ali's picture was more often than not featured with his famous sword, which had a name, *Dhu al-Fiqar* [the Two-Edged Sword]. Under the picture of Muhammad would be a phrase like *"La ilaha illa Allah, Muhammadan Rasul Allah"* [There is no God except Allah, Muhammad is his Messenger]; or alternatively *"Qulu La ilaha illa Allah wa Tuflahu!"* [Say! There is no God but Allah and be Saved!]. Ali's picture would have a caption like *"La fata illa Ali la Sayf illa Dhu al-Fiqar"* [There is no (more valiant) youth than Ali, and no (sharper) sword than Dhu al-Fiqar], or at times a Persian phrase like *"Ali: Nuri keh hargez khamush nemishavad"* [Ali: A Light that will never die out]. The Prophet's picture would rarely appear with a Persian phrase, but Ali's would more regularly.

A Traveler's Religion

Islam is a religion of travelers, voyagers, sojourners, people at home away from home; a migratory religion, for it began as a journey, a *hijra,* a migration, an emigration, a moving out of habitual comforts, with Prophet Muhammad's journeys, two journeys in particular that were definitive to his divine intervention. The first was when he ascended from Earth to the heavens [*Mi'raj*] to meet with Almighty the Creator, and the second soon afterward when he emigrated from Mecca to Medina to inaugurate the Muslim calendar and to establish his *ummah,* the community, the gathering of humanity to acknowledge and sing the praise of Almighty God, and to do right and be righteous. Islam was established by a Messenger [*al-rasul*], someone who had gone, traveled nocturnally somewhere else, and then came back with a message, a vision, a mission, a divine soghati. The first Muslims were those who traveled with the Prophet, the *Muhajirun* [the Emigrants], in the year 622, and then those who helped them adjust to their new environment in Medina, the *Ansar* [the Helpers]. Muhajirun and Ansar were the first Muslims, a band of brothers and sisters, the immigrants and those who helped them; and thus the metaphor of a journey, a pilgrimage, a *hijra,* a moving out, has remained definitive to Islam and to Muslims ever since. Muslims are those who travel, from *jahiliyyah* [pre-Islamic ignorance] to Islam, from *kofr* to *iman,* from disbelief to belief, from comfort to struggle, from the habitual to the engrossing.

Monotheistic prophets, Shi'i imams, and Sufi saints are ordinary people who have gone on a journey and come back with a gift, a soghati, with something to give, something to show, something to tell. A journey to Mecca, *Hajj* pilgrimage, is the highest aspiration and the most sublime duty of a pious Muslim—millions of them have done so on foot, over the centuries and from the four corners of the Earth. *Four Journeys* [*al-Asfar al-Arba'ah*] is the title of the most famous philosophical treatise of Mulla Sadra Shirazi (1571–1640), by far the most distinguished Shi'i philosopher.[1] Long before Mulla Sadra, Nasir Khusraw Qubadyani (1004–1088), a maverick Shi'i intellectual of the Isma'ili branch, wrote one of the earliest travelogues in Persian literature, *Safarnameh,* by way of recording the manner of his conversion from an idle and useless life to the committed work of a visionary philosopher, poet, and activist. Long after Mulla Sadra, Sohrab Sepehri (1928–1980), in a poetic register not too far removed from his cultural identification as an Iranian Shi'i, repeatedly used the metaphor of journey as the sacrosanct act of delivering himself to and from this world. *Safar, rihla,* both meaning journey in Persian and Arabic, and above all *hijra,* when with body and soul one moves from one state of being into another, is where Islam in motion has rested its case, where Shi'ism extends, amplifies, and multiplies the ritual pilgrimage to Mecca [*Hajj*] into the normative metaphor of what it means to be a Shi'i.

On the single most important earthly journey upon which Islam was founded, on the night of the Prophet's clandestine journey from Mecca to Medina (on Thursday, 9 September 622) to establish the Muslim community, the Shi'i tradition has it that his young and valiant cousin and son-in-law Ali slept in the Prophet's bed to disguise his flight. This night is so important for the Shi'is that they have given it a special name, *Laylat al-Mabiyt,* the night that Ali impersonated the Prophet. Shi'is believe that special verses of the Qur'an were revealed on that night about the virtue of Ali and in praise of his having endangered his life to save the Prophet's.[2] That nocturnal slipping into the Prophet's empty bed to cover for him as he went out to establish and propagate his divine mission is one among many inaugural moments when, for the Shi'is, Muhammad and Ali, their last Prophet and their first imam, become metamorphic. *"Ana Madinat al-'Ilm wa Aliun Babuha,"* says the Prophet on one occasion, according to the Shi'is: "I am the city of knowledge, and Ali is its gate." *"Man Kuntu Mawlahu fa-hadha Ali Mawlahu,"* says another tradition: "To whomever I am a Comrade/Leader, this Ali is a Comrade/Leader."[3] In the visual representations of Prophet Muhammad and Imam Ali, piously produced by devout artists in holy cities around the Shi'i world, Muhammad and Ali become pictorially metamorphic, symbolically metaphoric, one standing for the other. Persian miniature paintings show Archangel Gabriel descending upon Muhammad and Ali and wondering to which one it should give the divine message. An extremist branch of Shi'ism carried this metaphoric proclivity to its rhetorical conclusion and believed Ali to be a manifestation of divinity himself.[4] For the Shi'is prophets and imams are metamorphic, they fade in and out of each other, prototypically cast between Prophet Muhammad and Imam Ali.

Metamorphic Metaphors

The metamorphic characters of Muhammad and Ali in the Shi'i pious imagination, while upholding the strict doctrinal hierarchy of *Nubuwwah* [prophethood] over *Imamah* [imamhood], ultimately point toward the original charismatic disposition of Muhammad's prophetic mission. At the same time, the key question of charisma (how it is attained and what it means in an Islamic/Shi'i context) is central to our understanding of Prophet Muhammad's own authority as he first established Islam as a world religion. Shi'ism, in turn, will have to be understood as an attempt to perpetuate this charismatic moment of Muhammad's prophetic presence. An understanding of charisma in how Muhammad established his own authority over a period of more than twenty years is imperative to how the Shi'is understand their imams and how worldly struggle (which can extend from intellectual restlessness to political uprising) becomes definitive to Shi'ism.

"We shall understand 'prophet' to mean a purely individual bearer of charisma, who by virtue of his mission proclaims a religious doctrine or divine commandment," the German sociologist Max Weber observed.[5] Weber's famous turn to the concept of charisma was crucial in his sociology of religion, and in his typology of authority, which included traditional, rational/legal, and charismatic domains.[6] Equally important was this turn to an originally Christian concept (but through Max Weber radically recoded for a universal sociological use) for what Weber methodologically championed as a *Verstehendesoziologie.*[7] By methodically and comparatively recoding the Christian concept of *charisma* (or "gift of grace"), Weber enabled an entire generation of comparative sociology otherwise impossible and flawed. In crafting this crucial sociological concept and carrying it away from its doctrinal implication within the Christian dogma, Weber qualified his typology as not being (initially) "concerned . . . with the question [of] whether the followers of a prophet are more attracted to his person, as in the cases of Zoroaster, Jesus, and Muhammad, or to his doctrine, as in the case of Buddha and the prophets of Israel."[8] It is important to keep in mind at the outset, however, following Weber's own typology of two types of prophets—ethical and exemplary—that in the case of Muhammad the "doctrines" articulated in the Qur'an are as important for Muslims (if not more) as Muhammad's own character and his sayings and doings [*sunnah*].

Expanding on the notion of charisma, Weber emphasized the significance of "the personal call," which distinguishes the prophet from the priest. Whereas the priest's claim to authority results from services to an already established sacred tradition or ecclesiastical order, "the prophet's claim is based on personal revelation and charisma."[9] The manner in which the rabbinic class in Judaism or the priestly class in Christianity is in fact "authorized" by virtue of their moral and normative descent from their respective prophetic traditions is almost identical with the manner in which the class of *'ulama,* the learned clerical establishment known and honored for their knowledge of Islamic law, are authorized by virtue of their interpretative authority over Muhammad's exemplary conduct and his Qur'anic revelations. Weber makes a crucial connection between the prophet and the magician only by way of making an even more central distinction between them. "The prophet, like the magician, exerts his power simply by virtue of his personal gift. Unlike the magician, however, the prophet claims definite revelations, and the core of his mission is doctrine or commandment, not magic."[10] The structural link between the charismatic origin of the authority and the definite revelations that at once authorize and authenticate that charisma and thereby legislate the normative and moral mandates of the emerging community is where Muhammad's prophetic mission best fits a Weberian sociology of authority.

What exactly is the nature and function of this "charisma" that preoccupied Weber? "It was only under very unusual circumstances," he believed, "that a prophet succeeded in establishing his authority without charismatic authentication, which in practice meant magic."[11] This "authentication" effectively worked through an active (or even implicit) dialectic. The more successful a prophet was in his worldly (political) affairs, the more his claim to charismatic authority was verified and accommodated. "It is characteristic of the prophets," Weber believed, "that they do not receive their mission from any human agency, but seize it, as it were."[12] This "seizing" implicates a worldly context in which Muhammad's prophetic mission, as an example, had to be negotiated via a tightly adjacent set of parallels between political action and related (at times almost impromptu) divine revelation. The followers of Muhammad (as a Messenger of God) are thus put in a very peculiar position, for their obedience to him is given in hope of their own salvation and is not the source of the Prophet's charismatic authority—and yet (paradoxically) without that politically tangible and worldly obedience that authority becomes socially irrelevant.

Weber was quite conscious of Muhammad's charismatic authority and characterized it as "fundamentally political in its orientation . . . and his position in Medina, which was in between that of an Italian *podesta* and that of Calvin at Geneva, grew primarily out of his purely prophetic mission. A merchant, he was first a leader of pietistic conventicles in Mecca, until he realized more and more clearly that the organization of the interests of warrior clans in the acquisition of booty was the external basis for his missionizing."[13] What Weber calls "the external basis" of Muhammad's charismatic authority is one of the two major pillars of authority in general. (Weber called one "inner justification" and the other "external means.") Elsewhere Weber posited these two pillars as the *conditio sine qua non* of any form of (legitimate) authority.[14] The dialectic of these two forces—one internal to the message and the reception of a divine mission and the other worldly and external to it—morphs and amounts to a charismatic condition that can no longer distinguish between one and the other. The more the inner justification is powerful among the believers, one might argue, the less would be the need for external means, and the less convincing that inner justification might be or become the more need exists for those external means to act as an impetus for obedience. So far as Prophet Muhammad is concerned, some people were attracted to his divine message for purely religious reasons and others joined his cause out of sheer opportunism and material interests; the combination made his prophetic movement ultimately successful.

Weber was equally conscious of the role of Qur'anic revelations in authoring and authenticating Muhammad's charismatic authority. While suggesting differences between prophets and philosophers he maintained: "What primarily differentiates such figures [philosophers] from the prophets is their lack of that vital emotional preaching which is distinctive of prophecy, regardless of whether this is disseminated by the spoken word, the pamphlet, or any other type of literary composition (e.g., the *suras* of Muhammad)."[15] The *suras* [chapters] of the Qur'an are an integral element in the historical unfolding of Muhammad's charismatic authority and the formation of his expansive community. These revelations were not delivered in one act, but verse by verse and chapter by chapter, extended over a period of twenty-three years, each representing a particular phase in Muhammad's prophetic mission. The Qur'anic revelations map out Muhammad's prophetic mission and are instrumental in authoring his charismatic authority.

In his famous typology of prophets, Max Weber identified two distinct types, "one represented most clearly by the Buddha, the other with especial clarity by Zoroaster and Muhammad": the first type he called "exemplary," where "the prophet . . . [is] an exemplary man who, by his personal example, demonstrates to others the way to religious salvation, as in the case of Buddha"; the second type he called "ethical," where "the prophet . . . [is] an instrument for the proclamation of a god and his will, be this a concrete command or an abstract term. Preaching as one who has received a commission from god, he demands obedience as an ethical duty"—and the examples Weber provides are Zoroaster and Muhammad.[16] What is crucial in our understanding of Muhammad's charismatic authority, and the consequence of this charismatic disposition on the Shi'i conception of the divinely ordained charisma of their infallible imams, is that by Weber's definition Muhammad was both an ethical and an exemplary prophet. He was ethical by virtue of the Qur'anic revelations that were given to him and were communally believed to be of divine origin and quite independent of Muhammad's own character, except that he was a messenger who brought them to the Muslim community. But for Muslims the actual doings and sayings of their prophets—doings that were out of his earthly and worldly character and sayings that were not believed to be divine revelations—do in fact make him an exemplary prophet too, for Muslims seek in earnest to do and to say as he did. Above all, the compilation of these sayings and doings in the form of the canonical collection of *hadith* constitute the second most important source of Islamic law (after the Qur'an).

In retrospect, one might suggest that if the Sunnis (the overwhelming majority of Muslims) opted for the ethical dimension of the Prophet's mission and assimilated his exemplary conduct into the systematized doctrine of Islamic law [*shari'ah*] and jurisprudence [*fiqh*], the Shi'is did not want to let go of their Prophet's exemplary character and thus sought to extend his charismatic presence to their imams. For the Shi'is the ethical was necessary but not sufficient. They crafted their own law but sustained their insistence on the personal presence of an imam, investing him with *ilham* [inspiration] to continue with their Prophet's *wahy* [revelations]—a hermeneutic take on the textual evidence of a narrative that the Shi'is wished to prolong.

Weber's ultimate objective in his understanding of the character of the prophet is to assess the manner in which he facilitates a cosmic reading of the world. "Regardless of whether a particular religious prophet is predominantly of the ethical or predominantly of the exemplary type," he believed,

> prophetic revelation involves for both the prophet himself and for his followers—and this is the element common to both varieties—a unified view of the world derived from a consciously integrated and meaningful attitude toward life. To the prophet, both the life of man and the world, both social and cosmic events, have a certain systematic and coherent meaning. To this meaning the conduct of mankind must be oriented if it is to bring salvation, for only in relation to this meaning does life obtain a unified and significant pattern.[17]

This is where Weber yields his sociological language to a metaphysical underpinning of a religious visionary with enduring historical consequences: "The ultimate question of all metaphysics has always been something like this: if the world as a whole and life in particular were to have a meaning, what might it be, and how would the world have to look in order to correspond to it?"[18] That "meaning" for the Shi'is originates in an absolutist monotheism, of *Tawhid,* of a divine will to create and guide toward salvation, a corresponding *Nubuwwah,* whereby God sends charismatic emissaries to warn and make promises to humanity, and a further correspondence to *Imamah,* whereby these prophets appoint their successors, equally infallible and inspired to continue to lead the community on the right path. This trilateral root of a Shi'i belief—*Tawhid, Nubuwwah,* and *Imamah*—makes the characters of Prophet Muhammad and Imam Ali (as the prototype of all other imams) categorically metamorphic, and given the exemplary (in addition to ethical) disposition of Prophet Muhammad, Shi'is insist on preserving their Prophet's charismatic disposition by way of transmitting it to their imams, for that exemplary prophethood will continue to need the exemplary presence of an imam to sustain its charismatic condition.

The Life of a Prophet

Following this Weberian reading of the prophetic charisma at the heart of a religious visionary's manner of convincing his followers of his divine mission, let's now turn to a closer examination of Muhammad's career and see in what particular manner that category applies to him. Prophet Muhammad's charismatic authority was initiated, authenticated, and ascertained throughout his twenty-three years of active struggles to establish the veracity of his prophetic mission and the corroborating body of divine revelations that accompanied these struggles.[19] It is impossible either to imagine or to understand these revelations without those political actions, or to make sense of those political actions without these revelations. The combined force reveals the singular source of Muhammad's charismatic authority to have been his solitary soul assuming ever-expansive dimensions—in both political and metaphysical terms. The Muslim hagiographical preference for the Prophet's divine mission at the expense of his harsh political decisions is as much flawed as the Orientalist predilection to overemphasize his political acts in the absence of a recognition of his divine mission. At the core of Muhammad's charismatic character was an overwhelmingly solitary soul—he was an orphan—that began to fill itself with ever-expanding universes of his imagination, moral and normative, political and metaphysical, earthly and cosmic, mundane and divine, profane and sacred: a creative fusion of all such binaries to the point of overcoming them.

The life of the Prophet before his divine mission commenced in 610 is only of hagiographical interest to pious Muslims and of little significance for the historian or the sociologist.[20] Very little can be deduced from that early life, except the immediate detection of a solitary soul. Muhammad was born in 570 in Mecca to Abdullah ibn al-Muttalib and Amina bint Wahb, in the prominent but impoverished Banu Hashim clan of the Quraysh tribe.[21] Muhammad lost his father before he was even born, his mother by the time he was five, and he was subsequently raised by his paternal grandfather Abd al-Muttalib, a prominent member of the tribe, who also died a year later. The orphaned Muhammad was entrusted to his paternal uncle Abu Talib, the father of the First Shi'i Imam, Ali ibn Abi Talib.[22] His teenage years passed uneventfully as he began joining his uncle in various business trips as far north as Syria. During these business trips, as a young protégé of older merchants, Muhammad earned the epithet "al-Amin" (the Trustworthy). Losing his parents and grandfather cannot but implicate Muhammad in a life of sustained solitude and scarce reason to feel at home in the world—except in the company of a larger community that embraced and cared for him. His later habit of retreating to Mount Hira near Mecca is the outward expression of an introverted retreat into the solitary confinements of his soul from early childhood.

By 594, when Muhammad was a young and trustworthy man, the most significant event of his life was meeting and starting to work for a wealthy Meccan merchant, a prominent woman named Khadijah bint Khwaylid ibn Asad. A year later, in 595, when Muhammad was twenty-five and Khadijah forty, they married. This was Khadijah's third marriage and Muhammad's first. Six children were born to Muhammad and Khadijah—two sons died in their infancy and four daughters lived to become adults; only one daughter, Fatimah, survived her parents. Khadijah was the first person ever to believe in her husband's divine mission and to convert to Islam. She played an exceedingly important, even pivotal, role in the life of Muhammad and in persuading him of the veracity of his revelations when he was in severe doubt himself. Khadijah also undoubtedly provided Muhammad with financial security and social status, making it possible for him to retreat into his solitude and ready himself for his divine dispensations. Muhammad did attend to his wife's business matters, but the marriage was equally crucial in giving the Prophet the inner peace and that indispensable insularity of his soul on which would be written the divine revelations he was about to receive.

Beginning in 610, Muhammad became increasingly reclusive and hermitic, spending long retreats in the mountains adjacent to Mecca. During these long withdrawals of fasting and solitude, he was gradually convinced that he was in the presence of an overpowering divinity and that he was in fact the recipient of shattering revelations commanding him to rise and warn his tribesmen of a superior purpose in life—his and theirs. *"B'ism Allah al-Rahman al-Rahim"* (Muslims believe that the first six verses of the *Surah al-'Alaq* [96] are the very first revelations of the Qur'an to Muhammad),

> *Iqra'! B'ism Rabbik al-Ladhi khalaq.*
> [Read: In the name of thy Lord Who createth,
> Createth man from a clot.
> Read: And thy Lord is the Most Bounteous,
> Who teacheth by the pen,
> Nay, but verily man is rebellious.][23]

Qur'anic commentators are very particular about these inaugural verses of the Qur'an. Shaykh Abu al-Futuh al-Razi, among many other commentators, refers to the authority of the Prophet's later wife Ayeshah, among other authorities, in his assertion that these are the very first verses that were revealed to the Prophet.[24] The same sources, according to Abu al-Futuh al-Razi, report that initially the Prophet used to see "rightful dreams" [*al-ru'ya al-sadiqa*]—dreams that would come to pass, and that gradually he began to hear voices [*neda-ha*] when he was alone. These happened frequently until one day when the Prophet was sitting alone on Mount Hira, Archangel Gabriel appeared to him and told him "Recite!" to which the Prophet responds "I am not a Reader," or "I cannot read": *"Ma ana bi-Qarin!"* Gabriel then reaches out and holds the Prophet tightly and embraces and squeezes him closely, and again asks him to "Recite!" And again the Prophet tells him *"Ma ana bi-Qarin!"* This happens three times and three times Gabriel commands the Prophet to "Recite!" Shivering with fright, Muhammad goes to his wife Khadijah, and asks her to cover him with a blanket. He falls asleep. At this stage, Gabriel again appears to him and utters another verse of the Qur'an to him. The Prophet finally gets up and shares what has happened to him with Khadijah, and tells her that he thinks he is hallucinating. Khadijah assures him this is not a hallucination, for he is a good and righteous man. She tells the Prophet that they should both go to his uncle Warqah ibn Nawfal (died circa 610), for he is a learned man. His uncle assures Muhammad that he is indeed the bringer of the Great Law [*al-namus al-'azam*], as promised in earlier divine revelations—meaning the Hebrew Bible and the Gospels—and that Muhammad is indeed the last and the very seal of all other prophets.

For about three years, Muhammad kept these messages to himself, first divulging them to no one but his wife Khadijah, who instantly assured him these were not hallucinations and that he indeed was the recipient of divine dispensations. Muhammad's initial discussions of these messages were limited to his closest friends and allies. This period of gestation, reflection, revelation, and confidence building, mostly provided by the Prophet's wife Khadijah, were later instrumental in giving him a solid grounding in the veracity of his visions and revelations. As evidenced in the Qur'anic verses, there were serious periods of doubts, fears, and trembling for Muhammad in these years—an overwhelming sense of solitude in the presence of an ever-expansive divinity that his solitary soul now began to occupy.

From the moment that Muhammad began receiving his initial revelations in 610, his career is divided into two major periods, the Meccan (610–622) and the Medinan (622–632) periods. The dividing event is the migration of the Prophet from Mecca to Medina to establish his community [*ummah*] in September 622. These two periods are complementary phases of his career as a revolutionary leader, a community activist, and a religious visionary almost entirely devoted to building the foundations of the Islamic community, which will go through massive vicissitudes but survive to this day. In these public periods, his solitary soul begins to occupy the territorial domain of his political realm with the same tenacity and force as his mind and soul inhabit a celestial space of sublime assurances that what he did on Earth was a mere manifestation of what he was meant to do by divine providence. This is what he believed, and this is what those who believed in him believed.

The Medinan period is one of gradual dispensation of his divine messages to an ever larger audience consisting of a few prominent Meccans, but mostly the poor and the disenfranchised. The Meccan establishment is deeply troubled and antagonized by Muhammad's belligerent messages against patrimonial Arab paganism and increasing popularity among the Meccan poor and the disenfranchised. The significant event of this period is two successive waves of the so-called Abyssinian migrations in the year 615, when Muhammad was forced to dispatch small bands of his followers (first sixteen and then 103 recently converted Muslims) to Abyssinia to save them from the Meccan harassment and also to spread his word to a wider audience outside Arabia. The deaths of his beloved wife Khadijah and his protecting uncle Abu Talib in 619 finally forced him to leave Mecca for good—not to return until triumphantly toward the end of his life and career as the Prophet of Islam. The deaths of Khadijah and Abu Talib mark the final break of Muhammad from any earthly and familial connections that identified him with his childhood and youth. The Muslim traditions place Muhammad's famous *'Isra* and *Mi'raj* (his nocturnal journey from Mecca to Jerusalem and from there to the heavens to meet with previous prophets and God) right here after the death of Khadijah and Abu Talib and just before his historic migration from Mecca to Medina. Muslim commentators—philosophers, theologians, jurists, mystics, and poets—have been radically at odds as to how to interpret Mi'raj—as something the Prophet imagined or dreamed or as a physical ascent to the heavens. Some believe in the former and some in the latter. In part the problem has to do with the fact that Muhammad is not believed to have walked on water or split any sea. He is considered to have been an ordinary man, and his only claim to a miraculous act is the body of his revelations, the Qur'an, whose eloquence and beauty are believed to be inimitable. More than anything else, and if it were to be understood and interpreted within his prophetic career, this Mi'raj signifies the break of Muhammad from his earthly connections and his absolute and final sublation into a prophetic figure of celestial disposition, having been divinely ordained to perform an earthly mission. This is what Muhammad believed, and this what those who believed in Muhammad believed. Based on this belief a Muslim community was created that went forward to craft a world civilization and a massive empire.

The Medinan period begins in 622, when Muhammad finally leaves Mecca for Medina and begins the more aggressive and defiant proclamation of his prophetic mission. The opportunity to leave Mecca and move to Yathrib (soon to be renamed Medina, short for *Madinat al-Nabi,* or "The City of the Prophet") finally presented itself when two warring Medinan tribes—Aws and Khazraj—invited the Prophet to go to their city and act as an arbitrator between them. The most significant events of this latter period in the Prophet's career are a series of battles he waged against the Meccan establishment—of which the Muslims won the first (the Battle of Badr in March 624), lost the second (the

Battle of Uhud in March 625), and survived the third (the Battle of the Trench in April 627). This is the period of institution building for the Prophet, when he designates one group of Muslims who had emigrated with him from Mecca to Medina as Muhajirun (those who emigrated with the Prophet from Mecca to Medina) and another as Ansar (those Medinans who converted to Islam and helped the immigrants in Medina). He established the bond of brotherhood among them, from them created his *ummah,* and then led them in successive wars against the Meccans until he cut off the trade route that came down from Syria, passed through Mecca, and went toward Yemen—and thus paralyzed the Meccan commercial establishment.

The resolution of both the Meccan and the Medinan periods finally came in March 628 in the form of the Pact of al-Hudaybiyah between Muslims and the Meccans. According to this pact, Muhammad agreed not to attack Mecca that year and instead return the following year at the head of his army. The Meccans did not keep their part of the pact, but Muhammad had already won the moral high ground. In January 630, Muhammad marched triumphantly to Mecca at the head of the largest coalition of tribal forces ever witnessed in the recent history of the peninsula, and the Meccan establishment succumbed to his power and opened the gates of Ka'bah for him and his army. He and his comrades entered Ka'bah, smashed the idols that the Meccans had worshipped there since time immemorial, and proclaimed the Absolute Unity of God (Allah): his divine mission, his prophetic career, his solitary soul, and his universe of imagination all coming together in one cathartic act of liberation.

Before his death on 8 June 632, Muhammad had consolidated Arabia under his banner, established Islam as a unifying religion of the peninsula, and left a triumphant moral and imperial force to challenge the two superpowers of the time, the Sassanid and the Byzantine, and to overcome them within less than a century after the Prophet's death, creating an Islamic empire that stretched from the heart of Arabia to India and China in the east, the Atlantic Ocean in the west, and the southern coasts of Europe in the north.

The single most important aspect of the Prophet's career as a messenger of God and a statesman of steadfast political purpose is the simultaneous and spontaneous relationship between his political actions and his Qur'anic revelations. They prompt, corroborate, and correspond to each other. These Qur'anic verses are divided into two major subgroups:

the Meccan chapters and the Medinan chapters. The Meccan chapters are short, iconoclastic, revolutionary, and groundbreaking; the Medinan chapters are for the most part longer, more sober in tone, geared towards institution-building, and above all law-giving. The Meccan chapters proclaim; the Medinan chapters consolidate. One announces the opening of a sacred certitude while the other executes its normative and earthly mandates; one calls for defiance while the other commands obedience. These two sets of chapters contradict, and precisely in that contradiction, complement each other—and in the process give Muhammad's prophetic legacy an agitated and progressive disposition, at once destabilizing and forward-looking.

A triple dialectic ultimately defines and constitutes Muhammad's charismatic legacy: (1) the Meccan and Medinan chapters organically complementing each other in their thematic contradictions; (2) the Prophet's actions and revelations in the course of his life and career confirm and corroborate each other; and (3) the solitude he harbors and the society he keeps embrace and inform each other. The working of these three simultaneous dialectics narratively sustain and in the enduring terms of the Islamic sacred memory posit the inaugural moment of Islam as steadily iconoclastic, politically mutinous, normatively subversive, and consistently seditious.

Charisma Continued

The life of the Prophet and his career as a divine emissary introduced a new archetype of legitimate authority in Arabia—a charismatic revolutionary who revolted against the status quo and the patrimonial tribalism of his time and brought a divine message to sustain and support his movement. The death of the Prophet created a vacuum in that movement. Following his death, the overwhelming majority of Muslims opted to "routinize," as Weber called it, Muhammad's charismatic authority and establish various institutions to define and uphold the Muslim community based on his divine message and his enduring memory. A small band of his followers, however, thought that his moral presence was still needed to hold their community together. The majority gradually came to be known as the *Sunnis,* those who followed the Prophet's *sunnah* [path], and that small minority would later come to be known as the *Shi'is* [partisans], short for "the Partisans of Ali"—and, by extension, Ali's descendants. It took decades, if not centuries, for the theological positions of the Sunnis and the Shi'is to coagulate and contradistinguish themselves. But the seeds of their discord were sown early in Islamic history.

Shi'ism, one might thus suggest, is an attempt to sustain Muhammad's charismatic authority, prolonging his personal presence from generation to generation by extending it from an Islamic prophetology [*Nubuwwah*] to a Shi'i imamology [*Imamah*].[25] The Shi'i prophetology is articulated in a manner that anticipates, authenticates, and authorizes its own imamology.

A Deferred Defiance

To understand the pious veneration of the Shi'is for their imams and through that the dynamic effervescence of the Shi'i history we need grasp more closely Muhammad's prophetic mission, whereby the Prophet's charismatic presence is subsequently extended to embrace and include the Shi'i imams' infallible persona. In this respect, the ethical dimension of the Prophet's character (in its Weberian typology) is necessary but not sufficient for the Shi'is, and thus his exemplary presence is considered equally if not more palpable. The Shi'i imamology is thus deeply rooted in its prophetology and from there to its theology—all preludes to their soteriology, for without imams and the doctrinal stipulation of their intercessions no salvation is effectively possible. The result is a total narrative—from the divinity, through prophethood, and down to the sacred characters of the imams—in which the miasmatic charismatic presence of the Prophet and the imams extends to constitute a charismatic community as the tabula rasa of worldly salvation. If, as I have suggested, the combined effect of a "deferred obedience" (as Freud understood it) and filicide (as opposed to the Freudian patricidal origin of all religions and cultures) has cast Shi'ism into a state of permanent deferral, the charismatic condition of their infallible imams has made that deferral normatively combustible, ethically zealous, communally asocial, and above all politically explosive. So in Shi'ism what we have is in fact an always deferred defiance.

To Be or Not to Be Summoned

The summer after my senior year in high school was suddenly cut short. For months my father had been bringing up the matter of another summer trip to Mashhad, to which my mother gave her usual cryptic response that we would go if Imam Ali al-Rida were to "summon" us. The verb *talabidan* has a very peculiar declension in Persian. It comes from the Arabic *talaba,* which means "to demand," "to exact," "to require," or "to claim." As for many other Arabic words, we take this verb and throw it up into the machinery of Persian grammar and make a compound verb out of it: *talab-kardan* or *talabidan,* which in the context that my mother was using it here, meant that if Imam Ali al-Rida had decided to summon us to his shrine, he would facilitate our trip to Mashhad. It was out of our hands. In the sacred universe of my mother's habitual communion with our prophets, imams, and saints, there was a sacred will at work that made things happen or not happen according to an inner logic that always made sense to her, even though it left my father and the rest of us baffled and in our bafflement conscious of our earthly limitations. A divinity was shaping our ends, rough-hew them how we will, if Hamlet were to speak my mother's mind.

Imam Ali al-Rida had not talab-ed us that summer. Soon after my final exams were over in June—a few days after my eighteenth birthday on 15 June 1969—my father suddenly took ill and died (all his life he had suffered from chronic bronchitis). We did not go to Mashhad that summer. We stayed in Ahvaz and buried my father, and I postponed going to college in Tehran for a year so I could help sort out our family's finances. The most memorable thing I inherited from my father was a key chain with all his various keys and a nail clipper hanging from it. I never found out what all those keys were for, except for one that belonged to an old metal suitcase he had and which was kept locked and out of our reach. I had always had a mild but always passing curiosity about that suitcase, but nothing so overwhelming as to encourage mischief. One evening soon after my father died and we buried him, I took his keys and opened that suitcase and went through its contents. There was a strong and overwhelming sense of transgression about the act, and yet an even more compelling sense of open-ended liberation too. On top were mostly clothing items, especially, I remember, his National Railroad uniform, thick bluish in color with bronze buttons, with the official arm of the government marked on them. Then there was an assortment of things, but nothing in particular—and that was, and remains to this day, the strangest. That the suitcase was quite full of things I am sure, but full of exactly what I could not tell then and I can tell even less with the passage of time. Perhaps there were even more scattered keys to other unknown doors, locks, or suitcases; maybe a few pages of old newspapers and magazines with faded pictures; but nothing in particular, nothing noteworthy, nothing memorable, nothing to take out and keep. All I remember is that the smell of mothballs was growing ever stronger the deeper I excavated my father's suitcase. At some point I finally gave up, put back whatever I had taken out, covered it all with my father's uniform, closed and locked the suitcase, and later gave the key and that key chain to my mother. Years later, when I was a college student and my mother had moved to Tehran, I once saw the key chain wrapped inside a piece of black cloth with the twin picture of Prophet Muhammad and Imam Ali and the words *Allah, Muhammad, Ali, Fatimah, Hasan,* and *Hussein* written on it in a beautiful calligraphy—and placed gently in a corner of my mother's prayer rug, visible whenever she unfolded it to perform her ritual prayers.

2

BIRTH OF A REVOLUTIONARY FAITH

The Tehran of the early 1970s was the cosmopolitan capital of the universe. Everything happened in Tehran, and if it did not happen in Tehran, it happened nowhere; and if it did, it did not matter. There are many beautiful cities in Iran, but Tehran was something else. It shone. It glittered. It defied and defined you. The Tehran of the Constitutional Revolution from the early twentieth century on became the capital of a nation's best hopes and most agitated imagination. When I entered Tehran as a young undergraduate student in 1970, it was seductive, it was lascivious, and it was voluminous, with interwoven layers of interdictions and transgressions, and in it I was like a kid in a candy store: masses of people, multitudes of students from all over the country, Persian spoken in a symphony of accents, avant-garde art, cool and crazy art galleries, world literature, classical music, progressive politics, revolutionary zeal, European cinema, long hungry days with not enough money to buy food, Russian theater, Latin American soccer, Che Guevara posters painted with love and admiration and given to you on what you now discovered was your "birthday," Karl Marx in fluent Persian translation, Federico Fellini uncensored, working hard to make meager ends meet, pulsating with the poetic prurience of a world bursting with the erotic excitement of an adolescent touching the unfamiliar pastures of a stranger's body for the very first time. Tehran was urbane, suave, sophisticated; Tehran was stylish, elegant, debonair; Tehran was everything that the provinces were not—and the Tehranis knew it, flaunted it, formed and framed it. And you stood there: wide-eyed, beholden, bashful, dizzy.

Tehran, to be sure, was no Sodom or Gomorrah. Tehran was also pious, believing, at times even religiously sanctimonious, overbearing. Tehran had more than its share of mosques (and churches and synagogues and Zoroastrian temples), as well as its Hosseiniyehs (establishments exclusive to ritual remembrances of Imam Hossein), its rich and opulent but faithfully observant bazaars, its religious convictions, its moral codes, its fanaticism, asceticism, abstinence. Tehran had its supply of night clubs, movie theaters, sports facilities, and cafés and restaurants where young people of opposite sex comingled. But Tehran also had its Meydan Tajrish built around the shrine of a Shi'i saint; its more down-to-earth and even poor neighborhoods near Meydan Rah Ahan, Meydan Toup Khaneh, Bazaar Beyn al-Harameyn, Meydan-e Shush, Darvazeh Ghar, Shah Abd al-Azim; and the highway leading to Qom, a citadel of Shi'i piety, peopled with pious, observant believers, veiled women, bearded men, bewildered pilgrims, dishonest shopkeepers.

There was a hidden battle, a civil war, between the old Tehran—the religious Tehran, the Tehran of the persistent past, reluctant to yield in power and prestige—and the new Tehran—the burgeoning spectacles of the new cosmopolis, not just a window to the world, but in fact definitive to that world from just about any window through which you looked at it. Michelangelo Antonioni, the visionary prophet of Italian cinema, brought his *Passenger* (1975) to Tehran and, as a wide-eyed cineaste, I sat right in front of him during his press conference at the Tehran Film Festival. Now, how lucky could a boy be! But the divergent worlds crashed, and when push came to shove during the 1977–1979 revolutionary uprisings, the new cosmopolis joined the old capital but was in the end outmaneuvered by the wily schemata of the old. I have a cousin in Tehran, Abbas Parvizi, who was once a detective with the Tehran Police Department. He knew the subterranean Tehran, the criminal Tehran, the Tehran of thieves, drug pushers, addicts, pimps, and prostitutes. As an undergraduate student, I saw that hidden Tehran too, stretching wide and far under the thriving cosmopolis. During the violent Islamization of the Iranian revolution of 1979, these were all shoved under the carpet of a state-sponsored (false, fake, and forced) morality.

Two solitary souls defied this Manichean world, broke loose from its bastions of convictions and metaphors, and altogether challenged the bifurcated bone of contention in our innermost sanctities: one was one among a handful of poets who played our lives and sang our liberties like the troubadours of an ancient familiarity, and the other a maverick revolutionary visionary with Shi'ism of a new vintage and vantage point written all over his prophetic soul.

Among her contemporary master poets, iconic as they all were to our imaginative wherewithal, holding the soul of our nation together, Forough Farrokhzad was the only one to trespass that fictive barrier between the religiously musical and the atonal, between the sacred and the worldly—between the southern and the northern climes of Tehran. She accomplished all this in many enduring ways, above all in a single poem of astounding power and innocence: *Kasi keh mesl-e hich kas nist (Someone Who Is Like No One),* c. 1967. This is one of the very last poems of Forough Farrokhzad, published soon after her premature and tragic death in an automobile accident in 1967. It is a poem of irreducible simplicity and innocence, undergirded by the hallmark of her poetic gift for the uncanny, voiced from the vantage point of a second-grade girl, just about eight or nine years old. Here is the poem:

Kasi keh mesl-e hich kas nist (Someone Who Is Like No One)

I have dreamt that someone is coming:
I have dreamt of a Red Star—
And my eyelids keep fluttering,
And my shoes keep pairing,[1]
And I cross my heart and hope to die
If I lie:

I dreamt of that Red Star
When I was not asleep.

Someone is coming,
Someone is coming,
Someone else—
Someone better than everyone else,
Someone who is like no one else—
Someone who is not like Father, or like Ansi, or like Yahya, or like
Mother—

And he is just like the person that he ought to be:
And he is even taller than all the tall trees in the Architect's home,
And his face is even brighter than the face of Imam-e Zaman,[2]
And he is not even afraid of Seyyed Javad's brother—
And his fancy-schmancy police officer uniform—
And he is not even afraid of Seyyed Javad himself—
Who owns all the rooms in our house.

And His Name—
As Mother calls him at the end of her prayers is

Oh the Judge of all Judges!
Oh the Hope of all Hopes!

And He can read all the hard words of the Third Grade textbook
With His eyes closed!

And He can take one-thousand off twenty-million,
Without missing anything![3]

And He can buy on credit
All he wants from Seyyed Javad's store.

And he can make sure that the light of ALLAH—
Which was green, just like the early morning sky green—
Will light again
On the top of Masjed-e Meftahian.

Oh . . .
How light is beautiful,
How light is beautiful,
And how much I wish Yahya could afford a four-wheel cart, and a kerosene lamp,
And how much I wish I could ride on Yahya's cart,
Sitting among watermelons and cantaloupes,
Going for a ride around the Mohamadiyyeh Square—

Oh . . .
How beautiful it is to turn round the Mohamadiyyeh Square!
How beautiful it is to sleep on the rooftop!
How beautiful it is to go to the National Park!
How beautiful is the taste of Pepsi Cola!
How beautiful is Fardin's cinema![4]
And how much I love beautiful things—
And how much I wish I could just pull the hair of Seyyed Javad's nasty daughter!

Why is it that I am so small—
So small that I get lost in the streets?
Why is it that Father who is not so small—
And who won't get lost in the streets—
Doesn't do something so the person I have seen in my dream
Hurries up and comes soon?

And the people in the slaughterhouse district—
Whose small gardens are full of blood,
And whose small pools are full of blood,

And the sole of whose shoes are so soaked with blood—
Why is it that they don't do something?
Why is it that they don't do something?

Oh . . .
How lazy is the winter sun!

I have swept clean the stairs going up to the roof,
And I have also washed the windows—
Why should Father dream only in his dreams?

I have swept clean the stairs going up to the roof,
And I have also washed the windows—

Someone is coming,
Someone is coming,
Someone who in his heart he is with us,
Someone who in his breath he is with us,

Someone who in his voice he is with us.
Someone whose arrival no one can arrest,
Handcuff,
And throw into jail—
Someone who is born under Yahya's old trees,
And who every day grows up and gets bigger and bigger—
Someone from the rain,
Someone from the spattering sound of the rain,
Someone from whispering silence of the petunias.

Someone is coming from the sky of fireworks at night
Over Toup Khaneh Square[5]—
And he will spread the dining cloth wide and open:
And he will divide the bread,
And he will divide the Pepsi Cola,
And he will divide the National Park,
And he will divide the cough syrup,
And he will divide the registration day at public school,
And he will divide the waiting numbers at the hospital,
And he will divide the plastic boots,
And he will divide the tickets to watch Fardin's films,
And he will divide the trees in the house of Seyyed Javad's
   daughter,
And he will divide just about anything that has been amassed—
And he will give us our share too—

I have had a dream. . . .[6]

This poem is more powerful to me today than when I first read it decades ago. It is more convincing than ten learned metaphysical treatises, scores of juridical dissertations, and ten times as many philosophical tomes put together in Shi'ism—on Shi'i eschatology, imamology, prophetology, theology, theodicy—for what Shi'ism means, what these imams signify, and what power of conviction the innermost sanctities of a faith has invested in those who believe or even those who have long since abandoned belief. Forough Farrokhzad was no theologian, and for all people could tell had no particular religious faith up her sleeve. But in this single poem she planted in the inner innocence of a young girl's voice the very seed of expectation [*intizar*] at the heart of Shi'ism, a waiting, a yearning, a longing for an everlasting sense of justice that has been historically denied humanity at large. All Shi'i metaphors and convictions have been gently sublated in this poem into a fresh and bright rhapsody for which no religious affiliation or theological conviction is any longer necessary. The birth of Shi'ism as a religion of protest almost 1,400 years ago is given here a new nativity, a renewed significance, in the simple surface of a young girl's playful and defiant voice. No one was reading learned theological treatises that bearded men wrote in Qom, except for younger men at the mercy of their benevolence in secluded seminaries. Everybody, including those in the seminaries, was reading Forough Farrokhzad. The quintessence of Shi'ism, the soul of Shi'is, Shi'ism stripped of its scholastic paraphernalia surfaced in her innermost sanctity, the poetic moment of her self-revelation. That in the masculinist public eye that surrounded her, Forough Farrokhzad was made into a licentious harlot added even more potency to her prophetic voice.

Farrokhzad's poem generates its own metaphysics, at once Shi'i and universal, Islamic and cosmic, full of poeticized religious metaphors—from Allah to Imam Zaman—all reinvented for a resonance that they had all but lost. The poem is politically radical, revolutionary, incendiary even, but all in a distinctly human and tangible gesture, a gentility of perception and identification woven into its simple matter-of-factness. This was no Shi'ism with a marked turban on its clerical authority; this was Shi'ism renewed, revived, resurrected, with a pronounced voice of a woman, of a young girl, as the prophetic parlance of its revelatory power. No ayatollah, no mullah, no Islamist ideologue, no scholar could or did ever plainly say what the claim and call of Shi'ism was so simply, beautifully, convincingly, movingly. With Forough Farrokhzad's poetry in your heart and on your mind you need not have read any learned treatise on Shi'ism. You were walking it.

Forough Farrokhzad, however, was not alone in this metamorphosis of Shi'i metaphors into the narrative mannerism of her own time and place. In modern Shi'i revolutionary hagiography no one did more than Forough Farrokhzad's contemporary Ali Shari'ati to provide a universal revolutionary archetype that was modeled on the First Shi'i Imam, Ali ibn Abi Talib, but was propelled forward and backward in history to convince a far more diverse and evidently unbelieving audience. It is crucial to keep in mind that even Ali Shari'ati, a pronouncedly Shi'i thinker and revolutionary activist, modeled his rebellious archetype on Ali but yet again vicariously and through another historical figure, Abu Dharr al-Ghifari, who died in 652. Abu Dharr was an early convert to Islam, a devoted companion of the Prophet and after him a staunch Shi'i and a defender of Ali's cause. Through him Shari'ati crafted a model of an ascetic revolutionary for all ages and all cultures.[7]

As a Paris-educated revolutionary, Ali Shari'ati was very much in conversation with such leading Third World revolutionaries as Che Guevara and Frantz Fanon (with whom he carried on a correspondence).[8] The way Shari'ati reimagines Abu Dharr, the early Muslim comrade of the Prophet and Ali, is as "a great revolutionary, [set] against the nobility, against dictatorship, against capitalism, against poverty, and against racism—one who speaks more eloquently than [the French anarchist, Pierre Joseph] Proudhon."[9] Shari'ati was only too conscious of the fact that his contemporaries would be resistant to such characterizations, and would be baffled as to why a French-educated intellectual would choose to translate a book on an obscure early Muslim ascetic, originally written in Arabic, rather than something by Jean-Paul Sartre or other fashionable philosophers of the time. This, however, did not prevent Shari'ati from doing what he thought was most necessary in his country, and providing a free and expanded translation of a book on Abu Dharr, which he thought would initiate a revolutionary model that would best fit contemporary needs. The subtitle of Ali Shari'ati's book on Abu Dharr, *A Socialist Who Believes in God,* very much sums up how he wished to project and introduce his favorite Shi'i hero into a new world. Assimilating Abu Dharr forward to French philosophers like Blaise Pascal and Proudhon, Shari'ati projected the early Shi'i hero as a European figure of authority so that his contemporary Iranians would listen to him more attentively (and they did). Paramount in Shari'ati's remembrance of Abu Dharr for his immediate political causes is the fact that the early Muslim revolutionary became a believer in the Prophet's message some three years before Muhammad had even proclaimed his prophetic mission.[10] This had given Abu Dharr a certain aura of cosmic significance, an intuitive awareness of things to come, that best matched Shari'ati's conception of him. Abu Dharr was premonitory of the visionary prophet yet to come, devout, committed to social justice, vigorously against those Muslims who had soon abandoned the missionary zeal of their Prophet and had become worldly and wealthy. Abu Dharr, for Shari'ati, was a socialist revolutionary *avant la lettre*.

Between Forough Farrokhzad and Ali Shari'ati, a revolutionary poet and an elegiac revolutionary, Shi'ism had a renewed claim on a much wider spectrum of senses and sensitivities, allegiances and observances, pieties and politics.[11] One approached Shi'ism from the vantage point of a poetic cosmopolitanism that could generously embrace and re-signify, and the other from the perspective of a cosmopolitan Shi'ism that navigated freely between the mandates of the modern and the manners of the medieval sensibilities. Forough Farrokhzad and Ali Shari'ati, the oddest couple that any culture could claim and embrace, made sure Shi'ism had a new rendezvous with history. When everybody else was habitual in their ways, Farrokhzad and Shari'ati were "like no one else"—they were "Shi'is" in the most perfect sense of the term.

Years later, long after the deaths of Forough Farrokhzad and Ali Shari'ati, who died just before his revolutionary ideas and contagious zeal helped shape a massive social revolution in his homeland in 1977, the poet and the revolutionary were resurrected and brought together in the thoughts and prayers, visions and dreams of their kindred soul, a political revolutionary turned poetic visionary. Mohsen Makhmalbaf was already well established as a playwright, a novelist, an essayist, and above all a globally celebrated filmmaker when he published his essay on Forough Farrokhzad.[12] Makhmalbaf's "Forough Khahar-e ma bud" ["Forough Was Our Sister"] (1995) is a moving confessional that Makhmalbaf wrote on behalf of a group of Muslim revolutionaries, himself included, in which they all came together publicly to declare their love and admiration for Forough Farrokhzad. At that time, her already tarnished image as a promiscuous adulterer, scandalously manufactured during her own lifetime under the Pahlavi monarchy, was much exacerbated by the moral dogmatism of the Islamic Republic.[13] As the composer of the most erotic poems of her generation, written from the confident vantage point of a woman fully aware of her own sexuality, Forough Farrokhzad scandalized her generation and forever established an image and a reputation at once licentious and innocent, promiscuous and saintly. At the heart of Forough Farrokhzad's poetry was a contagious innocence that in turn became the tabula rasa of a renewed pact with the quintessence of existence. Speaking on behalf of his fellow Muslim revolutionaries and artists, Mohsen Makhmalbaf publicly confessed that they had regularly visited Forough Farrokhzad's gravesite, soliciting her blessings, and broke their fasts in her name. How he wished, he said, if he were to come back to this life, Farrokhzad would be his sister and Ali Shari'ati his cousin. As a devout Muslim revolutionary turned a visionary filmmaker, Mohsen Makhmalbaf embraced and celebrated Forough Farrokhzad and Ali Shari'ati as kindred souls. Makhmalbaf celebrated Farrokhzad above all for her masterpiece film, *Khaneh Siyah ast* [*The House Is Black*] (1963), but even more than that for her courage to imagine the unimaginable, and to search for light in the heart of darkness.[14]

In three thematic moves, Farrokhzad, Shari'ati, and Makhmalbaf—an iconoclastic poet, a firebrand revolutionary, and a rebellious filmmaker—at once defied and yet in their defiance paradoxically reaffirmed the hidden and obviated Shi'i that was in all of them, in their bodies and souls the distant echoes of foregone conclusions, dimmed memories of ancient convictions, a superlative vision of a common faith solidly reflected in three broken pieces of an honest mirror. So as Shari'ati contemporized Shi'ism for immediate and urgent political purposes, dragging it out of its medieval slumber and institutional complacency, Farrokhzad poeticized it into new metaphoric registers for people to read and respond to even beyond their confessional agnosticism, and then in turn Makhmalbaf aestheticized it into an even vaster body of visual narratives in his iconoclastic cinema, no longer even recognizable as evidently Shi'i. As three indexed expressions of their climes and cultures, Shari'ati, Farrokhzad, and Makhmalbaf—each in his and her own way, each in her and his own good time—pushed their ancestral faith one epistemic shift forward, sublating it into ever more global, ever more universal, and above all ever more cosmopolitan contexts. Shi'ism was now experiencing an epistemic transfusion, a schizophrenic split, with its aesthetics going one way and its politics another—but it was still too early to tell.

Shi'ism in Disguise

At the heart of Shi'ism, as a religion of protest written into the fabric of the history that it occupies, is the miasmatic manner of its inconspicuous transmutation into alternative modes of resignifying itself, of sublating itself, of disguising itself, of speaking in a multitude of languages. If for almost 1,400 years Shi'ism has sublated and cross-referenced itself in dogma, drama, law, theology, philosophy, mysticism, literature, poetry, metaphysics, and even painting and manuscript illustrations, as well as in voices of dissent, causes for uprising, and cries for revolution, then there is no reason for it to stop uplifting its metaphors. Above all, Shi'ism has a long cosmopolitan history of ritual, performative, and intellectual profusion—its charismatic agitation consistently *Aufgehoben,* as Hegel would say, into ever more historically sublated manners of registering itself. Rooted as it is in more ancient communal sentiments and historical manifestations, Shi'ism has always been a work in progress, thematically rescinding and narratively deferring itself, at once abrogating and prorating itself unto history. In Hegelian terms, if Shi'ism is the Idea, then its natural habitat in humanity results in the synthesis of its Spirit, at once rooted in that originary moment and yet sublated into more worldly manifestations. Within Shi'ism as a religion of protest and as the collective faith of historical communities, dogmas and principles, convictions and pieties, sentiments and aspirations overcome themselves—they are *Aufgehoben,* cancelled and raised at one and the same time, sublated by way of their own inner dialectic, for, as Hegel noted, the destiny of all identity is to be *Aufgehoben*—preserved via transcendence.[15] The clerical claim on Shi'ism is limited to a medieval jurisprudence with a very narrow margin of relevance to the globality of Shi'ism as an insurrectionary religion of protest.

In poems such as Forough Farrokhzad's *Someone Who Is Like No One,* in revolutionary zeal evident in rebellious souls like Ali Shari'ati's, and in visionary recitals of defiance and reaffirmation like those of Mohsen Makhmalbaf's cinema, an entire generation of lapsed or lasting Shi'is grew up seeking things otherwise silenced in their soul, whether in the ideas of Frantz Fanon; on the battlegrounds of Palestine, Vietnam, and Angola; through the pains of Latin America and sufferings in Africa, the actions of Che Guevara, the aspirations of Aimé Césaire, or the echoes of Langston Hughes's poetry. The charismatic dispensation once detected in the revolutionary uprising of a prophet and his immediate successors was now (across time and space, cultures and climes) remembered in terms both familiar and foreign to those who once defined and legislated the faith. The birth of Shi'ism as a revolutionary faith had Ali ibn Abi Talib as its inaugural figure of authority and an entire history to emulate that figurative authority of the unseen. The combined effect of a deferred obedience and infanticide has forever cast Shi'ism into a state of permanent deferral, both tropic and metaphoric, turned over to a deferred future, guilt-ridden not for having killed the father, but for having murdered the son—and this in more than just political terms has amounted to a state of permanent revolutionary defiance, in whatever language and diction most immediately accessible to the Shi'is' own trans-morphing into new clothing.

Birthing Shi'ism

The crisis of succession that ensued immediately after the death of Prophet Muhammad (570–632) ultimately resulted in a major split in the Muslim community—one group following the active routinization (as Max Weber called it) of Prophet Muhammad's charismatic authority into the institution of *caliphate,* and another (much smaller group) seeking to perpetuate that charisma first in the figure of Ali, the Prophet's cousin and son-in-law, and then after him in the institution of *Imamate.* The revolutionary figures of Ali, the First Shi'i Imam, and after him his son, Imam Hossein, the Third Shi'i Imam, provided the history of Shi'ism with its two most militant ideal figures—two "sons" murdered by their own father-figures. These two defiant figures have subsequently become definitive to the doctrinal basis of *Imamah* [*Imamate*] as the cornerstone of Shi'ism. The paradox definitive to Shi'ism takes shape and momentum right at this historical juncture, when two iconic figures in the early history of Shi'ism take up arms against tyranny and lead a band of revolutionaries in two historic battles. The charismatic nature of Shi'ism, as a result, rests on an attempt to institutionalize a constitutionally anti-institutional charismatic movement. The result of the paradox is the perpetual narrative deferral of the Shi'i metaphors of revolt from one set of significant signs to another, in a permanent semiotics of defiance and revolt, generation after generation, in whatever language necessary, metaphors metamorphosing to meet a renewed pact with history. As exemplified in the respective works of Ali Shari'ati (who contemporized Shi'ism), Forough Farrokhzad (who poeticized it), and Mohsen Makhmalbaf (who aestheticized it), the narrative deferral of Shi'ism has consistently sublated it into wider and vaster domains of global signification, where Shi'ism became ingrained in the cosmopolitan cultures it both occasioned and embraced.

For Shi'ism to be receptive of its own innate transmutations into newer metaphors, it must remember the point of its origin in ever-brighter terms. As a religion of protest, Shi'ism begins with the beginning of Islam itself, though its immediate causes are rooted in the crisis of succession that followed the death of the Prophet in 632.[16] But the political conditions that resulted in the crisis of succession might in fact be traced back to the origin of Islam, the nature of Muhammad's prophetic authority, and the paradoxical disposition of the Qur'an. The history of Islam as a political movement begins with the commencement of the Islamic calendar in September 622, when Prophet Muhammad led a band of revolutionaries from Mecca to Medina to establish the first Muslim community and launch his incessant attacks against the Meccan establishment. This crucial migration, the most significant political move of the Prophet at that time, followed from more than a decade of quiet revelations and passive recruitment in Mecca. By the time of his death in 632, Prophet Muhammad had consolidated his reign over Arabia, unified Arabs in what they believed to be a divinely ordained dispensation, and left them with a body of Qur'anic revelations to sustain the course of their pious remembrance of his legacy as they went around the world and conquered an unimaginable expanse of the habitable earth. Two paradoxes composed the fundamental crisis that surfaced upon the death of Muhammad, and that his community had to face. The first was Muhammad's charismatic authority—both revolutionary rebel and lawgiver. The second was the Qur'an that he revealed, which incites rebellion and commands obedience at the same time.

Who was to succeed the Prophet—and by what authority?[17] In Philip Rieff's theory of culture the latter critical question, which he borrowed from Max Weber and expanded into its biblical origins, is definitive to its normative character. In his own essay, "By What Authority? Post-Freudian Reflections on the Repression of the Repressive as Modern Culture," Rieff sought to characterize the advent of modernity as the inability (or unwillingness) to ask what has caused the Freudian repression.[18] Rieff identified this inability as a primary repression of the repressive, and the very *conditio sine qua non* of modernity. Rieff took this question of authority from the Bible, from Matthew 21: 23–24:

"And when he was come into the temple, the chief priests and the elders of the people came unto him as he was teaching, and said, By what authority doest thou these things? And who gave thee this authority? And Jesus answered and said unto them, I also will ask you one thing, which if ye tell me, I in like wise will tell you by what authority I do these things." By thus extending the Weberian theory of authority into its biblical predicates, Rieff's claim on both Weber and Freud exposed his predecessors' own repression, the repression of the repressive that Rieff took as the definition of modernity. The moment that we are now examining in early Islamic history, the birth of Shi'ism, is tantamount to this originary question, "By what authority?"

Muhammad had commanded both spiritual and political authority over his community, one indistinguishable from the other, and thus the charismatic character of his command and company. There was no immediate or wholly satisfactory response to this question, to the point that after Muhammad's death his community was on the verge of dissolution, of Muslims altogether abandoning their gathering and reverting back to their former tribal affiliations. "If you believed in Muhammad, Muhammad is dead, but if you believe in Muhammad's God, He is alive," is the famous statement (attributed to Abu Bakr)—a statement that ultimately saved the Muslim community.[19] The question of succession to Muhammad's authority was ultimately resolved via an impromptu tribal council that selected Muhammad's close companion and a respected elder of the community, Abu Bakr as-Siddiq, as his successor. Abu Bakr considered himself a *Khalifat al-Rasul Allah* (Representative of the Messenger of God), and reigned just two years, from 632 until 634. A similar tribal gathering decided the fate of leadership in the Muslim community after the death of Abu Bakr and concluded that Umar ibn al-Khattab, who reigned from 634 to 644, should succeed him, again as *Khalifat al-Rasul Allah*. Uthman ibn Affan then followed Umar in a similar manner, reigning from 655 until 656, and then after his death it was the turn of Ali ibn Abi Talib, reigning 656–661, who was selected via the same communal consensus. Through this chain of succession among the Prophet's immediate companions the institution of caliphate was established and has been honored by the overwhelming majority of Muslims for centuries since.[20]

A small but vociferous minority of Muslims differed at the time with this communal consensus, and in time developed and expanded their difference into a complete theology. They believed that the matter of leadership of the Muslim community was not for the community to decide, but that it was a matter of divine dispensation, which had, as they believed, already been pronounced by the Prophet himself at Ghadir Khum (among other occasions), and that Ali was in fact the rightful successor to the Prophet.

The significance of the Ghadir Khum incident for the Shi'is cannot be overstated. Shi'is believe that exactly ten years after his migration from Mecca to Medina, the Prophet led a major gathering of his followers in his last pilgrimage to Mecca [*Hajjat al-Wida'*]. On their way back from Mecca, at a place called Ghadir Khum, where Muslims were about to take different routes back to their homes, Shi'is believe that the following verse was revealed to the Prophet: "O Apostle! Deliver what has been revealed to you from your Lord; and if you do it not, then you have not delivered His message, and Allah will protect you from the people; surely Allah will not guide the unbelieving people" (The Qur'an, V: 67). When this message was received, according to the Shi'is, the Prophet ordered his followers to gather around him and delivered a speech, in which he said: "I leave for you two precious things, and if you adhere to them, you will never go astray. They are the Book of Allah and my Family." After this speech, Shi'is believe, Muhammad held Ali's hand and introduced him to everyone as his heir and successor. Soon after this event, again according to the Shi'i canonical beliefs, the following portion of the Qur'anic verse V: 3 was revealed: "This day have I perfected for you your religion and completed My favor on you and chosen for you Islam as a religion." Shi'is believe that everyone in that gathering listened to what the Prophet had to say and congratulated Ali, including Abu Bakr, Umar, and Uthman.[21]

The difference between the communal consensus of the majority of Muslims concurring on the authority of Abu Bakr and others that came after him, on one side, and a small band of dissidents who followed Ali, on the other, might be understood as two divergent forces: one (victorious) that stabilizes the Muslim community, encouraging external expansionism; and the other (overridden) that destabilizes it by continuing to persist on its prophetic legacy. The majority of Muslims united behind Abu Bakr and soon set their stupendous military machinery in motion to conquer half of the civilized world. Meanwhile, a small minority who dwelled on the theological speculation of "by what authority" ruled the Muslim community. The massive military success of Muslims in conquering the world to the east and west of Arabia soon became the central sign of their imperial claim to veracity, while the gradual emergence of Shi'ism as the dissident creed of insurrectionary movements against that empire emerged as the supreme symbol of its relevance and import for those left behind and disenfranchised by it. Short as it was, or perhaps paradoxically because it was so short and troubled, Ali's reign from 656 to his assassination in 661 remained at once celestial and symbolic, ethical and exemplary, for the rest of Shi'i history a sacrosanct model always to be emulated but never to be attained.

By virtue of its own charismatic disposition, Shi'ism itself was not to remain unitary or consistent. It soon began to splinter into a thousand pieces. The initial followers of Ali soon split into two groups after a major military confrontation, the so-called First Fitna (or civil war). In the Battle of Siffin (May-July 657), Ali ibn Abi Talib, as the Fourth Rightly Guided Caliph [*Khulafa' al-Rashidun*] faced his chief nemesis Mu'awiyah, who would soon succeed in establishing the first Muslim dynasty, the Umayyads (661–750). When Ali agreed to arbitration right at the moment when his army was about to crush Mu'awiyah's resistance, a group of his supporters violently disagreed with his decision on both political and theological grounds and splintered (*kharaja* in Arabic, and thus their name *Khawarij/Kharijites,* "those who revolted against Ali"). They formed one of the most radical early Islamic sects. Those who remained with Ali and formed the early nexus of the future Shi'is were not to stay put in their collective conception of who to follow and what to believe. Effectively, after the death of every Shi'i imam his followers splintered into two or more groups. When Ali was assassinated by one of the Kharijites in 661, his followers split into three factions. The first group thought that Ali had not died, that he would never die, and that he would remain alive until he established absolute and final justice on Earth. They were known as Saba'iyyah. Another group followed Ali's son Muhammad ibn Hanafiyah and were known as Kaysaniyyah. Yet a third group followed Ali's other son Hasan ibn Ali.[22] The same political and theological metastasis continued with every other Shi'i imam—as soon as he died his followers broke up into various opposing groups. Even the minor "imams'" followers broke up into more opposing groups, each giving rise to popular narratives of the most phantasmagoric detail as to the "imams'" whereabouts after death. When Muhammad ibn Hanafiyah died, some of his followers believed that "he is still alive, and that he resides in Razwi Mountains between Mecca and Medina, and that every morning and every evening deer go to him and he drinks from their milk and eats from their meat, and that two lions guard him on his left and right and they thus protect him until such time that he is again resurrected. Some say that on his right there is a lion and on his left a leopard."[23]

Because of this innate metastatic proclivity—a tendency to break away into opposing and factious sectarian cells—the Shi'is have been divided into one, two, three, all the way up to twelve Imami sects, of which only a few have played an important role in Islamic history: the Five-Imami or Zaydi Shi'is (thus named after their leader Zayd ibn Ali); the Seven-Imami or Isma'ili Shi'is (thus named after their leader Isma'il ibn Ja'far al-Sadiq); and the Twelve-Imami or Ja'fari Shi'is (thus named after the Sixth Shi'i Imam, Ja'far al-Sadiq). In the main Shi'i branch, the Twelve-Imami Shi'is *(Shi'i 'Ithna-'Ashari),* not all the imams had a politically rebellious character. The death of the Second Shi'i Imam, Imam Hasan, in 669 marks the quiet but short quiescence of the Shi'i community between the assassination of Ali in 661 and the uprising of Imam Hossein in 680. This can in part be explained by the communal shock at the cold-blooded murder of Ali, the forceful establishment of the Umayyad dynasty, and the peaceful and passive disposition of the Second Shi'i Imam. The martyrdom in 680 of the Third Shi'i Imam, Imam Hossein ibn Ali, marks the most significant archetypal moment of Shi'ism in the aftermath of Ali's assassination. Two consecutive revolts to revenge the murder of Imam Hossein, that of Tawwabun in 684 and that of Mokhtar in 686, identify the prototypical social revolutionary disposition of Shi'ism for centuries to come. The Fourth and Fifth Shi'i Imams, Imam Zayn al-Abidin (died 713) and Imam Muhammad al-Baqir (died 735), were pious and pacifist, and in no mood or position to continue with the revolutionary legacy of their father and grandfather, Imam Hossein. It was left to Zayd ibn Ali, another grandson of Imam Hossein, who established the Zaydi branch of Shi'ism, to continue with the revolutionary legacy of his grandfather. In the year 740, Zayd ibn Ali led a major uprising against the Umayyads. Less than a decade after the Zaydi revolt, the Umayyads fell under the onslaught of a new dynastic uprising, the Abbasids, led by Abu Muslim Khurasani (700–755), an Iranian convert.

Shi'ism of course has had more than its share of apolitical quietism. The Sixth Shi'i Imam, Imam Ja'far al-Sadiq (died 756), was a learned and pious man and refused to have anything to do with the Abbasid revolution. The earliest Shi'i uprising during the Abbasids was the revolt of Muhammad al-Nafs al-Zakiyyah in 758. But the Seventh Shi'i Imam, Imam Musa al-Kazim (died 799), very quietly succeeded his father Imam Ja'far al-Sadiq when his older brother Isma'il died during their father's lifetime. As usual, a group of Shi'is disagreed with this line of succession and remained true to Isma'il, forming the Isma'ili branch of Shi'ism, one of the most politically active and intellectually powerful medieval Muslim sects that has survived to this day. The Eighth Shi'i Imam, Imam Ali al-Rida (died 816), continued with the line of quietist imams and along with his progeny—the Ninth (Imam Muhammad al-Taqi, died 835), the Tenth (Imam Ali al-Hadi, died 868), and the Eleventh (Imam Hasan al-Askari, died 873)—commanded various degrees of communal but ultimately apolitical loyalty among the dwindling number of their followers. The Twelve-Imami Shi'ism finally came to a soteriological conclusion with the occultation [*ghaybah*] of the Twelfth Imam, al-Mahdi, who disappeared in 874. It is now a common belief among Shi'is that he will come back at the end of time to establish everlasting peace and justice. This is the imam to whom Forough refers in her poem as "Imam-e Zaman."[24]

Disappearance and Return

What can account for the historical success of *Ithna-'Ashari* (Twelve Imami; Ja'fari) Shi'ism? It has endured through all the vicissitudes of sectarian Shi'ism, outmaneuvered all its own splinter groups, and survives to this day. In two words: Shi'i jurisprudence. The occultation of the Twelfth Imam in 874 put an all but inevitable end to the cycle of violence and quietude of the splinter groups amassing around one or another descendent of Ali.[25] The idea of *ghaybah* of the last imam is something that emerged and developed over a long period of time, and most probably was not completely conceptualized until the time of Abu Jafar Muhammad ibn Hassan al-Tusi (995–1068), known by the honorific title of *Shaykh al-Ta'ifah* [The Master of the Community], arguably the most prominent Shi'i jurist of all time. More than anyone else, he is responsible for the comprehensive codification of Shi'i law, the systematization of its jurisprudence, and the comprehensive theorization of its theology—altogether the very backbone of Shi'ism as a communal faith and the single most important factor for its normative survival to this day.

The idea of the disappearance and return of a hidden imam does not begin with Twelve-Imami Shi'is. As early as the First Shi'i Imam, Ali ibn Abi Talib, some of his followers believed that he did not die and that he is hidden and will some day resurrect and come back.[26] The same belief was evident in just about any descendent of Ali who had stirred his community into a charismatic condition of devotion. As for the Twelve-Imami version of the idea, the Shi'i doctrine divides the disappearance of the Twelfth Imam into two metamorphic periods: *Ghaybah al-Sughra'* [the Lesser Occultation] and *Ghaybah al-Kubra'* [the Greater Occultation]. During the Lesser Occultation, the Hidden Imam is believed to have been in communication with his community through four successive deputies [*Nuwwab al-Arba'ah*]. Just before his death in the year 941, the last of these deputies, Abu al-Hasan Ali ibn Muhammad al-Samarri, informed the Shi'i community that the Hidden Imam had instructed him to tell his followers that he would be the very last channel of communication between the Last Imam and his community until he returns at the end of time to establish the reign of prophetic justice and everlasting peace. Al-Samarri died soon after this last communication and the gate of direct communication between the Hidden Imam and his community was closed.[27]

The period of the Four Deputies, between the disappearance of the Last Imam in 874 and the death of the last deputy in 941, is considered a transitional period whose end is commensurate with the appearance of a cycle of prominent Shi'i jurists that would hold the community together in the tight grip of a medieval jurisprudence of unsurpassed juridical precision and conceptual elegance. It is impossible to exaggerate the normative exactitude and the extraordinary juridical finesse with which Shi'i jurists have over the centuries collected the sayings of their prophets and imams, and then on that basis systematized, codified, and theorized the jurisprudential backbone of their communal faith. Three prominent jurists have between them produced four canonical sources, known as *Kutub al-Arba'ah* [The Four Books], which, ever since their composition in the tenth and eleventh centuries, have remained the vertebral columns of Shi'i jurisprudence. These four texts succeed those four deputies, and their gradual appearance and subsequent canonization mark by far the most stabilizing hermeneutic force in medieval Shi'i history. In a way, the disappearance of the Last Imam necessitates and facilitates the appearance of a scholastic tradition in Shi'ism in which the sanctity of the letter of law became a simulacrum of the charismatic presence of the Shi'i imams.[28]

First and foremost among the Four Books canonical to Shi'i law is Abu Ja'far Muhammad ibn Ya'qub ibn Ishaq al-Kulayni al-Razi's (died 940) *Kitab al-Kafi* [*The Compendium*]. A deeply respected jurist with an encyclopedic knowledge of Prophetic and Imami traditions, al-Kulayni was a contemporary of the last of the Four Deputies and thus in his lifetime he connects the end of the Lesser Occultation to the commencement of the Greater Occultation of the Hidden Imam. A Shi'i scholar of Iranian origin, al-Kulayni began his scholastic studies in Ray in central Iran and continued them in Baghdad at the seat of the Abbasid caliphate.[29] *Al-Kafi* is the most important work among a number of books written by al-Kulayni on Shi'i law. It is a compendium of more than 15,000 traditions (with full chain of transmission) attributed to Prophet Muhammad and the succession of Shi'i imams, and as such it provides the most basic conceptual and pragmatic foundation of the Shi'i law. The first part of this compendium provides canonical references to the Prophet's and imams' sayings and doings that collectively constitute the foundation of the *usual* [principles] of Shi'i jurisprudence.

Second in chronological order among the Four Books is the work of Abu Ja'far Muhammad ibn 'Ali ibn Babawaih al-Qumi (923–991), commonly known as Ibn Babawaih: *Man la yahduruhu al-Faqih* [*A Layman's Guide to Jurisprudence*]. A learned Shi'i also of Iranian origin, Ibn Babawaih (whose shrine near Tehran is a major attraction for Shi'i pilgrims) was the foremost jurist of his time. His honorific title of *al-Shaykh al-Saduq* [The Truthful Master] points to the high regard in which his legal opinions were held by the community.[30] This book too is basically a collection of hadith about the Prophet and imams, though this time around Ibn Babawaih opted not to include his chain of transmission in order to make the book of immediate use to a larger community of Shi'is. *Man la yahduruhu al-Faqih* as a result does not deal with the *usual* of jurisprudence, but with its *furu'* [derivatives] that are of immediate significance to the daily uses of the common Shi'is. In his introduction to the book, Ibn Babawaih reports an incident that led him to write the book and that speaks to the range and purpose of its reach. He says that once when he was in Balkh in Central Asia, he was shown a copy of *Kitab ila man la yahduruhu al-Tabib* [*A Layman's Guide to Medicine*] by the renowned philosopher and physician Abu Bakr Muhammad ibn Zakariya al-Razi (865–925). The friend who showed Ibn Babawaih this book asked him to write a similar book on Shi'i jurisprudence. Now, the title of both these books is quite peculiar. What al-

Razi's *Kitab ila man la yahduruhu al-Tabib* literally means is "book for someone who does not have access to a physician," just as Ibn Babawaih's means "[book for] someone who does not have access to a jurist." Both the location of this incident in Central Asia and the purpose of writing a book on Shi'i law for common people with no access to Shi'i jurists indicate the range and reach of Shi'ism far removed from the immediate circle of learned scholars in Baghdad. The composition and spread of the Shi'i communities around the Islamic world seems to be such that there are far fewer bona fide jurists to regulate the affairs of the community than the emerging communities need and demand, and thus the necessity of juridical manuals that function like a living jurist.

Third among the Four Books is Abu Jafar Muhammad Ibn Hassan al-Tusi's *Tahdhib al-Ahkam fi Sharh al-Muqni'* [*The Refinement of the Laws by Way of an Exegesis on (Shaykh al-Mufid's)* The Legally Sufficient]. *Al-Muqni'* [*The Legally Sufficient*] was the title of an important book on Shi'i law by al-Tusi's prominent teacher in Baghdad, Shaykh al-Mufid. The reverence with which Shaykh al-Tusi, or Shaykh al-Ta'ifah ("The Master of the Community," as he is called), is held among Shi'i jurists is impossible to exaggerate. A Shi'i of Iranian origin, al-Tusi was born and raised in Tus in Khurasan province, and went to Baghdad for his extensive scholastic learning, working directly under three luminary scholars of his time: Shaykh al-Mufid (948–1022), al-Sharif al-Murtada (965–1044), and al-Sharif al-Radi (970–1015). It would not be an exaggeration to suggest that it was al-Tusi who was chiefly responsible for the systematization of Shi'i law and jurisprudence. He had a long and illustrious scholarly career in Baghdad until the advent of the staunchly Sunni Seljuqid warlord Tughril Beg (990–1063), at which time al-Tusi's house and library were burned to the ground in Baghdad in 1055. Shaykh al-Tusi left Baghdad for Najaf, and there he laid the intellectual foundation of Shi'i scholastic learning that has survived to our time (though it remains to be seen if it survives the U.S.-led invasion and occupation of Iraq). Although Shaykh al-Tusi wrote on a wide range of subjects, from legal to theological treatises, it is mainly as a jurist that he is held chiefly responsible for the enduring systematization of Shi'i Law.[31] Al-Tusi's *Tahdhib al-Ahkam* contains almost 14,000 traditions and works as an extended commentary on the work of his teacher Shaykh al-Mufid. The authority of two jurists, a teacher and his student, al-Mufid and al-Tusi, are thus brought to bear on the authenticity, veracity, and exact practical implications of Shi'i beliefs and doctrines. By the time of al-Tusi and the writing of *Tahdhib al-Ahkam,* the discipline of Shi'i jurisprudence and the genealogy of prominent legal scholars had been solidly established, and Shi'ism as a religion had become independent of its political and revolutionary vicissitudes.

The fourth and final text among the Four Books is the same Shaykh al-Tusi's *al-'Istibsar fi-ma 'Ikhtalaf min al-Akhbar* [*Perspicacious Observations Concerning Variations on Received Traditions*]. *Al-'Istibsar* is basically an abridgment of *Tahdhib al-Ahkam,* meant to aid students and practicing Shi'is with the most basic mandates of a pious Shi'i life.

Thus, centered around four canonical texts and a small gathering of revered old men, came together the moral vertebrae of an otherwise youthful charismatic of revolutionary defiance. Their white beards and black turbans hovering over blank papers and sharpened reeds, these aging jurists became the sole indices of their brotherhood of juridical exactitude. In the long run they became the forceful counterbalance of armies of rabble-rousing young men placing their thin necks, boiling blood, and defiant souls against one tyrant or another and at the merciless edge of their sharp swords and dull wits. In due course of history, the imbalance of power between aging juridical exactitude and youthful revolutionary zeal, between fathers remembering the paternal generation of their faith and sons performing their delayed defiance, held Shi'ism together as a religion of protest. The imbalance of power navigated a corporeal site and held the youthful groins and the aging brains of a faith in balance. As a son-religion, Shi'ism remained youth-driven, insurrectionary, and destabilizing of the status quo for much of its history. But the central function of the scholastic tradition of learned jurists that emerged soon after the disappearance of the Twelfth Imam patiently moved toward the institutional stabilization of a doctrinal normativity immune to the vicissitude of the Shi'i political fate. As the youthful Shi'i revolutionaries destabilized, the aging scholasticism of the jurists stabilized, and the evident or implicit dialectic operative between the two opposing forces generated and sustained yet another, tertiary, dialectical space of its own. This is no mere medieval meandering of politics and knowledge. The most recent example of this dialectic is the current equilibrium between Grand Ayatollah Ali Sistani (b. 1930) and Seyyed Muqtada al-Sadr (b. 1973) in Iraq, an elderly scholastic jurist and a youthful revolutionary firebrand—two Shi'is at the two opposing but complementary ends of their faith, defending their cause and sustaining the historical fate of their community in two diametrically parallel but rhetorically divergent ways.

Shi'ism, Etcetera

The fragmentation of Shi'ism into even smaller splinter groups is not entirely due to its innate theological proclivities toward charismatic disintegration, nor is its endurance entirely because of the monumental scholasticism at the roots of its jurisprudence. There has been plenty of reason for revolt and revolution in the course of Islamic history over the last fourteen hundred years, and Shi'ism has contributed more than its share in leading these uprisings. There is a factor external to Shi'ism and yet coterminous in its importance in our understanding how and why Shi'ism has survived to this day. Even within Shi'ism, itself a profoundly destabilizing force in Islamic history, there have been systematic and repeated break-ups between stabilizing and destabilizing tendencies, between those Shi'is who wanted to settle down and let go of their Prophet and Ali's charismatic memory and codify their respective legacies in enduring institutions of authority, and those who have insisted on perpetuating it. To understand the destabilizing power at the root of Shi'ism and its successive collapses into ever smaller splinter groups, we must pull back from their closed-circuit sectarianism, place them next to non-Islamic revolutionary movements of the time (particularly proto-Zoroastrian movements in Iranian territories), and look at the larger picture of the rise of Islam as a universal religion and the massive imperial conquests of foreign territories that it occasioned.[32]

The early history of Shi'ism (and all other rebellious movements of the time) will have to be understood in the larger context of the Muslim territorial expansionism that immediately followed the death of the Prophet and ultimately resulted in two successive empires—the Umayyads (661–750) and the Abbasids (750–1258). Much of the reign of Abu Bakr (632–634) was spent on internal consolidation of forces, unification of various tribes, and the establishment of the institution of caliphate. During the reign of Umar (634–644), Muslim forces began to spread out of Arabia and challenge the two major superpowers of the time, the Sassanids and the Byzantines. The Battle of Bridge (634) and the Battle of al-Qadisiyyah (636) marked the onslaught of Muslim forces upon the Sassanid empire, whereas the Battle of Yarmuk (636) and the conquest of Syria (632) infringed on the boundaries of the Byzantine empire. By 643 Egypt was conquered, and by 644 the Fars, Kerman, and Sistan provinces of Iran were overrun by Muslim forces. Uthman's reign (644–656) commenced with the continuation of Muslim conquest all the way up to Khurasan, Armenia, and Transoxiana on one side, and North Africa and Cyprus on the other. The reign of Ali (656–661) was wrought with internal strife. Muslim forces began to attack each other in the Battle of Camel (656) and the Battle of Siffin (657). The assassination of Ali in 661 paved the way for the rise of the Umayyad Empire and the emergence of the Shi'ites and Kharijites as two revolutionary forces engaging the imperial domination of Muslim forces. The rise of Imam Hossein ibn Ali and the Battle of Karbala in 680 are the highlights of Shi'i revolts against the Umayyad establishment. The internecine civil wars notwithstanding, the Umayyads managed to extend their authority from their capital in Damascus all the way to Sicily, North Africa all the way to Tunisia, and as far east as Kabul and as far north as Oxus River and Bukhara. By 677 Constantinople was under Muslim siege. By 711 Muslims had crossed Gibraltar into Spain. It was finally in the Battle of Tours, also known as the Battle of Poitiers (732), that Charles "The Hammer" Martel put a stop to the evidently insatiable appetite of Muslim armies for territorial conquest and empire building.

Shi'ism was of course not the only set of sectarian movements within Islam that provided ideological banners to disenfranchised communities rebelling against these imperial conquests. The Kharijites were equally if not more important in defining a wide spectrum of rebellious uprising across the Muslim lands. There were even more Muslim sectarian movements when we look at the wider expanse of Islamic territories. Books such as *al-Farq bayn al-Firaq* by Abd al-Qahir ibn Tahir ibn Muhammad al-Baghdadi (died 1037) or *al-Milal wa al-Nihal* by Taj al-Din Abi al-Fath Muhammad ibn 'Abd al-Karim al-Shahrastani (1086–1153) are the best examples of Muslim scholars' attempt to categorize and systematize their understanding of their own sectarian movements. But not all revolutionary uprisings in the Islamic territories against the central caliphate in Damascus (under the Umayyads) and Baghdad (under the Abbasids) were of an Islamic nature. There were equally important non-Islamic, particularly proto-Zoroastrian, movements throughout Muslim lands and particularly in Iranian territories against their Muslim conquerors. These rebellious uprisings must be understood in the context of the Islamic imperial conquests and the social and political conditions that they occasioned—for most of these movements were launched by the impoverished peasantry and the urban poor, using Islamic or Zoroastrian leitmotifs as their revolutionary slogans.[33]

The formation of the Islamic Empire soon after the establishment of the Umayyad dynasty (661–750) and then in the course of the Abbasid dynasty (750–1258) created small but powerful pockets of beneficiaries as well as the masses that were disenfranchised by the empire. These were mostly the dispossessed peasantry and the urban poor (exacerbated under the Umayyads by their racist tribalism and the institutionalized humiliation of non-Arab Muslims, or the *Mawali*)—ordinary people who had been promised justice and peace but were abandoned to tyrannical local rulers and heavy taxation to provide for the wealth and power of the empire. The empire's beneficiaries, the Arab caliphs and the Persian and Turkish sultans, went about sponsoring and patronizing their political theorists, theologians, and eventually even philosophers and mystics. Meanwhile, those who were disenfranchised by it opted for revolutionary alternatives such as those offered by the Shi'ites and the Kharijites, which for centuries had mobilized massive rebellions shaking the Umayyad and the Abbasid dynasties to their foundations. The most influential medieval political theorist of the Muslim world during the Abbasid empire and the Seljuqid dynasty, Abu Ali al-Hasan al-Tusi, known as Nizam al-Mulk (1018–1092), wrote a political treatise, *Siyasatnama,* in which we read realpolitik details of ruling a vast empire. It anticipates Niccolò Machiavelli's *The Prince* (1532) by more than four centuries. Nizam al-Mulk even has a thing or two to teach his distant Italian progeny. The critical condition of sectarian movements, Islamic or non-Islamic, is thus the formation of two successive and massive Islamic empires, inheriting the territories of both the Sassanids and the Byzantines. Whereas dominant political theories, as well as scholastic theology and both Sunni and Shi'i jurisprudence, went about stabilizing the empire, Shi'i and Kharijite (Islamic) and proto-Zoroastrian (non-Islamic) movements offered liberation theologies that were dead set on destabilizing those empires.

Much of Shi'i history will have to be understood in the context of the excessive fragmentation of Islamic doctrines into opposing sectarian cells and movements, which in turn can only be comprehended within the larger imperial project of Islamic expansionism. As Muslim forces went about conquering massive territories—from the Indus Valley to the Iberian Peninsula and from Yemen to Central Asia, a colossal empire was crafted out of the remnants of its Sassanid and Byzantine precedents. The more the Islamic empire expanded, under both the Umayyads and the Abbasids, and the vaster the territories that came under Muslim control, the more the masses in impoverished communities rose up in revolt against the established authorities. Such revolutionary movements against the central caliphate invariably assumed both Islamic and non-Islamic ideological denominations.

The Tragic Hero and His Shadow

In the general context of Islamic history, Shi'ism is the archetype of revolt, as it tries (in vain) to capture the idealized reign of Ali, whose exemplary pious and ascetic character has been on Shi'i revolutionaries' mind ever since his short and tragic reign. The Shi'i archetype of revolt is based on the archetype of the tragic hero (Ali and Hossein in particular), a hero who is not a hero unless and until he is murdered and martyred, a hero who is not a hero unless and until he is a tragic hero. In Shi'ism the triumphant hero is a contradiction in terms, and that is why quintessential to Shi'ism is the ritual of mourning the tragically martyred heroes—the murder of a primordial son that is mourned forever. In his speech "Hossein: Vares-e Adam" [Hossein: The Inheritor of Adam], Ali Shari'ati in fact posits the Third Shi'i Imam as a cosmic figure whose murder weighs on the conscience of humanity.[34]

Like a Pigeon Hovering in Midair

Tehran of the 1970s, as it was being readied for the most massive social revolution in modern Shi'i history, was a self-alienated city—two moral sides at normative odds with each other. A triumphant monarchism claimed and conquered Shi'ism in its north, while in its south a rebellious Shi'ism defied and ultimately toppled it. But pushed aside under the southeastern shadow of the vast metropolis has always thrived, as if from time immemorial, the hustle-bustle of Shah Abd al-Azim shrine at the heart of the ancient city of Ray. The shrine is named after Shah Abd al-Azim (786–865), believed to be a descendent of Imam Hossein. But a number of other Shi'i saints are also buried in this much-revered complex of commerce and piety. In the shadow of Tehran, the shrine of Shah Abd al-Azim carries on with its own busy barometer of everydayness as if entirely oblivious to history. But if you were to sit in the main courtyard of Shah Abd al-Azim shrine under a late afternoon or early evening light and look around, you will notice, hidden and hanging from under the tall and inaccessible *mocárabe,* the honeycomb stalactites of its vaulted halls, or iwans [*muqarnas*], shades and shadows of uncertainty —one can never quite tell which one is which. The sculpted stalactites are carved and cornered in such a way that they generate and sustain their own shadows, irrespective of which way the light is hitting them. They become, they are, indistinguishable from their own shadows. Their being what they are morphs into their being other than themselves, their alterity. Here their matter becomes their manner; their terrestrial lifts their celestial claims on our fragile credulities. One is forever caught guessing which is which: forms or phenomena, earth or ether, doubt or certainty, faith or disbelief, blindness or insight. Right there and then reality is sublated into illusion—prophets, saints, and imams all the refracted lights of a will to believe, a desire to surrender. Revered old scholars and martyred young revolutionaries all hang in balance from those sculpted curvatures of stones and fantasies, amassing a resurrection of delivered delusions invading outward from the muqarnas and making their physical force factual, their imaginary interstices habitable. I once saw a pigeon hovering in the hollow of the hall under the muqarnas looking in vain for a place to land.

3

THE KARBALA COMPLEX

Had it not been for the public spectacle that the military tribunal made of his trial and subsequent execution, Khosrow Golsorkhi (1944–1974) would have been yet another name in the long annals of rebellious young Iranians who lost their lives fighting the Pahlavi monarchy to the end. But fate had decreed otherwise, for this public trial was early in 1974, soon after charges were brought against the defendants in October of the fateful year of 1973: the year of the Arab Oil Embargo (during the 1973 Arab-Israeli War). Mohammad Reza Shah Pahlavi (1919–1980; reigned 1941–1979) had opted not to participate in this embargo, and in return his oil revenues skyrocketed that year into billions of dollars. He, the king, seemed indispensable, indestructible, in power for good. There was an air of suspense, incredulity, even despair about the trial of Khosrow Golsorkhi during those fateful days. There had been a plot to kidnap the crown prince, and a number of radical groups had been involved. The two principal accomplices (we were told, and we were told to believe what we were told) were Khosrow Golsorkhi and Keramatollah Daneshian, and here they were on national television, being publicly tried in a military tribunal for the whole world to see, to watch, to learn, and never dare to repeat. People of the capital were transfixed watching the wide face, handsome demeanor, and heavily mustached lips of the young poet and journalist Golsorkhi, particularly when he stood up and spoke in his own defense, or more accurately not in his own defense, but in defense of his revolutionary ideas, ideals, and aspirations.[1] After reciting one of his own poems against colonialism and the ravages it had caused in his homeland, Golsorkhi (his name meaning *red rose,* by far the most potent metaphor, innocent sign, of revolutionary sacrifice and martyrdom for his generation of poets) began his defense with quite an unusual quotation—unusual, that is, given his own avowed ideological convictions):

> *"Ennema al-Hayat wa Aqidato Jahad!" (sic) Sokhanam ra ba gofteh'i az Mowla Hossein, Shahid-e Bozorg-e khalq ha ye khavar-e mianeh aqaz mikonam. Man keh yek Marxist-Leninist hastam bara-ye nakhostin bar edalat-e ijtema'i ra dar maktab-e Islam jostam va angah be socialism rasidam.*
>
> "Verily! Life is [naught but] conviction and struggle!" I begin my statement with a passage by Master Hossein, the great Martyr of the Middle Eastern masses. [Though] I am a Marxist-Leninist, for the first time I found social justice in Islamic ideology and then I became a socialist. In this court I do not [intend to] haggle for my life or for living. I am but an insignificant drop in the great . . . in the great suffering of the revolutionary Iranian masses.[2]

Why would Golsorkhi, a Marxist-Leninist revolutionary, begin his own last defense first and foremost by quoting a much-celebrated statement attributed to Imam Hossein, the Third Shi'i Imam, made politically potent once again by Golsorkhi's contemporary Ali Shari'ati, and then by confessing his admiration for the martyred Shi'i saint? That Golsorkhi's knowledge or practice of Islam and Shi'ism or of Imam Hossein for that matter is quite scant and scarce is immediately evident by his misquoting and mispronouncing the Arabic phrase at the commencement of his Persian speech. Nevertheless, Golsorkhi was consciously aware of the Shi'i origins of his revolutionary disposition—even (or as he put it, particularly) as a Marxist-Leninist.

"Sokhanam ra ba gofteh'i az Mowla Hossein, Shahid-e Bozorg-e khalq ha ye khavar-e mianeh aqaz mikonam." Arabic words have a peculiar resonance in Persian. They have their etymological roots in what they originally mean in Arabic, but they leave those roots behind and travel lightly and traverse sideways into a whole different emotive universe in Persian syntax and morphology (history and culture) and thus refract into a variety of ancillary sentiments. Golsorkhi refers to Imam Hossein as *Mowla Hossein,* meaning "Master Hossein," meaning an expression of Golsorkhi's deep love and admiration (devotion and dedication, one might even say) for the Shi'i imam—though not necessarily as a Shi'i imam, but as "the great Martyr of the Middle Eastern masses"—with the word "masses" underlying Golsorkhi's undying convictions in

a Marxist-Leninist frame of reference. The word for "martyr" *(shahid)* comes straight out of Shi'i doctrinal lexicography, since Imam Hossein is also known as the Prince of Martyrs, while the word "masses" *(khalq-ha)* is immediately rooted in the Third World socialist sentiments that Golsorkhi here best represented. The mixing and matching of these metaphors are all anchored on Golsorkhi's use of the two Arabic words of *mowla* and *shahid,* both balanced and fortified by that initial and courageous (but failed) attempt to utter a complete Arabic phrase. With that Arabic phrase, particularly in his innocent failure to pronounce it properly, Golsorkhi crosses both a psychological and an ideological barrier and reaches out to his revolutionary comrades, to Muslim revolutionaries, to Ali Shari'ati and his followers, to all those who shared his political ideals and aspirations, minus his historical materialism.

Just over a month after this trial began on 6 January 1974, Golsorkhi and Daneshian were executed, on 18 February 1974. In less than five years after their execution (their innocent but determined faces forever carved on a nation's collective memory), the Pahlavi dynasty would be toppled by precisely that combination of Marxist-Leninist, anticolonial nationalist, and militant Islamist sentiments that the young revolutionaries cried out loud before they were placed in front of the firing squad. But the resonance of a committed Marxist-Leninist revolutionary identifying with his "Mowla Hossein" echoed for decades to come, for it had been in the making for centuries past.

Martyrdom Prototyped

There is nothing odd about a Marxist-Leninist revolutionary identifying with the rebellious character of Imam Hossein. The word *shahid* that all revolutionaries—Marxist, nationalist, or Islamist—used for their heroes who had lost their lives in militant struggles against the monarchy is of an exclusively Islamic and particularly Shi'i origin and coinage. Icons and metaphors transfix and transmute across ages and cultures, ages and convictions. Years after Golsorkhi was executed, when I saw Francisco Goya's *The Shootings of May Third 1808* (1814) in the Museo Nacional del Prado in Madrid, I had an immediate affinity with the figure at the center of that iconic hallmark of Spanish nationalism. With the basilica of a cathedral in the dark background and the raised hands, enlightened centrality, dwarfed gatherings of both the other revolutionaries and Napoleon's firing squad, and above all the exaggerated height of the centerpiece Spanish revolutionary about to be executed (taller than everyone else though kneeling), Goya flaunted a heavily Christianized iconography and a Christlike figure to invoke the most sacrosanct sentiments in his audience. Goya was far more a Christian than Golsorkhi was a Shi'i.[3] But the figure of Imam Hossein had such a sacred and enduring resonance in Iranian and Muslim minds that there would scarce be any better metaphor (especially for a revolutionary poet like Golsorkhi) to invoke the sanctity of his ideals and aspirations, just a few steps before he too was to face his own firing squad. Like his Spanish counterpart in Goya's painting, he too, as legend has it, asked for his eyes not to be blindfolded.

Through successive thematic transformations, Imam Hossein comes back to a devout Marxist-Leninist like Golsorkhi via a circuitous mutation of metaphors and allegories—the paramount tragic hero, there to ennoble the age that gives him birth and meaning, the Karbala complex writ large. I offer the idea of a Karbala complex here via an interface between Freud's notion of the Oedipal complex (1926–1931) and Roland Barthes's reading of myth as a semiological system in his *Mythologies* (1957), with the obvious proviso that the Karbala complex is predicated on filicide, not patricide, and that in subsequent generations it mutates into multiple sites of symbolic (mythic) registrations. Barthes's reading of myth is also geared toward how it stabilizes the bourgeois society, but mine is in the exact opposite direction and toward a recognition of the manner in which Shi'ism becomes a mode of deferred defiance. Here I am after the traces of a transfusion of that deferred defiance in various sites, even those patently non-Shi'i.

By the time that the figure of a tragic hero, an exemplary revolutionary who sacrifices his life for a superior cause, reaches Golsorkhi's contemporary Ahmad Shamlou, the Iranian national poet of dissent and revolt, the Karbala complex is completely infused with the Crucifixion of Jesus of Nazareth. In Ahmad Shamlou's poetry the sublated figure of Jesus summons all his poetically distilled recollections (pieties and beliefs he has actively repressed), among which is a Shi'ism in whose doctrinal foregrounding he could not partake, but of which he was a reluctant inheritor. A rebellious figure of defiant disposition, a summoning of all his revolutionary heroes (including the Imam Hossein that had ceased to be a poetic metaphor for him but was transmuted into a Christological domain)—all are sublated into one Jesus of Nazareth, doing for Shamlou in effect what Mansur al-Hallaj, the prominent Persian mystic, did for Louis Massignon.[4] In *Marg-e Naseri* (Death of [the One from] Nazareth, 1965), Shamlou dwells on the figure of Christ precisely at the time of his Crucifixion, because for him the enduring image of Christ carrying his cross to Golgotha is the supreme sign of revolutionary responsibility:

> With a monotonous song—
> So monotonous—
> The end of the wooden burden
> Drew behind him
> A heavy and shaking line.
>
> "Put the Crown of Thorns on his head!"[5]

Shamlou ascribes much pain and suffering in this short but brutal journey:

> And the long and languorous song
> At the end of the burden
> Evenly
> Weaved
> A fiery lash
> Into the hallucinations of his pain
>
> "Hurry up, Nazareth, hurry up!"

A combination of pride and forgiveness carries Christ to his cross, as it must every revolutionary committed to a cause. The imagery is entirely Christian, descriptive of the carrying of the cross to Golgotha:

> He was relieved
> By the mercy he found in his soul
> And like a proud swan
> He looked into his own purity.
>
> "Lash him!"
>
> The leather lace came down
> And the endless red line
> Crossed through a big knot
> In its own length.
>
> "Hurry up, Nazareth, Hurry up!"

Treachery is always lurking from a corner, awaiting the revolutionary, who must endure the pain of treason—by which allusion Shamlou pushes the Christian imagery toward a more universal reading of sacrificial revolutionaries:

> From the roaring rank of onlookers,
> Eleazar
> Walked away,
> Clenching his hands behind him—
> His soul
> Released from a biting faith.
>
> "For He did not want, otherwise he could."

This for Shamlou can never be a final verdict, so a surging uprising is fast upon the world, whether it wants or knows it or not:

> The low
> Sky
> Heavy
> Fell
> Upon the silencing song of mercy—and
> Mourners ascended a mount
> And the sun and the moon
> Gathered.[6]

As Christ becomes for Shamlou what Mansur al-Hallaj *cum* Imam Hossein was for Massignon, no revolutionary poet like Golsorkhi could protest too much his Marxism-Leninism without a nod to Imam Hossein. For Golsorkhi and the entire generation of Marxist-Leninist revolutionaries, the rebellious figure of Imam Hossein (or Christ or Hallaj) represents the archetypal metaphor of a tragic hero, actively or implicitly identified with at once innocence and rebellion—pure and ready for self-sacrifice. What was paramount in Golsorkhi's reference to Imam Hossein and in Shamlou's sublating of his more immediate but repressed sacred figures into Jesus of Nazareth—a foreign figure made familiar in his poetry—was that cosmopolitan context of a living culture in which Shi'ism breathed naturally and left its creedal provincialism behind for a far more planetary claim on people's credulities.

Perhaps the best example of that cosmopolitan culture in which the

Karbala complex in Shi'ism had resumed a renewed significance in its visual and performative modernity is the staging of a Ta'ziyeh performance, *Moses and the Wandering Dervish,* at Trinity College in Hartford, Connecticut, in 1988 by the Iranian director Mohammad Ghaffari.[7] Adapting a classical sideshow of Ta'ziyeh about Moses and a wandering dervish, Ghaffari successfully incorporated contemporary scenes ranging from the iconic image of Eddie Adams's photo of General Nguyễn Ngọc Loan publicly executing a Viet Cong officer named Nguyễn Văn Lém, to the lashing of a pregnant woman under the Islamic Republic in his visual repertoire of Ta'ziyeh dramaturgy. The Karbala complex was now tuned in with the most traumatic moments and images of contemporary world history. This was still Ta'ziyeh, but its dramatic metaphors had been sublated, universalized, metamorphosed.

By the time that poets like Ahmad Shamlou, Marxist-Leninists like Khosrow Golsorkhi, or theater directors like Mohammad Ghaffari had co-opted their evident or sublated takes on the Karbala complex, Shi'i martyrology, and Ta'ziyeh dramaturgy in their respective universes, Imam Hossein as an iconic figure of revolt had been thoroughly reimagined within a contemporary cosmopolitan culture that at once embraced and reclaimed Shi'ism. What had happened over the long and arduous distance between a remote event early in Islamic history at the Battle of Karbala in 680 and these political, poetic, and artistic resurfacings of it in a more contemporary cosmopolitan context is the subject of further investigation in this chapter. Just keep in mind from the outset that in the most evidently modern and contemporary Shi'i country, a critical conversation took place between the most varied layers of revolutionary and aesthetic forms and by far the most traumatic moment of Shi'ism, with the former creatively adapting the latter to universal terms and transversal parameters. There is a universal transversalism in these obvious or hidden allusions to the Karbala complex that will require a very careful unfolding of Shi'i doctrinal and political history, from its medieval to its modern phases, to figure out its composition and composure.

Mazlumiyyat: Having Been Wronged

Khosrow Golsorkhi's announcement that he is a Marxist-Leninist and yet acknowledging *Mowla Hossein* as his revolutionary model points to an implicit semiological system that hinges on the principal function of the Karbala complex as a transformative mode of signification far beyond an identifiably Shi'i frame of reference. Here I need to explain in some detail what exactly I mean by this Karbala complex. What overriding parameters of conviction and belief come together to define and sustain it? First and foremost we need to remember the traumatic birth of Shi'ism into history. As the central trauma of Shi'ism, the Battle of Karbala in 680 has remained definitive to the rest of its history, an event and a phenomenon that has been raised to cosmic levels and made integral to the Shi'i sacred imagination. Two interrelated concepts have arisen from the post-traumatic stress syndrome of the Battle of Karbala and as such are definitive and integral to what Shi'ism has meant and what it has been over its long and arduous history: one is *mazlumiyyat* (innocence) and the other, deeply rooted in it, is *shahadat* (martyrdom).

The translations of these two concepts I give here are merely indexical, for their originals are not immediately translatable to non-Shi'i contexts. The etymological root of *mazlumiyyat* is ZLM, which means *tyranny* or *injustice*. So in the *mazlum* form, the word means a person who has been wronged or subjected to tyranny—and *mazlumiyyat* is the condition of being in that tyrannized state, having been subjected to it. The embedded conception of *innocence* is then actively implied in the sense that the person thus wronged is helpless, hopeless, and innocent not just in the sense of being tyrannized but in being metaphysically and by force of predestination fated to suffer injustice—so there is an element of fatality in the condition of mazlumiyyat, a sense of being innocently cast into that condition. A running leitmotif in the ritual remembrances of the Battle of Karbala is that, had Imam Hossein wished, so he would have had the armies of angels and demons all at his command to defeat Yazid's army—but he did not wish to do so because his sacrifice was predestined, so that his tragic end might be a source of salvation for all humanity. (The similarity between the Shi'i conception of Hossein and the Christian conception of Christ is quite striking.) *Hossein-e Mazlum* (Hossein the Innocent) is the single most cherished way of referring to the martyred imam for the Shi'is—particularly in conjunction with the memory of his having been beheaded while very thirsty.

As the principal doctrinal characteristic of Shi'ism that has forever signed and sealed its paradoxical character, the notion of mazlumiyyat (literally, "having been wronged") amounts to a condition that the veracity of the faith remains legitimate only so far as it is combative and speaks truth to power, and (conversely) almost instantly loses that legitimacy when it actually comes to power. This paradox of success in failure (the figure of Imam Hossein revolting against Yazid writ large into history) and failure in success (the figure of his father Imam Ali actually becoming a caliph writ large into history) is commensurate with Shi'ism as a religion that has employed an always delayed and deferred defiance—of the figurative sublation of Ali and Hossein in fact going against each other, cancelling each other out—a father and son negating and abnegating each other's sacred memory for their followers. Shi'ism came into being by a double paradoxical denial, a father and son cancelling each other's meaningful progeny. A social psychology of self-defeat awaiting revenge is thus at the very heart of Shi'ism. Shi'ism, as a religion of protest, is founded on a perceived political injustice, a wrong that can never be righted, but it must—that Ali was not allowed to succeed Prophet Muhammad as the ruler of the nascent Muslim community, that Hossein failed to achieve what was rightly his and his father's. "Justice," as a result, is central to the Shi'i theological disposition. To a Shi'i, the world is in a cosmic state of disarray, and he or she is here to set it right. But the tragic fate of Shi'is is that they are never to succeed. Their success defeats their purpose, for the instant the Shi'is have the illusion of having succeeded in establishing justice, they cease to be Shi'is, for the central trauma of their faith comes back to haunt them.

The historical denial that constitutes the paradigmatic prototype of the Shi'i state of perpetual defiance was the presumed right of Ali to succeed Prophet Muhammad as the leader of the nascent Muslim community. Shi'ism was thus born out of a traumatic "no" carved deeply into the bosom of the Shi'i historical consciousness. The problem is not simply a matter of the personal preference of Ali over Abu Bakr or any other companion of the Prophet. In the increasingly complicated Shi'i theology, the whole veracity of Islam as a faith depended on the nature and function of the Prophet's successor. The choice of Ali thus gradually emerges as a matter secondary to the more theological principle of who had to succeed the Prophet and how was the succession to be justified? It is not as much a question of whether or not Abu Bakr was qualified to lead the Muslim community as an objection by the succeeding generations of Shi'i theologians and revolutionaries (alike) as to the manner of his election via a tribal consensus. That "election," Shi'is later argued, was contrary to the very spirit of the Islamic revelation. Muhammad was a divine emissary, and the religion he established was divinely ordained. Humans had no business interfering in the divinity of that arrangement by electing someone through communal and tribal consensus. The election of Abu Bakr, the later generation of Shi'is maintained, categorically defied the nature of the Islamic revelation and altered its historical course. By altering that historical course, the Islamic community had gone wrong and they (the Shi'is) were the sole possessor of the "true" version of the faith. Their mission in life was thus to right the course of human history.

Far more important than the personal and familial connections between Ali and the Prophet is the continuity of their charismatic character, crucial in constituting the Shi'i claim to legitimate succession. To be sure, as his cousin and son-in-law, and the son of a man who effectively raised the Prophet, Ali was related and personally attached to the Prophet in any number of ways. But in the emerging Shi'i imamology, the character of Ali became the prototype of the very institution of Imamah, which was to carry forward the charismatic mission of the Prophet. A charismatic community thus emerged around the figure of Ali that in many historical instances has indeed been carried forward to extremes in attributing divine qualities to him. The more these qualities assume extra-historical proportions the more the Shi'i claim of his denied rights becomes superlatively doctrinal to the faith and traumatic to its history.

Right here and now we may consider the excruciating punctiliousness of Shi'i law and jurisprudence to be one particularly scrupulous manner of juridically overcompensating for the traumatic origin and precarious disposition of the Shi'i charismatic community. The more volatile, unstable, and impulsive the charismatic outbursts of revolutionary movements in Shi'ism have been throughout its medieval and modern history, because of its traumatic origin, the more precise the exactitude of the Shi'i law has sought to regulate, to the minutest details, the affairs of Shi'i believers—from their rituals of bodily purity to the dramaturgical particulars of their communal gatherings, to their political suspicions of anyone's claim to legitimate authority. This particular aspect of Shi'i jurisprudence is of course evident in Islamic law in general, though in a more relaxed manner in response to the death of the Prophet.

Equally if not more central in the charismatic characterization of the Shi'i social psychology of defeat, denial, and insurrection is the figure of the Third Shi'i Imam, Hossein ibn Ali. The ethic of insurgency is in fact far more identified with the figure of Hossein than with that of Ali—for Ali, after all, was in power and was killed; but Hossein was killed before he came to power. The revolt of Hossein ibn Ali against

Yazid ibn Mu'awiyah and his martyrdom in the Battle of Karbala is the very model of unsuccessful insurrection against tyranny at the heart of Shi'ism—glorious as it takes place, even more so if it does not succeed, for from its ashes the fire of future revolts will rise. Upon the ascension of Yazid to the Umayyad throne in the year 680, Hossein was encouraged by his supporters to revolt and claim his rightful place at the head of the Islamic community. Despite warning signs not to initiate a revolt against the reigning caliph, Hossein was encouraged by his supporters and moved from Mecca to Kufa to lead the uprising. The massacre of Hossein and his small army (symbolically fixed at the number seventy-two) that ensued has been carved in the Shi'i historical memory ever since.[8]

There are a number of key concepts that emerged in the aftermath of the Battle of Karbala and that collectively constitute the very nature of Shi'ism as a religion of protest, and thus anchor its paradoxical relationship to moral victory and political failure. First and foremost in the Battle of Karbala is the idea of *zulm* [tyranny]. Yazid, the Umayyad caliph who demanded Hossein's obedience or death, has emerged as the absolute personification of evil and injustice in the Shi'i historical memory. His reign is remembered as one of terror and injustice. Ever since Yazid, as it were, every ruler is an illegitimate ruler for the Shi'is unless provisionally proven otherwise. On the primordial model of Yazid, *zulm* is universally rampant and must be resisted by any means necessary. No political power is ever immune from a Shi'i accusation of tyranny—all are constitutionally illegitimate unless proven otherwise. Shi'ism is thus in effect an unending metaphysics of revolt against tyranny, with Imam Hossein and Yazid ibn Mu'awiyah as the archetypal representations of this cosmic battle. It is for that reason that Imam Hossein represents the ideal type: a revolutionary hero who revolts against *zulm*.

The Making of a Religion of Protest

An equally critical concept embedded in the Battle of Karbala is that of *qiyam* [insurrection]. Tyranny is not to be tolerated. Tyranny is to be resisted. Hossein's *qiyam* against Yazid is the archetypal model of a small band of revolutionaries rising against tyranny. *Zulm* and *qiyam* are thematically related in the moral universe of Shi'i political culture. If there is tyranny, then there must be revolt. Since there is always tyranny, then there must always be revolt. In that cosmic battle between Imam

Hossein and Yazid, Imam Hossein was defeated, and thus the idea of *defeat* becomes part of the archetypal presence of the Battle of Karbala in the Shi'i historical memory. *Zulm, qiyam,* and the historical fact of Imam Hossein's defeat become the triangulated pattern of a revolutionary event in the political subconscious of Shi'ism. If tyranny is not resisted, there will be something missing in the moral composition of the universe. Revolt is the "natural" state of a Shi'i historical presence. But the defeat of that revolt is almost a foregone conclusion because of the archetypal normativity of Imam Hossein's defeat in the Battle of Karbala.

What remains outside this triangular framing of history is the guilt of the Shi'i community for having abandoned Imam Hossein. All Shi'is, wherever and whenever they are, see themselves accused of being like the people of Kufa and having abandoned their imam, their Prince of Martyrs, their beloved Imam Hossein. Imam Hossein is the murdered son of the Shi'is, paradoxically identifying with a primordial murder of which they (seem to) stand accused. The guilt of having abandoned and in effect having killed their son has had a gripping effect on the rest of Shi'i history.

From this Karbala complex, which as I articulate it here amounts to a web of political subconscious underwriting the history of Shi'ism, the institution of *Imamah* as the defining fixture of Shi'i historical presence has been doctrinally defined and theologically established. The institution of Imamah carries the Shi'i collective sentiment of their historical denial to its logical conclusion. Islam, for the Shi'is, is in effect incomplete; the cycle of *Nubuwwah* [Prophethood] is historically interrupted if it is not carried forward in the institution of *Imamah*.

Considering that practically all Shi'i imams, with the exception of the twelfth who is hidden and in occultation, are commonly and doctrinally believed to have been martyred, killed in their youth by their adversaries, *shahadat* [martyrdom] becomes constitutional to the Shi'ite ideal of heroism. The only hero is the dead hero. This simultaneous celebration and condemnation of the hero is where the Shi'i community locates its primal guilt vis-à-vis its martyred son. The social psychology of this primal guilt is far more arresting than the one articulated by Freud. For the Shi'is, the figure of Imam Hossein is at once the founding father and the martyred son. So the guilt is dual—guilt for having killed both the father-figure of the faith and the son-substitute of the sacrifice. With one stroke the Shi'i community blames itself for having killed not only its founding father figure but also its martyred son, both its past and its future—and thus mapping out its premise for an always delayed and deferred defiance throughout its history. That mutually arresting grip is the cause of the constitutional paradox of Shi'ism and its moral success in political defeat, and moral defeat in political success (the complementary memories of Ali and Hossein becoming contradictory). The Shi'is by their own moral self-definition cannot be triumphant because at the primal point of entering their history they have killed their son, and they cannot forgive themselves because they have in him also killed their own founding father-figure. When the substitutional son becomes the founding father, the hero transmutes into the victim—and thus the Shi'i community both mourns and celebrates the death of its founding figure. It is precisely for that reason that the Shi'i imams must be *ma'sum* [infallible]. What could *infallible* mean here other than the constitution of the body of the martyred imam as the sacrificial lamb offered to cleanse a primeval guilt? But the assumption of the infallibility of the imam is also the figurative substitution of the body of the martyred, innocent son for the body of the community and thus the cleansing of a collective guilt.

In the primacy of mazlumiyyat as a key conceptual category in Shi'ism is thus operative the infallibility of the hero-imam, his having been subject to and then revolted against tyranny, and the paradoxical relation of the community toward its own moral and political presence in history. The imam, as the prototype of all saintly heroes, is mazlum (innocent) for having seen and identified tyranny, for having mobilized and fought against injustice, and for having been unjustly and brutally murdered in the act. The Shi'i community is implicated in the ensuing injustice for having instigated the imam to revolt and for having abandoned him on the fateful day of the battle. In the hero-imam is thus embedded both the defining moment and the inconclusive achievement of the faith, both the founding father and the martyred son. The result is that Shi'is must always fight against injustice and never be triumphant. They must fight because that is the mandate of their murdered father. They cannot be triumphant because they have already murdered their own son.

The last analysis completes the circle in my outline of the Karbala complex: the final Shi'i doctrine, one of *ghaybah* or occultation, the belief in the "disappearance" of the Twelfth Imam. What is this *ghaybah* supposed to mean? The doctrine of *ghaybah* is the historical seizure of Shi'ism within its own historical paradox. This is where Shi'ism detains itself in a cycle of repetition, a perpetual moment of everlasting expectation. *Ghaybah* is the Shi'i expectation of the final Return of the Twelfth Imam, *al-Mahdi al-Muntazir* [The Awaited Mahdi], who went into "hiding" in the year 874. He is to return and establish the Final Justice in the world. His occultation or *ghaybah,* as a result, brings Shi'i historical self-awareness to a grinding halt until such time that he is Returned. But before that Return, the Shi'is are in a permanent state of *intizar* [expectation], at a complete standstill in a history (otherwise filled with silence) that no longer has any place to go. It amounts to a Beckettian moment in *Waiting for Godot*—and the whole point is that Godot will never come. In that arrested moment dwells the first and the final paradox of Shi'ism as a faith that at its primal moment has witnessed the murder of its founding father and the slaughter of its martyred son at one and the same time—a false and falsifying guilt gathered into a theology of permanent revolution.

Karbala Complex

The Karbala complex is thus the gradual mutation of the central trauma of Shi'ism (the Battle of Karbala) into a nexus of emotive responses and political instincts that are then doctrinally codified and cast into a full panoramic history. This trauma is ultimately not just emotively untenable, but more important it is narratively untellable. It cannot be fully told to any Shi'i's full satisfaction, and thus there is a central mimetic crisis at the heart of Shi'ism. It has experienced a trauma, and that trauma is so overwhelming that it cannot be fully represented either theologically or dramaturgically. Thus jurisprudentially it has been overcompensated by a fastidious attempt to regulate the human body and the Shi'i community. This traumatic origin has in turn given rise to the Shi'i mimetic crisis (both in its politics and its aesthetics), a mode of suspended mimesis that is never complete (in the Aristotelian sense) and is always hovering in midair. As such it is the closest in dramaturgical terms to what the German dramatist Bertolt Brecht called *Verfremdungseffekt* [*distancing effect* or simply *alienation*]: the theatrical device that intentionally aborts passive compliance with the fictive narrative.[9] In the Shi'i dramaturgical case, however, this is a matter of doctrinal and historical development rather than a mere dramaturgical device, and in the case of Shi'ism as a semiotic system, the result of this incomplete mimesis is the splitting out and fragmentation of the central drama into multiple metamorphic parables—into multiple manners of telling the story of Imam Hossein, of the Battle of Karbala, sometimes conspicuously evident, and sometimes not so obviously detectable.[10]

Why would it be important to see the central trauma of Karbala and the formation of the Karbala complex in multiple metamorphic parables, in more than one way of saying or staging it?[11] My principal objective in detailing the originary contours of the Karbala complex and in making a case for its multiple metamorphic parables is geared toward the proposal that in the long and varied course of Islamic history, the domain of this defining moment of Shi'ism has not remained limited to Shi'ism alone. By varied acts of metaphoric and doctrinal osmosis it has in fact spread into any number of adjacent narratives and emotive territories—both Islamic and non-Islamic, theistic or agnostic, worldly or other-worldly. Shi'ism can disguise its central metaphors in varied forms. What I believe has happened is that in the course of time the pious remembrance of the Battle of Karbala has provoked more ancient themes in various regional cultures (ranging from Mesopotamian and Iranian to Indian, Central Asian, Arab, and perhaps even North and East African) and produced a more cosmic paradigm of charismatic revolt to emerge and coagulate. Because of its varied cultural sources, the Karbala complex has also charted variable narrative domains for itself and has in due course become parabolically metamorphic. It can easily metamorphose into multiple parables. A key factor in this transformation of the Karbala complex into multiple parables of mythic proportions, I believe, is the intermediary function of Islamic mysticism in sublating the Shi'i notion of shahadat into the Sufi conception of *fana* (annihilation).

But what exactly does this Karbala complex mean and signify in the political course of Shi'ism, and how does it help us understand its long and arduous history? By far the most crucial consequence of the Karbala complex is that heroic life in a Shi'i universe of sacred imagination loses its immediate and material significance by becoming signified into a superior moment and into mythic proportions. In this semiotics of reconfigured signification, life ceases to have any immediate meaning as it becomes a formal part of a metaphysics of ulterior significance.[12] Revolutionary figures all the way from Imam Hossein to Khosrow Golsorkhi (through Hallaj, Ayn al-Qudat, and many others) cease to be ordinary human beings in this mythic sublation of reality into myth. The ordinary lives of these revolutionary figures become iconic the instant that they are (body and soul) transfused into a mythic mode of mimesis.

This transfusion makes their physical lives insignificant precisely at the moment their being signifies something beyond its worldly meaning, as it assumes its sacred form.

The Karbala complex travels from an exclusively Shi'i register through the transmutation of its key concept of shahadat into the Sufi notion of *fana*. From there it splits into multiple metamorphic parables. This metamorphic transmutation of the Karbala complex follows from the particular mode of Ta'ziyeh mimesis in which there is no Aristotelian one-to-one correspondence between the person who does the representing (the actor) and that which is represented (the character). The Shi'i mimetic moment, as best evident in Ta'ziyeh performances, is of an entirely different nature, for it is rooted in an inability (not) to identify with the murdered son (Imam Hossein).[13] The result of this traumatic crisis is that Shi'ism is in a permanent state of suspended mimesis, looking for new and alternative parables to tell itself (from medieval to modern, from theological to dramaturgical, from political to poetic), just as in turn multiple parables of resistance and revolt as floating signifiers (including that of the Marxism-Leninism of Khosrow Golsorkhi's generation) look into Ta'ziyeh to retell themselves in alternative (more cosmically resonant) dramas.[14]

One immediate way to come to grips with this parabolic transmutation of the Karbala complex into varied forms of dramatic staging is to dwell on the manner in which Khosrow Golsorkhi refers to Hossein ibn Ali, not as *Imam* Hossein, which would have conceptually implicated him in the Shi'i theology (and as a Marxist-Leninist he could not have done so), but as *Mowla* Hossein, which implicates Golsorkhi in something entirely different. What does *mowla* mean? Derived from the word *wali* [friend], the term *mowla* oscillates between the two adjacent notions of *master* and *friend*. *Wali* and its plural *awlia'* [friends] have a long and illustrious history in Islamic mysticism.[15] The term *Awlia' Allah* [Friends of God], and the notion of *wilayat* [companionship] is on par with or even superior to *Nubuwwah* [Prophethood] among some Sufis. By calling Hossein ibn Ali "*Mowla* Hossein," Golsorkhi joins the Third Shi'i Imam in a mystical brotherhood of revolutionary camaraderie that transcends both his Marxism-Leninism and his hero's Shi'ism, for Sufism as an idea and a practice in effect transcends sectarian variations in Islam, though some scholars have persuasively demonstrated the enduring correspondence between Shi'ism and Sufism.[16] As two adjacent parables of revolt, Shi'ism and Marxism-Leninism become metamorphic through the Karbala complex and result in a revolutionary zeal that links Khosrow Golsorkhi and his Mowla Hossein (through such master martyr Sufis as Mansur al-Hallaj) together.

As a mystic, and one of the *Awlia' Allah,* Mansur al-Hallaj was of course not the first to flout the elements of juridical dogmatism and political tyranny and speak ecstatic utterances out of his conviction in *fana,* nor was he the last to be executed for that reason. Long before Hallaj, another Persian mystic, Bayazid Bastami (807–874), was famous for such intoxicated utterings; and generations after Hallaj, yet another major Muslim mystic, Ayn al-Qudat al-Hamadhani (1098–1131) was, like Hallaj, publicly executed for his "blasphemies."[17] The innocent, valiant, and defiant figure of Imam Hossein looms large over all these (and many other) mystics.[18] In all such cases, and because Shi'ism is in a permanent state of suspended mimesis and is always looking for alternative parables of telling itself, it is a fertile ground for sacrificial heroes who become the walking embodiment of that mimetic suspension, dwelling in a parabolic purgatory as they await their "second death"—for they have already experienced their first and put it behind them: passing as they have from insignificant *matter and meaning* into signified *myth and form* (if we were to read this with Barthes' theory of myth in mind). This notion of the "Second Death," instrumental in this transmutation, is based on a Prophetic tradition [*hadith*] that commands Muslims to "Go die before your death," on the basis of which Rumi says:

Ro bemir ay khwaja qabl az mordanat,
Ta nabashad zahmat-e Jan dadanat—
An chenan margi keh dar nuri ravi,
Ney chenan margi keh dar guri ravi.

Go die Sir before dying,
So you won't suffer death—
A kind of death that plunges you into light,
Not a kind of death that lowers you into a grave.[19]

Revolutionaries of mythic proportions from Hossein ibn Ali to Khosrow Golsorkhi seem to have already died and left their natural state and then come back to resignify their lives and the lives of others around them in a different manner. They are dead men walking, aware and communicating with their corresponding souls in those who love and admire them. They seem to be here to tell their contemporaries something, without fear of retribution and with total immunity from harm and harassment. The mystic notion of *fana* and the ecstatic utterance of *Ana al-*

Haq are there simply to shock and awaken their audience to that reality which has given a new significance to what they say. Martyrs become *Awlia' Allah fi al-Ard* [Friends of God on Earth], meaning those who in their lives have been sublated into an altered reality—living and dying in that state. That is why the Shi'i imams are always assumed not to be dead, because they have died before their death and they have resurrected into this life.

The Philosopher Martyr

Compensating for its absence of a complete mimesis, the Karbala complex thrives on multiple metamorphic parables—both medieval and modern in origin and disposition, sacred and profane in language, evident or implicit in their emotive universe. In Islamic and Iranian history, both modern and medieval (one in fact feeding on and exacerbating the other), the floating figure of a young, rebellious, and iconoclastic hero rebelling against the compromising mandates of a corrupt status quo has navigated a vast and varied topography. These figures, just like Imam Hossein, or Hallaj, or Ayn al-Qudat, are always remembered as young, impatient, rebellious, mazlum, idealist—always having seen a superior vision of reality, testaments of a better promise than the one allotted humanity. In order to see the full spectrum of this rebellious paradigm, it is imperative not to see or limit these revolutionary figures, or the Karbala complex they represent, to the realm of politics or rebellious uprising. As a semiotic system, the Karbala complex is even more evident in the domain of ideas. While from Imam Hossein to Khosrow Golsorkhi, the Karbala complex has been effectively present in a succession of political uprisings, neither Hallaj nor Ayn al-Qudat represents a particularly political figure in the ordinary sense of the term. It is their ideas and utterances, beliefs and thoughts, that have posed a narrative threat to the juridical discourse of domination. But even these two mystics partake in an iconoclastic Sufi parlance to which one might detect a political posturing. We need to move around and look at a particularly iconoclastic philosopher of unsurpassed intellectual brilliance and imaginative poignancy to see how the Karbala complex has far more than one way of revealing itself.

Shahab al-Din Yahya Suhrawardi (1155–1191), known also as *al-Shahid* [the Martyred] or *al-Maqtul* [the Murdered], appeared like a flash of light (just like his name) in Islamic intellectual history with such uncommon but short-lived brilliance that no one could tell what or where was his origin or to what point the domain of his influence extended after his death.[20] He is now known and remembered as the founder of the Illuminationist School of Islamic philosophy [*Hikmat al-Ishraq*]. He was born and raised in Maragheh in northern Iran and spent much of his short but dazzling intellectual life in Iraq and Syria, where he wrote a series of philosophical and allegorical prose narratives in philosophy (in both Arabic and Persian) that to this day have baffled historians, who have little idea as to where and how they originated. His iconoclastic ideas, deeply rooted in pre-Islamic Iranian sources, troubled his philosophical elders and the Muslim jurists of Aleppo, where Saladin's son Malik Zahir ruled during the Third Crusade (1189–1192). The juridical establishment demanded his execution from the sultan, and Suhrawardi was executed in 1191, at the age of thirty-six. Before his untimely death, and from the combined legacy of Zoroastrianism, Platonism, Neoplatonism, and Aristotelian-Avicenna philosophy, Suhrawardi single-handedly established the Illuminationist School of Islamic philosophy and challenged some of the most cherished principles of Aristotelian philosophy as Avicenna had expounded it. In the later history of Islamic philosophy, such major figures as the great Shi'i philosopher of the Safavid period Mulla Sadra Shirazi adapted and expanded Suhrawardi's ideas and sought to navigate an interface with Avicenna's philosophy.

The reach of Suhrawardi's philosophical influence was not limited to Safavid Iran and traveled as far east as India. The brutal end of Suhrawardi at the hands of his juridical elders and the iconoclastic nature of his philosophy are forever intertwined and point to the martyrological disposition of the Karbala complex far beyond its immediate Shi'i registers. What I am in effect proposing here is the location of Shi'ism as a religion of protest at the semiotic center of the Karbala complex, surrounded by the wide range of metamorphic domains in which the Karbala complex is parabolically operative at the heart of Islam in general: a delayed and deferred defiance that propels Islamic political and intellectual history forward.

Shi'ism Writ Large

The multiple parabolic metamorphoses of the Karbala complex are by far the most important guarantor of its endurance in varied and at times unrecognizable forms. The historical sublation of Imam Hossein into a tragic hero, an innocent idealist, was no exclusive proclivity of the Shi'i hagiography, nor was the operation of the Karbala complex limited to an Islamic frame of reference. As the distinguished Catholic historian of the Christian Church Jaroslav Pelikan has demonstrated in his *Jesus Through the Centuries,* it is a peculiar aspect of figures like Jesus Christ (or Imam Hossein, we might add) to be resurrected in various ways.[21] As Pelikan argues, Jesus has always been reconfigured ("resurrected," one might say) in various social circumstances, from a rebellious Jewish rabbi to a Latin American liberation theologian. So has an archetypal figure like Imam Hossein. We need not, in fact, look for the sublated figure of Imam Hossein only in Islamic, Christian, or even Marxist contexts—in Hallaj's mysticism, Massignon's Catholicism, Shari'ati's Shi'ism, or Golsorkhi's Marxism-Leninism. In the Persian national epic, Ferdowsi's *Shahnameh* (composed circa 1000), the mage of Seyavash is very much reminiscent of the tragic figure of Imam Hossein—as a supreme symbol of courage and innocence.[22] Heir to the throne, young, handsome, and valiant, the young Seyavash resists the persistent seductions of his stepmother Sudabeh, and when in revenge she accuses him of trying to rape her, he volunteers to go through a test of fire to prove his innocence. Once his honor is thus restored he leaves his father Kay Kavus's court and opts to live in the country of his arch-nemesis Afrasiab, where he is again suspected of treason, this time accused of plotting to overthrow the Turanian king. He is of course innocent of this charge as well. But this time around he is arrested and killed. The incestuous attraction of Sudabeh to Seyavash in Ferdowsi's *Shahnameh* thematically very much resonates with the necrophilic love that Salomé, the Daughter of Herodias, makes to Saint John the Baptist's severed head in Richard Strauss's *Salomé* (Dresden, 1905, based on Oscar Wilde's play). In modern Persian fiction, the three figures of Saint John the Baptist, Imam Hossein, and Seyavash all come together in by far the most famous and popular fiction in modern Persian literature, Simin Daneshvar's *Savashun* (1969).[23] In a key passage in the novel, the chief character, Zari, cannot tell which one of these three figures is depicted in a painting.

Along the same lines, perhaps no other story in the entire spectrum of Persian literature, modern or medieval, better represents the central trauma of filicide (son-killing) than the story of Sohrab in Ferdowsi's *Shahnameh.*[24] Sohrab is the son of Rostam, and Rostam is the principal hero of the *Shahnameh*. The story of Rostam and Sohrab begins with the Iranian epic hero wandering to the border between Iran and Turan, its chief nemesis in the *Shahnameh*. Rostam soon kills a wild animal, skewers and eats it, and then falls fast asleep. A number of Turanian soldiers chance upon Rostam's horse Rakhsh and capture and take him away. When Rostam wakes, he is angry and looks desperately for his horse. Night falls and he has not yet found his horse, but he comes across the fortress palace of the King of Samangan. Rostam is received royally at the palace, and upon his retreat to his private chambers, Tahmineh, the princess of Samangan, comes and expresses her love for the Iranian national hero. They marry right there and then, and from their single nocturnal encounter Tahmineh becomes pregnant. Rostam leaves the following morning and gives her a precious stone to remember him by and also to give to their son should their wedding bring fruit. Rostam soon finds his horse, packs his belongings, and goes back to Iran and to defending Persian monarchy against its enemies.

Nine months later Sohrab is born to Tahmineh, and every sign of a hero's son is written all over the young boy—he is valiant and courageous at a very young age. He soon demands to know who his father is. Tahmineh tells him and gives him the stone that Rostam had given her as a sign to find and identify his father. Sohrab leads an army of his supporters from Samangan toward Iran with the intention of deposing the reigning monarch King Kay Kavus (Seyavash's father) and placing his own father Rostam on the throne, and then using the Iranian army to defeat the Turanians and become their king himself. When Afrasiab hears that Sohrab is heading toward Iran to depose the Persian monarch, he sends an army to assist him in his battle, commissioning, meanwhile, two of his trusted generals, Human and Barman, to prevent Sohrab from recognizing his father, and then to kill him while he is asleep once he has defeated King Kay Kavus and killed Rostam. Sohrab's fortified army approaches Iran and reaches the White Fortress, whose lord Hajir engages Sohrab's army in battle. Hajir is defeated and arrested. But his daughter Gordafarid dresses herself in battle gear and attacks Sohrab's regiment. Gordafarid puts up a heroic resistance to Sohrab, but she is defeated—and upon recognizing his adversary Sohrab falls madly in live with Gordafarid. Gordafarid manages to escape from Sohrab, go back to the White Fortress, and subsequently escape altogether, sending a message to King Kay Kavus concerning Sohrab's approaching army.

Upon receiving Gordafarid's message, King Kay Kavus dispatches one of his chief generals, Give, to summon Rostam to defend him. After a short but nevertheless insulting delay, Rostam comes to the royal court and prepares to lead King Kay Kavus's army in battle against Sohrab. Both father and son (facing each other as enemies and unaware of their relationship) miss a number of opportunities to recognize each other, giving space to some of Ferdowsi's most powerful storytelling tropes. Rostam and Sohrab finally fight in prolonged single combat, neither knowing who the other combatant is. No one is initially victorious. Finally Sohrab defeats Rostam and is about to cut off his head when Rostam comes up with a trick and tells Sohrab that in Iran it is not customary to kill an enemy after the first defeat. The following day the father and son again face each other and this time Rostam is victorious, and without a moment of hesitation he plunges his dagger deep into his son's side and kills him. Upon his death, Sohrab warns Rostam that his father will avenge him. "Who is your father?" Rostam wonders. "Here is his sign," Sohrab says, and hands his father the precious stone he had given Tahmineh. Casting one look at the cursed sign, Rostam realizes he has just killed his own son. Rostam faints and wants to kill himself but is prevented by his comrades. He instantly sends a message to King Kay Kavus asking for *nushdaru* (a panacea that might cure Sohrab), but the treacherous king refuses, fearing that the father and son will conspire and it would be the end of him. And thus ends the tragic and short life of Sohrab—the valiant son of Rostam, killed by his own father.[25]

In the tradition of coffee house painting in Iran, the heroic figures of *Shahnameh* and those of the Battle of Karbala become narratively metamorphic and are often depicted together. So it would not be unusual to see the stories of Sohrab, Seyavash, and Imam Hossein reflecting each other in thematic and visual vocabulary. Equally evident in popular versions of the *Shahnameh* would be the imaginative encounters between the epic characters of Ferdowsi's masterpiece and the religious characters of Islamic history in general and of Shi'ism in particular.[26] There are in fact numerous epic narratives (in Persian poetry) that combine the spirit of Ferdowsi's *Shahnameh* with the heroic deeds of the Prophet and the Shi'i imams—among them *Khavaran-nameh* on the heroism of Ali ibn Abi Talib; *Saheb-qiran-nameh* on the valiant deeds of Hamza the Prophet's uncle; *Hamleh-ye Heydari* and *Khodavand-nameh,* both on the heroism of Prophet Muhammad and Imam Ali; *Mokhtar-nameh* on Mokhtar ibn Abi Ubaydah Saqafi, who rose in a major uprising to revenge Imam Hossein's death; and *Shahnameh Heyrati* on the heroic actions of Prophet Muhammad and all the Shi'i imams.[27] Most of these epic narratives were composed between the fifteenth and nineteenth centuries, namely in the aftermath of the establishment of the Safavid as a major Shi'i dynasty.

Modern Mutations of the Myth

In these epic narratives, which combine the Persian national epic with the Shi'i emotive universe, the Karbala complex assumes a renewed significance at a vastly popular level, which extends their narrative domain from medieval to modern as it does from sacred to worldly and cosmopolitan dispositions.[28] In modern Iranian annals of legendary heroes and martyrs, there can scarce be anyone as massively loved and showered with adoration as Gholamreza Takhti (1930–1968), the most widely celebrated wrestler in modern Iranian sports history, whose tale fits perfectly within the Karbala complex.[29] A combination of chivalry, humility, innocence, and sportsmanship come together to make Takhti a transcendent figure of mythical proportion in modern Iranian martyrology, particularly after his sudden and tragic suicide.

Born to a humble family in a poor neighborhood in Tehran, Takhti grew up to become by far the most globally famous Iranian wrestler. His charming and charismatic face for years during his own lifetime and then ever since his sudden and shocking death marked a sign of innocence and chivalry never matched in modern Iranian history. The worldwide adulation for the posters of Che Guevara is the closest example one can give for a similar adoration that Iranians have for the posters of Takhti sold in the remotest villages and towns around the country. Within the living memory of Iranians around the world there are iconic tales of Takhti's chivalrous behavior in and away from the wrestling arena. After a terrible earthquake in Bo'in Zahra, in Iran, Takhti is remembered for picking up a tray and walking down a main avenue in Tehran, where people from all walks of life and of massively divergent income brackets rushed to give him money for the victims of the earthquake. Such signs of humanity and humility abound about Takhti, particularly concerning his sportsmanship. The prominent Russian/Belarusian wrestler Alexander Medved is reported to have become a lifelong admirer of Takhti after a match in which Takhti refused to touch his opponent's hurting leg. Similar stories are told of his chivalrous and selfless behavior toward other world-renowned wrestlers. The image of Takhti accepting a gold medal in the 1956 Melbourne Olympics, standing on a platform above his Soviet and American rivals, soon assumed extraordinary anti-imperial importance, given the superpower rivalries of the time.

At the age of thirty-eight, happily married and the father of a young son named after Babak, an Iranian hero of the early Islamic period, and at the height of his success and popularity, Takhti was found dead on 7 January 1968 in a hotel room in Tehran. His millions of admirers simply refused to believe the official government report that this was death by suicide and collectively believed that there was some foul play at work. The myth finally took over reality, and people refused to believe that the shah's secret police had nothing to do with their hero's death.[30] Jalal Al-e Ahmad (1923–1969), a towering figure among twentieth-century public intellectuals, reflected on the death of Takhti in epic terms, embedded fully in Shi'i martyrology and the Karbala complex:

> It is always like that. They kill [heroes like] Seyavash and Sohrab. Because they cannot tolerate them . . . Don't you think this popular myth-making is a kind of defense mechanism for ordinary folks, by way of killing their own frightened persona in face of tyranny, so they can remain hopeful? Forget about Seyavash and Sohrab. In this land, even a common butcher can become a hero, or the leader of a revolutionary sect who plunges deep into a barrel of acid, or the other one who simply disappears, or still the next who ascends the heavens.[31]

Imam Hossein on Display

When Khosrow Golsorkhi was tried and executed under the Pahlavis in 1974; when a few years later in 1981 yet another revolutionary poet, Said Soltanpour, was executed under the Islamic Republic; when other Marxist revolutionaries like Bizhan Jazani (1938–1975) were murdered by the shah's secret police; when the famous Siahkal Marxist uprising happened in 1970; when the founding leaders of the Mojahedin-e Khalq organization were executed; when thousands of oppositional revolutionaries were killed in Khomeini's prisons during the Iran-Iraq War (1980–1988); when the student uprising of 1999 took place; when dissident intellectuals were serially murdered in the Islamic Republic in the same period; when millions of Iranians poured into the streets, discontented in the aftermath of the presidential election of June 2009—in all of these and on many other occasions, the enduring modulations of the Karbala complex metamorphosed into multiple parables and found renewed manners of telling and revealing itself: young men and women rising up against their corrupt elders to establish a better and more just society.

If there is one image that allegorically best represents the sublated figures of Imam Hossein and Jesus Christ combined, updates Goya's iconic representation of the Spanish revolutionaries, and with all of those hidden and obvious metaphors brings together all the youthful revolutionaries rising up against their paternal decay and corruption, it would be the picture of Ahmad Batebi on the cover of the 17 July 1999 issue of the *Economist* magazine—a young student raising the bloodied shirt of a friend during an antigovernment demonstration in Iran in July 1999. At once a crucifix and a public hanging, this was a picture that brought Christ, Che Guevara, Imam Hossein, Mansur al-Hallaj, Sohrab, Seyavash, and the whole archetypal master-form of revolt into full iconic view and galvanized a people, and with them the world. The raised bloodied shirt, the bandana, the long hair, and by an ingeniously serendipitous framing of the photograph, the mourning Madonna at the foot of the martyr (reminiscent of Goya's image)—all the details in this image gather together the diverse strands of martyred masters to represent a singular sign of revolt.

All of these youthful revolutionaries (sublated into an overriding image) were on the mind of the aging Ahmad Shamlou when he composed his by now legendary poem *Sorud-e Ebrahim dar Atash [The Song of Abraham in Fire]*, turning the biblical Jewish prophet into a supreme figure of ennobling revolt. Ahmad Shamlou (1925–2000) was the most cherished and celebrated poet of his lifetime. *Sorud-e Ebrahim dar Atash* was one of Shamlou's most famous and treasured poems, every line and every stanza of which, from beginning to end, is carved on our mind, memory, and soul—like grass-covered calligraphy on an immemorial rock! A fusion of what he considered revolutionary characters—from Abraham (against Nimrod) to Christ (against the Roman Empire) to Esfandiyar (against his royal father King Goshtasp, in Ferdowsi's *Shahnameh*) created the poetic prototype of a meta-historical revolutionary, which Shamlou in turn used to celebrate his own contemporary rebels.

The Song of Abraham in Fire begins like an epic, a pronouncement, a revelation—magnificent, spectacular, and visionary: "*Dar avar-e hhunin-e gorg-o-mish/Digar guneh mardi anak!*" (In the bloody battle of dawn/When wolf/Cannot be told from sheep—Behold: *Ecce Homo*). The rest of the poem is an ode in praise of revolutionary chivalry, rebellious uprising, using the conflated figures of Abraham, Christ, and Esfandiyar (all variations on a transcendent Imam Hossein) as the primordial archetype of sacrifice for decency and humanity. Here is the rest of the poem (in my own translation):

In the bloody battle of dawn
When wolf
Cannot be told from sheep—
Behold:

Ecce Homo
Who wished the earth green
And who deemed love the only thing
Worthy of the most beautiful women!

For this to him
Was no worthless gift
To deserve stoning
And burying under the earth.

What a man!
What a man—who
Used to say that
A heart
Is better bloodied
With seven swords of love;

And a throat
Worthier
Uttering the most beautiful names!

And a lion of a man thus made of iron—
And thus in love—
Traversed the bloodied domain of fate
With an Achilles heel!

An invincible man—
The secret of whose death
Was in the sorrow of love and
In the sadness of solitude.

"Ah, thou sad Esfandiyar!
You are better off with
Your eyes shut!"[32]

"Was it not enough?
Was one not just enough:

To pave my destiny?

I alone screamed:
No!
I refused to succumb—I
Was a voice—just a shape
Among other shapes—and I
Found a meaning.

I was and I
Became—
Not the way a blossom
Becomes a flower,
Or a root
A leaf bud,
Or a seed
A jungle.

No.

Exactly in the same way that
An ordinary man becomes a martyr—
So that the heavens will prostrate to him.

I was no little
Wretched creature—and the way
To my Everlasting Paradise
Was no solitary goat-path of prayers and servitudes:

I needed another kind of God
Worthy of a creature
Who does not bend
His neck in obedience
Just to get by—

And thus I created
Another God."

Alas!

The lion of a man thus made of iron
That you were—
And thus just
Like a mountain,
Long before you fell down
Upon the earth and died,
You had died standing up
Untiring and solid.

But neither God nor Satan—only an Idol
Had written your destiny,
An idol that others had glorified,
An idol that others glorified.[33]

II

HISTORICAL UNFOLDING

4

IN THE BATTLEFIELDS OF HISTORY

Hakim Nasir ibn Khusraw ibn Hares, al-Qubadyani, al-Balkhi, al-Marvazi, commonly known as Nasir Khusraw (1004–1088), was a maverick intellectual, an iconoclastic poet, a revolutionary Shi'i activist, and a renowned philosopher of uncommon brilliance, with a range and catholicity of learning rarely rivaled by his contemporaries—and the works of his contemporaries represented the most magnificent achievements of medieval Iranian and Islamic intellectual history.[1] First and foremost, Nasir Khusraw was a poet of unsurpassed brilliance, stylistic poise, and narrative felicity, a Neoplatonist philosopher with an exceptional command over Greek and Islamic philosophical discourses and (quite a rarity for his time) Persian philosophical diction in particular—to this day the wonder and unsurpassed philosophical joy of those who continue to read and admire him. But above all Nasir Khusraw was a committed Shi'i revolutionary activist who put his life, liberty, learning, and shining intellect at the service of a cause he deeply believed in and thus forever changed with his own indelible mark. In the starry sky of medieval Persian, Islamic, and Shi'i firmaments scarce a star has shined so brilliantly and for so long as that of Nasir Khusraw. Throughout his long and fruitful life, graced by a multitude of poetic and philosophical achievements, he commanded a probing and inquisitive intelligence, and for the most mature part of it he was a believing and practicing revolutionary Shi'i, and thus around his life and his world evolved a universe that forever defined what Shi'ism means—as a voice of dissent, as a moral cause, as a deeply rooted rebellion against the status quo, and as an intellectual project that emboldens all its claims to credulity.

Nasir Khusraw was born in Qubadyan in the Balkh region of Greater Khurasan, a major intellectual and political cosmopolis, in the year

1004 and lived for more than eighty years in that tumultuous century until his peaceful death circa 1088 during those otherwise dangerous times.[2] Much that is known about the various stages of Nasir Khusraw's turbulent and adventurous life—which was spent mostly in his native Khurasan and its environs except for a major journey around the Muslim world that lasted for some seven years (three of which were spent in Cairo)—is extrapolated from his mostly autobiographical poetry, the collection of which in fact reads like a detailed and regular journal of his life and thoughts.[3]

Almost four hundred lunar years had passed since Prophet Muhammad's death in 632 when Nasir Khusraw was born and raised in Khurasan. As a learned Iranian Shi'i, Nasir Khusraw was the product of a very particular political condition in the aftermath of the collapse of the Sassanids and the rise of Islamic empires.[4] Beginning with the earliest phases of Muslim conquests of Iran and Transoxiana, and taking full advantage of the Alborz mountain ranges, local and defiant dynasties in the northern and eastern Iranian plateau were staunchly resisting Arab advances and had established autonomous territories that remained more or less independent of the central Umayyad and Abbasid caliphates.

A succession of Iranian and subsequently (heavily Persianized) Turkish dynasties ruled over the Khurasan of Nasir Khusraw's parental birth, childhood, and youth.[5] When Nasir Khusraw was born, Khurasan was firmly under the rule of the Ghaznavids (977–1186) and soon after that the Seljuqids (1038–1194), two Turkish dynasties with deep and abiding Sunni convictions.[6] Just before the Seljuqids, and then simultaneous with them, the Ghaznavids ruled over a vast territory in Khurasan, Afghanistan, and northern Iran, but with the advent of the Seljuqids, from eastern Iran to western Syria and deep into Anatolia had all come under one massive Turkish dynasty. Despite (or perhaps because) of their tribal Turkish origins, both the Ghaznavids and the Seljuqids relied heavily on Persian administrative skills and on ancient Iranian theories and practices of political legitimacy to run two vast and multifaceted empires. Samarqand, Bukhara, and Ghazna for the Ghaznavids, Balkh and Isfahan for the Seljuqids, and Baghdad for the Abbasids emerged as major cosmopolitan centers of high Islamic culture and vast ecumenical learning, exquisite art and monumental architecture, exact sciences and competing philosophies, political thought and theological contestations. When Nasir Khusraw writes of missing his hometown of Balkh, he means missing the cosmopolitan urbanity and the literary humanism [*adab*] of his intellectual upbringing.[7]

It was during the reign of Sultan Mahmud of Ghazna (998–1030) that the Ghaznavids created an expansive empire that stretched from Central Asia through eastern Iran and contemporary Afghanistan, all the way down into the Indian subcontinent. Nasir Khusraw was born and then reached intellectual maturity during the reign of Sultan Mahmud, just as the Seljuqids were getting ready to take away a major chunk of the sultan's dynasty after his death. The Iranian and the Islamic world at large remember the reign of Sultan Mahmud first and foremost because of his conquest of India, but also for the fact that the greatest Muslim scientist of the time, Abu Rayhan al-Biruni (973–1048), accompanied Sultan Mahmud in this conquest in 1030 and wrote (among his other monumental works) an astonishing anthropological account of India, *Tahqiq ma li'l-Hindi* [An Investigation Concerning India], that to this day is used with wonder and confidence by scholars.[8] Ferdowsi's *Shahnameh* (circa 1000) was also completed during the reign of Sultan Mahmud and dedicated to him, without much reward or appreciation on the part of the Turkish warlord. After the reign of the Samanids, the Ghaznavid empire under Sultan Mahmud is usually considered the height of the Iranian cultural renaissance (the so-called *Shu'ubiyyah* movement) in the aftermath of the Arab conquest, when Persian language and culture, literature and the humanities, art and architecture, asserted its presence in the easternmost parts of the Abbasid empire. Nasir Khusraw's literary, poetic, and philosophical achievements and his confident and proud character are very much the results of this cosmopolitan environment.

The Poet Philosopher

These political developments had far reaching and unprecedented cultural consequences. The rise of Nasir Khusraw as a poet, a philosopher, and a revolutionary Shi'i activist occurred in the midst of an Iranian cultural renaissance (Shu'ubiyyah) in the aftermath of the Arab conquest—a renaissance that thrived on a magnificent and multifaceted *adab* (literary humanism) with an expansive emotive and aesthetic universe, and in particular the consolidation of an unprecedented Persian philosophical prose, adjacent to the more dominant and multifarious Arabic as the lingua franca of Islamic intellectual effervescence. This cultural renaissance had an effect on the urbanity of the Shi'i cosmopolitanism—its affiliation with the high court of the Buyids in particular, and an intellectual elite, which Nasir Khusraw best represented. It is imperative to have a full assessment of this cosmopolitan context in which Shi'i revolutionary intellectuals like Nasir Khusraw emerged, so that its juridical and sectarian disposition will not over-dominate our grasp of what medieval Shi'ism meant and signified.

Though first and foremost a committed Shi'i revolutionary activist of uncommon convictions and determination, Nasir Khusraw was a product of an cultural renaissance and of Persian literary humanism in particular. He was a maverick intellectual in the sense that he was not only a brave and iconoclastic poet (a major pillar of classical Persian poetry), but also a foremost philosopher of his time; not just a first-rank philosopher but also a revolutionary activist; and then not just that but also a social critic of uncompromising principles. The picture that emerges of Nasir Khusraw, the closer we look at him, is not limited to any one category—a poet, a philosopher, a theologian, a revolutionary activist, a social critic—but in effect he combines all these forces and factors together to forge a new intellectual character, who in turn becomes definitive to the kind of Shi'ism that he best personified. This multifaceted character, a cosmopolitan revolutionary and a worldly wise, determined, and driven man in both political and intellectual terms, indicates two significant facts about Nasir Khusraw in his medieval context: First, true to the restless and agitated spirit of Shi'ism, Nasir Khusraw could not be confined to any one overriding category, and the charismatic effervescence of Shi'ism animated his moral and intellectual imagination. Second, he was a bona fide product of a Persian literary humanism that embraced all these fields of knowledge and activity and yet was irreducible to any one of them. These two facts in turn characterize not just Nasir Khusraw personally but also the religion he had embraced after long periods of reading, reflection, travel, and activism. Nasir Khusraw, in short, is the personification of the cosmopolitan character of Shi'ism in its medieval gestation—derived from a cultural urbanity that extended from Balkh and Ghazna, through Ray and Isfahan, down to Baghdad and Cairo. Left to its own theological devices, Shi'ism would have been lost in the vacuous space between its historical battlefields and its juridical scholasticism. Placed in its cosmopolitan context, Shi'ism by osmosis permeated a cultural renaissance and a literary humanism in which it partook freely and subconsciously. Throughout its long and arduous history, Shi'ism has been the faith of the majority in its communities of believers with an overriding sense of a minority complex, for it has always been a numerical minority in the grand scheme of things, though a majority in the pockets of communal beliefs and resistance it has formed. The faith of a majority with a minority complex, Shi'ism has survived its otherwise tumultuous history by virtue of its ability to hide and seek solace in cosmopolitan contexts that at once conceal its anxieties and confirm its paradoxes.

Back in the Battlefields

Outside the courtly confidence of the Buyid dynasty and adjacent to the cosmopolitan urbanity of Nasir Khusraw's birth and breeding in Khurasan, Shi'ism continued to nurture and cultivate its revolutionary character in the battlefields of its tumultuous history. Both the Ghaznavids and the Seljuqids were staunch Sunni dynasties, and in conjunction with the central Abbasid caliphate they pretty much defined the religious, political, and intellectual domain of the Muslim universe. Yet revolutionary Shi'ism was very much alive and well, not just in the form of autonomous dynasties at the far edges of the Muslim world, but in fact more so in the range of revolutionary uprisings against the central caliphate and their Turkish sultanates.

Looking at the moral bankruptcy, political tyranny, tribal patrimonialism, clannish racism, and economic ravages of the Umayyad period (661–750) leaves no room for speculation as to why and how revolutionary messages like Shi'ism (among others) were popular, particularly with the increasingly impoverished peasantry, the displaced Bedouins, and the urban poor.[9] Above all else, a blatant and mightily flaunted sense of racialized supremacy, combined with a patrimonial tribalism writ imperially large, marked the ascendency of the Umayyads to power, translating, effectively, the metaphysical universalism of the Qur'anic message into political imperialism without the slightest regard for the consistent admonitions of the Prophet and his message on behalf of the poor, the weak, and the forsaken. In addition to the destitute peasantry and the urban poor, the Umayyads abused a third group of people, who they disdainfully called the *Mawali*, namely non-Arab Muslims who were treated with normalized, legalized, and systemic discrimination. Nothing of the initial and pervasive generosity of spirit that accompanied Muhammad's Qur'anic messages, his caring for and kindness toward the poor, and scarce anything of the social revolution that was meant to turn their lot around, remained remotely evident in the imperial arrogance and tribal hubris of the Umayyad dynasty as they went around the world emulating their superpower predecessors (the Sassanids and the Byzantines) with a clannish provincialism written to their imperialism.[10]

The first Islamic century witnessed the rise of the Umayyad caliphs presiding over a vast feudal fiefdom maintained mostly by Arab generals turned feudal warlords of the conquered and fertile territories—a development that resulted in a mass rural poverty breaking down under the burden of heavy and multiple taxations forced on the poor and weak peasantry in order to support and maintain an obscenely lavish court life and a world-conquering army. The tribal Arab chieftains (now nothing but nominally Muslim) soon assumed a position of superiority not just over non-Muslims but even more so over non-Arab Muslims, the Mawali. Beginning with the caliphate of Uthman (reigned 644–656), poor and disenfranchised Muslims became disgruntled with his favoritism towards the Banu Umayyad tribe and began to gather their sentiments and political force around Ali ibn Abi Talib. Devout ascetics like Abu Dharr a-Ghifari and Salman the Persian were attracted to Ali and his proverbial piety and began propagating his cause among the poor and the Mawali, namely the masses of impoverished Arabs and non-Arabs left disenfranchised by the rising tribal fortunes of the political elite.[11]

In 656, finally a group of Muslims disaffected by Uthman's rule conspired against the caliph and murdered him. By communal consensus, Ali succeeded Abu Bakr and became the Fourth Rightly Guided Caliph *(Khulafa al-Rashidun)*. Two Muslim generals, Talhah and Zubayr, in collaboration with the Prophet's youngest wife Ayeshah, revolted against Ali and accused him of having had a hand in the murder of Uthman. Ali defeated them in the Battle of Camel (so-called because Ayeshah participated in this battle, mounting a camel) near Basra in 656. A year later, in May-July 657, Ali faced yet another rebellious army, this one led by Mu'awiyah, again using the murder of Uthman as a pretext and challenging Ali's authority. Ali faced Mu'awiyah's army in the Battle of Siffin on the banks of the Euphrates. Ali was about to win this battle too when Mu'awiyah ordered pages of the Qur'an raised on lances, thereby asking for arbitration. Ali agreed, but a band of his followers became so angry at this decision that they parted ways [*kharaja*] with him and formed the radical sect of the Kharijites. One of these angry Kharijites, a man named Abd al-Rahman ibn Muljam, finally killed Ali on 27 January 661. Ali's son Hasan was in no mood to engage Mu'awiyah in any battle, and thus Mu'awiyah proceeded to establish the Umayyad dynasty, which lasted until the advent of the Abbasid revolution in 750. The battles of Camel and Siffin anticipated the Battle of Karbala and wrote the blueprint for the rest of Shi'i history.[12]

Beginning with the reign of Mu'awiyah, the Umayyad dynasty continued to exacerbate the emerging class differences between the small patriarchal network of the tribal elite and the masses of Muslims (both Arab and increasingly non-Arab). Under the banner of Shi'ism and now an even more revolutionary force, the Kharijites, resistance and revolt against the Umayyads became widespread. Attracted to both the Kharijites and the Shi'ites were four distinct groups of Muslims: the displaced and disenfranchised Bedouins, the impoverished peasantry, the urban poor, and the disaffected Mawali, which included landlords, peasants, and the merchant class. When Mu'awiyah died in 680, some of these disgruntled groups gathered around Hossein ibn Ali and expected him to lead them in an uprising against the Umayyads. He did, though without any effective mobilization of these forces, against the reigning caliph, Yazid ibn Mu'awiyah. Hossein and his small band of comrades were massacred in 680 in the Battle of Karbala, and soon after that Mokhtar ibn Abi Ubaydah Saqafi led a far more successful Shi'i uprising against the Umayyads and in revenge of Imam Hossein's murder.

It is important to keep in mind that the Shi'ites were not the only revolutionaries during the Umayyad period, and the general condition of poverty and destitution of the masses of both Arab and non-Arab Muslims in scattered parts of the expansive empire (to the east and the west of Arabia) attracted ordinary people to just about any ideology of revolt, which in this period inevitably assumed messianic (not all of it Islamic) overtones. The revolt of the Kharijites against the Umayyads was in fact far more radical than those of the Shi'ites and attracted more of the Mawali, the urban poor, and particularly the impoverished peasantry. By 686, a radical branch of the Kharijites called the Azraqites led a major uprising against the Umayyads in Iraq and southern Iran. It took the brutality of Hajjaj ibn Youssef (661–714), the governor of Iraq, to quell these Kharijite uprisings. For decades, the Kharijites remained the arch-nemesis of the Umayyads and appealed to a sense of equity and justice among Muslims of all sorts. Their revolutionary struggles were particularly attractive to the Mawali. The appeal and presence of the Kharijite revolts reached as far east as Sistan, Khurasan, and Transoxiana, relieving their insurrectionary followers, wherever they succeeded, from paying any taxes to the caliphal authorities.[13]

A major source of menace for the Umayyads that ultimately resulted in their demise was the Abbasids movement, led by Abu Muslim Khurasani, an Iranian general in charge of their military operation. The Abbasids claimed legitimacy to succeed the Prophet's rule based on their descent from Abbas ibn Abd al-Muttalib (566–622), one of the Prophet's younger uncles. Thus they opposed the Umayyads, who were from a completely different clan—one that was in fact initially hostile to Muhammad's prophetic mission. The Abbasid movement points to the dissatisfaction of not just the impoverished peasantry, the urban poor, and the Mawali, but also a rising class of Mawali merchants who saw the tribal racism of the Umayyads as an impediment to their increasingly lucrative business opportunities. Around Abu Muslim gathered masses of peasantry and urban poor from Khurasan as well as the Mawali—Shi'is and Sunnis, as well as Zoroastrians of various political persuasions. In successive battles in Tus, Neishabur, Gorgan, and finally Baghdad, the Abbasid movement, championed by Abu Muslim, managed to topple the Umayyad dynasty in 750.[14]

The Abbasid dynasty soon abandoned its initial multidenominational appeal, and before long a Sunni jurisprudence was consolidated as the juridical foundation of its state. The Abbasid dynasty further fortified the feudal system it had inherited from the Umayyads and incorporated Iranian elite into its ruling apparatus. The first action taken by the powerful Abbasid caliph al-Mansur (reigned 754–775) was to brutally murder Abu Muslim. Abu Muslim's connection to the masses of peasantry and urban poor (particularly in his home state of Khurasan) had something to do with his murder. The Abbasids used him to come to power, but then his appeal to the Muslim and Mawali masses became a liability for his ruling patrons. After his death, Abu Muslim gradually emerged as a legendary figure among his extended followers and further destabilized the authority of the Abbasids in Khurasan. A multiple taxing system increased the poverty and destitution of the peasantry and made them ready for revolt, whoever led them and under whatever messianic or sectarian idea.[15]

Under the Abbasids, Sunni theology in general and Sunni jurisprudence in particular became the ideological apparatus of the ruling feudal elite, whereas Shi'ism, having finally outlasted all other revolutionary movements, remained the principal ideological force of dissent and revolt, appealing to the impoverished peasantry and the urban poor as a way of protesting the status quo. The cosmopolitan imperialism of the Abbasids incorporated the Mawali (the Persian elements in particular) into their ruling ranks, as evident in the prominence of the Barmecides family of *wizirs* that served the Abbasids for generations. Within a year after the success of the Abbasids, the Shi'i revolt against them was well under way, particularly in Nasir Khusraw's home province of Khurasan.

The brutal murder of Abu Muslim was the prima facie cause of any number of revolts that took place in Khurasan and elsewhere to avenge his death. These were mostly proto-Zoroastrian in their ideological foregrounding. The revolt of Sunbadh in 755 in Khurasan was one such uprising. In his army, Sunbadh had Shi'i and Mazdakite followers alike.[16] There are reports that tens of thousands of Muslims and non-Muslims had gathered around him. He started his revolt in Neishabur but appealed to a much wider geographical domain. Al-Muqanna' was another such proto-Zoroastrian revolutionary who led a major uprising between 776 and 783 in Central Asia. Ustadhsis led yet another revolt in 767, with a massive body of Khurasani peasantry among his followers. By far the most important proto-Zoroastrian revolt of this period was the one led by the legendary Babak Khorram-din. In 816 Babak revolted against the Abbasids. Between 820 and 827 he launched a number of military campaigns against the Abbasids and freed a substantial territory from the caliphal administrators and local governors. Babak was finally arrested and brutally murdered by the caliph in 837. Similar revolts took place in Tabarestan, Bukhara, Gilan, Khurasan, and Sistan. Closer to home at the seat of the Abbasid caliphs there were even more determined revolts. Launched from Basra by way of an African-Arab alliance, the Zanj Revolt (869–883), which contrary to many assumptions was not an exclusively "slave revolt" but in fact a revolt led by seafaring merchants of African descent, shook the foundation of the Abbasid caliphate in the Persian Gulf area.[17]

The collapse of the central Abbasid caliphate and the rise of independent dynasties around the Muslim world were well under way as early as 755 in Spain, 868 in Morocco, and 909 in Egypt. Soon Armenia and Georgia followed suit, as did the eastern provinces in Iran, Central Asia, and Transoxiana. The Taherian, Saffarid, Samanian, and the Buyid were dynasties that were formed around local feudalism revolting against the central caliphate and its heavy taxation system.[18] When

Harun al-Rashid died in 809, the battle between his two sons, Amin (who was an Arabophile) and Ma'mun (who was an Iranophile, for his mother was Iranian), much weakened the authority of the Abbasids around their empire, to the point that Ya'qub Layth Saffar (840–879), an Iranian rebel and the founder of the Saffarid dynasty in Sistan, dared to challenge the caliphate. He moved to topple it altogether but failed.[19] Meanwhile Sunni theology, particularly the Ash'arite *kalam* (as opposed to its rationalist nemesis the Mu'tazilite school of theology), was systematized and consolidated as the ruling ideology of the dominant feudal caliphate.

These uprisings, mostly peopled and supported by the impoverished peasantry, urban poor, and disadvantaged merchant class, targeted the central caliphate and their feudal theology and jurisprudence, and the tribal culture of the Umayyads transposed into a metaphysical narrative, institutionalized into Sunni Kalam and the office of caliphate. The Abbasid dynasty very much addressed the disenfranchised Mawali by incorporating their elite into the ruling class of its cosmopolitan imperialism. But the Abbasids in turn produced their own inner contradictions by generating a mercantile class, who took advantage of the trade routes and became wealthy and yet were disenfranchised from partaking in the social apparatus of that wealth. Neither the central Abbasid caliphate nor the staunch Sunni Turkish dynasties of the Ghaznavids and the Seljuqids, and indeed not even the Twelve-Imami Shi'ism of the Iranian dynasties by the Caspian Sea, provided any satisfying normative or moral universe to which a restless intellectual like Nasir Khusraw could subscribe. It was now to an entirely different and differing fertile land, to the Fatimids in Syria, Palestine, and Egypt, that a man of his restless nature was most urgently drawn. He was now irresistibly attracted to the capital of the Fatimids in Cairo.

The Restless Poet

These Shi'i and non-Shi'i revolts during the first two centuries of Islamic history, between the death of the Prophet in 632 and the birth of Nasir Khusraw in 1004, shook both the Umayyad and the Abbasid caliphate to their foundations. They could not have been absent from the Persian poet and Shi'i revolutionary's mind and soul. Now in his twenties and thirties (between 1024 and 1034), Nasir Khusraw was growing up under the Turkish dynasties of the Ghaznavids and then the Seljuqids in

Khurasan—both regionally and militarily autonomous sultanates and yet entirely contingent on the central Sunni caliphate of the Abbasids in Baghdad.

All the indications are that Nasir Khusraw was from a prominent and learned family, and that he began his education at a very young age. In his twenties and thirties, he was employed at the court of the Ghaznavids and became quite wealthy and famous in the royal administrations, serving at the court of both Sultan Mahmud (reigned 998–1030) and his son Sultan Mas'ud (reigned 1031–1041). At this time, Nasir Khusraw enjoyed the lavish life of a highly educated and successful young man, who among his other talents was a gifted poet and a talented painter. (Years later we will learn that in Arabia he made a living as a painter, and in Jerusalem he sketched some of its monuments in his travel book.) Nasir Khusraw advanced to the highest positions in the Ghaznavid court in Balkh, and when the city fell to the Seljuqids in 1040 he advanced even higher as he moved from Balkh to Marv.[20]

As a young man, Nasir Khusraw became interested in non-Islamic religions and learned all he could about Judaism, Christianity, Zoroastrianism, and even Hinduism. He became an avid reader and a bibliophile and collected many books, which he carried with him in his journeys. He tells how during his travels he would mount his books and his younger brother on his camel and walk next to them. In his youth, Nasir Khusraw traveled throughout Central Asia and most probably went as far east as India. His tireless and adventurous soul was insatiable and even troubled. He confesses that he was a heavy drinker and indulged in all his carnal senses. Deeply curious and restive, he traveled widely in search of answers, debating religious scholars and Sufi saints, not satisfied with anything he read or heard. His perturbed mind kept the young rebel's nose to the moral grindstone. He was a cultivated rebel in search of a cause. Paramount in Nasir Khusraw's mostly autobiographical poetry, which he began writing at this young age and continued until his death, is an ethic of responsibility, a sustained celebration of reason, of rationality, of searching for truth, of a singular determination toward purposeful and meaningful knowledge.[21]

Shi'ism Splits

Three major revolutionary movements (among more scattered uprisings) mark the medieval history of Shi'ism after the Battle of Karbala in

680: one after the death of the Third Shi'i Imam (al-Hossein) in 680, which is known as the *Kaysaniyyah*, one after the death of the Fifth Shi'i Imam (al-Baqir) in 732, known as the *Zaydiyah*, and then by far the most radical and important of them all surrounding the death of the Seventh Shi'i Imam (Isma'il) in 754, known as *Isma'ilism*. The political conditions after the death of each of these three Shi'i imams in particular was such that their respective revolutionary momentum took off in powerful, poignant, and enduring ways. The Kaysaniyyah evolved from the followers of Mokhtar Saqafi who had revolted in revenge of Imam Hossein's murder. For a short period of time they in fact accounted for the majority of the Shi'is, until the advent of the Abbasids in 750. To the Kaysaniyyah were attracted a good portion of the Mawali, and among their doctrinal beliefs the positions of the Ghulat [extremists] found a hospitable space, among which was the attribution of divinity to the early Shi'i imams. In the wake of the Abbasid revolution, most of the Kaysaniyyah joined forces with Abu Muslim to topple the Umayyads. A similar, if not even more radical, group of Shi'is emerged after the death of the Fifth (quietist) Shi'i Imam, Muhammad al-Baqir. Zayd ibn Ali was a half brother of Imam al-Baqir and mostly identified not with his pacifist father, the Fourth Shi'i Imam Zayn al-Abidin, but with his grandfather Imam Hossein ibn Ali, and led an uprising against the Umayyads that was later known as the Zaydiyah movement. Zayd ibn Ali was reminiscent of his grandfather in his revolutionary appeal, and in his own charismatic appeal in fact renewed the Third Shi'i Imam's defiant character. Zayd altogether rejected the inherited notion of succession in Shi'ism and believed a leader must raise arms and by opposing tyranny claim his authority. Before his death in 740, Zayd had led a rebellion so successful that it outlasted his death. His work survived well into the Abbasid period and succeeded even in establishing two separatist states in Yemen and Daylam by the Caspian Sea. Central to both the Kaysaniyyah and the Zaydiyah movements was the notion of the Mahdi or Messiah, and their revolutionary messianism survived to define Shi'i insurrectionary spirit throughout the medieval period.[22]

Yet by far the most successful Shi'i revolutionary uprising of this period with enduring political and intellectual consequences was Isma'ilism, which emerged soon after the death of the Seventh Shi'i Imam Isma'il al-Mubarak. The traumatic origin of Isma'ilism commenced with the death of Isma'il in 754, only eleven years before his father Imam Ja'far al-Sadiq died in 765. His premature demise created a theological problem among some of the Shi'i followers of Imam Ja'far al-Sadiq. How could an imam appoint a successor who would die before becoming the leader of the community? That would not tally well with the assumption of the imams' *'ismah* (infallibility). So some of Imam Ja'far al-Sadiq's followers believed his initial decision was correct and that Isma'il had not died. Rather, they insisted (on the perennial Shi'i model) that he will come back to lead his community. The followers of Isma'il during his own lifetime were rooted in a community of Shi'is dissatisfied with Imam al-Sadiq's quietist, scholastic, and conciliatory actions and ideas. Isma'il himself was a politically engaged revolutionary who early on was involved in a plot against the Abbasid dynasty. Meanwhile the majority of the Shi'is followed Imam Ja'far al-Sadiq's eldest surviving son Abdullah al-Aftah, and when he died a few months later, most of his followers turned to his half-brother Musa al-Kazim (died 799) as their Seventh Imam and followed his line through to form the Twelve-Imami Shi'is, forever parting ways with the Isma'ilis, who remained Seven-Imami Shi'is, and who at this point opted to consider Isma'il's son Muhammad ibn Isma'il as their imam. A smaller splinter group of Imam Ja'far al-Sadiq's followers opted for the leadership of one of his other sons, Muhammad ibn Ja'far al-Dibaj (died 815), who led a successful revolt against the Abbasids in 815. The splintering of Shi'i groups provides another clear indication that the revolutionary disposition of Isma'il and the movement he initiated was rooted in fertile political fields. Rebellions broke out soon after the Abbasids used Shi'is (and other rebellious movements) for their own political ends against the Umayyads and then turned against them once in power.[23]

In the emergence of Isma'ilism as the most enduring revolutionary uprising of Shi'ism in its medieval register, we witness an active resurrection of the prototype of the "son-religion," in which a deferred defiance catches up with its communal history. The siding of the Shi'i community on a mass historical and geographical scale with the rebellious son (Isma'il) over and against the quietist father (Ja'far al-Sadiq) here assumes the added momentum of the son having died or disappeared before the father—signaling by far the most significant archetypal trauma of the faith. The fact that Isma'il's son Muhammad was subsequently considered the successor to his deceased father further exacerbates this proto-filial modulation of revolutionary Shi'ism, always siding with the deferred expectation of a future yet (though never) to come, a utopia based on a dystopic reading of reality—a reality which is yet to be, to become, to materialize. Always predicated on a deferred defiance, the Shi'i utopia is in fact a reverse-angle reading of a dystopia writ universally large upon the Earth.

If we follow through the traumatic moment of Isma'ilism in the aftermath of Imam Ja'far al-Sadiq's death, Muhammad ibn Isma'il, his grandson, cuts a particularly powerful posture as a son-figure. Born in 738, he was sixteen when his father Isma'il died and twenty-seven when his grandfather Ja'far died. Despite the fact that he was actually older than his uncle Musa al-Kazim, whom Twelve-Imami Shi'ism considers to be their Seventh Imam, he was imaginatively perceived as twice as young as him in generational terms. Soon after the death of his father and grandfather, Muhammad the son of Isma'il effectively disappeared into thin air, removing himself from the public eye. He "left Medina for the East and went into hiding to avoid Abbasid persecution, initiating the *dawr al-satr* or period of concealment in early Isma'ili history. Henceforth, Muhammad acquired the epithet of al-Maktum (the Hidden One), in addition to al-Maymun (the Fortunate One)."[24] If historians were to disregard the sacred memory of the forsaken son and follow his traces, then Muhammad the son of Isma'il must have died sometime after 795 during the reign of the Abbasid caliph Harun al-Rashid.[25] Not just around the figure of Isma'il, the rebellious son who died before his pacifist father, but also around Isma'il's own son Muhammad, who carried the memory of all Shi'is' sons into an unknown posterity, Isma'ilism charismatically constituted its institutional claim to an amorphous memory, a vicarious past, a precarious future.

The deferred defiance embedded in Shi'ism stayed in a state of suspended animation for almost a century and a half—between the disappearance and then death in anonymity of Isma'il in 754 and the rise of the Qaramita in 899 and the Fatimid dynasty in 909. For generations after Muhammad ibn Isma'il went into hiding for fear of Abbasid persecution, the leaders of the Isma'ili movement opted for quiet but effective organization of their doctrines and the mobilization of their followers until a certain Abdullah al-Mahdi (reigned 909–934) proclaimed himself an imam and in due course succeeded in establishing the Fatimid dynasty in Egypt.[26] The establishment of the Fatimids in Egypt followed a major doctrinal transmutation in Isma'ilism. Toward the end of the ninth century, Abdullah al-Mahdi suspended the notion of *Mahdiship*, namely the Shi'i expectation of the return of the Mahdi or "the Hidden Imam," in this case of Muhammad ibn Isma'il, and claimed Imamate directly for himself. At this point, Abdullah al-Mahdi also claimed that all the previous generations of Isma'ili leadership had in fact thought of themselves as *imam* and not as *hujjat,* or deputies of the hidden Imam. Rewriting the doctrinal history of the early Isma'ilism, Abdullah al-Mahdi so re-imagined Muhammad ibn Isma'il that his name became a generic moniker for all the descendents of Imam Ja'far al-Sadiq, himself included—thus altogether bypassing the doctrine of Mahdiship and claiming Imamah personally for himself, on his way to becoming the very first caliph and imam of the Fatimid imperial dynasty.[27]

Abdullah al-Mahdi's impromptu decision to write a revisionist history of Isma'ilism by way of proclaiming himself the imam did not sit well with all his followers, and his decision resulted in a major schism in the Isma'ili movement in the year 899. The first clandestine leader of the Isma'ilis during the period between the death of Muhammad ibn Isma'il in 795 and the rise of Abdullah al-Mahdi as the founder of the Fatimid dynasty was a certain Abdullah al-Akbar, who through one of his deputies, a revolutionary leader named Hamdan Qarmat, was converted to Isma'ilism in 874. Hamdan and his brother-in-law Abdan, originally from Ahvaz, were initially among the followers of Abdullah al-Mahdi until he decided to alter the doctrine of Mahdiship and call himself the imam. In the year 899, Hamdan dispatched his deputy Abdan to the Isma'ili headquarters in Salamiyyah in central Syria, where he met with al-Mahdi, and where "to his astonishment, Abdan discovered that instead of acknowledging the Mahdiship of Muhammad b. Isma'il, the new leader now claimed the Imamate for himself and his ancestors, the same individuals who had actually organized and led the Isma'ili movement after Muhammad b. Isma'il."[28] Abdan reported this change of doctrine to Hamdan in Iraq, and Hamdan in turn denounced al-Mahdi's decision and summoned Abdan to Iraq. Upon his return to Iraq, Abdan was soon murdered by a loyal follower of al-Mahdi. Hamdan went into hiding and soon emerged as the leader of the most radical offshoot of the Isma'ilis in their nascent stage.

Hamdan Qarmat's movement, away from the redirection of Isma'ilism by al-Mahdi toward the establishment of the Fatimid empire, later became known as the Qaramita, a utopian uprising that wreaked havoc on the Abbasids, established a proto-socialist commune in the Persian Gulf and eastern Arabia, and lasted for almost a century and a half. In the first half of the tenth century (roughly between 906 and 952), the Qaramita were the champions of a radical Shi'i movement, drawing their main support from the impoverished and landless peasantry, the tribal Bedouins, as well as the small seafaring merchants. So exactly at the moment when Abdullah al-Mahdi was about to abandon the messianic disposition of Shi'ism and establish a Shi'i dynastic empire, a son-figure was born from the bosom of their common revolutionary heritage and stayed the course for the charismatic zeal embedded in the Karbala complex. By 874, the Qaramita were on the move against the Abbasids, and by 880 Hamdan Qarmat tried to strike an alliance with the Zanj movement but failed. No later than 890 Hamdan Qarmat had built a fortress near Kufa as the headquarters of his revolutionary activities. As a revolutionary movement, the Qaramita were directly rooted among the impoverished Bedouins of eastern Arabia, the poor peasants of the same area, as well as city-based professional guilds in Syria and Iraq, all the way down to Yemen, and then in the other direction as far north as Khurasan, where they appealed in particular to the educated elite for their leadership. The Qaramita believed in and practiced a primitive form of socialism. By the middle of the tenth century, the Qaramita were the most powerful Shi'i-inspired insurrectionary force, launching relentless attacks against the political, theological, and commercial foundations of the Abbasid regime.[29]

The establishment of the Fatimid dynasty in 909, after almost a century and a half of secret mobilization, marked the first occasion when a family claiming descent (albeit circuitous) from Ali ibn Abi Talib established a major political dynasty in Egypt. They subsequently extended it into North Africa, Syria, and Palestine, right under the nose of the Sunni Abbasids. One must of course see the rise of the Fatimids early in the tenth century in Egypt in line with other separatist movements that had in fact preceded them by more than a century. Having assumed power in Egypt, the Fatimids soon sought to expand their Shi'i empire all over the Islamic world, sending propaganda officers or *da'is* to the farthest reaches of Muslim lands. The Fatimids (909–1171) ruled over North Africa, Egypt, Syria, and Palestine for more than two and a half centuries until given their deathblow by Saladin in 1171. The Qaramita, centered in Bahrain, controlled eastern and central Arabia roughly from 894 to the end of the eleventh century. While the Fatimids ruled over a vast and expansive empire, the Qaramita were limited to a small enclave of revolutionary Shi'is who sacked Kufa, attacked caravans, occupied Oman, and in 929 even invaded Mecca, taking *Hajar al-Aswad* [the Black Stone, sacred to all Muslims and central to the rituals of the Hajj pilgrimage] with them, not returning it until two decades later following the Fatimid Al-Mansur's request.[30]

The Kaysaniyyah, the Zaydiyah, the Qaramita, the Ghulat, and the Isma'ilis in general were various versions of grassroots proto-Shi'i movements of the first three Islamic centuries that increasingly assumed theological and even philosophical dispositions and doctrines. The Isma'ili appeal extended from Syria, Palestine, Iraq, and Arabia all the way north to Khurasan, Central Asia, and Transoxiana. In intellectual and philosophical terms, Neoplatonism and Christian Gnosticism heavily influenced the emerging Isma'ili doctrines, for more than a century the concealed preoccupation of a cadre of Shi'i thinkers and activists. The Isma'ilis believed in concentric gradations of creation, extending a hierarchical line of divine effusion through ascending and descending celestial spheres that came down from the Divine Absolute to what they called *'Aql-e Kol* [the universal intellect], passing down to *Nafs-e Kol* [the universal soul], and from there to *al-A'yan al-Thabitah* [Perennial Archetypes], before they finally reached the material world of sensible phenomena. The Isma'ilis further believed in a *batini* [esoteric] meaning of the Qur'an, hidden from the masses and known or knowable only to a select few.[31] Both the Isma'ili philosophical constitution of hierarchical, at once ascending and descending, spheres of creation and their doctrinal belief in the hidden meaning of the sacred word of God dovetailed perfectly with their secretive organizational needs and the strict disciplinary apparatus in their revolutionary activities. Their belief in hierarchical gradations had both a metaphysical and an even more immediate political purpose and function.

A Muslim Machiavelli

By the time the accumulated legacy and enduring effervescence of these revolutionary movements, mostly variations on Shi'i doctrines, reached Khwajah Nizam al-Mulk al-Tusi (1018–1092), the Muslim Machiavelli who quit this world over three centuries before his Italian counterpart was born, they required a thorough examination and an urgent theorization. Nizam al-Mulk, the omnipotent Seljuqid vizier who was ultimately murdered by an Isma'ili assassin, thought that Shi'ism and all its offshoots amounted to such a paramount threat to the security of the Seljuqid state that it required him to put them all together and theorize their troubling "menace." Reading the chapters of the *Siyasatnama* that he devotes to the revolutionary movements of his time is like reading a detailed intelligence report. He provides a detailed assessment of the threat—geographical locations, important leaders, doctrines and practices, their varied constituency, the danger they pose to the Seljuqid state apparatus. Further, he proposes harsh measures to deal with the revolutionary forces. "On Describing Those of Evil Religion Who Are the Enemy of This Kingdom and of Islam" is the descriptive title of the forty-third chapter of *Siyasatnama,* which Nizam al-Mulk wrote in 1076 for the Seljuqid warlord Malikshah (reigned 1072–1092). Nizam al-Mulk then proceeds to say that he intends to write a few chapters on the meaning of *khuruj* [revolt] in order to describe the great services he has performed for the Seljuqids. He calls those who revolt against their sovereign lord "dogs" that are hiding behind walls and waiting for the right moment to attack and dismantle the government and spread their infamy. These rebellious creatures, for Nizam al-Mulk, include the Kharijites, the Shi'ites, and the (proto-Zoroastrian) Khorram-dinan. There are, Nizam al-Mulk believes, Kharijite and Shi'i sympathizers quite close to Malikshah who are instigating him to topple the Abbasid caliphate. But thanks to Nizam al-Mulk and his good council the sultan has so far refrained from committing such a folly. He writes this book, he says, in order for it to remain a guide and a warning for the sultan once he is no longer alive to advise him in person.

Nizam al-Mulk's purpose in these chapters is to provide a genealogy of such rebellious behaviors, link them together, posit them as the enemy of the state, of religion, of morality, and above all as the enemies of private property. In order to drive home his point about the communistic disposition of these rebellious movements, Nizam al-Mulk makes repeated and scandalizing references to how these rebels wanted people to share their wives. Men will bring up to twenty guests home, he says, and their wives will be required to sleep with all of them. A hat will be hung at the door of a wife entertaining a male friend of her husband, so that other men passing by will know that she is busy and will not enter to expect services. "There is no sense of jealousy [*rashk*] or honor [*hamiyyat*]" among these rebels, Nizam al-Mulk reports.[32]

In the genealogy that he constructs for such rebellious behaviors against kings and their kingdoms, Nizam al-Mulk begins with the Iranian proto-socialist revolutionary prophet Mazdak the son of Bamdadan, who died circa 528, calling him the first person to have brought a degenerate [*mu'tallah*] religion. Mazdak revolted during the time of Sassanid king Qubad (reigned 488–531) and along with his followers was massacred by Qubad's son Khosrow Anushiravan, who reigned from 531 to 579. Nizam al-Mulk's vindictive, scandalized tone and abusive language in this and subsequent chapters consistently banks on offending the Islamic (patriarchal) sensitivities of his readers, turning Mazdak's proto-socialism into an amoral program of wife-sharing. From Mazdak, Nizam al-Mulk turns to the Khurasani revolutionary Sunbadh, and from him to *Batinian* and *Qarmatian* (for him, derogatory references to the Isma'ilis and the Qaramita), and from them to the Khorram-dinan. In each case he gives a full account of the regions in the Seljuqid empire where these movements have taken root. This part of *Siyasatnama* identifies the main traits of various revolutionary cells that the Seljuqid administrative apparatus had to watch carefully. Nizam al-Mulk left for posterity a perfect picture of who these revolutionary leaders were, who was their constituency, what sort of proto-socialist projects they espoused, and what menace they posed for the ruling political elite.

As Nizam al-Mulk was writing his *Siyasatnama* in 1076, a powerful branch of the revolutionary movement, now calling themselves the Fatimids, had succeeded in fulfilling the old Persian vizier's nightmare and established a Shi'i empire headquartered in Egypt, now ruled by al-Mustansir (reigned 1021–1094). Right toward the end of this Shi'i caliph and imam's reign, even as the proverbial ink had not yet dried on the pages of *Siyasatnama,* Nizam al-Mulk was stabbed and killed by an Isma'ili assassin, confirming and trespassing into his ministerial nightmares. Not too many years before, right in the middle of the long reign of al-Mustansir, the people of Cairo were visited by a traveler who had come a very long way to be with them in the capital of their insurrectionary dreams.

The Wandering Soul

Khwajah Nizam al-Mulk had just started his long and illustrious career in the Seljuqid courts in Khurasan when, late in December 1045, at the age of forty-two (though usually rounded to the proverbial forty), Nasir Khusraw had a troubling dream that changed his life forever. For months prior to this dream his soul was in turmoil—praying to God and asking for his guidance one day and then turning around and indulging in drinking wine on another. In this transformative dream, Nasir Khusraw sees a sage who tells him to stop drinking and wasting his life and go and find the truth. Where might that truth be, he asks the sage? The sage points toward Mecca and disappears.[33] At the time of this dream, Nasir Khusraw was a prominent member of the Persian literati in Khurasan and occupied a high-ranking position in the Seljuqid administration. On Thursday 19 December 1045, he tells us, he woke up from that path-breaking dream, went to a public bath, performed his ritual ablutions, prayed and asked God Almighty to help him stay away from things He has prohibited, and there and then decided to change his life radically. Upon making this decision, Nasir Khusraw embarked on a seven-year-long journey (from 1045 to 1052) toward Mecca, taking along his younger brother, a servant, and a selection of his books. He headed west from Khurasan and traveled through northern and western Iran into Armenia and Asia Minor, and then down to Syria, Palestine, and Arabia, going farther south to live in Egypt for some three years, performing his Hajj pilgrimage a number of times, and then traveling into Africa as far as Tunisia and Sudan before returning to Iran through its southern regions and heading north to Balkh. Nasir Khusraw kept meticulous notes during this journey and subsequently narrated them all in his *Safarnameh*.

There can be little doubt that while in Khurasan, Nasir Khusraw knew of Isma'ilism, but did he actually convert to it while still in his own homeland, or was this something that happened to him while he was in Cairo, the Fatimid capital? It is hard to say, though the description of his tumultuous soul and transformative dream (if not merely a narrative device) might be an indication of a major change in his moral disposition. What is certain is that by the time he reached Cairo, he converted to the Fatimid cause (if he had not done so earlier) and their brand of Isma'ilism. He subsequently met the caliph and imam al-Mustansir, who in due course appointed him as the *da'i,* or *hujjat* as he says, *Hujjat-e Khurasan,* a high-ranking position in the promulgation of the Fatimids. So he returned to Khurasan as a propaganda officer of the Isma'ili cause and soon as a major theorist of their theology and philosophy.[34]

The record of Nasir Khusraw from this journey, his famous *Safarnameh,* is one of the most astonishing documents of Iranian and Islamic intellectual history, and a masterpiece of social-scientific Persian prose.[35] Written centuries before the famous *Rihla* [Travels] of Ibn Battuta (circa 1304–1377), Nasir Khusraw's *Safarnameh* is a unique text of the medieval period in which we read the direct and telegraphic prose of a master Persian stylist with a sharp and unblinking critical eye for details. Everywhere that Nasir Khusraw goes—from Marv to Qazvin, to Tabriz, Aleppo, Beirut, Sidon, Jerusalem, Cairo, Mecca, Ta'if, al-Hasa, Basra, Abadan, Isfahan, and back to Khurasan—he seeks the leading authorities of every sect, Muslim or otherwise, and speaks with Sunni, Shi'i, Muslim, Jewish, Christian, and Hindu philosophers, theologians, and mystics; physicians and mathematicians; poets, members of the literati, and political leaders. He walks around towns and villages, measures their length and width, learns about their manufacturing products, laborers, slaves, artisans, and professional guilds. He is fascinated by city designs, architectural monuments, economy and polity; by roads, rivers, water resources, agricultural products, and markets. He learns and writes about their religious beliefs, cultural practices, and educational systems. He travels, he observes, he writes, he criticizes—all with an unsurpassed critical intelligence, good humor, and an insatiable thirst for knowledge.

When Nasir Khusraw finally reaches Egypt, he is gradually drawn to and deeply immersed in Isma'ili doctrines and converts to Isma'ilism, having gone through a systematic training and reaching the highest echelons of its propaganda machinery. Why, one may wonder, did Nasir Khusraw convert to the Fatimid version of Isma'ilism and not to that of the Qaramita? To be sure, by the time he reached Iraq, Syria, and Egypt, the heyday of the Qaramita (roughly from 894 to 977) was long since over. Nevertheless, on his way back from Cairo in 1051 he went to the capital of the Qaramita, al-Hasa, and wrote a couple of passages on that city and its history and inhabitants. He describes al-Hasa as a fortress city, surrounded by four watchtowers and heavily fortified. Inside the city, he reports, there are plentiful springs, each of which can turn the wheels of up to five mills. There are twenty thousand militia roaming in the city streets, he reports. He further adds that the original ruler of that city was "a noble man [*mardi sharif*]" who had exempted his followers from praying and fasting. "His name was Abu Sa'id," he says, which is an obvious reference to Abu Sa'id al-Hasan al-Jannabi (reigned 894–913), the founder of the Qaramita state of eastern and central Arabia (Bahrain). "If you were to ask the people of this city 'what is your religion,' they would say they are Abu-Sa'idian."[36] The city and the state, Nasir Khusraw reports, are run by a council of elders that consists of six leaders and their six viziers. They had purchased thirty thousand "Black and Abyssinian [*Zangi va Habashi*]" slaves, which they had set free and given land to cultivate, and who were not taxed. Nasir Khusraw reports of a form of socialist co-op at work in al-Hasa. "If someone becomes poor, or accumulates debt, they [the rulers] would support him until his fortune turned around."[37] They had abolished usury. If a foreigner entered that city and knew a craft, they would give him all the basic instruments that he needed in order to start working. If someone's land or house were damaged, they would send workers to fix it for him, without asking for anything in return. There were mills in al-Hasa, Nasir Khusraw reports, that belonged to the council of elders running the city, and they brought flour to the people for free. A mounted horse was always ready at the mausoleum of Abu Sa'id, waiting for him to return. Abu Sa'id had said to his followers that when he came back, they should verify his identity by cutting off his head, and if it were him, he would come back to life. "This doctrine," Nasir Khusraw observes, "he had established so no one would dare to come and claim to be Abu Sa'id." Nasir Khusraw even reports the fact that the ancestors of these people had once stolen *Hajar al-Aswad* and brought it there. His historical observations are matched by his eyewitness accounts. He gives a report, for example, of the butcheries in the city, where they sold the meat of cats, dogs, mules, cows, sheep, and so on. They would place the head and skin of the animal next to the meat so the customers would know what they were buying.[38] Despite his meticulous observations, Nasir Khusraw mentions nothing about these people being Qaramita, Isma'ilis, or related to the Fatimids. He only refers to them as Abu-Sa'idis, as they knew themselves.

Nasir Khusraw's attraction to the Fatimids seems to have been predicated on their revolutionary Isma'ili foregrounding, and on their having successfully established a dynasty that had lasted about a century and a half when Nasir Khusraw visited Cairo in the late 1040s and early 1050s. Nasir Khusraw's anger and rebellious disposition against both the Abbasids and the Seljuqids must have made the political success of the Fatimids ever more appealing to him for the mere possibility of one final and definitive victory of what for him was absolute right over absolute wrong—in effect a self-scripted defeat of a Shi'i intellectual. But by far the most significant achievement of this seven-year journey is not Nasir Khusraw's conversion to Isma'ilism, though for him this undoubtedly was a crucial turning point in his life. The most cherished achievement of this travel is in fact the travelogue he wrote, the notes he took, the narrative he almost unconsciously put together, and above all the Persian prose he so competently commanded and left for his posterity in his *Safarnameh*. The record of multiple cosmopolitan cultures he witnessed and reported to those who will read him generations into the future were incidental to the experience of his journey and the occasions of writing about them. He could have traveled to China instead of Egypt, or to India and back, and it would have made no difference, so far as the encounter between his agitated and probing soul and the wonders he witnessed occasioned a moment of reflection on what it meant to be human, all too human, in those perturbed years. Isma'ilism and the cause of the Fatimids may indeed have been the primary animus of Nasir Khusraw's life in the course of this journey and then for the rest of his life. But what ultimately remained from that life, this journey included, was his poignant prose and his soul-searching poetry, to which he would soon add a magnificent body of philosophical writing.

Heading Home to Philosophy

By the time he was almost fifty years old, Nasir Khusraw returned to Balkh after a long and transformative journey. Upon his arrival in Khurasan, he began promoting the Fatimid (Isma'ili) cause under harsh circumstances. He was very active, sending emissaries around to promote the Fatimids, which inevitably incited the anger and hostility of the local Sunni authorities and the Seljuqid establishment, who began to harass and intimidate him. His poetry at this point is full of bitter attacks against the Abbasids and the Seljuqids. Khwajah Nizam al-Mulk, in charge of the Seljuqid empire, and al-Ghazali, busy defending Sunni theology, both vehemently attacked the Isma'ilis at their doctrinal roots. In response to these pressures, Nasir Khusraw initially moved underground, but in 1061 he traveled to Mazandaran, where local Shi'i dynasties were more protective of his ideas and activities. He was now openly accused of being a Rafezi, a Qarmati, or a Mu'tazilite, all derogatory when used in such hostile circumstances, and the worst charges that could be brought against a person at the time. There are even indications that the notables of Khurasan were quite disappointed that a man of Nasir Khusraw's learning and poetic and philosophical gifts should fall into the trap of a misguided religion like Isma'ilism.[39]

Nasir Khusraw's escape to Mazandaran in 1061 did not make him any safer or more immune to Seljuqid and Sunni persecution. By about 1063, he finally left the public life of a revolutionary activist altogether and went into hiding in Yumgan in Badakhshan (today in Afghanistan), a highly fortified mountain fortress where he was safe from persecution, and where he lived in bitter exile from his friends and family until his death in 1088. Throughout his extended periods of exile he was deeply homesick and used poetry as a refuge to pour out his heart and complain about his exile. His poetry from these times reads like an extended autobiography, a travelogue in verse; and a detailed account of his convictions, aspirations, and struggles. In time he became fully confident about his status not only as a poet in both Arabic and Persian, but also as a philosopher. While in Yumgan, Nasir Khusraw resumed his revolutionary activities, though in a clandestine manner, by sending out his representative activists around the region, but most of his time was now devoted to writing. This was the most prolific period of his life, most of it spent writing his major philosophical treatises.

Most of Nasir Khusraw's philosophical work is from this period of exile in Yumgan, when he had plenty of time on his hands to read, reflect, and write. The philosophical writings of Nasir Khusraw that have survived are all in Persian, a perfectly logical choice given the fact that these treatises were targeted for his readership in greater Khurasan, and that many of them explain and elucidate the Isma'ili philosophical positions on major doctrinal issues to a wide audience. This does not mean that Nasir Khusraw saw himself as an Isma'ili philosopher, for he saw himself as a philosopher plain and simple, with Avicenna and Aristotle as his immediate predecessors, extending their respective work in Greek and Arabic into Persian. In the process, Nasir Khusraw advanced Persian philosophical prose to unprecedented levels. Relying on a vast body of learning in both Islamic and Greek philosophies, Nasir Khusraw's, however, is an entirely theo-ontological dwelling on the primacy and principality of God, Who remains absolutely inimitable, inexpressible, everlasting and quintessentially Other. As he points out in one of his major treatises, *Shish Fasl* [Six Discourses], the essence [*hoviyyat*] of God remains always aloof and indescribable to what is other than Him. In *Shish Fasl* Nasir Khusraw's absolute and unconditional monotheism assumes even semiological proportions when he dwells on the word *Allah,* the way it is written in Arabic, and performs a complete semiotic exercise on its shape and physiognomy.

The primary objective for Nasir Khusraw in practically all his philosophical treatises is to make sure that God's Essence remains untouched by His created beings—the world, the humanity, the heavens. As he says in *Goshayesh va Rahayesh* [Knowledge and Liberation], this is similar to a writer composing a book for which he needs certain instruments, but the composition of this book does not add or subtract from the essence of that writer.[40] The Absolute Unity of God, as he points out in some detail in *Jami' al-Hikmatayn* [Summation of the Two Philosophies], is not negotiable, the ontological cornerstone of the knowledge of the world. In this treatise, he takes issue with those who do not believe in God, or with those who believe in two or three gods. His monotheism really takes off, however, when he is engaged in denouncing the position of the literalists, even those with theological limitations in their perception of divinity, and assumes far more complicated hermeneutic dimensions. The purpose of the Creation is for humanity to learn how to praise this Absolute God absolutely, and for Nasir Khusraw, as he says in his *Zad al-Mosaferin* [The Pilgrims' Provisions], the singular objective of human reason is to learn how to praise God. The more humanity spends time reflecting on God's evident signs and created epiphanies, he points out in his *Khwan al-Ikhwan* [A Feast for the Brothers], the more he will be enlightened, able to see the purpose of the world better. Nasir Khusraw's philosophy reads like the summation of prolonged reflections on the nature of divinity and its worldly consequences, for as he says in his *Vajh-e al-Din* [The Case for Religion], his thirst for theological certainty led him into many debates with all sorts of religions, even with learned Hindus. Humans are made of both bestial and angelic qualities and attributes, as he says in *Vajh-e al-Din,* whereby they are enabled to know what they are doing, and by extension do as they reason.

Nasir Khusraw's philosophical system, as perhaps best represented in his *Goshayesh va Rahayesh,* consists of a cosmogony and an ontology, leading to a pronounced theocentric metaphysics, from there concluding with a theology and a theodicy. The narrative ploy of *Goshayesh va Rahayesh* is organized around thirty questions that are posed to Nasir Khusraw and to which he provides answers. The philosophical sophistication and articulated precision of these questions are clear indications that they are in fact narrative devices that give Nasir Khusraw an opportunity to expostulate on many issues he thinks important for a philosophical grasp of reality and for guiding his readership into asking the right sorts of questions. The first question, for example, posits the factor of time in creation. There is no doubt that the Creator was before the Created world, as Nasir Khusraw posits the question, but was there a lapsed time between the two; and if so then when the Creator had not yet created the world He was still a Creator and a Monarch. But if so, he was the Creator and the Monarch of what, when there was still no created world? In his cosmogony, Nasir Khusraw addresses the thorny issue of the incorporeality of God. In his ontology, he hinges his argument around the relation between the body and the soul; whereas in his physics, he dwells on the issue of form and matter and the way they are related. By far the most important cornerstone of Nasir Khusraw's theology is "the Word" of God, the *logos,* as the primary cause of existence. His theodicy ultimately turns to the enduring problem of free will and predestination. On this issue, he refers back to the authority of Imam Ja'far al-Sadiq, who said his position is neither *jabr* [predestination] nor *ikhtiyar* [free will], but something in between. Nasir Khusraw then interprets this saying by adding his own commentary, that humans are somewhere between beasts and angels. Beasts cannot be punished for their bestiality because they only have a carnal soul and no rational faculty; whereas angels cannot be rewarded for their obedience and good deeds because they have rational faculties but no carnal soul and thus are incapable of evil—so they are not even tempted to do wrong. It is only human beings who have both bestial and angelic qualities in them and in between them have a choice—tempted by evil, but held back by reason.[41]

It is imperative to see Nasir Khusraw's philosophical preoccupations (even or particularly as pure philosophy) in connection to his political activism as an Isma'ili and a Shi'i believer. His philosophy, the more abstract and metaphysical its language becomes, is deeply informed by his existential anxieties, social concerns, and political commitments. One cannot read his philosophy without having his persona, which emerges mostly from the pages of his travelogue, in mind, and neither makes any sense without having the character of his poetic compositions equally present in our reading of him. Nasir Khusraw is in fact the summation of all these factors and forces, irreducible to an absolutist abstraction. The metaphysical abstraction of Islamic, or Shi'i, or Isma'ili philosophy, of the sort that Henry Corbin and Seyyed Hossein Nasr are wont to do, categorically empties them of all their social and political dimensions and transforms them into a shapeless mass of meaningless ideas with no connection to reality. First and foremost Nasir Khusraw was a revolutionary activist, and his philosophy, poetry, and travelogue remain the textual evidence of the varied forms of his attempt not just to interpret the world but to change it.

Shi'ism Triumphant

Nasir Khusraw died in peace in 1088 in Yumgan in Badakhshan. He left a multifaceted body of poetry, philosophy, revolutionary activism, and social criticism as his enduring legacy. The splendor and majesty of the Fatimid empire and the revolutionary momentum of the Qaramita did not last after the death of Nasir Khusraw. Soon after he died, a major sectarian rift ripped the Fatimids asunder, split them into two competing factions and brought their house down. After the death of al-Mustansir in 1094, Nasir Khusraw's patron caliph and imam, the Fatimids were divided into a revolutionary Nizari branch and a corrupt court-based Musta'li branch, each following a different son of al-Mustansir, as the consequence of a palace coup lead by a conniving vizier named al-Afzal, who plotted to sustain his own power. The Musta'li Isma'ilis continued with their palace intrigues and dwindling prestige and power while the Nizari Isma'ilis found for their beleaguered faith far greener and more powerful pastures in the east.[42]

With the appearance of the Isma'ili *da'i* Hasan Sabbah (1034–1124), the center of Isma'ili revolutionary activism effectively left Egypt (if it was ever there), and retrieving its earlier radical Qaramita episode moved eastward into Iranian territories to wreak havoc on the Seljuqids. Hasan Sabbah's immediate support for the more radical Nizaris shifted the center of Isma'ili gravity into Iraq and Iran for a direct confrontation with the Abbasid establishment and their Seljuqid warlords. The Fatimid court in Egypt did not survive the palace coup that brought al-Musta'li to power. In less than a century its precarious rule came to an ignominious end by the combined force of regional uprisings, the invading Crusaders, and the rise of Saladin and the establishment of his Ayyubid dynasty, which lasted from 1169 until the end of the fifteenth century. Meanwhile, the Nizaris, under the powerful leadership of Hasan Sabbah, seized the mountain fortress of Alamut in northern Iran in 1090 and used the Nizari-Musta'li dispute to retrieve the revolutionary zeal of Isma'ilism, redirect it away from the palace intrigues of the Fatimids, and take the battle directly into the heart of the Abbasid/Seljuqid imperial alliance via a sustained, effective, and multifaceted armed rebellion. Hasan Sabbah used the Nizari cause as the modus operandi of his legitimation and moved on to reclaim the Shi'i and Isma'ili revolutionary zeal, mounting successive guerilla wars against the Seljuqids. He seized a number of strongholds like Alamut, Quhistan, and Gerdkuh, and these strategic gains shook the foundation of the Seljuqid empire and their Abbasid supporters and fully anticipated their final demise (while giving full momentum to the European myth of "the Assassins").[43]

The revolutionary zeal of Nasir Khusraw died with and in the Isma'ili cause, but his philosophical passion was further intensified and passed on to his kindred soul Khwajah Nasir al-Din al-Tusi (1201–1274), a monumental figure in medieval Islamic sciences and philosophy. It is also in the figure of al-Tusi that the philosophical and scientific effervescence of the Shi'i culture ultimately wins over its political convictions and revolutionary zeal.[44] In his prime in 1227, Nasir al-Din al-Tusi served the Nizari leader Abd al-Rahman ibn abi Mansur (died 1257) in his Quhistan stronghold in northern Iran. For almost thirty years, al-Tusi benefited from the patronage and hospitalities of the Nizari Isma'ilis and remained at the service of his patron, producing some of his most magnificent scientific and philosophical work.[45] In ethics, both his *Akhlaq-e Naseri* and his *Akhlaq-e Muhtashami* (two monumental works in medieval Islamic ethical philosophy) are dedicated to this patron. Nasir al-Din al-Tusi also composed a number of works in Isma'ili philosophy and hermeneutics. But in the wake of the Mongol invasion, al-Tusi abandoned the Isma'ili cause altogether (even sought to conceal his connection with them) and negotiated a peace treaty between his Isma'ili patron and Hulegu, the Mongol warlord, whom he now served as an advisor. He had an ulterior motive: he wished to save his fellow philosophers and scientists in Baghdad from the destruction wreaked by Hulegu in 1258.

The Mongols descended upon the Islamic lands with a divine vengeance and put an end to the Abbasids, the Seljuqids, and even to their enduring and most powerful nemesis the Isma'ilis. Thus they cleared the historical stage for the rise of a whole new set of players and parameters, sentiments and convictions, movements and maladies, with Shi'ism, as an enduring religion of protest, ready at hand to redefine and retool itself for its enduring historical saga.

A Summation of His Age

The full and bold embodiment of his age, and of rapidly aging but dearly held sentiments and certitudes, Nasir Khusraw personified the enduring paradox at the heart of his faith, of Shi'ism writ historically large, politically rabble-rousing. The Persian poet was drawn to the Isma'ili cause and the Fatimid caliphs, usurpers of the Shi'i revolutionary zeal as these presumptive caliphs and imams were. A poet who never spoke of love in his poetry, a philosopher who never found the truth in his philosophy, a revolutionary Shi'i who sold his soul to an established caliph and imam, Nasir Khusraw embodied his own thoughts and dreams only during those long and sonorous seven years that he wandered through deserts and mountains, cities and valleys, convictions and doubts, with all his books mounted on his camel and his younger brother there to watch over them. He faced mirages, watersheds of dreams he thought he saw, and long starry nights, during which he must have kept watch, gazing at the eternity of a dark sky. He could not have but fathomed the very depth of his own ultimate solitude—in search, always in search, of something too distant to reach, too close to see.

5

IN THE COMPANY OF KINGS, CALIPHS, AND CONQUERORS

Sadr al-Din Mirza Muhammad ibn Ibrahim ibn Yahya al-Qavami al-Shirazi, known honorifically and endearingly simply as Mulla Sadra Shirazi, or among his immediate readers and followers as Sadr al-Muti'allihin, or even more reverently and simply as "Akhond" (1571–1640), was a philosopher of monumental erudition, unsurpassed mastery over all the received and cultivated discourses of Muslim learning, who lived to see what he had sown sprout into an epistemic revolution in the long and revered history of Islamic philosophy.[1] His biography is very simply divided into four major journeys (to paraphrase the title of his most famous philosophical work): He was born, raised, and educated in his native Shiraz in 1571. He traveled to Isfahan to study with Mir Damad and other philosophical masters of his time. He left Isfahan soon after the completion of his studies and opted for a life of solitude, concentrating on his work in the village of Kahak near Qom. Finally, he accepted a teaching position in a prestigious college in his hometown of Shiraz, where he taught and continued with his writing until the end of his life in 1640. He died and was buried in Basra in Iraq while on a pilgrimage to Mecca.[2]

A cataclysmic conquest of global consequences (the Mongol invasion of the thirteenth century), two world conquerors (Genghis Khan and Tamerlane), and three simultaneous empires (the Ottoman in Anatolia, the Safavid in Iran, and the Mughal in India) separate the world of Mulla Sadra from that of his fellow Shi'i philosopher Nasir Khusraw. Without a reading of these intervening events, seismic and universal in their lasting consequences, we can neither read the foremost Shi'i philosopher of the sixteenth century properly nor fail to fall into the vacuous trap of fanciful Orientalism of one sort or another.[3]

Mulla Sadra is the author of numerous philosophical treatises, a number of shorter essays, a collection of letters to his principal teacher Mir Damad, and above all his magnum opus *al-Hikmah al-Muta'aliyyah fi al-Asfar al-'Aqliyyah al-Arba'ah* [The Transcendent Philosophy: The Four Intellectual Journeys]. In the history of Islamic philosophy, Sadr al-Muti'allihin is known and revered for his singular achievement in seeking to bring together all the hitherto competing, contending, but above all divergent epistemic forces within Muslim intellectual history. This history was first and foremost based on a juridical organization of the Muslim community along a *nomocentric* axis, where the letter and spirit of the word of God (the Qur'an) and the traditions (hadith) of his last chosen prophet were the normative foundations of Muslim characters and Islamic societies. Against those nomocentric proclivities of Islamic law soon emerged the *logocentricity* of Islamic philosophy, which sought to predicate a reading of reality on the basis of the primacy of reason. Against both Islamic law and Islamic philosophy soon emerged a reaction, an ascetic renunciation of both dry legality and even drier reason, and above all against the wealth and opulence of the caliphal or sultanate power that in one way or another sought its legitimacy from sponsoring the two dominant modes of Islamic knowledge production—law and philosophy. Sufism, or Islamic mysticism, or a homocentricity that went against the grain of both legislative law [*shari'ah*] and abstract reason [*'aql*], became the third thriving discourse of knowing or gnosis for Muslim mystics.[4] Each of these three discourses (manners of knowing God/Truth [*Haq*] and thereby existence or being [*wujud*]) was in turn divided along sectarian, scholastic, jurisprudential, or political axes and alliances. The result was the architectonic infrastructure of a variegated intellectual heritage that began to feed on its own epistemic modalities and generate all sorts of normative, moral, and political alliances. For primarily political reasons, these epistemic variations remained at discursive odds with each other and systematically developed into competing readings of reality, schools of jurisprudence, modes of philosophy, and mystical orders. The singular achievement of Mulla Sadra was to spend a lifetime trying to forge an existentially based [*wujudi*] epistemic alliance among all these discursive factors and forces—between Ibn Arabi's Sufism and Avicenna's philosophy in particular, all via Suhrawardi's *Ishraqi* [Illuminationist] philosophy, and all executed on the doctrinal premises of Shi'ism—in effect a monumental philosophical empire-building, a master narrative of truth-telling, akin in its imperial imagery to the Shi'i empire of the Safavids in which the seminal Shi'i philosopher lived. Isfahan as the imperial seat of the Safavids and Shiraz as a major Iranian cosmopolis were definitive to the triumphant urbanism, the urbane cosmopolitanism, and above all what we might even call the urban worldliness of Mulla Sadra's philosophical diction and vision. In that philosophy, first and foremost, is evident the ultimate defeat of the feudal scholasticism that had for centuries been definitive to Islamic juridical thinking—so triumphant in Mulla Sadra's creative courage and even audacity is the confident urbanity of a universal imagination, dwelling squarely in the making of a public reason.

The Sack of Baghdad: A Turning Point

For a clear understanding of the magnitude of Mulla Sadra's philosophical undertaking and the historical conditions of the rise of his philosophy, we need first to know what happened between the time of Nasir Khusraw's far less ambitious philosophical project during the heat of the Isma'ili appeal in the Muslim world and the time of Mulla Sadra. A preliminary reading of that span of almost five hundred years between the death of Nasir Khusraw in 1088 and the birth of Mulla Sadra in 1571 will leave very little room for the conjectures and speculations of an over-Orientalized metaphysics. The argument for historical foregrounding in this case does not mean that every philosophy is categorically reducible to its own history; but it does mean that a reading of philosophy stripped of its history is as flawed and incomplete as any conception of history devoid of a philosophy.

Nasir Khusraw's world came to an end with the final demise of the Abbasids, the Seljuqs, and that of their principal nemesis the Isma'ilis. Their demise is perhaps best symbolized by the sack of Baghdad in 1258 by Hulegu, the Mongol warlord. The conquest of Baghdad was a highlight among many similar spectacular expansions of the Mongol empire (1206–1405), which began in earnest in 1206 when the Mongol warlord Temüjin consolidated his control of Mongolia and received the honorific title of Genghis Khan [World Conqueror]. By 1211 the Mongol army had advanced deep into China, and by 1218 Genghis Khan was heading south toward Transoxiana and Khurasan, soon to overcome and defeat the Khwarazmids, a heavily Persianized Turkic dynasty that had succeeded the Seljuqs. By 1227, when Genghis died, the Mongol empire had extended from Asia into Europe and was already about four times the size of the Roman empire. By 1258 Baghdad fell to the Mongols.[5] At its height, the Mongol empire was the largest empire in human history, not to be surpassed in territorial size and political magnitude until the zenith of the British empire (1583–1945).[6]

The world that Mulla Sadra Shirazi inherited upon his birth in 1571 was still very much dominated (politically and imaginatively) by the extended shadow of the Mongol invasion, a moral, normative, and epistemic shift that instantly marked the nascent Islamic period that had come before it as ipso facto ancient history. "They came, they killed, they burned, and they looted"—that was the summation of how contemporary historians remembered and recorded the Mongol invasion, a political and psychological shock unprecedented since the Arab conquest of the Sassanid and Byzantine empires, and not to be matched until the commencement of the European colonial conquest in the eighteenth century. The Mongol invasion brought an abrupt end to the classical age of Islam, with Neishabur, Baghdad, and Cairo as perhaps the most significant cosmopolitan centers of its moral universe. Destruction of cities, of urbanism, and of urbanity was by far the most significant memory of the Mongol invasion—second only to Hulegu's killing in 1258 of al-Musta'sam, the last Abbasid caliph, which threw Sunni theology and jurisprudence into a spin. Sunnism and Shi'ism were on a similar footing after the Mongol invasion, equally shell-shocked; the Shamanist Mongols initially hardly cared to distinguish between them.

Yet not all was lost after the Mongols invaded: two monumental figures who flourished just a few decades before that cataclysmic event would have an enduring impact on the universe of Mulla Sadra's philosophical imagination. The first is Suhrawardi, who conceived and inaugurated the *Ishraqi* [Illuminationist] philosophy, and the other is his Andalusian counterpart Muhy al-Din ibn Arabi, known among his followers as al-Shaykh al-Akbar [The Great Master] (1165–1240). Suhrawardi's rebellious constitution of a mode of philosophical thinking defiantly set against the received Aristotelian-Avicennian heritage had widespread impact on the rest of Islamic intellectual history. By giving an ancient (pre-Islamic) Iranian genealogy to aspects of his Ishraqi philosophy, Suhrawardi exponentially expanded the epistemic domain and the analytical tropes of the Islamic transcendental vision of reality. Suhrawardi effectively changed the language of speaking philosophy from an Aristotelian-Avicennian peripatetic rationalism into an allegorical semiotics of light and perceptive luminosity as the source of knowing, and thus catapulted Greco-Islamic heritage in entirely unprecedented directions. Conducting his work entirely in Arabic (many of Suhrawardi's writings are in allegorical Persian), Ibn Arabi achieved a similar syncretic diction a generation later by (1) seeking to combine the divergent discourses of Islamic learning—from Qur'anic commentary to theology, philosophy, and mysticism; and (2) crafting a poetically pregnant language entirely his own and in categorical contradistinction with all other received and institutionalized discourses of legitimacy. In other words, just like Ayn al-Qudat and Suhrawardi before him, Ibn Arabi's writings cannot be reduced to philosophy (in the Aristotelian-Avicennian tradition), theology (following the Ash'arite-Mu'tazilite legacy), or even Sufism as it was established by the illustrious and canonical examples of the preceding generations of Sufi masters, practitioners, and theorists. Suhrawardi and Ibn Arabi would later become two instrumental figures in the formation of Mulla Sadra's own unique language as he sought to coordinate and consolidate the belligerently divergent discourses of Islamic learning before him. The unique and authorial voice of Mulla Sadra, in other words, follows in a tradition of such similar voices as Suhrawardi and Ibn Arabi, two kindred souls who in the wake of the Mongol invasion of the Muslim lands left two enduring imaginative edifices for Mulla Sadra later to identify and inhabit.

The moral and psychological effects of the Mongol invasion, the normative and social parameters it had at once agitated and set in motion, soon settled down in the formation of the first dynasty that descended from Genghis Khan's progeny. With the advent of the Ilkhanid dynasty (1256–1335)—founded by Hulegu and encompassing a territory that extended from Transoxiana to Afghanistan, the Caucasus, Iran, Iraq, and Turkey—Islam, renewed by Sunni and Shi'i jurists and theologians vying for a competitive edge, once again became the religion of the land. The Mongol invasion infused fresh imperial blood into the old Islamic body politic, and Shi'ism was the direct beneficiary of this historic event. When Hulegu invaded and conquered Baghdad in 1258, the monumental figure of Khwajah Nasir al-Din al-Tusi—a philosopher, an ethicist, a scientist, a vicarious Shi'i—was standing right next to him. The long shadow of the Mongol invasion influenced even the Shi'i dynasty of the Safavids and Mulla Sadra's universalizing philosophical project, his *al-Hikmah al-Muta'aliyyah* [metaphilosophy]. There is a direct link between Khwajah Nasir al-Din al-Tusi and Mulla Sadra Shirazi, two Shi'i philosophers who gave full metaphysical swing to the repressed Shi'i moral imagination under the shadow and as a discursive reflection of the world-conquering Mongol imperialism. The Mongol invasion gave political expression to the repressed Shi'i claim to universalism, and from Nasir al-Din al-Tusi to Mulla Sadra Shirazi, at the two ends of the Mongol conquest, were the philosophical expressions of that return of the Shi'i repressed.

There is no understanding Mulla Sadra without a historical grasp of the moral and psychological consequences of the Mongol invasion, nor would that understanding be complete without a simultaneous attention to Shi'i revolutionary uprisings occasioned by that very imperial conquest. It is perhaps only too obvious that an event of such monumental impact as the Mongol invasion and its political and psychological consequences would have an enduring effect on the moral and intellectual disposition of a world thus shaken to its foundations. What is not so obvious is that in the serene and confident labyrinth of Mulla Sadra's philosophy echo the cries and whispers of major rebellious uprisings that resisted that imperial conquest. The Mongols had scarce settled in Islamic lands as the Ilkhanid dynasty when rebellious Shi'i uprisings began to disrupt their reign, though this time with a major mystical twist to the Shi'i character of these revolts. The reign of the Ilkhanid Mongols sought to incorporate certain elements of official Shi'ism by employing the services of such high-ranking jurists as Allamah al-Hilli (1250–1325), but the revolutionary uprising identified as Sarbedaran (1332–1386) in Khurasan became the defiant pinnacle of a fusion of Shi'ism and Sufism, with enduring consequences for the rest of Shi'i history.[7] Sarbedaran was a Shi'i-Sufi revolutionary uprising with strong egalitarian proclivities launched in Khurasan by a dervish and preacher from Mazandaran named Shaykh Khalifah and after him by his immediate disciple Hasan Juri. "In the episode of the Sarbidars," notes one learned historian of the movement, "we encounter the phenomenon of Shi'ite Sufi militancy, which was to occur a century later with the Safavid order."[8] What scarcely anyone notes is that Mulla Sadra's learned and serene philosophical rapprochement between Shi'ism and Sufism during the Safavid period is rooted right here in the revolutionary uprising of the Sarbedaran. For long before the establishment of the School of Isfahan in the royal court of the Safavids, the major epistemic maneuvers in bringing Shi'ism and Sufism together, so evident in Mulla Sadra's philosophy, were already present in the agitating ideas of such rebellious movements as that of the Sarbedaran more than two centuries before Mulla Sadra or even his teachers put pen to paper.

Mystics, Ascetics, Poets, and Revolutionaries

It is necessary but not sufficient to trace the transcendental character of Mulla Sadra's philosophy to the metanarrative consequences of the Mongol invasion. It is equally important to see the origin of Mulla Sadra's later attempt to incorporate Shi'ism and Sufism into a third narrative space and craft a new transcendental language—called *al-Hikmah al-Muta'aliyyah*—in such revolutionary movements as the Sarbedaran.[9] Mulla Sadra's compelling ambition to bring philosophy and mysticism together into a Shi'i theological conversation of course ought to be traced back to Khwajah Nasir al-Din al-Tusi who wrote philosophical treatises while riding a horse next to the Mongol warlord Hulegu and effectively leading a flank of his army. Nasir al-Din al-Tusi's famous commentary on Avicenna's *al-Isharat wa al-Tanbihat* [Allusions and Examples] later became a cornerstone of Mulla Sadra's philosophy.[10] But that philosophical progeny is not sufficient. The syncretic character of Mulla Sadra's philosophy had one foot in such revolutionary uprisings as that of the Sarbedaran and their Shi'i-Sufi conversations in rebellious terms, and another in the philosophical mysticism of Nasir al-Din al-Tusi, whose writings were composed (literally) in the shadow of a world conqueror. Unless philosophers like Nasir al-Din al-Tusi, the most immediate intellectual ancestor of Mulla Sadra, suffered from severe schizophrenic maladies (for which we have no biographical indication), then they could not have avoided being influenced by their proximity to power. In juridical terms, the foremost authority among Mulla Sadra's generation was the same Allamah al-Hilli who was at the court of the Ilkhanid warlord Khodabandeh, converted him to Shi'ism, and consolidated the role of the *Mojtahed* [Most Learned Jurist] in Shi'i jurisprudence. Thus in juridical, philosophical, and mystical terms, Mulla Sadra's syncretic project is inconceivable without a world-conquering adventure that preceded him by two to three centuries. Both in the philosophical ambitions that it enabled (as enacted in Nasir al-Din al-Tusi) and in the revolutionary uprisings that it occasioned (as enacted in the Sarbedaran movement), the Mongol invasion influenced the metaphysical templates and historical antecedents of Mulla Sadra's future philosophy.

The revolutionary link between Shi'ism and Sufism that the Sarbedaran exemplified in action was further advanced in theory by such early Shi'i philosophers as Seyyed Haydar Amuli (1319–1385), the author of *Jami' al-Asrar* [The Compendium of Mysteries] and among the first philosopher-mystics who sought to reconcile the discursive differences among *shari'ah* [jurisprudence], *haghighah* [philosophical truth], and *tariqah* [mystical path]. Such prominent Sufi orders as the Kubrawiyyah, meanwhile, effectively converted from Sunnism to Shi'ism, following the logical progression of their combined belief in Ali as both an imam and a shaykh. None of these theoretical developments in theology and mysticism were aloof from their strong political consequences. The same Hasan Juri who was a founding figure of the Sarbedaran revolutionary movement in Khurasan was a prominent master of the Shaykhiyyah-Juriyyah branch of the Kubrawiyyah order.

As revolutionary resistance to the Ilkhanid dynasty unfolded in the form of the Sarbedaran so did the world-conquering projects that the Mongols had inaugurated. No sooner had the barbarities of the first world conqueror settled into the mannered civilities of the Ilkhanids than yet another world conqueror followed on his footsteps. Tamerlane (1336–1405), first ruler of the Timurid empire (1363–1506, becoming in India the Mughal empire, 1526–1857), was no less universal in his drive to claim a vast imperial territory. Like thunder Timur the Lame (and thus the Latinized form of his name as Tamerlane) trumped the world around him, conquering Transoxiana, Iran, Iraq, Russia, India, and Syria like a brushfire, and then advancing deep into Asia Minor by 1400, when he was barely thirty years old. It took Timur's entire lifetime of warfare and world conquering to produce a son like Shahrokh, who turned his court in Herat (in contemporary Afghanistan) into the most magnificent center of art and culture in medieval Islamic history. Between the reign of Shahrokh (1409–1447) and that of Sultan Hossein Bayqura (1470–1506, reigned from 1470), the last important monarch in this dynasty, Herat emerged as the most magnificent cosmopolitan center of Persian and Islamic learning and the arts. Like the Ilkhanids after Genghis Khan, the Timurids followed the reign of Tamerlane with an expansive cosmopolitanism that accommodated culture and industry, moral and intellectual imagination, within a territorial imperialism that could not but have its imaginative and epistemic consequences. The long reign of Sultan Hossein Bayqura, the last significant Timurid monarch of Central Asia, and the first Mughal emperor Sultan Babur, a descendant of both Tamerlane and Genghis Khan, who reigned from 1526 to 1530, brings us right to the doorstep of the Safavid dynasty and the birth of Mulla Sadra. The military imperialism of these latter two world conquerors would soon receive from the philosopher a sublated philosophical part in his journey toward a transcendental metanarrative in Islamic philosophical thinking.

Again we need to pull back from politics and turn to poetry right here and now in order to remember that the received heritage of two monumentally significant poets of the Mongol period will have to be kept in the forefront of our attention if we are to understand the moral universe of Mulla Sadra, whose mother tongue was, after all, Persian, though he wrote scarcely any major philosophical treatises in it. Mawlana Jalal al-Din Rumi (1207–1273) and Mulla Sadra's own fellow-Shirazi master poet and prose stylist Shaykh Muslih al-Din Sa'di Shirazi (1184–1291) cut two almost diametrically opposed figures: one whose style was other-worldly, paradisiacal, and sitting aloof upon the emotive majesty of his universe; the other utterly worldly, cosmopolitan, happy, humorous, and perpetually in love with the precious frailty of humanity. Two master lyricists of unsurpassed brilliance, with confident command over seemingly inexhaustible Persian possibilities, Rumi and Sa'di in two complementary manners defined the poetic universe that brought the Mongol world home to the learned Persian-speaking world from Central Asia to India and as far west as the Ottoman court and dominion. Mulla Sadra breathed the air of Rumi and Sa'di when he was born and raised in Shiraz.

The combined effect of Rumi and Sa'di, two master-poets of the Mongol period, comes to a crescendo with yet a third poet of similar rank but even superior serenity, composed and purposeful. Hafez (circa 1320–1389), by far the greatest Persian lyricist without any other qualification or hesitation necessary, casts a long and luminous shadow. It is impossible to exaggerate the significance of Hafez in Iranian (and thus Shi'i) history. His *Divan* has been the secret or flaunted companion of the most renowned philosophers, theologians, and mystics (and he is reducible to none of those categories) of post-Mongol Islamic and Shi'i history. He was and is above all discursive categories of reason or revelation, intellect or intuition, for he was a poet, first and foremost, last and lasting. He suspended the absolute ecstasy of his poetic vision of reality somewhere safe and sacred between Rumi's paradisiacal certitude and Sa'di's worldly cosmopolitanism. Hafez was purgatorial, suspenseful, dwelling and thriving in enabling and ennobling uncertainties. He gave every philosopher and every mystic he ever touched (and he touched and blessed them all—anyone who was fortunate to be born after him) an expansive universe, much as Bach, Mozart, and Beethoven mapped out the topography of the emotive cosmos of European philosophers and mystics. If Christianity is impossible to imagine without Bach and Titian, the Iranian sense of sanctity (Islamic in general or Shi'i in particular) is hard to fathom without Hafez. Consider what Søren Kierkegaard says about Mozart's *Don Giovanni,* or Friedrich Nietzsche about Georges Bizet's *Carmen,* or Theodor Adorno about music as such —and imagine Hafez doing the same for any Muslim philosopher and mystic who came after him. As a poet, Hafez was neither a philosopher nor a mystic, but he embraced, nourished, and graced the language and vision of them both. His is a tertiary domain, a poetic domain, the hidden haven of all philosophers and mystics who sought solace to assure themselves of their metaphysical whereabouts. Mulla Sadra was no exception.

It does a disservice to the story of Shi'ism to promote an insular view of the Shi'is—common or extraordinary—and analytically to sever their thinking reason from their feeling intellect, their doctrinal beliefs from their mystic mannerisms, their ritual practices from their poetic pauses, their innermost pieties from their impious indiscretions, their rebellious uprisings from their serene philosophies, or their homeless vagabonds from their royal patrons. In poetic diction alone, Rumi, Sa'di, and Hafez constitute a moral universe all their own—a Paradise, a Purgatory, and an ennobling doubt in between. They are above all sectarian divisions in Islam and offer a sanctity rooted exclusively in their poetic vision. When we remember them we scarce know or care if they are Sunni or Shi'i, nor does it matter. What does matter is the manner in which they hold together a moral universe called a culture, and they have affected the normative beliefs and behaviors of Muslims (Sunnis and Shi'is alike) in immediate but invisible ways ten times more enduringly than ten theologians and jurists put together. They are like the rosewater that people add to their drinks to quench their summer thirst—fragrant and entirely invisible. Rumi, Sa'di, and Hafez are evident but invisible in Mulla Sadra. But subtract them from the Persian poetic lexicon and something would be lacking in Mulla Sadra's philosophical Arabic.

From Rumi through Sa'di and Hafez and concluding with Jami (1414–1492), Persian poetic diction was coterminous with an aesthetic imagination that broke through glass houses of philosophical reflections, mystical mannerism, and theological contestations alike to re-craft an entirely different mode of being at once contiguous to these commanding abodes of meaningful existence and yet existentially different from them all.

What from the Mongol invasion of the thirteenth century to the dawn of the Safavid Empire in the sixteenth century defined the universe of moral and intellectual creativity was an urbanity of diction and imagination, a cosmopolitan universalism that effectively triumphed over (while incorporating and sublating) the scholastic feudalism of Islamic juridical thinking. The perfect example of this universalizing cosmopolitanism is evident in the ideas of Ibn abi Jumhur al-Ahsa'i (died circa 1501), who had studied Shi'i law and jurisprudence in Iraq and Lebanon. His attempt to unify Shi'ism, Sufism, and philosophy becomes the most immediate antecedent of the intellectual heritage that Mulla Sadra will soon inherit in Shiraz and Isfahan.[11] But even the ideas of Ibn abi Jumhur, a pacifist philosopher, correspond with and corroborate yet another revolutionary movement known as the Hurufiyyah, initiated and led by a certain Fazlullah Astarabadi (1339–1394), in combining Shi'ism and Sufism. With a central doctrine of messianic return at the root of its revolutionary uprisings, the Hurufiyyah movement challenged the power of Timur himself between 1384, when Fazlullah Astarabadi launched his movement, and a decade later, when Timur had him killed.

A clandestine, secretive, and urban-based guerilla movement, the Hurufiyyah were to the Timurids what the Sarbedaran were to the Mongols—both militant syncretic Shi'i-Sufi movements launched against the imperial underpinning of two empire-building world conquerors.[12] The Hurufiyyah movement might be identified also as a case of extreme hermeneutics, for they believed in the hidden meaning of the letters of the alphabet (or *huruf* in Arabic, and thus their name). "Hurufism," according to a historical sociologist who has studied them closely, "was a literate urban movement and gained widespread following above all among artisans and intellectuals."[13] It is imperative to locate the interface between Shi'ism and Sufism (as a cornerstone of Mulla Sadra's later philosophy) as much in the insular ideas of philosophers like Haydar Amuli or Ibn abi Jumhur as to see them in revolutionary practice in such rebellious movements as the Sarbedaran and the Hurufiyyah. Otherwise we may be tempted by metaphysical obscurantism about a philosophical tradition that was as much theorized in secluded royal libraries as practiced on militant battlefields of history, poised precisely against those monarchies. Anticipating the philosophy of Mulla Sadra on revolutionary battlefields, urban guerilla movements such as the Sarbedaran and the Hurufiyyah had precisely the same sort of syncretic intellectual disposition as the great Shi'i philosopher would develop a couple of centuries later. They shared also the urban and cosmopolitan foregrounding of a major epistemic shift in the Muslim intellectual disposition—a fact and a phenomenon that will soon define Mulla Sadra's philosophy and the social and intellectual history that will come after him.

Mystic Monarchs

The rise of the Safavid dynasty was to the revolutionary fusion of Shi'ism and Sufism in political terms what the appearance of Mulla Sadra would be to the same phenomenon in philosophical terms. The Safavid empire (1501–1722) can be traced to Shaykh Safi al-Din Ardabili (1252–1334), a pious and charismatic mystic in Azerbaijan. During the intervening century between Shaykh Safi al-Din and his descendant Shaykh Junaid, who assumed power in 1447, the Safavids were effectively incorporating and consolidating their Ghulat [extremist] Shi'ism with their Sufism, and beginning with Junaid and his son Haydar they went public and became radically militant. Both Junaid and Haydar were killed on the battlefield, and thus the leadership of the Safavid order was left to Haydar's youngest son Isma'il (1487–1524), who at the age of seven assumed the leadership of the Safavid order in 1494, and soon afterward in 1501 (when he was barely thirteen) founded the Safavid dynasty. From this point forward the Safavid rulers concealed their Sunni orthodox lineage and successfully manufactured a link between themselves and the Seventh Shi'i Imam Musa al-Kazim.[14]

The Safavids came to power at the logical conclusion of close to two centuries of active affiliation between Shi'ism and Sufism (founded on much earlier proximities in Islamic history), precisely in the same manner that Mulla Sadra's philosophy would soon emerge as the logical crescendo of a similar rapprochement in philosophical terms, with gnostic Shi'ism as the cornerstone of his existentialist metaphysics. For this connection to register, we need to keep in mind that there is a structural affinity among a number of concurrent trajectories that emerged in the aftermath of the Mongol invasion and the two imperial projects of Genghis Khan and Tamerlane that followed one another: (1) the establishment of the Safavid dynasty as the first post-Mongol Shi'i empire, (2) the ideological foregrounding of such revolutionary movements as the Sarbedaran and the Hurufiyyah in a syncretic reading of messianic Shi'ism and militant Sufism, and (3) the philosophical projects extending from Khwajah Nasir al-Din al-Tusi through Haydar Amuli and Ibn abi Jumhur al-Ahsa'i, and finally down to Mulla Sadra. None of these phenomena will make complete sense without a close reading of them in proximity to the others. The fusion between Shi'ism and Sufism that would later become a central preoccupation of Mulla Sadra was an equally compelling revolutionary (primarily messianic) ideology that was evident not only in the Sarbedaran, the Hurufiyyah, and ultimately the Safavid uprisings, but equally manifested in the more minor Musha'sha' movement of Seyyed Muhammad ibn Falah (died circa 1465) in 1436 in Khuzestan[15]—all of which point to the prevalence of a universal episteme of gnostic Shi'ism underwritten by messianic Sufism and cultivated in the aftermath of the Mongol invasion. In the same manner that the Safavid dynasty was only the successful version of the Sarbedaran and the Hurufiyyah movements before it, Mulla Sadra's project was the philosophical version of the same fusion and success in epistemic and theoretical domains, and thus equally rooted in the ideological foregrounding of those revolutionary uprisings.

Following the Mongol invasion, and in the aftermath of the global conquests of Genghis Khan and Tamerlane, and then the civilizing interludes of the Ilkhanids and the Timurids, finally three simultaneous empires emerged to map out the contours of premodern Islamic history: the Mughal in India, established by Babur Shah, a descendent of Genghis Khan and Tamerlane; the Safavid in Iran, established following the transmutation of their Sunni-Sufi order into a militant Sufi-Shi'i mystical movement; and finally the Ottoman in Asia Minor and Anatolia, with a nascent claim to pan-Islamic universalism. Having internalized a cataclysmic conquest of global consequence, two world conquerors and their respective dynastic progenies, and then three simultaneous empires in its historic vicinity, Shi'ism finally broke through its inaugurating trauma and let loose a massive imperial manifestation of its inner dreams and desires of world conquest. The Safavid empire was the return of the Shi'i repressed with a vengeance, and in its imperial domain and imagination, Mulla Sadra was the crowning achievement of its intellectual counterpart, seeking to conquer the scattered worlds of conflicting ideas with the same divine vision of a unified humanity—the paradoxical panning out of what was now a state majority religion with an enduring minority complex.

Shi'ism to the Safavids was what Persian literary humanism was to the Ghaznavids and the Seljuqs. The Safavid period in fact witnessed a sharp cultural decline from the golden age of Persian literary humanism as the Iranian literati left the inhospitable Shi'i domain of the Safavid for the much more welcoming and lucrative domain of the Mughal, where they gave rise to a magnificent new phase in Persian poetry, prose, and particularly historiography and social and intellectual history.[16] Meanwhile in Safavid Iran, an urbane cosmopolitanism of a far more universal appeal was taking shape, redefining Shi'ism in far more ambitious intellectual and artistic terms, overcoming the scholastic feudalism of the pre-Mongol era. Isfahan was the capital of this new providential dispensation of Shi'ism as a universalizing religion: Islam's seemingly unending dream of itself.

Isfahan Is the Center of the Universe

There is a popular Persian expression particularly favored by the Isfahanis that boasts: "*Isfahan Nesf-e Jahan,*" which is usually mistranslated as "Isfahan is half of the world." It actually means, "Isfahan is the center of the universe" (for *nesf* means both "half" and "center," and *jahan* is more "universe" than "world"). There is a reason for this expression that must be traced back to the Safavid period, when following its already significant place during the Seljuqid period Isfahan emerged as the urban showcase of the Safavids' imperial claim to glory. In lieu of Persian literary humanism, which left the Safavid court for better climes in India, three distinct domains in particular became the simultaneous sites of Shi'i aesthetic effervescence during the Safavids: art, architecture, and urban planning. The combined effect of these aesthetic sites accounts for the making of a cosmopolitan culture and a vision of the sublime and the beautiful unprecedented anywhere in Islamic history, with the possible exception of Islamic Spain and Ottoman Istanbul. Much can be said and indeed art historians have documented the most detailed minutiae of Safavid era art and architecture.[17] Founded on the courtly culture and patronage of art in the aftermath of the Mongol invasion,[18] the Safavid artists, architects, and city planners came together to redefine the city of Isfahan in the image of a global cosmopolis. But all the magnificence of Persian calligraphy, painting, manuscript illustration, and music—resting on a wide network of commerce, polity, economy, and industry—pales in comparison to one single event of unprecedented and unsurpassed significance in Islamic and Shi'i history, and that is the deliberate design and construction of public spaces, as distinct from markedly royal or religious sites, that marked the urban landscape of the Safavid capital.

Under the Safavids the city of Isfahan emerged as the urban site of the grandest manifestations of a renewed urbanity—confident, imperial, urbane. The centerpiece of the city, its main piazza, was (and remains) *Meydan-e Naqsh-e Jahan* [The Image of the World Square]. The rest of the city is organized around the logical and rhetorical implications of this vast public space.[19] On the western side of the square is the entrance to Ali Qapu Palace, one of the most splendid architectural masterpieces of the Safavid period, and where the ruling monarchs claimed their side of command over the Shi'i capital. Right in front of the palace on the opposite (eastern) side of the square is Masjed Sheikh Lotf Allah, a royal mosque and *madrasah* built between 1615 and 1618 by the order of Shah Abbas I, and where the Safavid royalty laid its claim on an Islamic (Shi'i) legitimacy. On the northern side of the square is the main portal of the Grand Bazaar, where the Safavid merchant class projected its commercial and financial power on the Shi'i capital. Facing it on the southern side of the square is Masjed-e Shah (now renamed after Khomeini), a grand public mosque that indicates the merchant class's sponsorship of public piety.[20] Right here on this square, the Safavid royalty and the merchant class competed for public space and civic attention while laying claim to Islam on the opposite side of where they stood (and could not do otherwise).

Far more important than each and every one of these monuments, and more critical even than all of them put together, is in fact the vacant space created among these buildings. Right there in the empty square is a public domain that will impact the rest of Iranian and Shi'i social and intellectual history in enduring ways. Art and architecture historians have rightly concentrated so much attention on those surrounding palaces, mosques, and bazaars that social and intellectual historians have neglected the significance of the open public space created among them. In that square, as the great Shi'i architects were busy building those magnificent palaces and mosques and bazaars, they were also crafting a far more eloquent abode, one where millions of Muslims would stand, and millions more to come after them, dwelling on the publicity of a domain that made the space and the opening for reason to become public, for intellect to leave the royal courts and the sanctity of mosques alike and to enter and face the urbane polity of a whole new conception of a people. If we forget about the significance of this public space and the public reason that it occasions then we will fall into the Orientalist trap of thinking of the majority of Muslims as ignorant fanatics with a handful of exceptional philosophers among (but scarce known to) them.

There are many palaces and mosques in Isfahan, but no other royal or religious space signifies the effervescence and triumph of urban cosmopolitanism over the court- and mosque-affiliated feudal scholasticism of the preceding ages better than Meydan-e Naqsh-e Jahan and its surrounding demarcations. Under the Safavids, Isfahan emerged as an imperial cosmopolis with definitive urban landscapes such as Meydan-e Naqsh-e Jahan constituting a civic and urbane public space in post-Mongol Islamic social history. As evident in Naqsh-e Jahan Square, the public space was decidedly confident in its social and symbolic demeanors of city-dwelling, embracing the hallmarks of science and technology, art and architecture, commerce and industry. Meydan-e Naqsh-e Jahan represents only the urban planning and architectural dimension of the Safavid renaissance, which was equally if not more evident in the realms of painting, manuscript illustrations, and calligraphy.[21] But the social and intellectual implications of Meydan-e Naqsh-e Jahan surpass all other monuments that surround it from near and far—for in this space the urban landscape of what Immanuel Kant calls "public reason" (as the defining moment of the European Enlightenment) becomes evident.[22]

The sheer size of the square, accommodating large crowds and a definitive public life, is by far its most important feature. As art and architecture historians Sheila S. Blair and Jonathan M. Bloom write, Meydan-e Naqsh-e Jahan is "an elongated rectangle (512 by 159 meters) which cover[s] eight hectares, a space far larger than contemporary European plazas." The construction of the square began in 1590, when Mulla Sadra was a young student of philosophy in Isfahan, and it was concluded in 1595, when he was deeply immersed in his studies with the master Safavid philosopher Mir Damad and most probably witnessed the construction of this square on a daily basis. In a subsequent phase, the commercial facilities of the square were expanded in 1602, "with two stories of shops around the perimeter, which were let at low rents to attract reluctant merchants from the old city center."[23] For all we know, Mulla Sadra could have been one of the first customers in those shops—on his way to and from his studies with Mir Damad and other philosophical luminaries of Isfahan.

Meydan-e Naqsh-e Jahan was the centerpiece of an extended map of public spaces that redefined the capital city from its Seljuqid years more in terms of its citizens than in terms of those who ruled in those palaces or issued fatwas in those mosques, or sold their merchandise in those bazaars. Extended from the square, from the west side of the palace of Ali Qapu, is Chahar Bagh, the Isfahan version of the Parisian Avenue des Champs-Élysées (1724), though preceding it by more than a century and offering twice the length. "This elegant boulevard, some four kilometers long," as Blair and Bloom write, "was flanked by the palaces of the nobles, who were encouraged by the shah to add fine buildings in the new capital, and divided into two lanes by a central canal punctuated by fountains and cascades and planted with flowers and trees." What is crucial about this magnificent public space is the idea of its design: "It is a realization," Blair and Bloom believe, "on an enormous scale and in three dimensions of the typical garden carpet." In other words, the private space of homes and other residences usually covered by (what foreigners call a "Persian") carpet was now formally transmuted and rendered public in urban design and social domain. The public space that was extended from the square to the Chahar Bagh does not end there: "The southern end of Chahar Bagh opens into the Si-o-se Pol [Bridge of Thirty-Three Arches], erected in 1602 by Allahvardikhan, favorite and generalissimo of [Shah] 'Abbas. Measuring a remarkable 300 meters long, it has a passage for beasts of burden flanked by raised lanes for pedestrians."[24]

If there were any doubts that from Meydan-e Naqsh-e Jahan, through Chahar Bagh, and over the Si-o-se Pol was an extended public space, Blair and Bloom further add, "at several points pavilions project from the main structure [of the bridge] to allow pedestrians to stop and enjoy the splendid view of the river basin. . . ."[25] We can well imagine Mulla Sadra walking from the Naqsh-e Jahan Square toward and through

Chahar Bagh, crossing Si-o-se Pol, and perhaps sitting in one of those pavilions with a copy of Nasir al-Din al-Tusi's commentary on Avicenna's *al-Isharat wa al-Tanbihat,* reading while behind him there was the hustle-bustle of the ordinary folks and their mules passing by, and in front of him would flow the calm and reassuring Zayandeh-Rud. The commercial and economic dimensions of these interconnected public spaces were quite evident from their designs: "As in Chahar Bagh itself, esthetics are joined to practical functions in a splendid ensemble, for the bridge crossed the Ziyanda [Zayandeh] river and linked the city to New Julfa, the economically important quarter of the Armenians, who had been recently relocated there from the war-torn borderlands."[26] The historians' overall assessment of the square:

> The maidan [Naqsh-e Jahan Square] represents an early example of a multifunctional space and was the most impressive feature of the new city for foreign travelers, who universally praised it for its sheer size and its architectural homogeneity and described it as a great square, overflowing with life from the bazaars, and a backdrop to pageantry and ceremonial splendor . . . The covered walkway and the outer arcades served as a bazaar. The great central space housed the stalls of merchants, craftsmen, barbers, and entertainers, but could be cleared for military parades, drill by the shah's personal militia, archery contests, polo matches, and festivals. At night fifty thousand earthenware lamps hanging from thin poles in front of the buildings illuminated the square."[27]

The School of Isfahan

Our understanding of the cosmopolitan context, social significance, economic foregrounding, political consequences, and intellectual implications of Meydan-e Naqsh-e Jahan in providing the centerpiece of a massive public space, and the *locus classicus* of what Immanuel Kant called "public reason," will not be complete if we do not walk through its spacious spectrum toward the most significant philosophical event of the period, which also carried the name of the city of Isfahan. The crowning intellectual achievement of the Safavid period is a particularly powerful transcendental philosophy, the School of Isfahan, a movement that best represents the urbane cosmopolitanism of the city that gave it its name. Mulla Sadra's work is the pinnacle of this philosophical movement, though in many significant ways he transcended, surpassed, and even altered certain defining particulars of that school. The School of Isfahan refers to a philosophical movement that was presided over by the monumental figure of Mulla Sadra's teacher, Mir Damad. It derives its name first and foremost from the fact that its principal founder, Mir Damad, and most of his students lived, at least for parts of their productive lives, in the Safavid capital and were patronized by Safavid kings. Thematically, though, the School of Isfahan refers to the syncretic language of a transcendental philosophy that sought to combine theology, philosophy, and mysticism into a master narrative and perform it on a specifically gnostic reading of the Shi'i doctrinal premises. As such the School of Isfahan has its most immediate antecedents in the writings of such pre-Safavid philosophers as Ibn Turkeh Isfahani, who, before he died in 1432, invoked Tamerlane's anger and was exiled to Samarqand, or Ibn abi Jumhur al-Ahsa'i, who was not even Iranian, or Qadi Meybudi (died 1504), who was not even Shi'i. All came before the establishment of this school. Then the movement continued in such figures as Mulla Sadra Shirazi, who quit the city of Isfahan for the most productive portion of his life to live in a small village called Kahak, near Qom. After him, the movement progressed through his immediate and distant students and disciples, who have carried his philosophical vision all the way to the twentieth and twenty-first centuries and all over the Shi'i and Muslim world. So the School of Isfahan in this expanded sense has a more philosophical and global significance.

Although the School of Isfahan is initially associated with the city after which it is named, at an epistemic level it is identified with a mode of transcendental thinking that both preceded and in turn outlasted its cosmopolitan location in the city of Isfahan (very much like the Frankfurt School in European philosophy, which was initially connected to a small group of philosophers gathered in the city of Frankfurt but later more specifically referred to a mode of neo-Marxist thinking that sought to salvage Marxism from its Stalinist predicament). Following from earlier developments in crafting a syncretic language that brought philosophy and mysticism closer together, the School of Isfahan sought to inoculate the result against theological and juridical charges of blasphemy, and thus performed it on the premises of Shi'i doctrinal beliefs. To achieve this end, Mir Damad and his School of Isfahan sought to bring Ibn Arabi and Suhrawardi's narrative experiments with alternative modes of writing the truth [*Haq*] to their logical and rhetorical conclusions and systematized a more cogent (*superlative,* they considered it) philosophical language distinct from the Aristotelian-Avicennian tradition. As such the School of Isfahan is the natural conclusion of many earlier developments in Islamic intellectual history, a monumental manifestation of (the repressed) Shi'i proclivity to metanarrative, and a solid expression of the urbane cosmopolitanism of the city after which it is named.[28]

The School of Isfahan can in part be explained as a natural outcome of centuries of divergent scholastic discourses finally demanding a synthesis—a predictable event that just happened to occur in Isfahan under the Safavids. But it can also be interpreted as an attempt by court-affiliated philosophers like Mir Damad to provide a philosophical school comparable in its magnitude and ambition with the Shi'i-Sufi foregrounding of the Safavid order, dynasty, and then empire. The three founding figures of the School of Isfahan—Mir Damad (died 1631), Mir Fendereski (died 1640), and Shaykh Baha'i (died 1610)—the Max Horkheimer, Adorno, and Walter Benjamin of the School of Isfahan—commenced their work during the reign of Shah Abbas I, who reigned from 1588 to 1629 and was by far the most prominent monarch of the dynasty after its founder Isma'il I. The philosophy of Suhrawardi looms prominently over the work of these three seminal philosophers, particularly his attempt to expand the operative faculties of philosophical thinking beyond its Aristotelian-Avicennian foundations and toward a syncretic awareness of an intuitive dimension of knowledge that he located on the tripartite poles of asceticism, mysticism, and gnosis. What Suhrawardi was effecting in this synthesis—particularly by invoking a proto-Zoroastrian angelology and a Neoplatonist cosmology—was exponentially to broaden the epistemic foregrounding of knowledge production beyond rational faculties. In this respect, Suhrawardi was the philosophical version of Babak Khorram-din in the revolutionary uprising against the Abbasid caliphate and the Aristotelian peripatetic legacy. They both—Babak and Suhrawardi—expanded the creative imagination of revolt, one in political and the other in philosophical terms. Through a creative reading of Suhrawardi and Ibn Arabi, the leading philosophers of the School of Isfahan in effect took the Isma'ili tradition of *ta'wil* [hermeneutics] in Qur'anic commentary and sought to bring the two evidently divergent languages of revelation and reason closer together. This language in turn enabled these philosophers to have a bird's-eye view of the enduring Ash'arite-Mu'tazilite disputation in speculative theology [*kalam*] and made it possible for them to reconcile between the two opposing camps. In all of these, the School of Isfahan was heavily influenced by Ibn Arabi's notion of *wahdat al-wujud* [unity of being/existential monism]. Next to Ibn Arabi, Rumi's poetic elevation of the existential experience of the divine to the status of presential knowledge was instrumental in their attempt to facilitate a poetic rapprochement between the two languages of revelation and reason.

Mir Burhan al-Din Muhammad Baqir Damad, reverentially known as the "Third Teacher" (after Aristotle and Alfarabi) and writing under the nom de plume of "Ishraq," was the founder of the School of Isfahan—a philosopher, mystic, jurist, and poet of uncommon learning, and a court philosopher to the Safavid kings Shah Abbas I and Shah Safi I, in whose company he died in 1631 on his way to Karbala. Born in Astarabadi, raised and educated in Mashhad, he completed his greatest intellectual works in Isfahan, the capital of Shah Abbas' Safavid empire. Mir Damad's most important philosophical work is *al-Qabasat* [The Sparkles], in which he is primarily concerned with the issue of the creation of the world in time and space and the theological problem it generates for the principle of the incorporeality of God. Central to Mir Damad's philosophy is a theory of time, which he divides into three interrelated and effectively ontological notions of *sarmad* (pertaining to the relationship between two permanent things), *dahr* (governing the relationship between the permanent and the changing) and *zaman* (operative between two changing phenomena).[29]

Mir Damad developed his philosophical system during the reign of Shah Abbas I and was the foremost philosopher at the Safavid monarch's court—and as such his philosophical project, summoned and articulated in the School of Isfahan, was in fact protected by two factors: first, a deliberately cultivated obscurantist language that not even his contemporaries understood properly, and second, the royal patronage of Shah Abbas. Under these protections, both safeguarding the Shi'i philosopher from his clerical adversaries, Mir Damad and his colleagues developed the School of Isfahan principally as an abstract philosophical project that in its imperial ambitions to unite all the hitherto conflicting Islamic intellectual discourses was coterminous with the Safavids' universal claims to an absolutist monarchy of reason, revelation, divinity, and messianic delivery.

In the emergence of the School of Isfahan, we witness the victory of cosmopolitan urbanism over the feudal scholasticism that was definitive to Shi'ism (and Islam in general) of the pre-Mongol and Mongol periods. This cosmopolitanism was as much evident in the School of

Isfahan as it was manifested in Safavid-era art and architecture, science and technology, commerce and industry, and foreign diplomacy and international relations.[30] After severe political suppression in the early Islamic period and long before the rise of the Safavids, Shi'i communities repeatedly rose in rebellion, occasionally assumed power, and on quite a number of occasions even established enduring dynasties in various parts of the Islamic world. The Fatimid Isma'ilis established a dynasty in Egypt that lasted more than two-and-a-half centuries (909–1171). The Twelve-Imami Buyids established yet another Shi'i dynasty in Iran and Iraq that lasted for close to a century and a half (923–1055). The Shi'i Hamdanids ruled in Iraq and Syria for close to a century (904–991). Other minor Shi'i dynasties have ruled over scattered territories of the Islamic world: from the 'Uqaylids in Iraq and Syria in the tenth century, to the Banu Ammar in Tripoli in the eleventh century, to Chupanids and Jalayirids in northern Iran in the fourteenth century, to Nizam shahs in Deccan, India, in the sixteenth century. But all these dynasties pale in comparison to what the Safavids achieved in Iran, which was to make a far-reaching cosmopolitan Shi'i culture definitive to the rest of Iranian, and by extension Shi'i, history. Before they crumbled under the invading Afghans in 1722, the Safavids had categorically transformed the cultural character of Shi'ism from its medieval scholastic feudalism into an urban cosmopolitanism of unprecedented moral and intellectual dimensions—all in the wake of the advance of European colonial modernity. Two historic sites were definitive to this Safavid cosmopolitan urbanism: one was the Naqsh-e Jahan Square as the centerpiece of Safavid art, architecture, urban planning, and above all the very idea of a public space, and the other the School of Isfahan as the crowning achievement of Islamic intellectual history. There was only one major problem with this cosmopolitan image: the royal patronage, monarchic affiliation, and courtly character of the School of Isfahan makes it a bit difficult to imagine its founding figure Mir Damad (who was physically quite overweight and hefty) bothering to cross the Meydan-e Naqsh-e Jahan, except in the company of his servants perhaps or carried by a horse, or at least a mule.[31] Mir Damad's "reason," even when catapulted into the urbane cosmopolitanism of the School of Isfahan, remained private to his clerical and courtly cliques. Convoluted into an idiosyncratic language of philosophical obscurantism, it lost all its public and political prowess the instant it dared to step out of its comfortable corners and walk into Naqsh-e Jahan Square. And so it is right here, where Mir Damad left off, that Mulla Sadra enters and signals a cataclysmic turning point in Shi'ism as an intellectual project *and* as a religion of protest.

The Making of a Monumental Philosophy

There is an imperial confidence and composure about Mulla Sadra's philosophy, an almost subdued arrogant awareness, flaunted only ever so imperviously, of having finally discovered and mastered a metanarrative that sums up and explains Islam to itself and for all posterity. Mulla Sadra was the most illustrious student of Mir Damad, Mir Damad was the court philosopher to the most powerful Safavid monarch, and the Safavid empire was the most powerful Shi'i claim to cosmopolitan politics in the aftermath of the Mongol invasion of the Muslim lands. The structural affinities between Mulla Sadra's transcendental philosophical project and the globalizing empire of the Mongols—the universal legacy they left behind, and in turn to the repressed Shi'i proclivity to a master narrative—are too obvious to need any further demonstration. There is a reason that ever since his death, Mulla Sadra has been considered the single most important Muslim philosopher of all time, effectively ever since his crowning achievements in the School of Isfahan and even before his full philosophical project was unfolded by his students in subsequent centuries. Mulla Sadra single-handedly synthesized the Peripatetic, Neoplatonist (gnostic), and Illuminationist traditions of Islamic philosophies and moved them toward a corresponding conversation with Shi'i doctrinal principles, basing them all on an existentialist (principium of *wujud* [being]) as opposed to an essentialist (principium of essence) reading of reality. The term that Mulla Sadra himself gave to his philosophy, *al-Hikmah al-Muta'aliyyah,* can in fact be best translated as metaphilosophy, superlative philosophy, or transcendent philosophy—a philosophy that had transcended all its previous mutations. Mulla Sadra became philosophically fixated on the mystery and principium of existence as the absolutely final and the very first site of being; one that needed deciphering and decoding.[32]

"*Being* [*wujud*] is the very first of the firsts imaginable," Mulla Sadra declares early in one of his most seminal philosophical treatises, "and the most knowable thing by its nature [*fitriyyah*], imagining it is predicated on an essence [*mahiyyah*], and not on what is the very 'thingness' [*inniyyah*] of things."[33] Ever so gently then Mulla Sadra's existentialist ontology begins to fade out and fade into a monotheist theology, for up until this point he has been talking about *wujud* as such, but then he starts a sudden transmutation of the thingness of *wujud* into the ipseity or selfhood of *God/Truth* [*Haq*]. "It [meaning *wujud*] is the being of *God/Truth* [*Haq*]—and It is the absolute Everlasting." From this point forward, Mulla Sadra's ontology and theology become indistinguishable, and he talks about the "thingness" of being as if he is talking about the "Whoness" of God, but the double entendre between God and being remains operative, enabling the Shi'i philosopher to unleash his radical ontological existentialism under the protective custody of his absolute monotheism (and thus remain immune to his theological and juridical detractors—who ultimately drive him out of Isfahan anyway):

> He is He Who He is/It is That Which It is. Indeed there is no he/it but He/It. For nothing exists in and of itself; nor is its innate annihilation [*halak*] separable from it, and it becomes evident only by virtue of its connection to God/Truth [*Haq*]. You ought to know that It is only He Whose Innermost Ipseity [*Dhat*] is contingent upon Itself; and whatever else positively exists it exists by virtue of being related to Him/It, added to Him/It, an aspect of Him/It, and an attribute of Him/It. For the essence [*mahiyyah*] of the Everlasting Being is within itself; and whatever else exists among the existent beings or existent things are [not but] aspects of Him/It that are abstracted from Him/It. He/It is the First Who/That is not in need of what is counted after Him/It; nor indeed is there anything other than Him. He is too sacred to have a likeness or similitude, for there cannot be a second to that absolute innermost ipseity of things. He is beyond perception [*wahm*] and beyond imagination [*khayal*], and higher than that which can be comprehended or exemplified.[34]

Although a product of the School of Isfahan in many significant ways, a number of key philosophical developments distinguish Mulla Sadra from his teacher Mir Damad, one of which (in a specifically Shi'i direction) is Mulla Sadra's progressive incorporation of Shi'i saints—the *Chahardah Ma'sum* [The Infallible Fourteen], who consist of the twelve Shi'i imams plus Muhammad and Fatimah—into Avicennian cosmology, replacing his *'Aql-e Fa'al* [Active Intelligence] as the sources of being. Equally important in Mulla Sadra's philosophy is the constitution of a semiology of existent beings via what he considered the *'Alam al-Mithal* [the world of images], which was cosmologically stipulated as located somewhere between the *intelligible* and the *sensible* worlds; as well as his signature doctrine of the transubstantial motion [*al-harakah al-jawhariyyah*]. But by far the most significant difference between the two Shi'i philosophers was Mulla Sadra's replacement of the principium of *wujud* [being] over Mir Damad's insistence on the principium of *mahiyyah* [essence]. While keeping Mir Damad's ambitious project of a metaphilosophy intact, Mulla Sadra went against his teacher's major philosophical premise and opted for the principium of *wujud* in his own ontology. This monumentally ambitious project made the task of a unified metaphysics holding his existentialist ontology together infinitely more difficult, for in this ontology we are no longer operating within the amorphous spectrum of shapeless quiddities, but dealing with concrete and evident existent beings.

The primacy of *wujud* became the most significant aspect of Mulla Sadra's philosophical project. Beginning with the Muslim reception and al-Farabi's reading of Aristotle the thorny question of the primacy of *wujud* or alternatively *mahiyyah* has been definitive to Islamic philosophy. Avicenna is the first Muslim philosopher to have suggested *wujud* as an accident of *mahiyyah* and thus constituted the dichotomy as a contentious nodal nexus among subsequent Muslim philosophers. The "*wujud-mahiyyah*" dichotomy progressed apace from Avicenna to Averroes, and by the time it reached Suhrawardi the primacy of Essence was thoroughly established and Existence was perceived as an entirely accidental aspect of the Essence of things. As late as Mulla Sadra's own teacher Mir Damad, the principium of Essence was very much the common philosophical lore. It was Mulla Sadra who radically reversed that position, upheld Mir Damad's syncretic epistemology, but turned his ontology upside down (becoming Marx to Mir Damad's Hegel) and argued persuasively for the primacy of *wujud* and the accidentality of *mahiyyah*.

Mulla Sadra had an equally transformative effect on Suhrawardi's philosophy, for he took Shaykh al-Ishraq's notion of the multiple intensity of mahiyyah and attributed it to wujud and called the phenomenon *tashkik al-wujud* [gradation of existence]. Mulla Sadra's existentialism is thus deeply rooted in the Avicennian constitution of the dichotomy, Suhrawardi's theorization of the varied intensities of quiddities, and a long generation of syncretic epistemology that culminated in Mir Damad's School of Isfahan—it is the combined effect of all these forces that Mulla Sadra called *al-Hikmah al-Muta'aliyyah*—the term that he used in the title of his magnum opus, *al-Hikmah al-Muta'aliyyah fi al-Asfar al-'Aqliyyah al-Arba'ah*. The theory of *tashkik al-wujud* in turn leads to Mulla Sadra's other signature theory of *al-harakah al-jawhariyyah* [transubstantial motion]. What in effect Mulla Sadra was offering in this idea was a theory of motion, whereby existent beings, or reality itself, or existence as such—both sublunar and celestial—are posited in a constant state of motion, some visible to the naked eye, some not. The existential reality of things is in motion, according to Mulla Sadra, and not merely a mental picture of their phenomenal appearances. The epistemological implications of this ontology are self-evident. Gradations of knowledge are coterminous with gradations of being. Based on the twin theories of *tashkik al-wujud* and *al-harakah al-jawhariyyah,* forms of being are not discarded but subsumed under (teleologically) more perfect forms of being, and so are modes of knowledge corresponding to those states of being. There is a spiral ascendency both of being and of corresponding knowledge toward a more perfect union of the two with the primacy of the Active Intelligence in full operation. Mulla Sadra's philosophical attraction to Sufism is precisely a result of this experiential dimension of knowing-as-being, which for him is at once graded and entwined.

Mulla Sadra's *Four Journeys,* as stipulated in his magnum opus, *al-Asfar,* can be seen as an epistemic-ontological mutation of the Sufi path of perfection with the philosophical passage of truth: The first journey is from *khalq* [people] to *Haq* [truth]: this is at once a cleansing of the soul of its carnal qualities and a departure from the masses toward the Source of truth. The second journey is into *Haq* in the company of *Haq:* this is when the intellect and that which is thought become one, and thinking and being are done in terms domestic to *Haq* and entirely distanced from *khalq*. The third journey is from *Haq* back to *khalq* in the company of *Haq:* this journey constitutes a circular spiritual/ontic path that in effect replicates the Mi'raj of the prophet, back from a truthful visitation with a mission, a vision, a perfection to perform. At this stage the passenger has become the passage, the messenger the message, speaking in terms of a transmuted being. The fourth and final journey is with *Haq* into *khalq:* this is where and when the human/divine soul has become one and the same, the message stripped of all worldly connections and yet worldly in its orientation.

The problem with the usual characterizations of Islamic philosophy or society dwells in the prevailing binary suppositions that separate the "good" Muslim philosophers from the "bad" Muslim revolutionaries. Islamic intellectual history does not allow for such bifurcations, for here the most serene, sedate, and sophisticated philosophers, safely tucked away at the comfortable courts of kings, caliphs, and conquerors, seem to have a running dialogue with rabble-rousing rebels, sleepless and wounded in the remote battlefields of history. By following that tumultuous history, we can come closer to the factual evidence supporting the formation of a public reason on the symbolic site of Meydan-e Naqsh-e Jahan in Isfahan and the solid space of Mulla Sadra's existentialist philosophy. The singular achievement of the Safavid period is thus the social and intellectual constitution of a public space and a corresponding public reason that urbanized and domesticated the revolutionary reason of Shi'ism. The constitution of this public reason during the Safavids catapulted Islamic philosophy from the heart of medieval scholasticism right into the bosom of colonial modernity.

6

AT THE DAWN OF COLONIAL MODERNITY

Late in the evening on Wednesday, 13 October 1852, a small band of drunken police officers in poorly made and clumsily worn uniforms were leading a beautifully groomed and dressed young woman from her private quarters to the dark and secluded corner of a garden. Though only in her late thirties, the young woman carried the signs of her long and battle-worn days gracefully. The short distance between the young woman's private quarters in the upper chambers of the official residence of Tehran's chief of police and the dark and secluded end of the nearby Ilkhani garden was quite dark and hard to navigate, especially following the haphazard steps of the drunkard police officers. Nevertheless, the bright and sparkling eyes of the young woman revealed her quiet and determined resignation to her fate. "The effulgence of thy face flashed forth and rays of thy visage arose on high"—she must have remembered there and then one of her own most celebrated poems: "Then speak the word, 'Am I not your Lord?' and 'Thou art, thou art!' We will all reply!" Once they reached the designated corner of the dark garden, one of the officers made a sudden and quick move toward the woman, dropped her on the ground and placed his two heavy and hurried thick hands on her thin neck and began to push and squeeze deep into her flesh. As the woman began flailing her limbs, the man shoved a dirty handkerchief he had readied before deep into her mouth and throat. "Thy trumpet-call 'Am I not?' to greet how loud the drums of affliction beat!" Her resistance was instinctive but feeble and futile. "At the gates of my heart there tramp the feet and camp the hosts of calamity." Within seconds the edgy gesticulations of her limbs stopped and a long and lasting cold and stilling peace descended upon her face. The quiet of the garden assured the men that the deed, the order, was done. A dog was barking in the distance, or so heard the bewildered officers. Assured of the silent completion of their mission, they reached for the dead woman's body and began lifting and dragging it to a well right where they had finished their grisly task. They lowered her body to the edge of the well and with a jolt pushed it into the hole. Their mission accomplished, the officers now collected their agitated wits and walked back to their posts, perhaps with a twinge of remorse, perhaps not, but assuredly unaware of the historic import of what they had just done.[1]

The long and tumultuous road that had brought the young woman to that dark end began innocuously some thirty-eight years earlier in the city of Qazvin, about 165 kilometers northwest of Tehran, where was born one Fatemeh Zarrin Taj Baraghani (1814–1852), endearingly known as Umm Salma, who would later be called *Zakiyyah* [the most intelligent], and *Qorrat al-Ayn* [the solace of the eye] by one revolutionary comrade, and *Tahereh* [the chaste] by another, and thus her nom de guerre Tahereh Qorrat al-Ayn. Nothing in that simple and inconspicuous birth of a girl to a prominent clerical family could have foretold the course of events that would cast the life of the infant into great historical turmoil. The infant's father Mulla Mohammad Saleh Baraghani, an accomplished and celebrated cleric, was blessed with a superior education and scholastic learning, a comfortable and opulent life, and two daughters, Fatemeh and Marziyeh, and also by two brothers, prominent uncles to these two infants, one Mulla Mohammad Taqi and the other Mulla Ali. The three learned and successful brothers had studied Islamic law and jurisprudence in Iraq, returned to their native Qazvin, and became prominent jurists in their city.[2]

No Longer Any Center to Any Universe

By the time of Fatemeh Baraghani's birth in Qazvin, Isfahan had long since stopped being "the Center of the Universe," and the magnetic field of Iranian gravity, of the Shi'i world and all its pious and impious imaginings, was moving north toward the advancing Russian threat in one direction and then south toward the British imperial dominance. Between the time we left Mulla Sadra teaching philosophy in Shiraz in the 1630s and the time of the birth of Fatemeh Baraghani in Qazvin, the Muslim world had witnessed the grandest days of its imperial dominations, with the Sunni Ottomans in the West, the Shi'i Safavids at the center, and the cosmopolitan, worldly, multicultural, rich, opulent, and vastly tolerant Mughals (particularly during the reign of Emperor Akbar, who ruled for almost half a century from 1556 to 1605) in the East. When we left Mulla Sadra Shirazi in his hometown in the middle of the seventeenth century, Muslims were the masters of their own destiny, for better or for worse. When we now record the birth of Fatemeh Baraghani, Muslims were either directly ruled by European colonial powers (in the British Raj), or seriously threatened with that paramount prospect (in Qajar Iran), or else quietly crumbling under their rising might (in what was left of the Ottoman empire).

The Ottoman empire (1299–1923) was the last great Muslim imperial design for global domination, ruling for more than six hundred years over a vast territory that covered three continents (Europe, Asia, and Africa). It was divided into twenty-nine administrative provinces (each later divided into two or three modern nation-states).[3] As in the West the rising star of European colonialism gradually outshone the fading firmament of the Ottomans, in the East the Mughal India between 1526 and 1858 experienced a much sharper rise to power. The descendents of Genghis and Tamerlane ascended, yet fell much faster to the might of the British imperialism.[4] Between the Sunni Ottomans and the multicultural Mughal were located the Shi'i Safavids.[5] Having ruled over a vast, prosperous, and cosmopolitan culture and clime for over two hundred years, the Safavids finally came to a crushing end early in the eighteenth century. The world of the Safavids that Mulla Sadra knew and the city in which he cultivated his ambitious philosophical project were both crushed under the boots of the Afghans and the hooves of their young and gallant horses. A combination of incompetent monarchs, heavy taxation, abused peasantry, urban poor, and ambitious merchant classes scattered on the peripheries of the Safavid empire gradually began to eat into its imperial authority, Shi'i legitimacy, territorial integrity, and regional standing. Initial revolts against the Safavids began in Armenia and Georgia in the northern provinces, banking on their Christian identities and appealing to the almighty Russian empire for support of their causes. Starting from 1700 these revolts assumed a more open and belligerent character, in full alliance with the Russians. Gradually these uprisings extended to other states in the Caucasus. By 1709 the people of Tabriz were up in arms, and soon after Dagestan broke loose. In many such cases the Sunni affiliation of these peripheral populations provided an ideological banner for their revolt against the Shi'i Safavids.

Hungry Wolves from East and West

Safavid Iran thus remained by and large immune to the vagaries of European colonialism, and while on its eastern and western borders the mostly Sunni Muslims were engaged in figuring out how to deal with their European conquerors, in predominantly Shi'i Iran, much more internal housecleaning needed to be done before the Shi'is too could join the battle against the colonial conquerors of their homelands.

One could argue that, all the peripheral uprisings and the evident disintegration of the Safavid empire notwithstanding, Mulla Sadra could have still recognized Isfahan and Shiraz if he were to come back and see them nearly half a century after his death. But soon after the beginning of the eighteenth century, one could no longer make that claim. The Sunni Afghans launched by far their most brutal assault against Safavid cosmopolitan Shi'ism. By 1709, under the leadership of an Afghan warlord named Mir Veis, the Sunni Afghans rebelled against the Shi'i Safavids and established their autonomy in Kandahar. The nineteen-year-old son of Mir Veis, Mahmud the Afghan, who reigned between 1717 and 1725, was destined to invade Iran, conquer Isfahan, and put an end to the Safavids and all their pomp and ceremony, glories and miseries. In a daring and bold venture, Mahmud the Afghan led his army through the fortresses of the eastern Iranian provinces and marched straight to Isfahan in 1721. He laid siege to Isfahan between March and October 1722. The magnificent Safavid city, and with it the Safavid dynasty, finally collapsed on 22 October 1722 when Shah Sultan Hossein marched with humility to Mahmoud's encampment and submitted his royal (Shi'i) power to the superior authority of his young Afghan (Sunni) adversary.[6]

The Safavid royalty having officially abdicated, soon a massive popular uprising against the Afghans ensued, at times engaging in guerilla warfare attacking the occupants of their homeland. Mahmud ruled Isfahan with a tight and brutal fist. But the revolts—scattered, disorganized, and certainly not led by any Safavid monarch—continued apace. Having just concluded his war with Sweden, the Russian emperor Peter the Great (who reigned from 1682 to 1725) sought to take advantage of the southern situation and strengthen his hold on the Caspian Sea. By 1722 Peter's army had advanced well into the Caucasus, at which time people of the Iranian northern provinces asked him to help them with the Afghans. On 23 September 1723, Shah Tahmasp II signed a treaty with Peter the Great soliciting his help in fighting the Afghans. Meanwhile the Sunni Ottomans, under Sultan Ahmet III (who reigned from 1703 to 1736), sought to carve a chunk of the Shi'i Safavid territories for themselves. By 1723, the Ottoman army was on the move toward Armenia and Georgia. The Orthodox Christian Russians and the Sunni Ottomans were now in open imperial competition for the Shi'i Safavid territories—left dispirited, soulless, ravaged.

The imperial rivalries between the Russians and Ottomans over the Iranian territories well under way, and the colonial machinations of the French and the British on the side, forging a national resistance was left to ordinary people, who in 1725 revolted in Tabriz against their imperial, colonial, and domestic tormentors alike. Meanwhile, to prevent any further revolt by any Safavid prince, Mahmud the Afghan had all the remaining members of the Safavid family safely gathered in one place and summarily slaughtered. This state of affairs continued until Mahmud the Afghan was succeeded by Ashraf the Afghan, who ended up fighting with the Ottomans, who now wanted to gobble up Safavid Iran in its entirety. By 1737, Ashraf the Afghan and Sultan Ahmet III had signed a treaty according to which Ashraf recognized Ahmet as the caliph of all Sunni Muslims and Ahmet acknowledged Ashraf the Afghan as the king of Iran.

Hungry wolves charging from east and west, north and south, all raced to subsume the dying carcass of the Safavid empire. The ordinary people's revolts against the Russians, the Ottomans, and the Afghans remained scattered and futile until they finally found a leader in a man named Nader Qoli Beig (circa 1688–1747), who by the year 1729 took the battle against the Afghans to their own backyard in Herat and severely punished and defeated the wandering warlords. Nader called himself Tahmasp Qoli Khan, literally "the Khan who is the servant of Tahmasp" (Tahmasp being the Safavid monarch at the time)—but in effect Tahmasp was the servant of Nader, used and abused by him to engineer his own drive to power.[7] The final and definitive defeat of the Afghans in Murchehkhort (near Isfahan) in 29 November 1729 put an end to the Afghan occupation of Iran. Ashraf the Afghan and his army looted the Isfahan Bazaar, killed Shah Tahmasp, and ran away to Shiraz. Nader chased after Ashraf, who ran to the borders, where a Baluch tribe captured and killed him.

Between 1730 and 1736 Nader cleared the Iranian territories of Afghan, Russian, and Ottoman forces. He installed Tahmasp's eight-month-old son Abbas III as king while ruling his homeland firmly himself. At this point something quite extraordinary, rather unprecedented, and in the long run utterly catastrophic happened to Iranian and Islamic political culture. Between January and March 1736, Nader ordered all the elders of various tribes as well as the religious authorities to come together in Dasht-e Moghan in Azerbaijan to appoint a new shah, for, he said, Abbas III was too young and he was too tired and wanted to retire. This bypassing of the Iranian and Islamic political culture, via a revival of the old Mongol practice of *Khuriltai* [council of tribal elders], was nothing more than a clever machination for Nader to become the king, though with the support, indeed the pleading, of the gathered convention. Everyone in the gathering of course got the point and voted for Nader—all except the Shi'is, who obviously did not like the abrogation of their absolutist juridical authority in this forum. But the first Shi'i leader who dared to utter a word against Nader was summarily executed. The rest remained quiet and saved their necks.

In due course, Nader finally declared that he would accept this "invitation" and become the shah on the condition that Shi'ism be dismantled as a bona fide religion and reduced to the status of a legal school, among the other four legal schools of Islam (Hanafi, Shafi'i, Hanbali, and Maliki). The Shi'i authorities in Dasht-e Moghan did not dare oppose the idea. Ultimately Nader Shah of course failed to reduce Shi'ism to a mere school of law, but the epistemic rupture occasioned by Nader Shah at Dasht-e Moghan would have cataclysmic consequences for the rest of Shi'i (and Iranian) history. None of this was of course registered at the time, for Nader Shah, who reigned between 1736 and 1747, was not content with securing the Iranian borders and soon began launching a more global conquest, invading India and looting Delhi in 1739, invading Dagestan in 1741, and attacking Ottoman borders in 1743. Beginning in 1742, Nader's thinly spread conquests began to come to pieces. The revolts of various provinces were in full swing in Central Asia, Armenia, Georgia, Azerbaijan, Gilan, and Khurasan. Half-crazed and pathologically suspicious, even of his own son Reza Qoli Mirza, whom he had brutally blinded, Nader's days finally ended on 19 June 1747 when a band of his servants successfully conspired to assassinate him.

A chaotic upheaval followed the murder of Nader Shah, from which a certain Karim Khan of the Zand tribe emerged as the unifying force. He established the seat of his government in Shiraz, where he restored

Shi'ism to its prominence without alienating other sects and religions and founded the Zand dynasty, which lasted from 1750 until 1794. The crisis of political culture that Nader had initiated in Dasht-e Moghan became immediately evident when the founding figure of the Zand dynasty did not know quite what to call himself, and so he simply called himself *Vakil al-Ro'aya* [the Deputy of the Subjects].[8] The crisis of authority in the Zand period coincided with the first attempt of the East India Company to find a colonial foothold in Iran, though with no success.

The Zand dynasty was effectively a one-monarch proposition and after the death of Karim Khan Zand in 1779, the early stages of the rise of the Qajars as the next major Shi'i monarchy in Iran were well under way. Aqa Mohammad Khan Qajar, who reigned for only one year, from 1796 to 1797, was castrated at birth and beheaded at death. Despite these setbacks he founded the Qajar dynasty. The cruel treatment he suffered at birth made the man psychotically murderous and the dynasty that he established pathologically diabolic. After he brutally murdered all his opponents, massacred or blinded people who dared resist his cruelty in the tens of thousands, Aqa Mohammad Khan proclaimed himself king in Tehran in 1796. His merciless and violent reign brought nothing but death and destruction to Iran and Iranians.[9] After he was murdered, his nephew Fath Ali Shah succeeded the Qajar throne, and it was during the long and languorous reign between 1797 and 1834 of this major Qajar monarch that the Russians, the French, and the British resumed their colonial interest in Iran. During his reign the first group of Iranian students were dispatched to Europe to learn European ways and come back, perhaps, to rescue their homeland from its endemic calamities—and it was also during the reign of this very same monarch that Fatemeh Baraghani was born in Qazvin, not too far from the long and extended shadow of the reigning Qajar warlord in his capital in Tehran.

The period between the death of Mulla Sadra in 1636 and the birth of Qorrat al-Ayn in 1814 was thus marked by the decline and collapse of the Safavids as the very last major Shi'i empire, the nomadic conquest of Iran by the Afghans, the onslaught of Russian and Ottoman territorial imperialism, and the epistemic rupture that Nader Shah introduced into Shi'i political culture in the Dasht-e Moghan gathering. At the dawn of the fateful nineteenth century, the rising Qajar dynasty was in no way ready—morally or materially—to face the challenge of the French and

British colonial interest in Iran. But Shi'ism, as a religion of protest, had a far more immediate rendezvous with history before it could turn its attention to European colonialism.

The Council of Tribal Elders

The fate of Iran, Shi'ism, and by extension the Muslim world that embraced them between the end of the Safavids in 1722 and the rise of the Qajars in 1796 was sealed by the singular events at the Dasht-e Moghan gathering ordered by Nader Shah in 1763, which catapulted all the Islamic, Shi'i, and Iranian theories of legitimate rulership back to pre-Safavid, Mongol-inspired *Khuriltai* [council of tribal elders] patrimonialism, and thus categorically dismantled more than two centuries of sustained development of a cosmopolitan Shi'ism with enduring implications in political theory, social institutions, and economic foregrounding. The Dasht-e Moghan tribal council—in which the world of Mulla Sadra, the legacy of the School of Isfahan, and the emergence of public reason in Naqsh-e Jahan Square all came to a crushing end—categorically and cataclysmically closed the era of cosmopolitan Safavid Shi'ism and ushered in a renewed complementary contestation between the pre-Safavid tribal patrimonialism (stripped naked of its courtly culture of literary humanism), on one hand, and Shi'i feudal scholasticism (stripped naked of its Safavid-era syncretic and cosmopolitan transmutations), on the other.[10] With the ousting of the last Safavid, ironically named Shah Abbas III, Nader also threw out the best of Safavid cosmopolitan Shi'ism attained under Shah Abbas I.

The road to Nader's nomadic tribalism was paved with a long history of clannish clashes, barbaric onslaughts, and colonial and imperial intrusions into the cosmopolitan urbanism of the Safavid era. The Afghan invasion ripped apart the cosmopolitan Shi'ism of Isfahan and with it the cosmovision of an entirely different world, and brought the vengeance of a banal banditry to bear on and dismantle the sustained urbanity of the Safavid legacy. After years of fighting with the Afghan warlords and Russian and Ottoman territorial imperialism, and even carrying his own peculiar combination of clannish tribalism and senseless nomadic conquest to India, Nader Shah effectively buried—bone, body, and spirit—the memory of the Safavid cosmopolitan Shi'ism and its effectively urbanized conceptions of public space deep into the ground of Dasht-e Moghan and revived what the distinguished sociologist of

Shi'ism Said Amir Arjomand calls "the pre-Safavid Turkman tribal principles of legitimacy,"[11] with even deeper roots in the Mongol period's *Khuriltai*—gathering of nomadic warlords. The same clannish predicament followed apace during the Zand period, where the founding monarch of the dynasty did not even know what to call himself. Meanwhile, if there were any unfortunate descendents of the Safavids foolish enough to claim monarchic descent, they would risk having their eyes gouged out, ears cut off, or some other vital organ on their person mutilated to make sure they would have no such illusion. The same clannish kind of patrimonialism remained the defining factor of the Qajars, who followed the Zands and Afshars precisely on the model of pre-Safavid tribalism that Nader had retrieved from the Mongol period at Dasht-e Moghan and that now became the modus operandi of "legitimate" leadership.

Here the fact that Nader had ordered the Dasht-e Moghan gathering in Azerbaijan, far away from any urban civility, is a telling indication of how far removed was his return to clannish tribalism from the cosmopolitan urbanism of the Safavid period. Soon after the murder of Aqa Mohammad Khan Qajar in 1797, his nephew and successor Fath Ali Shah, fully aware of the clannish disposition of their rule, turned to the Shi'i clergy, seeking their endorsement of the legitimacy of his kingship. Thus just as the Qajar rulership was stripped of the Safavid cosmopolitan character and reduced to a tribal patrimonialism, so the juridical Shi'ism to which Fath Ali Shah had turned for legitimacy was shorn of the Shi'i cosmopolitan character of the Safavid period and thrown back to the feudal scholasticism of the pre-Safavid period. Thus ironically instead of weakening and eliminating Shi'ism, Nader had in fact managed to strengthen and ossify it in its most recalcitrant feudal juridicalism, devoid of the slightest suggestion of its Safavid syncretic cosmopolitanism and the cultivation of a public space and a public reason in the bosom of its urbanity, Meydan-e Naqsh-e Jahan.

The tribal chieftainship of Fath Ali Shah, ceremoniously codified as "kingship," thus became coterminous with the re-emergence of the Shi'i clerical establishment, the 'ulama, and the resumption of its feudal scholasticism. Whereas the fusion of Shi'ism and Sufism in the idea of Safavid kingship had its revolutionary origins and counterparts in such movements as the Sarbedaran, the Hurufiyyah, and the Nuqtaviyyah, and its urbanized philosophical expression in the School of Isfahan and the philosophy of Mulla Sadra, the tribal disposition of the Qajar rulership and its theoretical reconnection with the old Iranian notion of the "Shadow of God" was stripped of any divine, mystic, or messianic disposition. It effectively followed on the model of Nader Shah's destruction of the Safavid cosmopolitan Shi'ism, thus vacating the position for the clerical class to resume its pre-Safavid feudal scholasticism, a status that was much compromised by the cosmopolitan Shi'ism of the School of Isfahan during the Safavids. The triumph of the nomadic tribalism that Nader had initiated in Dasht-e Moghan, and the Qajars continued in their capital in Tehran, necessitated a clerical class of turbaned jurists and their feudal scholasticism to shore up its precarious legitimacy. Between the two of them these retrograde institutions (clannish monarchism and feudal clericalism) arrested the natural growth of the Safavid syncretic Shi'ism in cosmopolitan directions. The onslaught of Russian and Ottoman territorial imperialism, underlined by the rise of European colonialism, further exacerbated this historic regression.

Instrumental in the exacerbated reversal of Qajar kingship to patrimonial tribalism and of the Shi'i clerical class to feudal scholasticism were various imperial and colonial intrusions—Russian, Ottoman, French, or British. To defend itself from these, the Qajar dynasty needed the clerical class to declare *jihad* [holy war] against these forces and to mobilize the masses. The clerics were only too eager to declare jihad, which elevated their political status and social significance by a return to pre-Safavid scholastic feudalism.[12] Said Amir Arjomand in fact credits a certain Aqa Seyyed Ja'far Ishaq Kashefi, who died in 1851, and his treatise *Tuhfat al-Muluk* [*Gift for the Kings*] (1817–1818) with having effectively systematized a Shi'i political theory in which the temporal authority of the Qajars (or any other monarchy) was theologically articulated in a manner that generated and sustained an equally supreme power and authority for the clerical class.[13] This retrograde development is a radical departure from the Safavid context, in which the urbane cosmopolitanism of the School of Isfahan embraced and contextualized the Safavid monarchy within a syncretic and cosmopolitan reading of Shi'ism.

In the re-emergence of feudal scholasticism of the Shi'i clergy, the memory of humiliated Shi'i notables in Nader's encampment in Dasht-e Moghan ensured that the legitimacy of the renewed reading of Persian monarchy was entirely contingent on the clerics' juridical approval and endorsement. In the process, the tribal chieftains of the Qajar dynasty received a modicum of precarious royal credentials from their Shi'i clerical establishment, while the principal power and authority of bestowing or denying that legitimacy remained with the Shi'i clergy itself. This power invested in the Shi'i clerics was completely absent in both the Afsharid and the Zand periods and utterly impossible under the Safavid kings, who claimed direct divine intervention and even status for their reign and thus by serendipity allowed for the emergence of a public space and a public reason through the syncretic cosmopolitanism of the School of Isfahan in Shi'ism, both epistemically and politically predicated on revolutionary uprisings from the Sarbedaran to the Hurufiyyah to the Nuqtaviyyah and their rebellious fusion of mysticism and Shi'ism. Other Shi'i jurists followed suit: Aqa Seyyed Ja'far Ishaq Kashefi legitimated the reign of Fath Ali Shah; Mulla Ali Kani, in a letter dated 1873, confirmed the next major Qajar monarch Nasser al-Din Shah, who reigned from 1848 to 1896. Launching the process, as Said Amir Arjomand notes, was the founder of the Qajar dynasty Aqa Mohammad Khan Qajar, who had summoned prominent Shi'i clerics to his court in Tehran in order to solicit from them a legitimation of his reign.

Thus in the history of Shi'i political culture the deserted landscape of Dasht-e Moghan stands as the polar opposite of the populated urbanism of Meydan-e Naqsh-e Jahan. In Meydan-e Naqsh-e Jahan, the locus classicus of a public reason was cultivated theoretically in the School of Isfahan and brought to fruition in the philosophical figure of Mulla Sadra, in whom the revolutionary reasoning of Shi'i uprisings from the Isma'ilis down to the Hurufiyyah was conceptually urbanized into a public reason. In Dasht-e Moghan, by contrast, that revolutionary or public reason was categorically destroyed and replaced by a reactionary, private reason, which Nader modeled on Mongol *Khuriltai* and passed on to the Zands and the Qajars—thus transmuting the rule of Iranian monarchs back to brute tribal practices unless verified and corroborated by the feudal reasoning and closed-door scholasticism of the Shi'i clergy that guarded its class interests with the tooth and nail of its juridical obscurantism and with an inbred hatred toward the syncretic cosmopolitanism of the Safavid era and what it ultimately entailed.

It is here that the significance of the final victory of the Usuli School of Shi'i jurisprudence over the Akhbari School becomes a key factor in furthering the institutional power of the clerical class (on the model of their return to their pre-Safavid feudal scholasticism). With Aqa Mohammad Baqir Behbahani (1704–1793) and Shaykh Morteza Ansari (1800–1864) as their chief theorists, the Usulis are ordinarily understood as the "rationalist" or even the "progressive" jurists, whereas the Akhbaris are thought to be "traditionalist," "literalist," or even "scripturalist."[14] These dubious designations conceal the fact that the triumph of the Usuli School of Shi'i jurisprudence in fact strengthened the institutional power of the custodians of a retrograde pre-Safavid feudal scholasticism that successively bypassed (or violently repressed) the Shi'i syncretic cosmopolitanism of the Safavid period and gave the Shi'i juridical establishment an inordinate amount of power, not just to keep themselves as the principal arbitrators in matters of politics, but also to legitimize an even more backward reading of supreme political leadership given to tribal chieftains and militant warlords masquerading as Qajar monarchs. What is even more troubling in this degenerative process is the aggressive transmutation of societal formations, intellectual cosmopolitanism, and economy and polity of a widespread urbanism—the crowning achievement of the Safavid period—into an exclusively juridical space in which the potentially free and autonomous citizens became the mere (or "naked" as Giorgio Agamben would say) subjects of a medieval jurisprudence.[15] The two major tenants of the Usuli School, *ijtihad* [juridical opinion] and *taqlid* [following the exemplary conduct of a high-ranking cleric] are in fact nothing but coded references to the manner in which the Shi'i clerics built up and institutionalized their own overwhelming power. Clerical power arose not just at the expense of the Qajar tribal chieftains but far more important as a result of the heavy cost of transforming the public space, the public person, and the public reason back to a private fraternity of the clerical class and their scholastic reasoning—a private fraternity in which human beings are stripped of their public agencies and reduced to mere tropic subjects of a feudal juridicalism.

The "reason" attributed to the Usulis is a scholastic reason, a juridically instrumental reason, a reason private to the class privileges of the clerical clique. It is not and in fact it is categorically hostile to public reason, a reason cultivated and categorized in the public domain. The clerical establishment, promoting the cause of the Usuli School, was celebrating their scholastic reasoning because the juridical use of that reasoning made their political position indispensable. The Akhbaris, however, were content with the Qur'an and the Prophetic traditions and did not wish to feed the insatiable appetite of the clerical establishment the claim and the office of "interpreting" the religious law, which is effectively a self-propelling hermeneutic that empowers the person who (and the institution that) thus uses that instrumental reason and disregards the masses (the potential public) at the receiving end of that reason. This use of reason is not public. This reason is yet again privatized.[16]

What the insecure and illegitimate Qajar monarchs did not know (or care to know) they were doing by effectively constituting the clerical class as the arbiter of their legitimacy was subjecting not just their own reign but the autonomous agency of potential citizens of their realm (which was all but evident in the public space of Meydan-e Naqsh-e Jahan) to the institutional whim and insatiable power of the clergy. They did so simply to secure a modicum of precarious legitimacy for their clannish claim to power. It would not be too long after the death of Aqa Mohammad Khan Qajar and in the course of the early-nineteenth-century Qajar encounters with Russian incursions into their northern territories, that in his *Awa'id al-Ayyam* Mulla Ahmad Naraqi (1771–1830), a leading Shi'i jurist, would fish out a prophetic tradition that claimed *"al-Muluk hukkam 'ala al-Nass wa al-'Ulama hukkam 'ala al-Muluk"* [Kings rule over the masses, and the clergy rules over the kings].[17] The common denominator of this hierarchy was of course *al-nass* [the people], who, deprived of their potential agency to become a public, became the mere subjects of a dual domination by brute force (of the *Muluk*) and the feudal clericalism of the Shi'i law (of the 'ulama).

The imperial aggressions of the Russians early in the nineteenth century, followed by the colonial interventions of the French and the British to advance their own commercial and strategic interests, further exacerbated the position of the 'ulama to push for their political power over both the Qajar monarch and more important the public at large, which had thereby been transformed to mere legal subjects of their medieval jurisprudence. As the 'ulama encouraged the masses for anticolonial mobilization and warfare—in effect bypassing the Safavids and going back to the earliest Shi'i sentiments, and thus putting the revolutionary character of Shi'ism vicariously at the service of the Qajar dynasty—by extension they consolidated their own (by now constitutionally retrograde) power.

Equally important in the consolidation of clerical power in this period, regaining their pre-Safavid juridical absolutism, was their expanded financial autonomy, which in turn resulted in a sizable increase in their numbers.[18] Equally instrumental in strengthening the respective offices of the Qajar kings and Shi'i clerics alike were the internecine rifts between them, culminating in the reformist premier Amir Kabir's (1807–

1852) attempt at administrative changes and the introduction of European education, both of which met with stiff resistance by the clergy.[19] Arjomand rightly notes that the rift that started here between the clerical ('ulama) and the clannish (Qajar) classes beginning with Muhammad Shah resulted in the monarchy increasingly seeking to fabricate a pre-Islamic "Persian" archeology for itself by way of bypassing the Shi'i clergy and connecting directly to pre-Islamic and non-Islamic (implicitly Zoroastrian) "origins" for the Persian monarchy. European Orientalists aided and abetted the Qajar and later the Pahlavi monarchy in this project. This, in fact, is the political origin of rediscovering and claiming a Persian imperial past for the Qajar and then Pahlavi shahs—a turn that further angered the clergy and exacerbated their power over the domain and the aggressive rejuridicalization of the public space. So whatever the Qajars did, including at times the patronage of Sufism, actually further ossified the jurists' power and self-propelling legitimacy.

Taking advantage of their renewed power during the Qajars, the Shi'i clerics went on a rampage: systematically destroying the cosmopolitan character of Safavid Shi'ism; dismantling its culture of tolerance; organizing frenzied masses against the Sufis, against the expatriate European communities, or against religious minorities (Armenians, Zoroastrians, and Jews). At the same time, the clerics took advantage of the Ta'ziyeh rituals and symbolism by identifying any sectarian or religious minority they did not like with Shimr and Yazid, and thus implicitly identifying themselves with Imam Hossein. The murder of the Russian diplomat, playwright, and composer Alexander Sergeyevich Griboyedov (1795–1829) occurred in an atmosphere of the same xenophobic agitation instigated by the Shi'i clergy. The more the Qajar princes and monarchs impotently failed to deal with colonial interventions, the more the Shi'i clerical establishment used the occasion to further its own institutional power.

The Dasht-e Moghan gathering interjected a violent epistemic rupture in the course of a syncretic and cosmopolitan Shi'ism that had been cultivated and institutionalized during the Safavid period and thereby urbanized the revolutionary reason of Shi'i uprisings—from the earliest periods through the Isma'ilis and the Qaramita, down to the Sarbedaran and the Hurufiyyah—into a public reason. In place of that cosmopolitan Shi'ism, the Dasht-e Moghan gathering ushered in a seismic reconstitution of the nomadic tribalism of the Qajar monarchs (on the one hand) and the clerical cliques (on the other), both partaking in a feudal scholasticism that robbed Iranians and with them all other Shi'is of their historic rendezvous with a societal modernity of their own accord, based on the constitution of a public reason and public space of their own architectonic making.

Shi'ism Resurgent

Between her birth in 1814 and her murder in 1852, Tahereh Qorrat al-Ayn lived a short but tumultuous life. Just about the time of her birth in Qazvin to a prominent and highly influential clerical family, the Qajar dynasty and the Shi'i scholastic establishment were busy destroying the syncretic and cosmopolitan achievements of the Safavid era and the legacy of the School of Isfahan. The same revolutionary logic that had initially given momentous occasion to the Sarbedaran and the Hurufiyyah movements (and many more like them before and during the Safavids), before they were urbanized in the School of Isfahan, re-emerged during the Qajar period in the form of first a messianic philosophical movement called Shaykhism, and then a revolutionary uprising deeply rooted in it called Babism. It is not accidental at all that while the Qajar monarchs and their clerical counterparts were carrying the implications of the meeting at Dasht-e Moghan to its logical conclusions and leading Iran and Shi'ism backward to medieval scholasticism, it was left to a distant student of Mulla Sadra, namely Shaykh Ahmad Ahsa'i (1753–1826), the founder of the Shaykhi school, to pick up where the School of Isfahan and Safavid-era Shi'ism had left off.

Even before the cataclysmic events that commenced with the rise of Shaykhism as a bold and progressive messianic re-constitution of the School of Isfahan and Mulla Sadra's philosophical legacy, a major challenge to the insatiable urge of the clerical order for power presented itself in the form of the popular Ne'matollahi Sufi order that became prevalent, particularly in Northern Iran, and alarmed the clerical establishment, which in turn appealed to Fath Ali Shah to repress them. Fath Ali Shah, ordered by the Shi'i clergy, did so. The popularity of the Sufi order rightly jeopardized the monopoly that the clerical establishment wanted to exercise over religious symbols, rituals, and doctrines, in a cozy and mutually beneficial arrangement with the Qajar dynasty. Above all, the rise of a Sufi order brought back the memory of the revolutionary fusion of Sufism and Shi'ism of the Sarbedaran and the Hurufiyyah, which had bypassed the clerical establishment and resulted in the

Safavid order, movement, and finally empire—an empire which encouraged the constitution of first a revolutionary and then a public space and reason.

The challenge of the Ne'matollahi Sufi order pales in comparison to the combined challenge that Shaykhism and Babism posed to the Qajar tribal dynasty and Shi'i scholastic clericalism alike. The combined effect of a daring and imaginative re-reading of the School of Isfahan and Mulla Sadra by Shaykh Ahmad Ahsa'i and the equally audacious and messianic appeal of Babism grabbed the retrograde Qajar tribalism and their clerical allies by the throat and all but destroyed their hold on the cosmopolitan legacy of the Safavid era. Soon after Fath Ali Shah ascended the Qajar throne, Shaykh Ahmad ibn Zayn al-Din ibn Ibrahim al-Ahsa'i (1753–1826), a deeply cultivated Shi'i philosopher from the Ahsa' region of the Persian Gulf island of Bahrain, moved from his native city to southern Iraq. He resided in the sacred Shi'i precincts of the region and began propagating his radical ideas about the principal foundations of Shi'ism. Of the five Pillars of Shi'ism [*Usul al-Din*], sacrosanct to the Shi'is, Shaykh Ahmad accepted only three (*Tawhid, Nubuwwah,* and *Imamah*) and discarded the other two (*'adl* [divine justice] and *Ma'ad* [bodily resurrection on the Day of Judgment]). He argued that justice, like any other divine attribute, is quintessential to God. There is no need to single it out as a principle of belief for a Shi'i Muslim, he stated, though he may have also had in mind the daring proposition that an unjust world could not be presided over by a just God. Far more radically, Shaykh Ahmad altogether rejected the idea of corporeal resurrection on the Day of Judgment. There is no returning to this or any other world after one's physical body dies. Instead of these two (in his judgment) superfluous principles, Shaykh Ahmad offered a Fourth Pillar [*Rokn-e Rabe'*], according to which a Perfect Shi'i [*Shi'a-ye Kamil*] is what is needed as the representative (*wakil* or *na'ib*) of the Hidden Imam among the Shi'i community.[20]

Shaykh Ahmad's bold and brilliant ideas posed an immediate danger to the Shi'i clerical establishment and threatened to put them out of their lucrative business of administering grief to frightened and fearful Shi'is. Humans had agency in Shaykh Ahmad Ahsa'i's theology, prophetology, and imamology—from all of which he put together a cogent, elegant, and worldly philosophy on the model of Mulla Sadra's but even more daring and imaginative. Human beings were not reduced in Ahsa'i's philosophy to mere (frightened) subjects of a medieval jurisprudence, waiting for ritual cleansing of their bodies or the salvation of their souls by one clerical intermediary or another. There was no longer any futile waiting for Time to end, Space to split open, or the Hidden Imam to come back and sort things out. Shi'is had to take arms and by opposing their worldly misery and injustice end them. It is not surprising at all that the origin of by far the most powerful revolutionary movement against both the Shi'i clerical clique and the Qajar aristocracy emanated from the teachings of Shaykh Ahmad Ahsa'i, a deeply cultivated Akhbari by juridical disposition who was radically opposed to the lucrative market that the Usuli jurists had manufactured for themselves ever since their humiliation in Dasht-e Moghan. He was a pathbreaking and worldly philosopher directly descended from the philosophical cosmopolitanism of the School of Isfahan and deeply inclined toward *Irfan* or gnostic Shi'ism—as rooted in it as Mulla Sadra but even more openly daring.[21]

As a student of Mulla Sadra, though with some major differences with him (chief among them the thorny question of bodily resurrection on the Day of Judgment), Shaykh Ahmad picked up the analytic dwelling on gnostic Shi'ism where Mulla Sadra had left off. Thus, in his pronouncedly messianic philosophical position, he posed a fundamental threat to the return of the dominant Shi'i clerical order to their lucrative zone of a feudal scholasticism they had now termed Usuli jurisprudence—a cozy and mutually beneficial arrangement with the Qajar kings and their tribal patrimonialism. Shaykhism disrupted that convenience for both the mullas and the monarchs. In his messianic philosophy, Shaykh Ahmad Ahsa'i was the living testimony to whatever was best and promising in the School of Isfahan, the urbane cosmopolitanism of the gnostic Shi'ism it represented, and potentially the most dangerous revolutionary threat that kind of Shi'ism could posit.

There is nothing in Shaykh Ahmad Ahsa'i's messianic philosophy that is not rooted in Mulla Sadra and the School of Isfahan in theoretical terms, and before them in the revolutionary fusion of Shi'ism and mysticism evident and extended from Isma'ilism to the Hurufiyyah. Though expressed more boldly and more imaginatively, Ahsa'i's urgently messianic philosophy was squarely rooted in Mulla Sadra's *al-Hikmah al-Muta'aliyyah* and his epistemic fusion of mysticism and philosophy on Shi'i jurisprudential and doctrinal grounds. The opposition of the Usuli jurists with Shaykhism was not that different from the opposition that Mulla Sadra faced while studying and writing in Isfahan, though by the time of Shaykh Ahmad Ahsa'i and because of the catastrophic consequences of Dasht-e Moghan, the Usulis were in a far more potent and powerful political position than the clerical establishment under the Safavids. Reading Shaykh Ahmad Ahsa'i in the middle of the nineteenth century is in direct correspondence with reading his fellow Bahraini philosopher and predecessor, Ibn abi Jumhur al-Ahsa'i, or Mulla Sadra Shirazi, or before both the founder of the Hurufiyyah movement, Fazlullah Astarabadi. All of them sought to unify Shi'ism, Sufism, and a transcendental and syncretic philosophy in either philosophical or in revolutionary terms. Even Ahsa'i's visionary dreams have much earlier roots in the works of Avicenna, Ibn Arabi, and above all Suhrawardi. Once you see Mulla Sadra in Shaykh Ahmad Ahsa'i, you see all of these earlier traces as well. By far the most revolutionary proposition of Ahsa'i was his constitution of *Hurqalya* as a celestial purgatory in which mortal bodies are transmuted (purified, sublated) before they resurrect on the Day of Judgment, and which in the process posits a radical theory of the corporeal body in Islamic philosophy.[22] Perhaps equally important in Shaykhism was its more pronounced and even urgent treatment of the messianic aspects of Shi'ism that reverted back to the cyclical theories of successive revelations in Isma'ilism and thus generated a more urgent sense of expectation about the appearance of a new divine dispensation.[23]

Shaykh Ahmad Ahsa'i traveled extensively in Iraq and Iran, refusing Fath Ali Shah's invitation to reside in Tehran. Wherever he arrived he drew huge crowds of admirers among the poor masses, the merchant class, and the intellectual elite alike—and thus inevitably invited the troubling wrath of the Usuli clerics, who sensed in him a deeply dangerous threat to their powerful status, cozy arrangements with the Qajars, and vested interests in the status quo. Among the cities Shaykh Ahmad visited while in Iran was Qazvin, and a chief Qazvini cleric named Mulla Mohammad Taqi Baraghani was among his staunchest and most pestiferous opponents. "In a particularly scandalous public debate with Shaykh Ahmad Ahsa'i," Mohammad Reza Fashahi reports, "Mulla Mohammad Taqi Baraghani charged him with being a student of Mulla Sadra, not believing in bodily resurrection, and with following the Greek and Muslim philosophers, and excommunicated him. In his official declaration of excommunication, Mulla Mohammad Taqi Baraghani declared Shaykh Ahmad to be an infidel and an apostate."[24]

This very belligerent Mulla Mohammad Taqi Baraghani had a brother named Mulla Mohammad Saleh, who was also a high-ranking Shi'i cleric, though with a slightly more tolerant disposition than his quarrelsome brother. It was to this brother that Fatemeh Zarrin Taj Baraghani was born in 1814—a momentous birth in a momentous time, a time thus out of joint, and cursed spite that she was ever born to set it right.

A Precocious Girl

Fatemeh Zarrin Taj Baraghani was a precocious child, endowed with a probing, restless, and agitated intellect, and for her time and age blessed with a liberally minded father, Mulla Mohammad Saleh Baraghani, a prominent member of the clerical class in Qazvin. He allowed his daughter the unusual luxury and the rare privilege of pursuing her studies beyond an elementary level. Her command of Arabic and Persian languages and literatures was soon evident in the beautiful poems she started composing in both.[25] Her primary interests, however, were jurisprudence, theology, and philosophy—particularly when they touched on the mounting contemporary political issues that agitated her family, her city, her country, and the Muslim world at large. Fatemeh Baraghani's father, Mulla Mohammad Saleh, was primarily interested in Qur'anic commentary, and toward the end of his life became somewhat apolitical, especially when compared with his elder brother Mulla Mohammad Taqi, who was a staunch Usuli cleric, a very ambitious powermonger, exceedingly belligerent, and violently anti-Shaykhi. Fatemeh Baraghani had a much more congenial relationship with her younger uncle, Mulla Ali, who (much to the chagrin of his elder brother) was a devotee of Shaykh Ahmad Ahsa'i and a committed Shaykhi.[26] Among these three father figures, Fatemeh Baraghani was well placed to grow up with a range of positive and negative, sympathetic and apathetic sentiments toward Shaykhism—which in effect amounted to the Marxism of the time in Iran (a creative combination of progressive philosophy and revolutionary politics). One might even compare Fatemeh Baraghani to Rosa Luxemburg.[27]

The scandalous behavior of Fatemeh Baraghani's elder uncle, Mulla Mohammad Taqi, effectively chased Shaykh Ahmad Ahsa'i out of Iran and back to Iraq. But the belligerent Qazvini mulla would not relent. Soon after Shaykh Ahmad Ahsa'i left Iran for Iraq, Mulla Mohammad Taqi wrote to his fellow Usuli jurists in Iraq, urging them to continue with their harassment of Shaykh Ahmad and his followers, which they did, to the degree that they even solicited the power of the Sunni Ottoman authorities to punish their fellow Shi'i Shaykhis.[28] Shaykh Ahmad did not tolerate this harassment well and was soon forced to leave Iraq for the holy cities of Mecca and Medina, where he died at the age of seventy-three, having constitutionally challenged the Shi'i doctrinal complacency, backed by Usuli jurisprudence and the monarchic feudalism of the Qajars.

Soon after the death of Shaykh Ahmad Ahsa'i in 1826 near Medina, the thirteen-year-old Fatemeh Baraghani had become quite a handful. Her father had cause to worry about his daughter and her sharply independent and probing mind. To put an end to all potential troubles, Mulla Mohammad Saleh married his daughter off to his nephew and her cousin Mulla Mohammad Baraghani, the son of none other than the same belligerent Mulla Mohammad Taqi who had chased Shaykh Ahmad Ahsa'i out of Iran and ultimately Iraq, possibly even hastening his death. Barely fourteen and deeply enmeshed in her studies, Fatemeh Baraghani was married in 1828 and the young couple was sent to Iraq so that Mohammad could continue with his advanced studies. Fatemeh was expected to bear children and be a good wife to her husband. The fourteen-year-old girl had much bigger dreams, however, and her poetic pulse already beat with the syncopations of entirely different, quietly militant melodies. A prophetic vision was growing in her, and she must have known it. Her dreams were real, and she saw reality with a dreamy determination. She must have known right there and then that she would not be husbanded by a benign fate, but that she would husband this world, that no feeble clerical piety would mount her superior intelligence—unnatural hags, she must have thought.

The progressive, provocative, and pathbreaking ideas of Shaykhism were not to end with the death of Shaykh Ahmad Ahsa'i himself. Soon after his death in 1826, one of his principal disciples, Seyyed Kazem Rashti (1798–1843), was communally recognized as the next *Shi'a-ye Kamil* [Perfect Shi'i]. He picked up his mentor's mantle and continued with his charged and pathbreaking teachings. Seyyed Kazem Rashti carried forward the revolutionary ideas of his teacher and just like him earned the vindictive anger of the clerical class. By the time Seyyed Kazem Rashti augmented Shaykh Ahmad Ahsa'i's writings with his own, a complete picture of Shaykhism as a philosophical project and millenarian movement was in full display.[29] In their eschatology they now fully returned to the Isma'ili and Neoplatonic positions first and best articulated by Nasir Khusraw, altogether rejecting corporeal resurrection of the physical body after death.[30] This eschatology had obvious implications for the Prophet's nocturnal journey to the heavens (the *Mi'raj*), which the Shaykhis believed not to have taken place with His physical body. The same implications were of course evident in the whereabouts of the Hidden Imam, and the impossibility of his having survived for hundreds of years with his physical body. The Shaykhis believed that his soul was alive, and that soul sought physical presence in just about any body, of anybody—and *there* was the dangerous political rub. The times were ripe for political change, people were waiting, and these ideas were bound to catch on like wildfire.

Fatemeh Baraghani and her cousin and husband Mulla Mohammad Baraghani traveled to Iraq and resided in the holy city of Karbala for thirteen years, between 1828 and 1841, where she gave birth to two sons (Ibrahim and Isma'il). During these long thirteen years, Fatemeh Baraghani did much more than be a wife to her husband (at which she was not particularly good) and bear him healthy sons. Through a maternal cousin, Mulla Javad Valiyani, she became acquainted with Shaykh Ahmad Ahsa'i's work during this period.[31] Much to her husband's horror she also attended the circle of Seyyed Kazem Rashti in Karbala. Her reading what effectively amounted to forbidden literature, attending the circle of Seyyed Kazem Rashti against the wishes of her husband and prominent and powerful father-in-law, put her at immediate odds with her elder uncle and the father of her children, but in effective alliance with her younger uncle Mulla Ali Baraghani and her maternal cousin Mulla Javad. Between the ages of fourteen and twenty-eight, Fatemeh Baraghani raised her two sons, quarreled with her husband, read deeply and widely into the Shaykhi literature, and attended the teaching circle of Seyyed Kazem Rashti, who carried the mantle of Shaykh Ahmad Ahsa'i, the most powerful liberation theologian and messianic philosopher of his time. The loving care of her father Mulla Mohammad Saleh, and the support and solidarity of her paternal younger uncle Mulla Ali and that of her maternal cousin Mulla Javad offer a set of corrective lenses when we observe the rise of a revolutionary marvel like Fatemeh Baraghani in nineteenth-century Shi'ism—without resorting to ahistorical hyperbole or revolutionary sandcastles. The fact that her powerful elder uncle and father-in-law Mulla Mohammad Taqi and her husband Mulla Mohammad were dead set against her interests in becoming a deeply cultivated and learned woman, let alone in increasing creative solidarity with the most revolutionary movement of her time, is just added seasoning to this extraordinary drama at the threshold of Shi'i entry into a colonial encounter with European modernity.

The long and arduous years in Karbala finally came to an end when Fatemeh Baraghani, her husband Mulla Mohammad, and their two children Ibrahim and Isma'il and a third yet unborn child finally collected their belongings and returned to their native Qazvin in 1841. She had barely arrived in her hometown when the collective wrath of her husband, father-in-law, and even now her mild-mannered father fast descended upon her, admonishing her for her devotion to the Shaykhi cause. But partially to balance the pressure, she found a new solid ally in her brother-in-law, Mulla Mohammad Ali Qazvini, husband to her sister Marziyeh, and soon to emerge as a major proponent of Shaykhism. An implicit pact between Fatemeh Baraghani, her younger uncle Mulla Ali, her maternal cousin Mulla Javad, and her brother-in-law Mulla Mohammad Ali created a modest zone of comfort in which Fatemeh could live and read and think through her ideas. The generational gap is clear, with the younger members of the Baraghani family increasingly attracted to a revolutionary cause and the older generation dead set against it. Soon after her return to Qazvin, Fatemeh Baraghani wrote a treatise on Shaykhism and dispatched it to Karbala to Seyyed Kazem Rashti, who in turn was deeply impressed by his young (twenty-seven-year-old) follower. He called her "the delight of my eye and the soul of my heart."[32] Toward the end of 1843, Fatemeh Baraghani finally persuaded her father that hers was a useless marriage, separated from her husband, left her children in the care of her family in Qazvin, and along with her sister Marziyeh set off for Karbala, where resided Seyyed Kazem Rashti and the heart of a confounding dream that had excited the slumber of an entire people, chief among them Fatemeh Baraghani and a few other kindred souls.

Fatemeh Baraghani was not to see Seyyed Kazem Rashti again, for just a few days before she arrived in Karbala, the grand Shaykhi master passed away. After the death of Seyyed Kazem Rashti, a number of his students sought to succeed him and claimed the status of *Shi'a-ye Kamil* for themselves. But none of them succeeded in persuading any sizable community of supporters, in part because of the very nature of the Shaykhi messianic philosophy, which was in full and imminent anticipation of a new divine dispensation. The philosophical messianism that had started with Shaykh Ahmad Ahsa'i had concluded with Seyyed Kazem Rashti, and yet another philosophical figure writing erudite glosses of the work of these two founding figures would not do.[33] They both had re-interpreted the world enough. It was now time to change it.

A Messianic Resurrection

It is right here, at this moment of great theoretical preparations and societal expectation, that the collective dream of the community, the Durkheimian *conscience collective,* in fact wills the appearance of that messianic resurrection, and finds that figure in the person of one young Shirazi merchant named Ali Mohammad Shirazi, known as the Bab or the Gate (1819–1850). Just as Seyyed Kazem Rashti was about to die, and as the expectations in Iraq and Iran were quite high after years of Shaykh Ahmad and Seyyed Kazem's persistent writings and activities, and while mediocre figures were plotting to succeed Seyyed Kazem Rashti in Karbala, a young Shirazi merchant suddenly stole the show and began quietly to let the world know of his positively disquieting and mysterious dreams and visions. Seyyed Ali Mohammad Shirazi was born and raised in Shiraz to a prominent merchant family, the profession he soon joined as a young man. He initially attended formal schooling for a few years but soon abandoned it for fear of the corporal punishment that his teacher inflicted on students.

The young Seyyed Ali Mohammad soon left Shiraz for the southern coastal town of Bushehr, and from there he went to Iraq, and for a while in Karbala he even attended Seyyed Kazem Rashti's circles.[34] Soon after Seyyed Kazem Rashti's death, Seyyed Ali Mohammad declared himself the *Rokn-e Rabe',* the Fourth Pillar or the Bab (the Gate) between the Hidden Imam and the world. Along with a number of Seyyed Kazem Rashti's students who began paying serious attention to him, Seyyed Ali Mohammad Shirazi, now reverently known as "the Bab," went to Mecca and then back to Bushehr. His followers soon began spreading all over the region, announcing him to be the promised Messiah. The Bab gradually abandoned any formal connection to Shaykhism and by 1844 (corresponding to the year 1260 on the Islamic calendar and thus exactly a thousand years after the Greater Occultation of the Hidden Imam that had occurred in the year 260 on the Islamic calendar, or 873 CE) thought of and proclaimed himself not only the Bab, but in fact the Hidden Imam Himself, and as such the prophetic visionary of a new cycle of revelations to be communicated in his book *Bayan* [Utterance].

The announcement generated both public excitement and official retribution. The governor of Shiraz, Mirza Hossein Khan Nezam al-Dowleh, soon had a group of the leading Babis arrested and punished and summoned the Bab himself to Shiraz, where he had him publicly tried, humiliated, and imprisoned.

The Bab's initial activities were limited to Bushehr and Shiraz, but soon a prominent Qajar prince named Manuchehr Khan Mo'tamed al-Dowleh summoned him to Isfahan and took him under his wing, just to score a power point with the clerical clique. For about three years the Bab was protected by Mo'tamed al-Dowleh until his death in 1846, and once the Bab resumed his public claims to be the Hidden Imam, the reigning monarch Muhammad Shah summoned him to Tehran and then dispatched him to Maku in Azerbaijan, where his fame and prominence grew even higher. There he completely abandoned the notion of being the Hidden Shi'i Imam and proclaimed himself a whole new prophet, whose book *Bayan* superseded the Qur'an, just as the Qur'an had superseded the Bible. This claim (which was nothing new, and was in fact as old as the claim of Ibn Habib al-Hanafi al-Musaylimah soon after Muhammad had established his prophetic authority in Arabia, or the revolt of Ustadhsis soon after the Arab conquest of Iran) drove the Shi'i clerics absolutely mad. They, in turn, demanded that Muhammad Shah's court arrest and punish the Bab. The Bab was arrested in Maku and sent to Chehriq Fortress near Tabriz in Azerbaijan, where he completed most of his subsequent writings.

Paramount in our understanding of Babism as a revolutionary movement will have to be its social and economic roots in a messianic culture now moving through major institutional transformation in face of European colonialism, and *not* undue emphasis on what could have remained the private fantasies of a young merchant with a particularly powerful imagination or even a historically irrelevant cult of personality. This is as much true about Muhammad ibn Abdullah, the Prophet of Islam (who also was a young merchant when he convinced people that God Almighty was talking to him) as it is about Ali Mohammad Shirazi, the Bab, the namesake of Babism, who also convinced a multitude, including a revolutionary vanguard and a politically significant population, ranging from illiterate peasantry and the urban poor to learned scholars and opulent and successful merchants, that he was in revelatory communication with God Almighty.[35] For a social historian it is utterly futile to dwell on the veracity of such messianic and revelatory claims. We are not qualified to judge. What matters for history is the overwhelming fact of the multitudes that believe in such prophetic voices and put their necks on the line.

That collective belief followed from a longstanding Shi'i doctrine of *intizar* [expectation] of a messianic figure, of a Mahdi, repeatedly manifested in varied Shi'i social revolutions in Islamic history, from the Kaysaniyyah and Zaydiyah early in Islamic history down to the Isma'ilis and the Hurufiyyah as the immediate predecessors of the Babi movement. The mode of messianism peculiar to Babism in the nineteenth century, however, was sifted through the messianic mysticism of Shaykhism, in militant and violent opposition to the Usuli School and its clerical custodians, and through Shaykhism back to the fusion of Shi'ism and Sufism in the making of the School of Isfahan and the philosophy of Mulla Sadra Shirazi. The revolutionary reason of the Hurufiyyah, and all other Shi'i uprisings before it, was urbanized by the School of Isfahan into a public reason. That public reason was displaced in the interregnum between the end of the Safavids in the middle of the eighteenth century and the commencement of the Qajars later in that century, through the catastrophic consequences of the Dasht-e Moghan gathering instigated by Nader Shah in 1736. This loss of public reason had resulted in a backward slide of the Shi'i political culture into feudal scholasticism of the Shi'i (Usuli) clerics and the monarchical tribalism of the Qajar dynasty. The singular significance of the Babi movement is that its revolutionary reason reconnected to that public reason of the Safavid era, re-revolutionizing it through a retrieval of the Hurufiyyah movement, all in light of a deliberate and conscious awareness of the onslaught of European economic colonialism, particularly in southern Iran, in Bushehr, where the Bab in fact commenced his messianic movement.[36] Just as in the formation of the Qajar dynasty after Dasht-e Moghan, a catastrophic symbiosis of feudal scholasticism (of the Shi'i clerics) and monarchic tribalism (of the Qajar kings) ipso facto destroyed the syncretic cosmopolitanism of the Safavid era, the Babi movement reignited the revolutionary reason at the heart of Shi'ism from its earliest history, but this time around through an active (Shaykhi) rearticulation of the School of Isfahan and its constitution of a public reason.

It is scarcely possible to exaggerate the central significance of Tahereh Qorrat al-Ayn in making the Babi movement possible and in re-revolutionizing the public reason it had retrieved from the Safavid period (via Shaykhism). She added to it a renewed public momentum as well. She was the key figure in pushing the messianic dimension of Shaykhism to its utter limits and thus turning Babism from the overwhelmingly active imagination of a young merchant visionary wandering between Shiraz and Bushehr, or Karbala and Mecca, into a massive revolutionary uprising that would define the history of Shi'ism in the nineteenth century. In recognizing Ali Mohammad Shirazi as the Bab, and ultimately as a prophetic and long-expected visionary, thus catalyzing Babism, two of his male followers are usually credited most: Mulla Hossein Boshru'i (1814–1849) and Mulla Muhammad Ali Barforushi, known as "Qoddus." Right next to these two military leaders of the Babi movement stood that very sharp and restless young woman from Qazvin, Fatemeh Baraghani, who was now known by her full honorific nom de guerre Tahereh Qorrat al-Ayn. Compared to her two male comrades, with whom she fought the Qajars and their clerical counterparts shoulder to shoulder, Tahereh Qorrat al-Ayn cuts a far superior figure in three significant and objective ways: She was far more learned in the theoretical foregrounding of the Babi movement (Shaykhism) than her two comrades put together. She was exceedingly eloquent and charismatic, a great public debater, exceptionally persuasive in her arguments, and fully conscious of her abilities to win over her audiences' minds and hearts. She was infinitely more daring, bold, and militant than her two male comrades put together. For these claims not to remain at rhetorical and hyperbolic levels, we need to pay closer attention to the active involvement of Tahereh Qorrat al-Ayn in the Babi movement.

Having left behind her husband and children in Qazvin, Tahereh Qorrat al-Ayn came to Karbala to claim her place in history. She resided at Seyyed Kazem Rashti's former home and between 1844 and 1847 cultivated a wider base of students, political activists, and local community leaders among her followers in Karbala and other shrine cities in southern Iraq. Supported by this community of followers, she radically interpreted Shaykhism to fulfill its revolutionary potential and wedded its messianic message to the figure and phenomenon of the Bab (with whom she corresponded but never met in person). During this nascent period, if we were to subtract Tahereh Qorrat al-Ayn from the southern Iraqi scene, Mulla Hossein Boshru'i from Khurasan, and Qoddus from northern Iran (as the revolutionary vanguard of Babism), the Bab would have remained yet another messianic visionary who thought he was God's gift to humanity. Tahereh Qorrat al-Ayn in particular championed and led a radical faction of Shaykhism, alienating both the conservative factions of the messianic movement and the Shi'i clerical establishment. She lectured widely to huge gatherings in Karbala (usually from behind a curtain), elucidating the messianic and political implications of Shaykhism, and soon began instructing women in the private quarters of Seyyed Kazem Rashti's household. Soon she developed a following, known as the Qorratiyah, in Iraq. In other words, she gave her name to a movement, or a particular faction of a movement, in much the same way that Shaykh Ahmad Ahsa'i had given his name to an interpretation of Mulla Sadra and the School of Isfahan, or in turn the Bab had given his name to a faction of Shaykhism. Historians of Babism refer to Qorratism quite differently than they refer to Shaykhism and Babism—and that is precisely the issue that needs to be kept in mind if we are to see in what particular way Shaykhism, Babism, and Qorratism revived and expanded the revolutionary and public reason that it had inherited from the Hurufiyyah and the School of Isfahan.[37]

Qorratism

In what particular way can we make a case for the phenomenon of Qorratism? Late in the summer of 1846, Qorrat al-Ayn left Karbala for the city of Kazemayn, running away from the more conservative followers of Shaykhism who thought she was carrying the implications of their beliefs, practices, and expectations too far—beyond their patience, courage, or imagination. Qorrat al-Ayn stayed in Kazemayn for the rest of that year, continuing to give public lectures and building the organizational basis of her movement, creating quite a sensation in that holy Shi'i city. People were attracted to her as a person, as a leader, and as a powerful rhetorician in full communion with the pulse of her time. "There she stayed," Amanat reports, "for the next six months as their guest, continuing her public sermons with greater vigor and freedom. An eyewitness confirms that 'a large number of people attended her teaching circles and prayed behind her. As she spoke, they listened with great astonishment in their hearts and were moved by her speeches.'"[38]

While in Karbala and Kazemayn, Tahereh Qorrat al-Ayn was chiefly responsible for politically radicalizing the Shaykhi movement and bringing it closer to the messianic claims of the Bab, and then calling for and actively preparing for armed rebellion in Iran and Iraq against both the Qajars and the Ottomans. Her strategic location was quintessential to the movement. She was residing on the site of the rise of Shaykhism, from where Shaykh Ahmad Ahsa'i had taught and Seyyed Kazem Rashti had lived. She was taking on the Ottomans and the Qajars directly. She was debating the Usuli clerics and defeating them eloquently and persuasively. She was winning masses of supporters, scores of clerical students, and major merchant sympathizers. She was building the revolutionary vanguard of the uprising, forming the party apparatus, sharpening the ideological foregrounding of a mass armed rebellion for an increasingly detailed awareness of what was to come. Mulla Hossein Boshru'i was doing no such thing. He was getting closer and closer to the Bab and becoming his propagandist and military lieutenant in generic and abstract terms, as did the Qoddus and other Babi leaders.

Tahereh Qorrat al-Ayn's groundbreaking activities in Iraq were much too much for the Shi'i clerical establishment or the Ottoman authorities (or the Qajars for that matter) to tolerate. The Ottoman authorities finally arrested Qorrat al-Ayn and deported her to Iran in March 1847. Instead of feeling defeated in her revolutionary activities, she used her passage from Iraq back to Iran to stop at some key strategic locations and promote her revolutionary cause. In every major and minor city in which she arrived (Kermanshah and Hamadan in particular), huge crowds would gather to hear her expound on the messianic philosophy of Shaykhism and the revolutionary cause of Babism—both from her own radical perspective. Among the rules she demanded and exacted for public debates with the aging Shi'i authorities (whom she debated from behind a curtain) was that no one was allowed to smoke in her presence or use foul language.[39] While on her way back to Qazvin in May 1847 Tahereh Qorrat al-Ayn was busy propagating the cause of Shaykhism and Babism and building a massive social basis for armed rebellion, the Bab was in the custody of Qajar officials. He had just arrived in Tabriz from Tehran, en route to Maku, awaiting his fate. Both the Bab and Tahereh Qorrat al-Ayn were now traveling, one to expound his messianic claims from his prison cell, the other to provide his messianic message with solid social grounding for militant mass uprising. For sure the Bab's and Qorrat al-Ayn's activities complemented each other, but the relationship had by now shifted far from that of a prophet and his disciple. At the head of a contingent of her devout, armed, and militant followers, Qorrat al-Ayn had earned the right and the power to interpret the Bab's message any way she wanted, and she wanted it in only one direction: the dismantling of the Qajar patrimonial monarchy and the dissolution of Shi'i clerical scholasticism—both fundamentally divorced from the changing historical circumstances that informed and agitated Qorrat al-Ayn's revolutionary zeal.

Qorrat al-Ayn finally arrived in Qazvin in July 1847 after three years of absence. She returned as a revolutionary leader at the head of a small band of militant followers ready to lay down their lives for her. Advancing the cause of her radical take on Shaykhism and Babism, she arrived in Qazvin almost exactly at the time that the Bab was incarcerated in his cell in Maku—an event that was now agitating Babi leaders and increasing the pressure for a collective uprising. Qorrat al-Ayn, meanwhile, had returned to her home in Qazvin an estranged daughter, wife, and mother. Much to her father's dismay she decided to stay at her parental home and refused to have anything to do with her estranged husband, from whom she now declared herself unilaterally divorced and *haram* [forbidden] by simply willing a superior reading of Islamic law. She cared little whether she angered her husband or alienated her prominent uncle and father-in-law Mohammad Taqi Baraghani, who was deeply offended and had a number of Tahereh's comrades arrested and punished. Qorrat al-Ayn stayed put in Qazvin for three months (July-September 1847), during which her massive popularity among her followers (the public at large, the young seminarian students, and segments of the merchant class) caused much anger and hostility above all in her uncle and father-in-law. The evident hostility between Qorrat al-Ayn and her father-in-law was finally too much for her devoted supporters to tolerate. During the holy month of Ramadan (August-September), a militant follower of Qorrat al-Ayn put a dagger to Mulla Mohammad Taqi's throat and killed him. Tahereh and her supporters were instantly arrested and dispatched to Tehran for further investigations.[40]

Did Tahereh Qorrat al-Ayn have anything to do with her uncle and father-in-law's assassination? Sources differ. Those with an anachronistic tendency to pacify the Babi movement, or that wish to turn Tahereh Qorrat al-Ayn into a Virgin Mary of their religion, seek to exonerate her, whereas the belligerent Qajar and clerical clerics paint her as a cold-blooded murderer. She was neither. She was a disciplined revolutionary leader. She could have very easily ordered the assassination of her uncle if she thought it politically expedient, and not if she thought it detrimental to the movement. One of her followers could have easily taken the matter into his own hands. Either way, accusing or exonerating Tahereh Qorrat al-Ayn can be prejudiced neither in terms of the bourgeois morality of North American converts to Baha'ism, nor in revenge of the wounded arrogance of Shi'i clerics. She was a disciplined revolutionary leader, and she advanced the movement in a measured and meaningful manner. She did or did not order the execution of her father-in-law only to further her revolutionary goals.[41]

By 1848, the Babi movement had spread well into Azerbaijan, Mazandaran, Zanjan, Khurasan, and Yazd. As a great Babi gathering took place between March and April 1848 in Khurasan, on 10 April 1848, the Bab himself was taken from Maku to Chehriq Fortress near Tabriz in Azerbaijan. By July of that year a great public spectacle and trial was organized by Qajar officials and their clerical cohorts in Tabriz in order to humiliate the Bab. His arrest and incarceration further radicalized the movement that was launched in his name. Babi leaders now saw it necessary to meet in one place and think through the state of their movement in general and their immediate strategies in particular. The historic Babi convention held in Badasht in northern Iran in June and July 1848 became a turning point in the history of the movement. Tahereh Qorrat al-Ayn left Tehran for the Badasht gathering knowing she had her work cut out for her. The movement was going nowhere. Scattered uprisings around Iran and Iraq (in Zanjan, Azerbaijan, Khurasan, and Karbala in particular) displayed astonishing heroism and massive sacrifices, but without any central organizing apparatus they were in danger of losing momentum and purposeful direction. The ideological and strategic apparatus of the movement was in dire need of re-assertion—and no one in the Babi movement was readier or more capable of attending to these urgent matters than Tahereh Qorrat al-Ayn.

Even worse for Tahereh Qorrat al-Ayn, there were signs that the Bab himself was seriously engaged in appeasing the Qajar monarchy. He had a long history of oscillating in his own messianic claims. First he had said that he was what Shaykh Ahmad Ahsa'i had called the *Rokn-e Rabe'* [The Fourth Pillar], then he said he was the Bab to the Hidden Imam. Next he thought he was the Hidden Imam himself, but then when he was arrested and tried in a kangaroo court, and beaten up by the Shirazi mullas, he altogether repented any claim he made. While still in Shiraz, and then from Isfahan, and while in Azerbaijan, he repeatedly wrote to the ruling Qajar monarch Muhammad Shah and his mystically minded prime minister, Hajji Mirza Aghasi, trying to ally himself with the monarchy against the mullarchy. While in Maku, he even composed a treatise, dedicated it to Hajji Mirza Aghasi, and sent it to him—one among many other indications that he wanted to endear himself to the Qajars.[42] Thus, as a leading historian of the Qajar period has rightly observed, "the development of Babism as a movement of revolt proceeded more or less independently of the Bab and his pronouncement."[43] In the making of that movement independent of the oscillations of its namesake, no one was more influential than Qorrat al-Ayn in wedding the logical (but what appeared to many Babis as extreme) implications of Babism to Shaykhism and pushing them toward a far more radical end than any anticipated.

During this extraordinary gathering of Shaykhi and Babi leadership at Badasht, the messianic inspiration of the movement was incarcerated in Azerbaijan and effectively irrelevant to the uprising. Tahereh Qorrat al-Ayn rose to the occasion and radically expanded on her previous positions, insisting on a collective armed rebellion. The time was ripe, and no more time should be wasted on hiding and dissimulating. In Badasht, Qorrat al-Ayn was in her element, in charge, and the most eloquent and powerful voice for a collective uprising. Perfectly evident in the Badasht gathering was the fact that Qorrat al-Ayn pushed the political implications of both Shaykhism and Babism far beyond what either Shaykh Ahmad Ahsa'i or the Bab had uttered or even anticipated. By all accounts, Qorrat al-Ayn was the Lenin of this "Marxism," the chief theorist and leader of revolutionary action, pushing the limits of the messianic message and then beyond. With Shaykh Ahmad Ahsa'i long dead and the Bab in prison, Tahereh Qorrat al-Ayn was the most forceful leader. She pushed the normative and political implications of their messianic utterances far beyond what her comrades were ready to accept. Mulla Hossein Boshru'i was absent from Badasht, and thus an immediate rivalry was evident between the other two luminaries, the comparatively conservative Mulla Muhammad Ali Barforushi ("Qoddus") and the far more daring and radical Tahereh Qorrat al-Ayn. In an iconoclastic gesture of defiance, at once shocking and scandalous, and thus deliberately designed to radicalize the movement, Qorrat al-Ayn threw off her veil in the middle of a fiery speech she was delivering at the convention—an act so troubling and outrageous to some members of the audience that among the gathered Babis "one Isfahani zealot cut his own throat."[44] Qorrat al-Ayn did not interrupt her speech.

Qorrat al-Ayn's position at this critical juncture was that this was a period of revolutionary interregnum, that the old social and ritual rules no longer held, and "when the Bab conquers the seven kingdoms and unites different religions, he will bring a new Shari'a and entrust his Qur'an to the community."[45] This provocative argument was made and attracted some attention. But it is crucial to keep in mind that only a small minority followed Qorrat al-Ayn and the overwhelming majority followed the far more conservative positions of Qoddus, who in turn accused Tahereh even of "heresy," a clear indication that the Babi movement was very much a Shi'i revolt and *not* the harbinger of "a new religion." Even Qorrat al-Ayn herself, by far its most radical (outrageous to her detractors) voice of the movement, still thought and argued in principally Islamic and Shi'i terms. She believed that the Bab would bring a new shari'ah and that he would entrust his Qur'an to his followers, proving that even in the most iconoclastic moments of the movement Qorrat al-Ayn still thought in doctrinally Islamic and Shi'i terms, confined to the limits of her normative imagination. To considering Babism as the harbinger of a new religion anachronistically attributed to Tahereh Qorrat al-Ayn categorically misses the crucial revolutionary disposition of the Babi movement. It demotes their armed uprisings, led by militant revolutionaries like Tahereh Qorrat al-Ayn, to modes of mere self-defense. True to the constituency they represented, the Babi leaders were social revolutionaries, with varied attachments to Islamic doctrinal principles ranging from steadfast and pious like Mulla Hossein Boshru'i and Qoddus to iconoclastic and rebellious like Tahereh Qorrat al-Ayn. "Heretical" is what Qoddus thought of Tahereh Qorrat al-Ayn. "He would have punished the transgressors with a sword," is what Mulla Hossein Boshru'i said of Tahereh Qorrat al-Ayn's rebellious behavior in Badasht when he heard of it later. Tahereh Qorrat al-Ayn led a band of revolutionaries who progressively overinterpreted the words of a messianic philosopher and a visionary dreamer to champion the cause of a justifiably violent and unabashedly armed uprising against a corrupt monarchy and their clerical supporters. Proving them "non-Islamic" or "anti-Islamic" or the bringers of "a new religion" (all anachronistically informed by a cult of personality) completely misses the point and distorts history.

The radical character and the provocative gestures of Tahereh Qorrat al-Ayn as the militant leader of the movement cannot be fully grasped unless her take on both Shaykhism and Babism is placed and understood within the context of Shi'i messianic movements throughout history. "Wrap up this spectacle," Amanat reports Tahereh Qorrat al-Ayn telling Qoddus while interrupting his ritual prayers, "sword in hand."[46]

These are symbolically provocative acts, deliberately designed to shock and awe the delegates into recognizing the revolutionary moment that they needed now to honor and follow. This was a rebellious vanguard that had gathered in Badasht, fully engaged in the doctrinal and iconic strategies of the uprising, not the masses of solid popular support that could not possibly have known or fully agreed with these gestures. Confusing the massive basis of a revolutionary uprising with the iconic and provocative acts of its leadership plays the horn of history from the wrong end. To outmaneuver Qoddus and his conservative faction (the majority), Tahereh Qorrat al-Ayn called for yet another public debate (her usual forté), and she managed, yet again, to convince the gathering of the superiority of her position and the necessity of armed rebellion.

To cast out any further doubt, Tahereh Qorrat al-Ayn finally interrupted the proceedings of the Badasht gathering one day "dressed in men's clothing, unveiled and mounted, wav[ing] her bare sword" and led the Babis in a series of battle cries against their enemies, the clerical establishment, and thus called for an armed rebellion that she would lead.[47]

The eloquence and provocative acts of Qorrat al-Ayn won the day. Qoddus relented.[48] Led by Tahereh Qorrat al-Ayn and endorsed by Qoddus, the gathering at Badasht decided to march toward Mazandaran. The two revolutionary leaders conversed comfortably, both in public and in the privacy of a *mahmel* [a mounted mobile chamber], while singing mystical and amorous revolutionary songs—an unveiled ("married") woman in the company of her chief male comrade, toward whom she "perhaps even [had] an unspoken affection."[49] What Amanat judiciously and with responsible circumspection calls "unspoken affection" here assumes scandalous dimensions in visceral anti-Babi sources that go wild with their vile fantasies about the orgy they think was taking place in Badasht in general and between Tahereh Qorrat al-Ayn and Qoddus in particular. "In one of the villages of Hezar-jarib," one anti-Babi historian who can scarce control his hatred of the movement reports, referring to a village through which the Babi caravan was passing, "he [Qoddus] took Qorrat al-Ayn to a public bath and fucked [*ham-khabeh*] her."[50] Here, again, Tahereh Qorrat al-Ayn is supported by an anachronistic bourgeois morality on one side and vilified by a vindictive anti-Babi narrative on the other. It is perfectly plausible that an amorous, perhaps even passionate relationship may have developed between Tahereh Qorrat al-Ayn, a young and by all accounts beautiful woman, and one of her comrades. It is only human. Even if we were to measure this by Islamic/Shi'i law, she no longer considered herself married to Mulla Mohammad (the father of her children), and there would be nothing wrong about her having an amorous relationship with one of her comrades. As in the assassination of her father-in-law, there is no evidence one way or another concerning a sexual relationship with Qoddus, and so dismissing the possibility with certainty is as flawed as giving it scandalous dimensions. A relationship or a lack of one would neither detract nor add to her already daring and imaginative take on the most powerful revolutionary uprising of her time.

Whatever the nature of the relationship between Qorrat al-Ayn and Qoddus, the sight of their combined leadership at the head of the Badasht delegation of the Babis deeply outraged a local mulla in Mazandaran, who led a frenzied mob of villagers against their caravan. Qorrat al-Ayn and Qoddus fled and went into hiding.

Soon after the Badasht convention, the reigning Qajar monarch Muhammad Shah died after a prolonged illness, and his son Nasser al-Din Shah succeeded him in September 1848. The imprisonment of the Bab and the death of Muhammad Shah further exacerbated tensions. By far the most significant uprising of the Babis took place between October 1848 and May 1849 at the Tabarsi shrine in Mazandaran—into which Qorrat al-Ayn tried in vain to smuggle herself. Similar uprisings took place in Zanjan and Neyriz. Qorrat al-Ayn's followers displayed unsurpassed courage and dedication, posing a major challenge to the young Qajar shah and his prime minister, Amir Kabir. The fateful battles raged in scattered parts of the Qajar realm—disparate, defiant, messianic, inconclusive.

After two years of hiding in northern Iran and continuing with her public and clandestine activities, in January 1850 Tahereh Qorrat al-Ayn was finally arrested in Mazandaran, charged with complicity in the murder of her father-in-law Mulla Mohammad Taqi, and dispatched to Tehran, where she was interrogated by Prime Minister Amir Kabir and met with the young king, Nasser al-Din Shah. She was asked to repent and be pardoned. She refused, and while in custody, she used the Babi women who came to pay her visits in various disguises to communicate with her followers. The major Babi uprising in Zanjan in central Iran and in Neyriz in Fars had by then prompted Amir Kabir finally to relent to clerical pressure to eliminate the Bab. Before these successive uprisings at the Tabarsi shrine and Zanjan in particular, the Qajar establishment had been far more tolerant of the Bab, and in fact used him to check the insatiable appetite for power of the court-affiliated Shi'i clerics. But the succession of violent revolutionary uprisings launched in his name clashed with the ideas and aspirations of the new prime minister. On the morning of 9 July 1850 the Bab was taken to the courtyard of the barracks where he was being held. A large crowd had gathered to watch his execution. Things partially quieted down soon after the execution of the Bab. But a failed assassination attempt against Nasser al-Din Shah in August 1852 renewed the Qajar suppression of the Babi movement and the elimination of its leadership. Already in custody in Tehran, Qorrat al-Ayn was finally issued a death sentence by a Shi'i cleric in September 1852.

Expanding the Political Community

Why insist on the singular significance of Tahereh Qorrat al-Ayn in the making of the Shaykhi/Babi messianic movement? Among the most illustrious leaders of the Babi uprising, by far the most significant social revolution of nineteenth-century Shi'ism, Tahereh Qorrat al-Ayn was the principal theorist of its radical faction and one of its top military commanders-in-chief. Far beyond that, she was one of the most remarkable women of all time. She left an indelible mark on the model of a revolutionary hero for all time. But to avoid truisms and hyperbole we must grasp what exactly she achieved through her revolutionary activities.

Because of the enormous historic significance of Qorrat al-Ayn and her extraordinary character, obviously many scholars and historians claim her for one cause or another—from anticolonial nationalism to Third World socialism, from radical Shi'ism to literary modernism, and of course from feminism to Baha'ism. None of these claims is unusual or strange, and Qorrat al-Ayn's green and growing memory is large, expansive, and generous enough to give a share of credibility to all of these. But I wish to claim her life and revolutionary career for something entirely different.

The critical significance of Tahereh Qorrat al-Ayn, as I see it, and her presence at the heart of both the Shaykhi messianic philosophy and the Babi revolutionary movement is in exponentially expanding the Islamic, Shi'i, and Iranian political community or *Gemeinschaft* to open up and embrace half of the humanity otherwise denied their social presence by the patriarchal foregrounding of Shi'i (and Islamic) feudal scholasticism, and thus encouraging that community toward the formation of an organic solidarity among its members, and thus toward the emergence of a modern society (*Gesellschaft*). In his groundbreaking study *Gemeinschaft und Gesellschaft* (1887), the German sociologist Ferdinand Tönnies had posited these two sociological categories by way of distinguishing between the communal (what he called *Gemeinschaft*) gatherings of individuals for a common purpose and the subsequent transmutation of these communities (under more advanced social and economic conditions) to a superior state of societal formation in which citizens and institutions would follow their own particular pursuits and yet fall within a larger frame of differential social formations and cultural mores.[51] Working almost at the same time as Tönnies, the French sociologist Émile Durkheim articulated two modes of mechanical and organic solidarity in his seminal study, *The Division of Labour in Society* (1893). Roughly corresponding to Tönnies's *Gemeinschaft,* Durkheim's notion of mechanical solidarity designates communal formations that are based on normative similarities and strong moral identifications, whereas his organic solidarity corresponds to Tönnies's *Gesellschaft* and identifies societal formations based on normative variations among the social actors and a far more subdued collective consciousness among them.[52]

What I propose here is the central significance of the figure of Tahereh Qorrat al-Ayn, through the doctrinal insurrection and widespread appeal of the Babi movement, in pushing the Iranian (Shi'i) society out of a communal, *Gemeinschaft,* mechanical solidarity toward a social, *Gesellschaft,* organic solidarity. The path she took—militantly transforming the juridical figure of the feminine as the mere subject of a medieval jurisprudence, converting what had been a private possession and proposition into a public persona and presence—constituted a development as important and historic as the formation (and subsequent suspension) of the notion of public reason during the Safavid period. In other words, I see and suggest the public figure of Tahereh Qorrat al-Ayn as singularly responsible for salvaging, rescuing, and retrieving the cosmopolitan constitution of public reason during the Safavids and, by reconnecting it to the pre-Safavid variations of revolutionary reason (now manifested in the Babi movement), pushing it toward an *Aufgehoben* formation of a Shi'i *Gesellschaft.* This is quite a claim and I need to articulate it with some patience.

Qorrat al-Ayn was an iconoclastic poet, a messianic theologian, and a revolutionary activist of unrivalled courage and imagination, with a deep sense of millenarian mission about her public demeanor—and she happened to be a woman. Her concerns were not defined or limited by being a woman. Her vision was the liberation of humans in general and humanity at large, of the human psyche, from what she believed to have been archaic mandates. That she did so by practice not by preaching brought the differential figure of the feminine into the predominant masculinity of Islamic, particularly Shi'i and Iranian, political culture. Although the introduction of the feminine was something entirely incidental to her revolutionary zeal, it is precisely in its accidental nature that it gains unprecedented importance in constitutionally altering the mechanical masculinity of Shi'i political culture. Casting off her veil in Badasht was above all an iconoclastic gesture. If she were a man, she might have shaven, cut off her right hand, put a veil on her face—whatever it took to shock and awe the public out of their habitual complacency. The gesture was integral, not definitive, to her feminine presence in an otherwise masculine and masculinist space, which she thus constitutionally shocked and altered. Because she was so central to the Babi movement, and because the Babi movement was by far the most widespread revolutionary uprising at the heart of Shi'ism and in Shi'i society in the nineteenth century, what she was effectively pushing forward was the expansion of a public space that now had to accommodate not just the public reason that was invested in it during the Safavids but the fact and phenomenon of a differentially modulated feminine force (a combination of Tönnies's *Gesellschaft* and Durkheim's organic solidarity toward the making of a new society from old communal or *Gemeinschaft* gatherings).

To be sure, this is not to suggest that before Tahereh Qorrat al-Ayn women had never been party to revolutions and warfare. Soon after the death of the Prophet, his young wife Ayeshah was chiefly responsible for the Battle of Camel in 656 against Ali, in which she personally participated and led a flank of her army. From the time of the Kharijite movement early in Islamic history women have had an active role in social revolutionary uprisings. Throughout medieval history and up to the famous Battle of Chaldoran (1514) between the Safavids and the Ottomans, Iranian women had a major role in joining men in battle. The figure of Gordafarid in Ferdowsi's *Shahnameh* predates and provides a perfect poetic template for that of Qorrat al-Ayn.[53] The character of Maral in Mahmoud Dolatabadi's modern epic *Klidar,* written between

1978 and 1983, comes after Qorrat al-Ayn and confirms that revolutionary persona.[54] Even among the Babis, Tahereh Qorrat al-Ayn was not the only woman who was integral to the movement. Beginning with philosophical attraction to Shaykhism and down to active membership in the Babi movement, there were many women who were thoroughly dedicated to the cause. In the famous Zanjan uprising against the Qajars led by Mulla Mohammad Ali Zanjani, known as "Hujjat," many female members of his family were active in the armed rebellion, including a sixteen-year-old girl named Zeynab who is reported to have worn men's clothing and participated in the battle, earning the nom de guerre of Rostam Ali.[55]

Qorrat al-Ayn, however, was a breed apart, and no one made herself so theoretically instrumental, publicly evident, politically indispensable, and iconoclastically definitive to the making of the Babi movement; and as such no other was responsible for the transfiguration of a Shi'i revolutionary uprising into a societal transformation and the renewal of that public reason that Nader Shah had buried in Dasht-e Moghan. *That* is a "resurrection and renewal" infinitely more important to the fate of a modern nation-state than the talismanic phantasms of a messianic prophet. Much time has been wasted on anachronistically insisting that Babism was something entirely new and unprecedented in Islamic and Shi'i history. Much more attention needs to be paid to the similarities, continuities, disruptions, and the enduring rootedness of Babism in its previous social and intellectual movements (that of the Hurufiyyah and the School of Isfahan in particular). Likewise, attention should be paid to the figure of Qorrat al-Ayn as the singular site where the differential force of the feminine public presence was inserted into the masculinist space of Shi'i social and intellectual history. This radically and exponentially expanded the societal basis of a revolutionary and public reason institutional to any reading of modernity. In other words, those millions of Muslim women who throughout the rest of the nineteenth and the twentieth centuries have poured into the streets of their cities inevitably become part of the citizenry. They demanded and exacted a share in the destiny of their homelands, and whether they knew it or not, they had a little bit of Tahereh Qorrat al-Ayn in them. But far more important, in making that public persona of the Muslim woman possible, Tahereh Qorrat al-Ayn is singularly responsible for retrieving the public domain of a public reason that was the crowning achievement of the School of

Isfahan and Mulla Sadra—all but lost in the aftermath of Nader's Dasht-e Moghan.

We need to understand Qorrat al-Ayn's flamboyant acts (discarding her veil, mocking her comrade's ritual prayers, perhaps even having an extramarital affair with one of her comrades) and many other transgressive gestures as the militant defiance of a thoroughly juridicalized subject that had been stripped of her humanity and reduced to a mere jurisprudential trope in the tyrannical labyrinth of medieval scholasticism. A committed and disciplined revolutionary, Tahereh Qorrat al-Ayn was a pioneering woman entirely oblivious to the magnitude of her own social significance, but fully conscious of her own transgressive acts. She personified by far the most radical wing of the Babi movement—a nightmare to the Qajar establishment and the Shi'i clerical clique alike—in the most momentous occasion of her nation's history, and in doing so she liberated the juridical subject and ushered her into the public domain of history. To her devoted followers, she personified the most progressive force within Babism when her radical brand of the movement scared the more conservative and compromising followers of the Shaykhi and Babi movement into both political and normative complacency. In her interpretation of Babism, Tahereh Qorrat al-Ayn gave far more significance to a radical messianic take on Shaykhism than the teaching of Shaykh Ahmad Ahsa'i or the uttering of the Bab would have warranted. If Shaykh Ahmad Ahsa'i took an idea of Mulla Sadra and ran away with it, and if Ali Mohammad Shirazi took an idea of Shaykh Ahmad Ahsa'i and thought himself the Gate to Divinity of one sort or another, Tahereh Qorrat al-Ayn took both those ideas and went into a third dimension, and thus we might as well heed the historical facts: there was a phenomenon at the time known as the Qorratiyah, namely the movement that had gathered behind Tahereh Qorrat al-Ayn. Much as the Bab initially gave lip service to Shaykh Ahmad Ahsa'i and Seyyed Kazem Rashti and then broke away from them and proclaimed himself a new prophet altogether, so did Qorrat al-Ayn to the Bab and Mulla Hossein Boshru'i. She simply did not live long enough to rest her own case with history. Just because she was a woman—an iconoclastic, bold, creative, and imaginative woman—does not mean that she is not entitled to a movement named after her. She was a witness to history and historically entitled. In Qorratism, then, the organicity of the Shi'i societal formations was sealed and its public reason evident and manifested, and thus the repressively juridicalized person differentially posited and politically liberated.

Qorrat al-Ayn's version of Shaykhism and Babism was far more radical than her contemporaries were ready to fathom or follow, though by asserting her position eloquently, forcefully, and above all publicly, she evidently and explicitly expanded the Shi'i political community into a societal organicity that had to come to terms with half of the humanity it had denied their full public presence. It is in those terms that we need to understand the social foundations of Babism, or more accurately Qorratism. The massive appeal of the Babi movement to the urban and professional classes speaks of its ideological disposition as a cosmopolitan phenomenon. "The Babi movement," Said Amir Arjomand has rightly observed, "did not . . . remain confined to young clerical circles. Proselytizing began very soon and was immediately successful, especially in the cities. Not unlike the Hurufi, many of the Babi converts were urban craftsmen and merchants, a fact reflected in the attention paid by the Bab to commerce in his writings. In fact, the merchants and guildsmen very soon came to constitute the second largest group [next to "young clerical circles"] of Babi converts, and in the long run, a more solid social basis for continued developments of the Babi religion."[56]

Here we ought to be careful not to confuse the intellectual elite and the revolutionary vanguard of the Babi movement, who came from progressive younger members of the clerical rank, with the followers of the uprising, who came from the merchant class and the artisans. Babism was the radicalization of Shaykhism in political terms in the same way that Shaykhism was the radicalization of the School of Isfahan and of Mulla Sadra in philosophical terms. If there is anything particularly important about Babism (and there is), then it is precisely in having Qorrat al-Ayn in its midst, and through her an active reconstitution of a public reason in a public space that now included the denied half of humanity—a fact that both Amanat and Arjomand do not mention. Although they recognize her heroism and extraordinary acts, they fail to notice the social and historic implications of this heroism.

Without detailed attention to the social implications of the figure of Qorrat al-Ayn, we fail to understand what was particularly important about Babism. Otherwise, as a messianic movement, Babism offered absolutely nothing doctrinally new or unprecedented in Shi'i history. Quite to the contrary, in its general contours it was entirely prototypical. *Beh har alfi alef qami bar ayo*—the piercing precision of a hemistich of Baba

Taher Oryan (died circa 1019) put it most succinctly: "For every three zeroes of a thousand years, the tall aleph of a number one will appear." There was nothing new in the Bab's claim that he was the Gate to the Hidden Imam, or even the Hidden Imam himself, or even the Gate to a new divine dispensation, or even a new prophetic vision. Far more provocative ideas than his and far more radical movements than Babism have been recorded in Islamic history, much earlier than the Babi movement. Sufi mystics like Mansur al-Hallaj (858–922) proclaimed in the middle of the bazaar that they were *Haq,* let alone just a new prophet. Sarbedaran stole *Hajar al-Aswad* [the Black Stone of Ka'bah] and it meant nothing. The Isma'ilis, the Fatimids, the Qaramita, the Sarbedaran, and the Hurufiyyah: Islamic history is inundated by such revolutionary claims, which have achieved varied degrees of success. When Mulla Hossein Boshru'i was fatally wounded in the course of the Tabarsi uprising and he told his followers that he would not die but come back in a few days, he was quoting almost verbatim a whole slew of messianic figures going back to the Persian revolutionary leader al-Muqanna'.

Practically from the time of the death of the First Shi'i Imam early in Islamic history, every time a Shi'i imam died, expectations of his return and corresponding messianic and millenarian movements were rampant in Muslim lands and among the Shi'is in particular. Even the Sunnis believed in the coming of a *Mojadded,* a Renewer of the Faith, once every thousand years. But they sought such figures in scholars, theologians, and philosophers like Imam Muhammad al-Ghazali (1058–1111). Shi'ism has been particularly prone to such messianic movements all through its long and arduous history. When Mulla Hossein Boshru'i declared in Shiraz: "I bear witness that Ali Mohammad is the Continuation [or Sign] of God [*Baqiyat Allah*]," something simply archetypal had taken place. With those words, the Babi movement reconnected to the Sarbedaran, the Hurufiyyah, the Nuqtaviyyah, and then back all the way to the Isma'ilis via a transfusion of the messianic aspects of Shi'ism with Sufism, but this time through a radical reading of the School of Isfahan and of Mulla Sadra through Shaykhism. As Said Amir Arjomand has noted, there is a remarkable similarity between Babism and the Hurufiyyah. But this similarity can in fact be extended to the Isma'ilis, the Qaramita, the Sarbedaran, the Musha'sha', and even the Safavid rebellion before it resulted in the formation of the Safavid empire. Every Safavid king thought of himself as *Morshed-e Kamil,* the Perfect Guide, long before Shaykh Ahmad Ahsa'i thought of himself as *Shi'a-ye Kamil.* Both of these titles were drawn from the Sufi notion of *Insan-e Kamil,* or the Perfect Human Being, a notion best articulated by the thirteenth-century mystic Aziz al-Din Nasafi. And so the Safavid monarchs thought they were a manifestation of divinity—not just the shadow of God, but the Sign of God, the *Baqiyat Allah.*[57] The Bab did not pull this out of his Shirazi hat.

In their doctrine of *huruf-e hay* [living letters], the Babis were the direct descendents of the Hurufiyyah movement, attributing cabalistic significance to letters and numbers. The similarity between the two revolutionary movements extends, as Arjomand has noted, to the honorific epithet of Qorrat al-Ayn, which was given to two prominent women: first to the daughter of Fazlullah Hurufi, and then to Fatemeh Baraghani.[58] Arjomand notes one significant difference between the Hurufiyyah and the Babis, and that is the fact that "*Bayan* contains detailed ethical regulations covering most areas of social and personal life."[59] The significance of this difference is in the fact that Babism is a post-Safavid revolutionary movement and the Hurufiyyah a pre-Safavid. Bab was a student of Seyyed Kazim Rashti, who was a student of Shaykh Ahmad Ahsa'i, who was a student (in the disciplinary sense of the term) of Mulla Sadra—and as a result the School of Isfahan and the public reason paramount in Mulla Sadra's philosophy finds its way into the revolutionary ideas of the Bab. Babism is no longer a mere revolutionary uprising limited to a battlefield, but in fact is the political expression of the normative disposition of the School of Isfahan, and as such, as Arjomand rightly notes, Babism appealed to "craftsmen and merchants," namely city-dwellers and artisans in particular.

Babism was not the last feudal uprising, as Fashahi and Arjomand suggest, or an entirely new and unprecedented phenomenon (anticipating the rise of a new Prophetology) the way Abbas Amanat consistently insists, but instead the very first modern Shi'i revolution. Though modern, it was deeply rooted in its historical antecedents in the transformation of a revolutionary reason into a public reason. Predicated on the ideas of Shaykhism, Mulla Sadra, and the School of Isfahan via a reconnection back to the Hurufiyyah and Sarbedaran movements, and in anticipation of the anticolonial Tobacco Revolt of 1891 and then the Constitutional Revolution of 1906–1911, Babism was the link that brought medieval Shi'i revolutionary reason to meet the evident fact of a public reason. Through the figure of Qorrat al-Ayn this linkage was differentially lifted toward the very first formation of a template for a Shi'i society *(Gesellschaft)*. There is a direct line from Shaykhism to Babism to the Tobacco Revolt of the late nineteenth century, and then to the Constitutional Revolution of the early twentieth century. Throughout the entirety of this history Qorrat al-Ayn remains a singularly significant figure.

As in the case of any other charismatic leader, after the death of the Bab his followers began to disintegrate around various claimants to his prophetic leadership, among them two brothers from the Nur region of Mazandaran: Mirza Yahya Sobh Azal (1831–1912) and his older brother Mirza Hossein Ali (1817–1889). The Bab had specifically nominated Sobh-e Azal as his successor. When the Babis were under severe persecution in the aftermath of an attempted assassination of Nasser al-Din Shah in 1852, the two brothers and the remaining Babis fled to Iraq in the Ottoman territories. Meanwhile, others claimed leadership of the Babis, though none were particularly successful. Soon the Babis were divided into two groups, those who followed the reticent but militant Yahya Sobh-e Azal (the Azalis), and those who followed the ambitious but pacifist Mirza Hossein Ali, who called himself *Baha'ullah* [The Glory of God] (the Baha'is). The internecine conflicts between the Azalis and the Baha'is finally forced the Ottoman authorities to split them and exile Baha'ullah to Acre and Sobh-e Azal to Cyprus. Baha'ullah now claimed to be the promised prophet that the Bab had anticipated and proceeded to establish a whole new religion named after himself, while the Azalis gradually diminished in number and significance.[60]

The transmutation of Babism into Baha'ism is a perfect example of the diminishing returns of a messianic movement and its transmutation back from societal organicity into cultic communalism. From Shaykh Ahmad Ahsa'i to Seyyed Kazem Rashti to Ali Mohammad Bab there is a clear and progressive crescendo of ideological and military dialectic within a mobilized community of believers, thus transforming into an organic society. One after the other, from Shaykh Ahmad through Seyyed Kazem to the Bab, they each upped the ante and pronounced a larger claim on messianic representation. All of these claims were corroborated *not* because they were just stated but because they were believed by a politically and socially significant population. In direct communication and in tune with the revolutionary expectations of Shi'is at large, Tahereh Qorrat al-Ayn and her comrades recognized Ali Mohammed Shirazi as the Bab, and made of the Bab a Babism that was politically potent and socially significant. This was no longer the case with Baha'ism. Though it also upped the ante and proclaimed a whole new prophethood, Baha'ullah could not gather any politically significant community of believers. Baha'ism thus emerged as a largely benign universalism with scattered adherents around the globe (more than 5 million in more than 200 countries, according to their own estimates), but entirely irrelevant to the political fate of any nation. As such it represents the effective dismantling of the societal *Gesellschaft* of a massive social revolution back to the communal *Gemeinschaft* of a cult of personality—theologically benign and harmless, politically innocuous and irrelevant.

The enduring legacy of Babism as a crucial social revolution, however, remains entirely immune to the vagaries of such inconsequential quibbling. Through the revolutionary mediation of Tahereh Qorrat al-Ayn, Babism picked up where the Hurufiyyah had left off, the School of Isfahan had resumed, and the Dasht-e Moghan had all but destroyed. If the School of Isfahan sublated the revolutionary reason of the Sarbedaran and the Hurufiyyah to public reason, and as the Qajar dynasty and its clerical counterpart sought to turn the historical clock back to pre-Safavid feudal scholasticism, the Babi movement re-sublated that very public reason back to a revolutionary reason. This time around, however, it proceeded with the philosophical heritage of the School of Isfahan and the Shaykhi radical re-reading of the legacy of Mulla Sadra as the very normative foundation of its movement. To put it in the vernacular of the physical spaces that marked these historic developments, what the School of Isfahan and Mulla Sadra had articulated in *Meydan-e Naqsh-e Jahan* and Nader sought to destroy in *Dasht-e Moghan*, the Babis revived in *Dasht-e Badasht*.

Toward the end of his book and in a moment of exasperation, Mohammad Reza Fashahi laments the legacy of Babism being handed over to Baha'ullah's successor Abd al-Baha, whose knighthood by the British Crown deeply troubles Fashahi's anticolonial sentiments. "*Chonin bud saranjam va noqteh-ye payan-e* [And thus it was]," Fashahi concludes, "that ended that glorious revolutionary uprising. As if that beautiful, pure, rolling, and thunderous river of an Iranian revolution was destined to end up into a rivulet rut carrying the rotten flow of quagmires and swamps, a filthy furrow that at its ending point would pour into the River Thames."[61] This is a harsh and misguided judgment of Baha'ism. The man that the Bab had designated as his successor, Yahya Sobh-e

Azal, ended up spending his retired days in Cyprus. Yahya Sobh-e Azal had two daughters, and as fate would have it, he married off these two daughters to two expatriate Iranian intellectuals, Mirza Aqa Khan Kermani (1853–1896) and Shaykh Ahmad Ruhi (1855–1896). These two brothers-in-law, sons-in-law to the Bab's designated successor, comrades-in-arms for a lifetime, would soon join forces and constitute the leading moral and intellectual edge of a massive Constitutional Revolution that would pick up from where Babism had left off and put an end to the Qajars. Their nation would see the dawn of a whole new day.[62]

VISUAL AND PERFORMING ARTS

7

SHI'ISM AND THE CRISIS OF CULTURAL MODERNITY

The camera blinks, the sequence starts, the actors act, and we are inside a bus full of passengers in downtown Tehran. The camera blinks again and we approach a row of seats, where we see a young bearded man and an older veiled woman sitting next to each other. From their body language we learn they are not related. The young man is reading a book; the older woman is looking idly around, and her gaze eventually falls on the cover of the book the young man is reading. We too get a closer look. It is a book by the leading Iranian Islamist revolutionary turned filmmaker and novelist Mohsen Makhmalbaf.[1] The book is called *Bicycle-Ran* [The Cyclist]. We know the film by that name, so this must be its script. The older woman strikes up a conversation with the young man. The young man offers his copy of the book to the older woman. She thanks him. He says he does not need it, because he is the author of that book. She is pleasantly surprised, but a bit incredulous. "Are you Mr. Makhmalbaf?" she asks. "Yes I am," the young man bashfully responds, keeping a straight face and a downcast gaze. He is lying. We know the author of that book. His name is Mohsen Makhmalbaf. We have seen pictures of the prominent filmmaker many times. This young man is not Makhmalbaf. He looks like him. But he is not the filmmaker. The older woman believes him, however, and continues the conversation based on the willingly credulous assumption that he is Mohsen Makhmalbaf. She says her children are fans of his films. He acknowledges the gesture with humility—bashful and humble. One thing leads to another, and the fake Makhmalbaf offers to come and pay the older woman's family a visit, perhaps even make a film about them. She is visibly excited, still a bit incredulous, positively baffled, but seems to will her credulity. Cut.

This is the opening sequence of one of the masterpieces of contemporary Iranian cinema—Abbas Kiarostami's *Close-Up* [*Nema-ye Nazdik*] (1990). We are now completely drawn into the unsettling labyrinth of fact and fantasy, reality and representation, which is the hallmark of the Iranian maestro's cinematic oeuvre. The film is based on an actual story, the cinematic chronicle of a certain Mr. Hossein Sabzian who went around Tehran pretending to be Mohsen Makhmalbaf. The man who plays Hossein Sabzian in Kiarostami's film, and there is the rub, is Hossein Sabzian himself, and the older woman and her family, the Ahankhah family, who were actually duped by Sabzian, believing him to be Makhmalbaf, reprise their real-life roles. They are not in fact acting. They are re-enacting. They are impersonating themselves, re-enacting when they were actually doing what they now pretend they are doing. When the event actually took place, Sabzian was pretending to be Makhmalbaf, while the Ahankhah family was not pretending, duped into believing they were dealing with Makhmalbaf. But when making this film version of that actual event—at the moment when Abbas Kiarostami stands behind his camera and says, "Action!"—now Sabzian pretends pretending to be Makhmalbaf while the Ahankhahs pretend to be themselves duped into believing they were facing Makhmalbaf. The two facing mirrors of fact and fantasy thus reflect each other ad infinitum.

Close-Up is a kaleidoscope of facts and fantasies, of reality and representation, vision and illusion. We see what we see, but what we see is not what we see, it is the simulacrum of truth, truth hidden and revealed only to be proven delusional. *Close-Up* is tunnel vision with mirrors, interspersed by floating beads and pebbles of fact and fantasy, of *factasy*.[2]

Abbas Kiarostami's *Close-Up* is the semiotic seal of the Iranian cinema, an artistic adventure that took the world by joyous and bewildered surprise soon after the Islamic Revolution in Iran (1977–1979). More than a decade after the Islamic Revolution, *Close-Up* led a global audience to ask how such thematically rich and visually sophisticated cinema could come out of an Islamic Republic. However legitimate on the surface, the question begged itself. Why should such films not come out of Iran? An explanation one could offer was that great works of art emerge out of deep historic traumas—out of the sorts of revolutions and wars Iran experienced in the 1970s and the 1980s.[3] In accord with this explanation, Iranian cinema emerged not despite the Islamic Revolution and the Islamic Republic it created but in fact because of the social and cultural turmoil that had occasioned and marked these cataclysmic events.[4]

There is another way of looking at the paradox, a complementary way, as to how good cinema could emerge out of (or adjacent to) bad politics. One might dwell on the moment of a categorical bifurcation between the evident binaries of politics and aesthetics in the contemporary consciousness of a Muslim (Shi'i) anticolonial imagination. The Islamic Republic of Iran, in which Kiarostami's cinema received global attention, was the result of an Islamic Revolution, and that Islamic Revolution was the penultimate outcome of a militant Shi'ism that had its most immediate roots in the nationalization of Iranian oil (1951–1953), the Constitutional Revolution (1906–1911), the Tobacco Revolt (1891–1892), and then all the way back to the Babi movement (1844–1852). This successive course of rebellious uprisings against European colonialism and the active emergence of an anticolonial modernity ultimately resulted in a radical bifurcation between a militant political Shi'ism, on one side, and an evident aesthetic formalism on the other. If we take Ayatollah Khomeini as the most recent figurehead of the former, representing a militant Shi'ism divorced of its creative imagination, we might consider Abbas Kiarostami as a hallmark of the latter, an aesthetic formalism with a distant and delayed connection to historical rootedness.

Kiarostami's *Close-Up* is a virtuoso performance and the best textual evidence of a radical bifurcation between reality (the real Makhmalbaf who is a filmmaker, the maker of fantasies) and representation (Hossein Sabzian, who pretends to be Mohsen Makhmalbaf the filmmaker, the maker of fantasies). As an iconic cinematic occasion, Abbas Kiarostami's *Close-Up* marks the semiotic representation of reality at the moment when it severs all its mimetic ties to reality under the overriding layers of ceaseless semiosis, an almost mimetic metastasis, when cinematic allegories become the agents of their own psychosomatic dispensations, when the acts of representation go rogue and frivolously feed on themselves, with nothing but an elusive relation to reality.

When and how did that happen, this semiotic bifurcation between reality and representation, between a militantly factual politics devoid of joyous mannerism and an affective aesthetics in want of factual worldliness?

The Making of a Politics of Despair

In this third part of my book, I wish to change my analytical register from historical to cultural—in both aesthetic and political terms. The reason for this necessary shift of focus is that in the course of the twentieth century something quite extraordinary has happened in the Shi'i collective consciousness, both creative and critical. A deeply traumatic split divides the matters of Shi'i politics from the manners of its aesthetic manifestations. Before we can resume any historical narrative of the fate of Shi'ism in our own time—its transition from medieval to premodern to modern—we will first have to come to terms with this paramount crisis of cultural modernity that has split the Shi'i collective consciousness into two divergent and conflicting halves: a politics of de-sedimented reality on one side, and an aesthetics of formalized representation on the other. Without a conceptual grasp of this split, nothing in contemporary Shi'i history will make much sense.

What I mean by an aesthetics of formalized representation is a mode of mimetic semiosis whereby the act of representing reality (history, politics, society, economics) assumes a reality sui generis and formally distances itself from the historical matters of that formality. In Abbas Kiarostami's *Close-Up,* for example, Hossein Sabzian pretends he is Mohsen Makhmalbaf, and this factually false representation is at the core of Abbas Kiarostami's cinema. But, one may say, all representations are factually false: Laurence Olivier, Kenneth Branagh, and Derek Jacobi are not Hamlet. They pretend they are Hamlet when they act in Shakespeare's play. But Hamlet was not a historical person. He was a dramatic persona. Mohsen Makhmalbaf is a real human being whom Hossein Sabzian impersonated in real life, and then Kiarostami asked him, once again, to re-enact this life in front of his camera—so this time around Hossein Sabzian got to act the role he had played for an unknowingly gullible family for a much larger and willingly gullible audience.

But who is this Mohsen Makhmalbaf, and why did Hossein Sabzian want to impersonate him? Well, Mohsen Makhmalbaf too is a filmmaker, a maker of fantasy. But his fame, and the reason that Hossein Sabzian wanted to impersonate him to those willing and eager to believe in him, was not just because he was a filmmaker. He was a public intellectual and activist, a Muslim Shi'i revolutionary who after spending almost five years in jail had come out first to support the revolution. Afterward, he radically changed his life mission and became an artist, a novelist, and a filmmaker. Kiarostami keeps that political point of

Makhmalbaf suspended in the air. He never addresses or introduces it in his narrative, paramount in which remains the mimetic moment of representation itself. It is that factastic mode of mimetic representation that I wish to consider and offer as an example of an aesthetics of formalized representation.

On the opposite side of this aesthetics of formalized representation is the politics of de-sedimented reality, or a politics of despair, by which I mean the gradual stripping of the Shi'i political culture from its vast and varied rootedness in a creative imagination that has throughout history given it moral dexterity, intellectual effervescence, and aesthetic agility in visual and performing arts (as best exemplified in Ta'ziyeh). The result of the stripping of Shi'i political culture of its moral imagination has been a steady transmutation of its politics into dry juridical and scholastic terms, further exacerbating the premodern (seventeenth through nineteenth centuries) emergence of Shi'i feudal scholasticism as the defining moment of its social functions. As the very last instance when Shi'ism sought to fuse its creative and critical (philosophical and political) dimensions together, the cathartic trauma of the Babi movement survived its diffusion into Baha'ism, now the pacifist faith of some 5 million people scattered over two hundred countries that began with a prophet who abandoned and pacified the Babi revolutionary heritage. Beginning with the Tobacco Revolt and continuing with the Constitutional Revolution, the insurrectionary heritage of Babism was handed over to the next generation of revolutionary theorists and activists. Such leading representatives of this new generation as Mirza Aqa Khan Kermani, Shaykh Ahmad Ruhi, Mirza Habib Isfahani, Mirza Fath Ali Akhondzadeh, and many others wedded the revolutionary heritage of Babism to a new Constitutionalist movement, into which was now actively infused anticolonial nationalism, Third World socialism, and a progressive political Islamism. Within this otherwise cosmopolitan context, militant Shi'ism assumed an increasingly single-sided ideological disposition, banking almost exclusively on the feudal scholasticism at its roots at the heavily expensive cost of denying, rejecting, or destroying its non-juridical heritage—from philosophical and mystical to literary, poetic, performative, and visual.

Split between Politics and Aesthetics

The tumultuous vicissitude of its own alternative modernity being well under way since the fifteenth century, Shi'ism was forcefully interrupted by the vagaries of European colonial modernity, which effectively and paradoxically strengthened the hand of the most retrograde forces of feudal scholasticism among the Shi'i clergy. During the Safavid period and the rise of the School of Isfahan, constitution of a public reason and space outside the private scholastic reasoning of the clergy put the Shi'i clerical establishment on the defensive. They experienced a vindictive ascendancy in the aftermath of the Nader Shah's Dasht-e Moghan, and were given a new lease on life during the Babi movement, the Tobacco Revolt, and the Constitutional Revolution. The epistemic split in Shi'i creative and critical consciousness takes place in the aftermath of these three events, with the creative going wayward and formal and the critical going clerical and vindictive.

In the course of the twentieth century this radical and self-alienating split between the politics and the aesthetics of the Shi'i critical and creative imagination was carried one step further soon after the Islamic Revolution in Iran, with domino effects in the Shi'i communities in Iraq and Lebanon. The same circumstances, I wish to argue, that occasioned the Islamic Revolution of 1977–1979 in Iran, and by extension the rapid rise of political Shi'ism in Iraq and Lebanon, also (and paradoxically) conditioned the rise of two totally globalized and globally celebrated Iranian artists—Abbas Kiarostami from Iran and Shirin Neshat from New York—the former operating from within a militantly Shi'i societal context and the other from within her deeply Shi'i creative imagination outside her homeland. It is not accidental, I would like to propose, that both these artists have been as universally celebrated by foreigners as deeply distrusted by Iranians and other Shi'is, who did not know quite what to do with these artists' radically formalized aestheticism outside the purview of their own urgent and mundane political predicament.

On the surface these two phenomena seem entirely unrelated and in fact autonomous from each other. But I wish to place this apparent anomaly into a single frame and historicize their evident estrangement. My argument is this: as Shi'ism was undergoing its own historical vicissitudes between the sixteenth and the nineteenth centuries, and in its own Arab, Persian, Turkish, and Indian neighborhoods, the violent onslaught of European colonialism tilted the balance and shocked its epistemic system. In historical terms, following the Arab and Muslim conquest of Asia and North Africa in the seventh through tenth centuries, only the Mongol invasion of the thirteenth century matched the enormity of its political and cultural consequences. After the Mongol invasion, the Russian and Ottoman empires were the key global players affecting the affairs of Shi'is in the seventeenth and eighteenth centuries until the rise of European colonialism and subsequently Soviet and American imperialisms in the nineteenth and twentieth centuries. European colonialism in particular brought along something it called *modernity,* which for the rest of the world inevitably meant a colonial modernity, and thus the only kind of modernity that the rest of the world could have in response to it (if it were not to succumb to a vacuous traditionalism) was an anticolonial modernity.[5] The shock of colonial modernity, and the anticolonial modernity that it occasioned, epistemically split Shi'ism into the dead-end of a politics without emancipatory hope, on one side, and an aesthetics without material worldliness, on the other. These consequences are thematically and constitutionally different from the way Max Weber has theorized the global phenomenon of modernity, and after him Jürgen Habermas has sought to further and sustain it.

The Break between the Critical and the Creative

Two prominent German thinkers are instrumental in our understanding of European modernity, Max Weber and Friedrich Nietzsche. The former embarked on a monumental comparativist project aimed at systematizing a global grasp of the capitalist mode of modernity, and the latter embodied a deadly serious frivolity aimed at discrediting and dismantling it. Whereas Max Weber's universalizing project was picked up by his fellow German philosopher Jürgen Habermas and projected into what he calls "the unfinished project of modernity," it was left to three French philosophers—Georges Bataille, Michel Foucault, and Jacques Derrida—to elaborate on Nietzsche's ideas and mount a postmodern and poststructuralist assault on the primacy of reason and the assumption of progress at the heart of European Enlightenment modernity.[6]

If we were to follow this particular reading of the universal phenomenon of modernity, the Weber-Habermas theoretical breakdown of the European project results in science, morality, and aesthetics as three normative and epistemic domains in "the West," while the selfsame phenomenon in the colonial world breaks, I wish to argue, into two competing, contesting, self-contradictory, and self-alienating domains of politics and aesthetics: as politics becomes increasingly nativized and absolutist, the aesthetics grows vacuously global and thrives on its crisis of mimesis because of its traumatic encounter with colonial modernity.[7]

This schizophrenic breakdown of the Shi'i collective consciousness, as an example of the more widespread phenomenon common to the colonized world, directs its creative consciousness toward the aesthetics with the same steadfast fixation as it leads its critical consciousness toward the politics. No understanding of the post/colonial condition of Shi'ism (or post/colonial consciousness across the Arab, Muslim, and the Third World in general) is possible without an initial grasp of the normative, creative, critical, and moral foregrounding of this traumatic tearing of the fabric of the Shi'i collective consciousness.

Max Weber believed, and Habermas elaborated the idea, that European modernity, which they both mistook for universal modernity, begins when constitutionally religious sentiments are broken down into rational, legal, and aesthetic domains. Weber's famous methodological preference for the *verstehende Methode* [interpretive method] was geared toward an understanding of those intersubjective meanings that are definitive to what he believed exclusively to be "Western modernity"—and the very cast of that intersubjective mode of knowledge production was predicated on this epistemic desedimentation. Weber considered instrumental rationality as definitive and integral to the *Kulturbedeutung* [cultural significance] of the selfsame modernity—and this instrumental rationality was impossible without the breakdown of the religious into rational, legal, and aesthetic domains. The entry of Shi'ism into colonial modernity, however, was a fortiori coterminous with a massive anticolonial uprising and a severe cultural crisis, both following from a major epistemic shift that split its collective consciousness into two dialectically self-negational halves: critically political and creatively aesthetic.

Through the category of disenchantment, Weber sought to explain the process by which religious worldviews had yielded to instrumental rationalization. This was not necessarily a welcome outcome for Weber, but it was nevertheless the historical development through which modern empirical sciences, economic institutions of advanced capitalism, an autonomous field of operation for art outside the ecclesiastical order and the courtly culture, a jurisprudence and legal apparatus based on rational argumentation, and modern state bureaucracies (among a host of other things, such as musical notation) had been made possible. Weber believed and later Habermas corroborated that such developments constituted the defining moment of modernity, which had occurred exclusively in what they both termed "the Occident."

The problem with such broad categorizations, partially insightful and revealing and partially blinded by universalizing Eurocentricity, is that even at the most comparative moments of universalism they remain (perhaps inevitably and necessarily) limited in their epistemic foregrounding, and the fact and phenomenon of the colonialism on which Western European modernity (including modern social sciences, of which Weber and Habermas are two prominent examples) is squarely based. In any understanding of the world outside the purview of that methodological and epistemic Eurocentrism, the factor of colonialism, as a principal catalyst of historical change, cannot be ignored. When we tilt our gaze and look at the Shi'i encounter with colonial modernity, we see how the cataclysmic event breaks it down—not into scientific, moral, and aesthetic rationalism as Max Weber thought and Jürgen Habermas elaborated, but into two major cross-alienating domains: politics and aesthetics. What Weber and Habermas saw and theorized about the European scene may very well be true and accurate, but the selfsame phenomenon of modernity, when it passes through the prism of colonialism and intercepts anticolonial modernity as its principal nemesis, breaks into two and not three shades of normative apparatus: the singularly political and the formally aesthetic.

This historic split in the Shi'i critical and creative consciousness in time results in the creation of a visual subconscious for the belligerent politics of Shi'ism, a subconscious that works through the mimetic consequences of an alienating aesthetics, which is tantamount (but not identical) to the Brechtian dramaturgical *V-effekt* (alienation or distancing effect). After this fateful split, and as the political goes native, nativist, and triumphalist, the aesthetics goes exactly in the opposite direction and becomes incessantly abstract and vacuous, working its way toward the formation of a visual subconscious that informs the Muslim polity and politics but remains visibly invisible to it. The force that mediates between the aesthetics and the politics, between the visual subconscious and the violent politics, is the mimetic consequences of the Shi'i version of the Brechtian *V-effekt*. As evident in the most performative aspect of Shi'ism, Ta'ziyeh mimesis is the force of that aesthetics amounting to "alterity" in action, as Emanuel Levinas would say. So after this split, the political side of Shi'ism is divorced from its cosmopolitan culture and alternate forces, while at the same time its alternate forces are radically stylized and aestheticized, and vanish to the point of no return into pure alterity, into abstract visuality.

In the making of that abstract visuality, there are many moments when Kiarostami's camera, for example, becomes overtly self-conscious, plunging into a visual solitude reminiscent of all Khayyamesque moments in the tradition of Persian poetic pauses and whispered meditations. In this case, however, Kiarostami's camera is *visibly* meditative, for the whole world to see—but to see what? To see us: the naked spectators, visually stripped of all our worldly and societal, cultural and political, whereabouts. We are face to face with the absolutism of reality now summarized in this rolling canister, coming from nowhere, going nowhere else. The rolling canister is there only as a ruse to see us undressed of all our existential claims to communions, gatherings, solitary and in the solitude of our own completely bared soul. Seeing that moment of visual solitude is the birth of an almost mystic elation, of self-revelation in the innermost sanctities of the spectator, who at this moment has stopped being the member of any communal audience and has been forced into a visual introspection of her or his own soul.

> *Na. In barf ra digar sar-e baz istadan nist . . .*
>
> No. This snow has no intention to stop
> Falling—the snow that falls
> On our hair and on our eyebrows
> So at the gate of the mirror
> We look at ourselves with fright—as if
> From the height of a cliff at the depth of a depthless gorge.[8]

It is precisely this poetic moment of pause and pondering, a poetic implosion, at once frightful and revelatory, evident anywhere from Omar Khayyam's quatrains to Ahmad Shamlou's lyricism, that Kiarostami has managed visually to fathom. But contrary to both Omar Khayyam and Ahmad Shamlou, Kiarostami's moment is visually posited and as such opens up (especially for the poetically cadenced mind of an Iranian filmmaker and poet) one's soul. Kiarostami's meditative camera concentrates on that pointless rolling of a depleted and discarded canister as a visual ruse, pulling along with it the unraveling *nafs-e nateqeh* [the loquacious soul] of anyone who dares to watch his or her own descent into nullity.

Oddly though, this particular shot in Kiarostami's magnum opus is not a moment of elegiac angst, death of the soul, or epicedial mourning in the Weberian iron cage, derived from a prolonged project of self-degenerative modernity in search of and in want of a charismatic deliverance. This is pure and unadulterated visual formalism assuming a *Kulturbedeutung* of its own, not through an epistemic desedimentation of cognition into instrumental reason in rational, legal, or aesthetic fragments, but into a moment of formalized bliss with no evident take on or break from reality—from the heart of which a renewed pact with reality can, might, and must be resurrected. In the absolute and last moment of the mimetic departure of Kiarostami from fact into factasy, a renewed pact with worldliness remains perfectly evident but always potential. I have, throughout my engagements with Kiarostami's cinema and through his cinema with the political pregnancy of the aesthetic he best represents, been concerned with the manner of critically liberating that creative potentiality from a necessarily formalized aesthetics into a liberating political necessity. If, in the shadow of anticolonial modernity, Shi'i politics is blinded by single-minded darkness, its alienated aesthetics is equally blinded by open-ended light. Liberation from the cyclical politics of violent despair will never dawn and shine unless and until the formal destruction of violence evident in its alienated aesthetics is once and for all dealienated, reawakened, and brought home to it.

The Naked Violence

The naked violence agitating the insularity of Shi'i politics is the return of its visual repressed—the more formalized the visual aesthetics that has been alienated from its politics, the more forcefully it conceals its violence, and the more it reveals the naked violence that remains solitary at the heart of the contemporary (post/colonial) Shi'i politics. The domain of radically formalized aesthetics, forming the visual subconscious of Shi'i politics, is a slippery danger zone on which an artist (like Abbas Kiarostami) can slide both ways: toward an aesthetics of emancipation in one direction, or toward a deeply alienating artwork that means specifically nothing to no one because it means generically everything to everyone. Before the fateful Shi'i encounter with colonial modernity, the correspondence between a prolonged historical course of vicarious reality and its varied representations in moral and imaginative manners sustained the course of a normative dialectic that enriched its politics and signified its art, and as such was integral to Shi'ism as a religion of protest. There is no better site to view this creative correspondence between reality and representation in the history of Shi'ism than in the Shi'i passion play, Ta'ziyeh.

As the locus classicus of Shi'i dramaturgical mimesis, where reality and representation have a convenient and procreative conversation, Ta'ziyeh has always thrived on the intersection of history and myth (evident reality and metaphoric representation). As such, it has been a paradigm of human redemptive suffering with the world as its site of citation, the material of its emerging evidence. Ta'ziyeh marks a mimetic dissonance between what it sees and what it shows—the memory of Karbala that it remembers and the streets and back alleys of a changing and traumatizing history that it thus resignifies. But it always does so with an open channel of creative communication between the evident reality and the sublating representation, enriching one while making the other worldly wise and significantly material. The mimetic dissonance that Ta'ziyeh marks leads to a suspended sense of history, where events mean more than meets the eye, and where, ipso facto, signs signify less than they invest in a posterity yet to come. The suspended sense of history (time and space) in Shi'ism is contingent on an expectant delivery, where an almost (but never completely) cosmic promise is made and remade, and where history can never end or begin. For history is but a mimetic trope in a story that is eternally to be told and retold by ordinary people who wage war and enact their own stories on the historical stage at one and the same time. The mimetic balance between thriving reality and its dramatic representation is what has hitherto made Shi'ism cosmically cogent, historically held together, dramatically worldly, mimetically resonant with reality—its art and politics embedded in and pregnant with each other.

If as a metaphor Ta'ziyeh fails narratively to absorb and aesthetically to sublate (at one and the same time) the rugged historical reality that it faces (from the Shah's monarchy in Iran to the U.S. occupation of Iraq to the Israeli invasion of Lebanon), then something far more crucial and precious than a people's home and habitat is endangered. A people's epic will come to a meltdown, and all its dwelling allegories will fade out and run away from its mimetic measures of meaning and significance. Nothing means anything anymore.[9] At that point people become moral zombies—*"homo sacer"* as Giorgio Agamben calls them, sleepwalking into a normative coma where nothing means anything any more—victims, or victimizers. As a dramaturgical paradigm, Ta'ziyeh is conjugated like an irregular verb that never exhausts its own impromptu grammatology. Mapped out on that paradigm, history is nothing but a passing exemplar, an illustration whose presence makes a dramatic point, that the world is but a stage and we the passing shadows that make it move and mean. The formation of mimetic dissonance at the heart of Ta'ziyeh suspends it in time, hangs it on the sense and sensibilities of a miasmatic location, a suspenseful conception of the history that it thus makes meaningful, trustworthy, and significant. Here the metaphor has come to meet naked aggression, where history attests to the veracity of the allegory. In deference to that allegory, history is always in a state of flux, waiting to be delivered, read, interpreted, as all Shi'is always are, awaiting the Expectant Deliverer, the Imam of the Age, to put his full stop and singular signature on one final reading of history.

As the single most performative evidence of Shi'ism as a religion of protest, Ta'ziyeh plays out as a theater of redemption inundated with sustained revolutionary potentials that consistently sublate reality into representation and sustain representation with reality. The asyncretic mimesis operative at the dramaturgical heart of Ta'ziyeh (that there is no one-to-one correspondence in its iconic acts of representation) corresponds to a mimetic dissonance that can read reality perfectly loudly and clearly but never succumb to it. Carrying within itself the very seed of Shi'ism as a religion of protest, Ta'ziyeh collapses the dual supposition of the moral and political communities into each other, disallowing the narrative and normative separation of the two. In the same vein, reality and representation are counter-narrated against each other, bringing the tragedy of Imam Hossein to bear on the contemporaneity of its actual performance. This in turn brings the creative and critical dimensions of the drama much closer together than ordinarily allowed. The two moments of the act, its historical roots and its momentary remembrance, are thus dramatically collapsed into each other, preventing an antipathetic distancing of the audience from the fact of the event. The diachronic separation and the synchronic fusion of history and reality are thus transmuted into each other, making art and politics almost impossible to separate, making the world its performative stage and battlefield at one and same time. It is precisely this mimetic fusion of art and politics that gets to be split in the extra-mimetic moments of the post/colonial condition.

This dramaturgical tension at the roots of Ta'ziyeh as ritual drama gives the nature of its mimesis an entirely different performative modulation from that of the Aristotelian mimesis or "imitation," which is immediately tantamount to onomatopoeia, or the actual making *(poiein)* of the naming *(onoma)* of the mimetic act. We have no such presumptions in Ta'ziyeh, where acting is not metaphysically mimetic but mimetically metamorphic—with something of a full contractual agreement, performatively stipulated, between the actors and the audience that they are just acting. If the Aristotelian mimesis is based on similitude, Ta'ziyeh is predicated on dissimilitude. The director of Ta'ziyeh is always present (and often deliberately visible) on the stage, not because the actors would not know what to do without him, but because the audience needs assurance that this is just acting. The stage is not really a stage, not because the villagers and townspeople who stage the Ta'ziyeh are poor and cannot afford a proper amphitheater, but because the stage must be an extension of the rest of the physical habitat of the actors and the audience—their ordinary realities fused into their acting. The actors often come on stage directly from their houses, alleys, streets, and markets. The stage never loses sight of its not-being-the-stage, of being a natural extension of reality. Nonactors can frequent the stage easily, while the actors fall in and out of character without any prior notice.

There is thus a transubstantial lucidity operative between reality and representation in Ta'ziyeh, for above all the actors are not acting a fiction. They are acting reality (just like Sabzian playing Makhmalbaf)—and *acting reality* is neither paradoxical nor oxymoronic here. Imam Hossein and his companions really were killed in the battle of Karbala in October 680 by Yazid and his cohorts. The actor cannot play-act, as if history never happened and he is just staging a work of fiction; and yet he cannot pretend that he is Imam Hossein either. That would be sacrilegious. This, as a result, necessitates an active vigilance on part of the audience. They must know when the actors are acting and when they are not. This is above all facilitated by the fact that Ta'ziyeh actors are not really actors. They ordinarily have other professions—greengrocers, butchers, carpenters, dentists, lawyers, or teachers. If we were to see a Ta'ziyeh performance with a built-in Aristotelian conception of mimesis, we would be terribly baffled and disappointed. In a doctrinally charged collapse of the *then* and the *now,* the moral and the political, the real and the ideal, the charismatic paradox at the heart of Shi'ism informs the dramatic tension inherent in Ta'ziyeh and all its suggestive symbols of acting, staging, showing, and representing.

Aware of this mimetic dissonance between the way a Shi'i audience watches and reacts to a Ta'ziyeh performance and the way a Western European or North American audience goes to watch the very same performance in a theater festival, Abbas Kiarostami has pulled off a quite dubious performative experiment with his audiences: his production of Ta'ziyeh for primarily European spectators comes with its own Iranian and Shi'i audience. The European audience not only watches a Ta'ziyeh performance but also watches, simultaneously, an Iranian and Shi'i audience watching the very same performance! Although in the initial version of his *Ta'ziyeh,* presented in Rome and Taormina (2002), he had arranged for a live performance by an Iranian theater group, in the subsequent Brussels (2004) and London (2006) versions the live performance was replaced by a videotape of the same Ta'ziyeh projected on a television screen. Whether they watch a live or recorded Ta'ziyeh performance, the European audience also watches two large screens placed behind the Ta'ziyeh, on which Kiarostami projects close-up shots of the faces of a Shi'i audience taken at a previous live performance in a village in Iran. The precise choreography of the performance and the close-ups of the faces are synched so that the European audience watches both the unfolding events in the Shi'i drama and the Iranians' responses to them. Not everything the European audience observes of the Iranian audience is about the play. They are seen casually conversing about other things before the Ta'ziyeh performance starts. Once the play starts, the Iranian audience is transfixed by the performance—laughing, sobbing, enrapt, and totally absorbed.

There is an obvious ethical issue here that conceals a larger theoretical problem. Making a European seasonal spectacle out of the ritual piety of the Shi'i spectators, who are participating in the sacrosanct moment of their collective faith, is all the more troubling when Iranian peasants caught in a moment of their sacramental rites are offered up for the passing entertainment of bored urban Europeans, who might attend a Russian circus next week and a film or theater festival the week after. This unethical act is of course not limited to this work of Kiarostami. When Japanese tourists were taken to Harlem to watch Gospel music in African-American churches, similar concerns were raised, just as when the Mevlevi (so-called "whirling") dervishes appeared on Broadway.

Along the same lines, and marking the dangerously slippery slope down which aesthetic formalism may slide, there is also an aggressive (violent even) anthropologization of rural areas for the benefit of urban spectators (whether in Tehran or Paris, it makes no difference). It runs through much of Kiarostami's and many other Tehran-based Iranian filmmakers' cinema in a general way and assumes darker dimensions in his *The Wind Will Carry Us* (1999). There is a scene in *The Wind Will*

Carry Us in which an obnoxious and nosy documentary filmmaker has chased a young rural woman to her house and is using the pretext of buying milk from her to subject her to a violent and humiliating verbal and visual abuse.[10] All the habitual care and confident balances of Kiarostami's camera here yield to the closest a scene in Iranian film can come to sexual violence. The camera movement, lighting, mise-en-scène, and the tight framing enclose the young woman as she milks a cow in a stable while the intruding Tehrani man watches her closely and recites a poem of Forough Farrokhzad in a thick and condescending Tehrani accent that the young girl cannot understand. Kiarostami's camera has framed her from his point of view in tight, dark, and miasmatic proximity to the cow's udder and genitalia—the closest approximation to a violent sexual scene—with perhaps even more troubling consequences than an actual rape scene.

What the unethical dimension of this particular scene conceals, and Kiarostami's version of Ta'ziyeh further documents, is something more fundamental in the radically formalized cinematic aesthetics that Kiarostami now practices. What happens in Kiarostami's *Ta'ziyeh* is the active and conscious transmutation of the whole performative nexus that is operative between the Ta'ziyeh as a theater of protest and its immediate and intended audience into a spectacle for a foreign, alien, and alienating audience. Kiarostami's *Ta'ziyeh,* in other words, is twice removed from the mimetic urgency of the performance when it is staged in Tehran, Sidon, or Karbala, where the audience is integral to the play. The entire Iranian Revolution of 1977–1979 can be seen as a massive Ta'ziyeh performance, as can the bloody resistance of the Iraqi Shi'is in Karbala and Najaf to the U.S. occupation of their homeland, or the Hezbollah defense of Lebanon against Israel.[11] Kiarostami takes this entire nexus—of piety, performance, and ritual; history, politics, and violence—and turns both Ta'ziyeh *and* its audience into a spectacle for the entertainment of his European audience, who by and large neither are Shi'is nor have a clue how to read the mimetic measure of a communal act of piety on stage. The heavily slanted relation of power between an ipso facto empowered European spectator and a disempowered Iranian spectacle is only one aspect of the event. It should not distract us from the more important transmutation of an entire mimetic nexus between a dramatic ritual and its immediately intended audience into a voyeuristic object of anthropological curiosity, not just for an alien audience but far more important in an alienating performance.

As the site of a creative correspondence between traumatic reality and liberating representation in Shi'ism, Ta'ziyeh is the dramatic citation of the moment when politics becomes creatively enriched and aesthetics critically significant. Abbas Kiarostami's *Ta'ziyeh,* a prime example of the excessively formalized aesthetics ushered in by the traumatic encounter with colonial modernity, breaks down this mimetic moment by making both the Ta'ziyeh performance itself *and* its Shi'i audience a spectacle for a curious European audience without an understanding of either the performance or the culture. Thus the placement of the dual screens, an attempt at double signification—one signifying the other—actually becomes doubly insignificant (or doubly "indifferent" as Jean Baudrillard would say). By turning the Shi'i act of communal piety into an anthropological object of curiosity, Kiarostami effectively stages the naked violence of a politics that has been visually repressed by paradoxically upstaging an aesthetics that has been politically vacated. But what remains constant in Kiarostami's work, as the best example of a larger phenomenon in visual arts, is the double indemnity of an aesthetic formalism that dwells on the dangerously slippery borderlines, that excessively overcompensates for a politics of desedimented reality that it tries to shun and disown. The result is the twilight zone of a hazardous event where the mimetic crisis can extend in liberating or alienating directions. If the canister scene in Kiarostami's *Close-Up* and the final sequence of his *Through the Olive Trees* are sublime examples of the former, the stable scene in *The Wind Will Carry Us* and his *Ta'ziyeh* performances in Europe are examples of the latter.

The Return of a Mimetic Crisis

The traumatic encounter of Shi'ism with European colonial modernity triggered its chronic mimetic crisis in the precarious correspondence it harbors between evident reality and evasive representation, best preserved in the Ta'ziyeh passion play. Contrary to the Aristotelian model of dramatic closure, the transitional and spontaneous mimesis at the heart of Ta'ziyeh is founded on the historical trauma of Karbala, which it does not quite know how to represent. That mimetic crisis, definitive to Shi'i history, was rekindled in the course of its encounter with colonial modernity following an aterritorial conquest of Muslim lands (from India to North Africa) unprecedented in Shi'i (Islamic) history. In part and in semiotic terms, because of that traumatic encounter and its mimetic crisis, Shi'ism splits its defining infinitive, with its politics going particularly parochial and its aesthetic bending universally global. Because of this historic trauma the mimetic resonance between reality and representation broke down, and as political reality lost its dialectic conversations with its creative and imaginative counterparts, manners of dramaturgical representation lost their rootedness in the daunting reality: the representational increasingly represented nothing, while reality ceased to think and feel its alterity.

Repeated but failed attempts at societal modernity over the last five hundred years, ranging from the School of Isfahan in the sixteenth century to the Babi movement in the nineteenth century, coupled with a debilitating encounter with European colonial modernity ultimately resulted in the final breakup of the endemic Shi'i mimetic crisis between the ever-changing reality and its corresponding representation, and thus as reality severs this historic nexus and goes its own way, so representation becomes autonomously iconic—politics becomes devoid of moral imagination, and aesthetics abandons its political interstices. If the Shi'i revolutionary leader Ayatollah Khomeini best represents one, the prominent Iranian filmmaker Abbas Kiarostami best represents the other: one deeply plunged into futile acts of political violence that defeat their stated purpose as they succeed, the other sublating that very reality into unrecognizable aesthetic formalism. Khomeini without Kiarostami makes as little sense in understanding contemporary Shi'ism as does Kiarostami's contemporary cinema without Khomeini. Long before Abbas Kiarostami finally turned to Ta'ziyeh, he (in the company of such luminary artists as Shirin Neshat and Bahram Beiza'i) had been incorporating latent Shi'i themes in his work, albeit in radically formalized and alienated terms. Ayatollah Khomeini and President Reagan (in the company of Margaret Thatcher) exacerbated each other's political parochialism and created a politics of despair that led to futile acts of violence, ultimately culminating in the events of 9/11. Meanwhile, as Guy Debord (1931–1994) anticipated in his *Society of the Spectacle* (1967), the fetishization of commodity was finally paired by the transmutation of politics into spectacle: Abbas Kiarostami took the spontaneous mimesis of Ta'ziyeh and went global with it, overcoming Aristotelian mimesis, matching the post-Nazi Brechtian *V-effekt* with an alienated post-Islamic reading of Ta'ziyeh.

The nature and function of this schizophrenic split between the sublime truth and the beautiful vision has hitherto been categorically disguised under the falsifying notion of "secularism." The binary opposition posited between "Islam and the West" or "Islam and modernity," or in more universal terms, between "tradition and modernity" has for the longest time mischaracterized and falsified this epistemic split between the formalized aesthetics and the alienated politics of the Shi'i collective consciousness. Abbas Kiarostami's *Ta'ziyeh* and Shirin Neshat's photography and video installations, as well as Bahram Beiza'i's cinematic and dramatic metaphysics and Forough Farrokhzad's poetics, all point to an alienating aesthetics that has gone rogue in its formal finitude—perhaps to build the momentum of a different significance, perhaps to indulge in the pure pleasure of a formal destruction of reality.

How does this split between politics and aesthetics bode for the future of Shi'ism in its effective history? The spontaneous mimesis at the heart of Shi'ism means that as a religion of protest it has now been emotively transmuted into visual and performative registers and is always ready for a renewed historical rendezvous with public reason in a global space via creative and ahistorical encounters with the pregnant works of such lapsed Muslims and avant-garde artists as Abbas Kiarostami and Shirin Neshat. By way of navigating its historical and doctrinal tropes in a much wider domain of creative imagination, barely even recognizable as "Shi'i art," the vast spectrum of the Shi'i visual and performing imagination is now capable of expanding the doctrinal, historical, and institutional dimensions of Shi'ism into its most public manifestation in formal rituals offering a whole new vista on the human condition, in which the central trauma of Shi'ism in the Battle of Karbala is barely remembered even as it is being re-enacted—always in allegorical tandem with its contemporary history.

Uniting the Fictive and the Factual

The penultimate scene and final sequence of Abbas Kiarostami's *Close-Up* is by now a classic study in the delight, wonder, joy, and magic of cinema. For the entire film the real Mohsen Makhmalbaf has been conspicuously absent. Everything in Kiarostami's film revolves around Makhmalbaf, but we never see him, for we are entirely preoccupied with the man who has impersonated him, pretended to be him, fooled an entire family into believing he is Makhmalbaf when he is not—he is a fake. Finally, in the very last sequence of the film, we find ourselves inside a truck with a camera, a camera crew, and the voice of Kiarostami himself (we never see him; we just hear his voice, and only those who have heard his voice before would recognize it). A telephoto lens points at the gate of a prison court where Hossein Sabzian is just about to be released into the busy hustle-bustle of the street, and right there and then we see Makhmalbaf himself, the real Mohsen Makhmalbaf, wearing army fatigues and sporting a beard and a pair of prescription eyeglasses. He is riding on a motorcycle, then walking toward the prison gate to greet Sabzian. Sabzian is flabbergasted and bursts into tears. "*Geryeh nakon, geryeh nakon*" ["Don't cry, don't cry"], we hear Makhmalbaf telling Sabzian. Makhmalbaf embraces Sabzian and takes him toward his motorcycle—and we are looking at all of this from the point of view of the camera crew inside Kiarostami's van.

Makhmalbaf mounts his motorcycle, Sabzian sits behind him and holds him tightly, and they start riding through the crowded streets of Tehran while we remain inside Kiarostami's van, looking at them from behind. In a move that has created much confusion and discussion but whose function is perfectly clear, we gradually notice that the sound engineer is having difficulty, and the audio of the conversation between Makhmalbaf and Sabzian keeps breaking up. This, followed by a discussion among Kiarostami, his camera crew, and the sound engineer leads the audience to believe that they are working with old and unreliable equipment. Using this ruse, Kiarostami keeps his camera rolling for the visual, altogether cuts the audio, and instead introduces a beautiful Persian melody by Kambiz Roshanravan. We listen to this melody while we watch Makhmalbaf and Sabzian riding a motorcycle together, navigating their way through the busy streets of Tehran.

The "faulty" audio equipment is wisely and prudently kept out of the conversation between Makhmalbaf and his body double, so we cannot eavesdrop on what they are saying to each other. Gently fading in a harmonic melody and lightly allowing his camera to watch from afar as the two ride away, Kiarostami allows a moment of soul-searching intimacy between the two men, the two entities, the two personae—one real and one fictive, both now indistinguishable: which one is now the real Makhmalbaf? Who is to tell, and what difference does it make, anyway? Here fact and fantasy, reality and representation, person and impersonation, politics and poetics, fuse, sublate, and become one—we are at the end of all mimetic acts here, of mimesis, of one representing the other, and thus we witness the beginning of a sublated reality, where reality is representation, representation reality. This final shot in Kiarostami's *Close-Up* makes up for a lifetime of cinematic lapses he may have committed. As the master visionary of what needs to be done, of what needs to be seen, he holds his camera steady for us to see. There they are, riding, Makhmalbaf and his body double, the thing itself and its fictive shadow, reality riding with its own fantasy embracing him tightly from behind, and the fantasy in turn holding the reality tightly in his bosom. Reality and representation have become one and the same, one embedded in the other, each one pregnant with the other, holding each other like Siamese twins in a fetal position, or even better, like yin and yang.

OTTOMAN EMPIRE
Constantinople
Cairo
Baghdad
SAFAVID EMPIRE
Kabul
Delhi
MUGHAL EMPIRE

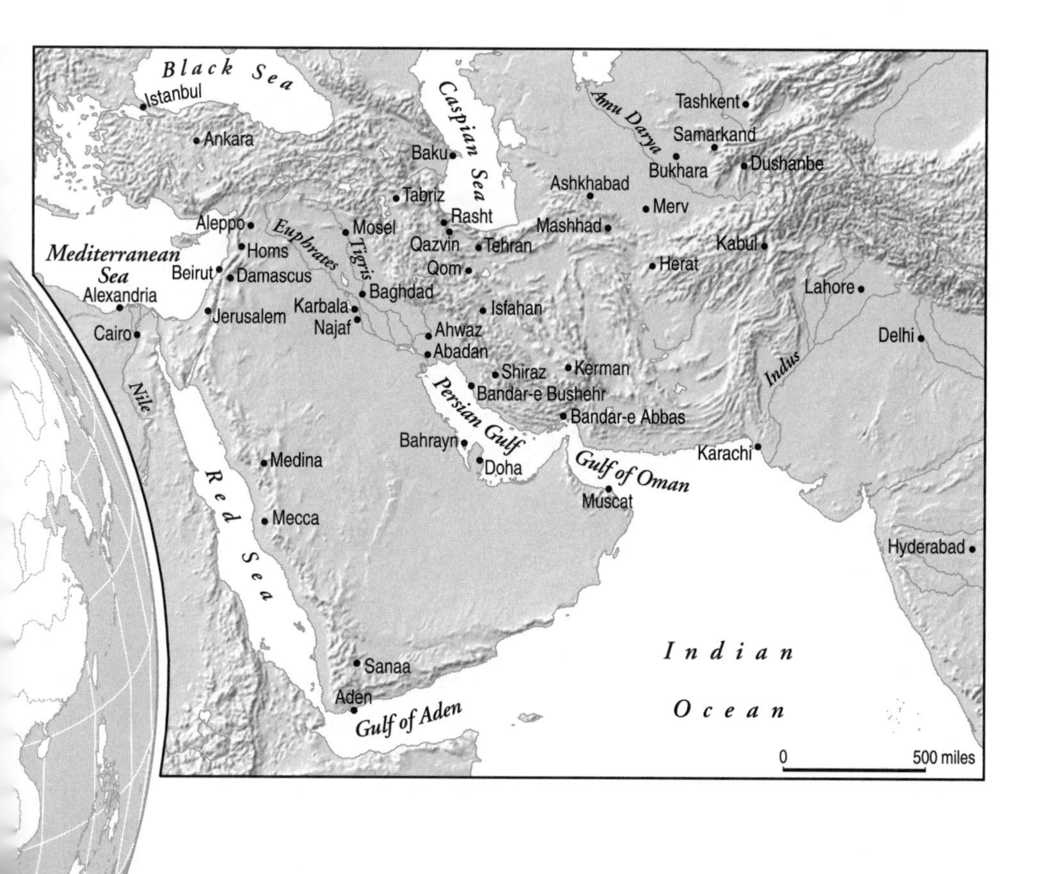

The Ottoman (c. 1550), Safavid (c. 1515), and Mughal (c. 1600) empires *(left)*; the Islamic world *(right)*.

Meridian Mapping, Inc.

On canvases like these various aspects of the story of Karbala and other significant sites of Shi'i memory were depicted by pious artists and then carried around towns and villages by professional storytellers, and from the iconic images stories were told to mesmerized audiences. At the center of the narrative is the valiant Imam Hossein, and around him various phases of the formative trauma of Shi'ism in the Battle of Karbala.

Abbas Al-Musavi, *Battle of Karbala*. Brooklyn Museum 2002.6. Gift of K. Thomas Elghanayan in honor of Nourollah Elghanayan. Reproduced with permission.

These pious and imaginary depictions of Prophet Muhammad and Imam Ali are examples of religious souvenirs sold in the bazaars built around imams' and saints' mausoleums, which cater to pilgrims from around the Muslim world. Although figurative painting is doctrinally prohibited in Islam, these acts of piety are widely popular among believing and practicing Shi'is.

Courtesy of Dr. Ingvild Flaskerud, private collection.

In a key scene from his film *Silence* (1998), Mohsen Makhmalbaf pays visual homage to a famous poem of Forough Farrokhzad, *Tavallodi Digar* [Another Birth], especially the stanza in which she says: "I will hang two earrings on my ears/ From two twin cherries/And the petals of dahlia I will attach to my fingernails." In poetic and visual terms, Forough Farrokhzad and Mohsen Makhmalbaf crossed sacred and profane divides to reach a higher understanding of the sublime—one rooted in Shi'ism but reaching far and wide into the contemporary worldliness of their respective art.

Maysam Makhmalbaf, courtesy of Makhmalbaf Film House, with permission of Mohsen Makhmalbaf.

The appearance of this photo of Ahmad Batebi, a student activist in Tehran, on the 17 July 1999 cover of *The Economist* catapulted him to global fame and landed him in jail in the Islamic Republic. The photo became the symbol of a renewed social uprising led by the vanguard of student activists, in effect appropriating the rebellious disposition of Shi'ism for themselves, as the leading clerics paradoxically lost their legitimacy.

Jamshid Bayrami/Reuters Pictures. Reproduced with permission.

A seat of high scholastic learning established by the Shi'i dynasty of the Fatimids in Egypt, al-Azhar University was one of the finest achievements of the Isma'ili branch of Shi'ism. For more than two centuries al-Azhar was the principal academic seat of Isma'ili scholasticism, providing peace and security for Shi'i doctors of law under a prosperous dynasty in search of legitimacy. It is to the Cairo that gave birth to this intellectual environment that Nasir Khusraw was drawn as a young poet, philosopher, and political activist.

Reprinted from E. Prisse d'Avennes, *L'Art Arabe* (Paris, 1877).

Surrounded by some of the most magnificent monuments in the history of Islamic architecture, Naqsh-e Jahan Square in Isfahan was and today remains an impressive site for Muslims and foreigners alike. An area of nearly 90,000 square meters, the space defied notions of art, history, and politics to inaugurate a whole new sense of urbanity. Although the origin of the site dates from the pre-Safavid period, construction was mostly completed during the reign of the visionary Safavid monarch Shah Abbas I (1588–1629).

Reprinted from M. Louis Dubeux's *La Perse* (Paris, 1841).

This apocryphal drawing of Tahereh Qorrat al-Ayn (1814–1852) captures the spirit of her enduring legacy as a valiant revolutionary for generations to come. A learned Shi'i theologian, gifted poet, and committed activist, Qorrat al-Ayn devoted her short but furious and flamboyant life to turning around the moral and intellectual disposition of her homeland, forever altering the vacuous assumption of Muslim women's passivity.

Reprinted from Yahya Aryanpour, *Az Saba ta Nima*, 4th ed. Tehran: Entesharat-e Jibi, 1350/1971.

Contemporary adaptations of Ta'ziyeh performances throughout the Muslim world are social events that commemorate and celebrate the locus classicus of Shi'i dramaturgical mimesis, with political realities as the immediate material of its renewed historical significance. At center stage is the valiant Imam Hossein mounted on his white horse, the eternal symbol of defiance and revolt, redemptive suffering and traumatic triumphalism, preparing himself for battle at the end of the Ta'ziyeh. In these performances, scattered around villages and towns in Iran, political realities and dramaturgical representations engage in a procreative conversation and reenact the intersection of history and myth. Shi'ism here comes back to life from within the communal experiences of the people who perform and practice Ta'ziyeh—against all doctrinal injunctions and clerical authorities.

Ta'ziyeh performance, Shiraz Art Festival, Husseiniyeh Mushir, Iran, 1976. Photo courtesy of Peter Chelkowski, private collection.

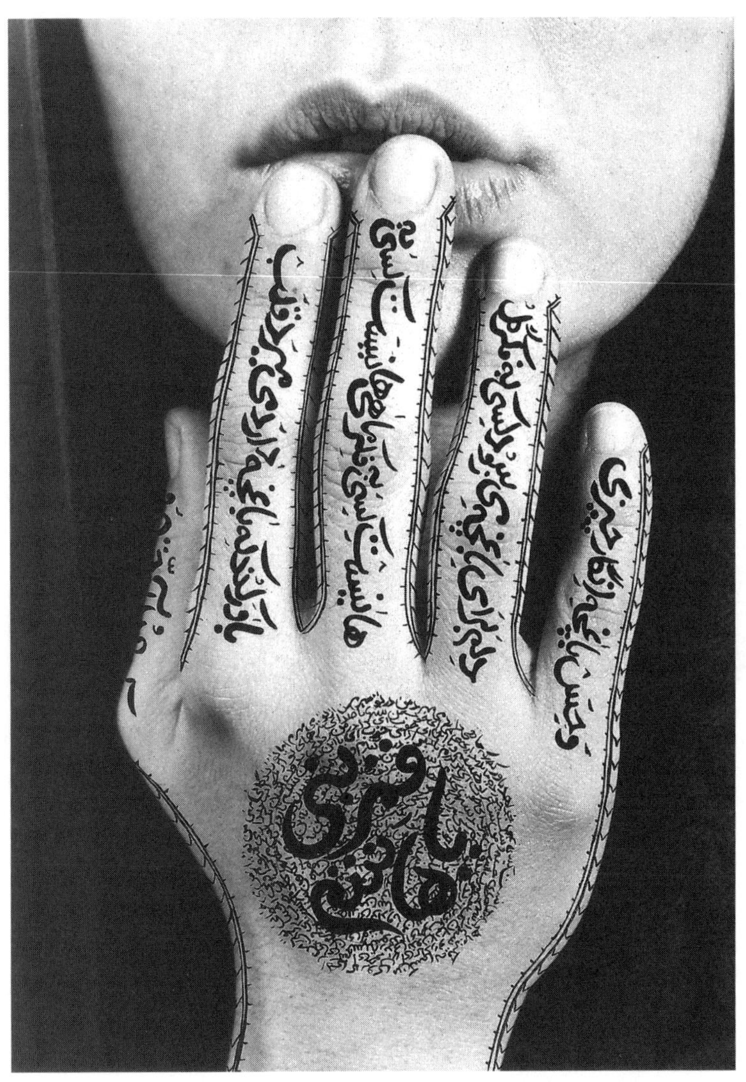

In the works of the contemporary Iranian artist Shirin Neshat, many palpable Shi'i themes are brought together in an emancipatory aesthetics in which piety and eroticism comingle. In staged photography, dramatic video installations, and cinematic magic realism, Shirin Neshat has been consistently tapping into the hidden experience of being a Shi'i Muslim woman. Filmmakers and artists like Shirin Neshat have crafted a visual aesthetics of the unseen beyond the received visual vocabulary of Shi'ism, and yet entirely in its revelatory spirit. The repressed aestheticism of Shi'ism is here on full display, as the artist as the emancipatory visionary announces and hides herself.

"Untitled" (1996), RC print & ink (photo taken by Larry Barns). Copyright © Shirin Neshat, courtesy Gladstone Gallery, New York; with permission of Shirin Neshat.

Shirin Neshat's video installation *Tuba* (2002) is a visual homage to a passage in the Qur'an. Although the reference is textual, the cinematic allusion is open-ended. This is globalized art from the vantage point of a liberated (and liberating) artist, wresting religion from its self-designated custodians and recasting it upon a vast, forgiving, and above all memoryless universe. Shirin Neshat has made Shi'ism lose in order to find itself—and in the act the artist as a visionary has sublimated the pact of the people with their faith into a universal register.

Film still from *Tuba*. Copyright © Shirin Neshat, courtesy Gladstone Gallery, New York; with permission of Shirin Neshat.

Iranian leader Ayatollah Ruhollah Khomeini (1902–1989) greets well-wishers before casting his vote in the final round of Iran's parliamentary elections on 13 May 1988. Khomeini cast his vote in a mobile booth outside his house at Hosseiniyeh Jamaran in northern Iran, and his appearance refuted rumors that he had died. Legalistic scholasticism, charismatic messianism, and totalitarian absolutism were the enduring results of Ayatollah Khomeini's Islamic Revolution—and as such he was the latest (perhaps the last) scholastic visionary that the venerable institution he represented and radicalized was capable of producing.

AP Photo/Sayaad. Reprinted with permission.

The figure of Jamal al-Din al-Asadabadi (known as al-Afghani; 1838–1897), photo taken in 1883, looms larger than life in the history of Muslim encounters with European colonialism. A born and raised Shi'i, he successfully disguised himself as a Sunni in order to have a wider frame of political reference and significance. Al-Afghani's enduring influence is felt today throughout the Islamic world, where his legacy dismantles the colonially manufactured myth of a perennial sectarian warfare within Islam.

8

ON *RESSENTIMENT* AND THE POLITICS OF DESPAIR

The many repeated but failed attempts at a Shi'i societal modernity over the last five hundred years have coincided with a violent Muslim encounter with European colonial modernity. Ultimately these failures have resulted in a definitive breakup of an enduring Shi'i mimetic nexus between reality and its representation. I have argued that following this split, reality parts company with this historic linkage and goes one way while its representation becomes almost entirely iconic and veers off in another direction. Both the politics of the mundane and the poetics of the sublime have suffered in the course of this formal fracture. As Shi'i politics became devoid of moral imagination, the poetics of the better angels attending its fate lost both poise and prosody: one plunged deeply into futile acts of speculative ideology and political violence, the other sublated those very realities into formalized aesthetic preoccupation.

How is the making of a politics without moral imagination possible? Shi'ism, now indistinguishable from Islam in general, soon after its encounter with European colonial modernity fell into the trap of a binary opposition, where it had to define itself in terms of a chimerical construction called "the West," for which it became a categorical, essentialized, militantly monological "Islam." Inside that trap, Shi'ism, and with it Islam, began to chase after its own tail with a dizzying speed, not seeing, not knowing what it was doing to itself and to its own multifarious moral and intellectual heritage. In the encounter with colonial modernity, the sectarian bifurcation between Shi'ism and Sunnism altogether disappears—not communally dissolved but politically overwritten by the more compelling cause of an anticolonial encounter with the West—thus robbing Muslims of one among many of their most potent dialectical latitudes in crafting regenerative worldly perspectives.

In this chapter I wish to discuss the active formation of a politics of desedimented reality, a politics of despair, predicated on a collective act of *ressentiment,* which carried the Shi'i critical consciousness (now integral to Islam in general) in one direction, while its creative consciousness was drawn in the opposite direction to an aesthetics of formalized representation decidedly divorced from its worldliness. This chapter is about an Islamic politics with a captured imagination trapped inside a useless binary ("Islam and the West"); the next chapter is about an aesthetics alienated from its material worldliness, its politics, though heavily pregnant with it. In this chapter I outline the particular parameters of modern Islamic (Shi'i) political thought and practice—in a manner that has tested to the fullest doctrinal extent the exposure of Islam (Shi'ism) to its contemporary colonial politics. The political breakdown of Islam in face of colonial modernity was inclusive of Shi'ism, and in this particular respect Shi'is have shared the fate of other Muslims, for in fact in the face of European colonial domination of the Muslim world, the medieval disposition of the Sunni-Shi'i divide went through a metamorphosis—communally evident, but politically overwritten.

With the British competing with the Portuguese in the Indian subcontinent, the Russians persistently pushing south toward the warm waters of the Persian Gulf, the French and Italians in control of North Africa, the British and the French dividing and conquering the Ottoman territories, and the Belgians and Dutch extending their domain of domination from sub-Saharan Africa to Indonesia and Malaysia, not a single site in the Muslim world was immune to European colonial rivalries and plundering. This colonial campaign of "shock and awe" paralyzed the Muslim world and demoralized their leaders to the point of submission. Muslim masses and their revolutionary leaders defied colonial rules, and along with all other colonized peoples, took up arms against their colonial occupiers. In anticolonial nationalism, in Third World socialism, and in militant Islamism, Muslims of various ideological colors and political persuasions fought back. The war was asymmetrical. Muslims lost—both Sunnis' and Shi'is' lands and liberties were either directly ruled by Europeans or else politically dominated by their superior military and commercial powers. As much as rebellion and resistance, so also resignation, disillusion, and *ressentiment* defined this colonial period—in both cases fueling a politics of despair that sent Muslims chasing after their own tails in fury and futility.

"Secularity": Between Territorial Conquests and Colonial Modernity

The Afghan invasion of Iran in the eighteenth century and the capture of Isfahan in 1722 may very well be marked as the beginning of a territorial and strategic groundswell in modern Shi'i history, the termination of its cosmopolitan confidence under the Safavids, and the commencement of its politics of despair. Following the downfall of the Safavids (1501–1722), the Russians from the north and the Ottomans from the west counterbalanced and complemented the Afghans from the east to bring the Safavid realm to the brink of complete moral and material dissolution. By 1736, Nader Shah of the Afshar tribe succeeded in defeating the Afghans in the east, pushing the Ottomans out of the western frontiers, and persuading the Russians to retreat in the north. Nader Shah valiantly safeguarded the territorial integrity of Iran as a country, but by seeking to combat Shi'i clerical power, he in fact achieved precisely the opposite, pushing Iranian political culture further back into a debilitating tribalism at the heavy cost of the worldly cosmopolitanism that had reached its peak during the Safavid period. The Shi'i clerical class survived Nader Shah's short-lived anti-Shi'ism and returned with a vengeance in the Qajar period, never again allowing the cosmopolitan disposition of the Safavid era to resume its worldly effervescence.

All these internecine rivalries among the Ottomans, the Russians, the Afghans, the Safavids, and the Afsharids suddenly assumed a bizarre "domestic" and even "medieval" disposition when much mightier military forces, prompted by groundbreaking economic changes in Europe, entered the scene. Precisely at the time that the Afghans and Nader Shah were putting an end to the Safavid cosmopolitan culture, by the middle of the eighteenth century, the British empire, at the time the single most powerful economic, military, and political force on the globe, faced its severest challenge in North America. The massive labor and capital migration into North America had created a new economic reality, far beyond anything the colonial administrators of the empire in London could conceive or control. Debates about the nature of North American colonies, their identities, and the very nature of the British empire became rampant. When in the summer of 1765 Lord Grenville's ministry passed the Stamp Act, these issues were at the top of the political agenda of the empire.[1] The Stamp Act of 1765 imposed a tax on legal documents throughout the empire. The colonies in the West Indies and North America reacted vociferously and convened a Continental Congress. An embargo on British goods was put into effect, and a full-fledged insurrection against the British was now under way. Between 1765 and 1775, North America posed a major challenge to the continued power of British colonialism, with official and popular protest spreading from Massachusetts to Rhode Island to New York.

As the year 1774 came to a close, the Zand dynasty (1750–1794) was in full control during the interregnum between Nader Shah's anti-Shi'i rule and the resurrection of Shi'i clerical power under the Qajar dynasty (1779–1925). The British empire was shaken to its foundations by rebellious events in North America. For all intents and purposes the British colonial officers were no longer in charge of their American colonies. Lord Dartmouth, the colonial secretary, was by then accustomed to receiving troubling letters from his representatives on North American soil. By April 1775, New Jersey, Pennsylvania, Maryland, Virginia, and South Carolina were in almost full control of the local committees of the Congress.[2] Between 1775 and 1776, the British depleted their garrisons in such places as Ireland, Gibraltar, and Minorca, and were actively recruiting soldiers in Britain for their wars in North America. The fear of the revolutionary outbreak reaching as far north as Canada was rampant. "The Canadians talk of that damned absurd word *liberty*," General Guy Carleton, the governor of Quebec, declared in exasperation.[3] By July 1776 the revolutionary Americans had drafted their Declaration of Independence from their British masters. The United States was now born and the British empire had to shift gears, and Muslims were about to bear the brunt of it.

The decline of British colonial interests in North America in the mid-eighteenth century was more than compensated in the Indian subcontinent, in what the British will now call the Middle East, and in Africa. Guided by Mercury, the god of commerce, Britannia was now looking eastward for further glories. The economic interests of Britain in India extended back as far as 1689: by 1740, the East India Company was in full control of commerce in Bombay, Madras, and Calcutta, totally unchallenged by the Indian principalities. The East India Company had such vast commercial interests in India that by 1815, it commanded the most powerful army in India and effectively governed Bengal and the upper Ganges basin, as well as vast territories in southern and eastern India.[4] The East India Company army was no ordinary band of mercenaries protecting the regional interests of an adventurous commercial enterprise. That army had experienced direct combat in such varied colonial outposts as Arabia, Mauritius, Malacca, and Java. Radically retheorized into its imperial economic prowess by Adam Smith (1723–1790), prompted by the Indian anticolonial rebellion of 1857, and through the Government of India Act of 1858, the British government soon began to take over the lucrative business of the East India Company and expand its commercial and economic interests in the subcontinent and beyond.

By the early nineteenth century, the Islamic world was thoroughly penetrated not only by the British, but also by the French and the Russians, who were competing for the lucrative and strategically vital regions extending from the Indus Valley to Central Asia and to the Levant and North Africa. Napoleon (1769–1821) was well poised to advance into Egypt in 1798 and even to seek to challenge the British interests in India, via the Qajar territories in Iran, before his defeat in Waterloo in 1815. Russia had defeated the Qajars in two successive wars early in the nineteenth century, and North Africa was the battlefield of British and French colonial rivalries. The Muslim world was now thoroughly entrenched in its colonial encounter with Europe, a mighty and purposeful force that would forever change the moral and material foundation of every clime it conquered.

It was at this crucial juncture that "Islam" was categorically coined (first and foremost by European Orientalists) as the civilizational "other" of "the West." "The West" now cast itself as modern and secular, in contrast to cultures it thus branded as ipso facto traditional and religious. "Islam" thus ceased to be a variegated reality, transitive and incandescent to itself, and became a solid symbol, a suggestive sign, a mimetic mantra, a designation, representation, a ruse, a chimerical construct alienated from and to itself. Planetary colonialism, wrapped around the globe, was the principal political power and economic force through which European modernity had found its way into much of the world—and the code name of this historic turning point was eventually christened as *Enlightenment, modernity,* or alternatively *secularism.* Colonizing Christianity in disguise, secularity, in particular, both constituted Islam (or Judaism for that matter) as other than itself and posited it as its defeated alterity. In a deconstructive move, at once dismantling the notion of the secular and placing it squarely at the foot of the modern history of Christianity in the course of colonial modernity, Gil Anidjar has suggested and persuasively argued that Western Christianity at one and the same time posited itself as religion par excellence and yet as the hidden mold of the secular.[5] The paradox that Gil Anidjar has outlined is a dialectical flip-flop that in a moment of psychoanalytic frivolity he terms "Munchausen-like," whereby Christianity outmaneuvers itself by bracing for a form of historical abnegation that requires it to become the prima facie religion, so that it can invent its own shadows and coin and call them "Judaism" or "Islam." Meanwhile, and here is Gil Anidjar's twisted insight, Christianity has camouflaged itself as secularism, so that anything non-Christian is identified as fanatical, religious, traditional, and outmoded. In this sense, Christianity had become the simulacrum of colonialism, the moral condition of domination, at once positing and subordinating its alterities as defeated, overrun, overwritten, and overcome. Islam became the doppelgänger of secularism, and secularism the new nomenclature of Christianity. Islam was thus put on the defensive, and with it Muslims, against the colonial might of secularity, underwritten by the missionary zeal of Christianity. A contradiction in terms, secular Muslims, if we follow through with Gil Anidjar's insidious insight, became the Trojan horse of colonial Christianity, unbeknownst to themselves.

The categorical collapsing of the colonial into the Christian of course has a number of obvious problems, and yet, surprisingly, it opens up a number of hitherto unknown possibilities. Christianity is not colonialism, but Christian missionaries did serve European colonialism's ends, though they also resisted them. Anidjar follows the history of colonialism beginning in 1492. Juan Ginés de Sepúlveda (c. 1490–1573) and Bartolomé de las Casas (1484–1566) serve as Anidjar's first examples, one wholeheartedly supporting European colonial conquests while the other vehemently opposes them. Ever since that crucial date, for every Sepúlveda condoning (in fact encouraging) European colonial conquests in the name of Jesus Christ, we have had a de las Casas opposing them, in the very same name. Gil Anidjar insists that what he means by Christianity is "Western Christianity." This is a moment of theoretical anxiety, for Western Christianity also produced Nietzsche and Kierkegaard, the supreme anti-Christian Christians. Then we also have the Latin American liberation theology: the Christianity of the poor people, from de las Casas to Gustavo Gutierrez, with its home in the poverty-stricken slums of Latin America in the backyard of U.S. imperial headquarters. From an Eastern orthodoxy that was Orientalized by Roman Catholicism, to anti-Christian Christians like Nietzsche and Kierkegaard, to the rise of Latin American liberation theology, exemplary model for all the rest, the colonial proclivities of Western Christianity have always been contested. Thus the categorical collapsing of the colonial into Christianity is quite untenable. Malcolm X and Jeremiah Wright speak the same liberation theology, one in a Muslim and the other in a Christian dialect.

But the selfsame collapsing is equally revealing in unearthing the hidden missionary disposition of colonialism. This we owe to Gil Anidjar, if we read him as revealing not so much the colonial character of Christianity as the Christian disposition of colonialism, two vastly different propositions. Another liberating aspect of the collapsing of the colonial into the Christian is the revelation of anti-Semitism as targeted not just against Jews but also against Muslims in equal and in fact identical measures. Here Gil Anidjar falls short of his own insight by positing the Jew and the Arab as the site of anti-Semitism. The Jew was the target of anti-Semitism not as a Semite but as a Jew, and the Arab is the target of anti-Semitism not because he is a Semite but because he is Muslim. The Muslim is upstream from the Arab—a Muslim may be South Asian, Turkish, Iranian, Indonesian, Malaysian, and so on—and that brings us back to the overriding presence of the European modernity that constitutes the Jew and the Muslim (not just the Arab) as the target of colonial desubjection.[6]

Put on the defensive by European colonial might and modernity, Islam and Muslims (Shi'is or Sunnis) were yanked out of their protracted and useless territorial conquests and forced to face the bugbear of secularism—a chimerical fabrication that borrowed the missionary zeal of Christianity to inform the colonial might of European military globalization of industrial power. At the heart of this anxiety-provoking encounter with secularism was the military force of a constitutionally colonial modernity. And thus it happened that in their confrontation with European colonialism, Muslims suddenly discovered that they were all very "religious," and that they should all become "secular" if they wanted to be saved. And thus it happened that they lost the terms of their own identities and alterities—who they were before they were discovered by European colonialists as "religious"—the parameters of their own ipseity and supplementarity, their sacred certitudes paramount and their profane worldliness in particular.

The Ups and Downs of a Cosmopolitanism

The general contour of the emergence of the politics of despair I propose commences with the proposition that during the Safavid period, Shi'ism was thoroughly urbanized and turned into a cosmopolitan project. It was taken out of its historical battlefields and its feudal scholasticism alike, and its revolutionary reason was urbanized into a public reason. I have then suggested that at the Dasht-e Moghan gathering, Nader Shah managed to dismantle not just the Safavid dynasty, but with it the civil societal possibilities it had made evident, and with the dismantling of these possibilities went the syncretic and cosmopolitan Shi'ism that it entailed. He thus managed to kill and bury not only Shi'i cosmopolitanism itself but its (potential and evident) public reason. The end of the Safavids also spelled the end of a possible Shi'i state apparatus and a corresponding conception of a civil society.

The Safavids had in effect internalized the revolutionary angst of Shi'ism, and in turn given space to a nascent public reason that would have made a civil societal turn in Shi'i political culture not just possible but perhaps even inevitable. Economic prosperity, increased volumes in foreign trade, participation in regional rivalries among the superpowers of the time, and a significant increase in urbanization might be considered chief among the reasons and causes for such a significant transformation from revolutionary reason to public reason. Nader Shah put an end to that process and to a gradual movement toward a sustained Shi'i theory of state and a corresponding conception of civil society. Thus the post-Safavid era, from the Afsharids to the Zands to the Qajars, can be described as a succession of tribal warlords and clannish kinships, with an increasingly evident appeal to a pre-Islamic conception of Persian kingship to camouflage that nomadic disposition.

The territorial expansionism of the surrounding areas was of course of crucial significance here. The Afghans, the Russians, and the Ottomans kept attacking the dying body of the Safavids, like three hungry dogs tearing it to pieces, but Nader Shah managed to save the territorial integrity of the country through militarism, warfare, clannish kingship, and even territorial expansion of his own. He retrieved a sense of geographical totality for the country. But from Nader's interlude emerged a clannish kingship of the tribal warlords that through the Afsharids and the Zands ultimately reached the Qajars at the dawn of colonial modernity. The Qajars opted for Shi'ism as their state religion but remained subservient to the Shi'i clerical whim to legitimize their precarious authority. In this context, the Babi movement of the mid-nineteenth century was infinitely more important for the future than both the Qajar monarchs and their clerical cohorts. The Babi movement was crucial because it effectively picked up from where the Hurufiyyah movement, including its urbanized and cosmopolitan version in the School of Isfahan and Mulla Sadra, had left off—in making a public reason in yet another revolutionary field. The Babis took the public reason of the Safavids, which they had inherited from Mulla Sadra through Shaykh Ahmad Ahsa'i, back to the revolutionary field, whereas Mulla Sadra had brought it from the revolutionary field into the public domain.

The Babis further differentiated and expanded the public reason they had retrieved from the Safavid period, particularly through Qorrat al-Ayn, who inspired incorporation of the feminine figure into the public domain. It is possible to see in this expansion of public reason the template of a revolutionary modernity, one that never actually resulted in what the German philosopher Jürgen Habermas calls societal modernity. From Shaykhism to Babism and then through the Azalis down to the Constitutional Revolution of 1906–1911, we have a consistent intensification of a Shi'i conception of *Gesellschaft.* As Baha'ism emerges as perhaps the best example of a benign universalism, a *Gemeinschaft* disposition writ large, a globality of sacred imagination with no significant social basis to sustain it or make it politically relevant, the enduring legacy of the Babi movement abandons it and proceeds to inform the rise of the Constitutional Revolution of 1906–1911, which in turn increases the stakes and further exacerbates the formation of a revolutionary public reason.

The constitutional drive toward the formation of a sustainable public domain early in the twentieth century is ultimately crushed under the boots of Reza Shah, the founder of the Pahlavi dynasty in the 1930s, who was the early-twentieth-century version of Nader Shah, a brutish military warlord who smashed the gradual formation of both public reason and public domain. His modern dictatorial monarchy did to the Constitutional Revolution of 1906–1911 what Nader Shah did to the similar legacy of public space and public reason in the Safavid era. The ranking elite of the Shi'i clerical establishment not only were not opposed to what Reza Shah did to that public domain but in fact wholeheartedly endorsed him. Further, they dissuaded him from following Mustapha Kemal Ataturk's example, establishing a republic in Turkey, and insisted on a renewal of the medieval Persian monarchy, in which they knew they had a confident and cozy corner carved out for themselves.

Before the advent of colonial modernity, Iran, as a model of Shi'i cosmopolitanism, could have achieved its own modernity (in the two crucial terms of a public reason and a public domain), but it did not for a number of interrelated reasons: its highest and most urbane cosmopolitanism was destroyed in Dasht-e Moghan; the Qajar kings and the Shi'i clerical class institutionally prevented its societal formations; Babism tried to retrieve it but ultimately failed to sublate its revolutionary reason back to public reason because the revolutionary rhetoric of the movement and its messianic mannerisms assumed a life of their own and were ultimately transmuted into the inconsequential universalism of Baha'ism. The reformist Qajar premier Amir Kabir soon emerged as the champion of (the colonial take on) European modernity. Thus as a grassroots and historic movement domestic to Shi'i doctrinal developments, Babism fell under Amir Kabir's more urgent agenda, for the Qajar premier had to attend to the mightier force of European colonialism, seeking to wrest from it the magic of its colonial might.

So what we witness in Shi'ism from the Tobacco Revolt forward is that colonialism supersedes and augments Qajar nomadic monarchism as the interlocutor of the clerical establishment. In effect, it globalizes and exacerbates the clerics' position of power, because they are now dealing with a more powerful and global force. Because of the Russian and Ottoman imperial incursions, the Shi'i clerics' role is reactivated, but this time with an added *ressentiment.* The Constitutional Revolution is the last pitched battle in which the Qajars and segments of the clerical force seek to prevent the active transformation of revolutionary reason into public reason. As with the Babi movement, the young and progressive segments of the clerical class broke rank with their more senior cohorts and sided with the revolutionaries. Their efforts constituted a final, historic attempt to retrieve syncretic Shi'i cosmopolitanism and constitute a public space for a public reason by retrieving the revolutionary reason of Shi'ism through Babism and wedding it to the best of a more global conception of cosmopolitanism that had come down to the constitutionalists through the Caucasus. The Constitutional Revolution succeeded in defeating and ultimately dismantling the Qajar dynasty but was itself ultimately defeated by a combination of colonial parochialism, monarchic tribalism, and clerical feudalism.

It is exactly at this point, the last attempt at securing a public space and reason, that I suggest the traumatic split in the modern history of Shi'i modernity takes place. The split divides the moral and imaginative universe of Shi'ism into an overtly militant nativism in politics, conditioned by a general Muslim anxiety with modernity and the commencement of a politics of despair, and an over-aestheticized formalism in art in an emancipatory direction. From the initial success but final failure of the Constitutional Revolution until the rise of Reza Shah's dictatorship, we witness a traumatic split in the struggle of Shi'is for their own take on cosmopolitan modernity—a split into aesthetic modernity on one side and militant Islamism on the other. I have devoted the last three chapters of this book to this traumatic split—defining its contours, giving an outline of its political aspects within a militant Shi'ism, as well as navigating through aspects of its aesthetic modernity. So what we witness in the aftermath of the Constitutional Revolution is an epistemic split of the template of modernity into two divergent and extremist directions: first, over-formalized aesthetics, and second, over-politicized Shi'ism. This critical development, I suggest, is rooted in the historic fact that when Mulla Sadra cultivated public reason, he philosophically domesticated the revolutionary reason he had inherited from the Hurufiyyah and other Sufi-Shi'i syncretic movements on a public space that was royally truncated. So what we in effect witness is that societal modernity (as Habermas calls it) yields to revolutionary modernity after the Safavids in Babism and to anticolonial modernity after the Qajars. Nader Shah did indeed manage to dismantle Shi'i cosmopolitan syncretism after all, compromising its urban and urbane disposition in the Safavid period because it was based on a public space that was royally truncated, a philosophical existentialism that had to urbanize a revolutionary reason on a royally manufactured and thus slanted public space, and absence of a societal modernity that could have emerged through economic productivity.

From Shaykhism to Babism to the Azalis, Shi'i revolutionary activism extended from Mulla Sadra to the Constitutional Revolution, but during the period between the reigns of Nader Shah and Reza Shah, it was aided and abetted by European colonialism, which supported the cause of nomadic monarchism with a fake and vacuous claim to a pre-Islamic imperial heritage of the Achaemenids to the Sassanids. The colonial condition of vicarious productivity imposed its own social class formation and societal modernity. Thus cultural modernity was taken up and catapulted into an age of abstract postmodernity, with no organic link to the economic logic of later capitalism. Shi'is remained peripheral to and parasitic on this colonial, capitalist system, while in the absence of societal modernity, militant Shi'ism reverted back to its rebellious disposition.

The circularity of territorial colonialism, tribal monarchism, and feudal scholasticism made for an aggressively provincialized conception and practice of overly political Shi'ism. So precisely at the moment when in artistic creativity, aesthetic formalism, and poetic liberation the formalized traces of cosmopolitan Shi'ism go transnational, and global, in politics precisely the reverse happens, and it becomes incessantly provincial. But this provincialization of Shi'ism (or Islam in general) is not entirely of its own making, neither totally in its own domestic terms nor completely out of a historic frustration with successive attempts at transforming its revolutionary reason and generating a public space and a public reason. The juridical disposition of Shi'ism (its Usulism) goes provincial also in part because its interlocutor, "the West" (European colonialism) is constitutionally provincial, and thus it provincializes every country, clime, or culture it touches. All colonial encounters are in fact provincial, because the vacuous globality of the colonial project conquers and provincializes the cultures it encounters at one and the same time.

Ayatollah Khomeini, the leader of the Islamic Revolution in Iran, carried forward the philosophical propositions of Mulla Sadra in theory, but in practice he promulgated an adversarial projection and negative identification with Reza Shah and Muhammad Reza Shah as a tribal chieftain in his own right. By the time of the Islamic Revolution, the belligerent Persian monarchy, inheriting a legacy from Nader Shah to Reza Shah, had made societal modernity impossible, and thus had atomized Muslims to the point that Khomeini could not see them as free citizens and autonomous agents of an emerging republic, but only as militant Shi'is on a battlefield or speculative subjects of Usuli jurisprudence [*fiqh*]. Precisely at the moment when Ayatollah Khomeini and his Islamic Republic were putting the final nail in the coffin of societal modernity, Abbas Kiarostami and Shirin Neshat went vicariously postmodern and excessively formal in their art and aesthetics. The result was the exacerbated condition of that split modernity that had thrived on a schizophrenic bipolarity: militant Islamism practicing a politics of despair on one side and artistic formalism dreaming of an aesthetic emancipation on the other—all because of the absence of a bona fide societal modernity, conditioned by an endemic economic vicariousness, caused and exacerbated by a global colonial economy. The paradoxical outcome of this schizophrenic partition between a politics of despair and an aesthetic of emancipation was the eventual substitution of a public art for a public reason that could not fully flower and develop in Shi'i social history. In effect the autonomy of a postcolonial aesthetics overcame and subverted the authority of a public reason that could not even fully emerge—and it is to that development that I will now turn.

9

AN AESTHETIC OF EMANCIPATION

In the face of European colonialism Shi'ism was doctrinally eclipsed and politically defaced, effectively dissolved into the larger Islamic context and its more fundamental predicament in facing colonial modernity. This effective political dissolution of Shi'ism into Islamism does not mean that, as a branch of Islam, Shi'ism lost its identity or that Shi'is forfeited their collective consciousness. Shi'is did respond to colonialism in specifically Shi'i terms, as Shi'is, and with Shi'ism. But in the face of the overpowering presence of European colonialism, in both moral and material terms the Shi'is were almost identical in their predicament to other Muslims, effectively losing their political composure and descending into a self-abnegating spiral of ideological resistance that in fact further exacerbated their politics of despair. Matching this collective politics of despair on the other side of the spectrum has been an overriding aesthetics of emancipation, a sublimated formalism that can go both ways—metaphorically transfused into bland abstractions, or alternatively tilted toward the formal destruction of politics. Today people look at and admire the artistic works of Abbas Kiarostami or Shirin Neshat, or alternatively the works of Ardeshir Mohassess or Nikzad ("Nicky") Nodjoumi, and yet their sense of aesthetics is baffled by what they see or by what they fail to see. If we read these artists in exclusively aesthetic terms, we will miss the hidden politics of their formal imagination, and if we read them in excessively political terms, we will overlook the overriding power of their aesthetic formalism. The more violent and defiant the Shi'i politics of despair became in opposing colonialism over the last two hundred years, the more an aesthetic formalism of abstracted sublimity escaped it and sought refuge in its opposite direction. In its politics of despair, Shi'ism invested, wasted, and lost everything it had; in this emancipatory aesthetics of the otherwise, Shi'ism did not even recognize the emerging terms of its own sublation, its own salvation, the transmutation of its own sacred into the sublime. As the Shi'i politics of despair became excessively expedient, its adjacent aesthetic of emancipation grew formally revelatory.

Renewed Mysteries, Forgotten Miracles

How did Shi'ism, as an emotive universe, eventually lose and yield its creative imagination to a pronouncedly post-Shi'i aesthetics? At the dawn of colonial modernity, I contend, the creative effervescence of Shi'ism effectively escaped—its theology, philosophy, and mysticism all summoned for one final bravura performance in Shaykhism, invested for a revolutionary uprising in Babism, but at the end lost in Baha'ism. Bereft of this creative effervescence, militant Shi'i clericalism of the twentieth century ultimately culminated in a militant Khomeinism that categorically collapsed into a juridical fanaticism of the most recalcitrant disposition. What thus remained in the Shi'ism that Khomeinism of the twentieth century best preached and practiced was the soulless body of the clerical establishment that stuck to a fanatical Usulism as its overriding ideology, the raison d'être of its class privileges, and the material base of its power. Shi'ism entered twentieth-century global geopolitics with its creative consciousness having escaped its doctrinal mandates, having left its dead and deadening body-politic behind to move clumsily toward a head-on collision with European colonialism and American imperialism. Thus leaving that dead body, to continue with the same metaphor, the soul of Shi'ism transmigrated, deeply rooted, and came to varied and colorful fruition in the creative consciousness of Shi'is (lapsed or believing, professing too little or protesting too much) for a whole new generation of sublimated dispensation. In its new habitat, this creative consciousness was in turn alienated and estranged from itself, going into the varied subterfuges of atheism, agnosticism, secularism, modernity, or laïcité—all successfully disguising the budding poetics, the suggestive aesthetics, of a whole new rendezvous with an emergent emancipatory politics. Working from their declared secularity, professed atheism, acknowledged agnosticism, lapsed piety, manifest impieties, or vaguely evident beliefs, these artists breathed in the air where their ancestral Shi'ism, even despite themselves, was to meet their emerging worldly cosmopolitanism.

To mark and measure this transition, we will have to move from the arid domain of Shi'i theology and jurisprudence to the fertile ground of its neighboring art and aesthetics. The fate of art in colonial modernity is of course predicated on the historical predisposition of art in any Islamic (Shi'i) context. From the privileged position of artistic creativity in royal courts, sites of commerce, and the sacred precinct of the mosque, Islamic art has always had an interface with the public face of power. From poetry to calligraphy to manuscript illustrations to architectural monuments and urban designs, the aesthetics of power, when art dwelled at the royal court, always matched the aesthetics of piety, when art sanctified itself in the mosque, and balanced the aesthetics of commerce, when it lent itself to architectural monuments and urban designs of commercial districts and vast bazaars. In its premodern context, however, Islamic art was never totally compromised by its alternate courtly, commercial, or sacred precincts. The creation of an open-ended public space for art has always been evident in coffee house paintings, public bath murals, and cemetery sites; also bazaar locations and street corners as the public stages for Ta'ziyeh and other performing arts. With the advent of colonial modernity, the privileged positions of art gradually disappeared and lost their momentum while the public spaces expanded exponentially to include movie houses, public theaters, and music halls. It is in this latter stage that public art is gradually transmuted into an almost autonomous aesthetics of wider abstractions. Art in this vein was inclined to become radically over-aestheticized, stylistically formalized, abstracted, and potentially alienated from itself. The more the aesthetic formalism of art was evidently pregnant with expansive hermeneutic possibilities, the less it yielded its paradoxically interpolated aporias—thus necessitating the rise of a whole new interpretative apparatus and class of interpreters distinctly separate from and at odds with the clerical custodians of Shi'i sacred lore.

As in the privileged spaces of court, commerce, and the mosque Islamic art dwelled and thrived in its visual and narrative delights for the fortunate few, in the more pronouncedly public spaces of coffee houses, village and city sites of Ta'ziyeh performances, communal monuments, and emerging urban domains, the publicity of visual and performing arts and architectures decoupled its emotive universe from its royal servitude and sacred certitude alike and expanded its autonomous aesthetics exponentially, eventually creating a new sacerdotal space of its own—formally and aesthetically irreducible to Islam, to Shi'ism, or to any other canonical convictions. The expanded domain of public art, which now accommodated and enabled a liberated and open-ended aesthetic landscape, in time crafted its own mysteries and miracles, moods and mannerisms, shades and shadows, techniques and prosodies, doubts and deliverances. A new horizon of visionaries was now upon Muslims and Shi'is—though not as one or the other, though not in denial of one or the other. The world had expanded, and in the making of its cosmopolitan domains, Islam and Shi'ism were integral but no longer definitive. The world was being (once again) re-enchanted with itself, and the new aesthetic experiments were the sinuous venues of this reenchantment. The gentle sublation of the sacred into the sublime was the chief operative apparatus of its global, nonsectarian appeal.

Where is the prophetic voice and vision of Shi'ism now? Distanced, estranged, and alienated from itself, the creative consciousness of Shi'ism escaped the Shi'i scholastic cul de sac (by now the exclusive fraternity of aging and belligerent clergy) and began breathing in wider, fresher, greener, worldlier, more sublime and beautiful pastures. "*Man beh mehmani donya raftam,*" in the poetic diction of Sohrab Sepehri: "I went to the great banquet of the world." Thus *Man* [I] was at once Muslim/Shi'i and yet transfused into a renewed cosmogony: "*Man Mosalmanan,*" Sepehri's poetic persona declares: "I am a Muslim," but (and there is the rub)

> I pray in the direction of a red rose,
> My prayer rug is the fountain—and
> I prostrate on light.
> The prairie is my prayer site—and
> I do my ablution with the palpitations of windows.
> In my prayer the moon flows . . .[1]

In the making of this cosmovision (Shi'ism sublated), with its terms of piety transpired, poets and filmmakers, playwrights and novelists, painters and photographers, satirists and graphic artists were all actively at work crafting the panorama of a miasmatic firmament upon which dwelled the emancipated vista of a new notion of humanity. Artists became the sublated transmutations of theologians, philosophers, and mystics; visionaries of the highest, of the otherwise, of the yet to come. In the making of this renewed imagery, a few artists became definitive, emotively alphabetical to the vision of the otherwise invisible site and citation of the sublime, which was standing in for the sacred. With the advent of colonial modernity, the visionaries of the highest had moved away from the realm of the prophetic into the site of the poetic. "Let these pure heavens," said Mehdi Akhavan Sales (1928–1990), a leading Persian poet of the twentieth century,

> Be the pasture
> Of such souls as Christ and others,
> For impurities like me
> Never know or knew
> Who the Father
> Of those Pure Ones
> Was
> Or else what was their Use.[2]

Paramount among these artists (emancipated visionaries of the otherwise) is a filmmaker like Bahram Beiza'i, whose magisterial cinema invariably revolves around an elegant and inexplicable mystery that is resolved at the end of the film but on an entirely different visual register, as perhaps best exemplified in one of his masterpieces, *Mosaferan* [Travelers] (1992). The Ma'arefi family is busy getting ready in Tehran for the wedding of their young daughter Mahrokh. Meanwhile, the bride's elder sister Mahtab Ma'arefi, her husband Heshmat Davaran, and their two children get into a car in the northern part of the country to drive south for the occasion. The Davarans put their children and their luggage, including a mirror they handle with special care, into their car and are now ready to leave. Just before getting into the car, Mahtab Davaran (née Ma'arefi) looks straight into the camera, which has now come to her for a close-up shot, and quite simply says, "We are going to Tehran to participate in my younger sister's wedding. We will not reach Tehran. We will have an accident and we will all die." Her prophecy comes to pass, her sister's wedding is marred and interrupted by the sad news. Only the mysteriously stubborn grandmother of the family refuses to believe the news and insists that the wedding preparations proceed as planned. In the very last sequence of the film, as the binary suspension between reality and representation sustains the mystery of the opening shot, the grandmother's prophecy comes to pass and Mahtab Davaran and her family slide into the wedding ceremony, bringing the old family mirror.[3] In between the two prophecies of the mother and daughter,

Beiza'i's cinema is a poetic interlude, paving a wide highway toward a vision of the invisible.

On an entirely different visual register, at the end of every film of Amir Naderi, another solitary soul in search of cinematic certitude, a small miracle happens. At the end of *The Runner* (1985), for example, the young Amiru turns a quickly melting piece of ice into a trophy and generously shares it with his thirsty friends; at the end of *Water, Wind, Dust* (1989), suddenly a fountain of water gushes out of the arid desert, otherwise dried out and withered away in utter desolation; at the end of *Manhattan by Numbers* (1993) someone comes to the desperate George Murphy and gives him a few dollars; at the end of *Marathon* (2002), a gentle and forgiving snow falls over the noisy madness of Manhattan; at the end of *Sound Barrier* (2005) the deaf-mute Jesse has a hint of a smile on his face, a sign that he can now finally hear. Amir Naderi's cinema of solitude cultivates a quiet obsession with the ordinary and the mundane, the arduous and untiring struggle of his characters finally yielding to a sudden miracle.

The visual key to Mohsen Makhmalbaf's cinema, to give a more recent example, is the transformative force of a virtual minimalism. Makhmalbaf's scenes are invariably vacated, cleaned of all but the absolutely necessary. Only a simple suggestion of things, ideas, peoples, and sentiments remains. There is a visual brevity about his cinema, an iconic simplicity, an aesthetic reduction of the absolutism of reality to a handful of visual props with which he can playfully manipulate reality. Makhmalbaf works with very few visual strokes, very few suggestive objects, very few overriding sentiments—and he allows them to grow on the screen, right in front of your eyes. As early as in his *Time of Love* (1990), these vacated scenes are evident in Makhmalbaf's cinema. Subsequently in his *Salam Cinema* (1994), *Gabbeh* (1995), *A Moment of Innocence* (1995), and *The Silence* (1997), they assume proverbial brevity and precision. The success or failure of all his subsequent films, from *Kandahar* (2001) to *Sex and Philosophy* (2005), depends on his ability to generate and sustain this visual brevity, his proverbial phraseology.

Running through the mystery that sustains Beiza'i's cinema, the miracle that concludes Naderi's, and the virtual minimalism that defines Makhmalbaf thrives a sense of aesthetic wonder, a visual veracity, in which factual illusions become compelling truths. These are not mere accidental virtuosities of great artists and individual filmmakers; they are also the elemental forces of a collective cosmovision that generates and sustains its own continuities in diverse and unpredictable directions. At his very best, Daryush Mehrjui, another leading Iranian filmmaker with consistent aesthetic sensibilities of his own, is the visual theorist of the uncanny, as perhaps best represented in his masterpiece, *Cow* (1969). Based on a story by the prominent Iranian psychiatrist and playwright Gholamhossein Saedi (1936–1985), and predicated on Freud's influential essay on "The Uncanny" (1919), Mehrjui's film revolves around the transmutation of a man into his cow soon after he discovers it has died. By tracing the paradoxical origins and contradictory implications of *Heimlich* (as known and familiar, yet secret and unknown) and *Unheimlich* (as unknown and unfamiliar, yet revealed and uncovered), Freud suggests in his pioneering essay that the two terms in effect turn on themselves so that the two binary concepts themselves become uncanny! In Mehrjui's *Cow,* the uncanny amounts to the return of the Freudian repressed, and thus the opening vista of the unknown, unknowable, and above all the invisible. Temporal and corporeal boundaries dissolve in the face of the uncanny, and the return of the repressed loosens up the corporeal boundaries between the hidden and the revealed, the denied and the permitted, the delusional and the emancipatory.

Culminating in Mehrjui's cinema of the uncanny, the visual hermeneutic of the knowable world posits the sovereignty of aesthetic reason over and above the primacy of instrumental reason. To top these all, Abbas Kiarostami's contemplative camera works through the almost complete visual takeover of the verbal, whereby socially saturated signifiers formally self-destruct into unruly signs, and a formal desedimentation of reality takes over. In Kiarostami's cinema all the constellations of *what-is* gradually change into a suggestion of *how-it-is.* The cinematic event thus becomes the simulacrum of a cinevision, a vision of reality that is quintessentially cinematic. This cinevision, however, is not a reality sui generis. It stands for a cosmovision of reality from within its worldly character.

If we add all of these defining moments of an emancipatory aesthetics together, we get a polyfocal cosmovision—lens by lens crafted by these and similar filmmakers and artists, all pointing to a visual aesthetics of the unseen where the sedimented reality and legislated social signifiers (the world as the artists have received it) are desedimented and let loose toward multi-significatory signs, dancing their way toward the ethereal irreality they thus imagine and form, like particles of dust in a patch of bright sunlight, like the aesthetically pleasing but verbally meaningless paintings of Hossein Zenderoudi in his *khattashi*—letters of the alphabet released from their legislated words and meanings and let loose to dance new, yet to be named, possibilities.

Citing the Sacred

The traveling metaphor definitive to Shi'ism ultimately casts the sacred memory into an exilic register that shifts the revelatory moment of the Qur'an away from merely memorial by making it palpable and worldly. Re/casting and re/citing the sacred upon the forgotten world marks the moment of the sacred memory when it is no longer even conscious of itself. I will now trace one such thematic transition of the sacred—from the Qur'anic to the literary to the visual—by way of excavating a representative archeology of it that scarce even conceals its earliest emotive layers. Paradoxically, the further it gets from the Qur'an, the closer it comes to its revelatory moment.

In the chapter of the Qur'an known as "The Thunder" there is a verse that reads: "Those who believe and do right: Joy is for them, and bliss [their] journey's end."[4] The word *joy* in this and all other English translations corresponds to the Qur'anic word *tuba* in the following original passage: "*Alladhina amanu wa 'amilu al-salihat tuba lahum wa husnu ma'abin.*"

Throughout the history of Qur'anic exegesis, Muslim commentators have elaborated extensively on what exactly this word *tuba* means. The twelfth-century Qur'anic commentator Shaykh Abu al-Futuh al-Razi, the Shi'i author of the voluminous Qur'anic commentary *Tafsir Rawda al-Jinan wa Ruh al-Janan,* has summarized all the preceding commentaries on this verse and on this word. According to al-Razi, "*Alladhina amanu wa 'amilu al-salihat*" ["Those who believe and do right"] is the subject of the verse and "*tuba lahum*" ["Joy is for them"] is its predicate. As to what exactly *tuba* means, al-Razi reports that Muslim scholars have differed. Some have believed that it means "they will be delighted"; others that "they will be generously rewarded"; others still have expanded on the same theme and believed that it means "they shall inherit goodness" or that "they will dwell in goodness forever," and so on.[5]

After this series of syntactical and etymological explanations, al-Razi proceeds to report alternative meanings, those that no longer take it as a verbal construct but instead as a proper noun, Tuba. He cites from the authority of Abdullah Abbas, an early Qur'anic commentator, that "Tuba is 'paradise' in the Abyssinian language." Other commentators have differed and suggested that it means *paradise* or *garden* in the Indian language. But in both cases, Tuba means *paradise*—so the meaning of the Qur'anic phrase is that "those who believe and do right" shall dwell in paradise.[6]

On the authority of Abu Said al-Khidri, al-Razi then reports that the Prophet Himself was once asked to define Tuba; to which he is reported to have said: "It is the name of a tree in paradise, toward which there is a road that takes one hundred years [to traverse]. The clothes that the inhabitants of paradise wear come from its calyx." Another reliable report claims, according to al-Razi, that the Prophet said: "Tuba is a tree in Paradise, which God Almighty has planted with the hands of his own power and then breathed His Soul into it, has allowed the inhabitants of Paradise to partake in its fruits, and whose branches are visible from behind the walls of Paradise." Yet another reliable source reports: "Tuba is a tree in Paradise, to which God Almighty says, 'Open up and give my created beings whatever they wish,' and that tree opens up and from it cometh forward steeds, garments, and whatever other permissible things that human beings demand." Still another reliable source, al-Razi reports, suggests:

> Tuba is a tree in Paradise that if someone were to mount a young or old camel and try to circumambulate it, he would get old and die before he is able to reach where he started; and there is no part of Paradise except a branch of that tree has reached it, and when the inhabitants of that part wish to have a fruit from that branch, the branch bends over so they can pick its fruits; and upon that tree there are birds the size of a Persian camel, and when the inhabitants of Paradise desire those birds, they will be skewered and prepared so that pious Muslims can eat and enjoy them, and then the birds will come back to life and fly away.[7]

Al-Razi quotes yet another reliable source—'Ubayd ibn 'Amir is his name—who said that Tuba is a tree whose roots and main trunk are in the Prophet's house,

> and there is no neighborhood, house, or room in Paradise except this tree has a branch in it; and God Almighty has not created any blossom or any fruit in any spring except they grow on those branches; and there is no color, except the color black, that does not appear on that tree, and from

> the roots of that tree two springs gush forth, one is called Camphor and the other Salsabil.[8]

Every leaf of this tree, al-Razi quotes a source saying, provides shade to a human being. Al-Razi then adds that once an angel approached the Prophet and asked Him if there were any fruits in Paradise. "Yes," the Prophet responded, "in Paradise there is a tree that is called Tuba, located right in front of the Upper Paradise [*Firdows A'la'*]," the Prophet specified. "Oh Messenger of God!" the angel asked, "Is there any tree on earth that resembles it?" "No," the Prophet responded, "but in Syria there is a walnut tree that is quite like it. It has a trunk, from which other boughs branch out and spread." "Oh Messenger of God!" the angel inquired further, "How big is the principal trunk of this tree?" "It is so big," the Prophet said, "that if a young camel from your tribe were to circumambulate around that tree, its hands and legs will be broken and [it will] fall down from weakness and old age before it is able to do so." That is what the Prophet is reported to have said to that angel. Then al-Razi proceeds to quote at length yet another reliable source who is reported to have given an even more elaborate account of this tree, and because of its storytelling quality I am going to translate in detail (for there is no translation of it and it is quite extraordinary):

> In Paradise there is a tree whose name is Tuba and if a swift rider were to ride in its shadow for a hundred years he would not be able to circumambulate it. Canopies and way stations are made of its blossoms. Rivers run through its leaves. Its branches are made of ambergris. It is planted on an earth made of ruby, its dust made of camphor. Its flowers are made of musk, while from its roots gushes forth a spring of milk and honey, by which sit the people of Paradise. Angels pay them a visit, while sitting there, accompanied by chaste creatures made of light, their faces lit like reflections of lanterns upon golden leaves; their wings are soft as feathers of birds; on their backs are tablets made of ruby, circles made of gold; their shirts are made of silk and brocade.[9]

Al-Razi then proceeds to report of other commentaries on this tree, quoting yet another reliable source in which Tuba is reported to be a tree in Paradise whose principal trunk is in fact in the house of Ali ibn Abi Talib, the Prophet's son-in-law (and according to Shi'is his rightful successor), from which the other branches spread out into the houses of all other pious Muslims. Al-Razi reports that the Prophet was once asked by yet another person what Tuba meant, to which the Prophet responded that it is "a tree in Paradise whose principal trunk is in my home, and from which other branches spread into the abodes of the inhabitants of Paradise." Someone else chances upon the Prophet and asks the same question, to which the Prophet responds that Tuba is "a tree in Paradise whose principal trunk is in the house of the Prince of Believers, Ali ibn Abi Talib, Peace and Benedictions be upon him, and from which other branches spread into the abodes of the inhabitants of Paradise." The man who had asked this question responded to the Prophet and said, "Oh Messenger of God! Just a while ago someone asked you 'What is Tuba?' and you said it is a tree in Paradise and its principal trunk is in your house, and now you say it is in the house of the Prince of Believers, Ali. How could that be?" The Prophet responded and said: "Don't you know that my home and Ali's home are one and the same in Paradise, and both of us live in the same house?"[10]

Sublimating the Sacred

What is evident in al-Razi's commentary on the word *tuba,* as it appears in the Qur'an, is an active Shi'i imagination in which a whole sacred memory is built around one particularly potent sacred sign, turning it into a symbol of cosmic proportions. Already evident in al-Razi is a storytelling urge, a fascination with the idea of a cosmic tree, about which he collects every bit of information he can, and around which he then builds a surreal story that Gabriel Garcia Márquez would covet. The Qur'anic word, the sacred symbol, and the cosmic universe they entailed were all very much the stuff of a medieval hermeneutic preoccupation for theologians and mystics alike—all but lost to subsequent generations of Muslims and Shi'is comfortably distanced from such surreal signs of bygone ages. But such sealed signatures of forsaken corners of a collective cultural consciousness have a way of coming back to be indulged in the creative imaginations of poets and novelists, who thrive on such distant echoes of melodious memories.

In 1988, when scarcely anyone outside the sullen seminaries of forgotten pieties cared to read Abu al-Futuh al-Razi anymore, Shahrnoush Parsipour, a prominent Iranian novelist, published *Tuba va Ma'na-ye Shab* [Tuba and the Meaning of Night] (1988). The story concerns a young woman, Tuba, who at a tender adolescent age marries a distant cousin more than twice her age. The story is initially set in the late nineteenth century and gradually moves all the way to the middle of the twentieth century, that is to say from when the Qajar dynasty is about to collapse (in 1926) until the Pahlavi dynasty is threatened by a major revolutionary uprising in 1979. Tuba soon divorces her first husband, marries another man, divorces him too, and finally loses her sanity when she witnesses the brutal murder of a young woman, Setareh, who is subsequently buried under a pomegranate tree, to which Tuba begins to attend. Other calamities eventually befall Tuba, until at the very end of the novel she and Leila, a friend and distant relative, join together and commence a conversation cast in the surreal realm of their imaginal universe.

At a frantic moment, Leila ecstatically shakes herself and suddenly explodes into small pieces of flesh, her blood splashing all over the surrounding walls. Tuba, sitting next to her, is covered by Leila's blood. But she hears Leila calling out to her: "Tuba!" Tuba looks around and sees Leila standing right in front of her, telling her: "With my death only descent is possible. We have to descend, go down into the depth. Only there is silence possible." The two women begin to descend into the roots of the pomegranate tree—the inferno, purgatory, and paradise of a whole different eschatology:

> First they dwelled at the roots of the pomegranate tree. Tuba could hear a melancholic chime, just as if a pear were a drop of water and dripped on the surface of a swamp. They needed to spend many moments in absolute silence in order to hear the sound. Tuba could hear the sound of dripping three times. She said: "These are the very last tremors of Setareh." The bell was now ringing from a very far distance, monotonously and slowly. The other one, Mariam, just like the thunder of a storm and whirlwinds were spinning around her own particles. She was like a flood under the earth, swirling and roaring. Leila said: "Let's descend farther down!" Here, it was all cries and moaning. She said: "These people have died dumb. Now they are speaking their mind."[11]

The descent of Tuba and Leila into the heart of the pomegranate tree, down deep into its roots, continues further, into even darker layers of memories, histories, mythologies: "Now a branch of light appeared. Leila said: 'This is enlightenment.' Tuba was in a desert now. Leila was inside her."[12] By now, Parsipour's narrative has completely abandoned its claim to realism, and with the twin tumbling of Tuba and Leila it seems that Parsipour's own prose has hit a high pitch of descending dizziness into subterranean territories, where History (not just specific histories) begins to find a mythic narrative in order to creatively remember itself. "Leila laughed and said: 'Do you remember when the eldest son became a hunter, you used to sit reverently a few steps away from him, with your kids all gathered around you?'"[13]

The mythic disposition of Parsipour's prose now begins to tell the story of humanity at large from the vantage point of two women, Tuba and Leila, two sisters hidden in the shadowy disposition of each other. Her prose is now entirely self-sustaining, suspended, revelatory. The narrative now simulates the biblical, the Qur'anic. It sublates the sacred into the mythic—a myth of creation so universal that it is as if Shahrnoush Parsipour (a contemporary Iranian woman living in California) is telling it for the very first time at the dawn of history. Gradually, as Parsipour's miasmatic narrative unfolds, and while Tuba and Leila descend ever deeper into the roots of the pomegranate tree, Leila becomes the simulacrum of a heavenly metaphor, the sky itself, while Tuba remains earthly. Their sons oscillate between the two of them. The heaven and the earth, Leila and Tuba, finally conspire and kill the wilder side of their elder son, driving him mad between sanity and savagery. By this time, Parsipour's narrative has hit yet another metamorphic pitch—at once mythic, revelatory, epiphanic. The journey deep into the heart of earth is as spatial as it is temporal, back to the tip of Creation. Leila's voice, speaking as if in a spell, is now completely parabolic, communicating from the depth of a history only she has excavated and accessed. Her symbolics are at once private and public, historical and mythic, factual and phantasmagoric. Where are we? What language is this—whence its origin, where its destination? Leila speaks to Tuba in the language of legends. These two women reminisce about a creation myth only they know, to which only they seem to have been eyewitnesses (they and their children, the preternatural though consistently sublunary parentage of humanity). These two women are eternally connected, one and the same, alternately giving birth to each other though disfigured and separated. Ultimately Leila, in her recounting of this story, goes to heaven, and Tuba remains on earth. Eventually we surmise a creation myth, with the figure of the divinity as feminine—Leila herself, the meaning of night. She speaks to her earthly half, the Mother Earth Tuba—mother and daughter, daughter and mother in succession, in reverse, all as if in an instant. The masculine and masculinist God—of the

Yahweh, of Allah, of the Father—has just been sublated into Mother Earth, and Mother Heaven, and Mother Child.

From the Qur'anic tree of Tuba to Tuba the tree-character at the heart of Shahrnoush Parsipour's novel passes a hidden thrust, through which the sacred has become mythic, the mythic sublime, the sublime narratively constituted, poetically poised—all in the hands of a present-day novelist.

À la Recherche du Temps Perdu

Almost similar accidents of life and cultural affinity that root Shahrnoush Parsipour's creative literary imagination in a distant memory of her ancestral faith brought her into contact with Shirin Neshat in New York. One conversation led to another, and soon Shirin Neshat made a video installation she too called *Tuba* (2002).[14] Detailed attention to the visual unfolding of this work brings everything I have sought to argue in this chapter together—the creative effervescence that sublimates the site of the sacred into the substance of the sublime, where an aesthetic of emancipation awaits on the opposing side of a politics of despair.

The extreme close-up of a closed eyelid juxtaposed against the extreme long shot of a landscape of a Nowhere opens Shirin Neshat's singular act of visual piety, *Tuba*. As one camera tilts from the sky down to a landscape of deserted and barren hills, another camera zooms out from the eye widely, gently. The landscape of our unfamiliarity is now fully drawn from the mind and imagination behind the closed eye—calm, quiet, foreclosed. Gradually, the camera draws the face of a person out of a rocky background, exactly at a moment when the other camera is fading out into a rocky landscape of hills so that the countenance of the by now androgynous figure we face turns into the face of a woman precisely when it perfectly matches the landscape of the rocky hills.[15] Now we see in the extreme long shot, the landscape of rocky hills, a crowd hurriedly approaching, dotted black figures on the surface of the deserted landscape. It is not until one camera has given a full view of the woman now integral to the bulky trunk of a huge tree (located precisely at the center of a short, rectangular wall) that the other camera gives a better view of the invading intruders—at once pilgrims, boisterous, and ominous. The rectangular, short wall around the open space surrounding the women/tree is now in full view. Now we know that we are witnessing the commencement of an invasion/pilgrimage toward a solitary sacred site in the geography of Nowhere. On one side stands a sacred solitude, serene in its paradisiacal absence of any witness except the unobtrusive camera, and observant of the privilege that it has been granted. On the other side looms the invading army of im/pious pilgrims, dead set on getting to the woman/tree. We are witnessing a desecration about to happen. The walled precinct marks the boundaries of a singular tree. This is Paradise, literally "walled garden." That tree is Tuba—literally and figuratively a woman, at once aging and ageless. Those intruding pilgrims are about to desecrate the sacred site, even as they seek sanctity.

On the side of the screen that draws the invading pilgrims, we the audience are now witnesses, unbeknownst to ourselves, to the circular commencement of a masculine piety as the seated source of that populated pilgrimage turned into an ominous invasion. Gradually, the visual registers begin to coalesce: what is frightful about *Tuba* is its sheer cosmic magnitude, its cosmogonic imagination, its articulation of a geography of Nowhere that is at the same time the topography of Everywhere. To say that *Tuba* is biblical or Qur'anic in its epic visuality is just to approximate it to the alphabetical verisimilitude of its formulations, and that will not do justice to its singular vision, which is a reality sui generis and *not* reducible to its constituent elements. Yet it is precisely through its constituent elements, in the traditions and trajectories it visually and deliberately invokes, that we may carefully approach its own universe, the sacred-turned-sublime space that it ipso facto generates, sustains, consecrates, and endangers at the moment of its sanctification of the sublime and its sublimation of the sacred—now being interrupted. In the span of only a few minutes a cosmic order is suspected, suspended, and threatened. From one Qur'anic word to Abu al-Futuh al-Razi to Shahrnoush Parsipour to Shirin Neshat now runs the image of a magnanimous tree that embraces, consecrates, and sublimates life (anything but "bare" if Giorgio Agamben were to worry) beyond any particular religion or tradition, history or biopolitics.[16]

The visual drama in Shirin Neshat's *Tuba* unfolds and culminates in two rectangular oppositions between an interior shot from the woman/tree out and an exterior shot toward the tree/woman shrine—everyone stopping at the sacred threshold of a prohibited space, defined hesitantly by a half-wall that is half inviting, half disinviting, creating a pause. The circle of men is engaged in a ritual act of agitated piety completely emptied of its central point of attention, matching a central point of attention around the tree with no one around it except the invading pilgrims, about to desecrate. The crowd gathers around the rectangular wall and there is a pause—fear of the sacred. The woman by now has disappeared from the heart of the tree into the heart of the tree: the grace is gone. Suddenly comes the moment of transgression: the pilgrims become pillagers, trespass the boundary, jump over the half-wall—half inviting, half disinviting. They trespass deliberating: one camera looking from the exterior of the transgression in, and the other looking from the interior of the invasion out. Thus two cameras record the transgression, one keeping a distance from the site of the transgression, the other engaging inside it.

The pilgrim pillagers keep a distance the size of their own shadow from the sacred center of the shrine—invasive, hesitant. The tree has lost its feminine figure, hidden it from the crowd. The tree remains the sacred center of the shrine, though emptied—the shrine itself is the tree, though its grace a memory. This is the tree from time immemorial, upon which people have hung objects of their desire, signs and symbols of their wishes hoping to be granted.

The shrine has been invaded, however. The camera becomes hesitant, caught between the crowd and the tree. It turns to the tree to mark the disappearance of the woman from the heart of the tree. Time and space are here suspended, metamorphic, interchangeable. The instance becomes instantaneous, metempsychosis visible, invisible. Time here is no longer chronic, teleological—it has no beginning, no duration, and no ending. The time is what medieval Persian philosophers called *sarmad* [the everlasting], when many become one, *tafreqeh* [diversion], and *hozur* [presence]. The camera begins to move, with a gentle, tender, noble, gracious zoom that is more sanctifying, more precious, more ennobling than the entire history of all theologies of all religions have foretold. It approaches with patience, pace, peace, grace, piety, and gentle nobility, taking one graceful, reverent, last look, its deferential parting bid to the sacred site of a memory right in the presence of so much violent transgression. Then it suddenly and courageously cuts (the glory of the cinematic blink!) into a long, lasting, forgiving long shot to show the peaceful abode of universe (the tree, the enclosed site, the invaders, the barren hills, the deserted landscape), and thus to forgive all. As soon as one's eyes settle in that long shot, suddenly an even longer shot moves in, a more expansive universe on one side, while on the other the grace of the tree has left, now surrounded by a pillaging crowd of pilgrims attending the vacated site of grace. On the other side, though, the camera, from God's point of view, has already embraced the universe—so hallowed and so sublime is that last shot!

Shirin Neshat's *Tuba* is no mere work of art. This is an entreaty, a prayer, a plea, flowing through a caring camera, a set of perceptive lenses—gracing what they see, forgiving what they show.

When the occasion is instant, the experiment is perilous. If time is horizontal across history, it is also vertical within the normative narratives that hold a culture together. The vertical insertion of time into the archeological site of a living culture taps on its hidden reservoirs, where the visual and performative staging of that culture show and tell in terms at once foreign to their immediacies and yet familiar to the layers of their historical amnesia. A culture may fancy itself "secular." But its sacred memories are nevertheless busy thinking its ideas and populating its dreams, suggesting its sublimities. A people may no longer remember (or may have successfully repressed) their horizontal past, but the vertical rootedness of their culture in the semiotics of their amnesia comes back to haunt their daydreams in pictures they take, stories they tell, and poems they recite. Cultural memories never die. They just change narrative venues, exchange their ceremonial sites, trade in their poetic licenses, their sacred for the sublime.

The surreal energy that sustains Shirin Neshat's visual reflection on Tuba—a tree, a woman, a tree/woman—draws from its distant (all but forgotten) Qur'anic origin. It reads through her contemporary (all but evident) literary rendition and brings it to a sustained visual act of piety, fully aware of the violent impieties it solicits to forgive, sins it seeks to absolve. This act of piety—out of place, untimely, perennial, desperate—is instantaneous, kinetic in bodies, momentary in time. The creative consciousness of Shirin Neshat's camera is the means of paying homage to her ancestral faith, whose falsely agitated memories are now cast globally onto an audience at home nowhere, with nowhere to call home anymore. *Tuba* was shot in Mexico. It might as well have been shot on the moon. It was shot in 2001, but it might as well have been shot in the year Zero—on any and on all, and thus on no calendar. But the untime of *Tuba* is no claim to timelessness. *Tuba* is timely. It is a search for grace in the midst of an otherwise graceless spectacle of violence now writ large upon the fragility of a seamlessly free-floating globe.

There is an old mystic saying that when there was Sufism there was no name for it, and when there was a name for it, there was no Sufism.

There is a contingent fragility about Shirin Neshat's art, and her visual reflection on piety (so belated and yet so befitting) in her *Tuba* operates on a similar paradox. Piety abounds in solitude, thrives in simplicity, dissipates in the crowd, degenerates in politics. Upon that paradox, Shirin Neshat envisions a world in dire need of grace, a grace that—in the absence of God in history—she solicits from the sinuous solace of her camera. She sees like a sublime visionary of our sacred incredulities—all despite ourselves, all against our will. In the untimely timbre of that certitude, she is a solitary monk praying for a universe turning at one of its darkest moments of despair.

The Sovereignty of Art

The exilic condition of an artist, shared between the Iranian artist Shirin Neshat and the late Iraqi artist Monkith Saaid, provides the remissive space where the formal destruction of instrumentalized reason, of the structural-functional reading of reality, is made creatively viable.[17] On that remissive site, we need to see how the formal reconnects with the factual. What I have sought to demonstrate in this chapter is a tenuous autonomy for the aesthetic site—whereby the sacred is sublimated into the sublime—in undermining the structural violence at the roots of both the colonial modernity that descended upon the Shi'is and all other Muslims and the "Islamic tradition" that it invented to oppose, denigrate, and overcome. Muslims became the primary practitioners of this "Islamic tradition," and in it they dug their own grave. The colonial reason, the reason for and of domination, the "objectivity" that (as Frantz Fanon used to say) always works against the colonized, had presented itself in a win-win situation. If Muslims converted to it, they were denied agency, and if they retreated to their "traditions" to safeguard their agential autonomy, they did not even see their domain as already colonially constituted. The aesthetic domain, on the contrary, and as decoupled from the doctrinal and political sites of Islam and Shi'ism alike, was immune both to the colonial modernity that was imposed on it and to the Islamic tradition that it had invented as its own negational shadow. On the site of the sublime, in which Islam was integral but not definitive, Muslims, even no longer as Muslims, were in charge of their own destiny, envisioning, imagining, projecting themselves as other than what they were. Here I augment much of the discussion about the autonomy of the aesthetic act with a substitution: colonial reason for an abstract (generic, self-Europeanized) conception of Reason. Based on the prior works of Theodor Adorno and Jacques Derrida, considering the aesthetic experience as overriding nonaesthetic reason with a superior sense of sovereignty, Christoph Menke has in fact upped the ante and suggested that the sovereignty of art is predicated on a genus sui generis and as such overpowers and subverts reason altogether. Menke places the domain of art completely outside any cognitive episteme of knowledge. "Art is not sovereign in that it tears down the boundaries separating aesthetic and nonaesthetic experience, thereby proving itself to be the direct overcoming of reason," he points out.

> It is instead sovereign in that . . . it represents a crisis for our functioning discourses. The aporias of the traditional romantic view of the sovereignty of art can only be resolved by combining two theses: (1) the deconstructive thesis that the aesthetic critique of reason is the subversion rather than the overcoming of reason: (2) the thesis . . . that it is not the contents but the effects, consequences, or repercussions of art that are the foundations of this critique. Taken together, these two claims outline an understanding of aesthetic sovereignty—as an aesthetically generated critique of reason—that not only does not violate the autonomy of enactment of aesthetic experience but is actually premised upon it.[18]

This proposition is doubly forceful if we replace the European Reason, thus self-proclaimed, for colonial reason. In the colonial corner of modernity, the sovereignty of the aesthetic overcomes and subverts colonial reason in emancipatory and enabling moves, and as such at long last aesthetic reason in public art will do for its audience what colonial reason in the public space had failed even institutionally to materialize, let alone politically to mobilize.

IV

CONTEMPORARY CONTESTATIONS

10

THE UN/MAKING OF A POLITICS OF DESPAIR

The cataclysmic encounter of Shi'ism with colonial modernity topped its repeated failures in the social construction of a public reason, *upped the ante,* and resulted in a politics of despair, in which the Shi'is were out of their element in facing the enormity of a world history that had just descended upon them. They had to reach deep and wide into their social and intellectual history for manners of coping with their predicament. The social and intellectual dimensions of Shi'ism have a long and varied history that includes political, juridical, theological, philosophical, and mystical dimensions. Although all these branches of Shi'i learning have continued and flourished apace from early Islamic history to the present time, it is only the political dimension of Shi'ism that has responded in significant and pronounced ways to the issues and problems posed by the advent of European colonial modernity. The unexamined metaphysics of reason and progress, defining the claims of colonial modernity on its extended history, came into direct and categorical conflict with the Islamic metaphysics that has doctrinally sustained and legitimized Shi'ism as a world religion. As a result, even the nonpolitical dimensions of Shi'ism—for example its juridical and philosophical traditions—have responded to colonial modernity with a fire and tenacity indicative of their political (not juridical or epistemological) crisis. Consequently, such issues in Shi'i juridical and philosophical discourses that do not address their epistemic problems in and with colonial modernity remain principally premodern in the terms and dispositions of their engagement. In addressing the political dimension of modern Shi'i thought, we will have to examine such points of contact and dialogue between

Shi'ism and colonial modernity that have been instrumental in placing it in its contemporary history. The making of a Shi'i politics of despair in the course of the nineteenth and twentieth centuries is embraced within the larger context of an anticolonial modernity that was commensurate with a cosmopolitan worldliness, which in turn was both the undoing and the remaking of Shi'ism in its enduring universal reaches.

At the Crossroads of History

The particular history of a Shi'i politics of despair, belligerently trapping itself against a juridical cul de sac, is long and laboriously crafted. Throughout the nineteenth centaury, the Shi'i *'ulama* [clerical class] gradually consolidated their position in a powerful relationship to the Qajar monarchy. The colonially besieged monarchy—pulled and pushed by the Russians, the Ottomans, the British, and the French—found its existence increasingly contingent on clerical support. Any court-initiated administrative reform that even smelled of curtailing their power was effectively stalled by the Shi'i clergy. By far the most powerful movement that challenged their authority was the Babi uprising of 1844–1852, which they helped the Qajar tyranny to suppress with unsurpassed brutality. The advent of the Constitutional Revolution of 1906–1911 created a major rift among the Shi'i clergy, with some supporting but many opposing it. Then a massive wave of cosmopolitan culture that had been long in gestation throughout the eighteenth and nineteenth centuries now was finally squeezing Shi'ism in a very uncomfortable embrace. The doors and windows of people in Muslim (Shi'i) lands had been forced open by European colonialism, and (as Said Amir Arjomand has judiciously put it) the political culture of the Shi'is was no longer an exclusively Shi'i political culture. In other words, Islam remained integral to Muslims' lives and thoughts but no longer (if it ever was) definitive to it.

For the first half of the twentieth century, Shi'ism had to contend with the multiple and conflicting forces of European colonialism, the rise of monarchic or (conversely) anticolonial nationalism, and above all Third World socialism. After the tumultuous period of the Constitutional movement, the 1910s was a decade of relative political inaction for Shi'i clerics. The occupation of northern Iran by the Russians did not engender much political concern on their part. Much of the clerical attention, as is evident in the work of a leading cleric, Seyyed Asadollah Kharaqani (died 1936), was directed against the clerics' declining moral authority, which was concomitant with the rapid rise of alternative modes of cultural and moral affiliation. In the 1920s, however, Iraqi Shi'i authorities were instrumental in the popular uprising against British colonialism. Mirza Muhammad Taqi Shirazi emerged as the leading clerical authority in Iraqi anticolonial struggles.[1] In collaboration with Shaykh al-Shari'ah al-Isfahani and other leading Shi'i authorities, Shirazi called for the establishment of "a theocratic government built upon one of the fundamental principles of the Shi'i doctrine."[2] The Iraqi Shi'is were much influenced by pro-Constitutional Shi'i authorities in Iran and many of them wished to emulate that system in Iraq.

A dialectic of reciprocity soon developed between Iran and Iraq as two complementary sites of contestation for the Shi'i clerics. Though the origin of this symbiotic relationship between Najaf and Qom is deeply rooted in history, it again assumed significance during the Qajar period and the Babi movement, and then again in the early decades of the twentieth century. Under British pressure, a leading Iraqi Shi'i authority, Shaykh Muhammad Khalesi (died 1963) went to Iran in 1922 and joined forces with his Iranian counterparts in an incipient war against a rising tide of antireligious sentiment in which Iran and Iraq found both a political and a moral danger. They saw a link between the decline of religious convictions and the growth of British imperialist influence, which sought to undermine clerical authority.[3] Soon the anticlerical agenda of the first Pahlavi monarch, Reza Shah, who reigned from 1926 to 1941, and the antiestablishment anger of the clerics came to a head in the late 1920s and scores of leading Shi'i clerical activists were arrested and severely punished.

From this symbiosis between Najaf and Qom, both seats of learning benefited intermittently, and the Shi'i 'ulama rose to even more actual and potential power. The 1930s and 1940s were decades of Shi'i polemical responses to the rising power of anticolonial nationalism and Third World socialism. Mirza Mohammad Hossein Na'ini (died 1936), Shaykh Abdolkarim Ha'eri Yazdi (died 1937), and Hajj Aqa Hossein Tabataba'i Qomi (died 1947) were the leading Shi'i jurists of these decades, chiefly responsible for elevating Qom to a position of prominence in juridical studies, on the same level as Najaf. It was the collective work of these leading jurists that paved the way for the increasing influence of Mohammad Hossein Tabataba'i Boroujerdi (died 1961), who enjoyed unprecedented power and prestige as a leading Shi'i authority. The political agenda of the 1940s was chiefly characterized by the continued anger of the clerical establishment against the relentless unfolding of alternative sites of political culture (of what in English is called *secularism,* though there is no word for it in Arabic, Persian, Turkish, or Urdu), such as nationalism and socialism. The enemy of the clerical authority now seemed to have disseminated from the tyrannical absolutism of the state to a widespread and hard-to-grasp diffusion of worldly and cosmopolitan ideas and practices. Khalesi's treatise on veiling in Islam, published in 1948, represents the dominant sentiment of the clerics in this period.[4] In this treatise, Khalesi tried to strike a balance between the radical traditionalists who denied women any social presence and status, and the rising worldly cosmopolitanism in which women were actively unveiled and socially present. That Reza Shah had appropriated aspects of such movements and affiliated them with the Pahlavi court did not diminish the fact that the phenomenon was far more universal in its appeal to the emerging urban middle class.

Shi'ism gradually had to enter creative or critical conversation with its ideological rivals. The rising tide of colonial and anticolonial modernity in the 1930s and 1940s, which in political terms ultimately led to the establishment of the Pahlavi state apparatus and opposition to it, also witnessed a contrapuntal mode of reform in Shi'i political thought. Mirza Reza Qoli Shari'at Sangalaji (1890–1944) is the chief representative of a rather radical notion of religious modernity. He tried to advance such subversive ideas as the total discarding of the institution of *taqlid,* or "the emulation of the exemplary conduct of the religious authorities."[5] What is detectable in Shari'at Sangalaji's thoughts is an almost Wahabi return to absolute monotheism, a rejection of the Shi'i cult of saint-worship. Such an emphasis allies Sangalaji's ideas with the proposed reforms of the noted historian and modernist reformer Ahmad Kasravi (1890–1946) and with a solid streak of anticolonial rationalism that was meant to rescue the Shi'i faith from medieval absolutism while equipping it for confrontation with the evils of "the West."

In the 1940s and early 1950s the Shi'i clerical establishment concentrated their attention on the Baha'is and the communists. The entirely misplaced clerical hostility against the Baha'is was a remnant of their active opposition to the Babi movement of the nineteenth century. The Baha'is at this point were an entirely pacifist sect with absolutely no revolutionary or even political agenda, and their persecution was (and remains) a hallmark of shame in the chronicle of the Shi'i clerical establishment. The opposition to communism, however, was more of a pronounced political rivalry. In 1951 Khalesi published *Bandits of Right and Truth, or, Those Who Return to Barbarism and Ignorance* in response to the antireligious tract published by the communist Tudeh Party, *Guardians of Magic and Myth*.[6] The two camps remained at each other's throats until the 1953 coup permanently weakened communist influence in Iran.

The 1950s also marked a reemergence of anticolonial nationalism in Iran, a movement chiefly identified with Mohammad Mossadegh (1882–1967), the champion of the Iranian nationalist resurgence. It was to nationalism that Shi'i political thought responded in the 1950s. Ali Akbar Tashayyod, a leading public intellectual, was chiefly responsible for an active coordination of Shi'i doctrines with the dominant themes of nationalism in the 1950s. While Tashayyod tried to assimilate nationalism into Shi'i political thought, Sayyed Mahmud Taleqani (1910–1979) sought to give an active rereading of such key Shi'i figures as Mirza Mohammad Hossein Na'ini by way of posing Shi'ism as an alternative to nationalism.[7]

All of these events pale in comparison with what the new decades had in store for the Shi'i clerical establishment and their communities alike. According to Said Amir Arjomand, "the 1960s was a decade of fateful change in Shi'ism."[8] The decade began with the death of Ayatollah Boroujerdi, the last mostly apolitical jurist in the tradition of Shaykh Abdolkarim Ha'eri Yazdi and Abu al-Hasan Isfahani. Boroujerdi's passive acknowledgment of the second Pahlavi monarch Muhammad Reza Shah, who reigned from 1941 to 1978, was reminiscent of Ha'eri Yazdi's passive acceptance of Reza Shah. This had limited Shi'i political activism to an anti–Tudeh Party agenda, with which the Pahlavi regime had much sympathy. The death of Boroujerdi, however, reopened the whole question of supreme political authority in the Shi'i community.[9]

At this crucial moment the leading Shi'i authorities gathered in Qom to ponder the future of religious and political authority. The proceedings of this conference were subsequently published in *Bahsi dar Bareh-ye Marja'iyyat va Ruhaniyyat* [A Discussion Concerning the Sources of Exemplary Conduct and the Religious Authorities]. Practically all the leading revolutionary ideologues of the late 1970s, with the notable exception of Ayatollah Ruhollah Khomeini (1902–1989), contributed to this volume in which such issues as the range of the *Marja al-Taqlid*'s religious and political authorities, the viability of the notion of following the most learned, the supervision of *Sahm-e Imam* revenue, and many other related issues were openly discussed and debated.

There were a number of major institutional developments following the death of Ayatollah Boroujerdi with enduring revolutionary implications, such as the emergence of Qur'anic commentary schools, chief among them the one established by Ayatollah Mahmud Taleqani in Tehran. Muslim student associations on many university campuses and Muslim professional associations of engineers, physicians, teachers, lawyers, and so forth were among the voluntary associations that began to emerge in the 1960s. These organizations provided the institutional bases for the propagation of contemporary political thoughts. Informal gatherings added momentum and energy to Shi'i political thought.[10] Weekly and monthly journals, such as *Maktab-e Tashayyu'* and *Goftar-e Mah*, propagated the ideas of the rising Shi'i ideologues. But ultimately the Hosseiniyeh Irshad, a religious institute established in 1965 in Tehran, must be considered the most successful institution of radical Shi'i thought.

Halfway through the twentieth century, Shi'ism had seen and endured much and was ready for more. Soon after the Constitutional Revolution of 1906–1911, it had to contend with the continued Russian and British colonial presence in the region. In the 1930s Reza Shah's monarchical nationalism and forced modernization projects were what the clerical establishment had to face. In the 1940s it was the turn of the Tudeh Party to test the patience and endurance of the Shi'i establishment, and then in the 1950s the anticolonial nationalism of the Mossadegh era stole the show. Come early 1960s, it was now the turn of militant Shi'ism to flex its political muscles.

Dress Rehearsals

The major event of the 1960s was Ayatollah Khomeini's leadership of the first revolutionary uprising inspired by militant Shi'ism. Since the 1940s, Khomeini had been active in Qom where he was busy pursuing his juridical studies under Ayatollah Ha'eri Yazdi. While such politically conscious and active clerics as Ayatollah Taleqani and Ayatollah Motahhari were busy debating Pahlavi legitimacy, Khomeini seized the moment by publicly calling for the ouster of the reigning shah. The June 1963 uprising shook the foundation of the Pahlavi monarchy, but it was severely crushed and Khomeini exiled first to Turkey and then to Iraq.[11]

As Said Amir Arjomand has noted, Khomeini's 1963 uprising put clerical reform on hold and gave added momentum to the continued validity of the institution of the 'ulama.[12] At least two high-ranking members of the 'ulama, Hasan Farid Golpayegani and Shaykh Ali Tehrani, carried forward the theoretical implications of Khomeini's 1963 uprising and in the 1970s wrote treatises in which ideas of supreme collective clerical rule for the Shi'i 'ulama were expounded.[13] The result of Khomeini's radical politicization of the institution of the 'ulama is so drastic that one can indeed speak of "an ideological revolution in Shi'ism," though predicated on enduring ideological traits dating from early in the nineteenth century.[14]

The greatest and most effective challenge to the authority of the 'ulama as an institution, however, came from Ali Shari'ati, the revolutionary thinker sketched earlier in this book. He was a threat to the Pahlavi monarchy and the Shi'i clerical establishment alike. In the 1960s and 1970s, Shari'ati singlehandedly reinvented a new, radically proactive political spectrum for Islam. In a series of effectively delivered and widely attended public lectures bolstered by massively distributed essays, Shari'ati generated an unprecedented energy and enthusiasm among politically committed intellectuals with a religious bent.[15] Educated in Mashhad and Paris, Shari'ati mastered an effective revolutionary language and then returned to his homeland, fully committed to transforming Shi'ism into a full-fledged political ideology. Shari'ati considered the institution of the clerical establishment fundamentally outdated and compromised. He sought to release the Shi'i sacred imagination from the authority of the 'ulama. With a barely concealed disdain for clerical quietism or what he considered irrelevant piety, or even limited revolutionary appeal, Shari'ati wed the sacrosanct memories of Shi'ism to the most serious problems of his time: cultural colonialism, social injustice, political repression, and the worldwide domination of European and American imperialism. Combining his own brand of Jean-Paul Sartre's existentialism and Frantz Fanon's anticolonialism, Shari'ati championed the ideal of an autonomous and independent person fully in charge of history. He also reconstructed outdated figures of Shi'i collective history, such as Fatimah, the Prophet's daughter and the wife of the First Shi'i Imam, Ali. He represented Fatimah as a devoted revolutionary woman to be emulated by his contemporaries.[16] Shari'ati redefined the role of revolutionary intellectuals, ridiculed and dismissed nonreligious intellectuals, and made faith and belief once again acceptable, even fashionable, among young Shi'is. In his major work, *Islam-shenasi* (1972), Shari'ati took upon himself the stupendous task of redefining what it means to be a Muslim. He explored the most sacrosanct corners of Shi'i and Islamic memories and brought back to life what he thought was "the true Islam," an Islam which was all but forgotten and yet waiting to mobilize its adherents to an active, radical, and revolutionary commitment in life. He redefined monotheism in classless, gender-equal, repressionless, antityrannical terms.

The person who facilitated much of what Ali Shari'ati accomplished in his radical repoliticization of Shi'i Islam was Jalal Al-e Ahmad (1923–1969), who in such works as *Gharbzadegi* [Westoxication] and *Dar Khedmat va Khiyanat-e Roshanfekran* [On the Services and Treasons of Intellectuals] had argued vociferously against the inordinate power and influence of "Western culture," including its revolutionary ideologies. He supported a local, domestically viable construction of a revolutionary ideology.[17] Al-e Ahmad pointed toward recent Iranian and Iraqi history, in which the only successful social mobilizations had occurred when the Shi'i clerics were actively involved in the process. Hailing from a prominent clerical family, initially intending to become a cleric himself, then subsequently becoming a disillusioned Marxist, Al-e Ahmad sought to rekindle a radical trait in Shi'ism. What Al-e Ahmad had barely noticed, however, Shari'ati took to its fullest potential, persuasively arguing for the revolutionary possibilities of a renewed reading of Shi'ism.[18]

By far the most erudite and relentless Shi'i ideologue who carried the revolutionary potential of a re-politicized Shi'ism to its logical conclusion was Morteza Motahhari (1920–1979), a leading clerical activist with a wide range of learning and unparalleled systematicity to his groundbreaking work in turning Shi'ism into a contemporary radical project. On some fundamental issues, particularly on the central role of the 'ulama in politics, Morteza Motahhari disagreed with Ali Shari'ati. Perhaps the unintended consequence of his ideas was the further consolidation of "Islamic ideology" as the most potent revolutionary machinery preceding the tumultuous events of 1979. Launching his revolutionary zeal from his solid place in the Shi'i clerical establishment, Motahhari mobilized Shi'i doctrines and institutions to argue against all other revolutionary alternatives, whether Marxist-materialist or nationalist-liberal. Islamic philosophy was his principal weapon in a deliberate attempt to dislodge historical materialism.[19] He shifted his attention from a popularization of the recondite language of Islamic philosophy to public lectures at various Muslim associations on a variety of issues, including the renarration of popular religious stories. He severely criticized the clerical establishment for its abandonment of politics, and in such works as *Akhlaq-e Jensi dar Islam va Jahdn-e Gharb* [Sexual Ethics in Islam and the West], or *'Ilal-e Gerayesh beh Maddi-gari* [Reasons for Attraction to Materialism], or *Islam va Muqtaziyat-e Zaman* [Islam and the Exigencies of the [Present] Time], he confronted all the vital issues of his time, preaching to and preparing a massive audience that ultimately joined him and other clerics in February 1979 to topple the Pahlavi monarchy. Soon after this, on 2 May 1979, he was assassinated by a splinter militia group.[20]

Motahhari's philosophical preoccupation with historical materialism and his concerns with popularizing a more readily accessible and politically relevant Islamic philosophy were largely indebted to his close association with Allamah Seyyed Mohammad Hossein Tabataba'i (1903–1981), a distinguished Shi'i scholar who was equally concerned with the erosion of Islamic doctrines and ideas. In his major philosophical contribution to the active engagement with Marxism and historical materialism, *Usul-e Falsafeh va Ravesh-e Ri'alism* [The Principles of Philosophy and the Realistic Method] (1953–1985), Tabataba'i took issue with those pervasive ideas. His concern was primarily for the seminary students in Qom who had apparently been drawn to radical, antireligious ideas.[21] But Motahhari's extensive commentaries on these texts made them accessible to a more diverse body of students at Tehran University. Throughout his Qur'anic commentaries and in his participation in questions of supreme juridical and political authority among the Shi'is, among other issues, Tabataba'i shared the concerns of his fellow high-ranking clerics about the rise of Marxism and historical materialism, and ultimately the future of the Shi'i faith and its social and political contexts.[22]

To address the specifics of those social and political contexts in a language that bore the sacred authority of the Qur'an, another major political thinker of this period, Sayyed Mahmud Taleqani, used the discourse of Qur'anic commentary as his preferred narrative. Through a succession of Qur'anic commentaries, published later as *Partovi az Qur'an* [A Reflection from the Qur'an] (1979–1983), Taleqani read an actively revolutionary message into the Islamic holy text. In and out of prison for his political activities over an extended period of time, Taleqani preached his radical, revolutionary reading of the Qur'an, linking its sacrosanct message to the most immediate and compelling problems of his time. Taleqani felt equally compelled to battle Marxism, especially its economic theory. He wrote a book, *Islam and Ownership* (1953), in which he countered the Marxist conception of the economic basis of social structure and then assimilated its principal terms and discourse in narrating an Islamic political economy.[23] Taleqani's ideological and political leadership was instrumental in the formation of the Mojahedin-e Khalq organization, an urban guerilla movement that paralyzed the Pahlavi regime, then joined the 1979 revolution but subsequently broke ranks with Ayatollah Khomeini's followers. Ultimately the Mojahedin was banned and forced into exile.[24]

The economic aspect of "Islamic ideology," as the Shi'i ideologues now actively identified their rallying cry, was more extensively elaborated by Seyyed Abolhasan Bani-Sadr (born 1933), a leading Muslim economist who joined the ranks of the Islamic Revolution in Iran. Long before he attained the distinction of becoming the first president of the Islamic Republic of Iran, Bani-Sadr actively participated in anti-Pahlavi movements and wrote extensively on the political economy of oil production in the Middle East in general and Iran in particular.[25] In such works as *Eqtesad-e Towhidi* [A Divine Unitary Economics] (1978) and *Naft va Solteh* [Oil and Domination] (1977), Bani-Sadr argued enthusiastically that the Pahlavi regime was plundering Iranian natural resources and selling them cheaply to the United States and Europe.[26]

Mehdi Bazargan (1907–1995), a quiet revolutionary with an unending admiration for Mahatma Gandhi, became the link between revolutionary ideologues and their targeted audience. Long before he had the precarious distinction of becoming the first (transitional) prime minister after the fall of the Pahlavi regime in 1979, Bazargan had been actively involved in the political mobilization of the professional classes. He was sent to Europe along with a group of other students by Reza Shah in 1929. After receiving an engineering education in France, Bazargan returned to his homeland determined to reawaken religious sensibilities against the rising tide of irreligious sentiments and thoughts and to mobilize the public toward his political ends. In 1961, Bazargan, Taleqani, and a number of other Muslim activists established the Liberation Movement of Iran.[27] Imprisoned for his political activities, Bazargan rewrote a history of the Indian independence movement to express his own wishes for a similar revolutionary movement in his homeland but escape censorship. Bazargan used the occasion of his defense at the Pahlavi court to issue a strong condemnation of tyranny and injustice. After his release from prison, Bazargan wrote and gave public lectures on a variety of issues, all targeted at an active resuscitation of a religious sensitivity conducive to revolutionary changes in the status quo.[28]

Throughout the 1960s and 1970s, the systematic repression of anticolonial nationalism and Third World socialism by a vindictive royal dictatorship paradoxically left its sworn enemy, militant Islamism, relatively free to cultivate a wide-ranging revolutionary agenda. Shi'i revolutionary thinkers, from Al-e Ahmad and Shari'ati to Motahhari and Taleqani, were all busy paving their way toward a revolutionary uprising against the Pahlavi regime while at the same time opposing and bypassing their principal revolutionary rivals—anticolonial nationalism and Third World socialism. In the process, however, and quite paradoxically, they had to internalize and digest the revolutionary projects of their rival ideologies and Islamize them. Islamize them they did, but in doing so they in fact sowed the seeds of their own future undoing by positing a civil society, a political culture, a societal organicity that no single ideology, Islamism or otherwise, could singularly claim and control. Dwelling at the heart of Islamism was the cosmopolitan culture that it had had to face and fathom, and in facing and fathoming it, it swallowed the seeds of its own future undoing.

An Islamic Revolution

By far the most rhetorically successful revolutionary Shi'i was Ayatollah Khomeini, who ultimately engineered the downfall of the Pahlavi monarchy. Born in the small village of Khomein, near Tehran, Khomeini grew up in the immediate aftermath of the Constitutional Revolution, which ushered in the rapid institutionalization of a colonial modernity in Iran. He received his early education in Khomein and Arak and then moved to Qom to pursue his higher scholastic studies, where he was aggravated by the rise to power of the Pahlavis and the even more rapid dissemination of court-initiated modernization. Khomeini watched with visceral contempt the shah's absolutist rule in the late 1950s and early 1960s. Khomeini's 1963 uprising against the shah was based on decades of resentful deliberation in religious and political terms. The increasing indifference of the Pahlavi monarchy to clerical authorities and the American domination of Iranian political, social, economic, and cultural life were the principal points of contention that moved Khomeini to open revolt. After the June 1963 uprising and exile, Khomeini launched a relentless campaign against the legitimacy of the Pahlavi regime and of the monarch's authority. The principal text that Khomeini wrote in this period was *Velayat-e Faqih* [The Authority of the Jurisconsult] (1970), in which he defined the major doctrines of his Islamic government.[29] The driving thesis of *Velayat-e Faqih* is quite simple: the Islamic government established by the prophet Muhammad and (according to the Shi'is) continued by the imams was not meant to be a transitional government. In the absence of the Twelfth Imam, who is now in occultation, the world is plunging deeply into corruption and despair. The Shi'is cannot know exactly when the Twelfth Imam is to appear. In the meantime, the responsibilities of leading Muslim nations cannot be entrusted to corrupt and tyrannical rulers like the shah, who simply aggravate the situation because they are deeply corrupt themselves. At this point, Khomeini accumulates a series of Qur'anic passages and prophetic traditions that he interprets to mean that the (Shi'i) jurists are to assume power, because, by virtue of having access to the specifics of the sacred law, they know how to regulate the daily affairs of Muslims so as to assure their other-worldly salvation. Other than *Velayat-e Faqih*, Khomeini wrote letters incessantly to Muslim student associations in Iran, Europe, the United States, and Canada, inviting and encouraging them to unite and revolt against the Pahlavi regime. Khomeini also wrote extensively on other issues—juridical, mystical, and philosophical in particular. Even some of his poetry has been published posthumously. But the main access to his political ideas remains in his letters, in his proclamations, and in *Velayat-e Faqih*.[30]

As Khomeini's leadership of the Iranian Revolution was gaining momentum late in 1970, in Lebanon another Shi'i cleric, Imam Musa al-Sadr (1928–1978), gave charismatic expression to the hopes and aspirations of the disenfranchised Shi'i community in that war-torn country. Musa al-Sadr was instrumental in turning the Shi'i minority of Lebanon into a major political force that not only the Sunnis and Maronite Christians had to take seriously, but that the two occupying powers, the Syrians and the Israelis, had to recognize. In the summer of 1978, Musa al-Sadr disappeared while on a short visit to Libya.[31]

In the meantime in Iran, after the success of the Islamic Revolution in February 1979, there followed a period of ideological institutionalization of Shi'i political ideas. In this respect, the constitution of the Islamic

Republic of Iran must be considered the latest document in the saga of modern Shi'i political thought.[32] The most prominent Shi'i political theorist after the success of the Islamic Revolution is Abdolkarim Soroush, whose theory of *Qabz va Bast-e Teoric-e Shari'at* [The Theoretical Contraction and Expansion of Religious Law] created much controversy in Iran. In a series of highly effective essays, Soroush worked the ideas of such major ideologues of the Islamic Revolution as Morteza Motahhari into a metanarrative of Islamic revolutionary revivalism. In the same breath he tried to elevate the level of ideological debate in Iran beyond the incessant factionalism of opposing parties that fought for the immediate fruits of their revolution. The result was of course a typical response to such highly effective propositions: while the entrenched clerical establishment smelled disenchantment and trouble from the writings of Soroush, a group of young and disenfranchised Muslim intellectuals began to gather around him. Soroush's serious engagement with the ideological and philosophical consequences of the success of the Islamic Revolution met with no serious critical judgment from those capable of engaging with it on its own terms. But as the most philosophically engaged ideologue of the period after the Islamic Revolution, Soroush has now emerged as the future systematizer of yet another master-dialogue of Shi'ism with its history.[33]

Hidden but still evident in the ideas and aspirations of Abdolkarim Soroush are the syncretic, worldly, and cosmopolitan ones of Ali Shari'ati, now given an even more rooted Islamic gestation. What such Islamist thinkers as Shari'ati and Soroush betray is the fact that what had happened in Iran between 1977 and 1979 was not an "Islamic" revolution but a revolution that was forcefully and violently "Islamized." Soroush himself, early in the course of the revolution, was in fact instrumental in purging the universities of "non-Islamic" elements, openly speaking of the necessity of the "Islamization" of the curriculum. Under two successive covers, the American hostage crisis of 1979–1980 and the Iran-Iraq War of 1980–1988, all the nationalist and socialist alternatives to Islamism were brutally crushed by Muslim militants. The constitution of an Islamic Republic was drafted and imposed on an ideologically and politically far more diversified constituency. The fears of the United States under the two terms of Ronald Reagan's presidency (1981–1988) and the aggressive construction of two bumper zones around Iran, Saddam Hussein and the Iran-Iraq War on its western front and the Taliban and inadvertently al-Qaeda in the east, were equally instrumental in further Islamizing the Iranian revolution. But as it would soon become evident during the Reform Movement and the presidency of Mohammad Khatami (1997–2005), the scarcely hidden, deliberately denied, and brutally suppressed polyvocality of Iranian civil society and political culture could be triggered to action given the slightest opportunity. The entrapment of Shi'ism in a politics of despair had paradoxically formulated its own *pharmakon* (both its remedy and its position, its cure and its kill) by contributing to the making of a larger cosmopolitan political culture and a corresponding civil society that it could not but inhabit via its prolonged contestations with its rival ideologies. The more Shi'ism protested, it protested too much, and even despite itself enriched that civil society. As the presidency of Khatami and the Reform Movement he spearheaded waned, three civil rights movements—women's rights, student uprisings, and labor unions—waxed powerfully, and these sustained the course of a cosmopolitan political culture that has been positively or paradoxically strengthened now for over two hundred years by its friends and foes alike.

11

TOWARD A NEW SYNCRETIC COSMOPOLITANISM

Toward the end of George W. Bush's presidency (2000–2008), a political scientist named Seyyed Vali Reza Nasr published a book about Shi'ism. Vali Nasr at the time was employed by the U.S. military and working at the Department of National Security Affairs at the Naval Postgraduate School in Monterey, California. His book, *The Shia Revival: How Conflict within Islam Will Shape the Future* (2006), was widely received and much celebrated—not just by its immediate military target but in fact by its wider American audience. Employed by a military academy committed to "provide relevant and unique advanced education and research programs in order to increase the combat effectiveness of U.S. and Allied armed forces,"[1] Vali Nasr had written *The Shia Revival* to explain to his students and those in the U.S. military and indeed to the American public at large that the fall of Saddam Hussein had acted as a catalyst, releasing the Shi'is from the Iraqi warlord's tyranny and also creating a "Shia Crescent" that stretched all the way from Lebanon and Syria to Iraq and Iran, through the Persian Gulf, and as far east as Pakistan and India.[2] Expanding on the thesis of an essay he had written two years earlier in 2004, and with a particular vengeance against Ayatollah Khomeini, whose Islamic Revolution in Iran had forced Vali Nasr's monarchist family to flee Iran, the professor of National Security Affairs further argued that prior to Khomeini, Shi'ism had been a rather quietist, spiritual, and ritualistic religion. The upshot of Nasr's argument was that an internecine sectarian opposition between the Sunnis and the Shi'is was not only the source of the carnage in Iraq but a more universal phenomenon affecting the entire region. American policymakers were thus advised to reconfigure their politics of the region, recognizing the Iranians as leading the Shi'i cause and the Saudis the Sunni cause in a deadly millenarian competition for power. Vali Nasr characterized this sectarian split as the single most important force in a region with vital implications for American national security interests.

As Vali Nasr saw the region, "the competition for power between the Shi'is and Sunnis is neither a new development nor one limited to Iraq. In fact, it has shaped alliances and determined how various actors have defined and pursued their interests in the region for the past three decades."[3] The principal point that Nasr was driving home in this thesis is that "the ascendance of Sunni militancy is at the forefront of anti-Americanism in Iraq today and, as such, is likely to spread anti-Americanism in tandem with sectarian tensions throughout the greater Middle East region."[4] For that reason, and to protect American military and strategic interests in the region, American policymakers had a whole new set of factors to consider, Nasr informed them, for "beyond Iraq, U.S. interests and objectives in the greater Middle East are ineluctably tied to the ebbs and flows of Shi'a-Sunni struggles for power. Policymaking must reflect this reality, both by responding to the threat posed by the broader Sunni reaction to Shi'a revival in Iraq and by exploiting the opportunities that the growing Shi'a power in the region presents."[5] With American military domination in the region thus at the forefront of his concerns, Vali Nasr further advised the U.S. military and diplomatic corps that "Shi'a revolutionary activism [as opposed to Sunni militant anti-Americanism] is essentially a spent force. Iran is currently a tired dictatorship teetering on the verge of collapse. The ideas emerging from modern-day Iran, similar to those that characterized the end of the Soviet era, do not support revolutionary fervor but rather demand liberal change."[6] On the basis of this assertion, Vali Nasr then has a number of key recommendations for American military and foreign policy decision makers: "Recognize that the Shi'a-Sunni balance of power is key to regional stability and U.S. regional interests"; "avoid confrontation with Iraq's Shi'a and, most importantly, al-Sistani"; "recognize that Shi'a-dominated countries of Iran and Iraq are better positioned to achieve economic growth and democracy than their Sunni neighbors."[7]

The timely publication of Nasr's essay and then book achieved two crucial objectives at the tail-end of George W. Bush's presidency: it diverted public attention from the catastrophic consequences of the illegal and immoral war in Iraq and the carnage it has caused; and it offered a reading of Shi'ism and Shi'i communities inimical to their historical experiences but in tune with an imperially mandated, sectarian reductionism of worldly and cosmopolitan cultures. *The Shia Revival* was strategically instrumental in redirecting public opinion from the principal and actual source of violence and of the mayhem that the U.S.-led invasion of Iraq had caused, namely George W. Bush's neoconservative ideology, which informed so much of his presidency. The Bush administration was anxious to find a sectarian scapegoat to justify their catastrophic actions in Iraq to an increasingly disbelieving U.S. public. By categorically disregarding the principal culprit of violence in Iraq, Nasr in effect informed his American audience that bloodshed in the region was not the result of an unjustifiable invasion and occupation by the U.S. military of a sovereign nation-state, but the expected result of internecine sectarian violence between the Sunnis and the Shi'is—domestic to Iraq and its neighboring countries.

This aspect of Vali Nasr's thesis hints at the importance of the domestic presidential agenda over the stated global peacekeeping efforts. Such propaganda and its associated Psychological Operations (PSYOP) projects have helped both the U.S. military and the public at large shift the unbearable burden of responsibility to Iraqi, Shi'i, and Islamic factors and forces, effectively exonerating the United States from any blame in the aftermath of the carnage in Iraq. But equally important to Vali Nasr's thesis is a reading of contemporary Shi'ism that is both analytically flawed and categorically detrimental to a historic grasp of Shi'ism and its cosmopolitan context. Given the position of power from which this book was published and disseminated, it helped reduce a polyfocal, cosmopolitan political culture to its sectarian denominator, to which it was of course integral but by no means definitive.

What Seyyed Vali Reza Nasr's book and its central thesis thus effectively demonstrated is the ascendency of a triumphant nativism, born and bred in the United States and aggressively projected against the worldly cosmopolitanism of people, their historical experiences, and their will to resist power. Above all, Nasr's argument shrinks the existing and evident syncretic cosmopolitanism of a world religion to one sectarian aspect. In so doing, he attempts to exonerate the United States from any wrongdoing, but also domesticates and nativizes worldly cultures of resistance to a pre-political, anthropological, and primitive status. The key question, of course, is how one can, under these circumstances, write about or speak of the syncretic cosmopolitanism of a world religion that has been reduced in such a manner to nothing more than sectarian violence. The will to power distorts reality in a manner compatible with its vision of the world, a vision that must dismantle people's will to resist power by first and foremost rewriting it as a primitive, anthropological, and outdated sectarianism.

The Making of a Fractured Imagination

No author is of course singularly responsible for the captured imagination of a public with a very limited vista on the historic experiences of a multifaceted religion, a variegated faith, a polyfocal culture, and its varied communal experiences throughout the ages and across a vast geography. Seyyed Vali Reza Nasr's book is integral to a mode of knowledge production about Islam and Muslims that can only be identified as knowledge under duress. With its roots in pre-9/11 variations on Orientalism and "Area Studies,"[8] what in the United States is now called "National Security Studies" operates on the surface (or else in the deep grammar) of a captured imagination that has come to full fruition in the post-9/11 state of war. At the time in the employ of the U.S. military, Nasr simply partakes in that captured imagination and exacerbates it, seeking to teach his employers how to divide the Muslims along their sectarian lines in order to rule them better (it's an old colonial practice). The standard, as evident in *The Shia Revival,* is to begin with a cursory account of early Islamic history, the Sunni-Shi'i split, a nod to the Battle of Karbala in the year 680, and then to run for a transcontinental jump to the aftermath of U.S.-led invasion of Iraq in March 2003 and the military and diplomatic strategies now facing it. What is lost in the act is not "the complexity" but in fact the simple phenomenological fact of these societies that are thus culturally fragmented and historically foreclosed in order to be politically ruled more effectively. For immediate strategic, military, propaganda, and public purposes such sectarian narratives might indeed be effective and satisfying. But a far more patient perspective is necessary if we are to contextualize and complicate the view of Shi'ism offered by native informers and political scientists from Monterey, California.

The sorts of triumphalist nativism that reduce multifaceted, polyvocal, worldly, transnational, and cosmopolitan cultures to their single-sided, divisive, sectarian, and factional denominators need to be recognized. In particular, we must understand why and how they are produced if we hope to lead them patiently to a much wider and more historically informed understanding of Shi'ism and the Shi'is (and by extension Islam and Muslims).[9] Triumphant nativism, posited against and effectively covering the worldly cosmopolitanism of these cultures, enables these native informers to apply sectarian blinders to others' view of their country of origin (usually the blinders consist of their own identity politics and scholarly interests). This nativism is of course not exclusive to native informers. It applies by extension to the anthropologists who do their "fieldwork" (an apt military term anthropologists use without the slightest hesitation) on Islam and Muslims. In addition, there is a much wider and more global insistence on sectarian identification that feeds on each others' essentialism and is exacerbated by the proximity of an Islamic republic, a Jewish state, a Christian empire, Hindu fundamentalism, and Buddhist nationalism. In the case of Shi'ism proper, the sorts of sectarian reductionism that Seyyed Vali Reza Nasr offers as the basis of his regional geopolitics, seeking to facilitate the U.S. military domination of a strategic area, in fact corroborates the clerical class in Qom and Najaf seminaries and confirms them in their belligerent clericalism, their juridical kidnapping of a polyfocal political world and the violent silencing of the syncretic cosmopolitan cultures to which they are of course integral but by no stretch of imagination definitive. Issued from a position of power, such as a military academy in the heart of an empire, such sectarian visions of the world persist on a myopic politics of despair, which is ultimately rooted in an entrenched mode of self-alienation. Whereas the liberating task of nations and their emancipatory cultures dwells in a recognition of that self-alienation (and the creative and critical *rapprochement* between their politics of despair and their aesthetics of emancipation), the sectarian tribalism that Seyyed Vali Reza Nasr and others propagate sustains and exacerbates it. And as analysts make a lucrative career out of that self-alienation, nations at large suffer the consequences.

Seyyed Vali Reza Nasr's imperial reinscription of the Sunni-Shi'i divide is nothing new in the arsenal of old-fashioned colonialism and its (Roman) logic of divide and conquer. In India, the British took full advantage of an exaggerated reading of the caste system, later systematically theorized by such social anthropologists as Louis Dumont (1911–1998) in his classic reading of the caste system, *Homo Hierarchicus: Essai sur le système des castes* (1966). As Nicholas Dirks has demonstrated in his *Caste of Mind: Colonialism and the Making of Modern*

India (2001), the Indian "caste system," so designated by British colonialism and their social anthropologists, is in fact not a fixed phenomenon in Indian history or society but a recent development stemming from the specific historic encounter between India and British colonialism. The point of Dirks's argument obviously is not that caste does not exist, but that it exists in a state of amorphous fluidity that is narratively solidified and legislated by colonial anthropology and British colonialism in tandem, all by way of facilitating the structural domination of India and its defiant cultures of resistance.[10] The same circumstances are applicable also to the Hindu-Muslim divide in India, or the Catholic-Protestant hostility in Northern Ireland, or the Hutu-Tutsi rivalries under French colonialism in Africa—and it is precisely the same with the Sunni-Shi'i divide in the Arab and Muslim world. It is not that this major sectarian division does not exist in Islam or that it does not matter to Muslims. But it has also existed in a state of historical fluidity, and the sectarian violence between Sunnis and Shi'is is always subject to external factors, which in the contemporary case of Iraq consist solely of the U.S.-led invasion and its campaign of "shock and awe." These external factors are kept *completely* out of Vali Nasr's diagnosis, in effect turning his analysis into a manual of domination, a position paper on how to consolidate and exploit this sectarian history in a manner that facilitates U.S. military ascendency in the region. The narrative consolidation of the sectarian divisions within Iraq is very much the colonial handiwork of the constitution that L. Paul Bremer III, U.S. viceroy to Iraq, (in collaboration with his legal advisor Noah Feldman) wrote for the Iraqis in 2003.[11] These American colonial officers are infinitely more sectarian in their own Orientalist imagination and thus their reading of Iraq than Iraq and the Iraqis are. Contemporary Iraq, like the rest of the region, is the result of, among other things, two hundred years of sustained anticolonial struggles, in which nationalism and socialism are as relevant as militant Shi'ism.

Breaking the Binaries

The active demonization of Islam and the concomitant manufacturing of nativized Muslims as the supreme enemy of "the West" are made possible only through the enduring governance of false binaries between the advanced and the primitive, the secular and the religious, the traditional and the modern, and the West and the Rest. These alienate cultures from themselves, subject their works of art to deadening anthropological curiosity, and posit the native informant as the marker of Man (in order to hide the Western Man's manufactured persona.)[12] So fractured, binary, invaded, and dominated go hand in hand with the act of "studying"—for such "studies" underline and exacerbate the inner logic and deep grammar of colonial domination. *Invading* and *occupying* are coterminous with *studying* and *examining*, which has been the case since Napoleon invaded Egypt and took along a platoon of French Orientalists with him to "study" the Egyptians. Contemporary anthropologists, particularly those of Iranian, Afghan, Palestinian, or Iraqi "origin," are thus instrumental in the paraphernalia of power they represent (but seek to hide). If an anthropologist sports a Latinized name like Pardis, Ali, Nadje, Mehdi, or Roxanne, the native informant's name in fact predisposes the anthropologist to override his or her anthropological pretensions and insecurities. The native informant turned anthropologist becomes the carrier of the male and masculinist colonial gaze into hitherto hidden corners of what Fanon thought were protected areas under the Muslim women's veil.[13]

The binary opposition is narratively manufactured between Sunnism and Shi'ism, divorcing sectarian denominations from the larger political cultures of these countries, including prolonged histories of Third World socialism and anticolonial nationalism. An equally compelling binary is posited between the sacred and the secular—this one categorically disregarding the aggressive globalization of a triumphalist U.S. imperialism or a Eurocentric arrogance that refuses to see the demographic emergence of new forces. All the existing national boundaries are systematically crossed by forces of internet nexus. Violent forces are yielding to nonviolent movements and the pathologies of a dual marginality are yielding to possibilities of amphibian intellectuals, those at home in two or more places, breaking the East-West binaries and creating multiple sites of critical citation. The result is the rise of a hermeneutics of alterity, with an adjacent semiotics of fluidity that allows for multiple sites of contestation against colonial conquest—with Iran, Iraq, and Lebanon as the multiple sites that inform the emergence of a new cosmopolitanism. Historically, from the preparatory stages of the Iranian Constitutional Revolution forward, Shi'ism has been cognitively fused into a worldly cosmopolitanism that is no longer limited to any given country, clime, or culture. By breaking such false binaries into which Islam is habitually trapped, we see through the struggles of millions of Muslims across history who have opposed and are opposing the domestication of their worldly cultures. By contesting such binaries we can tease out the hidden worldliness of cultures, thereby de-anthropologizing worldly cultures and undoing the harm that the army of ethnographers continues to perpetrate on the cosmopolitan world they have categorically failed to envision or inhabit. More than anything else, in this endeavor we need to restore and recognize the syncretic will to resist power that has historically sustained the worldliness of these cultures.

Shi'ism in Disguise

To dispel and dismantle the colonially manufactured myth of a perennial sectarian warfare within Islam, we can scarce do better than to remember Seyyed Jamal al-Din al-Asadabadi (known as al-Afghani; 1838–1897), a singularly significant revolutionary figure in the heat of the European colonial conquest of Muslim lands. It is impossible to exaggerate the significance of al-Afghani in the history of the Muslim encounter with European colonialism. One might in fact argue that the history of the Islamic response to colonial modernity in its entirety, from its philosophical to its political dimensions, is either in anticipation of al-Afghani or an extended commentary on his seminal positions and trailblazing anticolonial struggles. The figure and phenomenon of al-Afghani, as a paradigmatic Muslim revolutionary thinker and activist, looms large over everything that has happened in Muslim lands from the mid-nineteenth century to the present. His Egyptian disciples Muhammad Abduh (1849–1905) and Rashid Rida (1865–1935) in particular carried the legacy of al-Afghani's struggles to the most crucial sites of ideological and political encounters with European colonialism. But his enduring influence is felt today throughout the Islamic world.

By far the most significant aspect of al-Afghani's revolutionary career is his chameleon character. Throughout his tumultuous life—roaming from one end of the Muslim world to another, with regular excursions to European capitals—he consistently and systematically defied and trespassed all internal and colonially manufactured sectarian divisions and territorial boundaries in Muslim lands in a singular and steadfast pursuit of a unified Muslim response to European imperialism. Born and bred as an Iranian Shi'i, al-Afghani repeatedly reinvented himself, most famously as an Afghan Sunni but also as an Ottoman Turk and a South Asian Indian, and from then on became the touchstone of an anticolonial Islamic renaissance in the Arab and Muslim world. Al-Afghani moved freely from Iran to Afghanistan and India, where he pretended to be a Turk from Istanbul and agitated profound anticolonial sentiments. He challenged any sort of conciliatory response to the British. He then arrived in the Ottoman domains, presenting himself as an Indian reformer in order to do the same, and then moved on to Egypt where he posed as an Afghan Sunni. From there he traveled to Paris and London to produce and publish a pan-Islamic vision of anticolonial struggle unprecedented in a world brutalized by European colonialism. He had so successfully covered his Iranian and Shi'i origin, and yet so utterly baffled his principal nemesis, that foreign governments launched intelligence missions to find out his true origin. As Nikki Keddie, who has written a definitive biographical account of al-Afghani in English, has demonstrated, "both the British Foreign Office and the US Department of State at different times launched independent investigations to determine the question of Afghani's birthplace, and both decided unequivocally that he was Iranian."[14] But for the Muslim world at large, al-Afghani defied ethnicity, nationality, and sectarianism and remained a mythic figure beyond the divisive pale of any desperate and self-defeating politics of identity. He systematically and consistently kept up his multiple identities in order to delude his received or fetishized identity politics. In this way he could concentrate on what was most urgent to him: British colonialism, which he considered the principal culprit of the Muslim predicament in modernity.

Decades after his death and as a result of generations of scholarship, we can now view the full panorama of al-Afghani's life, and as we review that life we need to keep in mind that none of these chronological details were in fact all known at the same time to all his immediate followers and supporters. Al-Afghani was born to an Iranian Shi'i family in the village of Asadabad near Hamadan in central Iran in 1838.[15] He received his early education in his hometown and subsequently in Qazvin and Tehran before he went to the Shi'i shrine cities in southern Iraq, where he studied with the leading Shi'i jurists and theologians, became deeply attracted to Islamic philosophical and mystical teachings, and was exposed to the revolutionary ideas of Shaykh Ahmad Ahsa'i. He reached intellectual and political maturity in the heat of the Babi movement in Iran and Iraq. When the Badasht Convention and subsequently the Fort Tabarsi uprising took place in 1848–1849, al-Afghani was a ten-year-old impressionable student. The bloody Babi uprising of Zanjan and Neyriz a couple of years later in 1850–1851 could not have left al-Afghani unimpressed, or the public execution of the Bab himself in 1850. Although he was a very young boy when many of these key events took place, by the time he reached southern Iraq in his late teens or early twenties the remnants of the Babis who had fled Iran were all gathered in the Shi'i shrine cities, and there they undoubtedly made an impression on the young al-Afghani. When the great massacre of the Babis took place in the aftermath of an assassination attempt against Nasser al-Din Shah in 1852, there are reports that al-Afghani left Iran precisely at the same time that many Babis fled their homeland as well. Nikki Keddie also persuasively argues for the similarities between al-Afghani's innovative ideas and those of Shaykh Ahmad Ahsa'i. "Both Afghani's later messianic tendencies," Keddie points out, "and his advocacy of reinterpreting religious doctrines seem to have a basis in Iranian Shi'i traditions." Keddie also correctly links al-Afghani's penchant for philosophical rationalism, in any meaningful encounter with European colonial modernity, to his early exposure to Islamic philosophical sources that were more readily available in Shi'i Iran than in the Sunni Arab world.[16]

After his early education in Shi'i jurisprudence, theology, philosophy, and mysticism in Iran and Iraq, al-Afghani spent a considerable part of the decade between 1856 and 1866 in India, which means the great anticolonial Indian uprising ("mutiny") of 1857 happened when he was on the subcontinent. Keddie suggests this experience accounts for al-Afghani's emergence as "a champion of Muslim struggle against British imperialist encroachments and a violent critic of British rule over Muslims."[17] He may thus be considered as the key and critical factor in the ideological transformation of Shaykhism and Babism from a domestic Shi'i and Iranian issue into a global ideology of resistance against European colonialism in general and British imperialism in particular. "It was in India," Keddie points out, "and specifically from contacts with Indian Muslims under British rule, that al-Afghani first developed his lifelong hatred of the British."[18] The two formative periods of his early life must thus be located in Iran, Iraq, and India. In the first two countries he was raised as a learned Shi'i thinker, young and fresh out of the most significant Shi'i revolutionary movement of the nineteenth century; and in the third country he experienced firsthand the brutality of British colonial domination and the heroic possibilities of taking up arms and opposing it. If he left Iran and Iraq a born and convinced Shi'i, he came to full political fruition in India, cognizant of the larger revolutionary task that all Muslims (Sunni and Shi'i) now faced. The brute vulgarity of the British colonial domination of India must have cured al-Afghani of any sectarian attachment to Shi'ism he may have harbored at the time. There was a much harsher reality and a more urgent task at hand.

After he finally left India, al-Afghani traveled through the Muslim lands, visited Mecca, went to Istanbul, and then sometime in 1866 traveled through Iran and went to Afghanistan. His principal objective while in Afghanistan, between 1866 and 1868, was to encourage Afghan leaders to ally themselves with the Russians against the British. His political sentiments at this point "have the fiercely anti-British tone that was to characterize most of his life."[19] So whatever strategy he devised to defy the politics of identity remained constant throughout his steadfast struggles against domestic tyranny and colonial domination of Muslim lands. His experiences in India and Afghanistan, the two major sites of British colonialism, now focused his anticolonial struggles in wider and more globalized terms. Not only did he conceal his Shi'ism but in fact traded in his Sunni or even Afghan masks for whatever proved politically most expedient at the specific sites he visited.

Al-Afghani's anti-British agitations finally got him expelled from Afghanistan in 1868. He went for another tour of Muslim lands, traveled to Bombay and Cairo, and a year later in 1869 arrived in Istanbul, where he stayed until his expulsion from the Ottoman capital in 1871. While in Istanbul, al-Afghani made the acquaintance of a few high-ranking Ottoman officials and was invited to give a public lecture on modern sciences and industry. The speech, infused with philosophical allusions, incensed the Ottoman 'ulama who in turn forced the officials to expel him. It was by now quite clear that al-Afghani worked on two simultaneous fronts: first, colliding head-on with European colonialism, encouraging Muslim leaders to raise arms against their colonizers; and second, addressing what he believed to be the root cause of Muslim backwardness in science and technology.

His next stop was Egypt, where he spent eight years, between 1871 and 1879, lending political zest and intellectual effervescence to young Muslim militants and their anticolonial aspirations. During this period al-Afghani attracted most of his Egyptian disciples and devotees, chief among them the distinguished reformer Muhammad Abduh. Nikki Keddie rightly attributes aspects of al-Afghani's popularity among young Egyptians to his emphasis on Islamic philosophy, but stops short of suggesting that his turn to Islamic philosophy, deeply rooted in his Shi'i scholastic learning in Iran and Iraq, was in and of itself a transsectarian move, for on the site of philosophy the Sunni-Shi'i bifurcation, or even the emerging ethnic nationalisms, meant very little, if anything at all.[20] The near-decade that al-Afghani spent in Egypt was instrumental the formation of Egyptian anticolonial nationalism, which ultimately led to the Urabi movement. But at the commencement of the movement in 1879, and before the British occupation in 1882, al-Afghani was expelled from Egypt. His sojourn in Egypt was instrumental in turning him into a universal icon of resistance to and struggle against British colonialism. During his time there he won energetic and committed young Egyptian devotees and acquired philosophical momentum to his transsectarian appeal for a Muslim uprising against European colonialism.

It was again time for al-Afghani to change his identity and venue. From Egypt he traveled to Bombay and from there to Hyderabad, where he spent two years, between 1879 and 1882, comingling with Indian Muslims and seeking to affect their perceptions of and reactions to British colonialism. Though the great Indian reformists Sir Seyyed Ahmad Khan (1817–1898) and his followers were very receptive to al-Afghani and welcomed him in India, al-Afghani found their passive submission to scientific rationalism, or "naturism," as it was known, highly objectionable and spent his years in India writing a devastating critique of it. This "critique of materialism" has led such historians as Keddie to speculate that perhaps al-Afghani went through a "religious conversion" back to Islam, which is contradicted, as Keddie herself notes, by signs of freethinking evident in al-Afghani's writings two years after he left India.[21] All such confusions and questions arise if we fail to follow the singular line of al-Afghani's moral, intellectual, and political thrust: steadfast opposition to British colonialism. Everything else was incidental and tangential to that objective. Championing a pan-Islamism that united Muslims against their British occupiers did not need, mean, or amount to a "religious conversion." It comfortably banked on an Islamic cosmopolitanism and scientific culture that had been the defining factors of Muslim culture almost from its very imperial origin. The opposition of al-Afghani to Sir Seyyed Ahmad Khan's colonized mind was all but inevitable from that vantage point. Al-Afghani was after restoring agential autonomy and revolutionary defiance in and about Muslims—and a moral and intellectual self-confidence was definitive to that objective.

Late in 1882 al-Afghani left India for Europe heading to France, where he intended to launch an anti-British campaign to oppose their crackdown on the Urabi movement in Egypt. After a short stop in London, early in 1883 he went to Paris, where he took advantage of inter-European colonial rivalries and began a sustained journalistic career writing against British colonialism and the moral stagnation of Muslim countries. His work culminated in a public debate with the prominent French philosopher and political theorist Ernest Renan (1823–1892). It was in Paris that his chief Egyptian disciple Muhammad Abduh joined him, and together they published their famous periodical *al-'Urwah al-Wuthqa* [The Solid Link] in 1884, an organ of pan-Islamism that remained widely popular and deeply influential for generations to come. Between 1884 and 1885, Wilfrid Blunt (1840–1922), the British poet, essayist, and political polemicist, was instrumental in seeking to implicate al-Afghani in British colonial policies in Egypt and Sudan. His overture toward the British did not succeed in any measurable way, but his pan-Islamist views inevitably endeared him to Sultan Abdülhamid II, emperor of the Ottomans (1842–1918, reigned 1876–1909). His affinity with people in positions of power, Muslim or European, is an obvious extension of his ambitious projects in leading Muslims in their anti-colonial struggles, a goal he achieved as much by way of revolutionary agitation as by diplomatic and political maneuvering among various Muslim and European powers.

From Europe, al-Afghani traveled back to Iran and spent almost two years between 1886 and 1887 trying to agitate anti-British sentiments at the Qajar court and with Nasser al-Din Shah directly. He failed, and soon he departed for Moscow, responding to an invitation from Mikhail Nikiforovich Katkov (1818–1887), the prominent Russian conservative journalist. Katkov died soon after his arrival, but al-Afghani managed to stay put in Russia and continue with agitation against the British in high diplomatic circles in St. Petersburg, where he also met with Nasser al-Din Shah, who was on his way to Europe, and accompanied him to Munich. Trying to appease the Russians, who were incensed by his recent commercial concessions to the British, Nasser al-Din Shah invited al-Afghani to Iran, to which he returned in 1889. This was a period of stagnation in al-Afghani's mass appeal. The more he convinced himself that he had to initiate anticolonial sentiments and actions from the top down, the more he was trapped in superpower rivalries and the internecine intrigues of Muslim courts. In hindsight it is quite obvious that although al-Afghani thought he was influencing high-ranking officials in Ottoman, Russian, French, and Iranian circles, he was himself being manipulated by these powers for their own interests. It is also quite obvious that by now he had all but lost his contact with grassroots revolutionary movements or even their vanguard elite and had become a pawn in high European Realpolitik.

While in Iran, al-Afghani tried to rectify this flaw and reconnect with his followers, especially with a small clique of revolutionary activists, who in turn began agitating against both the Qajars and their connections to the British. Under pressure from the government to leave the country, al-Afghani sought refuge in Shah Abd al-Azim shrine in southern Tehran and continued with his revolutionary agitations. Early in January 1891, he was forcibly removed from the shrine and deported from the country. On his way to London, via Basra and Baghdad, he openly called for revolt against the Qajars and their British supporters. By now, al-Afghani was reconnecting with his Shi'i roots and actively using the Shi'i clerical apparatus in southern Iraq as a springboard for his anticolonial activities. He was instrumental in forcing the Shi'i clerical establishment to issue a *fatwa* [religious edict] against economic concessions to Europeans, particularly in the events leading to the Tobacco Revolt of 1891–1892.

While in London in 1892, he collaborated with a leading Iranian intellectual dissident, Mirza Malkam Khan, and the seeds of revolt he had sown in Iran were quickly sprouting to fruition. Nevertheless, he was once again duped by power and went back to Istanbul on the invitation of Sultan Abdülhamid II, again thinking, in vain, that he would continue with his anti-British activism from the top down. In Istanbul the Ottoman sultan effectively used al-Afghani, and through him other revolutionary activists, to further his own pan-Turkic and pan-Islamic agenda, in which al-Afghani's anticolonial sentiments had little or no place. When in May 1896 one of al-Afghani's Iranian followers, Mirza Reza Kermani, assassinated Nasser al-Din Shah, the Ottoman sultan extradited for immediate execution three prominent Iranian intellectuals residing in Istanbul (Mirza Aqa Khan Kermani, Shaykh Ahmad Ruhi, and Khabir al-Molk) to Iranian authorities, but kept and protected al-Afghani on the pretext that he was an Afghan, but in reality because

"Afghani knew too much about what was going on at the Sultan's court, and particularly about his pan-Islamic activities."[22]

In 1897, al-Afghani died in Istanbul a broken and disillusioned man. But the anticolonial legacy he left behind, the vastly cosmopolitan revolutionary life he led, and the steadfast defiance of identity politics he best exemplified posthumously gave him mythic proportions. After sustained perseverance in historical biography, systematically and successfully dismissing all the fanciful myth manufactured about al-Afghani, Nikki Keddie herself indulges in a bizarre set of speculations about his sexual life, including his supposed "hostility towards relations with women," suggesting that perhaps he was a homosexual.[23] Referring to Harold Lasswell's study, *Psychopathology and Politics* (1960), Keddie even suggests certain common traits of "hyperactivity, high verbal ability, a desire to control others and sway crowds, and delusions of grandeur and of persecution, which Lasswell related to their latent homosexuality or fear of impotence."[24] From these unsupported speculations, Keddie even ventures further and suggests that these "Afghanian features," as she calls them, are in fact common among "many other modern Muslims"—though she does not specify if by this she means modern Muslims are all latent homosexuals or just paranoid schizophrenics.[25]

One need not diverge from verifiable historical inquiry or indulge in such fanciful speculations about a man's sexual proclivities in order to understand what al-Afghani was doing in the latter part of the nineteenth century. The bizarre tendency to pathologize dissent against European colonialism inevitably follows from the assumption that to bend backward and accommodate colonial power is a more "normal" course of behavior. Homosexualizing al-Afghani, castrating him, or positing him as sexually impotent, all speak much more directly to the fanciful anxieties of the self-Westernized historian than the object of her study. At the root of the historian's anxiety is the attribution of homosexuality as a "pathology" to a Muslim revolutionary. There would have been nothing wrong or pathological about al-Afghani even if he were a homosexual—and there is not a shred of evidence that he was, or he was not, or that even if he was, he was a "homosexual" in a generic Euro-American sense of the term.[26] But by creating a psychopathology around homosexuality and then attributing it to a Muslim revolutionary to better explain his steadfast anticolonial struggles over the span of a lifetime, Keddie thus inevitably normalizes others' passive and obsequious acceptance of colonialism. Keddie's outlandish remarks about how al-

Afghani's young male admirers' letters to him are filled with "adoring phrases," or that in a moment of hyperbolic exasperation he threatened he "would cut off his own sexual organs" are, alas, nothing other than indications of a prosaic knowledge of Persian prose and its narrative proclivity to hyperbole.[27] Casting the Muslim male as an infantilized, beardless "nonman" is an old-fashioned visual and emotive trope evident throughout Orientalist paintings.

To this day, al-Afghani is remembered as the founding father of a militant Islamism that dates back to the middle of the nineteenth century and continues to reverberate throughout the Muslim world. The Arab, Iranian, Turkish, and Indian worlds—reformers and revolutionaries alike—claim him with pride and prejudice. The reason for that persistence is that what we see in the figure of al-Afghani is the example par excellence of a politics of revolutionary cosmopolitanism through a Shi'ism in willing and capable disguise. A panoramic look at his life and career shows the ease with which a revolutionary spirit can run like a brushfire across the Muslim lands, defying all the inherited and manufactured politics of identity and despair. Al-Afghani's opting to present himself as an Afghani Sunni obviously was an attempt to account for his mother tongue being Persian and yet to avoid being bogged down by a minority status as a Shi'i or a Persian. Such a label might have worked against the more global anticolonial project he had in mind even early in his career. In his person and in his ideas, in his cosmopolitan character and transnational politics, al-Afghani was the link between the revolutionary spirit of Babism and the geopolitics of anticolonial struggle. It is now important to remember the phenomenon of al-Afghani and his defiance of a limiting politics of identity. British colonialism then sought to accomplish what American imperialism now seeks to achieve in Iraq through such influences as that of Seyyed Vali Reza Nasr—dividing Muslims into Sunnis and Shi'is just as the British divided Indians into Muslims and Hindus, or the Irish into Catholics and Protestants. In Africa, the colonial French divided Hutu from Tutsi. Al-Afghani was a leading revolutionary figure who defied this trap and reached for the core critical issue of his time: colonial domination through fomenting sectarian divisions on one side and writing ethnographic primitivization of them on the other. Al-Afghani's history is the Muslim response to Seyyed Vali Reza Nasr, more than a century before the U.S. military hired Vali Nasr to help it divide the Muslim world in order to rule it better.

In a remarkable way, al-Afghani kept reinventing himself as a work of political art—from an Iranian Shi'i into an Afghan Sunni, then an Indian, and then a Turk, and then trespassing them all into a cosmopolitan revolutionary beyond the pale of his Muslim identity.[28] What ultimately accounted for his transsectarian activism was the presence of British colonialism, which transcended such amorphous divisions and changed the terms of engagement. Today, U.S. imperialism and the presence of Israel, as the last enduring European colonial settlement in the region, act precisely in the same way and transcend sectarian proclivities to become the defining factor in the asymmetric warfare that has ensued. The reason that "the entire first thirty years of his [al-Afghani's] life have been shrouded in mystery, and even his later life has been enveloped in a mythology," or that his disciples in all parts of the Muslim world, particularly in Afghanistan, the Arab world, Iran, and South Asia, claim him all to themselves, is precisely the iconic significance he has assumed in battling colonialism beyond the divisive traps of sectarian politics—to the point that not just anticolonial nationalists but even Third World socialists have found inspiration in his life and achievements. The reason that his memory has not yielded to "an accurate picture of either his life or his thought" is precisely because it is necessary for his transversal image to remain potent, enabling, and mobilizing.[29]

As Nikki Keddie has argued, al-Afghani deliberately and consciously made up stories about his life, and admirable as Keddie's meticulous attempt is to sort out the details of his life, she entirely misses the point of why he kept reinventing himself. The two early biographers of al-Afghani, his disciple Muhammad Abduh and the prominent member of the Egyptian literati Jurji Zaidan, have been instrumental in maintaining the mythical figure of the revolutionary leader by way of sustaining his transversal significance beyond sectarian domains. As Keddie rightly notes, al-Afghani's disguises can be read as a particular marker of his practice of *taqiyeh* [dissimulation].[30] His defiance of sectarian politics is so effective that many of his contemporary critics even accused him of *ilhad* [blasphemy], a charge that even an astute historian like Keddie approvingly reiterates.[31] This accusation stems from a completely Christian conception of "religion" and "irreligion" and disregards the cosmopolitan context of Islam in which no exclusionary orthodoxy, juridical or otherwise, can exclusively limit the definition of what Islam is or what it means to be a Muslim.

A crucial consequence of al-Afghani's creative assumption of multiple identities is to disallow any sort of binary opposition—Sunni-Shi'i, Arab-Iranian, Iranian-Indian, Arab-Turk, or Eastern-Western—to distract from critical attention paid to the central problem of colonialism, foreign domination, and the plunder of weak peoples' natural resources. Equally important in the fact and figure of al-Afghani is a defiant revolutionary agency that preempts the ethnographic primitivization of Muslims as the objects of colonial gaze, a process begun by European and American anthropologists and now carried out by native informants turned anthropologists.

The Formal Destruction of the Politics of Despair

Al-Afghani did in his prolonged battles against European colonialism what today art is harboring for history: a poetics of possibilities in defiance of a politics of despair. The alienated aesthetics that left the estranged Shi'i politics to its own limited devices is definitive to a formal destruction of the politics of despair through varied artistic forms that dwell on the creative consciousness of artists and literati. There is a passage from an aesthetics of emancipation to a renewed syncretic cosmopolitanism that puts everything we see and know about contemporary Shi'ism in perspective. The bifurcated and formalized aesthetics that I have outlined in the previous chapters has effected—through a creative osmosis—a formal destruction of the ideological determinism of the politics of despair that has sustained and defined much of what has happened to Shi'ism over the last two hundred years. Unless and until we can see Abbas Kiarostami as the hidden light behind Ayatollah Khomeini's imposing darkness, a light always pregnant with the otherwise of that darkness, scarce anything in modern Shi'i history will make complete sense.

Working its way toward a new syncretic cosmopolitanism, Shi'ism has relied on that formal aesthetics and has had to navigate its way around its two principal nemeses: Third World socialism and anticolonial nationalism. Positing a militant Islamism beyond sectarian subdivisions, Shi'ism has had to content itself with a modest share in comparison and competition with its two nemeses. Thus predicated on that concomitant aesthetic of emancipation, Shi'ism finally has had to come to terms with a renewed syncretic cosmopolitanism. Shi'ism has thus dwelled in a sublated art form it could not (but) claim as its own. The aesthetics and poetics that informed the alienated self of Shi'ism have had to hide themselves from its politics of despair. In visual, performing, and literary arts, the hidden dream of Shi'ism has formally dismantled nativized sectarianism from within and sustained its cosmopolitanism from without. But globalized imperialism—with its native informers and platoon of anthropologists—has kept positing Shi'ism and the Shi'is as subordinate sectarian and nativist shadows of a protracted modernity. This is the central function of native informers like Seyyed Vali Reza Nasr and the platoon of native and nativist anthropologists that go to Iran, Iraq, Lebanon, or Palestine "to study" them in one way or another. The formal destruction of the politics of despair, through an aesthetics that has consistently worked toward a renewed syncretism, is where Shi'ism is poised to face the world enriched and fortified by the shadow of its own presence in the world. To achieve this full realization, Shi'ism will have to confront and acknowledge its own cosmopolitan context, for without it, Shi'ism is once again reduced to a faded feudal scholasticism with nothing to show for itself.

12

CONTEMPORARY SITES OF CONTESTATION

In mid-April 2009, the British Broadcasting Corporation reported that Egyptian security forces were "scouring the Sinai Peninsula for 13 alleged Hezbollah operatives."[1] These men were apparently identified during the interrogation of some forty-nine Hezbollah suspects that Egypt had arrested. The Hezbollah leader Hassan Nasrallah had confirmed in Lebanon that at least one of the forty-nine arrested in Egypt was in fact a member of his guerilla organization. Whether these Hezbollah activists were in Egypt to engage in guerilla operations against Egyptian targets or just to smuggle weapons and other items into besieged Gaza, or whether they were all Lebanese or Egyptians or perhaps even Palestinians was not quite clear, nor was there any indication of whether they were Sunni or Shi'i. What is clear is that by far the most powerful Shi'i guerilla organization in the Arab world was actively involved in helping Palestinians in Gaza to defend themselves against the Israeli military occupation of their homeland.

Earlier in the year the BBC also reported that Cyprus officials had searched a cargo ship "suspected of smuggling weapons from Iran to the Gaza Strip."[2] The BBC further elaborated: "suspicions that the ship was carrying arms from Iran to Hamas in Gaza were reportedly raised by the US military." The American navy had earlier spotted the Iranian vessel, suspected that it was carrying arms for Palestinians, and made it sail to Port Said, but it had no legal authority to search it. The issue ended inconclusively, except for the fact that the Shi'i leadership of the Islamic Republic was actively involved in helping Palestinians trapped inside their own homeland to fight back against their Israeli occupiers—a situation that had become particularly acute in the aftermath of the Israeli invasion of Gaza in December 2008–January 2009, with massive civilian casualties on the Palestinian side.

The fact that a powerful Shi'i guerilla organization in Lebanon (Hezbollah) and the state apparatus of a Shi'i nation-state (the Islamic Republic of Iran) were actively involved in helping out the overwhelmingly Sunni and in fact Christian Palestinians defend their homeland against colonial occupation is now the defining moment of what Shi'ism means and does in the context of its geopolitics of convictions, commitments, sentiments, and solidarities. In this final chapter I intend to map out the manner in which an emancipated Shi'i politics has now yielded to the possibilities of a renewed syncretic cosmopolitanism, predicated on a state of asymmetric warfare in three major and a number of subsidiary sites of contestation. In Iran, Iraq, and Lebanon, with the non-Shi'i sites of Palestine and Afghanistan as the catalytic forces of everything positive and progressive that might happen in the interlude, Shi'ism is now poised to embrace its renewed, syncretic, and cross-sectarian cosmopolitanism on an asymmetric battlefield of its history.[3]

Looking at the three major sites of combative contestations between Shi'ism and a U.S.-led globalized politics of intervention, occupation, and domination, far beyond the Shi'i doctrinal, normative, allegorical, and metaphoric limits, we see modern Shi'is in direct confrontation with the radical contemporaneity of their own history. From its periodic sectarian propensities, and out of its innate paradoxes of success-in-failure and failure-in-success, and most immediately after two centuries of a self-defeating politics of despair, Shi'ism is now poised, once again, to embrace its cosmopolitan character. The terms of that cosmopolitanism in the Safavid period, before it was aborted by Nader Shah, were domestic to the Shi'i cosmovision. The domain of that cosmopolitanism in the course of the Babi movement in the mid-nineteenth century, before it was crushed by the Qajar aristocracy and their clerical establishment, was limited to an Iranian frame of reference. The terms and domains of this renewed cosmopolitanism are strategically regional and potentially global. The triumph of scholastic clericalism, after the abortion of Safavid cosmopolitanism, has now run its course and a renewed politics of emancipation is fast upon Shi'ism and the Shi'is. The key question is whence this prognosis and wherefore its politics?

A Parting Gift of Grace

Shi'ism entered the nineteenth century trapped inside its historic paradoxes and arrested in a scholastic clericalism devoid of moral courage and creative imagination. The greatest gift at the heart of Shi'ism in the nineteenth century was Babism, a massive social revolution based on a sublime emancipatory theory that restored to Shi'ism its defiant and liberating disposition. Belligerent clerics and their Qajar supporters succeeded in destroying Babism and entrusting the dead corpse of Shi'ism to its clerical custodians. Eventually outwitted by two robust rivals, anticolonial nationalism and an emerging Third World socialism, and while the gift of grace had been finally lost on the remnants of Babism, Shi'ism faced European colonial modernity trapped inside an endogamous juridicalism.

Anticolonial nationalism early in the nineteenth century and Third World socialism later in the same century emerged as far more potent and mobilizing forces than Shi'ism or Islam throughout the Muslim world. As the Shi'i clerics presided over a dead and deadening Shi'i scholasticism, the intellectual and artistic elite of nations at large were drawing their worldly aspirations from moral forces already aroused by anticolonial nationalism and transnational socialism. The eventual appearance of a simplified and far-reaching prose, the introduction of printing machines, the emergence of newspapers and magazines, a rise in literacy, the dispatch of students and travels of merchants around the world and the publication of their travelogues, a massive translation movement from European sources, the formation of a widespread public space, the eventual levitation of such modern literary forms as novels, novellas, and short stories, the daring introduction of groundbreaking changes in Arabic, Persian, Turkish, and Urdu poetics and dramaturgy were chief among institutional and narrative developments that redefined Muslim nations at large and opened up much wider and more inviting horizons for them.

The political adventures and ideological daring of Seyyed Jamal al-Din al-Afghani toward the latter part of the nineteenth century shows, more than anything else, how under colonial duress the best of Shi'ism, always hidden in its sinuous scholastic labyrinths, can emerge in disguise and wed its creative forces with the most timely, the most progressive, and the most acutely historical. With Afghani's Shi'ism in disguise, the Shi'i aesthetic gift of grace had also gradually abandoned it, as the creative and critical souls of Shi'ism sought formal emancipation from all forms of inherited dogmatism. At the height of its aesthetic confidence, Shi'ism was definitive to Safavid art and architecture, but nothing of the sort can be said of the Afsharid, Zand, or even Qajar periods, when the true and the beautiful wandered for decades and finally came to magnificent fruition in entirely altered worlds. In prose, poetry, and drama, the best of the Shi'is, just like Afghani in his transsectarian politics, went into hiding and sought greener creative pastures to roam. This is the great period of *al-nahda,* the moral and intellectual awakening in the Arab world that began late in the nineteenth century, with its counterparts in the rest of the Muslim world.[4] Widespread exposure to European colonial modernity had opened Muslims' moral imagination to new horizons, and they were partaking in it in generous and emancipatory portions. Meanwhile the false and falsifying binary between the sacred and the secular soon descended upon Muslims and distorted the nature and disposition of this awakening. The most progressive and emancipatory dimensions of Muslims' thoughts and creativity were branded as secular, Western, or modern while ipso facto manufacturing a falsely sanctified domain in which were seized and arrested certain doctrinal or institutional dimensions of Islam now branded immutable and immune to history. The false binary was self-alienating and divisive, casting one group of Muslims against another, distancing one fragmented vision of Islam from the next. This self-alienation of Muslims in general and the Shi'is in particular from their own moral and aesthetic imagination is by far their most significant historical trauma in the course of colonial modernity.

But by now the selfsame alienating colonial forces that had caused a schizophrenic split in Shi'ism (and Islam in general) were afoot and instrumental in manufacturing a figure like Afghani, who delivered Shi'ism in disguise: the overtly juridicalized faith abandoned its endemic sectarian politics of desperation and faced the colonial reality of its current history. Thus in disguise, Shi'ism leaves its endogamous clericalism behind and meets the challenges of its contemporary history face to face. The figure of Afghani remained relevant and forceful at the turn of the century in such massive social movements as the Urabi Revolt of 1879–1882 in Egypt and the Constitutional Revolution in Iran, in which a progressive and forward-looking Islam (Shi'ism) joined forces with anticolonial nationalism and transnational socialism, which now commanded considerable force in the region. As Baha'ism ran the revolutionary legacy of Babism aground and lent to it a jaundiced pacifism at best or complicity with British colonialism at worst, in the figure of Afghani and the range of revolutionary sentiments he generated and sustained, the Babi movement was successfully resurrected and wedded to the worldly aspirations and noble struggles of millions of human beings across the Muslim lands. In the figure of Afghani, one might in fact suggest, the revolutionary Shi'ism embedded in Babism was sublated into a much larger global Islamic space, where the aborted project of a public space was once again resumed and finally given a far more worldly domain and cosmopolitan character. Afghani is the link between the precolonial revolutionary disposition of Babism and the anticolonial phase of Shi'ism—effectively rescuing the Babi revolutionary spirit from the pacifism of the Baha'is and updating it to face the brutalities of the colonized world. In the figure of Afghani also dwells the creative effervescence of Shaykhism and Babism, which he creatively retrieved and wedded to a renewed syncretic cosmopolitanism beyond borders and national or sectarian identities. In this respect his identification with Afghanistan, a manufactured colonial concoction, was positively ingenious.

Thereafter, a beleaguered and outdated juridical Shi'ism was entangled in a prolonged battle with anticolonial nationalism and socialism, vying for power in a collective struggle against domestic monarchical tyranny and European colonial incursion. The creative soul of Shi'ism left it behind and resumed an autonomous life of its own. Left a soulless body, Shi'ism was trapped in a politics of despair. Decades after the Constitutional Revolution of 1906–1911, only Ali Shari'ati can be noted for trying to rescue it from its sectarian cul de sac by wedding it to wider emancipatory movements around the globe. It was in Paris, after connecting with progressive European anticolonial movements as well as actively partaking in African and Latin American revolutionary uprisings, all underlined by his correspondence with Frantz Fanon, that Shari'ati learned the manner and mode of rescuing Shi'ism from its sectarian trap.

My contention is that it is only through coming to terms with Shi'ism's ideological rivals, the shadows of its claims on universality, through a reinvocation of its theodicy, that Shi'ism can also come to terms with its own collective creative unconscious. For the body and soul of Shi'ism—its scholastic learning and its creative ego—to come together, first and foremost it has had to come to terms with its ideological rivals. With that creative ego having left it soulless and entrapped in a politics of despair, Shi'ism realizes its creative soul—now soaring freely in art and poetry, cinema and drama—only in the alienated faces of its ideological others. Under U.S. stratagems to abort the Islamic Revolution and prevent its universal appeal, the worst came out of Shi'ism. It devoured all its own children, killed its rivals, reenacted itself as a son-religion, killing its own sons and daughters and mourning them by sitting on the soulless belligerence of a politics of despair. Facing the United States and Israel, with the nobility of the Palestinian cause and the desperation of the Afghan people on two adjacent horizons as its catalyst, the hidden universalism of Shi'ism can emerge for another historic visitation. What I suggest is not a wish or an imposition on Shi'ism. It is for Shi'ism to fully realize its own historic *Geist,* if Hegel were to describe it. Without embracing the non-Shi'i causes of Palestine and Afghanistan, the Shi'i causes of Iran, Iraq, and Lebanon will degenerate into self-defeating sectarianism of the worst kind, which will best benefit the beleaguered mullas in Iran and the aging potentates of Saudi Arabia. Such sectarian violence is precisely what feeds the militarist analytics of U.S. strategists like Seyyed Vali Reza Nasr or the U.S. Iraqi viceroy L. Paul Bremer III.

By virtue of their demographic diversities, in Iraq and Lebanon Shi'ism has already been forced to face its syncretic disposition—and so could these two countries effectively embrace the multiculturalism of Palestine and Afghanistan. It is through those adjacent sites that the emerging geopolitics of the region will restore the syncretic cosmopolitanism of Iran—and this is precisely what military strategists like Vali Nasr wish to dismantle and prevent. U.S. strategists seek to finish what Bremer and his legal advisor Noah Feldman have already started by drafting an Iraqi constitution in a manner that robs Iraqis of not only their natural resources and strategic significance, but also their historic cosmopolitan character, a character that has endured as one of the crowning achievements of Arab cultural renaissance.

Shi'is now have the option of pursuing sectarian defeatism, following the desires of the Bush presidency, or else retrieving, restoring, and resuming their historic march toward a full-bodied self-recognition—in body and soul—of their embedded doctrinal proclivities. Syncretic cosmopolitanism is evident in the doctrinal DNA of Shi'ism throughout its long and varied history. Every time Shi'is have come close to recognizing it fully they have been a beacon of hope for the poor, the weak, and the forsaken, and every time they have been furthest away from it they have been the damnation of the earth. From the archetypal figures of Ali and Hossein down to the revolutionary movements of Zaidism, Isma'ilism, the Qaramita, the Hurufiyyah, and the Sarbedaran, and on to the Safavid cosmopolitanism and their School of Isfahan and ultimately to the Babi movement, Shi'ism has been the vanguard of hope and inspiration for revolutionary uprising and the restoration of earthly justice. The phenomenal figure of Afghani linked the very last of these movements, that of Babism, to the fate of Muslims around the world under the cutting edge of European colonialism. Now a compelling globalized condition has given the syncretic cosmopolitanism of Shi'ism a renewed promise—from its scholastic reason to its public reason to its alienated aesthetic reason, now Shi'ism faces the possibility of a full-bodied recognition of the moral and normative reunification of its body and soul.

Shi'ism in Dissolution

Shi'ism, with a prolonged history of militant political activism, reentered the regional political scene in the late 1970s with the advent of the Islamic Revolution. Once again it wrote itself into the larger transformative domains of a global claim on Islam and Muslims and into the making of a massive social revolution. The anticolonial postures of Shi'ism during the Perso-Russian wars of 1804–1813 and 1826–1828, the Babi revolution of 1848–1850, the Tobacco Revolt of 1891–1892, the Constitutional Revolution of 1906–1911, the anticolonial uprising of the 1920s in Iraq, and the June 1963 uprising led by Ayatollah Khomeini ultimately culminated in the Islamic Revolution of 1977–1979 and placed Shi'ism on an entirely unprecedented regional and global stage.

The appeal and significance of the Islamic Revolution went far beyond Iran or Shi'ism and reached farthest into the heartland of the Arab and Muslim world. This Iranian revolution has never been called a "Shi'i" revolution, always an "Islamic" revolution, for not a single ideologue, militant or moderate, turbaned or tied, thought of himself as a Shi'i revolutionary before thinking himself a Muslim. It is imperative now to keep in mind that Shi'is have never considered themselves Shi'is who happen to be Muslims, but exactly the opposite, Muslims who happen to be Shi'is. Shi'ism for the Shi'is is a take on their Islam, not Islam a take on their Shi'ism. Undue emphasis is put on the distinction between orthodoxy and heterodoxy in Islam or any other religion. Every religious orthodoxy is a politically successful heterodoxy. The political logic of that medieval fact transcends any single world religion and has a larger claim on universality. What ultimately emerged as the Islamic Revolution in Iran was never branded a "Shi'i revolution" in its character or disposition, political aspirations or institutional foregrounding.

That revolution always had a global claim on Islam and the world it inhabited. From its very first rumbles, the Islamic Revolution had regional, cross-sectarian, and even trans-Islamic aspirations. Ali Shari'ati was dead by the time the revolution broke out, but he and his universal conception of a global revolution against domestic tyranny and transnational colonialism were integral to the massive social uprising he in part anticipated. The same is true about Ayatollah Khomeini or any other leading revolutionary of the movement. Khomeini never thought of himself as an exclusively Shi'i leader after the interests of the Shi'is. He had a global revolutionary mission—as did Jalal Al-e Ahmad, Morteza Motahhari, Mahmud Taleqani, Mehdi Bazargan, and other leading ideologues of the Islamic Revolution in Iran. Shari'ati took his inspirations from Che Guevara and Frantz Fanon, Al-e Ahmad from Antonio Gramsci, Bazargan from Mahatma Gandhi, Motahhari from Allamah Iqbal. To the degree that Islam was instrumental in the making of the Iranian revolution of 1977–1979—a claim it must always equally share with anticolonial nationalism and Third World socialism—that Islam was never overtly branded as Shi'i. In the modernity of its current history, Shi'ism has worked best in disguise—from Seyyed Jamal al-Din al-Afghani to Ruhollah Khomeini, but perhaps best represented in the global vision of Ali Shari'ati. Shari'ati injected a deeply rooted anticolonial nationalism, a wide spectrum of Third World socialism, and a deeply humanist reading of European existentialism into the making of his revolutionary Shi'ism. His Shi'ism was thus a camouflage for all the revolutionary traits he encountered in Europe, and those in turn he disguised into their collective sentiment, which was in extra-Shi'i registers.

The Shi'is have always thought of themselves as Muslims. Sectarian thinking in and out of Muslim communities is always a matter of external political manipulation of internally dormant doctrines. Throughout history, every single revolutionary uprising for or against Shi'ism has had more immediate material and political causes and consequences. Today only the United States, Saudi Arabia, and al-Qaeda speak of Shi'is as Shi'is, for Shi'is themselves think of their identities as integral to the Muslim world at large. The reason for Iranian support for the Lebanese Hezbollah is not because they are Shi'is; nor do Iranians withhold their even more active support for Hamas because they are not Shi'is. What do American military strategists like Seyyed Vali Reza Nasr, Saudi shaykhs and military warlords, and violent al-Qaeda operatives have in common? A common interest in dividing the Muslim world along sectarian lines to better dominate it. Bremer and Feldman wrote a bitter sectarian factionalism into the very fabric of the Iraqi constitution (very much on the model of the French in Lebanon), and then Nasr theorized the strategy and put a larger strategic spin on it. The Saudis detest the Shi'is not just because their minority status exposes the medieval potentates for what they are but because a Sunni-Shi'i divide gives them, as well as the other Arab tribal chieftain King Abdullah II of Jordan, an inroad into Iraq.

The transnational politics of the region can never be assayed in singularly sectarian terms. The Iran-Iraq War (1980–1988) placed two overwhelmingly Shi'i populations against each other, and for eight long and bloody years Shi'is were slaughtering Shi'is—but their being Shi'i had scarcely anything to do with the causes, the catastrophe, or the consequences of the war. The United States and its allies militarily fed and fortified Saddam Hussein's megalomaniacal tyranny as a ploy to prevent the spread of the Iranian revolution westward. Saddam Hussein fought his war not with Shi'ism but with a strong sense of messianic Arab nationalism, launching a war against "Persians." He considered this war the second Qadisiyyah, named after the famous Battle of al-Qadisiyyah in 636 in which the Muslim Arab army defeated the Sassanid dynasty in a decisive encounter. Hussein commissioned the prominent Egyptian filmmaker Salah Abouseif (1915–1996) to make a propaganda film, *Al-Qadisiyyah* (1982), on that theme. On the Iranian front, the war had nothing to do with Shi'ism. This was a battle for Qods, for Jerusalem, for Palestinians, as most of the battle cries, slogans, and warfront billboards testify.[5]

A similar scenario holds true in Afghanistan in the aftermath of the Soviet invasion and occupation of that country (1980–1988). The United States, during the Reagan administration, created the Afghan Mojahedin from the same pool from which the Taliban would later emerge in order to forge a force to fight against the Soviets and (given the Wahabi disposition of the Mojahedin and Taliban) to manufacture a Sunni front as a buffer for the Islamic Revolution in Iran, which now suddenly assumed a Shi'i disposition in the eyes of its American and Saudi beholders.[6] But the fact is that before the Americans, the Saudis, and the Pakistanis conspired to manufacture the Afghan Mojahedin, the Islamic Revolution in Iran was just that, *Islamic*—in addition to its anticolonial nationalist and socialist dimensions. It was the manufacturing of the Mojahedin/Taliban as a Sunni (Wahabi) force that suddenly gave the Islamic Revolution a Shi'i denomination. Add to that phenomenon the fact that before its militant Islamization, the Iranian revolution of 1977–1979 was not even exclusively Islamic, though Islamism was integral to it. A wide range of political sentiments and forces from anticolonial nationalism to transnational socialism were equally integral to that revolution. Militant Islamism ultimately succeeded in outmaneuvering nationalist (the National Front) and socialist (the Tudeh Party and the Fedayeen Guerrilla Organization) forces not just by brutally suppressing them but also by subsuming their respective ideologies into its own parlance and practices. The exclusive Shi'i reductionism of the massive social revolution was almost entirely a U.S. project—attained by active collaboration among American, Saudi, and Pakistani regional interests.

If we now turn to a wider circle of regional politics, the rise of Hezbollah in Lebanon in the 1980s is a direct result of the Israeli invasion of 1982, adding fuel and momentum to the historically disenfranchised Shi'i community of Lebanon. The origin of the sectarian divisions in Lebanon goes back to its colonial history in the aftermath of the First and Second World Wars. In 1943, the political foundations of the modern Lebanese state apparatus were established, and based on a 1932 census it was colonially mandated that the president of the new republic would be a Maronite Christian, the prime minister a Sunni Muslim, and the Speaker of the Chamber of Deputies a Shi'i Muslim.[7] A typical colonial manufacturing of sectarian politics, this division put the increasingly expanding Shi'i community at a political disadvantage. It was in the aftermath of the September 1982 Israeli invasion of Lebanon and subsequently the October 1983 bombing of U.S. and French headquarters, in which 241 U.S. marines and 56 French paratroopers were killed, that militant Shi'i groups entered the Lebanese political scene in earnest. By 1993, the threat of Hezbollah to Israeli military superiority in the region was powerful enough for the Jewish state to launch yet another attack into Lebanon. The same targeting of Hezbollah was repeated in 1996—again to no avail, and in fact strengthening their position even more. By the year 2000, Hezbollah had forced the Israeli forces to withdraw from Lebanon, thus emerging as a champion of Lebanese national liberation from colonial conquest and military occupation. The July 2006 invasion of Lebanon with the specific intent of destroying Hezbollah had exactly the opposite effect: it exponentially strengthened its military potency and made it, as a Shi'i guerilla operation, infinitely more powerful in the Lebanese context than ever before. But even today, it is impossible to understand the regional significance of Hezbollah without first and foremost placing it within the Lebanese body-politic in which it has to share power with not only non-Shi'i (Sunni) forces but even non-Islamic (Christian) and nondenominational (nationalist and socialist) forces. The assassination of Prime Minister Rafik Hariri and then of the prominent journalist Samir Kasir in 2005 has in fact galvanized a significant portion of Lebanese against the Hezbollah.[8]

The rise of Hezbollah in Lebanon must of course be read along with the rise of Hamas in Palestine, and that in turn in the context of the First and then the Second Intifada as two key catalytic factors in the regional politics that has scarce anything to do with either Shi'ism or the Shi'i-Sunni hostility.[9] Hamas, *Harakat al-Muqawamat al-Islamiyyah,* was formed in 1987 by Shaykh Ahmed Yassin (1937–2004)—an almost blind paraplegic invalid that the Israeli military assassinated in 2004—and his comrades at the beginning of the First Intifada.[10] The increasing popularity of Hamas was proportionate to the emerging unpopularity of Fatah and other components of the Palestinian national liberation movement, who had been unable to secure any concession from Israel since the 1967 appropriation of even more Palestinian territories into the Jewish state. As a widespread network of social, humanitarian, and civic administrations, adjacent to a committed determination in civil uprising and resistance operations against the colonial domination of Palestine, Hamas soon outmaneuvered Fatah and gained the confidence, admiration, love, and ultimately the vote of Palestinians in a general election in 2007. Despite its immense popularity, Hamas still does not represent the entirety of the Palestinian population or even electorate and is but one component of the Palestinian national liberation movement, which remains consistently polyvocal, cross-sectarian, and in fact global in its appeal to a wide range of people around the world. To the degree that Muslims, let alone Shi'is, actively or passively support the Palestinian cause in general or Hamas in particular the entire movement ipso facto casts the resistance in the region into a transnational and cosmopolitan syncretic force engaged in an asymmetric warfare against the United States and Israel.

Iran has an overwhelmingly Shi'i population, and significant percentages of people in Iraq and Lebanon are also Shi'is. Integral as Shi'ism is to the political culture of these nations, it has never been singularly definitive to it. Israel as a colonial settlement on Palestinian territories and the United States as a superpower now seeking to secure its military, economic, and strategic domination in the region have perforce created hostile conditions in which a cross-sectarian regional alliance of resistance forces is all but inevitable—and this resistance cannot be divided along sectarian lines. This is how throughout the decade of the 1990s Iran—in active collaboration with oppositional forces inside Iraq, Lebanon, Afghanistan, and Palestine—was locked in a confrontational posture vis-à-vis Israel and the United States. In the making of this regional geopolitics, Shi'ism was almost completely sublated into either nationalist registers or else disguised in transnational Islamism, anticolonial struggles, and an expansive opposition to the American imperial take on a New World Order. However different their domestic policies might have been, in terms of their global and regional policies, presidents Ronald Reagan (1981–1988), George H. W. Bush (1989–1992), and William Clinton (1993–2000) shared a common, belligerent, pro-Israeli militancy in the last quarter of the twentieth century that deeply offended many and widely aggravated anti-American and anti-Israeli militancy. In the general configuration of that emotive universe, Shi'ism was but one mobilizing force whose color and character was present and palpable only by being dissolved into the admixture of a much more diversified and pluralist culture of resistance.

9/11 and the Emerging Politics of Resisting an Empire

The events of 9/11 in 2001 thoroughly shifted the political language and landscape of global conversation about "Islam and the West" and gave it a decidedly civilizational tonality. The violent acts of a band of militant adventurers were narrated into a grand metanarrative of an Armageddon encounter between forces of Good ("the West") and Evil ("Islam"). In the writing of this scenario there was no provision or special role made or assigned to Shi'ism. It in fact took quite some time for American neoconservative ideologues to convey to President George W. Bush that there was this Sunni-Shi'i division among Muslims that they could exploit for immediate and far-reaching purposes. The triumphalist tribalism of the American neoconservative movement thus projected itself onto its principal nemesis and sought and secured an equally tribal sectarianism among Muslims. By the time L. Paul Bremer, Noah Feldman, and Seyyed Vali Reza Nasr had written a divisive sectarianism into Iraqi and by extension regional politics—to divide Muslims to rule them better—the geopolitics of resistance to American and Israeli militarism had far more emancipated and enabling parameters informing it than evident in the texture and tenure of this presumed and imposed sectarianism.

In the long and arduous years of George W. Bush's War on Terror, Iran, Iraq, Lebanon, Afghanistan, and Palestine were interlocked in a regional geopolitics of asymmetric warfare. With Iranian military and paramilitary forces in conjunction with Hezbollah and Hamas on one side, and Israel and the United States on another, and the wild card of al-Qaeda in the middle, the im/balance of power has now completely bypassed the parameters of conventional warfare. A turbulent world now forces Shi'ism into a renewed pact with the contemporaneity of its history. In this renewed pact, from Seyyed Jamal al-Din Afghani in the late nineteenth century to Ali Shari'ati in the late twentieth century, a sublated Shi'ism has a historic rendezvous with its history. In this sublation, Ali Shari'ati remains a paramount figure, accomplishing what Seyyed Jamal al-Din Afghani achieved almost a century before him but in precisely the opposite direction. Shari'ati remains a revolutionary model of staying put within Shi'ism, wearing his Shi'ism on his sleeve, and yet ever so successfully opening the moral and imaginative wings and vistas of the faith to embrace emancipatory forces from Latin America to Asia, from Africa to the Arab World, from Che Guevara to Frantz Fanon. The contemporary sites of historic contestation between the will to power and the will to resist power are poised to save and rescue Shi'ism from its inherited paradox of success-in-failure and failure-in-success, as well as from its politics of despair, all through a dissolution of the defiant tenets of Shi'ism into the transformative force of its contemporary history. Only through this dissolution does Shi'ism dissolve into the world, reading its own innate paradox of being at odds with itself into the parallax of being at odds with an unjust world that is at odds with itself. Released from its politics of despair, the historically emancipated Shi'ism has yielded to the widespread possibilities of a renewed syncretic cosmopolitanism that once again embraces the world and allows its sublated forms to engage its history. Predicated on a state of asymmetric warfare in three major and a number of subsidiary sites of contestation, Shi'ism has now reached its originary character as the hidden soul of Islam, its sigh of relief from its own grievances against a world ill at ease with what it is. From a religion of protest at odds with itself, Shi'ism is now a cry of freedom in a world at odds with itself.

CONCLUSION

I have taken my time and laid out in extended detail a schematic theory of Shi'ism as a religion of perpetual protest. I have asked for and indulged in your generous patience in order to lead you in a leisurely but purposeful journey from the very inception of Shi'ism early in Islamic history in the mid-seventh century to the dawn of colonial modernity in the eighteenth century, and then to our own contemporary sites of militant contestations in the first decade of the twenty-first century. In this journey I have intended for you to serve as a witness to the prolonged and persistently unfolding soul of a people and the measures and manners that have moved and mobilized them. That I am one of these people by birth and breeding, as you might or might not be, has placed me in the paradoxical position of both showing you things you would not have otherwise seen and yet doing so through and not despite the blind spots that enable my own vision of things. Visions, as you must know, are made possible not despite our blind spots but in fact because of them.

I commenced this journey by first detailing for you the doctrinal foundation of Shi'ism as a son-religion, a religion that began not by the proverbial Freudian murder of the father and the civilizing guilt that it entails but by the murder of an archetypal son and the collective guilt that subsequently becomes definitive to a paradoxical revolutionary reason as an unending compensation for that guilt. Then I moved on to give you a reading of Shi'ism in its variegated history. The historical unfolding of the Shi'i doctrines, in their full defiant dimensions, has worked the paradoxically posited revolutionary reason through successive social uprisings and, alternatively, through the formation of vast and powerful dynasties. Finally, I have argued, in the makeup of the Safavid dynasty in the sixteenth century we witness the possibility of that revolutionary reason transmuting into what we might today call a public reason. That long and arduous process, I demonstrated in some detail, ended in failure following first the Afghan invasion that put an end to the Safavid empire in 1722 and then Nader Shah's categorical resumption of a tribal political culture. I have also demonstrated that through the massive revolutionary uprising of Babism in the mid-nineteenth century this public reason was re-linked to its revolutionary origin and then sought to be thematically expanded and socially multiplied.

The way I read Shi'ism, for this move from revolutionary reason to public reason to be historically grounded, makes it inseparable from and entirely contingent on how we understand Islam in its entirety. Following this line of argument, my principal thesis in this book has been that Shi'ism is both a festive and a furious occasion of ritually remembering its murderous myth of origin in ever more forgetful ways. I have suggested that the combined effect of a "deferred obedience" (as Freud understood it) and infanticide (as opposed to patricide) has cast Shi'ism into a state of permanent deferral, a deferred future, guilt-ridden not for having killed the father but for having murdered the son, which has in political terms caused a state of permanent revolutionary defiance. If, as I have suggested, the combined effect of a "deferred obedience" and infanticide has cast Shi'ism into a state of permanent deferral, the charismatic condition of their infallible imams has made that deferral normatively combustible and politically explosive. I have thus offered Shi'ism as the Shadow of Islam, never allowing it to accept or believe in its own victories, its affirmations of the world. I believe that for a long time Shi'ism has been considered a mere sect within Islam, alienated from its natural habitat not just by its historians but by Muslim heresiographers themselves. Instead I have sought to offer Shi'ism as the deferred Shadow of Islam *supplementing* Sunnism as the triumphant doubt of Islam. Meanwhile, the compliant Sunnism protests too much, denying the return of its own repressed as Shi'ism. In this sense, I have offered a reading of Shi'ism that makes it inseparable from Islam, a not-so-hidden hole in its soul that sustains its emotive membranes.

Halfway through my book I moved by necessity from a historical perspective to a theoretical one. I addressed a normative dislocation that occurs in Shi'ism via a schizophrenic split between its politics and its aesthetics. With its quest for a public space and a public reason successively denied and aborted, and under pressure from the onslaught of a colonial modernity that manufactured its own public space and public reason, the Shi'i schizophrenic split takes place between an urgent politics of despair and a meandering aesthetic of formal destruction, causing a deep alienation in the Shi'i collective consciousness. The advent of European colonialism, I argued, ultimately aborts altogether the possibility of public reason in specifically Shi'i terms. This in turn causes a traumatic epistemic shift in Shi'ism after which its politics of despair becomes endogamous and excessively self-indulgent, and as such exponentially distanced from its alienated aesthetics of emancipation. The serendipitous but auspicious outcome of an otherwise alienated aesthetics, I suggested, amounts to an internal transmutation of public reason into an aesthetic reason.

Why, you might ask, has it taken so long for us ("us" meaning Shi'is) to see through this schizophrenic split at the heart of Shi'ism—with its politics getting recalcitrant while an emancipated aesthetics carries on a cosmopolitan culture of critical creativity? This question will have to be answered by way of the falsifying delusion of "secularism." As a false category, secularism (or Westernization, or modernization) has hitherto concealed this split and alienated Shi'ism and the Shi'is from themselves and their formalized and estranged aesthetics in visual, literary, and performing arts. It is as if the soul of a person has vacated its body and wandered away while the body lies about, not knowing what to do with itself. After this schizophrenic split takes place, an alienated aesthetic formalism goes one way, and a compelling politics of despair goes another. One is falsely branded "secular" and the other "religious." A deeply schizophrenic culture convinces and divides a people in utter desperation. They dream their best in their art and then they damn themselves in their politics—and yet (strangely) they don't seem to see the link. Except in the dramaturgical attraction of artists and literati to Ta'ziyeh, I have argued, this link between the two Janus faces of Shi'ism has been kept hidden and denied. Filmmakers like Bahram Beiza'i, theater directors like Mohammad Ghaffari, novelists like Mahmoud Dolatabadi, and dramatists like Akbar Radi have been directly involved with the Karbala theme in their respective work. But even prominent poets like Forough Farrokhzad, Sohrab Sepehri, Mehdi Akhavan Sales, or Ahmad Shamlou, each in his or her own particular way, divulged the link between a sublated Shi'i martyrology or eschatology and their visions of the true, the beautiful, and the sublime. Through a releasing of the collective repression and the de-fetishization of the alienated labor one might thus both see and reverse the historic split that has happened and alienated Shi'ism from itself. The body and soul, to continue with the same metaphors, can thus recognize and come back to inhabit and animate each other in a wholesome return.

This move was thus necessary to demonstrate the syncretic reunification of Shi'ism with its alienated aesthetic reason—now fully blooming and triumphant. The historical process, or (nonteleological and entirely accidental) evolution, from a revolutionary reason to a public reason had historically faced a cul de sac. But now it was rescued via the creative formation of an aesthetic reason. This aesthetic reason I offered as the dream of Shi'ism of itself, which now finally triumphs and expands the faith to the frontiers of a renewed cosmopolitan syncretism. At the culmination of this trajectory the aesthetic reason informs the revolutionary reason that it has retrieved and preserved in its heart, and informs the now globalized public reason in which Shi'ism finds and recognizes itself. What is important in this process is how as the self-defeating Shi'i politics of despair (we can code-name it "Khomeini") faced a cul de sac, its formally pregnant aesthetic formalism (we can code-name it "Kiarostami") went global. It paved its own way, informing revolutionary reason and making a globally public space and thus a public reason. This renewed public space was occasioned not by public reason but by public art—an art that has come out of both the monarchs' courts and the mullas' mosques, and yet kept its sacred serenity intact. Facilitated by public art, a syncretic cosmopolitanism emerged out of medieval Adab literary humanism and joined the premodern to late Ottoman cosmopolitanism. This conjunction led to the new globalized cosmopolis in which Shi'ism now finds itself. Shi'ism is now ready for a renewed syncretic cosmopolitanism, practicing a public reason of an entirely different and more global sort.

As I was making my closing arguments, I introduced you to the phenomenal figure of Seyyed Jamal al-Din Afghani, whose adventurous career looms prominently in the latter part of the nineteenth century. I identified Afghani as a prominent case of Shi'ism in disguise, a key figure who connects the spirit of precolonial Babism to anticolonial political culture at the turn of the twentieth century, a feat made possible only by his transfusion of Shi'ism into a larger Islamic (regional and global) concern. I then linked the figure of Afghani to that of Ali Shari'ati as the case par excellence of the thematic dissolution of Shi'ism into larger global concerns. The rise of asymmetric warfare in contemporary regional politics, I then suggested, radically changes the balance of power and reasserts the political condition of a renewed syncretic cosmopolitanism for Shi'ism. The world in which Shi'ism now finds itself demands and exacts such syncretic cosmopolitanism.

Having offered you a Shi'i lens of how to see the world, I concluded this leisurely walkabout by arguing that the contemporary sites of contestation between the imperial will to power and the collective will to resist that power are well poised to save and rescue Shi'ism from its inherited paradox of success-in-failure and failure-in-success through a dissolution of the defiant tenets of Shi'ism into the transformative force of its contemporary emancipatory history. Only through this dissolution, I argued, can Shi'ism dissolve itself into the world and thus succeed in overcoming its central crisis by reading its own innate paradox of being at odds with itself into the parallax of being at odds with an unjust world. The Shi'i paradox, in other words, is dialectically self-referential and thus thematically insoluble except in being dissolved into the world at large, the world that is patently at odds with itself. The dissemination of Shi'ism into the world, from faith to force, from a self-defeating paradox to a self-effacing parallax, is the *conditio sine qua non* of its cosmopolitanism. This is my conclusion.

Shi'ism Triumphant

How does the theory I have outlined in some detail fare in light of the most important historical event of Shi'ism over the last two hundred years—namely the Islamic Revolution of 1977–1979 in Iran? As you might expect, the Shi'is in their most recent history have had to deal with the acute anxiety of success in the aftermath of this cataclysmic event.[1] Because Shi'ism has doctrinally and historically been a religion of protest, I have offered, as soon as it is politically successful it loses its moral legitimacy. In order to remain morally potent, Shi'ism must always be in a posture of protest. The success of the Islamic Revolution of 1977–1979 thus ushered in yet another occasion in which the inner contradiction of Shi'ism as a religion of protest came to be historically visible. Once again Shi'ism began by assuming its constitutional posture of protest. In the course of the revolution, a Shi'i cleric, Ayatollah Khomeini, emerged as the leader of the revolutionary movement against the Pahlavi regime.[2] He developed a theory of Islamic government on the basis of Shi'i doctrinal positions and subsequently mobilized the masses of Iranians. Other revolutionary leaders had already joined the chorus of the Shi'i ideological protest. Ali Shari'ati, Morteza Motahhari, Ayatollah Sayyed Mahmud Taleqani, and scores of Shi'i revolutionary ideologues closed rank, lay and clergy alike, and mobilized a massive revolutionary movement of outrage against tyranny, injustice, and corruption.[3] The enormous arsenal of Shi'i rebellious symbolism was put to effective political use. God Almighty, the Prophet, the Twelve Infallible Imams, and all other major and minor Shi'i saints were all mobilized in the service of the revolution against tyranny.[4] Shi'ism was in full insurrectionary posture—back in its originary form, substance, essence, and attributes. Shi'ism held moral sway. Shi'ism was not the only revolutionary game in town, but at this moment it was powerful enough to flex its symbolic and institutional muscles.

So far as the Shi'is were concerned, the revolution was successful. Shi'ism won, and tyranny disappeared. The shah, the Yazid made incarnate, fled in shame and died in exile, in indignity. All the enemies of the Twelve Infallible Imams fled in disgrace, died in infamy. The Shi'is were happy; their religious leaders were now in charge, and everything would now be fine. Justice would finally prevail. But would it? Soon Shi'ism had to rule. And it began to rule with a vengeance. First it had to eliminate all other claimants to the revolution. The nationalists, the socialists, even the alternative Islamists, they all had to conform to the official Shi'ism or else be made silent. The intellectuals, the literati, filmmakers, dramatists, anyone who did not agree with the official version of Shi'ism had to be silenced, put under house arrest, imprisoned, forced into exile, or killed. Even further, Shi'ism had to be institutionalized, made into a ruling government, written into a constitution. The clerical revolutionaries assembled. The Qur'an and the *hadith,* the sayings of the imams and the judgments of the jurists, the wisdom of the foregone ages and the vision of a Shi'i utopia were all brought together, and a constitution was written for the Shi'i state. Any opposition to this constitution had to be silenced. No one was to oppose this Shi'i constitution. The American diplomatic corps in Tehran was taken hostage by Shi'i students in November 1979. While a long diplomatic ordeal paralyzed the nation, the Shi'i constitution was written and ratified; all objections to it were ignored, suppressed, silenced, and condemned to hell. The moderate opposition was silenced; the radicals killed. Massive numbers of Iranians were forced into exile to allow for a unified Shi'i state. Then the war with Iraq began. Eight years of brutal, inconsequential war followed, with many opportunities to end its atrocities missed precisely in the name of an Islamic (Shi'i) triumphalism.

The war ended. Hundreds of thousands were killed. The country was in ruins, but Shi'ism was triumphant. The clerics were in charge; all opposition pacified. Not a single sign of protest or even deviation from the mandated rules of the custodians and interpreters of the sacred was tolerated. Religious minorities were severely repressed. A cultural revolution was launched, seeking actively to sanctify the country, Islamize it. Women became the target of the most brutal and humiliating restrictions, from their social behavior to their mode of dress. Universities were "cleansed" of anyone with the slightest ideological "impurity." The body-politic was treated like the human body—it had to be ritually cleansed. It was cleansed, with cruel precision. Islam was triumphant: Shi'ism was in full charge; Shi'ism was politically successful; Shi'ism had to be saved from itself.

To face that task, by far the most prominent public intellectual in post-revolutionary Iran, Abdolkarim Soroush (born 1945), sought to navigate an intellectual integrity for Shi'ism over and above its history. The magnitude of the Islamic Revolution in Iran and its region seems to have produced a man of monumental intellectual prowess to ponder how to save Shi'ism from itself. Born and raised as Hossein Haj Faraj Dabbagh in Iran, and initially trained as a pharmacologist in England in the 1970s, Abdolkarim Soroush emerged as the leading Shi'i metaphysician and hermeneutician of the post–Islamic Revolution era. Initially he was deeply involved in the cultural warfare of the post-revolutionary period, a key figure in the cultural revolution that sought to radically Islamize Iranian society. Very soon after the successful institutionalization of the Islamic Republic, however, Soroush diverted from revolutionary orthodoxy and began to articulate theoretical positions on Islam in general and Shi'ism in particular that have come up against severe criticism from the clerical establishment, forcing him to leave his homeland and live in exile in Europe and the United States. He is the author of numerous books and countless essays, writing with astonishing facility in his elegant (if at times too self-absorbed and floral) prose. Soroush soon developed a sizeable following in and out of Iran. He has a calm and mystic demeanor, writing from within the glow of a self-assured serenity that seems to have enveloped his mind and thinking. He has the facility of Rumi with words and the monumentality of Mulla Sadra's philosophical strokes—and the two virtues, overwrought, often have the better of the man. But despite his intellectual effervescence Abdolkarim Soroush lives in a bubble, and from there he seeks to suck Shi'ism, what he calls "Islam Itself," into the safe confinement of his hermetic haven.[5] But this is exactly where Shi'ism should *not* be, if it is to resolve its paradox by absolving itself into the world—a cosmopolitan world that has always embraced it.

The World Is Our Home

Throughout this book I have been writing about something I keep calling *syncretic cosmopolitanism.* Now perhaps the time has arrived to explain what I mean by it. In his *Cosmopolitanism: Ethics in a World of Strangers,* Kwame Anthony Appiah has written quite eloquently about the moral imperative of a globalized cosmopolitanism. He urges his readers to redraw the hostile and imaginary boundaries in a manner that brings humanity together. He celebrates the Greek origin of cosmopolitanism and world citizenship that has in turn characterized the cosmopolitanism of the European Enlightenment. Appiah is quite persuasive in providing a Greek and European pedigree for the term *cosmopolitanism* and settles for an understanding of it on "two strands that intertwine": "One is the idea that we have obligations to others . . . The other is that we take seriously the value not just of human life but of particular human lives, which means taking an interest in the practices and beliefs that lend them significance."[6] Meanwhile, another distinguished philosopher, Seyla Benhabib, in her *Another Cosmopolitanism* (2006) argues that "since the UN declaration of Human Rights in 1948, we have entered a phase in the evolution of global civil society, which is characterized by a transition from international to cosmopolitan norms of justice." What she means by this transition is that "norms of international justice most commonly arise through treaty obligations and bilateral agreements among states and their representatives. . . . Cosmopolitan norms of justice . . . accrue to individuals as moral and legal persons in a worldwide civil society."[7]

As two prominent examples of thinking about a cosmopolitanism that is ipso facto a vacuous disguise for globalization, Appiah and Benhabib disregard the persuasive argument that Timothy Brennan put forward in his *At Home in the World: Cosmopolitanism Now* over a decade ago. Brennan argued that the emerging emphasis on hybridity, transnationalism, globalization, and thus "cosmopolitanism" is in fact a ploy in the service of U.S. imperialism. Such ideas, he believes, have paved the way and were in effect facilitating the operation of transnational capital on a global and cross-cultural level. He sees the floating ideas of "cosmopolitanism" a condition for the crushing of local cultures of resistance to globalized capital and its cultural foregrounding. "Nationalism is not dead," Brennan declares, "and it is good that it is not."[8] In the opposite direction of a "cosmopolitanism" that supersedes nationalism Brennan emphasizes their centrality in safeguarding cultures of resistance. "There is only one way to express internationalism: by defending the popular sovereignty of existing and emergent third-world politics."[9] The key to this systematic elimination of national cultures is their ethnographic subjugation to anthropological "studies." Concentrating on the field of cultural studies, by which the reference is also to cultural anthropology, Brennan insists, "cultural studies . . . has maintained a hold in the universities in part because . . . it leaves the U.S. national sense of preeminence untouched."[10] A key target of Brennan's criticism is the network of academics, journalists, policymakers, and public intellectuals who are instrumental in pacifying national liberation movements by way of reading them as dying, exotic, or ethnically charted cultures now outdated by globalized capitalism and its varying visions of itself. Such theorists of "hybridity" as Homi Bhabha would have a difficult time reading Timothy Brennan when they go about "problematizing" national cultures or the manner in which they have narrated themselves. The same holds true for cultural anthropologists who keep "studying" what are called and branded "third-world cultures."

The syncretic cosmopolitanism I have sought to articulate in this book is neither the ideal cosmopolitanism that Anthony Appiah celebrates nor the potential cosmopolitanism that Seyla Benhabib recommends; nor indeed is it the postnational cosmopolitanism that Timothy Brennan rightly criticizes. My notion of cosmopolitanism is neither ideal, nor potential, nor even postnational. By the term *cosmopolitanism* I simply wish to unpack the layered folds of national consciousness within which already dwell the hidden, forgotten, repressed, or violently denied traces of a worldly presence in history. The cosmopolitanism I have espoused in this book is neither new nor ideal, neither globalized nor emerging. The problems with Appiah's and Benhabib's notions of cosmopolitanism, as Brennan had anticipated, are self-evident; they are subservient to a globalized imperialism that seeks to pacify all its cultures of resistance.

The problem with Brennan's notion of cosmopolitanism is that he seems to think that the United States possesses the only culture capable of a worldly claim—and that all other cultures are merely national. This is a false and paradoxically imperial assumption, of course. All national cultures, in my reading of cosmopolitanism, are always already cosmopolitan by virtue of their worldly presence in history. Mine is a conception of cosmopolitanism that already exists in the domain of the nationalized cultures by virtue of the worldly experiences of those cultures—cosmopolitanism from the ground up. What I have in mind by cosmopolitanism is very much akin to what Edward Said calls *worldliness*. Cultures are cosmopolitan not by virtue of a wish, a recommendation, or even a denial. Cultures are cosmopolitan by virtue of the factual evidence they have lived, endured, or celebrated. What even Brennan does not recognize is the fact that people in all four corners of the globe did not have to wait for a vacuous globalization in order to experience and inhabit the world. Every home has plenty of abroad in it. Many worlds, happily or haphazardly, inhabit every home. Shi'is, as all other Muslims living in a vast part of the globe, carry in their national and communal consciousness the layered polyfocality of many worlds that have come their way. Even Timothy Brennan, otherwise an astute critic of the sort of ethnicization anthropologists enact on non-European cultures, robs these non-"Western" cultures of the worlds that have inhabited by thinking them exclusively "national" and resistant to American globalizing imperialism. They are not. These "national" cultures inhabit their own worlds and are, and have been, equally capable of imperial proclivities. The syncretic cosmopolitanism of which I have written is the worldly disposition of peoples' active knowledge of themselves. It stands entirely independent of both the globalization of the nativist disposition of one empire or another and the denial or ignorance of other worlds by theorists who either ethnicize or else nativize them.

Against the grain of the particular cosmopolitanism in which Shi'ism now finds itself, Abdolkarim Soroush is the best contemporary example of how a particularized Shi'i case produces a particular Shi'i attempt at resolution of its endemic crisis rather than seeing its thematic dissolution into a worldly parallax. The problem with Soroush's efforts stems from the insularity of his thoughts. He is by far the best and the most prominent metaphysician that Shi'ism has produced at its worst and most nativist disposition. Soroush is conscious of nothing. Nothing matters in his hermetically hermeneutic universe. He is a take-it-or-leave-it proposition. His is a totalizing project, the man a mystic unto himself, a finalizing meta-narrating metaphysician—quite eloquent and attractive if you enter his pages, entirely useless and vacuous if you leave them. He is a metaphysician who sublates into theoretical sublimity the nativist juridicalism of his arch-nemesis—the clerical class. He does not rescue Shi'ism from clericalism; he in fact sublates that clerical scholasticism into a very attractive hermeneutic entrapment.

The world outside Soroush, the world in which we live, forces the Shi'i paradox into a worldly parallax and resolves it, redesigns its minuscule self-indulgence into a mosaic pattern, to which it contributes but over which it cannot preside. The act forces Shi'ism and the Shi'is to face correlations not abstractions, dynamics not mechanics, tolerance not absolutism, and thus by expanding the particulars into the comparative it leads the particulars into its embedded universals and the universals into a syncretic cosmopolitanism they have always entailed, and that perforce leads back to the revelatory moment of Islam. Not the fragmented history but the moment of cosmic revelation is at the heart of any divine claim on our mundane realities, reverting the fragmented history and consciousness to the revelatory moment when the heavens embrace the earth. History is the site of fragmentation, or *iftiraq* as the old Sufis used to say, and the task facing humanity, and to the Shi'is and Shi'ism that are integral to it, is what they called *jam'* or a gathering-together.

Abeer, Fatima, and Marjane

Abeer Qassim Hamza al-Janabi (1991–2006) was a young Iraqi girl who lived with her parents and three siblings near the village of Yusufiyah on the outskirts of the city of Mahmudiyah. Three years into the U.S.-led invasion and occupation of her homeland, the fourteen-year-old Abeer and her parents were petrified by the placement nearby of a U.S. Army checkpoint. She spent much of her time at home for fear of violence. On 12 March 2006, a gang of American soldiers from the 502nd Infantry Regiment stationed at the checkpoint walked to Abeer's home, separated her from the rest of her family, and as one of them, Private First Class Steven Green, killed her parents and younger sister in an adjacent room, his friends gang-raped Abeer. Steven Green then emerged from the next room, declared to his friends that he had just killed Abeer's parents and younger sister, and proceeded to join them in raping Abeer.

After they were done, Steven Green shot Abeer in the head and killed her. Before the soldiers left, they set fire to all the dead bodies and burned their house, too. When the neighbors discovered the dead and burned bodies of Abeer and her family, they told reporters: "The poor girl, she was so beautiful she lay there, one leg was stretched and the other was bended and her dress was lifted to her neck."[11]

Fatima Ali was a Pakistani undergraduate student at Columbia University who in the late 1990s and early 2000s was my research assistant. Over the decades I have never known a more dedicated and conscientious assistant, among scores of them who have helped me with my work at Columbia or other universities. I would on occasion send her email late in the evening with a request for a book or an article from the library. She would check her emails soon after her early morning prayers, and by the time I would get to my office by 9 or 10 AM, whatever I had requested she had already checked out or photocopied and placed on my desk. When a number of my colleagues and I put together a Palestinian film festival in January 2004, Fatima Ali was a miracle of efficiency and persistence—without whom I very much doubt we would have managed to pull the festival together. Soon after her graduation we all lost track of Fatima. Our understanding was that she soon married after her graduation and got absorbed in her private life.

Marjane Satrapi was a precocious child born to an elite Iranian family just about a decade before the advent of the Islamic Revolution in Iran. Soon after that cataclysmic event, her family sent her to Europe, where she received her high school education. She returned briefly to Iran for her college years, married and divorced within a couple of years, and returned to France soon after she finished her college degree in graphic arts. Initially published in Europe in French and subsequently in the United States and the United Kingdom in English, Marjane Satrapi's graphic novel *Persepolis: A Story of Childhood* (2003) and its sequel *Persepolis 2: The Story of a Return* (2004) were followed by *Embroideries* (2005). These became international bestsellers, and by the time that the film version of her *Bande Dessinée* appeared in 2007 she was quite a global phenomenon—and deservedly so.

Abeer Qassim Hamza, Fatima Ali, and Marjane Satrapi represent three faces of contemporary Muslim women. One murdered at the prime of her life, the other lost in the sanctity and anonymity of her private life, and the third made globally known and celebrated by her gift of showing and telling the tales of her nation at large. Abeer was born and raised and murdered in a small village in Iraq. Fatima was born in Pakistan, raised in Queens, New York, and attended Columbia University before she married and resumed her private life. Marjane Satrapi was born and raised in Iran, grew to artistic and political maturity in Europe, and became a global celebrity with a gifted capacity for visual storytelling. Fatima I know for sure was a Shi'i. Marjane was born and raised in a nominally Shi'i family but now has the privilege of providing a sophisticated frivolous answer if she were asked about her faith. Abeer's young and precious life was too brutally cut short to matter if she were a Sunni or a Shi'i—and who except military strategists in Monterey, California, would care to know, and what difference would it make?

I am father to four children, all born and raised in the United States. Every time I look at the face of my youngest daughter Chelgis I can see a Marjane Satrapi confidently growing up in her, and I can see a Fatima Ali deep in her bashful moments, and then I feel a shiver in my spine when I imagine the picture of my little daughter in the frightened face of Abeer Qassim Hamza when she was violated and murdered. What holds these names and universes together? A perished innocence, the absolution of a private life, and the celebratory cast of a public figure all fade away in face of a history that transcends identity and ascends to a fragile and frightened humanity that underlies them all. Lived lives and perished innocence inhabit the world alike, and no faith, no metaphysics of assured strokes, has ever exhausted the simplest moments of which life histories are made.

Shi'ism is an abstraction. Shi'is are real people. They perish or persist, like everyone else, in the world they inhabit by measures and moments they make by volition or by force of circumstance. The Iranian revolution of 1977–1979 was the very last time the Shi'i paradox worked itself out and climbed and collapsed from political victory to moral defeat. As evident from its most illustrious metaphysical mind, Abdolkarim Soroush, it has sought to deny or camouflage that defeat but instead has plunged ever deeper in it. The only way for Shi'ism to resolve its enduring paradox is to absolve it into the world at large and transform it from being at odds with itself to being at odds with a world at odds with itself. That absolution is possible only if Shi'ism embraces the syncretic cosmopolitanism that has always defined and embraced it throughout its history in one way or another. An asymmetric warfare of disproportionate imbalance now holds the world together uneasily. The only

Shi'ism that now matters is the one that can fade in and out of history in caring communion with it, where the three figures of Abeer Qassim Hamza, Fatima Ali, and Marjane Satrapi coalesce and give birth to a new visionary recital in the world. The "Shi'ism" of the three images of my little daughter Chelgis is once and for all found and lost in a universe that sees the world as the site of a cosmic battle between two mutually exclusive visions of the lonely planet we inhabit: one that inadvertently seeks to destroy it, and the other that must purposefully decide to save it. The rest is commentary.

Neda Aqa-Soltan

The cataclysmic events and spectacular demonstrations that occurred during and after the presidential election of June 2009 in Iran once again put a national uprising in a Shi'i country on the moral compass of the globe. The Shi'i Islamic republic that was popularly established and violently consolidated some thirty years earlier seemed to have unraveled in a matter of weeks, with massive security forces killing scores of protestors; arresting, incarcerating, and torturing the demonstrators; and forcing them to make confessions to bogus charges. My central thesis in this book has much to say about and much to learn from this dramatic unfolding in a major Shi'i country. Has the face and visage of Neda Aqa-Soltan (1982–2009), one among scores of other young Iranians who were killed by the security forces during these demonstrations, opened up a new vision of Shi'ism not embedded in any other young person carrying the call of the faith in affirmation or denial—and if so in what particular way?

My central thesis in this book has unfolded in the following terms: (1) There is a central paradox in Shi'ism—its political success equals its moral collapse, and conversely its political failure equals moral authority. (2) This paradox was about to be resolved in the formation of a public space during the Safavid period, but the collapse of the Safavid and the tribalism of Nader Shah preempted it. (3) A renewed attempt at crafting that public space was launched in the nineteenth century with the Babi movement, but that too was crushed by the Qajar and the Ottomans and above all by the advent of European colonialism, which created its own public space, a globalized public space in terms alien to Shi'ism and hostile to Shi'ism. (4) A cosmopolitan constitution of that public space in anticolonial terms was posited by Jamal al-Din al-Afghani, a Shi'i in disguise, which led to the militant Shi'ism of the nineteenth and twentieth century, a belligerent political Shi'ism devoid of its aesthetic and formal creativity. This Shi'ism had meanwhile become self-alienated, excessively formal, and autonomous, paradoxically creating a global public space, though one alienated from Shi'ism. Despite this setback, Shi'ism's aesthetic reason finally posited a Shi'i public reason in disguise. (5) Political Shi'ism culminated and exhausted itself in the Islamic Revolution, but it is now about to be reunified with its creative effervescence and historically realize itself on the battlefield of an asymmetric warfare in Iran, Iraq, Lebanon, and Palestine, which demands and exacts a formal and theological creativity that I have termed a "liberation theodicy," namely a mode of theological worldliness that does not demonize and dismiss but in fact embraces and accepts the shades and shadows of its own alterities.

What I believe is happening in Iran today begins with the simple fact that, predicated on the bedrock of my thesis, the ruling Shi'ism has lost its moral legitimacy. It has lost it simply by being in power and trying in vain to remain in power by maiming and murdering its own people. The source of moral legitimacy has now completely shifted from the clerical class back to the people themselves, demonstrating in the masses of millions in the streets. It is they who may bestow that legitimacy to one leader or another. Meanwhile another thing that is happening is the organic completion of the Shi'i body-politic—the unification of its exhausted body and its alienated soul, its depleted politics and its vagrant poetics, coming together to form a robust and whole polity in body and soul—a fact perhaps best evident in the operatic spectacle of massive demonstrations, of millions of people pouring into the streets in choreographed rallies, singing their slogans, chanting their hymns, dancing while holding hands. In one such symbolic move, the supporters of the oppositional candidate Mir Hossein Moussavi held hands and formed a human chain from the northernmost part of Tehran to its southern neighborhoods. Joyous and melodic hymns and chants and slogans were perhaps the most significant part of these public spectacles, as were young men and women brandishing green bandanas and wristbands, evocatively worn on their faces and figures. By all accounts, this was a public spectacle on a massive scale, where the participants were in fact the reporters, taking snapshots of their own acts and relaying them around the globe. The alienated, formal defiance of art had now come back to inform the making of a whole new kind of politics.

But what kind of politics? Much of my final analysis in this book was based on expanding the national content of all Shi'i communities within a larger transnational geopolitical context—thinking that it was in that larger playing field that this reunification of Shi'ism in body and soul would become possible. The events surrounding the presidential election of June 2009 in Iran have reintroduced a complementary bend to that context, which is the uplifting of the national scene into the regional and global. What this resurrection of national politics in the regional geopolitics has made possible is to make that theodicy, the tolerance of alterity, not only contextual to a constellation of Shi'i countries but in fact equally textual to any one of them. In other words, the contextual resolution of the paradox at the heart of Shi'ism is now aided by its organic sublation within a national body-politic. As Shi'ism absolves its central paradox by being resolved in the parallax of the geopolitics of its region, whereby it is forced to sublate its theology into a theodicy, it is now equally absolved from partaking in the ideological battlefields of its nationalized histories by being resolved into a civil rights movement beyond the contours of ideological warfare.

By virtue of their demographic diversities, Iraq and Lebanon draw our attention as the active sites of forcing Shi'ism to face its syncretic disposition—and so would be their effective embracing of Palestine and Afghanistan. But in the aftermath of June 2009, we see how this horizontal geopolitical context also has a vertical national parameter whereby we observe a transubstantial motion from the ideological into the postideological, from the political into the civil. As Shi'ism was escaping sectarian defeatism by way of retrieving, restoring, and resuming its historic march toward a full-bodied self-recognition (in body and soul) of its embedded doctrinal proclivities—from the side, by way of a catalytic impact of one country on the other—to this external catalytic factor is added an internal transmutation of the political into the public, the ideological into the civil.

In the last part of my book I had argued that the contemporary sites of historic contestation between the will to power and the will to resist power were now poised to save and rescue Shi'ism from its inherited paradox of success-in-failure and failure-in-success, and from its politics of despair—all through a dissolution of the defiant tenets of Shi'ism into the transformative force of its contemporary history. Only through this dissolution, I suggested, does Shi'ism dissolve into the world, reading its own innate paradox of being at odds with itself into the parallax of being at odds with an unjust world that is at odds with itself. Released from its politics of despair, I argued, the historically emancipated Shi'ism had now yielded to the widespread possibilities of a renewed syncretic cosmopolitanism that once again embraced the world and allowed its sublated forms to engage its history. After the June 2009 presidential election in Iran, we can also see how this innate paradox has a complementary mode of resolving itself by way of sublating its paradox *within* a national consciousness that posits the public domain and its contingent civil liberties as the modus operandi of the political project. If through the figure of Ali Shari'ati, Shi'ism was prepared to face the world and resolve its central paradox by way of absolving itself into the larger world, through the June 2009 uprising, which has (fortunately) no charismatic leader, it has become clear that the collective will of Iranians, as a Shi'i nation, has already united in its own creative soul that alienated bifurcation between form and fact, between art and politics. It has made itself whole via an aesthetic reason that has now gone completely public, through a carnivalesque staging of a national epic—with symbolic color, incandescent chanting, choral hymns, and choreographed dancing. It has staged an operatic comeback, an epic reclaiming of its body and soul. Shi'ism is at home—as always, in disguise.

NOTE ON TRANSLITERATION

In this book I have followed a very simplified transliteration system. By and large I have preferred the anglicized versions of common Arabic and Persian names and words—such as Muhammad, Ali, Hossein, Fatimah, Shi'ism, Isma'ilis, and so on. For the same reasons, I have dispensed with all diacritical marks that distinguish between similar sounding but different Arabic and Persian letters. For the specialists among my readers the original words are immediately evident, and for the general reader they are of no concern. For unfamiliar and rarely anglicized names and words I have kept that rule of simplicity and closest approximation to Arabic or alternatively Persian pronunciations in mind. My primary concern has been the ease and convenience of a pleasant reading experience for an educated audience, whether familiar or unfamiliar with the subject matter.

ARABIC AND PERSIAN GLOSSARY

adab: literary humanism

'Adl: divine justice; one of the five Shi'i Pillars

'alam al-mithal: the world of images; a key concept in Mulla Sadra's philosophy

alamdaran: standard bearers. These powerful men carry huge masts with flags or other religious icons in religious parades.

al-Amin: the Trustworthy; one of the many epithets for the Prophet Muhammad.

Ana al-Haq: "I am the Truth/I am God"; an ecstatic utterance in Sufism.

Ansar: the Helpers; Medinans who converted to Islam and helped the immigrants from Mecca

'aql: intellect

'Aql-e Fa'al: Active Intelligence. Mulla Sadra offered this idea as the source of Being, in lieu of the Infallible Fourteen (see *Chahardah Ma'sum*), distinguishing himself from his teacher Mir Damad. The idea has a much longer pedigree in Shi'i thought—all the way to Avicenna and even earlier.

'Aql-e Kol: The Universal Intellect. In Isma'ili thought, this is one of the celestial spheres through which the divine is effused on its way to the material world. (See also *Nafs-e Kol* and *al-A'yan al-Thabitah.*)

Ashura: tenth day of the Islamic month of Muharram. It is a holiday that commemorates the day in 680 when Hossein was martyred at Karbala.

Avesta: the principal sacred texts of Zoroastrianism

awlia': friends (see also *Awlia' Allah*)

Awlia' Allah: Friends of God. A Sufi concept of closeness to God through companionship, often signifying a Sufi saint.

al-A'yan al-Thabitah: Perennial Archetypes. In Isma'ili thought, these represent celestial spheres through which the divine is effused on its way to the material world. (See also *'Aql-e Kol* and *Nafs-e Kol.*)

ayatollah: the title given to high-ranking Twelve-Imami Shi'i clerics. They are considered experts and the highest authorities in Islamic jurisprudence.

al-bab: Gate, door; used as a metaphor for the connection between the Hidden Imam and the world. Seyyed Ali Mohammad Shirazi, founder of Babism, took this as his title.

Banu Hashim: Muhammad's clan

Baqiyat Allah: God's Reserved One. This title was claimed for the Hidden Imam and later claimed for Seyyed Ali Mohammad Shirazi, *al-Bab,* which linked him to earlier Shi'i/Sufi (Isma'ili) thoughts. The Safavid monarchs also considered themselves *Baqiyat Allah.*

batini: esoteric; used to describe the hidden meanings of the Qur'an

caliph: representative; a leader of the Muslim community after Muhammad's death, claimed by many Muslim dynasties.

caliphate: succession of the prophet; the lineage of rulers after Muhammad's death

Chahardah Ma'sum: the Infallible Fourteen, composed of the Twelve Shi'i Imams plus Muhammad and Fatimah. These fourteen also make up Mulla Sadra's incorporation of Shi'i saints into his philosophical system.

dahr: time; a key concept in Mir Damad's philosophy, overturning the relationship between the permanent and the changing

da'i: deputy (of the imam). These men were propaganda officers with the aim of converting Muslims to Isma'ilism.

dammam: a bass drum made from wood, rope, and animal skin, commonly used in southern Iran.

dawr al-satr: period of concealment; the period in Isma'ili history when Muhammad ibn Isma'il disappeared to avoid Abbasid persecution after the death of his father, Isma'il

dhat: ipseity, selfhood

Dhu al-Fiqar: This two-pronged sword belonged to Ali and is an important Shi'i symbol.

Eid al-Adha: the Festival of Sacrifice; a commemoration of Abraham's willingness to sacrifice his son, as commanded by God. In the Muslim tradition, Ishmael is the son who is to be sacrificed, whereas it is Isaac in Jewish and Christian traditions.

fana: annihilation (into God); a Sufi concept

fatwa: a religious edict

fiqh: Islamic jurisprudence

fitriyyah: the nature of a thing

furu': derivatives (of jurisprudence); the rules, or positive law, that have been derived from the principles, *usul,* of jurisprudence.

Ghadir Khum: the location where Muhammad allegedly decreed Ali his heir and successor

ghaybah: disappearance, occultation

Ghaybah al-Kubra': the Greater Occultation. This occultation is marked by the end of communication between the Hidden Imam and his community until the end of time when he will return to establish justice and peace on Earth.

Ghaybah al-Sughra': the Lesser Occultation. During this transitional period, the Hidden Imam remained in communication with his community through four successive deputies.

Ghulat: extremists, exaggerators. This proto-Shi'i movement within the first three centuries of Islam included the attribution of divinity to the first Shi'i imams.

hadith: prophetic tradition; a canonical collection of Muhammad's sayings and doings. The *hadith* are considered the second most important source of Islamic law after the Qur'an.

haghighah: truth

Hajar al-Aswad: Black Stone. A relic sacred to all Muslims, this stone is located on the side of the Ka'bah in Mecca and plays a central ritual role in the Hajj.

Hajj: an annual holy pilgrimage to Mecca; one of the five pillars of Islam

Hajjat al-Wida': the Farewell Pilgrimage; Muhammad's last pilgrimage to Mecca *halak:* annihilation

hamiyyat: honor

al-Haq: Truth, God

al-harakah al-jawhariyyah: The transubstantiation motion (of being). Mulla Sadra's theory of motion says that all of existence is constantly in motion, even if invisible to the naked eye. In this way, gradations of knowledge (of the divine) are coterminous with gradations of being. (See also *tashkik al-wujud.*)

haram: forbidden

hijra: migration, emigration. (See also *safar, rihla.*)

Hijra: Muhammad's flight from Mecca to Medina with his followers in 622; the starting point of the Muslim Hijri calendar.

Hossein-e Mazlum: Hossein the Innocent; an epithet for Imam Hossein.

Hosseiniyeh: establishments exclusive to ritual remembrance of Imam Hossein

hoviyyat: essence of God

hozur: presence

hujjat: deputies of the Hidden Imam. They were considered the living proof of the Hidden Imam and served as the imam's connection to the community. A *hujjat* is higher in rank than a *da'i.*

Hurqalya: In this celestial purgatory, human bodies are transmuted before they resurrect on the Day of Judgment. This was one of the revolutionary principles of Shaykhism.

huruf: letters of the alphabet

huruf-e hay: living letters. These honorary letters were assigned to the earliest converts to the Babi cause, most probably descending directly from the Hurufiyyah movement in attributing cabalistic significance to letters and numbers.

iftiraq: fragmentation; part of a Sufi saying that history is the site of fragmentation. (See also *jam'.*)

ijtihad: juridical opinion; a major tenet of the Shi'i Usuli school of thought

ikhtiyar: free will

ilhad: blasphemy

ilham: inspiration

Imamah: Imamhood/Imamate; the leadership of Ali and his descendants. *Imamah* is also one of the five Shi'i Pillars.

iman: belief

inniyyah: thingness of things

Insan-e Kamil: the Perfect Human Being

intizar: expectation; the Shi'i expectation of the return of a messianic figure, the Mahdi.

Irfan: Knowing; used to refer to Islamic, especially Shi'i, mysticism or Gnosticism

'ismah: the infallibility of the imams

'Isra: Muhammad's Night Journey from Mecca to Jerusalem to Heaven. This is considered by some to have been a physical journey and by others to be a spiritual one. (See also *Mi'raj*.)

jabr: predestination

jahiliyyah: pre-Islamic ignorance

jam': gathering together. This is the answer to fragmentation. (See also *iftiraq*.)

jamal: camel; the Battle of Jamal is so called because Ayeshah rode a camel in this battle.

ja-namaz: prayer rugs

jihad: holy war

Ka'bah: a cube-shaped building in Mecca; the destination of the annual *hajj* pilgrimage

kalam: speculative theology

Karbala: A city in modern-day Iraq and the site of the Battle of Karbala in the year 680, when Imam Hossein was martyred there.

Khalifat al-Rasul Allah: Representative, or institution of representatives, of the Messenger of God, Muhammad

khalq: people

kharaja: to break, splinter. This is how the Kharijites got their name as "those who splintered off from Ali."

khayal: imagination

Khulafa al-Rashidun: Rightly Guided Caliphs. This refers to the first four caliphs after the death of Muhammad: Abu Bakr, Umar, Uthman, and Ali.

Khuriltai: Council of Tribal Elders. This Mongol council maintained a practice of election.

khuruj: revolt

kofr: disbelief

Kutub al-Arba'ah: the Four Books. Four canonical sources produced by three prominent jurists in the tenth and eleventh centuries have remained the vertebral columns of Shi'i jurisprudence. These books succeeded the Four Deputies. (See *Nuwwab al-'Arba'ah.*)

Laylat al-Mabiyt: the night that Ali impersonated the Prophet to cover up his historic flight from Mecca to Medina

Ma'ad: bodily resurrection on the Day of Judgment; one of the five Shi'i Pillars.

Mahdi: Messiah. Shi'is believe that the Mahdi will return at the end of time to instill justice and peace on Earth.

al-Mahdi al-Muntazir: The Awaited Messiah; an epithet for the Twelfth Imam who went into hiding in 874.

mahiyyah: essence of things

mahmel: mounted mobile chamber; a mode of transportation

al-Maktum: the Hidden One; an epithet given to Muhammad ibn Isma'il after his period of concealment.

al-Maqtul: the Murdered One; an epithet given to Shahab al-Din Yahya Suhrawardi (1155–1191), founder of the Illuminationist School. (See also *al-Shahid.*)

masjed: mosque; a gathering spot to pray as well as a social institution. A mosque is also a spatial extension of one's peace and comfort zones.

ma'sum: infallible; used to describe Shi'i imams

Mard-e sharif: a noble man

Marja al-Taqlid: Source of Emulation; a label of Shi'i religious authority

Mawali: the Clients; non-Arab Muslims who were treated with normalized, legalized, and systemic discrimination.

al-Maymun: the Fortunate One; an epithet given to Muhammad ibn Isma'il after his period of concealment *mazlumiyyat:* the state of having been wronged; the condition of innocently being in a tyrannized state, having been subjected to it, as Hossein was.

Mi'raj: Muhammad's mystical ascension to heaven to meet the previous prophets and God. Some believe Muhammad's physical body went, and others believe that his soul went. (See also *'Isra.*)

Mithraism: an Iranian religion; an offshoot of Zoroastrianism and a strong rival of Christianity that flourished in Asia Minor in general and Rome in particular between the first and fourth centuries.

Mojadded: Renewer of the Faith; a figure believed to return to Earth and renew humanity's faith

mojtahed: an Islamic scholar; a title for the most learned jurists in Shi'i jurisprudence

Morshed-e Kamil: the Perfect Guide. Every Safavid king considered himself *Morshed-e Kamil.* The title is predicated on the Sufi notion of the Perfect Human Being (see also *Insan-e Kamil*).

mowla: master, friend

Muhajirun: the Emigrants; those who emigrated with Muhammad in 622 from Mecca to Medina.

Muharram: one of the Shi'i holy months. Ashura is the tenth day of this month, the day on which Imam Hossein was murdered in the Battle of Karbala.

muluk: kings

muqarnas: lattice-work structure that provides shade and privacy in a pattern where light and shadows or light and negative are indistinguishable

mu'tallah: degenerate

Nafs-e Kol: the Universal Soul. In Isma'ili thought, this is one of the celestial spheres through which the divine is effused on its way to the material world. (See also *al-A'yan al-Thabitah* and *'Aql-e Kol.*)

nahda: awakening

na'ib: representative (of the Hidden Imam). (See also *wakil.*)

al-Namus al-'Azam: the Bringer of the Great Law; an epithet for the Prophet Muhammad

al-nass: the people

noheh khanan: cantors

Nubuwwah: belief in the prophethood of Muhammad and other prophets sent by God; one of the five Shi'i Pillars.

Nuwwab al-'Arba'ah: the four successive deputies to the Hidden Imam with whom he is believed to have been in communication between 874 and 941.

qameh: saber

qameh zanan: those who cut themselves on their heads in ritual acts of self-mutilation to commemorate the martyrdom of Hossein

qiyam: insurrection

Qorrat al-Ayn: The Solace of the Eye; an epithet for Umm Salma, the revolutionary Babi leader. (See also *Tahereh.*)

Qur'an: The Recitation. This text is the collection of revelations that Muslims believe God gave to Muhammad.

Quraysh: Muhammad's tribe

rashk: jealousy

al-rasul: messenger (from God). Muhammad is known as the *rasul* of God.

rihla: journey

Rokn-e Rabe': In Shaykhism, *Rokn-e Rabe'* is the fourth principle or pillar of Shi'ism, the gate between the imam and the rest of the world, which Shaykh Ahmad used to replace two other Shi'i principles, *'Adl* and *Ma'ad.*

al-ruya al-sadiqa: rightful dreams; Muhammad's revelatory dreams

safar: journey

Safar: one of the Shi'i holy months on the Islamic calendar

sahm-i imam: revenue collected by Shi'i clerics in the name of the Hidden Imam

saqqa-khaneh: a Shi'i institution; a small water station where passersby can stop and have a drink of water for free

sarmad: the everlasting; part of Mir Damad's theory of time, pertaining to the relationship between two permanent things

shahadat: martyrdom

al-Shahid: the Martyred One; an epithet for Shahab al-Din Yahya Suhrawardi (1155–1191), founder of the Illuminationist School. (See also *al-Maqtul.*)

Shahnameh: Book of Kings; an epic Persian poem by Ferdowsi written around 1000

shari'ah: Islamic law, jurisprudence

Shi'a-ye Kamil: the Perfect Shi'i. This title is predicated on the Sufi notion of the Perfect Human Being. (See also *Insan-e Kamil.*)

Shi'is: the Partisans of Ali

Shu'ubiyyah movement: This Iranian cultural renaissance began soon after the Arab conquest and reached its height under the Samanids and then the Ghaznavids, when Persian language and culture asserted its presence in the easternmost parts of the Abbasid empire.

sineh zanan: those who rhythmically beat their chests to commemorate the martyrdom of Hossein

soghati: gifts for friends and family

Sufism: A mystical, spiritual branch of Islam that can overlap with Sunnism or Shi'ism.

sunnah: the Path of the Prophet; Muhammad's character, his sayings and doings

suras: chapters of the Qur'an

tafreqeh: diversion

Tahereh: the Chaste; an epithet for Umm Salma. (See also *Qorrat al-Ayn.*)

taqiyeh: dissimulation; concealing your identity to protect yourself

taqlid: following the exemplary conduct of a high-ranking cleric; a tenet of the Shi'i Usuli school of thought

tariqah: mystical path

tasbih: rosaries

tashkik al-wujud: gradation of existence. This key concept in Mulla Sadra's philosophy says that essence comes from existence. In this way, gradations of knowledge are coterminous with gradations of being. (See also *al-harakah al-jawhariyyah.*)

Tawhid: unity of God, absolute monotheism; one of the five Shi'i Pillars.

ta'wil: hermeneutics

Ta'ziyeh: theatre of redemption; the Shi'i passion play based on the Karbala narrative.

temsal: likeness; images of the prophet or imams printed on pieces of cloth or woven into carpets

tuba: a tree in Paradise

'ulama: the clerical establishment in Islam

ummah: the Muslim community

Usul al-Din: the five pillars of Shi'ism (See *Tawhid, Nubuwwah, Imamah, 'Adl,* and *Ma'ad.*)

Vakil al-Ro'aya: the Deputy of the Subjects; the title of the authority of the Zand dynasty

wahdat al-wujud: unity of being, existential monism

wahm: perception

wahy: revelations

wakil: representative (of the Hidden Imam). (See also *na'ib.*)

wali: friend, especially in Sufism

wilayat: companionship

wizir: official, minister

wujud: being, existence

Zakiyyah: the Most Intelligent; an epithet for Umm Salma

zaman: span of time; part of Mir Damad's theory of time, operative between two changing phenomena

zanjir zanan: those who rhythmically beat their backs with chains to commemorate the martyrdom of Imam Hossein

Zohr-e Ashura: noon on Ashura. At exactly 12 PM on Ashura in 680, when the sun was perpendicular over the Earth, Imam Hossein was reportedly beheaded.

Zoroastrianism: a Persian religion based on the teachings of the prophet Zoroaster

zulm: tyranny

SCHOOLS OF THEOLOGY, PHILOSOPHY, AND POLITICAL THOUGHT

This list highlights the schools of thought mentioned in this book and should not be considered complete.

Sufism: A mystical, spiritual branch of Islam that can overlap with Sunnism or Shi'ism.

Sunnism: The overwhelming majority of Muslims are considered Sunnis, those who follow the Sunnah or path of the Prophet. They follow the Four Rightly Guided Caliphs: Abu Bakr, Umar, Uthman, and Ali ibn Abi Talib. The Sunni schools of jurisprudence are named after the legal theorists who established them: Hanafi, Shafi'i, Hanbali, and Maliki. Sunni theologies include Ash'arites, founded by Abu al-Hasan al-Ash'ari (died 936). This group was considered the most "traditional" of Sunni theology. It was the historic foe of the Mu'tazilite School, the "rationalists" in terms of speculative theology.

Shi'ism: The second largest denomination of Muslims are Shi'is. Shi'is follow Ali ibn Abi Talib as the first imam and the first rightful caliph/successor to the Prophet Muhammad.

Kharijites: Most Sunnis and Shi'is credit Ali ibn Abi Talib as a rightful caliph (whether the first rightful one or the fourth). During Ali's life, a group of Muslims splintered off from his leadership and became known as the Kharijites ("those who splintered off from Ali"). A Kharijite eventually assassinated Ali in 661.

Azraqites: A radical branch of Kharijites.

Mu'tazilites: A distinctive school of speculative theology. They favored reason over tradition and were the historical foe of the Sunni Ash'arite School of speculative theology.

Ghulat: A minority of Muslims who took extreme views about the divinity of some of the early Shi'i Imams.

In 680, at the Battle of Karbala, Hossein, the third imam, was martyred. Upon his death, the Shi'i community was again divided:

Zaydiyah (Five-Imami Shi'is): In 732, one group disputed the succession of Muhammad al-Baqir as the fifth imam, and instead followed his brother Zayd ibn Ali as the fifth imam. This group rejected the notion of inherited succession in Shi'ism and believed an imam must raise arms and claim his authority by opposing tyranny. The majority of Zaydis live in Yemen today.

Isma'ili (Seven-Imami Shi'is): In 754, Isma'il was killed before the death of his father Jafar al-Sadiq. While other Shi'is followed his brother Musa al-Kazim, one group believed that Isma'il was the final imam and that his son Muhammad ibn Isma'il, who went into hiding, was his representative who would eventually return as the Mahdi. Finally, one Isma'ili leader, Abdullah al-Mahdi, proclaimed himself an imam and established the Fatimid dynasty in Egypt. He also claimed that the previous generations of Isma'ili leadership had in fact thought of themselves as true imams and not just deputies of the Hidden Imam.

Qaramita: In 899, those who opposed Abdullah al-Mahdi's claims were led by Hamdan Qarmat. This group was one of the most radical offshoots of Isma'ilism in its nascent stage, and they practiced an early form of socialism, with their center in Bahrain.

Musta'li: A court-based branch, in 1094 the Musta'li broke from the Fatimid Isma'ilis and then dwindled quickly.

Nizari: At the same time the Musta'lis broke from the Fatimid Isma'ilis in 1094, a revolutionary branch broke off too. This group was uninterested in court politics and revived the Shi'i/Isma'ili revolutionary zeal. They shifted the Isma'ili center of gravity east to Iraq and Iran. Nizaris make up the majority of Isma'ilis today.

Ithna-'Ashari (Twelve-Imami Shi'is or Ja'fari Shi'is): In 874, the twelfth imam, Muhammad al-Mahdi, went into occultation at only five years of age. Ithna-

'Ashari Shi'is believe the Mahdi will return at the end of time to restore peace and justice on Earth. This is the most popular version of Shi'ism in the world today and the official religion of Iran.

Within Ithna-'Ashari Shi'ism, there exist two major schools of jurisprudence:

Akhbari: This group was historically considered literalist, traditionalist, and scripturalist. This is the minority school of jurisprudence among the Ithna-'Asharis today.

Usuli: This group makes up the majority of Ithna-'Ashari Muslims today and was historically considered rationalist.

Islamic philosophy combined with other major forces in Islamic intellectual history to create new schools of thought and theology:

Illuminationist School: Founded by Shahab al-Din Yahya Suhrawardi (1155–1191), this school of thought draws from Avicenna and Neoplatonism and had an iconoclastic nature deeply rooted in pre-Islamic Iranian sources.

School of Isfahan: Founded by Mulla Sadra's teacher, Mir Damad, this philosophical movement best represents the urbane cosmopolitanism that gave the city its name. Mulla Sadra's work represents the crowning achievement of this movement. It brings philosophy and mysticism together in the ultimate combination of Shi'ism and Sufism.

Irfan: gnostic Shi'ism, based on Mulla Sadra's philosophies. Mulla Sadra single-handedly synthesized the Peripatetic, Neoplatonist, gnostic, and Illuminationist traditions of Islamic philosophy and then moved them toward a corresponding conversation with Shi'i doctrinal principles, basing them on an existential (rather than essential) reading of reality.

Musha'sha': A minor branch of gnostic Shi'ism founded by Seyyed Muhammad ibn Falah in 1436.

Sarbedaran: An early fourteenth-century revolutionary uprising that fused Shi'ism and Sufism for the rest of Shi'i history.

Hurufiyyah: This group began as a resistance movement against the Timurids.

The Hurufiyyah is named after *huruf* [letters of the alphabet] because they believed in a hidden meaning of the letters of the alphabet in the Qur'an.

Nuqtaviyyah: Another group with a rebellious fusion of mysticism and Shi'ism.

Ne'matollahi: Another revolutionary fusion of Shi'ism and Sufism. This group challenged the monopoly of the clerical establishment over religious symbols, rituals, and doctrines.

Kubrawiyyah: This Sufi group converted from Sunnism to Shi'ism following the syncretic belief in Ali as both an imam and a shaykh.

Shaykhism: This group began through a combination of Sufism and Shi'ism. Founded by Shaykh Ahmad Ahsa'i (1753–1826), the Shaykhis discarded two of the five Shi'i pillars, 'Adl and Ma'ad, and replaced them with a different fourth principle of the Perfect Shi'i as the representative of the Hidden Imam. This philosophy encouraged Shi'is to take arms and oppose injustice in the present because there was not going to be an other-worldly resurrection. Shaykhism was in violent opposition to the Usuli school of thought.

Qorratiyah: A radical branch of Shaykhism led by Tahereh Qorrat al-Ayn. This radical interpretation of Shaykhism highlights its fullest revolutionary potential and wedded the messianic message to the figure of al-Bab (with whom Qorrat al-Ayn corresponded, but whom she never met in person). This group called for and actively prepared for armed rebellions against the Qajars and Ottomans and therefore established the social cause for both Shaykhism and Babism.

Babism: Founded by Seyyed Ali Mohammad Shirazi (1819–1850), who was originally a Shaykhi. He took the title al-Bab, the Gate, and proclaimed himself the Hidden Imam, breaking his connection to Shaykhism. He claimed that his book *Bayan* [Utterances] surpassed the Qur'an as the Qur'an surpassed the Bible. Babism was the link that brought medieval Shi'i revolutionary reason to meet public reason, forming a template for Shi'i society.

Azali: After al-Bab's death, one group followed the reticent but militant Yahya Sobh-e Azal because they opposed the claims to divinity of al-Bab's successor, Baha'ullah.

Ba'hai: The group who followed Mirza Hossein Ali, Baha'ullah [the Glory of God], who eventually claimed to be the prophet that al-Bab had anticipated. Baha'ullah established a new Prophethood while retaining the unity of God.

These combinations of Shi'i thoughts eventually produced many modern thinkers, including but not limited to:

Mirza Muhammad Taqi Shirazi (d. 1896): Emerged as the leading clerical authority in Iraqi anticolonial struggles, including the Tobacco Revolt.

Seyyed Jamal al-Din al-Asadabadi (al-Afghani) (d. 1897): A revolutionary figure who opposed British colonialism in Muslim lands. He championed a pan-Islamism that united Muslims against their British occupiers. His ideas helped launch the Tobacco Revolt of 1891–1892.

Mirza Mohammad Hossein Na'ini (d. 1936): A leading Shi'i jurist of the Constitutional and early Pahlavi period in Iran who lent religious legitimacy to anticolonial nationalism.

Shaykh Abdolkarim Ha'eri Yazdi (d. 1937): A leading Shi'i jurist who helped elevate the city of Qom to the same level as Najaf in terms of juridical studies.

Mirza Reza Qoli Shari'at Sangalaji (d. 1944): The chief representative of a rather radical notion of religious modernity who tried to advance such subversive ideas as the total discarding of the institution of *taqlid,* or following the exemplary conduct of a high-ranking cleric.

Mohammad Hossein Tabataba'i Boroujerdi (d. 1961): Enjoyed unprecedented power and prestige as a leading Shi'i authority. Under his authority, the Shi'i clerical establishment enjoyed the widest range of its institutional legitimacy.

Jalal Al-e Ahmad (d. 1969): A leading public intellectual who helped facilitate what Ali Shari'ati would later accomplish in terms of repoliticizing Shi'ism. Al-e Ahmad argued against the power and influence of Western culture in favor of a domestic revolutionary ideology.

Mohammad Mossadegh (d. 1967): The champion of Iranian nationalist resurgence. Mossadegh served as prime minister and led the nationalization of Iranian oil. He was deposed by a CIA-engineered coup in 1953.

Ali Shari'ati (d. 1977): A lay- and Paris-educated revolutionary thinker who threatened both the Iranian Pahlavi monarchy and the Shi'i clerical establishment. He posed Shi'ism against cultural colonialism, social injustice, political repression, and Western imperialism, and turned outdated Shi'i figures into modern revolutionary models.

Imam Musa al-Sadr (d. 1978): A Lebanese Shi'i cleric of Iranian origin who gave charismatic expression to the hopes and aspirations of the disenfranchised Shi'i community in war-torn Lebanon. He was instrumental in turning the Lebanese Shi'i minority into a major political force.

Morteza Motahhari (d. 1979): A major ideologue of the Islamic Revolution in Iran. He disagreed with Ali Shari'ati and placed emphasis on the radical revolutionary zeal of the Shi'i clerical establishment.

Sayyed Mahmud Taleqani (d. 1979): A radical cleric who wrote Qur'anic commentaries expounding a revolutionary message and posed Shi'ism as an alternative to nationalism. He established a new Qur'anic commentary school of thought.

Allamah Seyyed Mohammad Hossein Tabataba'i (d. 1981): A distinguished Shi'i scholar who was as concerned as Morteza Motahhari with the erosion of Islamic doctrines and ideas. He and Morteza Motahhari joined forces in meeting the philosophical challenge that young seminarians in Qom faced from modern European philosophy.

Ayatollah Ruhollah Khomeini (d. 1989): A leading clerical authority who led a revolutionary uprising inspired by militant Islam in 1963 and eventually led the Iranian revolution of 1977–1979. Ayatollah Khomeini established the Islamic Republic on the basis of his ideas and the doctrine of *velayat-e faqih* [the supreme authority of the jurist].

Mehdi Bazargan (d. 1995): A quiet revolutionary with an unending admiration for Mahatma Gandhi, Bazargan became the link between revolutionary ideologues and their targeted audience.

Seyyed Abolhasan Bani-Sadr (b. 1933): A leading Muslim economist who joined the ranks of the Islamic Revolution in Iran and used Shi'ism to argue against the Pahlavi regime's closeness to Europe and the United States. He was the first president of Iran following the 1979 revolution.

Abdolkarim Soroush (b. 1945): The most prominent Shi'i thinker after the success of the Islamic Revolution. He engaged with the ideological and philosophical consequences of the revolution.

CHRONOLOGY

224–651	The Sassanid dynasty in Iran; Zoroastrianism is the state religion.
570	Muhammad is born in Mecca.
610	Muhammad's revelations begin.
622	Migration of Muslims from Mecca to Medina
632	Muhammad dies; Abu Bakr becomes the first caliph; a small band of Ali's supporters do not concur; the seed of Shi'ism is planted.
632–661	The reign of the Four Rightly Guided Caliphs: Abu Bakr, Umar, Uthman, and Ali
636	Muslim armies defeat the Byzantines and the Sassanids.
656	During the reign of Uthman, the Qur'an is compiled and standardized.
661–750	Umayyad dynasty
711	Muslims conquer Spain.
732	Charles Martel defeats Muslims in France.
750–1258	The Abbasid dynasty
755–1031	The Umayyads rule in Spain.
819–1005	The (Iranian) Samanid dynasty rules in Khurasan and Transoxiana.
894–977	The Qaramita Shi'is in Arabia and the Persian Gulf
905–1004	The Hamdanid Shi'i dynasty of al-Jazira and Syria
909–1171	The Fatimid Shi'i dynasty rules Egypt and North Africa.
932–1062	The Buyid Shi'i dynasty rules western Iran and Iraq.
977–1186	The Ghaznavids rule eastern Iran and Afghanistan.
1037–1194	The Seljuq dynasty
1090–1256	The Isma'ilis
1097–1291	The Crusades

1171–1250	The Ayyubid dynasty in Egypt
1220	The Mongol invasion
1250–1517	The Mamluk dynasty in Egypt
1256–1353	The Ilkhanids rule Iran.
1258	The Mongols sack Baghdad.
1299–1923	The Ottoman empire
1369–1506	The Timurid empire
1501–1722	The Safavid empire
1526–1858	The Mughal empire
1600	Shah Abbas establishes Isfahan as the capital of the Safavid empire.
1722	Afghans put an end to the Safavid empire.
1736	Nader Shah becomes monarch and establishes the Afsharid dynasty.
1736–1795	The Afsharid dynasty
1750–1794	The Zand dynasty
1779–1925	The Qajar dynasty
1798	Napoleon conquers Cairo.
1828	The Qajar dynasty cedes control of Caucasus to Russia after two successive wars.
1830	French occupy Algeria.
1844	The rise of Seyyed Ali Mohammad Shirazi and the commencement of the Babi movement
1875	The British rule in Egypt.
1881	The French occupy Tunisia and the first Zionists settle in Palestine.
1890	The Tobacco Revolt in Iran
1906–1911	The Constitutional Revolution in Iran
1913	The Young Turk Revolution in Turkey
1914–1918	World War I
1917	Balfour Declaration; British favor a Jewish state in Palestine.
1920	Iraq placed under British mandate; the State of Greater Lebanon is proclaimed.
1921–1926	Reza Shah leads successful coup in Iran, establishes Pahlavi dynasty.
1924	The establishment of the Turkish Republic
1932	Iraq gains independence.
1939–1945	World War II

1941	Reza Shah is deposed in Iran; his son Muhammad Reza Shah ascends the Pahlavi throne.
1947	The UN partition plan for Palestine is approved.
1951	Prime Minister Mohammad Mossadegh nationalizes the Iranian oil industry.
1953	A CIA-sponsored coup restores the shah to his throne.
1958	The Iraqi monarchy is overthrown.
1963	Military coup by Arab Socialist Ba'th Party; Ayatollah Khomeini first attempts a revolt against the shah.
1968	A Ba'thist-led coup brings General Ahmad Hasan al-Bakr to power in Iraq.
1970	Anwar Sadat becomes the Egyptian president.
1972	Iraq nationalizes the Iraqi oil industry.
1973	Arab-Israeli War
1975–1990	Lebanese Civil War, and the rise of Lebanese Shi'is to power
1979	The Islamic Revolution in Iran; President Sadat is assassinated in Egypt and Hosni Mubarak succeeds him; President Hasan al-Bakr resigns and is succeeded by Vice-President Saddam Hussein in Iraq; Soviets invade and occupy Afghanistan.
1980–1988	The Iran-Iraq War
1982	Israel invades Lebanon; Iran helps create Hezbollah.
1983	241 U.S. marines and 56 French paratroopers are killed in Beirut; responsibility is claimed by militant Shi'i groups.
1988	The first Palestinian Intifada
1989	The Salman Rushdie affair; Ayatollah Khomeini dies.
1990	Iraq invades Kuwait.
1991	The U.S.-led invasion of Iraq; the Kuwaiti royal family is restored to power.
1996	Israel attacks Lebanon; the Lebanese Hezbollah resists and is empowered.
1997	Mohammad Khatami wins the presidential election in Iran; a reform movement begins.
1999	Students lead a major uprising in Iran.
2000	Israel withdraws from Lebanon; it is considered a victory for the Shi'i Hezbollah.
2001	Terrorist attack on the United States; U.S.-led invasion of Afghanistan
2003	The U.S.-led invasion of Iraq
2004	Massive carnage in Iraq

2005 Conservative Mahmoud Ahmadinejad becomes the Iranian president.

2006 Israel invades Lebanon; according to the UN, an average of more than 100 civilians are killed each day in Iraq; on 30 December, Saddam Hussein is hanged.

2007 The United States announces sweeping sanctions against Iran, concerned about its nuclear program.

2009 Post-electoral crisis in June presidential election in Iran and the commencement of the Green Movement

NOTES

Introduction

1. For an excellent collection of essays on the events of Karbala at the roots of the Shi'i Passion Play (Ta'ziyeh) see the classic edited volume, Peter J. Chelkowski, *Ta'ziyeh: Ritual and Drama in Iran* (New York: New York University Press, 1979). For a more recent study of drama in Iran see Willem Floor, *The History of Theater in Iran* (Washington, DC: Mage, 2005). Equally informative is the collection of essays in *TDR: The Drama Review* 49, no. 4 (2005), *Special Issue:* Ta'ziyeh, guest editor Peter J. Chelkowski. See also Jamshid Malekpour, *The Islamic Drama* (London: Routledge, 2004) for a comprehensive study of Ta'ziyeh. Two recent studies are equally excellent: Kamran Scot Aghaie, *The Martyrs of Karbala: Shi'i Symbols and Rituals in Modern Iran* (Seattle: University of Washington Press, 2004); and Kamran Scot Aghaie, *The Women of Karbala: Ritual Performance and Symbolic Discourses in Modern Shi'i Islam* (Austin: University of Texas Press, 2005).

2. For a recent study of the history of Ta'ziyeh rituals in Islam see Ali J. Hussain, "The Mourning of History and the History of Mourning: The Evolution of Ritual Commemoration of the Battle of Karbala," *Comparative Studies of South Asia, Africa and the Middle East* 25, no. 1 (2005): 78–88. An equally good account is Yitzhak Nakash, "An Attempt to Trace the Origins of the Rituals of 'Ashura,'" *Die Welt des Islams* 33, no. 2 (1993): 161–181.

3. For an excellent eyewitness account of Ta'ziyeh rituals in India see David Pinault, *The Shiites: Ritual and Popular Piety in a Muslim Community* (New York: Palgrave, 1992). The best general account of the Iraqi Shi'is before the U.S.-led invasion of March 2003 is Yitzhak Nakash, *The Shi'is of Iraq*, rev. ed. (Princeton: Princeton University Press, 2003). For a firsthand ethnographic account of the Lebanese Shi'is see Lara Deep, *An Enchanted Modern: Gender and Public Piety in Shi'i Lebanon* (Princeton: Princeton University Press, 2006). See

also an excellent take on the globality of Ta'ziyeh: Peter Chelkowski, "From Karbala to New York City: Ta'ziyeh on the Move," *TDR, The Drama Review* 49, no. 4 (2005): 12–14; and Peter Chelkowski, "From the Sun-Scorched Desert of Iran to the Beaches of Trinidad: Ta'ziyeh's Journey from Asia to the Caribbean," *TDR, The Drama Review* 49, no. 4 (2005): 156–170.

4. For more on this aspect of the drama see the pioneering work Mahmoud Ayoub, *Redemptive Suffering in Islam: A Study of the Devotional Aspects of Ashura in Twelver Shi'ism* (The Hague: Mouton, 1978).

5. See, for example, Ehsan Yarshater, "Ta'ziyeh and Pre-Islamic Mourning Rites in Iran," in *Ta'ziyeh, Ritual, and Drama in Iran,* ed. Chelkowski, 88–94.

6. Ibid., 93.

7. Sigmund Freud, *Totem and Taboo: Some Points of Agreement between the Mental Lives of Savages and Neurosis,* in *The Origins of Religion: Totem and Taboo, Moses and Monotheism and Other Work,* ed. Albert Dickson, trans. James Strachey et al., The Pelican Freud Library 13 (London: Penguin Books, 1985), 208.

8. Ibid., 201. Equally important in this regard are Mikhail Bakhtin's theories of *carnivalesque.* See Bakhtin, *Rabelais and His World,* trans. Hélène Iswolsky (Bloomington: Indiana University Press, 1993).

9. Freud, *Totem and Taboo,* 208.

10. Ibid., 210.

11. Ibid., 202.

12. Ibid.

13. Ibid., 203.

14. Ibid., 205.

15. Ibid., 206.

16. Ibid., 215–216. Mithraism was an Iranian religion, an offshoot of Zoroastrianism and a strong rival of Christianity, that flourished in Asia Minor in general and in Rome in particular between the first and fourth century CE. For an excellent source on Mithraism see Franz Cumont, *Mithraism and the Religions of the Empire* (New York: Kissinger Publishing, 1910/2005).

17. Freud, *Totem and Taboo,* 216.

18. Ibid., 217.

19. Ibid. Freud refers to J. G. Frazer, *Spirits of the Corn and of the Wild,* vol. 2, *The Golden Bough* (London: Macmillan, 1912).

20. The dramatic similarities between Ta'ziyeh and the Christian Passion play (the Oberammergau Passion Play in particular) are quite remarkable. For an account of Oberammergau see Michael Collins Piper, *The Passion Play at Oberammergau* (New York: National Institute for Christian Solidarity, 2005).

21. For more on these tribal feuds preceding the rise of Shi'ism as a religion of protest see Hamid Dabashi, *Authority in Islam: From the Rise of Muham-*

mad to the Establishment of the Umayyads (New Brunswick, NJ: Transaction, 1989). For even more details see Wilferd Madelung, *The Succession to Muhammad: A Study of the Early Caliphate* (Cambridge: Cambridge University Press, 2008).

22. For a full script of this play see Colonel Sir Lewis Pelly, K.C.B., K.C.S.I., Revised with Explanatory Notes by Arthur N. Wollaston, *The Miracle Play of Hasan and Husain: Collected from Oral Tradition* (London: Wm. H. Allen, 1879), 1:171–205 (Scene X: "The Martyrdom of Muslim, the Envoy of Husain," and Scene XI: "Murder of the Sons of Muslim").

23. For an English version of Ferdowsi's *Shahnameh,* including these stories, see Abolqasem Ferdowsi, *Shahnameh: The Persian Book of Kings,* trans. Dick Davis (New York: Viking, 2006).

24. For more detail, see Gilles Deleuze's opening of the path for this line of thinking in Gilles Deleuze, *Masochism: Coldness and Cruelty* (New York: Zone Books, 1991), ch. 5, esp. pp. 60–61.

25. For more on this and other visual and performative aspects of the Islamic revolution in Iran see Peter Chelkowski and Hamid Dabashi, *Staging a Revolution: The Art of Persuasion in the Islamic Republic of Iran* (New York: New York University Press, 1999).

26. Philip Rieff, *Freud: The Mind of the Moralist* (Chicago: University of Chicago Press, 1959), 362.

27. A wonderful exception is the rare attention that Allan Megill gives to Philip Rieff's reading of Freud and the notion of "psychological man," in Alan Megill, *Prophets of Extremity: Nietzsche, Heidegger, Foucault, Derrida* (Berkeley: University of California Press, 1985), 323–325.

28. Rieff, *Freud: The Mind of the Moralist,* 370.

29. Ibid., 372.

30. See ibid.; Rieff, *The Triumph of the Therapeutic: Uses of Faith after Freud* (1966); *Fellow Teachers* (1973); and the collection of essays that his student Jonathan Imber prepared as *The Feeling Intellect* (1990).

31. Rieff, *Freud: The Mind of the Moralist,* 372.

32. Ibid., 373.

33. Ibid., 380–381.

34. Ibid., 387.

35. Ibid., 275–276.

36. Ibid., 276–277.

37. See in particular Luce Irigaray, *Speculum of the Other Woman* (Ithaca: Cornell University Press, 1985) for a critical correction of Freud and Lacan's theory of sexuation. Irigaray's emphasis on the child's pre-Oedipal phase is of crucial significance here.

38. For more on my notion of "colonial modernity" see Hamid Dabashi, *Iran: A People Interrupted* (New York: New Press, 2007), epilogue.

39. For a reading of the transcendental triumphalism operative in American imperialism see Hamid Dabashi, "American Empire: The Triumph of Triumphalism," *Unbound: Harvard Journal of the Legal Left* 4 (2008).

40. The Battle of Karbala took place on and around 10 Muharram 61 AH, which corresponds to 9–10 October 680 CE, which means early in autumn, when it can still be quite hot in that region (my hometown Ahvaz in Iran is not too far from Karbala in central Iraq). But the metaphor of thirst is so powerful in Shi'ism that one always has an impression of hot summer days in Ashura.

1. Death of a Prophet

1. For more on Mulla Sadra Shirazi see Muhammad Kamal, *Mulla Sadra's Transcendent Philosophy* (New York: Ashgate, 2006); and Christian Jambet, *The Act of Being: The Philosophy of Revelation in Mulla Sadra* (New York: Zone, 2006). For more on the school of philosophy that Mulla Sadra and his followers established see Hamid Dabashi, "Mir Damad and the School of Isfahan," in *A History of Islamic Philosophy,* ed. Oliver Leaman (London: Routledge, 1994).

2. For more details see Muhammad Ibrahim Ayati, *Tarikh-e Payambar-e Islam* [The History of the Prophet of Islam], revisions and additional notes by Abu al-Qasem Gorji (Tehran: Tehran University Press, 1366/1987), 216.

3. For these and other similar sayings attributed to the Prophet about Ali see the Shi'i canonical source Shaykh al-Mufid, *Kitab al-Irshad: The Book of Guidance,* trans. I. K. A. Howard, preface by Seyyed Hossein Nasr (London: Balagha Books, 1981), 18–43.

4. See Matti Moosa, *Extremist Shiites: The Ghulat Sects* (Syracuse, NY: Syracuse University Press, 1988).

5. See Max Weber, *The Sociology of Religion,* trans. Ephraim Fischoff, introd. by Talcott Parsons (Boston: Beacon Press, 1922/1963), 46. I have used Max Weber's notion of "charismatic authority" within an early Islamic context in Hamid Dabashi, *Authority in Islam: From the Rise of Muhammad to the Establishment of the Umayyads* (New Brunswick, NJ: Transaction, 1989).

6. For Philip Rieff's critique of the Weberian notion of "charisma," via a return to its originating significance in the New Testament, see Philip Rieff, *Charisma: The Gift of Grace, and How It Has Been Taken Away from Us* (New York: Vintage, 2007).

7. The idea of the *Verstehendemethode* extends from the works of Max Weber and includes those of Wilhelm Dilthey and Georg Simmel, and thus embraces the whole tradition of German sociological thinking, moving away from French positivism and British utilitarianism toward an understanding of the motives and meanings of social actions. For more on Max Weber's sociological

methodologies see the excellent work Sven Eliaeson, *Max Weber's Methodologies: Interpretation and Critique* (New York: Polity, 2002).

8. Max Weber, *Sociology of Religion,* 46.
9. Ibid.
10. Ibid., 47.
11. Ibid.
12. Ibid., 51.
13. Ibid., 51–52.
14. See Max Weber, "Politics as a Vocation," in *From Max Weber: Essays in Sociology,* ed. Hans Gerth and C. Wright Mills (Oxford: Oxford University Press, 1946), 78.
15. Max Weber, *Sociology of Religion,* 53.
16. Ibid., 55.
17. Ibid., 58–59.
18. Ibid., 59.
19. For an extensive discussion of Prophet Muhammad's charismatic authority, via an extension of the Weberian notion into Islamic domains, see Dabashi, *Authority in Islam.*
20. For an excellent study of Muslim pious veneration of their prophet see Annemarie Schimmel, *And Muhammad Is His Messenger: The Veneration of the Prophet in Islamic Piety* (Chapel Hill: University of North Carolina Press, 1985).
21. The earliest and best primary source on the life of Prophet Muhammad is Ibn Ishaq (d. 761), *Sirat Rasul Allah* as it was abbreviated by Ibn Hisham (d. 833). For a translation of this source see A. Guillaume, *The Life of Muhammad* (Oxford: Oxford University Press, 2002). Many excellent biographies of the Prophet are available in English, among them the two-volume set, W. Montgomery Watt, *Muhammad at Mecca* (Edinburgh: Edinburgh University Press, 1988), and Watt, *Muhammad at Medina* (Oxford: Oxford University Press, 1956). Now a classic in this field is Maxime Rodinson, *Muhammad* (New York: New Press, 2002). For a biography of Muhammad in English see Karen Armstrong, *Muhammad: A Biography of the Prophet* (New York: Harper, 1993). All these recent biographies by European and American scholars benefit from the obvious advantage of detached scholarship and yet (at the same time) suffer from the very same apathetic distance that enables that scholarship.
22. A work of monumental scholarship and detailed primary source archiving on the life of Prophet Muhammad is Ayati, *Tarikh-e Payambar-e Islam* [The History of the Prophet of Islam]. This book is also important for the manner in which a Shi'i historian consistently and in detail assimilates the lives of the Prophet and Ali into each other. Many of these details are of a hagiographical nature, but they do reveal the metamorphic character of Muhammad and

Ali. For example, when Muhammad is born, Fatima bent Asad, Ali's future mother, went to her husband Abu Talib to tell him about the birth of Muhammad, to which her husband immediately responded, "Wait for thirty years, and I will give you the good tiding of a son exactly like him [Muhammad], except for being a prophet"; in another tradition he tells her, "Why are you amazed at this news? You too will get pregnant, and will give birth to his [Muhammad's] successor" (56).

23. This is from *The Meaning of the Glorious Koran,* trans. Mohammed Marmaduke Pickthall (New York: Everyman's Library, 1992).

24. Shaykh Abu al-Futuh al-Razi, *Tafsir Ruh al-Jinan wa Ruh al-Janan,* 5 vols. (Qom: Mar'ashi Library Publications, 1404/1983), 5: 555–558.

25. For a more detailed account of this idea see Dabashi, *Authority in Islam,* ch. 6.

2. Birth of a Revolutionary Faith

1. Eyelids fluttering and shoes pairing (when you take them off before entering a room) are folkloric signs of having had a dream that will soon come true. People might fake such signs by way of suggesting that their dreams will come true, and thus, "I cross my heart and hope to die/If I lie."

2. "Imam-e Zaman" [The Imam of the Time] is the most common way of referring to the Twelfth Shi'i Imam, the Mahdi, who is believed to be in occultation now and expected to come back at the end of time and bring about everlasting peace and justice.

3. Iran was commonly believed to be ruled by not more than one thousand families *(hezar famil),* and the population of Iran at the time of this poem was commonly thought to be 20 million. This line was read as a surreptitious reference to the common belief that if the one thousand useless ruling families were to be taken out of Iran, people would have lost nothing.

4. Mohammad Ali Fardin (1930–2000) was a very popular actor in Iranian melodramatic movies at the time of this poem.

5. Toup Khaneh is a popular and crowded square in downtown Tehran.

6. My translation of Forough Farrokhzad's *Kasi keh mesl-e hich kas nist,* from the original Persian in her posthumously published volume, *Iman bi-avarim beh Aghaz-e Fasl-e Sard* [Let Us Believe in the Commencement of the Cold Season] (Tehran: Morvarid Publications, 1352/1973), 55–66. For more on my take on Forough Farrokhzad's poetry see Hamid Dabashi, "Forough Farrokhzad and the Formative Forces of Iranian Culture," special issue *Forough Farrokhzad: A Quarter Century Later,* ed. Michael C. Hillmann, *Literature East and West,* 24 (1988). For a biography of Forough Farrokhzad see Michael C. Hillmann, *A Lonely Woman: Forough Farrokhzad and Her Poetry* (Wash-

ington, DC: Mage, 1987). For a collection of her poetry in English see Forough Farrokhzad, *Sin: Selected Poems of Forough Farrokhzad,* trans. Sholeh Wolpé (Little Rock: University of Arkansas Press, 2007).

7. Ali Shari'ati's book on Abu Dharr, which was published for the first time in 1955 in Mashhad, when Shari'ati was twenty-two years old, is actually a free and much expanded Persian translation of an original Arabic work by Abd al-Hamid Jawdah al-Sahhar, an Egyptian writer. For the details of the translation see Shari'ati's own introductory remarks in Ali Shari'ati, *Abu Dharr* (Solon, OH: The Office of Editing and Publishing the Collected Works of the Martyred Brother Doctor Ali Shari'ati, 1357/1978), 7–8.

8. For more on Ali Shari'ati see Hamid Dabashi, *Theology of Discontent: The Ideological Foundation of the Islamic Revolution in Iran* (New Brunswick, NJ: Transaction, 1993/2006), ch. 2. For an excellent study of his life and thoughts see Ali Rahnema, *An Islamic Utopian: A Political Biography of Ali Shariati* (London: I. B. Tauris, 2000).

9. Ali Shari'ati, *Abu Dharr,* J.

10. Ibid., 250.

11. Ali Shari'ati's version of Forough Farrokhzad's *Kasi keh mesl-e hich kas nist* [Someone Who Is Like No One] is his lecture *Entezar: Mazhab-e I'teraz* [Expectation of Mahdi: The Religion of Defiance], in which he interpreted the Shi'i doctrinal expectation of the return of the Mahdi as a revolutionary momentum that restores agency to humanity. See Ali Shari'ati, *Hossein: Vares-e Adam* [Hossein: The Inheritor of Adam] (Tehran: Qalam Publications, 1367/1988), 253–304.

12. For more on Mohsen Makhmalbaf and his cinema see Hamid Dabashi, *Makhmalbaf at Large: The Making of a Rebel Filmmaker* (London: I. B. Tauris, 2008).

13. See Mohsen Makhmalbaf, "Forough Khahar-e ma bud" [Forough was our sister] in Makhmalbaf, *Zendegi Rang ast: Gozideh Neveshtar va Goftar, 1370–1375* [Life Is Color: A Collection of Speeches and Essays, 1991–1996] (Tehran: Nashr Ney, 1377/1998), 75–95.

14. For more on Forough Farrokhzad's *Khaneh Siyah ast* [House Is Black] (1963) see Hamid Dabashi, *Masters and Masterpieces of Iranian Cinema* (Washington, DC: Mage, 2007), ch. 1.

15. For more on this logic of transmutation and progress in history see G. W. Hegel, *Reason in History,* trans. Robert S. Hartman (Indianapolis, IN: Library of Liberal Arts, 1953).

16. For a comprehensive study of the crisis of succession to Prophet Muhammad see Wilferd Madelung, *The Succession to Muhammad: A Study of the Early Caliphate* (Cambridge: Cambridge University Press, 1998).

17. For more details of the conflicts that ensued concerning the question of

succession to Prophet Muhammad see Hamid Dabashi, *Authority in Islam,* chs. 2 and 3.

18. The essay is published in John P. Diggins and Mark E. Kann, eds., *The Problem of Authority in America* (Philadelphia: Temple University Press, 1981), 225–255.

19. For more details of these conflicts see Dabashi, *Authority in Islam,* chs. 2 and 3.

20. For a critical examination of the institution of the early caliphate see Patricia Crone and Martin Hinds, *God's Caliph: Religious Authority in the First Centuries of Islam* (Cambridge: Cambridge University Press, 2003). In this study, Crone and Hinds argue that the comprehensive authority afforded the early caliphs was identical with the authority that the Shi'is gave their Imams, and that the subsequent Sunni politicization of the institution of caliphate is a later development that emerged out of conflict between the caliphs and the learned community of the 'ulama.

21. For more details and variations on these narratives see Moojan Momen, *An Introduction to Shi'i Islam* (New Haven: Yale University Press, 1987), 11–17; and for even more details see S. H. M. Jafri, *The Origins and Early Development of Shi'a Islam* (London: Librairie du Liban, 1979), 19–21, 27–57.

22. For more details in this early period see Abu Muhammad Hasan ibn Musa al-Nowbakhti, *Firaq al-Shi'a,* ed., trans., and annotated by Muhammad Javad Mashkur (Tehran: Markaz Entesharat 'Ilmi va Farhangi, 1361/1982), 42–44. Al-Nawbakhti's (died c. 922) text is a major source of Shi'i heresiography. The best source of detailed information on Islamic heresiography available in English is Ignaz Goldziher, "The Sects," in Goldziher, *Introduction to Islamic Theology and Law,* trans. Andras Hamori and Ruth Hamori (Princeton: Princeton University Press, 1981), 167–229.

23. See Al-Nawbakhti, *Firaq al-Shi'a,* 50–51.

24. The idea of the Messiah (the Shi'i Mahdi) is of course much older than Shi'ism and is deeply rooted in the Hebrew Bible, particularly in such key passages as Isaiah 2, 11, 42, 59:20; Jeremiah 23, 30, 33, 48:47, 49:39; Ezekiel 38:16; and Hosea 3:4–5, among other places. It is also one of Maimonides' "Thirteen Principles of Faith" in Judaism. The prophesies of Saint John the Baptist before the appearance of Jesus of Nazareth, and then the anticipated return of Jesus Christ, His Second Coming, are also part of the Christian Christology. In this regard, one might compare Forough Farrokhzad's poem *Kasi keh mesl-e hich kas nist* with W. B. Yeats's *Second Coming* (1920).

25. For a thorough examination of this crucial period in Shi'ism see Hossein Modarressi Tabataba'i, *Crisis and Consolidation in the Formative Period of Shi'ite Islam: Abu Ja'far ibn Qiba al-Razi and His Contribution to Imamate Shi'ite Thought* (Princeton: Darwin Press, 1993).

26. See al-Nowbakhti, *Firaq al-Shi'a,* 40.

27. For an extensive study of the early history of the idea of Hidden Imam see Jan-Olaf Bleichfeldt, *Early Mahdism: Politics and Religion in the Formative Period of Islam* (Leiden: E. J. Brill, 1985). For an even more elaborate study of the idea in Shi'ism see Abdulaziz Abdulhussein Sachedina, *Islamic Messianism: The Idea of the Mahdi in Twelver Shi'ism* (Stony Brook: State University of New York Press, 1981).

28. No one has studied this phenomenon over the long expanse of Shi'i history better and with more consistent insights than Said Amir Arjomand in his extraordinary work, Said Amir Arjomand, *The Shadow of God and the Hidden Imam: Religion, Political Order, and Societal Change in Shi'ite Iran from the Beginning to 1890* (Chicago: University of Chicago Press, 1987).

29. For more on al-Kulayni see Ali Akbar Ghaffari, introduction to al-Kulayni, *al-Kafi* (Tehran, 1388/1968), 1:9–13.

30. For more on Ibn Babawaih see Seyyed Hassan al-Musawi al-Khurasani, introduction to his critical edition of *Man la yahduruhu al-Faqih* (Tehran, 1390/1970), 1:h–w.

31. For more on al-Tusi's life and significance see Robert Gleave, "al-Tusi," in *Encyclopedia of Islam and the Muslim World,* ed. Richard C. Martin et al. (New York: MacMillan, 2003).

32. For a concise account of the early Muslim conquest see Hugh Kennedy, *The Prophet and the Age of Caliphates: The Islamic Near East from the Sixth to the Eleventh Centuries* (London: Routledge, 1986).

33. For more on non-Islamic, proto-Zoroastrian rebellious movements in Iran after the early Muslim conquests see Roy Mottahedeh, "The Abbasid Caliphate in Iran," in *The Cambridge History of Iran,* ed. R. N. Frye, vol. 4, 57–89 (Cambridge: Cambridge University Press, 1975). For a more extensive treatment see Elton L. Daniel, *The Political and Social History of Khurasan under Abbasid Rule, 747–820* (New York: Bibliotheca Islamica, 1979). Equally informative is Wilferd Madelung, *Religious Trends in Early Islamic Iran* (New York: Bibliotheca Persica, 1988).

34. See Shari'ati, *Hossein: Vares-e Adam* [Hossein: The Inheritor of Adam].

3. The Karbala Complex

1. For more on Khosrow Golsorkhi and other leftist revolutionaries of this period see Maziar Behrooz, *Rebels with a Cause: The Failure of the Left in Iran* (London: I. B. Tauris, 2000); and Afshin Matin-Asgari, *Iranian Student Opposition to the Shah* (Costa Mesa, CA: Mazda, 2002).

2. This defense is now available at www.youtube.com/watch?v=buTIBLGdUfo. Accessed 30 June 2010. The transcription of Golsorkhi's speech and its translation from the original Persian are mine. The public trial of

Khosrow Golsorkhi and Keramatollah Daneshian began on Sunday 16 Dey 1352/6 January 1974. They were both condemned to death on Thursday 20 Dey 1353/10 January 1974, and executed early in the morning of Monday 29 Bahman 1352/18 February 1974. For more details see Anush Salehi, *Ravi Baharan: Mobarezat va Zendegi Keramatollah Daneshian* [The Narrator of Springs: The Struggles and Life of Keramatollah Daneshian] (Tehran: Qatreh Publishers, 1382/2003). I am grateful to Afshin Matin-Asgari for lending me his copy of this invaluable book.

3. For an excellent piece of scholarship on Goya, weaving together his personal traumas, social conditions, and a detailed reading of his works, see Robert Hughes, *Goya* (New York: Knopf, 2003).

4. Louis Massignon, the French Orientalist and scholar of Islamic mysticism, wrote a monumental biography of Mansur al-Hallaj (858–922). Al-Hallaj was legendary for his famous iconoclastic phrase *"Ana al-Haq"* ["I am truth"], for which he was executed.

5. The term that Shamlou uses for Christ in the title of his poem is the adjectival noun "Naseri," meaning "He who is from Nazareth." I have substituted the noun for the adjective here.

6. My translation of the original Persian of Ahmad Shamlou, *Marg-e Naseri* [Death of (the One from) Nazareth], in Ahmad Shamlou, *Majmu'eh Ash'ar* [Collected Works], 2 vols. (Hissen, Germany: Bamdad, 1989), 2:845–848.

7. For more on this performance see Milla C. Riggio, "Moses and the Wandering Dervish: Ta'ziyeh at Trinity College," *TDR: The Drama Review* 49, no. 4 (2005): 100–112.

8. The most recent and detailed study of the Battle of Karbala and its social, political, and economic contexts is Seyyed Ja'far Shahidi, *Qiyam-e Hossein* [Hossein's Uprising] (Tehran: Daftar-e Nashr-e Farhang e Islami, 1365/1986).

9. For more on Brecht's notion of *Verfremdungseffekt* see John Willet, ed., *Brecht on Theatre: The Development of an Aesthetic* (New York: Hill and Wang, 1977).

10. Ta'ziyeh has a fascinating story of traveling from Iran to India and from India to Trinidad and, after mixing there with elements from Latin American carnivals, assuming renewed symbolic significance. Peter Chelkowski has examined this phenomenon in some detail. See Chelkowski, "From the Sun-Scorched Desert of Iran to the Beaches of Trinidad: Ta'ziyeh's Journey from Asia to the Caribbean," *TDR: The Drama Review* 49, no. 4 (2005), *Special Issue:* Ta'ziyeh, Peter J. Chelkowski, guest editor. In another study of the traveling of Ta'ziyeh rituals from India to Trinidad, Gustav Thais, "Contested meanings and the politics of authenticity: The 'Hosay' in Trinidad," in *Islam, Globalization and Postmodernity,* ed. Akbar Ahmed and Hastings Donnan (London: Routledge, 1994), 38–62, Gustav Thais has rightly pointed out the multiple sites of contes-

tations among the Shi'is, the Sunnis, and the non-Muslims in that Caribbean island as to what *Ta'ziyeh* in this context could mean. Thais's analysis, however, is predicated on the false assumption that in its Indian, Iranian, Iraqi, or Lebanese context, the commemorations of Karbala lack such elements of festivity and carnivalesque. They are there—but hidden to the anthropologists' eyes.

11. This notion of multiple metamorphic parables includes the fact that in each Muslim region, Ta'ziyeh performances assume local colorings for otherwise opposing factions, such as in India among the Sunnis and the Hindus who participate equally in an otherwise exclusively Shi'i ritual. For more details see Juan Cole, *Roots of North Indian Shi'ism in Iran and Iraq: Religion and State in Awadh, 1722–1859* (Berkeley: University of California Press, 1988); and David Pinault, *The Shiites* (New York: St. Martin's Press, 1992).

12. I offer this reading of the Karbala complex via Roland Barthes's theory of myth. "The signifier," Barthes says in his *Mythologies* (1957), "can be looked at, in myth, from two points of view: as the final term of the linguistic system, or as the first term of the mythical system. We therefore need two names. On the plane of language, that is, as the final term of the first system, I shall call the signifier: *meaning* . . . on the plane of myth, I shall call it: *form.*" Roland Barthes, "Myth Today," in *A Barthes Reader,* ed. Susan Sontag (New York: Hill and Wang, 1982), 103.

13. I have developed this Shi'i mimetic disposition in some detail in Hamid Dabashi, *Islamic Liberation Theology: Resisting the Empire* (London: Routledge, 2008), 171–195.

14. See Peter Chelkowski, "From the Sun-Scorched Desert of Iran to the Beaches of Trinidad," for a more detailed study of the geographical traveling of Ta'ziyeh around the globe. Again, even within its *locus classicus* in Iraq and Iran, the Karbala commemorations had extensive carnivalesque qualities long before they reached Trinidad. Nevertheless, the sorts of geographical traveling that Chelkowski and others have documented exacerbates and corroborates the active transmutation of the Karbala complex into multiple metaphoric parables.

15. For an extensive discussion of the term *wali* in Islamic mysticism see the pioneering essay Ignaz Goldziher, "Veneration of Saints in Islam," in Goldziher, *Muslim Studies,* ed. S. M. Stern, trans. C. R. Barber and S. M. Stern, with an introduction by Hamid Dabashi (New Brunswick, NJ: Transaction, 2006), particularly pp. 263–270.

16. See, for example, the extraordinary work Kamil Mustafa al-Shibi, *Tashayyu' va Tasawwuf* [Shi'ism and Sufism], trans. and annotated by Alireza Zakavati Qaraguzlu (Tehran: Amir Kabir, 1359/1980).

17. For more on Ayn al-Qudat al-Hamadhani see Hamid Dabashi, *Truth and Narrative: The Untimely Thoughts of Ayn al-Qudat al-Hamadhani* (London: Curzon Press, 1999).

18. See William C. Chittick, "Rumi's View of the Imam Hossein," *Alsarat* (The Imam Husayn Conference Number) 12 (1984): 3–12 for a concise study of the presence of Imam Hossein and the tragic events of Karbala in the works of Jalal al-Din Rumi and other Persian mystic poets. An equally relevant essay is Annemarie Schimmel, "Karbala and the Imam Husayn in Persian and Indo-Muslim Literature," *Alsarat* 12 (1984): 29–42.

19. The poetic rendering of this Prophetic tradition appears many times and in various forms in Rumi's *Masnavi.* See for example verse VI: 739 in Jalal al-Din Rumi, *Masnavi,* ed. R. A. Nicholson (Tehran: Amir Kabir, 1363/1984), 3:315.

20. For an introductory essay on the character and ideas of Shahab al-Din Yahya Suhrawardi see S. H. Nasr, *Three Muslim Sages* (New York: Caravan Books, 1964/1976); and S. H. Nasr, "Shahab al-Din Suhrawardi Maqtul," in *A History of Muslim Philosophy,* ed. M. M. Sharif (Wiesbaden: Otto Harrassowitz, 1963). For a more extensive treatment of Suhrawardi's philosophy see Mehdi Amin Razavi, *Suhrawardi and the School of Illumination* (London: Curzon, 1997); and H. Ziai, *Knowledge and Illumination: A Study of Suhrawardi's Hikmat al-Ishraq* (Atlanta: Scholars Press, 1990). By far the most extensive study of Suhrawardi's philosophy is H. Corbin, *En Islam iranien: aspects spirituels et philosophiques,* 4 vols. (Paris: Gallimard, 1971).

21. See Jaroslav Pelikan, *Jesus through the Centuries: His Place in the History of Culture* (New Haven: Yale University Press, 1999).

22. For an English translation of the story of Seyavash see Abolqasem Ferdowsi, *The Legend of Seyavash,* trans. Dick Davis (London: Penguin Classics, 1992). For the connection between the figure of Imam Hossein in Ta'ziyeh and that of Seyavash in Shahnameh see Ehsan Yarshater, "Ta'ziyeh and Pre-Islamic Mourning Rites in Iran," in *Ta'ziyeh: Ritual and Drama in Iran,* ed. Peter Chelkowski, 88–94 (New York: New York University Press, 1979).

23. For an English translation of this novel see Simin Daneshvar, *Savashun: A Novel about Modern Iran,* trans. M. R. Ghanoonparvar (Washington, DC: Mage, 1991).

24. For an English translation of the story of Sohrab and other events in Rostam's life, see Abolqasem Ferdowsi, *Rostam: Tales of Love and War from Persia's Book of Kings,* trans. Dick Davis (Washington, DC: Mage, 2007). Another full English translation of this story is Abolqasem Ferdowsi, *The Tragedy of Sohrab and Rostam: From the Persian National Epic, the Shahname of Abol-Qasem Ferdowsi,* trans. Jerome W. Clinton (Seattle: University of Washington Press, 1996).

25. Matthew Arnold has a famous poem, "Sohrab and Rustum," based on this story of the *Shahnameh.* For more details on this translation see John D. Yohannan, *Persian Poetry in England and America: A 200-year History* (Delmar, NY: Caravan Books, 1977), 78–85. For a recent edition of the translation

see Matthew Arnold, *Sohrab and Rustum and Other Poems* (New York: BiblioBazaar, 2007).

26. One such popular story, collected by the Iranian folklorist Seyyed Abolqasem Anjavi Shirazi, produces an imaginative and anachronistic encounter between Ferdowsi and Ali, whereby the first Shi'i Imam miraculously restores the Persian poet's eyesight. See Seyyed Abolqasem Anjavi Shirazi, *Mardom va Ferdowsi* [People and Ferdowsi] (Tehran: 2535/1355/1976), 10–11.

27. For more on these mostly Shi'i epic narratives see Zabihollah Safa, *Hamaseh-sara'i dar Iran* [Epic Narratives in Iran] (Tehran: Amir Kabir, 1321/1942), 377–390.

28. One of these epic narratives on Hamza, the Prophet's valiant uncle, has now been capably translated into English from original Urdu. See Ghalib Lakhnavi and Abdullah Bilgrami, *The Adventures of Amir Hamza,* trans. Musharraf Ali Farooqi, introduction by Hamid Dabashi (New York: Modern Library, 2007).

29. There is a very useful site devoted to Gholamreza Takhti's lifetime achievement at: http://parssport.ir/wrestling/yademan/takhti.htm [accessed 10 July 2008]. For an excellent article in English on Gholamreza Takhti see Houchang E. Chehabi, "Sport and Politics in Iran: The Legend of Gholamreza Takhti," *International Journal of the History of Sport* 12 (1995): 48–60.

30. The prominent Iranian filmmaker Ali Hatami started shooting a film based on Takhti's life but died before he finished the film. A younger Iranian filmmaker, Behrouz Afkhami, finished the film, in which various conspiracy theories surrounding Takhti's death are examined.

31. My translation of Jalal Al-e Ahmad's remarks. For the full text of the original see http://parssport.ir/wrestling/yademan/takhti_from_ale_ahmad.htm [accessed 10 July 2008].

32. In Ferdowsi's *Shahnameh,* Esfandiyar is immortal, except for his vulnerable eyes (because, according to later, post-*Shahnameh,* traditions he closed them when Zoroaster poured holy water on his body in order to seal it against harm). Rostam targets Esfandiyar's eyes in their fateful battle. For a complete English translation of the story see Abolqasem Ferdowsi, *In the Dragon's Claws: The Story of Rostam and Esfandiyar from the Persian Book of Kings,* trans. Jerome W. Clinton (Washington, DC; Mage, 1999). For the details of the secret of Esfandiyar's immortality see Mahmoud Omidsalar, "Raz-e Ru'in-tani-ye Esfandiyar" [The Secret of Esfandiyar's Immortality], in Omidsalar, *Jostar-ha-ye Shahnameh-Shenasi* (Tehran: Afshar Endowment, 1381/2002), 3–30.

33. My translation of Ahmad Shamlou, *Sorud-e Ebrahim dar Atash* [The Song of Abraham in Fire], in Shamlou, *Majmu'eh Ash'ar* [Collected Works], 2:1001–1006. The poem is dedicated to the memory of an Iranian revolutionary named Mehdi Reza'i, a member of the Mojahedin-e Khalq organization who at the age of twenty was tried in a military tribunal and then executed in

1972. For more on the history and development of the Mojahedin-e Khalq organization see Ervand Abrahamian, *The Iranian Mojahedin* (New Haven: Yale University Press, 1992).

4. In the Battlefields of History

1. The most recent general introductory book on Nasir Khusraw is the excellent monograph Alice C. Hunsberger, *Nasir Khusraw, the Ruby of Badakhshan: A Portrait of the Persian Poet, Traveler and Philosopher* (London: I. B. Tauris, 2000). For a shorter essay on Nasir Khusraw's life and thoughts see also Alice C. Hunsberger, "Nasser Khusraw: Fatimid Intellectual," in *Intellectual Traditions in Islam,* ed. Farhad Daftary (London: I. B. Tauris, 2000), 112–129.

2. In this biographical sketch I follow the narrative of Seyyed Hassan Taqizadeh, as augmented by Mojtaba Minovi, with additional notes by Ali Akbar Dehkhoda in their introductions and commentaries on the Hajji Seyyed Nasrallah Taghavi's edition of *Divan-e Nasir Khusraw* (Tehran: 1305/1926). Among its other virtues, this volume brings together the exemplary work of four giant Iranian scholars of their time in facilitating an accurate understanding of Nasir Khusraw.

3. For a good reading of Nasir Khusraw's poetry as a source of his biography see the samples in Hunsberger, *Nasir Khusraw, the Ruby of Badakhshan,* chs. 3 and 4. A selection of Nasir Khusraw's poetry is also edited with extensive commentary in Nasir Khusraw, *Sharh-e Si Qasideh az Hakim Nasir Khusraw Qubadyani,* ed. and annotated by Mehdi Hohaqqeq (Tehran: Tus Publications, 1369/1990). For a translation into English of a selection of Nasir Khusraw's poetry see Nasir-i Khusraw, *Make a Shield from Wisdom: Selected Verses from Nasir-i Khusraw's Divan,* trans. Annemarie Schimmel (London: I. B. Tauris, 2001). For a detailed study of one of his poems see Julie Scott Meisami, "Symbolic Structure in a Poem by Nasir-i Khusraw," *Iran* 31 (1993): 103–117.

4. For a recent study and re-interpretation of the collapse of the Sassanid empire and Arab conquest see Parvaneh Pourshariati, *Decline and Fall of the Sasanian Empire: The Sasanian-Parthian Confederacy and the Arab Conquest of Iran* (London: I. B. Tauris, 2008).

5. For a close study of Khurasan in the aftermath of the Muslim conquest see the excellent study Elton L. Daniel, *The Political and Social History of Khurasan under Abbasid Rule, 747–820* (Chicago: Iran-America Foundation, 1979). Equally informative is M. A. Shaban, "Khurasan at the Time of the Arab Conquest," in *Iran and Islam: In Memory of the Late Vladimir Minorsky,* ed. C. E. Bosworth (Edinburgh: Edinburgh University Press, 1971): 479–490.

6. For more details on the history of the Ghaznavids see Clifford Edmund Bosworth, *The Ghaznavids: Their Empire in Afghanistan and Eastern Iran, 994–1040* (Edinburgh: Edinburgh University Press, 1963). For more on the

Seljuqids see Clifford Edmund Bosworth, *The History of the Seljuq Turks: From the Jami al-Tawarikh* (London: Routledge Curzon, 2000).

7. The best introductory text on Arabic literary humanism *(adab)* is George Makdisi, *The Rise of Humanism in Classical Islam and the Christian West: With Special Reference to Scholasticism* (Edinburgh: Edinburgh University Press, 1990). A similar book on Persian, Turkish, or Urdu literary humanism is yet to be written.

8. For an English translation see Alberuni, *Alberuni's India* [abridged] (New York: W. W. Norton, 1993).

9. For a study of the rise of caliphate as a political institution see Patricia Crone and Martin Hinds, *God's Caliph: Religious Authority in the First Centuries of Islam* (Cambridge: Cambridge University Press, 2003).

10. For a close examination of the Umayyad period see G. R. Hawting, *The First Dynasty of Islam: The Umayyad Caliphate* AD *661–750* (London: Routledge, 2000).

11. For more on the immediate aftermath of the death of the Prophet and the early history of the caliphate, including tribal and sectarian revolts, see Hugh Kennedy, *The Prophet and the Age of the Caliphates: The Islamic Near East from the Sixth to the Eleventh Centuries* (London: Routledge, 1986).

12. For more on this first civil war in early Islamic history see M. A. Shaban, *Islamic History: A New Interpretation,* 2 vols. (Cambridge: Cambridge University Press, 1971), vol. 1, chs. 4 and 5.

13. The insurrectionary appeal of the Kharijites throughout medieval history was such that it became proverbial in subsequent generations; by the time Khwajah Nizam al-Mulk wrote his *Siyasatnama,* he used the expression *Khariji/Kharijite* to mean any kind of rebellion against government, all the way back from the Mazdakites in pre-Islamic Iran to various revolutionary uprisings in his own time. See Khwajah Nizam al-Mulk al-Tusi, *The Book of Government or Rules for Kings: The Siyar al Muluk or Siyasat-nama of Nizam al-Mulk,* trans. Hubert Darke (London: Routledge Curzon, 2001), ch. 43. For my references I use the original Persian. Nizam al-Mulk, *Siyar al-Muluk (Siyasatnama),* ed. Hubert Darke (Tehran: Amir Kabir, 1340/1961).

14. For more details of the Abbasid Revolution see M. A. Shaban, *The Abbasid Revolution* (Cambridge: Cambridge University Press, 1970).

15. For further details on the aftermath of the murder of Abu Muslim see Shaban, *Islamic History,* vol. 2, ch. 1. For a reading of the rise of Abbasid empire see Albert Hourani, *A History of the Arab Peoples* (Cambridge, MA: Harvard University Press, 1991), ch. 2.

16. Mazdakites were followers of the pre-Islamic, proto-socialist Persian prophet Mazdak (died circa 528).

17. For a long time the Zanj Revolt was considered a "slave revolt" by many

historians since the German Orientalist Theodor Nöldeke (1836–1930) identified it as such. M. A. Shaban has seriously challenged this assumption and argued that this was "not a slave revolt. It was a *zanj,* i.e., a Negro, revolt. To equate Negro with slave is a reflection of nineteenth-century racial theories; it could only apply to the American south before the civil war" (Shaban, *Islamic History,* 2:101). But that at least some of the people involved in the Zanj revolt were slaves is perfectly evident in a passage from Nizam al-Mulk's *Siyasatnama* (composed in 1076—long before Theodor Nöldeke!) where he talks about the Isma'ilis and the Qaramita. Referring to the Zanj revolt in Khuzestan, which was simultaneous with that of the Qaramita, Nizam al-Mulk adds, "*Hameh-ye Zangian Khwajegan-e khish ra bekoshtand*" [and all the Zanjis killed their masters] (Nizam al-Mulk, *Siyar al-Muluk (Siyasatnama),* 306). Furthermore, an eyewitness account dates back even earlier than 1076 (when Nizam al-Mulk was writing his *Siyasatnama*) by Nasir Khusraw sometime in 1050 when on his way back from Egypt he visited al-Hasa, the capital of the Qaramita in Bahrain, where he reports in his *Safarnameh* that the rulers of the city had purchased "thirty thousand *Zangi va Habashi* [Black and Abyssinian] slaves and let them free to work in agriculture without taxing them." Nasir Khusraw Qubadyani, *Safarnameh,* ed. and annotated by Nader Vazinpour (Tehran: Jibi Publications, 1350/1971), 114. Thus, that there were black slaves in the Persian Gulf area is not in doubt, and some or all of them may have participated in the Zanj revolt, though the revolt indeed did include non-slaves as well.

18. For an overview of the Islamic taxation system at this time see Hossein Modarressi Tabataba'i, *Kharaj in Islamic Law* (London: Anchor Press, 1983).

19. For more on Ya'qub and his historical and symbolic significance see S. M. Stern, "Ya'qub the Coppersmith and Persian national sentiment," in *Iran and Islam,* ed. Bosworth, 535–556.

20. For more details of Nasir Khusraw's early life see Hunsberger, *Nasir Khusraw, the Ruby of Badakhshan,* ch.1. As early as E. G. Browne, "Nasir-i Khusraw: Poet, Traveler, and Propagandist," *Journal of the Royal Asiatic Society* (1905): 313–352, Nasir Khusraw's life has been the source of many scholarly investigations.

21. For an excellent essay on the central significance of "Reason" in Nasir Khusraw's poetry see Shahrokh Meskoob, "The Origin and Meaning of *'Aql* (Reason) in the View of Nasser Khusraw," *Iran Nameh* 6 (1989): 239–257.

22. For more on the centrality of the idea of *Mahdi/Messiah* in these early Shi'i movements see Jan-Olaf Blichfeldt, *Early Mahdism: Politics and Religion in the Formative Period of Islam* (Leiden: E. J. Brill, 1985); and Said Amir Arjomand, *The Shadow of God and the Hidden Imam: Religion, Political Order, and Societal Change in Shi'ite Iran from the Beginning to 1890* (Chicago: University of Chicago Press, 1987), ch. 2.

23. By far the most detailed and comprehensive study of the Isma'ilis at this early stage and in its later developments is by Farhad Daftary, *The Isma'ilis: Their History and Doctrines* (Cambridge: Cambridge University Press, 1990). For a shorter version of this book see Farhad Daftary, *A Short History of the Isma'ilis: Traditions of a Muslim Community* (Edinburgh: Edinburgh University Press, 1998).

24. Daftary, *Short History of the Isma'ilis,* 36.

25. For further details see Daftary, *Short History of the Isma'ilis,* 35–36.

26. For a detailed study of the Fatimid dynasty see Paul E. Walker, *Exploring an Islamic Empire: Fatimid History and Its Sources* (London: I. B. Tauris, 2002). Equally informative is Heinz Halm, *The Fatimids and their Traditions of Learning* (London: I. B. Tauris, 2001).

27. See Daftary, *Short History of the Isma'ilis,* 45–46.

28. Ibid.

29. For more on the Qaramita see Wilferd Madelung, "Karmati," in *Encyclopedia of Islam,* 2nd ed., 4:660–665; see also Farhad Daftary, "Carmatians," in *Encyclopedia Iranica,* ed. Ehsan Yarshater (London: Routledge and Kegan Paul, 1982–), 4:823–832.

30. The relationship between the Fatimids and the Qaramita is the subject of a pioneering study, Wilferd Madelung, "Fatimiden und Bahrainqarmaten," *Der Islam* 34 (1959): 34–88. For an English translation of this essay see Farhad Daftary, *Medieval Isma'ili History and Thought* (Cambridge: Cambridge University Press, 1996), 21–73.

31. For more on Isma'ili philosophy see Henry Corbin, *Cyclical Time and Ismaili Gnosis* (London: Kegan Paul, 1983); and Paul E. Walker, *Early Philosophical Shiism: The Ismaili Neoplatonism of Abu Ya'qub al-Sijistani* (Cambridge: Cambridge University Press, 1993). Walker's study is a far more reliable study of philosophical Isma'ilism; Corbin's work is marred by his larger projects on Islamic intellectual history, categorically deboning it of all its social and political dimensions and transmuting it into a bodiless mass of somnambulated ideas. Henry Corbin has done extensive work on philosophical Shi'ism in general and, facilitated by Seyyed Hossein Nasr, he had a major intellectual impact in Iran, and no one more than he and his circle are responsible for an aggressive mystification of Islamic intellectual history. This crucial phase in Iranian (Islamic) intellectual history is the subject of a forthcoming book by Afshin Matin-Asgari.

32. Nizam al-Mulk, *Siyar al-Muluk,* 260.

33. Alice C. Hunsberger has done an excellent comparison of the narrative of this dream with a poem of Nasir Khusraw in which he describes his spiritual crisis in more detail. See Hunsberger, *Nasir Khusraw: The Ruby of Badakhshan,* ch. 4.

34. For more on the link between Nasir Khusraw and the Isma'ilis see Henry Corbin, "Nasir-i Khusrau and Iranian Isma'ilism," in *The Cambridge History of Iran,* vol. 4: *The Period from the Arab Invasion to the Saljuqs,* ed. R. N. Frye (Cambridge: Cambridge University Press, 1968–1991), 520–542; though Corbin's account ought to be balanced with Vladimir Ivanov, *Nasir-i Khusraw and Isma'ilism* (Bombay: NP, 1956), and Hunsberger, *Nasir Khusraw: The Ruby of Badakhshan,* chs. 11 and 12.

35. For an English translation of Nasir Khusraw's *Safarnameh* see *Nasir-i Khusraw's Book of Travels: Safarnamah,* trans. Wheeler M. Thackston (Costa Mesa, CA: Mazda, 2001). For my references I use the original Persian, Nasir Khusraw Qubadyani, *Safarnameh,* ed. and annotated by Nader Vazinpour (Tehran: Jibi Publications, 1350/1971).

36. Nasir Khusraw Qubadyani, *Safarnameh,* 113.

37. Ibid., 114.

38. Ibid., 115.

39. For more on this period of Nasir Khusraw's life see Hunsberger, *Nasir Khusraw, the Ruby of Badakhshan,* ch. 11.

40. For a critical edition and translation of *Goshayesh va Rahayesh* [Knowledge and Liberation] with a detailed introduction to Nasir Khusraw's philosophy see Nasir Khusraw, *Knowledge and Liberation: A Treatise on Philosophical Theology,* ed. and trans. Faquir M. Hunzai, with an introduction by Parviz Morewedge (London: I. B. Tauris, 1998).

41. For more details of the Isma'ili philosophical traditions preceding Nasir Khusraw's work see Walker, *Early Philosophical Shi'ism.*

42. For more on the history of the Fatimids and the Nizari-Musta'li split see Daftary, *A Short History of the Isma'ilis;* and Walker, *Exploring an Islamic Empire.*

43. For a superb historical investigation into the origin of the myth of "the Assassins" in the time of the Crusades and the writings of Marco Polo (subsequently exacerbated by European Orientalists), see Farhad Daftary, *The Assassin Legends: Myths of the Isma'ilis* (London: I. B. Tauris, 1995).

44. For more on Khwajah Nasir al-Din al-Tusi see Hamid Dabashi, "Khwajah Nasir al-Din al-Tusi: The Philosopher/Vizier," in *A History of Islamic Philosophy,* ed. Seyyed Hossein Nasr and Oliver Leaman (London: Routledge, 1994); and Hamid Dabashi, "The Philosopher/Vizier: Khwajah Nasir al-Din al-Tusi and His Isma'ili Connection," in *Studies in Isma'ili History and Doctrines,* ed. Farhad Daftary (Cambridge: Cambridge University Press, 1996).

45. For more on the scientific achievements of Nasir al-Din al-Tusi in mathematics and astrophysics see the groundbreaking work George Saliba, *Islamic Science and the Making of the European Renaissance* (Cambridge, MA: MIT Press, 2007).

5. In the Company of Kings, Caliphs, and Conquerors

1. The term "Akhond" has assumed a pejorative connotation in contemporary Persian for a number of class-related and political reasons. But rarely are those who use the term "Akhond" pejoratively aware of its unsurpassed implication of reverence and honor when applied to Mulla Sadra.

2. For a general introduction to Mulla Sadra's life and thought, plus an extensive bibliography of his writings, see Seyyed Hossein Nasr, *Sadr al-Din Shirazi and His Transcendent Theosophy: Background, Life and Works* (Tehran: Imperial Academy of Philosophy, 1978). For an introduction to his philosophy see Muhammad Kamal, *Mulla Sadra's Transcendent Philosophy* (London: Ashgate, 2006).

3. The link between Mulla Sadra and Nasir Khusraw is no mere heuristic device here. Mulla Sadra was very much aware not only of Nasir Khusraw's philosophy but even of his Persian poetry, which he quotes appropriately in its original Persian in order to make a point in his usually Arabic prose; for example, Mulla Sadra, *al-Waridat al-Qalbiyyah fi Ma'rifat al-Rububiyyah* [Divine Inspirations in Understanding the Divinity], ed. Ahmad Shafi'iha (Tehran: Anjoman Falsafeh, 1358/1979), 65.

4. I have given a more detailed outline of this epistemic theory of Islamic intellectual history in various places, among them in Hamid Dabashi, *Truth and Narrative: The Untimely Thoughts of Ayn al-Qudat al-Hamadhani* (London: Routledge, 1999).

5. For more on Mongol conquests see J. J. Saunders, *The History of the Mongol Conquests* (Philadelphia: University of Pennsylvania Press, 2001).

6. For more on the Mongol Empire see Michael Prawdin, *The Mongol Empire: Its Rise and Legacy* (New Brunswick, NJ: Transaction, 2005).

7. The best study of the relationship between Shi'ism and Sufism is in Arabic, translated into Persian: *Tashayyu' va Tasawwuf* [Shi'ism and Sufism], trans. Kamil Mustafa al-Shibi, annot. Alireza Zakavati Qaraguzlu (Tehran: Amir Kabir, 1359/1980).

8. See Said Amir Arjomand, *The Shadow of God and the Hidden Imam: Religion, Political Order, and Societal Change in Shi'ite Iran from the Beginning to 1890* (Chicago: University of Chicago Press, 1984), 70.

9. *Al-Hikmah al-Muta'aliyyah* has also been translated as "transcendental theosophy" by Seyyed Hossein Nasr and others. But, along with many other scholars, I prefer "metaphilosophy," or even "transcendental philosophy," because I think they better correspond to Mulla Sadra's philosophical project, and do not attribute to him an anachronistic Pahlavi-era theosophical neologism of which Henry Corbin and Seyyed Hossein Nasr were particularly wont. There is definitely a certain theo-ontological element in Mulla Sadra's philosophy, but that does not mean that his entire philosophical project is theosophical.

10. For more on the mystical dimensions of Khwajah Nasir al-Din al-Tusi's philosophical project see Hamid Dabashi, "Khwajah Nasir al-Din al-Tusi: The Philosopher/Vizier and the Intellectual Climate of his Time," in A *History of Islamic Philosophy,* ed. Seyyed Hossein Nasr and Oliver Leaman (London: Routledge, 1994), ch. 32; and Hamid Dabashi, "The Philosopher/Vizier; Khwajah Nasir al-Din al-Tusi and His Isma'ili Connection," in *Studies in Isma'ili History and Doctrines,* ed. Farhad Daftary (Cambridge: Cambridge University Press, 1996).

11. For a thorough examination of Ibn abi Jumhur al-Ahsa'i's ideas see Sabine Schmidtke, *Theologie, Philosophie und Mystik im Zwolferschiitischen Islam Des 9./15. Jahrhunderts: Die Gedankenwelten Des Ibn Abi Gumhur Al-Ahsa'i* (Um 838/1434/35–Nach 906/1501) (Leiden: Brill, 2000). There is also a short but excellent chapter on him in al-Shibi, *Tashayyu' va Tasawwuf,* 331–340.

12. Al-Shibi has a detailed account of the theological origin and social implications of the Hurufiyyah movement. See al-Shibi, *Tashayyu' va Tasawwuf,* 157–231.

13. Arjomand, *The Shadow of God and the Hidden Imam,* 72. So radical were the ideas of the Hurufiyyah that Said Amir Arjomand believes that its founder Fazlullah had actually "created a religious revolution. He transformed Shi'ism into a new religion, which, in marked contrast to Twelver Shi'ism, rested upon knowledge and mystery as opposed to piety and faith" (74). Alternatively one might argue that this messianic disposition has always existed in Shi'ism, and with the Sarbedaran and Hurufiyyah movements it becomes pervasively urbanized, with a particular appeal to the urban intellectual elite.

14. For an introductory study of the Safavid dynasty see Roger Savory, *Iran under the Safavids* (Cambridge: Cambridge University Press, 2007). Equally thorough is Charles Melville, *Safavid Persia: The History and Politics of an Islamic Society* (London: I. B. Tauris, 1996). Andrew J. Newman, *Safavid Iran: Rebirth of a Persian Empire* (London: I. B. Tauris, 2006) is a groundbreaking work in the field of Safavid studies. By far the best study of Shi'ism under the Safavids remains the monumental work Arjomand, *Shadow of God and the Hidden Imam.*

15. Although Said Amir Arjomand dismisses the Musha'sha' movement as "an obscurantist religious tyranny" (*The Shadow of God and Hidden Imam,* 77), the movement that Ibn Falah led shared the essential features of the messianic rebellions that mixed doctrinal and mystical dimensions of Shi'ism. Ibn Falah and his son Mawla Ali believed themselves to be the manifestations or reincarnations of the First Shi'i Imam.

16. For more details of this transference see E. G. Browne, *A Literary History of Persia* (Oxford: Oxford University Press, 1924), 4:24–31.

17. See, for example, the chapters on Safavid art and architecture in Sheila S.

Blair and Jonathan M. Bloom, *The Art and Architecture of Islam 1250–1800* (New Haven, CT: Yale University Press, 1994).

18. For a detailed set of studies of the post-Mongol society, art, and culture see Linda Komaroff and Stefano Carboni, eds., *The Legacy of Genghis Khan: Courtly Art and Culture in Western Asia, 1256–1353* (New York: Metropolitan Museum of Art, 2002).

19. For more on the social dimensions of the Safavid architecture see Stephan B. Blake, *Half the World: The Social Architecture of Safavid Isfahan, 1590–1722* (Costa Mesa, CA: Mazda, 1999).

20. For more on the urbanization under the Safavids see Masashi Hamada, "The Character of the Urbanization of Isfahan in the Later Safavid Period," in *Safavid Persia: The History and Politics of an Islamic Society,* ed. Charles Mill-ville (London: I. B. Tauris, 1996), 369–388.

21. For the courtly and royal dimensions of the Safavid art see James Allan, Sheila Canby, and Jon Thompson, *Hunt for Paradise: Court Arts of Safavid Iran 1501–76* (Milan: Skira, 2004).

22. "All that is required for enlightenment," says Kant, "is *freedom;* and particularly the least harmful of all that may be called freedom, namely, the freedom for man to make *public use* of his reason in all matters." Immanuel Kant, "What Is Enlightenment," in *The Philosophy of Kant,* ed. Karl J. Friedrich (New York: Modern Library, 1992), 147.

23. Blair and Bloom, *Art and Architecture of Islam 1250–1800,* 185.

24. Ibid.

25. Ibid.

26. Ibid.

27. Ibid. For more descriptions of the public scene in the Safavid capital see Newman, *Safavid Iran,* 68–71, though Newman, like all other social and intellectual historians of the period, fails to see the link between this public scene and the emergence of a "public reason."

28. For more on the history of the School of Isfahan see Seyyed Hossein Nasr, *Islamic Philosophy from Its Origin to the Present: Philosophy in the Land of Prophecy* (Albany, NY: State University of New York Press, 2006), chs. 12–13. As a term, "the School of Isfahan" was coined by Seyyed Hossein Nasr and Henry Corbin. Nasr also posits such similar terms as "School of Shiraz" and "School of Tehran," which have been far less convincing, and he remains the only one who uses them; whereas the term "School of Isfahan" has assumed a far more global acceptance. For alternative views on the School of Isfahan see Hamid Dabashi, "Mir Damad and the School of Isfahan," in *A History of Islamic Philosophy,* ch. 34; for a different perspective see Andrew J. Newman, "Towards a Reconsideration of the Isfahan School of Philosophy: Shaykh Baha'i and the Role of the Safavid Ulama," *Studia Iranica* (Paris), vol. 15, fasc. 2 (1986), 165–199.

29. I have discussed Mir Damad's philosophy in some detail in Dabashi, "Mir Damad and the School of Isfahan."

30. For a study of the Safavid era foreign relations see Michel M. Mazzaoui, *Safavid Iran and Her Neighbors* (Salt Lake City: University of Utah Press, 2003).

31. For more details of Mir Damad's problems with his weight in the royal company of Shah Abbas see Dabashi, "Mir Damad and the School of Isfahan," 606–607.

32. For an excellent introduction in English to Mulla Sadra's philosophy see Fazlur Rahman, *The Philosophy of Mulla Sadr (Sadr al-Din al-Shirazi)* (Albany: State University of New York Press, 1975); see also Hossein Ziai, "Mulla Sadra: His Life and Works" in *History of Islamic Philosophy,* ed. Nasr and Leaman (London: Routledge, 1996), 635–642. For an excellent translation of one of Mulla Sadra's seminal works, plus an extensive introduction to his philosophy, see J. W. Morris, *The Wisdom of the Throne: An Introduction to the Philosophy of Mulla Sadra* (Princeton, NJ: Princeton University Press, 1982).

33. Mulla Sadra, *al-Waridat al-Qalbiyyah fi Ma'rifat al-Rububiyyah* [Divine Inspirations in Understanding the Divinity], 56. Translation from the original Arabic is mine.

34. Ibid.

6. At the Dawn of Colonial Modernity

1. For these and other details of Tahereh Qorrat al-Ayn's life and death I use a combination of three sources. The unsurpassed and judicious study of Babism, Abbas Amanat, *Resurrection and Renewal: The Making of the Babi Movement in Iran, 1844–1850* (Ithaca, NY: Cornell University Press, 1989), 328–330; the vituperative but insightful account, Mohammad Reza Fashahi, *Vapasin Jonbesh-e Qorun-e Vosta'i dar Doran-e Feodal* [The Last Medieval Uprising in the Feudal Period] (Tehran: Javidan Publications, 1355/1976), 132–133; and the sedate and punctilious study, Yahya Aryanpour, *Az Saba ta Nima* [From Saba to Nima] (Tehran: Zavvar Publications, 1350/1971), vol. 2, 130–133. Qorrat al-Ayn's poem is quoted and translated in E. G. Browne, *Materials for the Study of the Bábí Religion* (1918; Cambridge: Cambridge University Press, 1961), 349. "Am I not thy Lord" is a famous phrase from the Qur'an (VII: 171), particularly dear to the Muslim mystics, for in it God is soliciting a positive response from His created beings that He is their Lord.

2. For additional details of Tahereh Qorrat al-Ayn's life I also sift through a particularly hostile source by a contemporary Qajar historian, I'tezad al-Saltaneh, *Fetneh-ye Bab* [The Menace of the Bab], ed. and annotated by Abd al-Hossein Nava'i (Tehran: Babak Publishers, 1333/1954). This book is only a segment of a larger volume, I'tezad al-Saltaneh, *al-Mutinabb'iyn* [Pretenders to

Prophethood], that begins with pre-Islamic prophets Mani and Mazdak and concludes with Ali Mohammad Shirazi, the Bab. Abd al-Hossein Nava'i's commentaries in this volume are equally hostile to Babism and sardonic and scornful towards Qorrat al-Ayn. But nevertheless these commentaries contain many valuable details. To balance these belligerent sources I also use another contemporary account by a European traveler, Carla Serna, *Hommes et Choses en Perse* (Paris: G. Charpentier et Cie, Editeurs, 1883), translated into Persian, Ali Asghar Sa'idi, *Adam-ha va A'in-ha dar Iran* [Human Beings and Rituals in Iran] (Tehran: Zavvar Publications, 1362/1983), which gives an extraordinary eyewitness account of the Babi movement. Carla Serna was an Italian traveler who had gone to Iran (among other places) and written her travelogue during the years 1877–1878, not too long after the Babi uprising, and writes in detail and somewhat sympathetically about Qorrat al-Ayn. Whatever source I have used on Babism and Qorrat al-Ayn I have checked against the exemplary scholarly diligence of Abbas Amanat, *Resurrection and Renewal,* in which he carefully navigates between sympathetic Babi sources and hostile Shi'i and Qajar sources. In this chapter I will have a few major points of interpretative differences with Amanat. But in terms of his due diligence in a field fraught with political land mines and sectarian fanaticism he remains singularly trustworthy in his scholarship.

3. For the most recent study of the late Ottoman period see Sukru Hanioglu, *A Brief History of the Late Ottoman* (Princeton: Princeton University Press, 2008).

4. For an account of the British rule in India see Lawrence James, *Raj: The Making and Unmaking of British India* (London: St. Martin's, 2000). For a critical account of the same period see Nicholas B. Dirks, *The Scandal of Empire: India and the Creation of Imperial Britain* (Cambridge, MA: Belknap Press of Harvard University Press, 2008).

5. For an excellent account of the Safavid dynasty in the context of its region see Michel M. Mazzaoui, *Safavid Iran & Her Neighbors* (Salt Lake City: University of Utah Press, 2003).

6. For more on the last years of the Safavid Empire see Roger Savory, *Iran under the Safavids* (Cambridge: Cambridge University Press, 1980), 226–254.

7. For a comprehensive study of Nader's ascendancy to power in this period see Ernest S. Tucker, *Nadir Shah's Quest for Legitimacy in Post-Safavid Iran* (Gainesville: University Press of Florida, 2006). Tucker's major thesis in this book—that Nader Shah's mode of political legitimacy represents a "modern" political practice—is categorically flawed, for reasons that I explain in this chapter. An earlier study by Laurence Lockhart, *Nadir Shah, Shah of Iran, 1688–1747* (London: Luzac, 1938), is still reliable.

8. For more on Karim Khan Zand and his period see John R. Perry, *Karim Khan Zand* (London: Oneworld, 2006).

9. For a set of pioneering studies on the Qajar period see Ann K. S. Lambton, *Qajar Persia: Eleven Studies* (Austin: University of Texas Press, 1988). For a more recent study see Nikki R. Keddie, *Qajar Iran and the Rise of Reza Khan 1796–1925* (Costa Mesa, CA: Mazda, 1999).

10. Nader's *Khuriltai* was decidedly modeled on that of Genghis Khan, convened at the source of the Onon River in the spring of the Year of Tiger (1206). Nader also imitated Genghis Khan's timing by convening his own *Khuriltai* in Dasht-e Moghan in spring of 1763 (with his coronation scheduled on 24 Shawwal 1148, twelve days before the Persian New Year at the vernal equinox). For more detail on Genghis' *Khuriltai* see Paul Ratchnevsky, *Genghis Khan: His Life and Legacy* (London: Blackwell, 1991), 89–96. Quite contrary to Ernest S. Tucker's assessment in Tucker, *Nadir Shah's Quest for Legitimacy in Post-Safavid Iran,* Nader's legacy was anything but "modern"; in fact it was decidedly anti-modern, tribal, feudal, patrimonial, and nomadic—destroying the cosmopolitan legacy of the Safavid period, with catastrophic consequences, as I will argue in this and subsequent chapters, for the rest of Iranian and Shi'i history.

11. Said Amir Arjomand, *The Shadow of God and the Hidden Imam: Religion, Political Order, and Societal Change in Shi'ite Iran from the Beginning to 1890* (Chicago: University of Chicago Press, 1984), 221.

12. See Arjomand, *Shadow of God and the Hidden Imam,* 224–225, for more details of this argument.

13. Ibid., 225.

14. For more on the Akhbaris see Robert M. Gleave, *Scripturalist Islam: The History and Doctrines of the Akhbari Shi'i School* (Leiden: Brill, 2007).

15. For more on Giorgio Agamben's notion of "naked life" see Giorgio Agamben, *Homo Sacer: Sovereign Power and Bare Life* (Palo Alto, CA: Stanford University Press, 1998).

16. So, contrary to Said Amir Arjomand, I do not see the rationalism of the Usuli as "world-embracing" (Arjomand, *Shadow of God and the Hidden Imam,* 232)—quite the opposite, I believe it to be positively world-rejecting and a radical mode of privatization of reason against the world. For more on the Usulis see Arjomand, *Shadow of God and the Hidden Imam,* 234–237.

17. For a more detailed discussion of this early articulation of the notion of the absolute authority of the jurist *(wilayat-e faqih)* over that of the reigning monarch, see Hamid Dabashi, "Early Propagation of *Wilayat-e Faqih* and Mulla Ahmad Naraqi," in *Expectation of the Millennium: Shi'ism in History,* ed. S. H. Nasr, H. Dabashi, and S. V. R. Nasr (Albany: State University of New York Press, 1988).

18. Arjomand, *Shadow of God and the Hidden Imam,* 245–246.

19. Ibid., 248–249.

20. The notion of a *Shi'a-ye Kamil* [Perfect Shi'i] has its roots in the Sufi fig-

ure of *Insan-e Kamil* [Perfect Human Being]. For more details on the sources and significance of this concept see Hamid Dabashi, "The Sufi Doctrine of 'The Perfect Man' and a View of the Hierarchical Structure of the Islamic Culture," *Islamic Quarterly* 30, no. 2 (1986).

21. The most extensive discussion of the Shaykhism is available in Henry Corbin, *En Islam iranien: aspects spirituels et philosophiques* (Paris: Bibliothèque des Ides, 1971–1972), vol. 4. A representative sample of Shaykh Ahmad Ahsa'i and his students' writings are also available in Henry Corbin, *Spiritual Body and Celestial Earth: From Mazdean Iran to Shi'ite Iran* (Princeton: Princeton University Press, 1977), 180–270.

22. I have discussed extensively Ahsa'i's theory of the body in a reading of Shirin Neshat's photography in Hamid Dabashi, "Bordercrossings: Shirin Neshat's Body of Evidence," *Catalogue of Castello di Rivoli Retrospective on Shirin Neshat* (Turin, Italy, January 2002).

23. For a cogent discussion of Shaykhism in anticipation of Babism see Amanat, *Resurrection and Renewal,* 48–69. Here Amanat rightly observes that "in spite of its pronounced messianic overtones, Shaykhism remained a theological school, close in many ways to Orthodox Shi'ism though not in harmony with the interpretation of prominent jurists" (58). For this very reason, Amanat's earlier attempt to show a major epistemic shift in the ideas of Shaykhism that were not already evident in Mulla Sadra and the School of Isfahan (15–18) is not convincing. As I will argue in this chapter, there is nothing in Ahsa'i (except for a bolder expression and more receptive historical circumstances) that is not already evident in Mulla Sadra in philosophical terms, and by extension nothing in Babism (except for its extended roots in Shaykhism, Mulla Sadra, and the School of Isfahan) that was not already evident in the Hurufiyyah and other syncretic Shi'i revolutionary movements before it, going all the way back to Isma'ilism, the Zaydiyah, and the Kaysaniyyah.

24. Fashahi, *Vapasin Jonbesh-e Qorun-e Vosta'i dar Doran-e Feodal* [The Last Medieval Uprising in the Feudal Period], 60.

25. Tahereh Qorrat al-Ayn's significance as a poet is recognized and admired by the prominent literary historian Yahya Aryanpour in his monumental three-volume study, Yahya Aryanpour, *Az Saba ta Nima* [From Saba to Nima], 2:130–133.

26. See Moojan Momen, "Usuli, Akhbari, Shaykhi, Babi: The Tribulations of a Qazvin Family," *Iranian Studies* 36, no. 3 (2003): 317–337, for more details on the trials and tragedies of the Baraghani family, in the political context of their time.

27. In her travelogue Carla Serna refers to Shaykhism/Babism as "a kind of Socialism and Nihilism" (Serma, *Hommes et Choses en Perse/Adam-ha va A'in-ha dar Iran* [Human Beings and Rituals in Iran], 31), which ought to be taken both seriously and symbolically. The European traveler had rightly sensed some-

thing revolutionary and iconoclastic about Babism, and her "Socialism and Nihilism" (in that contradictory combination) was her manner of registering it.

28. Mohammad Reza Fashahi pays detailed attention to the Usuli clerical establishment and their varied plots and visceral attacks against the Shaykhis. See Fashahi, *Vapasin Jonbesh-e Qorun-e Vosta'i dar Doran-e Feodal* [The Last Medieval Uprising in the Feudal Period], 57–62.

29. For a cogent discussion of Seyyed Kazem Rashti's messianic ideas in continuation of Ahsa'i's, see Amanat, *Resurrection and Renewal,* 58–69.

30. For more details, see the relevant passages of Shaykh Ahmad Ahsa'i's *Kitab Sharh al-Ziyarah,* as translated in Henry Corbin, *Spiritual Body and Celestial Earth,* 180–221.

31. For more details on Mulla Javad Valiyani, his relationship with Tahereh Qorrat al-Ayn, and his political oscillations, see Amanat, *Resurrection and Renewal,* 256, 297, and 301–306.

32. For more details of this exchange see ibid., 298.

33. Henry Corbin has collected these successive philosophical treatises of the subsequent generations of Shaykhi philosophers in Corbin, *Spiritual Body and Celestial Earth,* 222–270.

34. Every aspect of Bab's biography is a matter of heated contestation between Qajar chroniclers and the orthodox clerical sources (vehemently hostile), on one hand, and the Babi sources (categorically hagiographical), on the other. The most balanced assessment of these two sources available in English is the judicious account in Amanat, *Resurrection and Renewal,* 136–152. Amanat's account, however, errs on the side of occasionally overemphasizing the Bab's prophetic claims at the expense of losing sight of the movement as a social revolution, and thus borders on a study in a cult of personality. While categorically at odds with Babi (and Baha'i) hagiography and an exemplary model of balanced scholarship, Amanat's account still shares certain epistemic assumptions of an anachronistic reading of Babism. A far more neutral reading of these sources is that of Mohammad Reza Fashahi, though his account is at times vituperatively anti-Baha'i, from an anticolonial and Marxist perspective. Said Amir Arjomand's account remains the model of scholarly neutrality, entirely devoid of any animus toward one side or another; his success stems from having predicated his study on a pioneering application of Weberian sociology of religion to Shi'ism. None of these perfectly legitimate academic contestations of historical facts and their interpretations has the slightest bearing on the unconscionable persecution of the Iranian Baha'is in their own homeland, and however they may wish to interpret the history of their own religion. As all other Iranians, the Baha'is are entitled to their lives and liberties, in a land now ruled by people the least concerned with such sacrosanct principles. My account of Babism basically follows Amanat's, with occasional emendations from other sources, and sporadic (but crucial) interpretative disagreements, via an insistence on a *longue*

durée approach to Shi'i history which, like that of Said Amir Arjomand, includes Babism. However, my intepretation insists on similarities and variations, rather than proclaimed epistemic ruptures, as in the case of Babism.

35. Abbas Amanat provides a detailed account of the social and economic background of the Babis in Amanat, *Resurrection and Renewal,* 332–371.

36. Amanat, *Resurrection and Renewal,* 121–122 provides details of the trade routes in southern Iran during the five years that the Bab spent in Bushehr (1835–1840 CE), routes that extended from Shiraz and Yazd, to Bushehr and Bandar Abbas, down to the ports of Muscat and Bahrain, and from there to Bombay, Madras, and Calcutta, and all the way to Zanzibar and Java. Amanat also notes the colonial presence of the British in southern Iran and its confrontation with regional merchants and the clerical class. But from there he turns to the Bab's family connections and makes no effort to link the Bab's messianic messages with his mercantile background, in particular his confrontation with British colonialism in the area.

37. Amanat, *Resurrection and Renewal,* 300, notes that Tahereh Qorrat al-Ayn's followers were known as the Qorratiyah, but does not develop the formation of this group into its logical conclusions.

38. Amanat, *Resurrection and Renewal,* 300.

39. Ibid., 314.

40. Ibid., 316–323. For more gory details of Mulla Mohammad Taqi's assassination see Abd al-Hossein Nava'i's angry and vindictive essay on Qorrat al-Ayn in his edition of 'al-Saltaneh, *Fetneh Bab* [The Menace of the Bab], 174–175.

41. Abbas Amanat's judicious conclusion (in Amanat, *Resurrection and Renewal,* 322–323), minus any attention to Qorrat al-Ayn's disciplined revolutionary disposition, is that she was not involved in the assassination. In my judgment, Amanat is too hasty in that conclusion. Qorrat al-Ayn could have, in terms perfectly justifiable to her revolutionary cause, ordered the assassination of Mulla Mohammad Taqi, the most pestiferous enemy of the Shaykhis and the Babis in Qazvin. But as with any other secret communication in a political assassination, there is no way to ascertain this one way or another.

42. For more details of such appeasements see Hamid Algar, *Religion and State in Iran: 1785–1906* (Berkeley: University of California Press, 1969): 139.

43. Algar, *Religion and State in Iran,* 139.

44. Amanat, *Resurrection and Renewal,* 326.

45. Ibid.

46. Ibid., 326.

47. Ibid., 327. For an excellent essay on the symbolic implications of the unveiling of Qorrat al-Ayn see Negar Mottahedeh, "The Mutilated Body of the Modern Nation: Qurrat al-'Ayn Tahirah's Unveiling and the Massacre of the

Babis," *Comparative Studies of South Asia, Africa, and the Middle East* 18 (1998): 38–50.

48. Amanat's proposal (Amanat, *Resurrection and Renewal,* 327–328) that Mirza Hossein Ali Nuri's intermediary role in Badasht between Tahereh Qorrat al-Ayn and Qoddus was instrumental in bringing forth a "third approach" that offered "a break with the past but nonviolent moderation in its implementation" is anachronistic, untenable, and unsupported by the facts of the Badasht moment. If the public debates between Qorrat al-Ayn and Qoddus were not premeditated to radicalize the movement—and there are indications that they might have been—then the plain fact is that Qorrat al-Ayn and her faction persuaded Qoddus and his faction and pushed the movement forward in a more militant way. Whatever pacifist ideas Mirza Hossein Ali may have had at the time or developed later is entirely irrelevant to this particular historic moment of Babism and its revolutionary outcome.

49. Amanat, *Resurrection and Renewal,* 328.

50. Abd al-Hossein Nava'i's essay on Qorrat al-Ayn in 'al-Saltaneh, *Fetneh Bab* [The Menace of the Bab], 186.

51. For more on the theory of *Gemeinschaft* and *Gesellschaft* see Ferdinand Tönnies, *Community and Society* (New York: Dover, 2002).

52. For more on the binary notions of *mechanical* and *organic* solidarity see Emile Durkheim, *The Division of Labor in Society* (New York: Free Press, 1997).

53. The *Shahnameh* heroine Gordafarid, standing up to the valiant Sohrab, is the poetic prototype of a courageous young woman who wears men's clothing and goes to war. Her story is part of the "Rostam and Sohrab" tragedy. For more see the English translation in Fardowsi, *Rostam: Tales of Love & War from Persia's Book of Kings,* trans. Dick Davis (Washington, DC: Mage, 2007). As a trope, Qorrat al-Ayn wearing men's clothing and waging war is figuratively in line with the epic image of Gordafarid, but it has far more serious societal implications.

54. For more on the character of Maral and other figures in Mahmoud Dolatabadi's epic *Klidar* see Hamid Dabashi, "Who's Who in Klidar: Society and Solitude in the Making of a Character," in *Iranica Varia: Papers in Honor of Professor Ehsan Yarshater,* ed. Manuchehr Kashef, *Acta Iranica* 30, vol. 26 (Leiden: Brill, 1990), 48–59.

55. For more on this woman, though in hostile and derogatory terms, see Abd al-Hossein Nava'i's note in 'al-Saltaneh, *Fetneh Bab* [The Menace of the Bab], 261–262, note 77.

56. Arjomand, *Shadow of God and the Hidden Imam,* 255.

57. For more on the life and thoughts of Aziz Nasafi see Lloyd Ridgeon, *Aziz Nasafi* (London: Routledge Curzon, 1998).

58. Arjomand, *Shadow of God and the Hidden Imam,* 254.

59. Ibid.

60. For an account of this period that is sympathetic to the Azalis see Fashahi, *Vapasin Jonbesh-e Qorun-e Vosta'i dar Doran-e Feodal* [The Last Medieval Uprising in the Feudal Period], 151–153; and for an account sympathetic to the Baha'is see Peter Smith, *The Babi and Baha'i Religions: From Messianic Shi'ism to a World Religion* (Cambridge: Cambridge University Press, 1987), 57–71.

61. Fashahi, *Vapasin Jonbesh-e Qorun-e Vosta'i dar Doran-e Feodal* [The Last Medieval Uprising in the Feudal Period], 165.

62. For more on Mirza Aqa Khan Kermani and Shaykh Ahmad Ruhi and their influence on the Constitutional Revolution of 1906–1911 see Hamid Dabashi, *Iran: A People Interrupted* (New York: New Press, 2007), ch. 2.

7. Shi'ism and the Crisis of Cultural Modernity

1. For more on Makhmalbaf see Hamid Dabashi, *Makhmalbaf at Large: The Making of a Rebel Filmmaker* (London: I. B. Tauris, 2008).

2. I have used this made-up word by way of explaining Kiarostami's cinema in both Hamid Dabashi, *Close Up: Iranian Cinema, Past, Present and Future* (London: Verso, 2001); and Hamid Dabashi, *Masters and Masterpieces of Iranian Cinema* (Washington, DC: Mage, 2007).

3. For more on this explanation see Dabashi, *Makhmalbaf at Large,* ch. 1.

4. One could offer similar explanations for the rise of Russian, Cuban, or Chinese cinema as well. For a thorough examination of Palestinian cinema from this perspective see *Dreams of a Nation: On Palestinian Cinema,* ed. Hamid Dabashi (London: Verso, 2006).

5. I have given a detailed account of this anticolonial modernity in Dabashi, *Iran: A People Interrupted,* Epilogue.

6. For a series of reflections on Jürgen Habermas's notion of modernity as an unfinished project see Maurizio Passerin d'Entreves and Seyla Benhabib, eds., *Habermas and the Unfinished Project of Modernity: Critical Essays on the Philosophical Discourse of Modernity* (Cambridge, MA: MIT Press, 1997).

7. For Weber's own formulation of what he called "Occidental Rationalism," see the Introduction to Max Weber, *The Protestant Ethic and the Spirit of Capitalism,* trans. Talcott Parsons (New York: Charles Scribner's Sons, 1958), 13–31. For an excellent collection of essays by the leading Weber scholars on aspects of his conceptions of *rationality* and *modernity* see Scott Lash and Sam Whimster, eds., *Max Weber, Rationality and Modernity* (London: Routledge, 1987/2007). For Habermas's take on Weber see Jürgen Habermas, *The Philosophical Discourse of Modernity: Twelve Lectures,* trans. Frederick G. Lawrence (Cambridge, MA: MIT Press, 1990), 1–23.

8. My translation of the first two stanzas of Ahmad Shamlou's "*Va Hasrati*" [And a Regret], in Ahmad Shamlou, *Majmu'eh-ye Ash'ar* [Collected Poems], 2 vols. (Giessen, Germany: Bamdad, 1989), 2:919–921.

9. I have developed this theme extensively in a chapter on Ta'ziyeh in Hamid Dabashi, *Islamic Liberation Theology: Resisting the Empire* (London: Routledge, 2008), 171–195.

10. I have addressed this scene in some detail in Dabashi, *Close Up*.

11. I have made this case extensively in Peter Chelkowski and Hamid Dabashi, eds., *Staging a Revolution: The Art of Persuasion in the Islamic Republic of Iran* (New York: New York University Press, 1999).

8. On *Ressentiment* and the Politics of Despair

1. See Lawrence James, *The Rise and Fall of the British Empire* (New York: St. Martin's Griffin, 1994), 98.

2. Ibid., 107.

3. Ibid., 113.

4. Ibid., 123.

5. See Gil Anidjar, "Secularism," *Critical Inquiry* 33, no. 1.

6. Thus the more logical title of Gil Anidjar's book *The Jew, the Arab: The History of the Enemy* (Palo Alto, CA: Stanford University Press, 2003) should really be titled "The Jew, the Muslim: The History of the Enemy"—following the logic of his own insight.

9. An Aesthetic of Emancipation

1. Sohrab Sepehri, "Seda-ye Pa-ye Ab" [The Footsteps of Water], in *Hasht Ketab* [Eight Books] (Tehran: Tahuri, 1363/1984), 272–273.

2. See Mehdi Akhavan Sales, "Chavoshi" [A Caravan Ballad] in *Zemestan* [Winter] (Tehran: Morvarid, 1335/1956), 144 (my translation).

3. For more on Bahram Beiza'i's cinema see my chapter on him in Hamid Dabashi, *Masters and Masterpieces of Iranian Cinema* (Washington, DC: Mage, 2007).

4. The Qur'an, 13: 29. From Mohammed Marmaduke Pickthall, *The Meaning of the Glorious Koran: An Explanatory Translation* (New York: Mentor Books, 1985).

5. See Shaykh Abu al-Futuh al-Razi, *Tafsir Rawdhah al-Jinan wa Ruh al-Janan* (Qom: Ayatollah Mar'ashi Najafi Publications, 1404/1983), 3:192.

6. Ibid.

7. Ibid.

8. Ibid.

9. Ibid., 193.

10. Ibid. The notion of a "tree of life" is of course not limited to Islamic sources and is widely present in all major world religions and multiple myths of creation—from India, Assyria, Armenia, China, and Egypt, all the way to Germanic and Mesoamerican sources.

11. Shahrnoush Parsipour, *Tuba va Ma'na-ye Shab* (Tehran: Esparak, 1368/1989), 502. Shahrnoush Parsipour wrote the first draft of this novel while she was in jail in the Islamic Republic in 1982–1983 for entirely unstated reasons. Her jailers confiscated her completed manuscript. When she was released from jail, she burned that manuscript and started writing a new draft of the novel afresh. She wrote this draft between 1986 and 1987, while trying to run a bookstore as a source of income. She finished this second draft in May–June 1988, and it was published soon after that—first 5,000 copies, then 8,500, and after that 15,000 copies. After the publication of her prison memoir, the book was banned in Iran and appeared in scattered versions in Europe and the United States. I am grateful to Ms. Parsipour for giving me these details during an interview in April 2005. There is now an English translation of this novel: *Touba and the Meaning of Night,* trans. Havva Houshmand and Kamran Talattof, afterword by Houra Yavari, biography by Persis M. Karim (New York: Feminist Press at CUNY, 2006). (Translations used in this chapter are all my own.)

12. Parsipour, *Tuba va Ma'na-ye Shab,* 503.

13. Ibid., 504.

14. Shirin Neshat has chosen to transliterate the Arabic/Persian word as *Tooba,* in order to avoid confusion with the English word *tuba* (a brass wind instrument). For the sake of consistency, however, I transliterate it as *Tuba*—corresponding to the Arabic/Persian word that is written with ta, waw, ba, and ya.

15. The woman in the tree is Maria de Los Angeles; the cast is men and women of the village of Tiracoz and Cuilapan de Guerrero, Oaxaca, Mexico; the cinematographer is Darius Khondji. I am grateful to Shirin Neshat for her diligent efforts to make it possible for me to get to know behind-the-scene events of her work, including *Tuba.*

16. For the crucial distinction that Giorgio Agamben makes between *zoë* and *bios* see Giorgio Agamben, *Homo Sacer: Sovereign Power and Bare Life,* trans. Daniel Heller-Roazen (Stanford, CA: Stanford University Press, 1998).

17. For a biographical account of Monkith Saaid see Rebecca Joubin, *Two Grandmothers from Baghdad: And Other Memoirs of Monkith Saaid* (The Netherlands: De Weideblik Press, 2004).

18. Christoph Menke, *The Sovereignty of Art: Aesthetic Negativity in Adorno and Derrida,* trans. Neil Solomon (Cambridge, MA: MIT Press, 1998), xiii.

10. The Un/Making of a Politics of Despair

1. For more details see Yitzhak Nakash, *The Shi'ites of Iraq* (Princeton: Princeton University Press, 1994), 66–72.

2. Ibid., 68.

3. For more details see Said Amir Arjomand, ed., *Authority and Political Culture in Shi'ism* (Albany: State University of New York Press, 1988), 178–200.

4. Ibid., 188.

5. For more details see Abolhasan Bigdeli, ed., *Beh Monasebat-e Yeksadomin Sal-e Rehlat-e Shari'at* (Tehran: 1323/1944); and Yann Richard, "Shari'at Sangalaji: A Reformist Theologian of the Rida Shah Period," in *Authority and Political Culture in Shi'ism,* ed. Arjomand, ch. 7.

6. See Arjomand, *Authority and Political Culture in Shi'ism,* 188–189.

7. For more on Taleqani see Hamid Dabashi, *Theology of Discontent: The Ideological Foundation of the Islamic Revolution in Iran* (New York: New York University Press, 1993), ch. 4.

8. See Arjomand, *Authority and Political Culture in Shi'ism,* 189.

9. For further details of this crucial transitional period see Dabashi, *Theology of Discontent,* 264–265.

10. For further details on these gatherings see Dabashi, *Theology of Discontent,* chs. 3 and 5.

11. For more on the long career of Ayatollah Khomeini see Dabashi, *Theology of Discontent,* ch. 8. For a collection of Khomeini's writings see Ruhollah Khomeini, *Islam and Revolution: Writings and Declarations of Imam Khomeini,* ed. and trans. Hamid Algar (Berkeley, CA: Mizan, 1981).

12. Arjomand, *Authority and Political Culture in Shi'ism,* 190. See also Karl-Heinrich Göbel, *Moderne Schiitische Politik und Staatsidee* (Opladen, Germany: Leske und Budrich, 1984), ch. 3.

13. Arjomand, *Authority and Political Culture in Shi'ism,* 191.

14. See Said Amir Arjomand, *The Shadow of God and the Hidden Imam: Religion, Political Order and Societal Change in Shi'ite Iran from the Beginning to 1890* (Chicago: University of Chicago Press, 1984), ch. 10; and Arjomand, *Authority and Political Culture in Shi'ism,* 192.

15. For a comprehensive study of Ali Shari'ati's life and thoughts see Ali Rahnema, *An Islamic Utopian: A Political Biography of Ali Shari'ati* (London: I. B. Tauris, 1988); and for a sample of Ali Shari'ati's writings see Ali Shari'ati, *What Is to Be Done* (Baltimore: Islamic Publications International, 2005); and Ali Shari'ati, *On the Sociology of Islam: Lectures,* trans. Hamid Algar (Berkeley, CA: Mizan, 1979).

16. For a comprehensive analysis of Shari'ati's revolutionary ideas see Dabashi, *Theology of Discontent,* ch. 2.

17. See Jalal Al-e Ahmad, *Occidentosis: A Plague from the West,* trans. R. Campbell (Berkeley, CA: Mizan, 1984). For a cogent critic of such nativist thinking see Mehrzad Boroujerdi, *Iranian Intellectuals and the West: The Tormented Triumph of Nativism* (Syracuse, NY: Syracuse University Press, 1996).

18. For more detail on Al-e Ahmad's life and work see Dabashi, *Theology of Discontent,* ch. 1.

19. For samples of his writing see Morteza Motahhari, *Fundamentals of Islamic Thought: God, Man, and the Universe,* trans. R. Campbell (Berkeley, CA: Mizan, 1985); and Morteza Motahhari, *Social and Historical Change: An Islamic Perspective,* trans. R. Campbell (Berkeley, CA: Mizan, 1986).

20. For more on Motahhari and his ideas see Dabashi, *Theology of Discontent,* ch. 3.

21. For more on Tabataba'i's ideas and a sample of his writings see Mohammed Hossein Tabataba'i, *Islamic Teachings: An Overview,* trans. R. Campbell (New York: Mizan, 1989).

22. For more on Tabataba'i's life and thought see Dabashi, *Theology of Discontent,* ch. 5.

23. For an English translation, see Mahmud Taleqani, *Islam and Ownership,* trans. Ahmad Jabbari and Farhang Rajaee (Lexington, KY: Mazda, 1983). For more on Taleqani's life and thoughts see Dabashi, *Theology of Discontent,* ch. 4.

24. For further details on the Mojahedin see Ervand Abrahamian, *Radical Islam: The Iranian Mojahedin* (London: I. B. Tauris, 1989).

25. For Bani-Sadr's political views, see Abolhassan Banisadr, *Fundamental Principles and Precepts of Islamic Government,* trans. Mohammad R. Ghanoonparvar (Lexington, KY: Mazda Publishers, 1981).

26. For more on Bani-Sadr see Dabashi, *Theology of Discontent,* ch. 7.

27. For a comprehensive study of the Liberation Movement see Houchang E. Chehabi, *Iranian Politics and Religious Modernism: The Liberation Movement of Iran under the Shah and Khomeini* (Ithaca, NY: Cornell University Press, 1990).

28. For more on Bazargan's career and thoughts see Dabashi, *Theology of Discontent,* ch. 6.

29. For a translation of this and other texts by Ayatollah Khomeini see Khomeini, *Islam and Revolution.*

30. For more on Khomeini's life and thoughts see Dabashi, *Theology of Discontent,* ch. 8.

31. For more details see Fouad Ajami, *The Vanished Imam: Musa al Sadr and the Shia of Lebanon* (Ithaca, NY: Cornell University Press, 1986).

32. For a translation, see *Constitution of the Islamic Republic of Iran,* trans. Hamid Algar (Berkeley, CA: Mizan Press, 1980).

33. For more on Abdolkarim Soroush see Mahmoud Sadri and Ahmad Sadri,

eds., *Reason, Freedom, and Democracy in Islam: Essential Writings of Abdolkarim Soroush* (Oxford: Oxford University Press, 2002).

11. Toward a New Syncretic Cosmopolitanism

1. This according to the mission statement of the Naval Postgraduate School's Web site, www.nps.edu/Aboutnps/index.html (accessed 6 March 2009).

2. See Vali Nasr, *The Shia Revival: How Conflict within Islam Will Shape the Future* (New York: W. W. Norton, 2006). This book is the expanded version of the essay published two years earlier through the auspices of the Center for Strategic and International Studies and the Massachusetts Institute of Technology, Seyyed Vali Reza Nasr, "Regional Implications of Shi'a Revival in Iraq," *The Washington Quarterly* 27 no. 3 (2004): 7–24.

3. Nasr, "Regional Implications of Shi'a Revival in Iraq," 7.

4. Ibid., 8.

5. Ibid.

6. Ibid., 20.

7. Ibid., 21–22.

8. For more details on these variations see Hamid Dabashi, *Post-Orientalism: Knowledge and Power in Time of Terror* (New Brunswick, NJ: Transaction, 2008).

9. For more on the nature of this imperial triumphalism see Hamid Dabashi, "American Empire: Triumph of Triumphalism," *Unbound: Harvard Journal of the Legal Left* 4, no. 82 (2008): 82–95.

10. Sudipta Kaviraj has made a similar argument in his pioneering essay, "The Imaginary Institutions of India," in *Subaltern Studies VII: Writing on South Asian History and Society,* ed. Partha Chatterjee and Gyanendra Pandey (Delhi: Oxford University Press, 1992), 2–39. Based on what he calls the "colligatory function" of narratives, Kaviraj demonstrates in this essay the power of the colonial discourse in manufacturing institutional grounds for its domination of conquered cultures.

11. For Paul Bremer's own account of his mission in Iraq see L. Paul Bremer III, *My Year in Iraq: The Struggle to Build a Future of Hope* (New York: Simon and Schuster, 2006).

12. See Gayatri Chakravorty Spivak, *A Critique of Postcolonial Reason: Toward a History of the Vanishing Present* (Cambridge, MA: Harvard University Press, 1999), 6; also see Mahmut Mutman, "Writing Culture: Postmodernism and Ethnography," *Anthropological Theory* 6 (2006), 165–167.

13. See Frantz Fanon, "Algeria Unveiled," in *A Dying Colonialism,* trans. Haakon Chevalier (New York: Grove, 1967), 35–63.

14. See Nikki R. Keddie, *An Islamic Response to Imperialism: Political and*

Religious Writings of Sayyid Jamal al-Din "al-Afghani," with a new introduction: *From Afghani to Khomeini* (Berkeley: University of California Press, 1983/1968), 7. In my account of al-Afghani's life I will mostly follow Keddie's chronology, which is the best and most reliable.

15. The Iranian origin and Shi'i background of al-Afghani are now incontrovertibly documented by Iraj Afshar and Asghar Mahdavi, *Documents inédit concernant Seyyed Jamal-al-Din Afghani* (Tehran, 1963), as thoroughly examined and discussed in detail and corroborated by additional material in Keddie, *An Islamic Response to Imperialism;* see particularly pp. 6–12.

16. Keddie, *An Islamic Response to Imperialism,* 10–11. Quotation from p. 9.

17. Ibid., 11.

18. Ibid., 12.

19. Ibid., 15.

20. Ibid., 17–18.

21. Ibid., 22–24.

22. Ibid., 32.

23. Ibid., 33–34.

24. Ibid., 34, note 49.

25. Ibid., 34.

26. For a cogent critique of what he calls "gay international" see the groundbreaking work Joseph Massad, *Desiring Arabs* (Chicago: University of Chicago Press, 2008).

27. See Keddie, *An Islamic Response to Imperialism,* 34.

28. Nikki Keddie believes that there are reasons to doubt even al-Afghani's commitments to orthodox Islamic doctrines. See Keddie, *An Islamic Response to Imperialism,* 4. For a similar argument made before Keddie see also Elie Kedouri, *Afghani and Abduh: An Essay on Religious Unbelief and Political Activism in Modern Islam* (London: Routledge, 1966). Both these observations are based on a very strict juridical interpretation of "Islam," and ignore the cosmopolitan context of Islamic culture in which a much wider interpretation of the faith is evident and obvious.

29. See Keddie, *An Islamic Response to Imperialism,* quotations from pp. 4, 5.

30. Ibid., 9.

31. Ibid., 12–14.

12. Contemporary Sites of Contestation

1. See "Egypt 'hunts Hezbollah suspects,'" BBC News, 13 April 2009, available at http://news.bbc.co.uk/go/pr/fr/-/2/hi/middle_east/7996665.stm [accessed 13 April 2009].

2. See "Cypress searches 'Gaza arms' ship," BBC News, 3 February 2008, available at http://news.bbc.co.uk/go/pr/fr/-/2/hi/middle_east/7868726.stm [accessed 1 April 2009].

3. The emerging parameters of asymmetric warfare are now very much engaging American military strategists. See, for example, Roger W. Barnett, *Asymmetrical Warfare: Today's Challenge to U.S. Military Power* (Washington, DC: Potomac Books, 2003).

4. For an account of *al-nahda* see George Antonius, *The Arab Awakening: The Story of the Arab National Movement* (New York: Simon Publications, 2001).

5. For an extended discussion of these iconic dimensions of the Islamic revolution in Iran see Peter Chelkowski and Hamid Dabashi, *Staging a Revolution: The Art of Persuasion in the Islamic Republic of Iran* (New York: New York University Press, 1999).

6. For more details on the Taliban see Ahmed Rashid, *Taliban: Militant Islam, Oil and Fundamentalism in Central Asia* (New Haven: Yale University Press, 2001).

7. For more on the history of modern Lebanon see Fawwaz Traboulsi, *A History of Modern Lebanon* (London: Pluto, 2007).

8. For the most recent study of Hezbollah see Naim Qassem, *Hizbullah: The Story from Within* (London: Saqi Books, 2005). See also Hala Jaber, *Hezbollah* (New York: Columbia University Press, 1997).

9. On the First Intifada see Mary Elizabeth King and Jimmy Carter, *A Quiet Revolution: The First Palestinian Intifada and Nonviolent Resistance* (New York: Nation Books, 2007). On the Second Intifada see Ramzy Baroud, *The Second Palestinian Intifada: A Chronicle of a People's Struggle* (London: Pluto, 2006).

10. For more on Hamas see Azzam Tamimi, *Hamas: A History from Within* (Fowlerville, MI: Olive Branch Press, 2007). See also Zaki Chehab, *Inside Hamas: The Untold Story of the Militant Islamic Movement* (New York: Nation Books, 2008); and Paul McGeough, *Kill Khalid: The Failed Mossad Assassination of Khalid Mishal and the Rise of Hamas* (New York: New Press, 2009).

Conclusion

1. I have addressed this particular point in detail in Hamid Dabashi, "The End of Islamic Ideology," *Social Research* 67, no. 2 (2000): 475–518.

2. For more on Ayatollah Khomeini see Hamid Dabashi, *Theology of Discontent: The Ideological Foundations of the Islamic Revolution in Iran* (New York: New York University Press, 1993), ch. 8.

3. On all these revolutionary figures see Dabashi, *Theology of Discontent.*

4. For more on the ideological formation of the Islamic revolution in Iran see Mansoor Moaddel, *Class, Politics, and Ideology in the Iranian Revolution* (New York: Columbia University Press, 1994).

5. For a brief account in English of Soroush's thought see the useful essay John Cooper, "The Limits of the Sacred: The Epistemology of 'Abd al-Karim Soroush," in *Islam and Modernity: Muslim Intellectuals Respond,* ed. John Cooper, Ronald Nettler, and Mohamed Mahmoud, 38–56 (London: I. B. Tauris, 1998). For a more extensive exposure to his ideas see Ahmad Sadri and Mahmoud Sadri, eds., *Reason, Freedom, and Democracy in Islam: The Essential Writings of Abdolkarim Soroush* (Oxford: Oxford University Press, 2000). For a critical assessment of his ideas see Hamid Dabashi, *Islamic Liberation Theology: Resisting the Empire* (London: Routledge, 2008), 99–142.

6. See Kwame Anthony Appiah, *Cosmopolitanism: Ethics in a World of Strangers* (New York: W. W. Norton, 2006). Quotation on p. xv.

7. Seyla Benhabib, *Another Cosmopolitanism* (Oxford: Oxford University Press, 2006), 15–16.

8. See Timothy Brennan, *At Home in the World: Cosmopolitanism Now* (Cambridge, MA: Harvard University Press, 1997). Quotation on p. 317.

9. Ibid., 316.

10. Ibid., 313.

11. For these and other details see Ghaith Abdul-Ahad, "'We have been silent about many crimes but we will not stand rape,'" *The Guardian,* 20 October 2006. For additional reports see "US soldier admits murdering girl," BBC News, 22 February 2007, http://news.bbc.co.uk/2/hi/americas/6384781.stm (accessed 16 April 2009).

FURTHER READING

The academic study of Shi'ism has gone through two surges: the first following the Iranian revolution of 1977–1979 when political Shi'ism became definitive to the state apparatus, and the second following the U.S.-led invasion of Iraq in March 2003 and the consequent rise of the Iraqi Shi'i community in revolt. Quite possibly we may see a new surge of contemporary Shi'i studies in the aftermath of the June 2009 presidential election in Iran.

In the first academic surge period, the two decades following the Islamic Revolution in Iran, an impressive and unprecedented body of scholarly literature appeared, mostly on the political but extending to the religious and cultural dimensions of Shi'ism. Some of the best examples of the scholarship on Shi'ism that was produced in the aftermath of and, partly, in direct response to the Islamic Revolution in Iran are (in chronological order): Abdulaziz Abdulhussein Sachedina, *Islamic Messianism: The Idea of the Mahdi in Twelver Shi'ism* (Albany: State University of New York Press, 1981); Said Amir Arjomand, *The Shadow of God and the Hidden Imam* (Chicago: University of Chicago Press, 1984); Nikki R. Keddie, *Religion and Politics in Iran: Shi'ism from Quietism to Revolution* (New Haven, CT: Yale University Press, 1984); Roy P. Mottahedeh, *The Mantle of the Prophet: Religion and Politics in Iran* (New York: Pantheon Books, 1985); Juan R. Cole and Nikki R. Keddie, eds., *Shi'ism and Social Protest* (New Haven, CT: Yale University Press, 1986); Moojan Momen, *An Introduction to Shi'i Islam: The History and Doctrines of Twelver Shi'ism* (New Haven, CT: Yale University Press, 1987); Martin Kramer, ed., *Shi'ism, Resistance, and Revolution* (Boulder, CO: Westview Press, 1987); Said Amir Arjomand, ed., *Au-*

thority and Political Culture in Shi'ism (Stony Brook: State University of New York Press, 1988); Abdulaziz Abdulhussein Sachedina, *The Just Ruler in Shi'ite Islam* (New York: Oxford University Press, 1988); J. R. I. Cole, *Roots of North Indian Shi'ism in Iran and Iraq: Religion and State in Awadh, 1722–1859* (Berkeley: University of California Press, 1989); H. Halm, *Shiism* (Edinburgh: Edinburgh University Press, 1991); Farhad Daftary, *The Isma'ilis: Their History and Doctrines* (Cambridge: Cambridge University Press, 1992); E. A. Kohlberg, *Medieval Muslim Scholar at Work: Ibn Tawus and His Library* (Leiden: E. J. Brill, 1992); H. Moddarressi, *Crisis and Consolidation in the Formative Period of Shi'ite Islam* (Princeton, NJ: Darwin Press, 1993); Y. Richard, *Shi'ite Islam: Polity, Ideology, and Creed,* trans. Antonia Nevill (Cambridge: Blackwell, 1995); A. K. Moussavi, *Religious Authority in Shi'ite Islam: From the Office of Mufti to the Institution of Marja'* (Kuala Lumpur: International Institute of Islamic Thought and Civilization, 1996); W. Madelung, *The Succession to Muhammad: A Study of the Early Caliphate* (Cambridge: Cambridge University Press, 1997); D. J. Stewart, *Islamic Legal Orthodoxy: Twelver Shiite Responses to the Sunni Legal System* (Salt Lake City: University of Utah Press, 1998); Andrew J. Newman, *The Formative Period of Twelver Shi'ism: Hadith as Discourse Between Qum and Baghdad* (London: Routledge/Curzon, 2000); and Mangol Bayat, *Iran's First Revolution: Shi'ism and the Constitutional Revolution of 1905–1909* (Oxford: Oxford University Press, 2001). Two of my own earlier works also belong to this period: *Authority in Islam* (New Brunswick, NJ: Transaction, 1989); and *Theology of Discontent: The Ideological Foundations of the Islamic Revolution in Iran* (New York: New York University Press, 1993; with a new introduction, New Brunswick, NJ: Transaction, 2006).

In the second academic surge period, soon after the U.S.-led invasion of Iraq, a number of far less competent and worthy (with a couple of notable exceptions), but far more popular—even bestselling—books appeared on the more urgent and combative dimensions of Shi'ism in action. A representative sample of post–9/11 books on Shi'ism includes: Juan Cole, *Sacred Space and Holy War: The Politics, Culture and History of Shi'ite Islam* (London: I. B. Tauris, 2002); Houchang Chehabi, *Distant Relations: Iran and Lebanon in the Last 500 Years* (London: I. B. Tauris, 2005); Yitzhak Nakash, *Reaching for Power: The Shi'a in the Modern Arab World* (Princeton: Princeton University Press, 2006); Seyyed Vali Reza Nasr, *The Shia Revival: How Conflicts within Islam*

Will Shape the Future (New York: W. W. Norton, 2007); and Patrick Cockburn, *Muqtada: Muqtada al-Sadr, the Shia Revival, and the Struggle for Iraq* (New York: Scribner, 2008).

In addition, a body of literature about the Lebanese Shi'i community following the 1982 Israeli invasion of Lebanon and the rise of Hezbollah to political prominence has also been steadily produced. The best recent book on Lebanon is Fawwaz Traboulsi, *A History of Modern Lebanon* (London: Pluto, 2007); an equally excellent collection of writings on Lebanon is Rashid Khalidi and Nubar Hovsepian, eds., *The War on Lebanon: A Reader* (New York: Olive Branch, 2007). Robert Fisk, *Pity the Nation: The Abduction of Lebanon* (New York: Nation Books, 2002) is now a classic in the field, as is Kamal Salibi, *Crossroads to Civil War: Lebanon 1958–1976* (New York: Caravan, 1976). All of these books include extensive treatments of the Lebanese Shi'is. Rodger Shanahan, *The Shi'a of Lebanon: Clans, Parties and Clerics* (London: I. B. Tauris, 2005) is a general treatment of the subject; more specifically on Hezbollah is Augustus Richard Norton, *Hezbollah: A Short History* (Princeton: Princeton University Press, 2007); see also Fouad Ajami, *The Vanished Imam: Musa Al Sadr and the Shia of Lebanon* (Ithaca, NY: Cornell University Press, 1986).

There is nothing unusual about a succession of studies produced following major political events that have aspects of Shi'ism at their focal center. Soon after the Babi movement (1844 to 1852) of the mid-nineteenth century, the distinguished Hungarian Orientalist Ignaz Goldziher (1850–1921) wrote his *Zur Literaturgeschichte der Shi'a* (1874); during the Constitutional Revolution of 1906–1911, his British counterpart Edward G. Browne (1862–1926) wrote extensively on the revolution's doctrinal and social causes in Edward G. Browne, *The Persian Revolution of 1905–1909* (1910).

A few of the best studies of Shi'ism prior to the 1977–1979 Iranian Revolution are: Marshall Hodgson, "How Did the Early Shi'a Become Sectarian?" *Journal of the American Oriental Society,* 75 (1955): 1–13; Alessandro Bausani, *Persia Religiosa, da Zaratustra a Bahá'u'lláh* (Rome, 1959); Hamid Algar, *Religion and State in Iran, 1785–1906: The Role of the Ulama in the Qajar Period* (Berkeley: University of California Press, 1969); Henry Corbin, *En Islam Iranien: Aspects spirituels et philosophiques,* 4 vols. (Paris: Gallimard, 1971–1973); S. Husain M. Jafri, *Origins and Early Development of Shi'a Islam* (London: Librairie du Liban, 1979); and a collection of previously published essays, Ann K.

S. Lambton, *Continuity and Change in Medieval Persia: Aspects of Administrative, Economic and Social History, 11th–14th Century* (New York: State University of New York Press, 1988).

The body of scholarship that has been produced on Shi'ism in the aftermath of 9/11 and the U.S.-led invasion of Iraq in March 2003 pales in comparison with that produced in the aftermath of the Iranian Revolution of 1977–1979. Much of this post-9/11 work is of an immediate and disposable significance. Very few works of enduring scholarship have come out of this latter period that are comparable to earlier works such as: Said Amir Arjomand, *The Shadow of God and the Hidden Imam: Religion, Political Order, and Societal Change in Shi'ite Iran from the Beginning to 1890* (1987); Abdulaziz A. Sachedina, *Islamic Messianism: The Idea of the Mahdi in Twelver Shi'ism* (1981); Farhad Daftary, *The Isma'ilis: Their History and Doctrines* (1992); Wilfred Madelung, *The Succession to Muhammad: A Study of the Early Caliphate* (1997); Andrew Newman, *The Formative Period of Twelver Shi'ism: Hadith as Discourse Between Qum and Baghdad* (2000). All of these are exemplary masterpieces deeply rooted in an impressive body of scholarship and all were prompted by the events of the Iranian Revolution of 1977–1979.

Two books on Shi'ism that have appeared in the aftermath of the U.S.-led invasion of Iraq sum up the condition of post-9/11 studies of Shi'ism: Seyyed Vali Reza Nasr, *The Shia Revival: How Conflicts within Islam Will Shape the Future* (2007); and Patrick Cockburn, *Muqtada: Muqtada al-Sadr, the Shia Revival, and the Struggle for Iraq* (2008). The first book is produced by a young scholar with an impressive academic background yet it reads like a propaganda handbook produced by the U.S. military seeking to shift the responsibility for the carnage that followed the U.S.-led invasion of Iraq to the chronic Sunni-Shi'i hostilities. The other book is written by a seasoned and courageous journalist who defies such military "psychological operations" (PSYOP) and reaches for the heart of the war-torn Iraq, producing by far the best book on the subject that has appeared in the post-9/11 flea market of publishing. The urgency and massive global concerns regarding the issues facing the world following the U.S.-led invasion of Iraq in March 2003 have invariably contributed to the production of shallow and hasty insights regarding the social and political disposition of Shi'ism.

My goal in this book has been threefold: (1) produce a narrative of contemporary significance for the educated public, responding to deep concerns about the rise of violence in the post-9/11 world, with particular attention to Shi'ism in three hotly contested areas: Iran, Iraq, and Lebanon; (2) construct arguments on solid scholarship of the last two hundred years and the primary sources of Shi'ism, and present them in easily accessible language; and, most significantly, (3) wed the latest generation of Shi'i studies to the earlier social, cultural, and psychoanalytic theories typically overlooked by the isolated and insular chronicles of Shi'ism that now define the field. My hope is to contribute to a renewed interest in a major world religion, its dramaturgical spectacles, epic narratives, doctrinal foundations, historical unfolding, social and intellectual disposition, moral and aesthetic dimensions, political urgency, and its contemporary sites of revolutionary contestation, and now above all its civil liberties.

ACKNOWLEDGMENTS

The idea of writing this book for Harvard University Press emerged over the course of a number of delightful conversations with Sharmila Sen, General Editor for the Humanities. It is to her patient and gracious coaching and stewardship that I am most indebted for seeing this book come to fruition. I am equally grateful to two anonymous readers who generously endorsed my work and enthusiastically recommended its publication. This is a time-honored process from which scholarly endeavors have consistently benefited. Having the seal of their caring intellect behind it, I let my book meet the public and posterity with much more confidence. To Harvard University Press goes my most humble and heartfelt thanks for awarding my book the prestigious Belknap imprint. I am honored. Ian Stevenson, Assistant Editor in the Humanities, corralled and cared for the many details of the manuscript with skill and aplomb. I deeply appreciate his meticulous care. I thank Philip Schwartzberg for the marvelous maps he created based on my suggestions. They are perfect for the book! Working with Katherine Brick, a senior editor at Harvard University Press, to prepare the final draft of this book has been a delightful experience. She has a gentle but firm hand in making sentences behave.

I wrote most of this book during a precious parental leave, cozily ensconced in an inconspicuous corner of a Dunkin' Donuts on the corner of Amsterdam and 106th Street in New York—far from the madding crowd by hiding in its belly. I am grateful to my good friend and then chair of my department Shelly Pollock, the William B. Ransford Professor of Sanskrit and Indian Studies at Columbia, for graciously affording me that leave. Co-teaching with my dear and distinguished friend and colleague Gayatri Chakravorty Spivak, University Professor and a founding member of the Institute for Comparative Literature and Society at Columbia University, has been a sustained course of inspiration for me. My writing is sharper and my mind steadier for the privilege of being in the close vicinity of her exceptional brilliance.

A work of theoretical ambition such as mine is impossible to conceive or achieve without the generations of sound scholarship that came before it. In my case I have particularly benefited from the extraordinary scholarship of such friends and colleagues as Ervand Abrahamian, Hamid Algar, Abbas Amanat, Said Amir Arjomand, Houchang Chehabi, Peter Chelkowski, Farhad Daftary, Nikki Keddie, Rudi Matthee, Mojan Momen, Negar Mottahedeh, Roy Mottahedeh, Andrew Newman, and Roger Savory. If, at times, I have had occasion in my book to differ with their scholarly positions, it has always been with an abiding sense of respect, admiration, and gratitude for their having made my own perspectives possible.

Procuring the illustrations for my book has been a particularly prolonged and detailed task. My diligent research assistant Ashley McKannon has been extraordinarily helpful in tracking them, procuring the correct format, and acquiring permission to print them. I am very grateful to her. She has made life in this and all other aspects of my teaching and scholarship much easier and more pleasant. The staff of the Avery Library at Columbia University has also been instrumental in procuring illustrations. My dear friend and distinguished artist Shirin Neshat has generously given me open access to her extraordinary work. My book is graced with her beautiful photographs. The same goes for my old friend Mohsen Makhmalbaf (and his son Maysam Makhmalbaf) for giving me immediate access to a photograph from one of his most beautiful films. I am equally indebted to another distinguished Iranian photographer, Rana Javadi, for her indispensable help earlier in the course of my research into the visual dimensions of Shi'ism. Through the kind assistance of my good friend Layla Diba I was able to approach the Brooklyn Museum to procure a copy and permission to print a picture in their collection. I am grateful to her, as well as to Katie Apsey and Ruth Janson of the Brooklyn Museum, for friendly and collegial support. My dear friends Mahmoud Omidsalar, Negar Mottahedeh, and Touraj Daryaee have been exceedingly generous with their time and assistance in getting me illustrations from around the globe. I am honored by their friendship. I offer many thanks to Ahmad Batebi for chasing after a copy and permission to reproduce his own now legendary portrait, taken by the prominent Iranian photographer Jamshid Bayrami during a student protest in July 1999 in Iran, which I needed for a crucial discussion in my book. Mr. Nader Motallbi Kashani has kindly helped by procuring an old picture of Naqsh-e Jahan Square for me from Isfahan, for which I am much obliged. My old friend Peter Chelkowski has, as always, munificently allowed me access to his extraordinary collection of slides and photographs from Ta'ziyeh performances. He was also instrumental in connecting me to Dr. Ingvild Flaskerud, who in turn generously shared with me her collection of Shi'i iconography from Iran. I am grateful to them both. Kaoukab Chebaro, Middle East and Islamic Studies librarian at Columbia University, has also been gracious and helpful in this and many other library-related matters. I have benefited from the professional courtesy and competence of my contacts at both AP and Reuters for photographs I have needed in their collection. From Isfahan to Oslo, from Cairo to California, "*Abr-o bad-o mah-o khorshid-o falak*" [The cloud, the wind, the moon, the sun, and the firmament], as Sa'di says in a poem—all had to come together for me to procure these illustrations, collect them in this book, and tell you what they mean. My "show and tell" would not have been possible with any less liberal shades and shadows of friendship and collegiality—and a bit of divine intervention too.

To my wife Golbarg, to my children Kaveh, Pardis, Chelgis, and Golchin, and of course to the conspicuously self-absorbed feline extensions of our domestic gathering, Bashu and Dazzle, I have dedicated this book for the canopy of joy and peace with which they have graced my life.

INDEX

Abbas, Abdullah, 249
Abbas (half brother of Hossein ibn Ali), 3
Abbas I, Shah, 146, 151, 152, 166, 369n31
Abbasid dynasty, 65, 68, 104, 105, 107, 113, 120, 124, 125, 129; revolts against, 62–63, 69, 111, 117–118, 129, 151; establishment of, 70–71, 110, 114, 115, 362n15; end of, 110–111, 130, 134, 135; Mawali under, 111, 112; Harun al-Rashid, 112, 116
Abbas III, Shah, 163, 164, 166
Abd al-Azim, Shah, 71
Abd al-Baha, 202
Abd al-Karim al-Shahrastani, Taj al-Din Abi al-Fath Muhammad ibn: *al-Milal wa al-Nihal,* 69
Abd al-Muttalib, 38
Abd al-Qahir ibn Tahir ibn Muhammad al-Baghdadi: *al-Farq bayn al-Firaq,* 69
Abd al-Rahman ibn abi Mansur, 130
Abd al-Rahman ibn Muljam, 109
Abduh, Muhammad, 284, 287, 289, 293
Abdülhamid II, Sultan, 289, 290–291
Abdullah al-Akbar, 117
Abdullah al-Mahdi, 116–118, 339
Abouseif, Salah: *Al-Qadisiyyah,* 304
Abraham: sacrifice of Ishmael/Isaac, 16; as revolutionary figure, 97–100
Abu al-Futuh al-Razi, 39
Abu al-Hasan Isfahani, 267
Abu Bakr al-Siddiq, 59, 60, 68, 81–82, 108, 338
Abu Dharr al-Ghifari: and Ali, 53, 108; and Shari'ati, 53–54, 354n7
Abu Muslim Khurasani, 62, 110, 111, 114, 362n15
Abu Sa'id al-Hasan al-Jannabi, 123, 124
Abu Talib, 38, 41, 353n22
Abyssinian migrations, 40–41
Achaemenid empire, 239
Adab [literary humanism], 105, 106, 145, 166, 312
'Adl [divine justice], 174, 341
Adorno, Theodor, 141, 151, 259
Aesthetic reason, 247, 258–259, 302; vs. public reason, 240, 310–311, 312, 323, 325
Afghani, al-, 284–294, 308; British colonialism opposed by, 284–285, 286–287, 288, 289–290, 291, 293, 298, 299–300, 312, 323, 342; multiple identities assumed by, 284–285, 287, 292–294, 303, 323; Keddie on, 285, 286, 287–288, 291–292, 293, 381n14, 382n28; and Shaykh Ahmad Ahsa'i, 285, 286, 300; early life, 285, 293; and Babism, 285–286, 292, 299–300, 302, 312; views on science and technology, 287; and Qajars, 289, 290; and Ottoman Empire, 289, 290–291; sexuality of, 291–292

Afghanistan, 104, 105, 297; Yumgan, 125–126; Herat, 139, 163; and Safavid dynasty, 153, 161, 162–163, 165, 166, 230, 235, 310; Kandahar, 162; Taliban in, 275–276, 304–305, 383n6; al-Afghani in, 287; British colonialism in, 287; U.S. invasion and occupation, 301, 307, 308, 324; Mojahedin in, 304–305; Soviet invasion and occupation, 304–305
Afsharid dynasty, 167, 169, 230, 235, 236, 298
Aftah, Abdullah al-, 115
Afzan, al-, 129
Agamben, Giorgio, 170, 255; *Homo Sacer,* 218, 371n15, 378n16
Aghasi, Hajji Mirza, 188–189
Ahankhah family, 207–208
Ahmad, Jalal Al-e, 96
Ahmad Naraqi, Mulla: *Awa'id al-Ayyam,* 171
Ahmet III, Sultan, 163
Ahvaz, 351n40; Bushehri residents of, 1–2; Isfahani residents of, 1–2; Masjed-e Isfahani-ha in, 1–2; Masjed-e Bushehri-ha in, 1–4, 5–6; Ahvaz Jadid, 2; Ahvaz Qadim, 2, 5
Akbar, Emperor, 161
Akhondzadeh, Mirza Fath Ali, 211
Alamdaran, 4–5
Al-e Ahmad, Jalal, 273, 303, 342; *Dar Khedmat va Khiyanat-e Roshanfekran* [On the Services and Treasons of Intellectuals], 270; *Gharbzadegi* [Westoxication], 270; *Occidentosis,* 380n17
Alfarabi, 152, 156
Al-Hasa, 123
Ali, Fatima, 320–321, 322
Ali, Mirza Hossein, 201, 202, 341, 375n48
Ali al-Hadi, Imam, 63
Ali al-Rida, Imam, Eighth Shi'i Imam, 29, 45, 63
Ali Asghar, 15, 16
Ali ibn Abi Talib, 68, 85, 94, 195, 301, 341, 351n3, 360n26; as First Shi'i Imam, 3, 38, 53, 57, 64, 139, 199, 269, 338, 367n15; assassination of, 14, 16, 61, 62, 69, 82, 109, 199, 338; as legitimate successor to Muhammad, 23, 43, 57, 60–61, 81–82, 250, 338, 353n23; likenesses of, 29–30, 32, 46; as Holy Prince of Believers, 30; sword of, 30; on night of the *hijra/Laylat al-Mabiyt,* 31–32; exemplary and pious character of, 37, 61, 71; as Fourth Rightly Guided Caliph, 59, 61, 69, 81, 108–109, 338; and Ghadir Khum incident, 60; as tragic hero, 71; and the poor, 108; and Tuba/tree in Paradise, 250, 251
Ali ibn Mahziyar, 4
Ali Kani, Mulla, 169
Allahvardikhan, 148
Al-Muqanna', 111
Al-Qadissiyyah, Battle of, 68
Al-Qaeda, 275, 303–304, 308
Amanat, Abbas, 198, 200; on the Bab, 185, 373n34, 374nn35,36; on Qorrat al-Ayn, 190–191, 375n375; *Resurrection and Renewal,* 369n1, 370n2, 372n23, 373nn29,31,32,34, 374nn35–41,44–47, 375n49; on Shaykhism and Babism, 372n23; on Mulla Mohammad's assassination, 374n41
Amina bint Wahb, 38
Anidjar, Gil, 233, 234, 377n5; *The Jew, the Arab: The History of the Enemy,* 377n6
Ansar, 31, 42
Ansari, Shaykh Morteza, 169–170
Anthropologists, 281, 282–283, 294, 295, 317, 357n10
Antiauthoritarianism, 22, 23, 83
Anticolonial nationalism: and Shi'ism, 25, 211, 229, 264, 265, 273, 282, 283, 294, 298, 299, 300, 303, 304, 305; and Qorrat al-Ayn, 193; Mossadegh, 267, 268, 342; in Egypt, 288; and al-Afghani, 293
Anti-Semitism, 234
Antonioni, Michelangelo: *Passenger,* 48

Appiah, Kwame Anthony: *Cosmopolitanism,* 316, 317
Aqa-Soltan, Neda, 322
Arab-Israeli War of 1973, 73
Arab Oil Embargo, 73
Aristotle, 91, 126, 135–136, 151, 152, 154, 156, 340; on mimesis, 219–220, 223, 224
Arjomand, Said Amir: on tribal principles of legitimacy, 167; on Qajar dynasty, 168, 169, 172; on Babism, 198, 199, 200, 373n34; on the Hurufiyyah, 199, 200, 367n13; on colonialism, 264; on Shi'ism in 1960s, 267; on Khomeini's 1963 uprising, 269; *The Shadow of God and the Hidden Imam,* 356n28, 363n22, 366n8, 367nn14,15, 371nn11–13,16,18,19, 375n56, 376nn58,59, 379n14; on Usuli School, 371n16; *Authority and Political Culture in Shi'ism,* 379nn1–6,8,13,14
Armenians, 172
Artisans/craftsmen, 123, 142, 149, 198, 200
Asadabadi, Seyyed Jamal al-Din al-. *See* Afghani, al-
Ash'arite School of theology, 112, 136, 151, 338, 339
Ashraf the Afghan, 163
Ashura, 4–9, 351n40; Zohr-e Ashura, 6–7, 9–10, 13; feast on, 6–7, 9–10, 13, 16; pleasure felt during, 7–9. *See also* Muharram ceremonies; Ta'ziyeh
Assassin myth, 130, 365n43
Asymmetric warfare, 293, 297, 306, 308, 312–313, 321–322, 323, 383n3
Ataturk, Mustapha Kemal, 237
Averroes, 156
Avicenna, 91, 126, 133, 135–136, 151, 155, 176, 340; *al-Isharat wa al-Tanbihat* [Allusions and Examples], 138, 149; on being [*wujud*] and essence [*mahiyyah*], 156
Ayeshah, 108, 195
Ayn al-Qudat al-Hamadhani, 87, 89, 90, 136, 358n17
Ayyubid dynasty, 129
Azalis, 201, 202–203, 236, 238, 341, 376n60
Azerbaijan: Dasht-e Moghan tribal council, 164, 165, 166–173, 175, 176, 183, 196, 197, 202, 212, 235, 237, 371n10; Maku, 182, 188–189
Aziz al-Din Nasafi, 200, 375n57
Azraqites, 109, 338

Babak Khorram-din, 111, 120, 151
Baba Taher Oryan, 199
Babism, 174, 181–203, 209, 212, 224, 265, 310, 322, 374n35; relationship to Shaykhism, 173, 183, 184–186, 189, 197–198, 201, 236, 238, 242, 341, 372nn23,27; *Bayan* [Utterance], 181, 182, 200, 341; al-Bab (Seyyed Ali Mohammad Shirazi), 181–185, 186, 187, 188–189, 192–193, 197, 198–199, 200, 201, 202–203, 286, 373n34, 374n36; and Shi'i clergy, 182, 186–187, 188–189, 192, 193, 197, 212, 237, 264, 266, 297, 298, 373n34; relationship to Hurufiyyah, 183, 185, 196, 198, 199, 200, 202, 236, 301, 372n23; relationship to School of Isfahan, 183, 185, 196–197, 198, 199, 200, 202, 236, 301, 372n23; and Qorrat al-Ayn, 183–187, 189–191, 193, 194–199, 200, 201–202, 236, 341, 370n2, 375n48; Badasht convention, 188, 189–192, 195, 202, 285, 375n48; Zanjan uprising, 192–193, 196, 285–286; Tabarsi uprising, 192–193, 199, 285; relationship to Baha'ism, 201, 202–203, 211, 237, 242, 266, 299, 300, 341, 373n34; and al-Afghani, 285–286, 292, 299–300, 302, 312
Babur, Sultan, 140, 144
Badasht: Babi convention in, 188, 189–192, 195, 202, 285, 375n48
Badr, Battle of, 41
Baghdad, 104, 112, 135; Shi'i jurists in, 23, 65, 66–67; Mongols in, 130, 134, 135, 136

Baha'ism, 188, 236, 376n60; Baha'ullah [the Glory of God], 201, 202, 341; relationship to Babism, 201, 202–203, 211, 237, 242, 266, 299, 300, 341, 373n34
Bahrain, 118, 123, 174, 339, 363n17
Bahsi dar Bareh-ye Marja'iyyat va Ruhaniyyat [A Discussion Concerning the Sources of Exemplary Conduct and the Religious Authorities], 267–268
Bani-Sadr, Seyyed Abolhasan, 343; *Eqtesad-e Towhidi* [A Divine Unitary Economics], 272; *Naft va Solteh* [Oil and Domination], 272; *Fundamental Principles of Islamic Government*, 380n25
Banu Ammar dynasty, 153
Baqir, Imam Muhammad al-, 62, 114, 339
Baraghani, Fatemeh Zarrin Taj. *See* Qorrat al-Ayn, Tahereh
Baraghani, Mulla Ali, 160, 177, 179, 180
Baraghani, Mulla Mohammad Saleh, 160, 177, 178, 179, 180, 187
Baraghani, Mulla Mohammad Taqi, 160, 176, 177–178, 179–180, 187–188, 192, 374nn40,41
Barforushi ("Qoddus"), Mulla Muhammad Ali, 184, 186, 189, 190, 191–192, 375n48
Barmecides family, 111
Barthes, Roland: *Mythologies*, 76, 89, 358n12
Bastami, Bayazid, 89
Bataille, Georges, 213
Batebi, Ahmad, 97
Baudrillard, Jean, 223
Bazargan, Mehdi, 272–273, 303, 343
Bedouins, 107, 109, 118
Beg, Tughril, 66
Behbahani, Aqa Mohammad Baqir, 169–170
Being/existence [*wujud*], 133, 154–155, 156
Beiza'i, Bahram, 224, 225, 311; *Mosaferan* [Travelers], 245–246
Belgian colonialism, 229
Benhabib, Seyla: *Another Cosmopolitanism*, 316, 317; *Habermas and the Unfinished Project of Modernity*, 376n6
Benjamin, Walter, 151
Bhabha, Homi, 317
Binaries, false: Islam and the West, 225, 228–229, 232, 282–283, 299, 307; and European colonialism, 280–284; the sacred and the secular, 283, 299, 311; Sunnism and Shi'ism, 283–284, 303–304
Biruni, Abu Rayhan al-: *India, Tahqiq ma li'l-Hindi*, 105
Blair, Shelia S.: *Art and Architecture of Islam*, 147, 148, 149, 367n17
Bloom, Jonathan M.: *Art and Architecture of Islam*, 147, 148, 149, 367n17
Blunt, Wilfred, 289
Boroujerdi, Mohammad Hossein Tabataba'i, 3, 265, 267, 268, 342
Boshru'i, Mulla Hossein, 184, 186, 189, 190, 197, 199
Brecht, Bertolt: on *Verfremdungseffekt*, 86, 215, 224, 357n9
Bremer, L. Paul, III, 282, 301, 304, 307, 381n11
Brennan, Timothy: *At Home in the World*, 316–318
Bridge, Battle of, 68
British colonialism, 135, 160; in India, 161, 229, 231–232, 281–282, 285, 286–287, 288–289, 292, 370n4; and Iran, 163, 165–166, 168, 171, 264, 268, 374n36; East India Company, 165, 231–232; in North America, 230–231, 232; in Iraq, 265, 302; opposed by al-Afghani, 284–285, 286–287, 288, 289–290, 291, 293, 298, 299–300, 323, 342
Buddha, 33, 35
Bukhara, 111
Bush, George H. W., 307–308
Bushehr, 1–2, 4, 181, 182, 183, 374n36
Buyid dynasty, 106, 111, 153
Byzantine empire, 42, 68–69, 70–71, 108, 135

Caliphate, 68, 71, 362nn9,11; relationship to *Imamah/Imamate,* 57, 59–61, 355n20
Camel, Battle of, 69, 108, 109, 195
Capitalism, 239, 316–318
Carlton, Guy, 231
Caspian Sea, 114
Césaire, Aimé, 56
Chaldoran, Battle of, 195
Chelkowski, Peter J., 349n3, 357n10, 358n14; *Ta'ziyeh,* 348n1, 359n22; *Staging a Revolution,* 350n25, 377n11, 383n5
Christianity, 113; vs. Islam/Shi'ism, 1, 12, 13–14, 33, 40, 58–59, 80, 92, 97, 119, 141, 232–233, 293, 349n20, 355n24; vs. Mithraism, 12; Trinity, 12; Christ as redeemer/savior, 12, 80; Freud on, 12–14; as son-religion, 12–14; communion/Eucharist, 13, 21; charisma in, 33; priestly class in, 33; Gospels, 40; Christ's authority, 58–59; Matthew 21:23–24, 58–59; Crucifixion, 76–78; Christ as revolutionary figure, 76–78, 92, 97–100; and secularism, 232–233; and European colonialism, 232–234; Anidjar on, 233, 234; liberation theology, 233–234; Oberammergau Passion Play, 349n20
Chupanid dynasty, 153
Clinton, William, 307
Colonialism, 172, 183, 209, 228–235, 238–239, 240, 311, 322; colonial modernity, 24, 153, 158, 211, 212, 213–214, 215, 223–224, 228, 232, 233, 234, 241, 242, 243, 245, 258, 263–264, 273, 284, 298, 299; anticolonial modernity, 209, 213, 214, 215, 223–224, 228–230, 238, 258, 263–264, 266; and Shi'i clergy, 237, 264–265; and art, 243, 245, 258–259; colonial reason, 258–259; and politics of despair, 263–264; divide and rule strategy of, 280–284, 292; and anthropologists, 281, 282–283, 294, 295, 317; and Muslim self-alienation, 281, 299. *See also* Anticolonial nationalism; British colonialism; French colonialism
Corbin, Henry, 128, 365n34, 366n9, 368n28; *En Islam iranien,* 359n20, 372n21; *Cyclical Time and Ismaili Gnosis,* 364n31; *Spiritual Body and Celestial Earth,* 372n21, 373nn30,33
Cosmopolitanism, 106–107, 235–240, 242, 264, 276, 283–284, 382n28; of Safavid dynasty, 24–25, 134, 149, 151, 152–153, 154, 161, 162, 166, 167–168, 169, 170, 172, 175, 183, 194, 230, 235, 297, 301, 340, 371n10; and opposition to U.S. and Israeli policies, 25, 296–297, 301–302, 305–308, 311–312, 323; and art, 78–79, 244–245, 294–295, 312; of Timurid dynasty, 139–140; as syncretic, 167, 168, 169, 170, 172, 173, 183, 235, 237, 238, 279–280, 294–295, 297, 300, 311–313, 316–319, 321–322; and women, 266; Appiah on, 316, 317; Benhabib on, 316, 317; Brennan on, 316–318; definition of syncretic cosmopolitanism, 316–319
Craftsmen/artisans, 123, 142, 149, 198, 200
Crusades, 129, 365n43
Cyprus, 69

Dabashi, Khodadad, 1, 29, 44–46
Dagestan, 161, 164
Daneshian, Keramatollah, 73, 75, 356n2
Daneshvar, Simin: *Savashun,* 92
Dasht-e Moghan: Nader Shah's *Khuriltai* [council of tribal elders] at, 164, 165, 166–173, 175, 176, 183, 197, 202, 212, 235, 237, 371n10
Daylam, 114
Day of Judgment: bodily resurrection on, 174, 175, 176, 179, 341
Debord, Guy: *Society of the Spectacle,* 224
Deferred defiance, 23, 44–45, 76, 81, 85, 91, 115–116, 310
Deferred obedience, 11, 12, 22–23, 44, 57, 310

De las Casas, Bartolomé, 233
Deleuze, Gilles: *Coldness and Cruelty,* 16–17; *Masochism,* 350n24
Derrida, Jacques, 213, 259
Dirks, Nicholas: *Caste of Mind,* 281–282; *The Scandal of Empire,* 370n4
Divide and rule strategy, 280–284, 292, 307–308
Dolatabadi, Mahmoud, 311; Maral in *Klidar,* 195–196, 375n54
Dumont, Louis: *Homo Hierarchicus,* 281
Durkheim, Émile: on mechanical vs. organic solidarity, 194, 195, 375n52; *The Division of Labour in Society,* 194, 375n52; on *conscience collective,* 181
Dutch colonialism, 229

East India Company, 165, 231–232
Egypt: Muslim conquest of, 69; Cairo, 104, 106, 112, 121, 122, 124, 135; Napoleon's invasion, 283; al-Afghani in, 285, 287–288; Urabi movement, 288, 289, 299. *See also* Fatimid dynasty
Eid al-Adha, 16
Eighth Shi'i Imam, 7, 29, 45, 63
Eleventh Shi'i Imam, 63
Essence [*mahiyyah*], 154–155, 156
European Enlightenment, 147, 213, 232, 316
European existentialism, 269, 303
Expectation [*intizar*], 52, 85–86, 218, 219, 354n11

Fanon, Frantz, 53, 56, 258, 269, 283, 300, 303, 308
Farabi, al-, 152, 156
Fardin, Mohammad Ali, 50, 353n4
Farooqi, Musharraf Ali: *The Adventures of Amir Hamza,* 360n28
Farrokhzad, Forough, 222, 225, 311; *Kasi keh mesl-e hich kas nist* [*Someone Who Is Like No One*], 49–53, 63, 353nn1–3, 354n11, 355n24; vs. Shari'ati, 54, 55, 56, 57–58; Makhmalbaf on, 54–55; *Khaneh Siyah ast* [*The House Is Black*], 55
Fars: Neyriz, 192
Fashahi, Mohammad Reza, 176, 200, 373n34; on Baha'ism, 202; *Vapasin Jonbesh-e Qorun-e Vosta'i dar Doran-e Feodal* [The Last Medieval Uprising in the Feudal Period], 369n1, 372n24, 373n28, 376nn60,61
Fath Ali Shah, 165, 167, 173, 174, 176
Fatimah, 38, 155, 269
Fatimid dynasty, 199, 364n26, 365n42; and Nasir Khusraw, 112, 122, 123, 124, 125, 129, 130–131; and Isma'ilism, 116–117, 122, 123, 124, 125, 130–131, 153, 339; end of, 118, 129
Fazlullah Astarabadi, 142, 176
Fedayeen Guerilla Organization, 305
Feldman, Noah, 282, 301, 304, 307
Ferdowsi, *Shahnameh:* 94–95, 105; Seyavash, 8–9, 16, 92, 94, 96, 97, 359n22; Sohrab and Rostam, 16, 92–94, 96, 97, 359nn24,25, 375n53; Esfandiyar, 97–100, 360n32; Gordafarid, 195, 375n53
Fifth Shi'i Imam, 62, 114
First Fitna, 61
First Shi'i Imam. *See* Ali ibn Abi Talib
Five-Imami Shi'is, 62, 114, 119, 183, 339
Foucault, Michel, 213
Four Deputies period, 64, 65
Fourth Shi'i Imam, 62, 114
Frankfurt School, 150, 151
Frazer, J. G., 13, 349n19
French colonialism, 229, 232; and Iran, 163, 165–166, 168, 171, 264; and Hutu-Tutsi rivalries, 282, 292; in Lebanon, 304, 305
Freud, Sigmund: *Civilization and Its Discontents,* 9; *Future of an Illusion,* 9; *Moses and Monotheism,* 9; on festive rejoicing, 9; on guilt, 9, 11, 12, 13, 14, 17, 19, 20–21, 22, 84; on the primal father, 9–13, 15, 16–17, 21, 22, 44, 309; on totemism, 9–14, 15,

16–17; *Totem and Taboo,* 9–14, 15, 16–17, 18–19; on incest taboo, 11; on murder taboo, 11; on deferred obedience, 11, 12, 22–23, 44, 310; on repression, 11–12, 20, 58, 59; on Christianity, 12–14; Rieff on, 17–21, 58, 59; on culture, 18–19; on morality, 21; on Oedipal complex, 76; "The Uncanny," 247

Gabriel, the Archangel, 32, 39
Gandhi, Mahatma, 272, 303, 343
Genghis Khan, 132, 134–135, 139, 140, 144, 371n10
Ghadir Khum incident, 60
Ghaffari, Mohammad, 79, 311; *Moses and the Wandering Dervish,* 79
Ghazali, Imam Muhammad al-, 125, 199
Ghaznavid dynasty, 104, 105, 107, 112–113, 145, 361n6
Ghulat, 114, 119, 143, 339
Gilan, 111
Globalization, 316–318
Gnosticism, Christian, 119
Gnostic Shi'ism [*Irfan*], 175, 340
God: Absolute Unity of, 37, 42, 126, 127, 155, 266; Essence [*hoviyyat*] of, 126–127; incorporeality of, 128, 152; human knowledge of, 133; justice of, 174, 341
Goftar-e Mah, 268
Golpayegani, Hasan Farid, 269
Golsorkhi, Khosrow: trial of, 73–76, 96, 356n2; and Hossein, 74–76, 78, 79–80, 87, 88, 89–90; as Marxist-Leninist, 74–76, 78, 79–80, 88, 92, 356n1
Goya, Francisco, 357n3; *The Shootings of May Third 1808,* 75–76, 97
Gramsci, Antonio, 303
Green, Steven, 319–320, 384n11
Grenville, Lord, 231
Griboyedov, Alexander Sergeyevich, 172
Guevara, Ernesto "Che," 3, 53, 56, 95, 97, 303, 308
Guilt: for killing Hossein/infanticide, 7, 10, 14–15, 16, 22–23, 57, 84–85, 309, 310; Freud on, 9, 11, 12, 13, 14, 17, 19, 20–21, 22, 84; as civilizing, 17–21, 309; Rieff on, 18, 19, 20–21, 22

Habermas, Jürgen: on modernity, 213–214, 236, 238, 376nn6,7; *The Philosophical Discourse of Modernity,* 376n7
Habib Isfahani, Mirza, 211
Hadith, 36, 65, 89, 133, 314
Ha'eri Yazdi, Shaykh Abdolkarim, 265, 267, 268, 342
Hafez's *Divan,* 140–142
Haghighah [philosophical truth], 139
Hajar al-Aswad [the Black Stone], 118–119, 124, 199
Hajjaj ibn Youssef, 109
Hajj pilgrimage, 31, 118–119
Hallaj, Mansur al-, 87, 89, 90, 92, 97; and Massignon, 76–77, 78; and phrase "Ana al-Haq" ["I am truth"], 199, 357n4
Hamas, 296, 303, 306, 308, 383n10
Hamdanid dynasty, 153
Hamleh-ye Heydari, 94
Hamy ibn Urwah, 15
Hamza al-Janabi, Abeer Qassim, 319–321, 322, 384n11
Hariri, Rafik, 306
Harun al-Rashid, 112, 116
Hasan, Imam, 62
Hasan al-Askari, Imam, 63
Hasan ibn Ali, 61, 109
Hasan Juri, 137, 139
Haydar Amuli, Seyyed, 143, 144; *Jami' al-Asrar* [The Compendium of Mysteries], 139
Hegel, G. W. F., 56; *Reason in History,* 354n15
Hezbollah, 24, 222, 296–297, 303, 305–306, 308, 383n8
Hidden Imam, 63–64, 65, 116–117, 174, 179, 356n27; and the Bab, 181–182, 188, 199, 341. *See also* Mahdi, the; Occultation [*ghaybah*]

Hijra, the, 30–32, 40, 41, 42, 58
Hilli, Allamah al-, 137, 138
Hinduism, 113
Horkheimer, Max, 151
Hossein Bayqura, Sultan, 139, 140
Hossein ibn Ali: death at Karbala, 3, 6, 13–16, 17, 22–24, 25–26, 69, 79, 83, 84, 86–87, 94–95, 109, 113–114, 218, 219, 220, 223, 225, 311, 339, 359n18; as Prince of Martyrs, 3, 7, 25, 75, 84; vs. Seyavash, 8–9, 16; and Kufans, 14–16, 17, 23–24, 84; weapons of, 15; vs. Sohrab, 16; thirst of, 25–26, 80, 351n40; as Third Shi'i Imam, 57, 62, 71, 74, 88, 114; as tragic hero, 71, 92; as revolutionary figure, 74–76, 78, 79–80, 81, 82–84, 85, 87–88, 89–90, 90, 97–100, 114, 301; and salvation, 80; as innocent, 80, 92
Hosseiniyehs, 48
Hulegu, 130, 134, 135, 136, 138
Hurufi, Fazlullah, 200
Hurufiyyah, the, 238, 340–341, 367n12; Fazlullah Astarabadi, 142, 176; vs. the Sarbedaran, 142–143, 144, 167, 169, 172, 173–174, 199, 200, 202; and fusion of Sufism and Shi'ism, 142–143, 144, 167, 169, 173–174, 175; relationship to Babism, 183, 185, 196, 198, 199, 200, 202, 236, 301, 372n23; Arjomand on, 367n13

Ibn Abd al-Muttalib, Abbas, 110
Ibn abi Jumhar al-Ahsa'i, 142, 143, 144, 150, 176, 367n11
Ibn al-Muttalib, Abdullah, 38
Ibn 'Amir, 'Ubayd, 249–250
Ibn Arabi, Muhy al-Din, 133, 135, 136, 150–152, 176; on *wahdat al-wujud* [united of being/existential monism], 152
Ibn Babawaih al-Qumi, Abu Ja'far Muhammad ibn 'Ali, 356n30; *Man la yahduruhu al-Faqih* [A Layman's Guide to Jurisprudence], 65–66
Ibn Battuta, *Rihla,* 122
Ibn Falah, Seyyed Muhammad, 144, 340, 367n15
Ibn Habib al-Hanafi al-Musaylimah, 182
Ibn Isma'il, Muhammad, 115, 116–117, 339
Ibn Ja'far al-Dibaj, Muhammad, 115
Ibn Turkeh Isfahani, 150
Ilham, 36
Ilkhanid dynasty, 136, 137, 138, 139, 144
Illuminationist [*Ishraqi*] School, 154; Suhrawardi, 90–91, 133, 135–136, 150–151, 156, 176, 340, 359n20
Imamah: relationship to *Nubuwwah,* 32, 37, 44, 84; relationship to caliphate, 57, 59–61, 81–82, 355n20
Imperialism, 24, 25, 295; of Soviet Union, 213; of United States, 213, 242, 269, 273–274, 283, 293, 303–304, 317–318, 351n39
India: Mughal Empire, 132, 139, 140, 144, 145, 161; Nizam shahs in Deccan, 153; British colonialism in, 161, 229, 231–232, 281–282, 285, 286–287, 288–289, 292, 370n4; and Nader Shah, 164, 166; anticolonial uprising of 1857, 232, 286; Gandhi, 272, 303, 343; caste system in, 281–282; al-Afghani in, 285, 286–287, 288–289; Ta'ziyeh performances in, 357n10, 358n11
Indonesia, 229
Infanticide, 14–15, 22–23, 57, 310
Intizar [expectation], 52, 85–86, 183, 218, 219, 354n11
Iqbal, Allamah, 303
Iran: Ahvaz, 1–4, 5–6, 351n40; Mashhad, 7, 29–30, 45; Constitutional Revolution of 1906–1911, 47, 200, 201, 203, 209, 211, 212, 236, 237–238, 264, 268, 273, 283, 299, 300, 302, 376n62; Fars province, 69; Kerman province, 69; Sistan province, 69; Bo'in Zahra, 95; Arab conquest of, 105, 182; Shiraz, 132, 134, 142,

160, 161, 162, 164–165, 181, 182; and British colonialism, 163, 165–166, 168, 171, 264, 268, 374n36; Zanjan, 192–193, 196, 285–286; nationalization of oil, 209, 342; Muslim professional associations in, 268; Muslim student associations in, 268, 274; Qur'anic commentary schools in, 268, 343; al-Afghani in, 285–286, 288. *See also* Isfahan; Islamic Republic of Iran; Islamic Revolution of 1979; Khurasan; Pahlavi monarchy; Qajar dynasty; Qom; Safavid dynasty; Tehran
Iran-Iraq War, 96, 275–276, 304, 314–315
Iraq, 119, 123, 129, 139, 160; Shi'is in, 8, 24, 25, 153, 277, 278, 297, 301, 304, 306–307, 308, 324, 348n3, 358n14; Mahdi's Army in, 24; artists in, 25; U.S. invasion, 66, 218, 222, 277–279, 282, 292, 301, 304, 319–320, 348n3; Najaf, 66, 222, 265, 281, 342; Karbala, 184, 185, 188, 222; uprising against British colonialism in, 265, 302; Saddam Hussein, 275, 277, 304; constitution written by Americans, 282, 301, 304, 307; al-Afghani in, 285, 286, 288
Irigaray, Luce, 22; *Speculum of the Other Woman,* 350n37
Isfahan, 145–154, 368n20; Mulla Sadra in, 132, 134, 142, 147–150, 161, 162, 175–176; urban planning in, 145–149, 153; art and architecture in, 145–149, 153, 298, 368n19; Masjed-e Shad/Khomeini, 146; Masjed Sheikh Lotf Allah, 146; merchants in, 146; Ali Qapu Palace, 146, 148; Grand Bazaar, 146, 163; Meydan-e Naqsh-e Jahan [Image of the World Square], 146–149, 153, 158, 166, 167, 169, 171, 202, 368n27; Chahar Bagh, 148–149; Si-o-se Pol [Bridge of Thirty-Three Arches], 148–149; captured by Afghans, 162. *See also* Safavid dynasty; School of Isfahan
Isfahani, Shaykh al-Shari'ah al-, 265
Islamic expansionism, 60–61, 68–71, 104, 212
Islamic jurisprudence [*fiqh*]. *See* Shi'i jurisprudence; Sunni jurisprudence
Islamic law [*shari'ah*], 33, 36, 82, 139; vs. Islamic philosophy, 133
Islamic Republic of Iran: and Hezbollah, 24, 296–297, 303, 308; moral dogmatism in, 54; execution of Soltanpour under, 96; student uprising of 1999, 96, 97; presidential election of 2009, 97, 322, 323–324; constitution of, 274–275, 314, 380n32; women in, 79, 276, 315; and Gaza, 296–297; relations with United States, 300–301, 304–305, 307; relations with Israel, 307; repression in, 314, 315, 322, 323, 378n11
Islamic Revolution of 1979, 54, 75, 252, 313–316, 321, 323; and Khomeini, 3, 15–16, 239, 272, 273, 274, 277, 303, 313–314, 343; and Kufans, 15–16, 17; Tehran during, 48; and cinema, 208–209, 212, 224; and Islamic ideology, 270, 272; and Motahhari, 270–271; American hostage crisis, 275, 314; significance of, 302–303, 313; and Shari'ati, 303, 314, 325
Isma'ilism, 114–119, 121, 172, 175, 176, 183, 199, 301, 363n17; and Isma'il ibn Ja'far al-Sadiq al-Mubarak, 62, 63, 114–115, 339; and Muhammad ibn Isma'il, 115, 116–117, 339; and Fatimid dynasty, 116–117, 122, 123, 124, 125, 130–131, 153, 339; and Nasir Khusraw, 122, 123, 124, 125, 126, 128, 129, 130–131, 134, 179; Musta'li Isma'ilis, 129, 339, 365n42; Nizari Isma'ilis, 129–130, 339, 365n42; and Shaykhism, 178–179; relationship to Babism, 372n23. *See also* Qaramita, the
Isma'il I, 143, 151
'Isra, 41

Israel: Arab-Israeli War of 1973, 73; Lebanon attacked by, 218, 222, 274, 305–306; as European colonial settlement, 293, 306–307; Gaza policies, 296–297; relations with Iran, 307. *See also* Palestine
Italian colonialism, 229

Ja'far al-Sadiq, Imam, 62–63, 114–115, 116, 117, 128
Ja'fari Shi'is. *See* Twelfth Imam
Jahiliyyah [pre-Islamic ignorance], 31
Jalayirid dynasty, 153
Jami, 142
Jazani, Bizhan, 96
Jews and Judaism, 113, 172, 232, 234; vs. Islam, 12; prophets of Israel, 33; rabbinic class, 33; Hebrew Bible, 40, 355n24. *See also* Israel
Jihad [holy war], 168
John the Baptist, 92, 355n24
Jordan, King Abdullah II, 304
Junaid, Shaykh, 143
Justice, 81, 97, 302, 314, 316; to be brought by the Mahdi, 63, 64, 330, 333, 340, 353n2; *'Adl* [divine justice], 174, 341

Ka'bah, 42
Kabir, Amir, 171–172, 192, 193, 237
Kant, Immanuel: on public reason, 147, 149, 368n22
Karbala, 184, 185, 188, 222
Karbala, Battle of: death of Hossein at, 3, 6, 13–16, 17, 22–24, 25–26, 69, 79, 83, 84, 86–87, 94–95, 109, 113–114, 218, 219, 220, 223, 225, 311, 339, 359n18. *See also* Ashura; Muharram ceremonies; Ta'ziyeh
Karim Khan Zand, 164–165, 370n8
Kashefi, Aqa Seyyed Ja'far Ishaq, 169; *Tuhfat al-Muluk* [Gift for the Kings], 168
Kasir, Samir, 306
Kasravi, Ahmad, 266
Katkov, Mikhail Nikiforovich, 289
Kaysaniyyah, the, 61, 114, 119, 183, 372n23
Keddie, Nikki: on al-Afghani, 285, 286, 287–288, 291–292, 293, 381n14, 382n28; *Qajar Iran and the Rise of Reza Khan,* 371n9; *An Islamic Response to Imperialism,* 381n14, 382n15
Kermani, Mirza Aqa Khan, 203, 211, 290, 376n62
Kermani, Mirza Reza, 290
Khadijah bint Khwaylid ibn Asad, 38
Khalesi, Shaykh Muhammad, 265, 266; *Bandits of Right and Truth, or, Those Who Return to Barbarism and Ignorance,* 267
Khalifah, Shaykh, 137
Khan, Mirza Malkam, 290
Khan, Sir Seyyed Ahmad, 288–289
Kharaqani, Seyyed Asadollah, 264–265
Kharijites, 14, 61, 69, 70, 108–110, 120, 195, 338, 362n13
Khatami, Mohammad, 276
Khavaran-nameh, 94
Khayyam, Omar, 216
Khidri, Abu Said al-, 249
Khodabandeh, 138
Khodavand-nameh, 94
Khomeini, Ayatollah Ruhollah, 96, 209, 224, 242, 267, 294, 312; and Islamic Revolution of 1979, 3, 15–16, 239, 272, 273, 274, 277, 303, 313–314, 343; vs. Kiarostami, 224, 294, 312; and uprising of 1963, 268–269, 273–274, 302, 343; and doctrine of *velayat-e faqih* [the supreme authority of the jurist], 274, 343
Khorram-dinan, 111, 120, 121, 151
Khosrow Anushiravan, 121
Khurasan, 69, 110, 111, 119, 134, 184, 188, 361n5; Mashdad, 29; Tus, 66; and Nasir Khusraw, 103–105, 112–113, 122, 125, 126. *See also* Sarbedaran, the
Khusestan. *See* Ahvaz
Khusraw, Nasir, 103–107, 111, 112–113, 121–131, 361n2, 363n20; as revolutionary activist, 103, 105, 106, 125, 126, 128; and Fatimids, 112, 122, 123, 124, 125, 129, 130–131;

and reason, 113, 128, 363n21; dream of, 121–122, 364n33; and Isma'ilism, 122, 123, 124, 125, 126, 128, 129, 130–131, 134, 179, 365n34; *Safarnameh,* 31, 122–125, 363n17, 365n35; on al-Hasa, 123–124; exile in Yumgan, 125–126, 129; on God's Essence [*hoviyyat*], 126; *Shish Fasl* [Six Discourses], 126; *Goshayesh vs Rahayesh* [Knowledge and Liberation], 126–127, 365n40; *Jami' al-Hikmatayn* [Summation of the Two Philosophies], 127; *Khwan al-Ikhwan* [A Feast for the Brothers], 127; on God's Absolute Unity, 127; *Vajh-e al-Din* [The Case for Religion], 127; *Zad al-Mosaferin* [The Pilgrims' Provisions], 127; on human beings, 127, 128; on God as Creator, 127–128; on God's incorporeality, 128; on "the Word" [*logos*] of God, 128; theodicy of, 128; and Mulla Sadra, 132–133, 366n3

Khwarazmid dynasty, 134–135

Kiarostami, Abbas: compared with Neshat, 24, 212, 224, 225, 239–240, 241; *Close-Up* [*Nema-ye Nazdik*], 208–209, 210–211, 216–217, 220, 223, 225–227; *Ta'ziyeh,* 220–223, 224, 225; *The Wind Will Carry Us,* 221–222, 223; *Through the Olive Trees,* 223; compared with Khomeini, 224, 294, 312; compared with Mehrjui, 247

Kierkegaard, Søren, 19, 141, 233, 234

Kubrawiyyah order, 139, 341

Kufans, 14–16, 17, 23–24, 84

Kulayni al-Razi, Abu Ja'far Muhammad ibn Ya'qub ibn Ishaq al-: *Kitab al-Kafi,* 65

Kutub al-Arba'ah [The Four Books], 64–68

Labor unions, 276

Lasswell, Harold: *Psychopathology and Politics,* 291

Lebanon: Shi'is in, 8, 24, 25, 212, 222, 274, 277, 296–297, 301, 303, 305–307, 308, 323, 324, 342, 348n3, 383, 383n8; Hezbollah, 24, 222, 296–297, 303, 305–306, 308, 383n8; Israeli attacks into, 218, 222, 274, 305–306; Syrian occupation, 274; Maronite Christians in, 274, 305, 306; Sunnis in, 274, 305, 306; French colonialism in, 304, 305; Hariri and Kasir assassinations, 306

Levinas, Emanuel, 215

Liberation Movement of Iran, 272–273, 380n27

Literary humanism [*adab*], 105, 106, 145, 166, 312

Ma'ad [bodily resurrection on Day of Judgment], 174, 175, 176, 179, 341

Machiavelli, Niccolò: *The Prince,* 70

Mahdi, the, 24, 114, 355n24, 363n22; expectation [*intizar*] of, 52, 85–86, 183, 218, 219, 354n11; peace and justice to be brought by, 63, 64, 330, 333, 340, 353n2; Twelfth Imam as, 63, 85–86, 353n2; Muhammad ibn Isma'il as, 116–117, 339. *See also* Hidden Imam

Mahmoud of Ghazna, Sultan, 105, 113

Mahmud the Afghan, 162, 163

Makhmalbaf, Mohsen, 56, 57; "Forough Khahar-e ma bud" ["Forough Was Our Sister"], 54–55; and Kiarostami's *Close-Up,* 207–208, 209, 210–211, 220, 225–227; *Gabbeh,* 246; *Kandahar,* 246; *A Moment of Innocence,* 246; *Salam Cinema,* 246; *Sex and Philosophy,* 246; *The Silence,* 246; *Time of Love,* 246; visual minimalism of, 246

Maktab-e Tashayyu', 268

Malaysia, 229

Malcolm X, 234

Malikshah, 120

Malik Zahir, 91

Mansur, al- (Abbasid), 110

Mansur, al- (Fatimid), 118, 119

Marja al-Taqlid, 267

Martel, Charles "The Hammer," 69

Martyrdom [*Shahadat*], 8, 80, 84–85, 87; Hossein as Prince of Martyrs, 3, 7, 25, 75, 84
Marxism, 177, 272; Marxism-Leninism, 74–76, 78, 79–80, 88, 92, 356n1; Siahkal uprising, 96; Stalinism, 150; Tudeh Party, 267, 268, 305; historical materialism, 270, 271. *See also* Third World socialism
Mashhad, 7, 29–30, 45
Massignon, Louis, 77, 78, 92, 357n4
Mas'ud, Sultan, 113
Mawali: under Umayyad dynasty, 70, 107, 108, 109, 110, 114; as merchants, 109, 110; under Abbasid dynasty, 111, 112
Mazandaran, 125, 137, 188, 191, 192, 201; Tabarsi uprising, 192–193, 199, 285
Mazdak, 111, 120–121, 362nn13,16, 370n2
Mazlumiyyat [innocence], 79–83, 85
Medved, Alexander, 95
Mehrjui, Daryush: *Cow,* 247
Menke, Christoph: on sovereignty of art, 259
Merchants, 111, 112, 118; Prophet Muhammad as merchant, 34, 38, 182; Mawali merchants, 109, 110; during Safavid dynasty, 146, 161; and Babism, 181, 182, 184, 186, 187, 198, 200, 374n36
Metamorphic parables, 86–90, 91–97
Mi'raj, 30, 41, 157, 179
Mir Damad, 150–151, 152, 153–154, 369n31; relationship with Mulla Sadra, 132, 133, 148, 154, 155–156, 340; *al-Qabasat* [The Sparkles], 152; on time, 152; on essence [*mahiyyah*], 156
Mir Fendereski, 151
Mir Veis, 162
Mithraism, 12, 349n16
Mohassess, Ardeshir, 241
Mojahedin-e Khalq, 96, 272, 360n33, 380n24
Mokhtar ibn abi Ubaydah Saqafi, 62, 94–95, 109, 114
Mokhtar-nameh, 94–95
Molk, Khabir al-, 290
Mongols: Genghis Khan, 132, 134–135, 139, 140, 144, 371n10; invasion by, 130, 132–133, 134–139, 142, 144, 154, 212–213, 366nn5,6
Monotheism, absolute, 37, 42, 126, 127, 155, 266
Mosques: Muharram ceremonies in, 1–2; as social institution, 1
Mossadegh, Mohammad, 267, 268, 342
Motahhari, Ayatollah Morteza, 268, 273, 275, 303; on historical materialism, 270, 271; and Islamic Revolution of 1979, 270–271, 314, 343; *Akhlaq-e Jensi dar Islam va Jahdn-e Gharb* [Sexual Ethics in Islam and the West], 271; *'Ilal-e Gerayesh beh Maddi-gari* [Reasons for Attraction to Materialism], 271; *Islam va Muqtaziyat-e Zaman* [Islam and the Exigencies of the (Present) Time], 271; *Fundamentals of Islamic Thought,* 380n19; *Social and Historical Change,* 380n19
Mo'tamed al-Dowleh, Manuchehr Khan, 182
Motlaq, Zahra Parvizi, 2, 45, 46
Mount Hira, 38, 39
Moussavi, Mir Hossein, 323
Mu'awiyah, 61, 108–109
Mughal Empire, 132, 139, 140, 144, 145, 161
Muhajirun, 31, 42
Muhammad, the Prophet, 3, 22, 68, 94, 95, 155, 351n3; exemplary conduct of, 14, 33; divine revelations of, 14, 33–34, 35–36, 37, 38–40, 41, 42–43, 58, 60, 107–108, 133, 182; weapons of, 15; likenesses of, 29–30, 32, 46; and the *ummah,* 30, 40, 41, 42, 43, 58, 59–60, 81–82; *Mi'raj* of, 30, 41, 157, 179; as Messenger of God, 30–31, 33–34, 36; *hijra* of, 30–32, 40, 41, 42, 58; charismatic authority of, 32–37, 43–44, 56–57, 58, 59–60, 68, 81–82, 352n19; character, 33, 36, 37;

sayings and doings [*sunnah*] of, 33, 36, 43; during Medinan period, 33, 40, 41–42; as merchant, 34, 38, 182; as orphan, 37; early life, 37, 38; as solitary soul, 37, 38–39, 40; political actions of, 37, 42–43; as "al-Amin," 38; relationship with Khadijah, 38, 39–40, 41; relationship with Ayeshah, 39; and tribal patrimonialism, 40, 43; and the poor, 40, 107–108; during Meccan period, 40–41, 58; *'Isra* of, 41; relationship with Abu Dharr, 53–54; crisis of succession after death, 57–59, 60–61, 81–82; and Ghadir Khum incident, 60; on Tuba/tree in Paradise, 249, 250–251
Muhammad al-Nafs al-Zakiyyah, 63
Muhammad ibn Hanafiyah, 61–62
Muhammad Shah, 172, 182, 188, 192
Muharram ceremonies, 1–9, 357n10; music during, 3–5, 6; and guilt, 7, 10, 17, 21–23; pleasure felt during, 7–9, 21–22; and political revolution, 8; pre-Islamic origins for, 8–9; and totemism, 9–13. *See also* Ashura; Ta'ziyeh
Mulla Sadra Shirazi, 239, 315, 351n1, 369n32, 372n23; *al-Hikmah al-Muta'aliyyah fi al-Asfar al-'Aqliyyah al-Arba'ah* [The Transcendent Philosophy: The Four Intellectual Journeys], 31, 133, 136, 154, 156–157, 175, 366n9; and Safavid dynasty, 91, 134, 137, 145, 158, 161, 167, 236; relationship with Mir Damad, 132, 133, 148, 154, 155–156, 340; in Isfahan, 132, 134, 142, 147–150, 161, 162, 175–176; in Shiraz, 132, 134, 161, 162; in Kahak, 132, 150; as "Akhond," 132, 366n1; and Mongol invasion, 132–133, 134–140; and Nasir Khusraw, 132–133, 366n3; and Ibn Arabi, 133, 135, 136; and Suhrawardi, 133, 135–136, 156; on being [*wujud*], 133, 154–155, 156–157; on God/Truth [*Haq*], 133, 155; and public reason, 134, 158, 166, 169, 183, 197, 202, 236; and Nasir al-Din al-Tusi, 136–137, 138, 144, 149; fusion of Shi'ism and Sufism by, 137–138, 142–144, 157, 175, 176, 183, 340; and the Sarbedaran, 137–138, 144; and Rumi, Sa'di, and Hafez, 140–142; on thingness [*inniyyah*], 154–155; on essence [*mahiyyah*], 154–155, 156; on the *'Alam al-Mithal* [world of images], 155; on transubstantial motion [*al-harakah al-jawhariyyah*], 155–156, 157; on gradation of existence [*tashkik al-wujud*], 156–157; on people [*khalq*], 157; on truth [*Haq*], 157; and Shaykh Ahmad Ahsa'i, 173, 174, 175–176, 185, 197, 198, 199, 200, 202, 372n23; *al-Waridat al-Qalbiyyah fi Ma'rifat al-Rububiyyah* [Divine Inspirations in Understanding the Divinity], 366n3
Muqanna', al-, 199
Murtada, al-Sharif al-, 66
Musa al-Kazim, Imam, 63, 115, 116, 143, 339
Musha'sha' movement, 144, 199, 340, 367n15
Muslim ibn Aqil, 14–16
Musta'li Isma'ilis, 129, 339, 365n42
Mustansir, al-, 121, 122, 129
Mu'tazilite School of theology, 112, 136, 151, 338, 339

Naderi, Amir: Manhattan by Numbers, 246; Marathon, 246; Sound Barrier, 246; The Runner, 246; Water, Wind, Dust, 246
Nader Shah, 163–164, 183, 196, 231, 235–236, 238, 297, 370n7; Dasht-e Moghan council, 164, 165, 166–173, 175, 176, 183, 197, 202, 212, 235, 237, 371n10; and tribal patrimonialism, 166–168, 230, 235, 310, 322, 371n10
Nahda, al-, 299, 383n4
Na'ini, Mirza Mohammad Hossein, 265, 267, 342
Najaf, 66, 222, 265, 281, 342
Napoleon I, 232, 283

Nasr, Seyyed Hossein, 128, 364n31, 366n9; *Three Muslim Sages,* 359n20; *Sadr al-Din Shirazi and His Transcendent Theosophy,* 366n; *Islamic Philosophy from Its Origin to the Present,* 368n28
Nasr, Seyyed Vali Reza: *The Shia Revival,* 277–282, 292, 295, 301, 304, 307, 381n2; "Regional Implications of Shi'a Revival in Iraq," 381nn2–7
Nasrallah, Hassan, 24, 296
Nasser al-Din Shah, 169, 192, 193, 201, 286, 289, 290
National Front (Iran), 305
Neishabur, 135
Ne'matollahai order, 173–174, 341
Neoconservatism, 279, 307
Neoplatonism, 103, 119, 151, 154, 178–179, 340
Neshat, Shirin: vs. Kiarostami, 24, 212, 224, 225, 239–240, 241; *Tuba,* 254–258, 378nn14,15
Neyriz uprising, 286
Nezam al-Dowleh, Mirza Hossein Khan, 182
Nietzsche, Friedrich, 19, 141, 213, 233, 234
Ninth Shi'i Imam, 63
Nizam al-Mulk, Khwajah, 125; *Siyasatnama,* 70, 119–121, 362n13, 363n17
Nizari Isma'ilis, 129–130, 339, 365n42
Nodjoumi, Nikzad "Nicky," 241
Noheh khanan [cantors], 4–5, 6
North Africa, 69, 118
Northern Ireland, 282, 292
Nubuwwah, 174; relationship to *Imamah,* 32, 37, 44, 84; vs. *wilayat,* 88
Nuqtaviyyah, the, 167, 169, 199, 341

Occultation [*ghaybah*]: of Twelfth Imam, 63, 64, 65, 67, 85–86, 174, 179, 181, 182, 188, 199, 274, 339–340; Greater Occultation [*Ghaybah al-Kubra'*], 64, 65; Lesser Occultation [*Ghaybah al-Subhra'*], 64, 65
Orientalism, 37, 133, 147, 172, 232, 282, 292, 357n4, 363n17, 365n43
Ottoman empire, 132, 144, 160, 165, 166, 178, 213, 285, 312; Istanbul, 145, 287; and Safavid dynasty, 161, 163, 195, 230, 235; Ahmet III, 163; and Qajar dynasty, 168, 237, 264; and Babism, 185–186, 322, 341; end of, 229, 237; Abdülhamid II, 289, 290–291; al-Afghani in, 289, 290–291

Pact of al-Hudaybiyah, 42
Pahlavi monarchy, 54, 75, 96, 172, 218; Reza Shah, 2, 236–237, 238, 239, 265, 266, 268, 272; and Shi'i clergy, 2–3, 265, 266, 267, 268–269, 271, 273–274, 313–314; Muhammad Reza Shah, 73, 239, 267, 314; coup of 1953, 267, 342
Pakistan, 277, 304, 305
Palestine, 112, 118, 119, 301, 304, 307, 323, 324; Hamas, 296, 303, 306, 308, 383n10; Gaza, 296–297, 303; Fatah, 306; First Intifada, 306, 383n9; Second Intifada, 306, 383n9
Paradox of moral success in political failure and moral failure in political success, 80–81, 85, 297, 308, 313, 321, 322, 323–325
Parsipour, Shahrnoush: *Tuba va Ma'na-ye Shab* [Tuba and the Meaning of Night], 251–254, 255, 378n11
Parvizi, Abbas, 48
Patrimonialism, tribal: of Umayyad dynasty, 14, 107, 109; opposed by Prophet Mohammad, 40, 43; and Nader Shah, 166–168, 230, 235, 310, 322, 371n10; of Qajar dynasty, 175, 183, 186–187, 235
Pillars of Shi'ism [*Usul al-Din*]: *Imamah,* 32, 37, 44, 57, 59–61, 84, 174, 355n20; *Nubuwwah,* 32, 37, 44, 84, 88, 174; *Tawhid,* 37, 42, 126, 127, 155, 174, 266; *Ma'ad,* 174, 175, 176, 179, 341; *'Adl,* 174, 341
Platonism, 91. *See also* Neoplatonism

Poitiers, Battle of, 69
Politics of despair, 263–276, 297, 300–301, 308, 324–325; vs. aesthetic formalism, 55, 209, 210–217, 223–225, 228, 229, 238, 239–240, 241–242, 254, 281, 294–295, 310–312, 323; defined, 211; and *ressentiment,* 229–230
Poor, the, 70, 109, 110–111, 118, 182, 233–234; and the Prophet Mohammad, 40, 107–108
Portuguese colonialism, 229
Postmodernism, 213, 239–240
Poststructuralism, 213
Proudhon, Pierre Joseph, 53
Public reason: and Mulla Sadra, 134, 158, 166, 169, 183, 197, 202, 236; during Safavid dynasty, 146–147, 158, 167, 172, 174, 194, 196–197, 212, 368n27; relationship to public space, 146–147, 158, 195, 198, 200–201, 225, 237–238, 368n27; Kant on, 147, 149, 368n22; transformation of revolutionary reason into, 158, 169, 172, 183–184, 185, 194, 200–201, 202, 235, 237–238, 239, 309–310, 312, 341; vs. scholastic reasoning, 170–171, 172–173, 212, 239–240; vs. aesthetic reason, 240, 310–311, 312, 323, 325
Public space, 167, 174, 300, 310–311, 322–323; relationship to public reason, 146–147, 158, 195, 198, 200–201, 225, 237–238, 368n27; Naqsh-e Jahan Square in Isfahan, 146–149, 153, 158, 166, 167, 169, 171, 202, 368n27; Islamic art in, 243–244

Qadi Meybudi, 150
Qadisiyyah, Battle of al-, 304
Qajar, Aqa Muhammad Khan, 165, 167, 169, 171
Qajar dynasty, 161, 167–174, 235, 265, 371n9; and Russian empire, 165, 168, 171, 232, 237, 264, 268, 302; establishment of, 165–166, 169; and Shi'i clergy, 167, 168–174, 175, 176, 178, 183, 188, 193, 202, 230, 231, 236, 237–238, 264, 297, 298; and Ottoman empire, 168, 237, 264; Nasser al-Din Shah, 169, 192, 193, 201, 286, 289, 290; Muhammad Shah, 172, 182, 188, 192; and Babism, 185–187, 188–189, 192–193, 197, 203, 322, 341, 373n34; end of, 203, 252; and al-Afghani, 289, 290
Qameh zanan, 6, 7
Qaramita, the, 116, 117–119, 121, 123, 129, 172, 199, 301, 363n17, 364nn29,30; Hamdan Qarmat, 117, 118, 339
Qarmat, Abdan, 117, 118
Qazvin, 160, 173, 176–177, 180, 187
Qazvini, Mulla Mohammad Ali, 180
Qiyam [insurrection], 83–84
Qoddus, 184, 186, 189, 190, 191–192, 375n48
Qom, 59, 271, 343; Hazrat-e Ma'sumeh's shrine in, 29; juridical studies in, 265, 268, 342; and Najaf, 265, 281; Khomeini in, 267, 268, 273
Qorrat al-Ayn, Tahereh, 369nn1,2, 372n25, 374n47; execution of, 159–160, 193; birth of, 160, 161, 165, 173, 177; and Shaykhism, 177, 179–180, 184–186, 189, 193, 197–198, 341; early life, 177–181; relationship with Mulla Mohammad Baraghani, 178, 179–180, 187, 192; and Babism, 183–187, 189–191, 193, 194–199, 200, 201–202, 236, 341, 370n2, 375n48; in Karbala, 184, 185–186; in Kazemayn, 185–186; and assassination of father-in-law, 187–188, 192, 374nn40,41; at Badasht gathering, 188, 189–192, 195, 375n48; relationship with Qoddus, 189, 190, 191–192, 375n48; armed rebellion advocated by, 189–191; arrest of, 192–193; and Iranian political community, 193–203; historical significance of, 193–203; as woman, 194–197, 198, 236; vs. Gordafarid, 195, 375n53

Qubad, king, 121
Quietism, 62–63, 114, 115
Qur'an: and the *hijra,* 32; revelations in the, 33–34, 35–36, 37, 38–40, 41, 42–43, 58, 60, 107–108, 133, 182, 314; *Surah al-'Alaq,* 39; Meccan chapters, 43; Medinan chapters, 43; V: 3, 60; V: 67, 60; esoteric [*batini*] meaning, 119; *ta'wil* [hermeneutics], 151; and Akhbari School, 170; *tuba* in "The Thunder," 248–251, 254, 255, 257; VII: 171, 369n1
Qur'anic commentary schools, 268, 343
Quraysh tribe: Banu Hashim clan, 38

Radi, Akbar, 311
Radi, al-Sharif al-, 66
Rank, Otto, 21
Rashti, Seyyed Kazem, 178–179, 180–181, 184, 186, 197, 200, 201, 373n29
Razi, Abu Bakr Muhammad ibn Zakariya al-: *Kitab ila man la yahduruhu al-Tabib* [A Layman's Guide to Medicine], 65–66
Razi, Shaykh Abu al-Futuh al-: on meaning of *tuba,* 248–251, 255; *Tafsir Rawda al-Jinan wa Ruh al-Janan,* 248–251
Reagan, Ronald, 224, 304, 307
Reality vs. representation, 228; in Ta'ziyeh performances, 15–16, 88, 218, 219–220, 223–224; in cinema, 209, 210–211, 217, 226–227, 245–246
Reason: and Nasir Khusraw, 113, 128, 363n21; vs. revelation, 151–152; instrumental reason, 170–171, 214, 217, 247, 258. *See also* Aesthetic reason; Public reason; Revolutionary reason
Reform Movement, 276
Renan, Ernest, 289
Revolutionary defiance, 23, 24, 57, 67, 310
Revolutionary reason: transformation into public reason, 158, 169, 172, 183–184, 185, 194, 200–201, 202, 235, 237–238, 239, 309–310, 312, 341
Rey, 71
Rida, Rashid, 284
Rieff, Philip: on culture, 8, 17–21, 22, 58; on Freud, 17–21, 58, 59; political conservatism of, 18; *Sacred Order/Social Order,* 18; *Freud: The Mind of the Moralist,* 18, 19; on the psychoanalytic industry, 18, 19, 20; on guilt, 18, 19, 20–21, 22; *Charisma,* 18, 351n6; on repression, 18–19, 20, 21, 22, 58–59; *The Triumph of the Therapeutic,* 19; on modernity, 19, 58–59; *Fellow Teachers,* 19–20; on morality, 21; "By What Authority?" 58–59
Roshanravan, Kambiz, 226
Rostam Ali/Zehnab, 196, 375n55
Ruhi, Shaykh Ahmad, 203, 211, 290, 376n62
Rumi, Mawlana Jalal al-Din, 89, 140, 141–142, 152, 315, 359nn18,19
Russian empire, 139, 160, 166, 213, 229, 268, 289, 290; and Safavid dynasty, 161, 162–163, 230, 235; and Qajar dynasty, 165, 168, 171, 232, 237, 264, 268, 302

Saaid, Monkith, 258, 378n17
Saba'iyyah, 61
Sabbah, Hasan, 129
Sabzian, Hossein, 208, 209, 220, 226–227
Sacher-Masoch, Leopold von, 17
Sacred and sublime, the, 242, 245, 254, 255, 257
Sa'di Shirazi, Shaykh Muslih al-Din, 140, 141–142
Sadr, Imam Musa al-, 274, 342
Sadr, Seyyed Muqtada al-, 24, 67–68
Sadr al-Mut'allihin. *See* Mulla Sadra Shirazi
Saedi, Gholamhossein, 247
Safar, 2, 21
Safavid dynasty, 132, 136, 140, 160–161, 212, 367n14, 368n20, 370nn5,6; establishment of, 8, 95, 142, 143–145, 173–174, 199–200;

cosmopolitanism of, 24–25, 134, 149, 151, 152–153, 154, 161, 162, 166, 167–168, 169, 170, 172, 175, 183, 194, 230, 235, 297, 301, 340, 371n10; and Mulla Sadra, 91, 134, 137, 145, 158, 161, 167, 236; urban planning during, 145–149, 153; art and architecture during, 145–149, 153, 298, 367n17, 368nn19,21; universal claims of, 152, 154; end of, 153, 161, 162–163, 165, 166, 183, 230, 235, 310; and public reason, 158, 194, 309–310; and Ottoman empire, 161, 163, 195, 230, 235; and Russian empire, 161, 162–163, 230, 235. *See also* Isfahan; School of Isfahan
Saffar, Ya'qub Layth, 112
Saffarid dynasty, 111, 112
Safi al-Din Ardabili, Shaykh, 143
Safi I, Shah, 152
Saheb-qiran-nameh, 94
Sahme-e Imam revenue, 268
Said, Edward, on worldliness, 318
Saladin, 118, 129
Sales, Mehdi Akhavan, 311; "Chavoshi" [A Caravan Ballad], 245
Salman the Persian, 108
Salvation, 8, 33, 36, 37, 44, 80, 274
Samanian dynasty, 111
Samanid dynasty, 105
Sammarri, Abu al-Hasan Ali ibn Muhammad al-, 64
Sangalaji, Mirza Reza Qoli Shari'at, 266, 342
Saqqa-khaneh, 25–26
Sarbedaran, the, 301, 367n13; and Mulla Sadra, 137–138, 144; and fusion of Sufism and Shi'ism, 137–139, 142–143, 144, 167, 169, 173–174, 340; vs. the Hurufiyyah, 142–143, 144, 167, 169, 172, 173–174, 199, 200, 202
Sarmad [the everlasting], 256
Sartre, Jean-Paul, 269
Sassanid empire, 42, 71, 108, 120–121, 239; fall of, 68, 104, 135, 304, 361n4
Satrapi, Marjane, 320–321, 322
Saudi Arabia, 278, 301, 303–304, 305
School of Isfahan, 149–158, 167, 173, 174, 224, 368n28; cosmopolitanism of, 149, 151, 152–153, 168, 175, 340; and public reason, 158, 166, 169, 183, 202, 212, 236; relationship to Babism, 183, 185, 196–197, 198, 199, 200, 202, 236, 301, 372n23. *See also* Mir Damad; Mulla Sadra Shirazi
Second Shi'i Imam, 62
Secularism, 232–233, 234–235, 242, 266, 311
Self-alienation, Muslim, 281, 299, 311–312
Self-knowledge, 26
Seljuqid dynasty, 104, 105, 107, 112–113, 122, 124, 145, 148, 362n6; revolts against, 129–130; end of, 130, 134. *See also* Nizam al-Mulk, Khwajah
Sepehri, Sohrab, 31, 311; "Seda-ye Paye Ab" [The Footsteps of Water], 244
September 11th attacks, 224, 280, 307–308
Sepúlveda, Juan Ginés de, 233
Seven-Imami Shi'is. *See* Isma'ilism
Seventh Shi'i Imam, 63, 114–116, 143
Shah Abd al-Azim shrine, 71–72
Shahadat [martyrdom], 8, 80, 84–85, 87; Hossein as Prince of Martyrs, 3, 7, 25, 75, 84
Shahnameh Heyrati, 95
Shahrokh, 139
Shamlou, Ahmad, 76–78, 79, 216, 311; *Marg-e Naseri* (Death of [the One from] Nazareth), 77–78, 357n5; *Sorud-e Ebrahim dar Atash* [The Song of Abraham in Fire], 97–100; "Va Hasrati" [And a Regret], 377n8
Shari'ati, Ali, 74, 75, 92, 273, 300; *A Socialist Who Believes in God,* 53–54; and Abu Dharr, 53–54, 354n7; vs. Farrokhzad, 54, 55, 56, 57–58; and Makhmalbaf, 55; "Hossein: Vares-e Adam" ["Hossein: The Inheritor of Adam"], 71; on Fatimah, 269; views on Shi'i clerics, 269, 270, 342, 343; views on Shi'ism and politics,

Shari'ati, Ali *(continued)* 269–270, 303, 314; vs. Al-e Ahmad, 270; *Islamshenasi,* 270; vs. Soroush, 275; and Islamic Revolution, 303, 314, 325; vs. al-Afghani, 308, 312; *Entezar: Mazhab-e I'teraz* [Expectation of Mahdi: The Religion of Defiance], 354n11; *Hossein: Vares-e Adam* [Hossein: The Inheritor of Adam], 354n11; *On the Sociology of Islam,* 379n15; *What Is to Be Done,* 379n15

Shaykh Ahmad Ahsa'i, 174–176, 186, 189, 201, 236, 341, 373n29; and Mulla Sadra, 173, 174, 175–176, 185, 197, 198, 199, 200, 202, 372n23; on God's justice, 174; on corporeal resurrection, 174, 175, 176, 179, 372n22; on Perfect Shi'i [*Shi'a-ye Kamil*], 174, 178, 180–181, 200, 341, 371n20; on Fourth Pillar [*Rokn-e Rabe'*], 174, 181, 188, 341; on *Hurqalya,* 176; and Mulla Mohammad Taqi Baraghani, 176, 177–178; death of, 178; and al-Afghani, 285, 286, 300; *Kitab Sharh al-Ziyarah,* 373n30

Shaykh Baha'i, 151

Shaykhism, 177–180, 286, 372n21, 373n28; relationship to Babism, 173, 183, 184–186, 189, 197–198, 201, 236, 238, 242, 341, 372nn23,27; and Qorrat al-Ayn, 177, 179–180, 184–186, 189, 193, 197–198, 341; and Seyyed Kazem Rashti, 178–179, 180–181, 184, 186, 197, 200, 201, 373n29

Shi'i clergy: and Pahlavi monarchy, 2–3, 265, 266, 267, 268–269, 271, 273–274, 313–314; as *'ulama,* 33, 167, 171, 264, 269, 355n20; feudal scholasticism among, 152, 166, 167, 168, 169–170, 172–173, 175, 183, 187, 194, 197, 202, 211, 212, 235, 239, 295, 297, 298; legitimation of political leaders by, 167, 168–171, 236, 323; and Qajar dynasty, 167, 168–174, 175, 176, 178, 183, 188, 193, 202, 230, 231, 236, 237–238, 264, 297, 298; and Fath Ali Shah, 167, 169, 173; and Shaykism, 175–176, 177–178, 183, 185, 186–187, 373n28; and Babism, 182, 186–187, 188–189, 192, 193, 197, 212, 237, 264, 266, 297, 298, 373n34; and colonialism, 237, 264–265; and Constitutional Revolution, 237–238, 264, 265; views on women, 266; Baha'is persecuted by, 266–267; Tudeh Party opposed by, 267, 268; and Soroush, 319

Shi'i imams, 31, 36, 90, 94, 95; Eighth Imam, 7, 29, 45, 63; as infallible [*ma'sum/'ismah*], 35, 85, 114, 155, 310, 314; Second Imam, 62; Fourth Imam, 62, 114; Fifth Imam, 62, 114, 339; Sixth Imam, 62–63, 114–115; Eleventh Imam, 63; Ninth Imam, 63; Tenth Imam, 63; Seventh Imam, 63, 114–116, 143. *See also* Ali ibn Abi Talib; Hossein ibn Ali; *Imamah;* Twelfth Imam

Shi'i jurisprudence, 56, 63; in Baghdad, 23, 65, 66–67; *Kutub al-Arba'ah* [The Four Books], 64–68; relationship to Shi'ism's traumatic origins, 82, 86; the *Mojtahed* [Most Learned Jurist] in, 138; Akhbari School, 169–171, 175, 340, 371n14; Usuli School, 169–171, 175–176, 177–178, 183, 186, 239, 242, 340, 341, 371n16; in Qom, 265; and Khomeini, 274

Shi'i paradox of moral success in political failure and moral failure in political success, 80–81, 85, 297, 308, 313, 321, 322, 323–325

Shi'i saints, 71, 266; as *Chahardah Ma'sum* [The Infallible Fourteen], 155

Shimr ibn Dhi al-Jawshan, 4, 172

Shiraz, 142, 160, 164–165, 181, 182; Mulla Sadra in, 132, 134, 161, 162

Shirazi, Mirza Muhammad Taqi, 265, 342

Shu'ubiyyah movement, 105–106

Siffin, Battle of, 61, 69, 108, 109
Sineh zanan, 2, 4–5, 6
Sistan, 110, 111
Sistani, Grand Ayatollah Ali, 67–68
Sixth Shi'i Imam, 62–63, 114–115
Sobh-e Azal, Mirza Yahya, 201, 202–203, 341
Soltanpour, Said, 96
Son-religion: Christianity as, 12–14; vs. father-religion, 13–14; Shi'ism as, 13–17, 22–23, 44, 57, 67, 71, 84–85, 115–116, 309
Soroush, Abdolkarim, 315–316, 318–319, 321, 343, 380n33, 384n5; *Qabz va Bast-e Teoric-e Shari'at* [The Theoretical Contraction and Expansion of Religious law], 275
Soviet Union, 213
Strauss, Richard: *Salomé,* 92
Sufism, 133, 136, 172, 257; Sufi saints, 31; *fana* [annihilation], 87, 88, 89–90; *wilayat* [companionship], 88–89; *Awlia' Allah* [Friends of God], 88–89, 90; *Ana al-Haq,* 89–90; fusion with Shi'ism, 137–139, 142–144, 151, 157, 167–168, 169, 173–174, 175, 176, 183, 199, 338, 340, 341, 366n7; Kubrawiyyah order, 139, 341; Ne'matollahai order, 173–174, 341; *Insan-e Kamil* [Perfect Human Being] in, 200, 371n20. *See also* Hallaj, Mansur al-
Suhrawardi, Shahab al-Din Yahya, 90–91, 150–151, 176, 340, 359n20; and Mulla Sadra, 133, 135–136, 156
Sunbadh, 111, 121
Sunni jurisprudence, 36, 135, 136; Hanafi school, 164, 338; Hanbali school, 164, 338; Maliki school, 164, 338; Shafi'i school, 164, 338
Sunnis: vs. Shi'is, 36, 43–44, 110–111, 135, 141, 161, 162, 199, 228–229, 234, 277–279, 282, 310, 355n20; Sunni dynasties, 104, 107, 110–111, 135, 160; *Mojaddad*/Renewer of Faith, 199; Wahabism, 266, 304–305; and Saudi Arabia, 278
Sunni theology, 125, 135; Ash'arite School, 112, 136, 151, 338, 339; Mu'tazilite School, 112, 136, 151, 338, 339
Syria, 104, 112, 118, 119, 123, 139, 153; Muslim conquest of, 68–69; Damascus, 69; Lebanon occupation, 274

Tabarestan, 111
Tabarsi uprising, 192–193, 199, 285
Tabataba'i, Allamah Seyyed Mohammad Hossein: *Usul-e Falsafeh va Ravesh-e Ri'alism* [The Principles of Philosophy and the Realistic Method], 271, 343
Tabataba'i Qomi, Hajj Aqa Hossein, 265
Taherian dynasty, 111
Tahmasp II, Shah, 162, 163
Takhti, Gholamreza, 95–96, 360nn29,30
Taleqani, Ayatollah Seyyed Mahmud, 267, 272, 273, 303, 314; and Qur'an commentaries, 268, 271–272, 343; *Partovi az Qur'an* [A Reflection from the Qur'an], 271–272; *Islam and Ownership,* 272, 380n23
Tamerlane, 132, 139, 140, 144, 150
Taqi, Imam Muhammad al-, 63
Taqlid, 266, 342
Tariqah [mystical path], 139
Tashayyod, Ali Akbar, 267
Tawhid [absolute monotheism], 37, 42, 126, 127, 155, 174, 266
Ta'wil [hermeneutics], 151
Tawwabun, revolt of, 62
Taxation, 70, 108, 110, 111, 161, 363n18
Ta'ziyeh, 9, 172, 211, 215, 217–225, 243, 311, 348nn1–3, 349nn3,20, 359n22; reality vs. representation in, 15–16, 88, 218, 219–220, 223–224; Ghaffari's *Moses and the Wandering Dervish,* 79; Kiarostami's *Ta'ziyeh,* 220–223, 224, 225; in India, 357n10, 358n11; in Trinidad, 357n10, 358n14

Tehran: in early 1970s, 47–48, 71; during Islamic Revolution, 48; Toup Khaneh Square, 51, 353n5; Hosseiniyeh Irshad, 268; Tehran University, 271; American hostage crisis of 1979–80, 275, 314
Tehrani, Shaykh Ali, 269
Tenth Shi'i Imam, 63
Thingness [*inniyyah*], 154–155
Third Shi'i Imam. *See* Hossein ibn Ali
Third World socialism: "Che" Guevara, 3, 53, 56, 95, 97, 303, 308; and Shi'ism, 25, 74–76, 75, 78, 79–80, 88, 211, 229, 265, 273, 282, 283, 294, 298, 299, 300, 303, 304, 305; and Qorrat al-Ayn, 193, 264; Tudeh Party, 267, 268, 305; and al-Afghani, 293
Timurid empire, 139–140, 142, 144, 340
Tobacco Revolt of 1891–92, 200, 201, 209, 211, 212, 237, 290, 302, 342
Tönnies, Ferdinand: *Gemeinschaft und Gesellschaft,* 194, 195; *Community and Society,* 375n50
Traboulsi, Fawwaz: *A History of Modern Lebanon,* 383n7
Transoxiana, 69, 104, 110, 119, 134, 139
Trench, Battle of the, 42
Trinidad: Muharram ceremonies in, 8; Ta'ziyeh performances in, 357n10, 358n14
Truth [*Haq*], 133, 150–151, 155, 157, 199
Tudeh Party, 268, 305; *Guardians of Magic and Myth,* 267
Turkey, 237
Tusi, Abu Jafar Muhammad ibn Hassan al-, 63, 356n31; *Tahdhib al-Ahkam fi Sharh al-Muqni'* [The Refinement of the Laws by Way of an Exegesis on (Shaykh al-Mufid's) The Legally Sufficient], 66–67; *al-'Istibsar fi-ma 'Ikhtalaf min al-Akhbar* [Perspicacious Observations Concerning Variations on Received Traditions], 67
Tusi, Khwajah Nasir al-Din al-, 365nn44,45, 367n10; *Akhlaq-e Muhtashami,* 130; *Akhlaq-e Naseri,* 130; and Mulla Sadra Shirazi, 136–137, 138, 144, 149
Twelfth Imam: as "Imam-e Zaman" [The Imam of the Time], 49, 52, 63, 353n2; Twelve-Imami Shi'is [*Shi'i 'Ithna-'Ashari*], 62, 63, 63–68, 112, 116, 153, 339–340, 367n13; occultation [*ghaybah*] of, 63, 64, 65, 67, 85–86, 174, 179, 181, 182, 188, 199, 274, 339–340; as Mahdi, 63, 85–86, 353n2; and jurisprudence, 63–68
Tyranny, 83–84, 114, 314, 339

Ubaydullah ibn Ziad, 15
Uhud, Battle of, 42
Umar ibn al-Khattab, 59, 60, 68, 338
Umayyad dynasty, 14–15, 69, 104, 107–110, 112, 362n10; tribal patrimonialism of, 14, 107, 109; establishment of, 61, 68, 70–71, 108–109; end of, 62, 115; Mawali under, 70, 107, 108, 109, 110, 114. *See also* Yazid ibn Mu'awiyah
Ummah and the Prophet Muhammad, 30, 40, 41, 42, 43, 58, 59–60, 81–82
United States: invasion of Iraq by, 66, 218, 222, 277–279, 282, 292, 301, 304, 319–320, 348n3; imperialism of, 213, 242, 269, 273–274, 283, 293, 303–304, 317–318, 351n39; September 11th attacks, 224, 280, 307–308; Reagan administration, 224, 304, 307; American Revolution, 231; CIA-engineered coup of 1953 in Iran, 267, 324; relations with Pahlavi monarchy, 273–274; Naval Postgraduate School, 277, 381n1; George W. Bush administration, 277–280, 301, 307–308; relations with Islamic Republic of Iran, 300–301, 304–305, 307; invasion of Afghanistan by, 301, 307, 308, 324; during Iran-Iraq War, 304; George H. W. Bush administration, 307; relations with Israel, 307
Unity of God. *See* Monotheism, absolute

'Uqaylid dynasty, 153
'Urwah al-Wuthqa, al-, 289
Ustadhsis, 111, 182
Uthman ibn Affan, 14, 59, 60, 69, 108, 338

Valiyani, Mulla Javad, 179, 180, 373n31

Wahabism, 266, 304–305
Wali [friend], 88, 358n15
Warqah ibn Nawfal, 40
Water and thirst, 25–26, 80, 351n40
Weber, Max, 373n34; on prophetic charisma, 32–37, 351n6, 352n19; on magicians, 33; on priests, 33; on typology of authority, 33; on ethical vs. exemplary prophets, 33, 35–36, 37, 44; on the interpretive method (*Verstehendemethode*), 33, 214, 351n7; on Muhammad's charismatic authority, 34–35, 43, 57, 58, 59; on philosophy, 35; on the Qur'an, 35; on modernity, 213–215, 376n7; on disenchantment, 214; on instrumental rationality, 214; introduction to *Protestant Ethic and the Spirit of Capitalism,* 376n7; on occidental rationalism, 376n7
Wright, Jeremiah, 234
Wujud [being/existence], 133, 152, 154–155, 156

Yarmuk, Battle of, 68–69
Yassin, Shaykh Ahmed, 306
Yazd, 188
Yazid ibn Mu'awiyah, 3, 17, 80, 81, 83–84, 109, 172, 220, 314
Yemen, 114, 339
Yohannan, John D.: *Persian Poetry in England and America,* 359n25
Yumgan, 125–126, 129

Zaidan, Jurji, 293
Zaidism, 301
Zand dynasty, 164–165, 167, 169, 231, 235, 236, 298, 370n8
Zanjani, Mulla Mohammad Ali, 196
Zanjan uprising, 192–193, 196, 285–286
Zanjir zanan, 4
Zanj Revolt, 111, 118, 362n17
Zarer, 8–9
Zayd ibn Ali, 62, 114, 339
Zaydiyah, 62, 114, 119, 183, 339, 372n23
Zaynab (sister of Hossein ibn Ali), 3
Zayn al-Abidin, Imam, 62, 114
Zehnab/Rostam Ali, 196, 375n55
Zenderoudi, Hossein, 248
Zoroastrianism, 9, 68, 69–70, 91, 113, 172, 349n16, 356n33; Zoroaster, 33, 35, 360n32; Babak Khorram-dinan revolt, 111, 120, 121, 151